Chancery
Order Room (filing) 708.
Tel 071 936 6000 x 6148

Chancery Practice and Orders

© Longman Group Ltd 1991

ISBN 0 85121 7036

Published by
Longman Law, Tax and Finance
Longman Group UK Ltd
21-27 Lamb's Conduit Street, London WC1N 3NJ

Associated Offices
Australia, Hong Kong, Malaysia, Singapore, USA

All rights reserved. No part of this publication may be reproduced, stored in a retrieval system, or transmitted, in any form or by any means, electronic, mechanical, photocopying, recording or otherwise, without either the prior written permission of the publishers or a licence permitting restricted copying issued by the Copyright Licensing Agency Ltd,
90 Tottenham Court Road,
London W1P 9HE.

No responsibility for loss occasioned to any person acting or refraining from action as a result of the material in this publication can be accepted by the authors or publishers.

The material herein which is Crown Copyright is reproduced with the permission of the Controller of Her Majesty's Stationery Office

Official forms are reproduced by kind permission of the Solicitor's Law Stationery Society Ltd.

A CIP catalogue record for this book is available from the British Library.

Phototypeset by Kerrypress Ltd, Luton
Printed in Great Britain by Mackays of Chatham PLC

Chancery Practice and Orders

Robert Blackford
Barrister and former Solicitor

Colin Jaque
Solicitor of Jeffrey Green Russell

and

Francesca Quint
Barrister

Contents

Preface	ix
Table of Cases	xi
Table of Statutes	xvii
Table of Statutory Instruments	xxi
Abbreviations	xxvii

Part I: Chancery Practice Generally

1 Chancery Chambers—Introduction   3
1. Breadth of jurisdiction   3
2. The structure of Chancery chambers   4
3. Masters and judges—general   7
4. Judges   7
5. Masters   8

2 Commencement and Conduct of an Action   14
1. Introduction   14
2. Selection of originating process   15
3. General provisions relating to writs and originating summonses   21
4. The sequence of proceedings   24
5. Service   37
6. Amendments   42
7. Default judgments   45
8. Time   47

Commencement and Conduct of an Action—Orders   49

3 Intitulement and Parties   60
1. Intitulement   60
2. Parties   63

Intitulement and Parties—Orders   69

4	**Interlocutory and Enforcement Applications**	75
1.	Application by summons	75
2.	Applications *ex parte* by affidavit	76
3.	Applications on motion	77
4.	Summary judgment	82
5.	Applications to determine procedural questions	83
6.	Treating as trial	83
	Interlocutory and Enforcement Applications— Orders	85
5	**Injunctions**	99
1.	Injunctions—general	99
2.	Mareva injunctions	99
3.	Anton Piller orders	100
4.	Preservation orders	104
	Injunctions—Orders	107
6	**Orders and their Issue**	118
1.	Orders—general	118
2.	The drawing up of orders	121
3.	Representation orders	128
4.	Declarations	129
	Orders and their Issue—Orders	130
7	**Listing, Obtaining Appointments, Setting Down and Place of Trial**	151
1.	General	151
2.	Lists	152
3.	Obtaining appointments and directions for hearing	156
4.	Setting down	162
5.	Place of trial	164
	Listing, Obtaining Appointments, Setting Down and Place of Trial—Orders	169
8	**Proceedings under Orders and Judgments**	170
1.	The 'accounts and inquiries section'	170
2.	The enforcement of orders and judgments	170
3.	Procedures	172
4.	Accounts and inquiries	172
5.	Receivers	175
6.	Sales by order of the court	177
7.	Funds	181
8.	After judgment	191

Contents

	Proceedings under Orders and Judgments—Orders	193
9	**District Registries**	227
1.	District registries	227
10	**County Court Jurisdiction and Transfer of Actions**	231
1.	County court jurisdiction	231
2.	Transfer	232
	County Court Jurisdiction and Transfer of Actions—Orders	236
11	**Appeals**	240
1.	Appeals—general	240
2.	Appeals from the master	240
3.	Appeals from the judge	241
4.	Leave to appeal	244
	Appeals—Orders	248
12	**Bundles of Documents; Affidavits; Exhibits**	263
1.	Bundles	263
2.	Affidavits	264
3.	Exhibits	266
13	**Costs**	269
1.	Liability	269
2.	Bases	273
3.	Costs on claim and counterclaim	274
4.	Stage of proceedings at which costs to be taxed	275
	Costs—Orders	280
14	**Post and Telephone**	298
1.	Issue of writ or originating process	298
2.	Acknowledgment of service	299
3.	Issue of summons	299
4.	Agreed orders	300
5.	Appeals from masters	300
6.	Adjournment by consent	300
7.	Legal aid taxation	300
8.	Filing documents by post	300
9.	Office copies	301
10.	Drawing up of orders	301
11.	Telephone	301
12.	Telex	301
13.	Fax	302

Part II: Particular Chancery Actions

15 Intellectual Property — 305
1. Copyright — 305
2. Patents and registered designs — 308
3. Trademarks — 312
4. Passing off — 315
5. Breach of confidence — 316

    Intellectual Property—Orders — 319

16 Land and Other Specific Property — 336
1. Joint property — 336
2. Specific performance — 348
3. Boundary disputes — 366
4. Easements — 368
5. Summary applications for possession: trespass cases — 370
6. Summary applications for possession: Ord 113 not applicable — 373
7. Landlord and Tenant Act 1954, Part II — 378
8. Leasehold enfranchisement — 388
9. Mortgages — 390
10. Registered land — 396

    Land and Other Specific Property—Orders — 403

17 Partnerships: Winding Up and Receivership — 455
1. Winding Up and Receivership — 455

    Partnership: Winding Up and Receivership—Orders — 468

18 Rectification and Rescission — 474
1. Rectification — 474
2. Rescission — 476

    Rectification and Rescission—Orders — 480

19 Trusts: General — 483
1. Introduction — 483
2. Determination of questions and orders directing acts to be done or abstained from — 484
3. Applications by trustees, personal representatives or beneficiaries for the exercise of the court's jurisdiction — 485
4. Actions by beneficiaries against trustees or personal representatives — 486
5. Appointment and removal of trustees — 487
6. The judicial trustee — 491

7.	Variation of trusts	495
8.	Vesting orders	498

Trusts: General—Orders   500

20 Wills and Succession   525
1. Contentious probate   525
2. Family provision   531
3. Construction of wills (deeds and other written instruments)   536
4. Administration actions   540

Wills and Succession—Orders   550

21 Charities   571
1. Introduction   571
2. Charity proceedings   571
3. Appeals under Charities Act 1960   574
4. Enforcement of Charity Commission orders   576

Charities—Orders   578

22 Companies   581
1. Companies   581

Companies—Orders   584

23 Insolvency   603
1. Individual insolvency   603
2. Corporate insolvency   605

Appendix A: Practice Directions   609
Appendix B: Thomas More Building   620

Appendix C: Supreme Court Fees Order 1980   621

Index   633

Preface

This book combines and updates *Chancery Practice Handbook* by Robert Blackford and Colin Jaque and *Chancery Orders* by Edmund Heward, formerly Chief Chancery Master. Its purpose is to give practical guidance in day to day Chancery practice. Text describing the workings of the Chancery Division is combined with specimen orders and the design of the book is such that it can be used without necessarily having to refer elsewhere.

The scope is wide reaching and includes all Chancery actions and applications likely to be met with. The procedure in each instance is given in sequence, with a short section indicating possible hazards and pitfalls, so that the reader may avoid them. Relevant forms of order appear at the end of chapters.

Reference is made to all Practice Directions currently in use, the book is entirely up to date, and includes a comprehensive listing of the powers of masters and judges, and introduces all recent changes in the Rules. However, the 'illustrations' provided are intended to be referred to only in terms of general content and layout—care should be taken not to include any factual statements they contain which do not accord with the practitioner's own cases.

We are grateful to HMSO and the Lord Chancellor's Department for permission to use the forms of order in use in the Chancery Division drafting section and to Mr W R Heeler, the head of that section, and his colleagues for their considerable help.

Robert Blackford

Colin Jaque

Francesca Quint

August 1991

Table of Cases

Alpha Co Ltd, *Re* [1903] 1 Ch 203...502
American Cyanamid Co v Ethicon Ltd [1975] AC 396; [1975] 2 WLR 316; [1975]
   1 All ER 504...308, 314
Anton Piller KG v Manufacturing Processes Ltd [1976] Ch 55, CA..........100, 313
Arthur v Consolidated Collieries (1905) 49 SJ 403..............................79
Artoc Bank & Trust v Prudential Assurance Co [1984] 1 WLR 1181; [1984]
   3 All ER 538; (1984) 128 SJ 737...412
Bacharach's Will Trusts, *Re*, Minden v Bacharach [1959] Ch 245; [1959]
   2 WLR 1; [1958] 3 All ER 618..538
Bartlett v Barclays Bank Trust Co Ltd [1980] Ch 515; [1980] 2 WLR 430; [1980]
   All ER 139...483, 487
Beddoe, *Re*, Downes v Cottam [1893] 1 Ch 547...........................485, 501
Bedson v Bedson [1965] 2 QB 666; [1965] 3 WLR 891; [1965] 3 All ER 307
   ....179, 339
Benjamin, *Re* [1902] 1 Ch 723..548
Berliner Industrie Bank AG v Jost [1971] 2 QB 463; [1971] 3 WLR 68H; [1971]
   2 All ER 1519d..248
Birchall, decd, *Re*, Wilson v Birchall (1980) 16 Ch D 41......................145
Braybrook, *Re*, Braybrook v Wright [1916] WN 74..............................128
Brown's Will, *Re*, (1884) 27 Ch D 179...128
Buckbod Investments v Nana-Otchere [1985] 1 WLR 342; [1985] 1 All ER 283;
   (1985) 129 SJ 172...253
Bullock v London General Omnibus Co [1907] 1 KB 264; 216 LT 280; 103
   LJ 507; CA..271, 275
CBS United Kingdom Ltd v Lambert [1983] Ch 37; [1982] 3 WLR 746; [1982]
   3 All ER 188; CA..307
Cadogan and Hans Place Estate (No 2) Ltd, *Re*, (1906) WN 112..................84
Campbell (Donald) & Co v Pollak [1927] AC 732.................................272
Cassell & Co Ltd v Broome [1972] AC 1027; [1972] 2 WLR 645; [1972] 1 All
   ER 801, HL..315
Chetwynd's Settlement, *Re*, Scarisbrick v Nevison [1902] 1 Ch 692; 71 LJ
   Ch 352; 86 LT 216...488
City Construction Contracts (London) Ltd v Adam, *The Times*, 4 January,
   1988, CA...36
Clitheroe's Settlement Trusts, *Re*, [1959] 1 WLR 1159; [1959] 3 All ER 789;
   103 SJ 961..496
Collins and Tuffley v Elstone [1893] P1.......................................538
Covell Matthews & Partners v French Wools [1978] 1 WLR 1477; [1978]
   2 All ER 800; (1977) 122 SJ 79...412
Davies v British Gear Ltd [1957] 1 QB 1; [1956] 3 WLR 679; [1956] 3 All ER
   389..64
Dennis v Malcolm [1934] Ch 244; [1933] All ER Rep 293.........................397
Donib v Isoz [1980] Ch 548; [1980] 2 WLR 565; [1980] 1 All ER 942, CA.........477

Drewe's Settlement, *Re*, Drewe v Westminster Bank [1966] 1 WLR 1518; [1966]
  2 All ER 844 496
EMI Records Ltd v Wallace (Ian Cameron) Ltd [1983] Ch 59; [1982] 3 WLR
  245; [1982] 2 All ER 980 274
English Exporters (London) v Eldonwall; Same v Same [1973] Ch 415; [1973]
  2 WLR 435; [1973] 1 All ER 726 381
Evers' Trusts, *Re*, Papps v Evers [1980] 1 WLR 1327; [1980] 3 All ER 399;
  (1980) 124 SJ 562 178
Foxon v Gascoigne (1874) LR 9 Ch App 654; 43 LJ Ch 729; 31 LT 289 340
Fritz v Hobson (1880) 14 Ch D 542; [1874-80] All ER Rep 75; 49 LJ Ch 321 172
Goodwin, *Re*, Goodwin v Goodwin [1969] 1 Ch 283; [1968] 3 WLR 558; [1968]
  3 All ER 12 .... 533, 535
Harrison & Another v Tew [1990] 2 WLR 210; [1989] QB 307, CA 294
Harrison's Share under a Settlement, *Re*, Harrison v Harrison William's Will
  Trusts, *Re*, Williams v Richardson, Ropner's Settlement Trust, *Re*, Ropner v
  Ropner [1955] Ch 260; [1955] 2 WLR 256; [1955] 1 All ER 185 122
Harter and Slater v Harter (1873) LR 3 P & D 11; 42 LJP & M 1; 27 LT 858 538
Hatt & Co (Bath) v Pearce [1978] 1 WLR 885; [1978] 2 All ER 474; (1978)
  122 SJ 180, CA 232
Hatton v Harris [1892] AC 547 123
Hollis v Burton [1892] 3 Ch 226; 67 LT 146; 40 WR 610, CA 45
Hytrac Conveyors Ltd v Conveyors International Ltd [1983] 1 WLR 44; [1982]
  3 All ER 415; (1982) 126 SJ 728 100
IRC v Hoogstraten [1985] QB 1077; [1984] 3 WLR 933; [1984] 3 All ER 25 220
Jay v Budd [1898] 1 QBD 12; 66 LJQB 863; 77 LT 335, CA 24
Jennery, *Re*, Jennery v Jennery [1967] Ch 280; [1967] 2 WLR 201; [1967]
  1 All ER 691 534
Johnson v Agnew [1980] AC 367; [1979] 2 WLR 487; [1979] 1 All ER 883,
  HL 348, 350
Jones v Challenger [1961] 1 QB 176; [1960] 2 WLR 695; [1960] 1 All ER
  785, CA 178, 339
Jones v Davies [1940] WN 174; 84 SJ 334 488
Ker's Settlement Trusts, *Re*, [1963] Ch 553; [1963] 2 WLR 1210; [1963]
  1 All ER 801 497
Langton, *In the Estate of* [1964] P163; [1964] 2 WLR 585; 108 SJ 96 527
Learoyd v Whitely (1887) 12 App Cas 727; 57 LJ Ch 390 483
Lewis v Green [1905] 2 Ch 340; 74 LJ Ch 682; 93 LT 303 538
Lidington, *Re*, Lidington v Thomas [1940] Ch 927; [1940] 3 All ER 600;
  163 LT 280 532
Littler dec, *Re*, Littler v Rowland 1973 W 3853 559
Mareva Compania Naveria SA v International Bulk Carriers SA [1975] 2 Lloyd's
  Rep 509; 119 SJ 660, CA 100
Marley Laboratory Ltd's Application, *Re*, [1952] 1 All ER 1057; [1952] WN 195;
  69 RPC 156, CA 122
Masters' Practice Directions No 13 .... 62, 127
Masters' Practice Directions No 15 45
Masters' Practice Directions No 31 [1970] 1 WLR 472 67
Medway Oil and Storage Co v Continental Contractors [1929] AC 88 274
National Westminster Bank v Stockman [1981] 1 WLR 67; [1981] 1 All ER 800;
  (1980) 124 SJ 810 192
Paget's Settlement, *Re*, Baillie v De Brossard [1965] 1 WLR 1046; [1965]
  1 All ER 58; 109 SJ 577 497
Pooley's Trustee v Whetham (1884) 28 ChD 38 65
Practice Direction [1945] WN 80 619
Practice Direction (1946) WN154 125
Practice Direction [1950] WN 279 160
Practice Direction [1972] 1 All ER 286 166
Practice Direction 5, December 1975 618

TABLE OF CASES xiii

Practice Direction 18, May 1983 [1983] 2 All ER 416 241
Practice Direction (No 6 of 1988) [1988] 3 All ER 1086 614
Practice Direction (No 4 of 1989) 5 December 1989 [1990] 1 All ER 255 12
Practice Direction 16, May 1990 [1990] 2 All ER 318 244
Practice Direction (Affidavit Evidence) [1969] 1 WLR 974; [1969] 2 All ER 639
 .... 266, 609, 610
Practice Direction (Affidavits: Cross Examination) [1969] 1 WLR 983; [1969]
 1 Lloyd's Rep 484 .... 26, 611
Practice Direction (Applications) [1955] 1 WLR 36; [1955] 1 All ER 30 609
Practice Direction (Applications by post or telephone) [1983] 1 WLR 791;
 [1983] 2 All ER 541 .... 23, 119, 120, 250, 301, 309, 310, 617
Practice Direction (Application for the Rectification of the Register of
 Patents or Designs: Agreed Directions), 10 December 1984 [1985] 1 All ER
 192 .... 80, 617
Practice Direction (Applications and Change of Name) (No 1 of 1984),
 16 February, 1984 [1984] 1 WLR 447; [1984] 1 All ER 720; (1984) 128 SJ 156
 .... 15, 62, 73, 82, 127, 610, 618
Practice Direction (Assessment of Case: Substance) [1972] 1 WLR 3; [1972]
 1 All ER 288 152
Practice Direction (Central Office: Description of Parties) [1969] 1 WLR 1259;
 [1969] 2 All ER 1130 .... 20, 126, 611
Practice Direction (Central Office: First and Second Class Mail) [1968] 1 WLR
 1489; [1968] 3 All ER 319; 112 SJ 660 38
Practice Direction (Chancery: Consent Orders in Court) [1985] 1 WLR 593;
 [1985] 1 All ER 1040 .... 121, 611
Practice Direction (Chancery: District Registries) [1972] 1 WLR 53 616
Practice Direction (Chancery: Lists) (No 1 of 1982) 164
Practice Direction (Chancery: Lists) (No 1 of 1983) [1983] 1 WLR 436; [1983]
 1 All ER 1145 .... 152, 161, 613
Practice Direction (Chancery: Masters' Powers) [1971] 2 All ER 215 383
Practice Direction (Chancery: Masters' Powers) [1975] 1 WLR 129; 1 All
 ER 255 .... 11, 145, 176, 490, 497, 515, 517, 524, 543, 613
Practice Direction (Chancery: Masters' Powers) (No 2) [1975] 1 WLR 405,
 [1975] 1 All ER 640 .... 11, 534, 613
Practice Direction (Chancery: Masters' Powers) (No 3) [1976] 1 WLR 637;
 [1976] 2 All ER 610 .... 8, 11, 613
Practice Direction (Chancery: Masters' Powers) (No 4) [1977] 1 WLR 1019;
 [1977] 3 All ER 121 .... 11, 490
Practice Direction (Chancery: Originating Notice of Motion: case stated and
 similar proceedings) [1984] 1 WLR 1216 .... 17, 616
Practice Direction (Chancery: Originating Summons) [1974] 1 WLR 708 379
Practice Direction (Chancery: Originating Summons) (No 2) [1976] 1 WLR 201 .. 609
Practice Direction (Chancery: Powers of Masters) [1971] 1 WLR 706 613
Practice Direction (Chancery: Procedure No 2 of 1982) [1983] 1 WLR 4
 .... 11, 60, 240, 241, 278, 371, 610, 613, 614, 617, 618
Practice Direction (Chancery: Procedure) [1983] 1 All ER 131 .... 125, 145
Practice Direction (Chancery: Proceedings outside London) [1972] 1 WLR 1
 .... 165, 615
Practice Direction (Chancery: Proceedings outside London) [1984] 1 WLR 417 ... 616
Practice Direction (Chancery: Proceedings outside London) [1985] 1 WLR 109 ... 616
Practice Direction (Chancery: Setting Down) [1975] 1 WLR 321 609
Practice Direction (Chancery: Setting Down for Trial) [1981] 1 WLR 322;
 [1981] 1 All ER 752 .... 162, 618
Practice Direction (Chancery: Speedy Trial) [1979] 1 WLR 204 .... 163, 609
Practice Direction (Chancery: Transfer of Business) [1988] 1 WLR 741; [1988]
 2 All ER 639 233

Practice Direction (Chancery Chambers) (No 1 of 1982) [1982] 1 WLR 1189;
 [1982] 3 All ER 124 .... 4, 118, 120, 121, 123, 148, 157, 159, 160, 161, 165, 167,
 .... 174, 228, 229, 301, 610, 612, 614, 615, 616, 620
Practice Direction (Chancery Chambers) (No 2 of 1982) [1983] 1 WLR 4
 .... 20, 21
Practice Direction (Chancery Chambers: Expedition) [1970] 1 WLR 95; [1970]
 1 All ER 11 .... 25, 157
Practice Direction (Change of Surname) [1965] 1 WLR 541; [1965] All ER 928;
 109 SJ 260 127
Practice Direction (Costs: Assessment in Chambers) [1975] 1 WLR 1202 351
Practice Direction (Costs: Assessment in Chambers) (No 3 of 1985) [1985]
 1 WLR 968; [1985] 2 All ER 1024 278
Practice Direction (Description of Parties) [1969] 1 WLR 1259; [1969]
 2 All ER 1130 21
Practice Direction (Documents for Use Abroad) [1971] 1 WLR 604; [1971]
 2 All ER 160 611
Practice Direction (Drawing up of Orders made on Motion) 15 January, 1970
 [1970] 1 WLR 249 121
Practice Direction (Estate Agents' and Auctioneers' Fees) [1983] 1 WLR 86 612
Practice Direction (Estimated Length of Hearing) [1963] 1 WLR 326 26
Practice Direction (Evidence: Documents) [1983] 1 WLR 922 .... 17, 611
Practice Direction (Exchange of Witness Statements and the Lodging of
 Pleadings) (No 1 of 1989), 23 January 1989 [1989] 1 WLR 133; [1989]
 1 All ER 764 29
Practice Direction (Expedited Trial) [1974] 1 WLR 339 618
Practice Direction (Family Provision: Application) [1978] 1 WLR 585 .... 536, 612
Practice Direction (Family Provision: Endorsement of Order) [1979] 1 WLR 1
 .... 566, 612
Practice Direction (Hearing Dates for Originating Summons Expedited Form)
 [1974] 1 WLR 708 609
Practice Direction (Index) (No 1 of 1986) 8 December 1986 [1987] 1 WLR 93;
 [1987] 1 All ER 879 609
Practice Direction (Judgment: Foreign Currency) [1976] 1 WLR 83 611
Practice Direction (Land Register: Inspection) [1983] 1 WLR 150; [1983]
 1 All ER 352 611
Practice Direction (Limited Companies' Change of Name) [1965] 1 WLR 120;
 [1965] 1 All ER 43; [1965] 1 Lloyd's Rep 48 127
Practice Direction (Minutes of Order) [1960] 1 WLR 1168; [1960] 3 All ER 416;
 104 SJ 866 .... 119, 611, 614
Practice Direction (Miscellaneous Directions) [1970] 1 WLR 520 .... 609, 612
Practice Direction (Miscellaneous Provisions) [1970] 1 WLR 977 .... 549, 609
Practice Direction (Motion: Agreed adjournment) (No 2 of 1988) 29 April 1988
 [1988] 1 WLR 632; [1988] 2 All ER 510 80
Practice Direction (Motions: Agreed adjournment) [1976] 1 WLR 441; [1976]
 2 All ER 198; 120 SJ 284 614
Practice Direction (Motions: Procedure) 18 January 1985 [1985] 1 WLR 244;
 [1985] 1 All ER 384 .... 77, 78, 80, 160, 614, 617
Practice Direction (Motions: Procedure) (No 2) [1985] 1 WLR 244 614
Practice Direction (Motions: Revision of Procedure) [1980] 1 WLR 751; [1980]
 2 All ER 750; [1980] FSR 590 77
Practice Direction (Patents Actions) [1973] 1 WLR 1425; [1974] 1 All ER 40;
 [1973] FSR 587 .... 309, 617
Practice Direction (Patent Summonses) [1970] 1 WLR 94 310
Practice Direction (Possession Order: Issue of Execution) [1972] 1 WLR 240 612
Practice Direction (Principal Clerks' Function) [1974] 1 WLR 461 77
Practice Direction (Probate Actions) [1973] 1 WLR 627 615
Practice Direction (Probate: Contentious Actions) [1974] 1 WLR 1349
 .... 528, 529, 615

TABLE OF CASES xv

Practice Direction (Probate: Compromised Action) [1972] 1 WLR 1215 530
Practice Direction (Queen's Bench Division Postal Service) [1985] 1 WLR 489
....39, 617
Practice Direction (Termination of Proceedings by Consent) [1963] 1 WLR 246;
[1965] 1 All ER 416..610
Practice Direction (Title of Proceedings) [1959] 1 WLR 743..............20, 21, 609
Practice Direction (Trustee under Disability) [1948] WN 273 ....490, 517, 618
Practice Direction (Trustee's Costs) [1953] 1 WLR 1365, [1953] 2 All ER 1159 ...609
Practice Direction (Vacation of Masters' Appointments) 614
Practice Direction (Variation of Trusts: Counsel's Opinion) [1976] 1 WLR 884
....497, 619
Practice Note (1904) WN 203 81
Practice Note [1907] WN 44 609
Practice Note [1927] WN 290 611
Practice Note [1929] WN 105 609
Practice Note [1940] WN 155 ....265, 609
Practice Note [1945] WN 210 609
Practice Note [1949] WN 441 616
Practice Note 3 October 1982 [1982] 3 All ER 376 242
Practice Note (Business Tenancy: Joint Applications) [1973] 1 WLR 299
....383, 613
Practice Note (Chancery: Deposition) [1981] 1 WLR 1560 ....61, 126, 618
Practice Note (Claims for Interest) (No 2) [1983] 1 WLR 377..............36, 37, 613
Practice Note (Revenue Paper: Abolition) [1982] 1 WLR 1474....................613
Practice Note (Trustee's Costs) [1953] 1 WLR 1452; [1953] 2 All ER 1408;
97 SJ 832..609
Practice Note (Variation of Trusts: Stamp Duty) [1966] 1 WLR 345; [1966]
1 All ER 672; 110 SJ 132 ....497, 619
Preston Banking Co v William Allsup & Sons [1895] 1 Ch 141 123
Pritt, Re, Marton v National Church League (1915) 85 LJ Ch 166................126
R v Wandsworth County Court, ex parte, Wandsworth London Borough Council
[1975] 1 WLR 1314; [1975] 3 All ER 390; 119 SJ 529 372
Rayner, Re, Rayner v Rayner [1904] 1 Ch 176; [1900-3] All ER Rep 107;
73 LJ Ch 111, CA..538
Reed v Gray [1952] Ch 337; [1952] 1 All ER 241; [1952] 1 TLR 114..............297
Robertson's Application, Re, [1969] 1 WLR 109; [1969] 1 All ER 257; (1968)
112 SJ 943..389
Royal Trust Co of Canada v Markham [1975] 1 WLR 1416; [1975] 3 All ER
433; 119 SJ 643 390
Royscott Trust Ltd v Rogerson [1991] The Times 3 April 479
Sainsbury's Settlement, Re, Sainsbury v First CB Trustee (Practice Note)
[1967] 1 WLR 476; [1967] 1 All ER 878; 111 SJ 177 496
Salmon, decd, Re, Coard v National Westminster Bank [1981] Ch 167; [1980]
3 WLR 748; [1980] 3 All ER 532 535
Salter Rex & Co v Ghosh [1971] 2 QB 597; [1971] 3 WLR 31; [1971] 2 All
ER 865, CA..244
Samuels v Linzi Dresses [1981] QB 115; [1980] 2 WLR 836; [1980] 1 All
ER 803, CA..48
Sanderson v Blyth Theatre Co [1903] 2 KB 533; 72 LJKB 761, CA 271, 274
Schering Chemicals Ltd v Falkman [1982] QB 1; [1981] 2 WLR 848; [1981]
2 All ER 321, CA..316
Seale's Marriage Settlement, Re, [1961] Ch 574; [1961] 3 WLR 262; [1961]
3 All ER 136...497
Siebe Gormon & Co v Preupac [1982] 1 WLR 185 (1981) 125 SJ 725..............48
Stretton, Re, Stretton v Clegg [1942] WN 95....................................488
Suedeclub Co Ltd v Occasions Textiles [1981] 1 WLR 1245; [1981] 3 All
ER 671; (1981) 125 SJ 589 37
Swire, Re, Mellor v Swire (1885) 30 ChD 239 123

The Trustee of the Property of the Bankrupt v Solomon, *Re*, Solomon
  (A Bankrupt), *ex parte* [1967] Ch 573; [1967] 2 WLR 172; [1966] 3 All ER
  255 126
Till v Till [1974] QB 558; [1974] 2 WLR 447; [1974] 1 All ER 1096 340
Tuck-Murch v Loosemore, *Re*, (1906) 1 Ch 693 144
Walker v Boyle [1982] 1 WLR 495; [1982] 1 All ER 634; (1981) 125 SJ 724 478
Wallersteiner v Moir [1974] 1 WLR 991; [1974] 3 All ER 217; 118 SJ 464 129
Weston's Settlements, *Re*, Weston v Weston [1969] 1 Ch 234; [1968]
  3 WLR 786 497
Whitaker, *Re*, Denison-Pender v Evans [1911] 1 Ch 214; 80 LJ Ch 63;
  103 LT 657...547
Williams & Glyn's Bank v Boland; Same v Brown [1981] AC 487; [1980]
  3 WLR 138; [1980] 2 All ER 408 391
Yap v Williams (1901) WN 91 79

Table of Statutes

Prescription Act 1832 368
Judgments Act 1838 425
   s 17 .... 36, 195, 196
Land Clauses Consolidation Act 1845
   181
Court of Probate Act 1858, ss 23, 26
   529
Bill of Sale Act 1878 .... 626, 627
Conveyancing Act 1881 394
Bill of Sale Act 1882 .... 626, 627
Partnership Act 1890 455
   s 23 192
   s 32 456
   ss 32-4 457
   s 35 456
Stamp Act 1891, s 13 136
Judicial Trustees Act 1896 .... 485, 491,
   .... 492, 495
Public Trustee Act 1906 522
   s 4 .... 512, 522
      (3) 492
   s 5(2)(*i*) 513
   s 9 521
Limited Partnerships Act 1907 455
Bankruptcy Act 1914—
   s 76 125
   s 130(1) 547
Electricity (Supply) Act 1919 18
Administration of Justice Act 1920,
   Part II 625
Maintenance Orders (Facilities for
   Enforcement) Act 1920 625
Administration of Estates Act 1925
   .... 231, 484, 541
   s 7 71
Land Registration Act 1925 ....
   .... 3, 11, 396, 425
   s 5 518
   ss 15(2), 17(1), 56(1), 57(3) 397
   s 82 .... 397, 480, 481
      (*b*) 481
   ss 83(8), 138(3) 397

Law of Property Act 1925
   .... 3, 231, 337, 394, 419, 484
   s 12(1) 336
   s 30 ....
   ...20, 21, 177, 178, 233, 336, 338, 342
   s 40 363
   s 50(2), (3) 10
   s 58(1) 366
   s 64 ....
   .... 437, 438, 440, 444, 445, 451-3
   ss 85, 86 419
   s 87 392
   s 90 ....
   .... 180, 196, 418, 420, 426
   s 115 420
   s 146(3) 407
   s 172 479
   s 203(B) 342
Settled Land Act 1925 ....
   .... 3, 231, 484, 488, 518
   s 12 517
   s 36(3) 520
   s 64 .... 9, 485, 496-8, 515
   s 113(1) 484
Supreme Court of Judicature Act 1925—
   s 45 175
   s 50(1) 547
   s 51 21
Trustee Act 1925 .... 3, 5, 181,
   231, 337, 450, 484, 506, 508, 511, 513
   ss 31, 32 8
   s 36 .... 487, 517
   s 40(4) 517
   s 41 .... 487, 488, 491
   s 42 490
   s 44 .... 178, 181, 498
   ss 44-48 488
   ss 44-51 487
   s 47 .... 436, 499
   s 48 499
      (*a*) 454
   s 50 .... 181, 436
   s 50-53 488

xviii   TABLE OF STATUTES

Trustee Act 1925—*contd*
  s 51(1) 198, 424
  s 57 9,
  .... 180, 336, 342, 483,
  .... 485, 496-8, 515
  s 58 488
  s 59 .... 9, 510, 512, 516, 544
  s 61 .... 486, 515
  s 63 .... 182, 618
    (1), (2) 181
  s 68(17) 483, 541
Landlord and Tenant Act 1927 227
  s 1 405
  s 3(1),(6) 406
  Part I 3,18
Foreign Judgments (Reciprocal
  Enforcement) Act 1933 625
Leasehold Property (Repairs) Act 1938
  .... 3, 10, 18, 231, 407
  s 1 227
Trade Marks Act 1938 312
  s 9 333
Land Clauses Consolidation Act 1945...
  5
Crown Proceedings Act 1947—
  s 17 64
  s 20(2) 233
Exchange Control Act 1947 190
Patents Act 1949 .... 3, 308
  s 23 310
  s 30 331
Registered Designs Act 1949-61
  .... 166, 308
Maintenance Orders Act 1950 625
Landlord and Tenant Act 1954 ....
  .... 133, 228, 231
  ss 23-46 8
  s 24 411
    (a) 378, 380
  s 24A 12, 411
  ss 24-28 .... 412, 613
  s 25 .... 378, 384, 385, 410, 411
  s 26 .... 378, 382, 411
  s 30 .... 380, 381
    (1) 379, 409, 410
    (a) 409
  s 31 409
    (2) 410
    (a) 411
    (b) 410, 411
  s 34 381
  s 36(2) 408, 409
  s 37(4) 410
  s 38 .... 383, 412
    (4) 9, 12
  s 40 .... 386, 387
    (1) 383, 386
  s 54 9

Landlord and Tenant Act 1954—*contd*
  s 63(4) 382
  s 64 383
  Part II ....
  .... 3, 18, 232, 233, 378, 384, 387
Copyright Act 1956 .... 305, 307
Public Trustee (Fees) Act 1957 521
Defence Contracts Act 1958 166
Variation of Trusts Act 1958 ....
  .. 8, 18, 231, 483-5, 495, 496, 498, 523
  s 1(1) 9, 11
  s 24 231
County Courts Act 1959—
  s 51A 367
  s 174 190
  s 192 232
Charities Act 1960 .... 18, 571, 577
  s 5(2) 574
  s 18 .... 488, 575
    (2) 579
    (3) 573
    (9) 572
    (10)-(12) 575
  s 21 575
  s 28 578
    (1), (3), (5) 572
    (5) 573
    (8) 571
  s 41 576
Trustee Investments Act 1961 ....
  .... 495, 496
Commons Registration Act 1965 ....
  .... 134, 251
  s 8 244
  ss 14, 18 .... 250, 251
Compulsory Purchase Act 1965 5
Finance Act 1965—
  s 91 262
Leasehold Reform Act 1967 .. 3, 133, 389
  s 9 417
  s 19 12,388
  s 27 .... 9, 388, 389, 416, 613
  Part I 384
Matrimonial Homes Act 1967 .. 179, 339
Misrepresentation Act 1967 477
  s 2 477
    (2) 477, 478
  s 3 .... 477, 478
Civil Evidence Act 1968—
  ss 2 6(3)(*a*), 9(3), (4) 367
Administration of Justice Act 1969—
  s 12 253
  Part II 253
Family Law Reform Act 1969 .... 62, 66
Law of Property Act 1969 413
  s 5 383
  ss 21,25 12

Table of Statutes

Administration of Justice Act 1970—
  s 1(4) 526
  s 4 627
  s 8 391
  s 36 390
  s 37(1) 391
  Sched 2 391
Taxes Management Act 1970—
  s 53, (2) 260
  s 56 ....136, 255, 257, 258, 261
  s 100 260
Courts Act 1971—
  s 25 237
Civil Evidence Act 1972 311
Land Charges Act 1972 .....12, 231, 425
  s 1(6), 3(1), 5(4), (10) 114
Landlord and Tenant Act 1972 12
Education Act 1973 576
Powers of the Criminal Courts Act 1973—
  s 3(1) 217
  s 19(1) 214, 217, 219
  s 31(3) 217
    (4) 226
Consumer Credit Act 1974—
  s 25 ....398, 400
Legal Aid Act 1974 ....145, 147, 281,
    ...430, 551, 553, 555, 556, 565-7, 570
  s 2 271
  s 2A 273
  s 8(1)(e) 272, 281
  s 9(b) 340
  s 10(1) 273
Solicitors Act 1974......................
    ....275, 276, 293, 294, 629
  s 35 18
  s 70................291-3, 295, 296
  s 73 192
  Sched 1, Part II, paras 10, 11 11
  Part III....................394, 621
Trade Unions and Labour Relations Act 1974............................456
Finance Act 1975 257
  s 19 18
  Sched 4, para 7 136
Inheritance (Provisions for Family and Dependants) Act 1975 ...3, 10, 11, 18,
    ....129, 137, 228, 231, 233,
    ....531, 532, 564-7, 612
  s 1 ....532, 536
  ss 1-4 535
  s 2 570
    (1)(a), (3) 568
    (4) 570
  s 4 613
  s 7(1) 569
  s 9 570

Inheritance (Provisions for Family and Dependants) Act 1975—contd
  s 21(a)-(f) 569
  s 22(1) 231
Patents Act 1977 .....134, 308, 309, 311
  s 5(2) 325
  s 40 18
  s 75 331
Rent Act 1977 59
  s 123 449
Unfair Contract Terms Act 1977—
  s 11 477
Interpretation Act 1978—
  s 7 39
Changing Orders Act 1979—
  s 2 192
Housing Act 1980—
  ss 140-2 388
Contempt of Court Act 1981—
  s 4(19) 213
  s 14(1) 219
    (3)......................214, 219
  s 16(1)(a) 215
    (b) 216
Stamp Act 1981—
  s 13 261
    (4) 262
Supreme Court Act 1981 72
  s 3A 37
  s 18 244
  s 20(2) 233
  s 33 18
    (2) 621
  s 34(2) 621
  s 35A ....
    ....36, 354, 356, 464, 467
  s 37(3) 175
  s 39................181, 435, 436
  s 40 191
  s 40A 212
  s 49 388
  s 51(1) 271
  s 54 312
  s 61(1).....................474, 477
  s 65 235
  s 68 237
  s 117 550
  s 140(1), (a).....................225
    (b).............................226
  s 151 72
  s 152(4) 233
  Sched 1 ....3, 474, 477
    para 1(g) 526
  Sched 7 233
Criminal Justice Act 1982—
  s 9 214
Insurance Companies Act 1982 ....
    ....597, 598

Merchant Shipping (Liner Conferences)
Act 1982 625
Mental Health Act 1983 .....18, 66, 488
Part VII 166
Capital Transfer Act 1984—
s 225 255
County Court Act 1984—
s 23 231
s 32 232
s 40 ....232, 233
s 41 236
s 56 622
s 105(1) 232
Inheritance Tax Act 1984—
s 221 259
s 222 258
  (1), (3).......................259
s 225 257
ss 249(3), 251(2) 260
Trade Marks (Amendment) Act 1984
.................................312
Administration of Justice Act 1985—
s 15 36
s 20 ....526, 538
s 48 12
s 49(1)(b) 551
s 50 233
s 55 212
s 57 ....174, 491
Sched 1 36
Charities Act 1985................576
Companies Act 1985 ....
.............18, 37, 40, 581, 582, 588,
......589, 594, 595, 597, 598, 601, 605
s 138(1) 594, 596, 599
s 139(2) 594, 596, 599
s 425 ....591, 592
ss 456, 459 631
s 651 589
s 725 38

Companies Act 1985—*contd*
s 726 63
  (1) 35
Company Directors Disqualification
Act 1986 589
ss 2-4, 6 590
Drug Trafficking Offences Act 1986
.................................589
Family Law Act 1986—
Part I 626
Insolvency Act 1986 ....
......479, 581, 584-7, 590-3, 600, 631
s 8 ....591, 592
ss 8-27 600
s 18 594
ss 46(1),48 606
s 76 65
ss 122-130 605
s 127 588
s 132 606
s 231 ....591, 592
s 235 600
s 268(1)(a), (b) 603
s 287 603
Part I 591, 592
Landlord and Tenant Act 1987 ...413-6
s 22 414
s 27 415
Part II 415
Copyright, Designs and Patents
Act 1988 ....305-8, 312
s 51 307
s 100 306
ss 115, 152, 205..................307
Sched 1, para 19 307
Finance Act 1988—
s 6 422
Legal Aid Act 1988 ....271, 287
s 12 ....281, 282
Companies Act 1989 581

Table of Statutory Instruments

Land Registration Rules 1925 (SR & O No 1093) r 299 397
Trade Marks Rules 1938 (SR & O 661) 312
Design Rules 1949 (SI No 2368) 308
Rules of the Supreme Court 1965 (SI No 1776) 12, 51, 495
Ord 1, r 4(1) 237
    (2) 75, 228
Ord 3 48
    rr 2(2), (3), (5) 48
    r 3 .... 28, 30, 48
    rr 4, 5(1)–(3) 48
    r 6 .... 37, 46, 122, 162, 618
Ord 4, r 3 235
    r 5 235
    (1), (2) 234
    (4) 227–8
    r 9 238
Ord 5, r 2(a)–(c) 18
    r 3 18
    r 4 474–5
Ord 6 298
    r 1 19
    note 4 126
    r 2 20–21
    r 3 .... 62, 125
    r 6 23
    r 7 391
    r 8 .... 24, 76, 118, 379
Ord 7 .... 28, 51, 298
    r 3 .... 20–21.25
    r 4 .... 23, 76
    r 5(2) 227
    r 6 .... 24, 76, 118
Ord 8, r 2 17
    r 3(1) 250
    r 5 99
    r 35 228
Ord 9, r 2 17
    r 3 17
    (1) 228
    r 4 17

Rules of the Supreme Court 1965—*contd*
Ord 10 37
    r 1 23
    (2) 56
    (4) 38
    (11) 39
    r 4 371
    r 5 .... 23–4, 371
    r 10(3) 56
Ord 11 41
    r 1 .... 21, 44
    (a) 44
    r 4 76
    r 5 56
Ord 12, r 1(5) 47
    r 3 .... 30, 38, 299
    r 7 272
    r 9 25
Ord 13 528
    r 1 57
    (2) 37, 59
    (9) 275
    rr 2, 3 58
    r 4 .... 58, 373–4
    r 7 374
Ord 14 .... 16, 82, 234, 242, 282, 289, 311, 348, 352, 544, 618
    r 2(1) 82
    (3) 83
Ord 15, r 1 21
    (1) 61
    r 2(4) 270
    r 5 239
    (2) 528
    r 6 .... 31, 61, 74
    r 6A 72, 130
    (1) 129
    r 7 .... 10, 61, 65, 73–4, 126
    (4) 73
    r 8 126
    (1) 61
    r 12 .... 63, 65, 128

Table of Statutory Instruments

Rules of the Supreme Court 1965—
contd
- Ord 15, r 12(3) 63
  - r 13...65, 128, 485-6, 532, 538
    - (4).....................128
  - r 14 128
    - (1) 485, 486
  - r 15.....................72, 129
  - r 16......366, 474, 477-8, 537
  - r 20 30
- Ord 16.........................30
  - r 1 31
    - (1), (2) 31
  - r 2 76
    - (2).................31-2, 34
  - r 4(1) 31
  - r 8 132
- Ord 17, r 1 35
  - (1), (A) 34
  - r 2 35
    - (4)......................93
  - r 3 19
  - r 5(2) 97
- Ord 18, r 1 22-3
  - r 8(4)..................37, 59
  - r 19 45
- Ord 19.........................528
  - r 2 57
  - rr 3-5 58
- Ord 20, r 2 42
  - r 3 45
    - (*a*) 42
  - r 5 ....51, 61, 118
    - (1)......................42
    - (5)......................45
  - r 7 51
  - r 8 61
  - r 11 ....122-3, 148
  - r 12(1) 42
    - (2)......................45
- Ord 21 ....47, 530
  - r 2 153
    - (3A) 47
  - r 6 47
- Ord 22, r 1..............186, 189
  - r 2 189
  - r 3 188
  - r 4 182
  - r 14 273
- Ord 23, r 1(1) 63
  - (*a*).......................35
  - (3) 63
  - (19), (B) 35
- Ord 24, r 1(2) 75
  - r 2.....................29, 86
  - r 9 113
  - r 16 46

Rules of the Supreme Court 1965—
contd
- Ord 24, r 16(3) 46
- Ord 25 ....16, 29, 65, 128, 234, 299
  - r 1(7) 29
  - r 2(4) 162
  - r 7 134
    - (1), (*e*)..................29
  - r 8 ....30, 162
  - r 9(1), (3) 29
- Ord 26.........................85
  - rr 1,3.....................85
- Ord 28 ....21, 28, 51, 163
  - r 1 ....26, 51
  - r 1A 22, 25
    - (1).........24-5, 27, 157
    - (2).........24-5, 27-8
    - (3)-(5) 27-8
- Ord 28, r 2 22
  - (2) 28
  - (3) 121
  - r 4 16
    - (1) 26, 51, 56
    - (2)-(4)...................51
    - (5)......................16
  - r 5 51
  - r 7 ....51, 380
  - r 8 ....19, 51
    - (2).......................52
  - r 9.................51, 164
- Ord 29, r 1 176
  - r 1A 51
  - r 2 112
  - r 4 25
  - r 7A 18
  - Pt II......................275
- Ord 30, r 1 176
  - r 2(1), (3) 192
  - r 4(1)....................192
  - r 5 ....174, 177, 472
- Ord 31 ....178, 337-8
  - r 1..............177-8, 336
  - r 2(2) 430
- Ord 32, r 1 134
  - r 4(2)................26, 158
  - r 5 26
  - r 9.................9, 18, 21
    - (2).......................227
  - r 12...11, 159, 228-9, 234, 545
  - r 14 ....8, 11, 228
    - (2) 229, 234
    - (3) 7, 8, 11
    - (4) 7
  - rr 23-6 228
- Ord 33, r 1 ....162, 165
  - r 7 98
- Ord 34, r 2(1), (2) 162
  - r 3(3)....................162

Table of Statutory Instruments

Rules of the Supreme Court 1965—
contd

Ord 35, r 2	606
Ord 36, r 3(2), (4)	237
r 11	91-2
Ord 37	194
r 2	194
Ord 38, r 1(3)	275
r 2(3)	77, 90
r 2A	16, 29
r 9	87
r 11	489, 512
r 13	350
Ord 39, r 1	87
r 2(*a*)	88
Ord 41, r 1, paras 4-8	265
rr 2, 4	265
Ord 42, r 1	57-8
r 2	46, 408
(1), (2)	144
r 4	57, 121
r 6(1)	122
r 7	99
(3)	123
r 9(*b*)	148
Ord 43	14, 170-71, 173, 307, 456
r 2(2)	140
rr 7-9	174
Ord 44	170, 172-3, 180, 192, 241, 337, 456, 486, 530, 538, 541
r 2	546, 561
r 3	545-6
(1)	172-3
(*c*)	539
(2)	172
rr 4,5	545-6
rr 6, 7	545-6, 548
r 8	539, 545-6, 549
rr 9,10	545-6
r 11	120, 545-6
Ord 45, r 3	374
(2)	199, 403
r 5	39, 46, 458
r 7	39
(3)	39
(4)	39, 81, 124
Ord 47, r 7(1)	124
Ord 48	200
Ord 49	191-2, 209, 211
r 1	191
(1)	191
r 2	76, 191
r 3	211
r 10	212
r 11	5
rr 14(4), 15	19
Ord 52, r 1(3)	41
(4)	576

Rules of the Supreme Court 1965—
contd

Ord 52, r 4(3)	213
Ord 53	622
Ord 56	250
rr 7, 10	250
Ord 58, r 1	160, 240, 248, 250
r 2	241
(*b*)	194
r 3	241
rr 6, 7	244
Ord 59	241, 244, 312
r 3	242
r 4(1)	249
r 5	243
(1)	249
r 6(1)	243, 629
r 13	246
r 15	242, 249
r 17	312
r 20(2), (8)	224
Ord 62	289
r 2(4)	547
r 3(2)	272
(3)	42, 272-3
(6)	270
r 5	273
r 7(4)	272
r 8	275, 284
(1), (3)	275
r 9(*d*)	272
r 11	279
r 12	273
r 13	276
note 1	289
rr 14(1), 15(1), 16	273
rr 21-7	275
r 28	547
r 30	68
r 31	547
App 1	275
App 3	212, 289
Ord 63, r 11	228
Ord 65	38
r 4	24, 40, 76
Ord 66, rr 1,2	163
Ord 75, r 5(1)	629
Ord 76, r 1	526
r 2	10, 21
(1)	18, 227
r 4(2)	529
rr 5(2), 7	528
r 12	530
r 13	529
r 14	550
Ord 77, r 9	64
r 13	167
Ord 78, r 2	234

Table of Statutory Instruments

Rules of the Supreme Court 1965— contd
Ord 80 ....40, 66, 70
  r 2(3) 66
  r 3..........................68-9, 76
  rr 4, 5 69
  r 10..........................20, 67
  r 11(3) 227
  r 12 190
Ord 81, rr 1, 2 64
  r 3(6), (8) 66
  rr 4(1), 9 127
  r 10 192
Ord 85 ....145, 502, 541
  r 1..........................486, 540
  r 2..........................
  ....484-6, 537, 541, 546-7, 563
    (3) 177-8
    (d) 515
  r 3..........................537
    (2) 501
  r 5..........................485, 546
Ord 86 ...7, 14, 16, 76, 82-3, 119, 163,
  228-9, 242, 266, 348-9, 352, 357, 618
  r 2 349
  r 3 228-9
Ord 88 ....4, 10, 19, 41,
  59, 163, 199, 227, 391, 395, 398
  r 1(1), (b) 180
    (e) 184
  r 3 391
  r 6 59
Ord 91 256
  r 2 ....18, 259
    (5) 259
  r 4 256
  r 5 260
Ord 92 ....6, 182, 184
  r 2 182
  r 5..........................20, 76
    (3) 182
Ord 93.........................337
  r 3 18
  r 4 ....337, 484, 488
  r 6 ....18, 484, 496
  r 10(2) 166, 244, 396
  r 15 388
  r 16 250
Ord 97, r 2 378
  r 3 ....18, 227, 405-6
  rr 4, 5 405
  r 9 410
  r 9A..........................383
  r 10(1) 411
  r 11(2) 382
Ord 99, rr 1, 2.....................532
  r 3 ....18, 532
    (1) 228

Rules of the Supreme Court 1965— contd
Ord 99, r 4 532
  r 5 532-3
  r 6 532
  r 7 ....5, 532, 565
  r 8 ....10, 532, 534
  rr 9, 10 532
  r 11 532-3
Ord 100, r 3 312
Ord 102.........................581-2
  r 1, para 4 582
  rr 2, 3 ....18, 582
  r 4 582
  r 5 18
  rr 6, 9-11 582
Ord 103.........................308
Ord 104.........................308
  r 2(1) 12
  r 3..........................311, 326
  4 5(11) 18
  r 11 319
  r 13 18
  r 14 331
Ord 106, r 5 18
Ord 107.........................232
  r 1 234
    (4) 233-4
Ord 108.........................576
  r 1 18
  r 3(1) 573
  r 4 576
Ord 113 ......4, 7, 10, 18-20, 24-5, 41
  134, 157, 163, 229, 372-3, 617
  r 1..........................370, 372
  r 2 370
  r 3 370-71
  r 4 ....24, 370
Ord 114.........................254
Appendix A 19
County Courts Jurisdiction (Inheritance: Provisions for Family and Dependants) Order 1978 (SI No 176).......................536
Patents Rules 1978 (SI No 216) 308
Rules of the Supreme Court (Writ and Appearance) 1979 (SI No 1716).....19
District Registries Order 1980 (SI No 1216).......................227
Legal Aid (General) Regulations 1980 (SI No 1894)—
  r 84 277
  r 127(a) 281
  r 127(b) 282
  r 143 281
County Court Rules 1981 (SI No 1687) 232, 235
Ord 13, r 1 233

County Court Rules 1981—*contd*
  Ord 18, r 1 47
  Ord 24, rr 1-11 373
  Ord 25, r 11 232
Rules of the Supreme Court
  (Amendment No 2) 1982
  (SI No 1111)........167, 227, 229, 240
  r 53 ......172, 486, 530, 538, 541, 546
  Sched 1 529
Rules of the Supreme Court
  (Amendment No 3) 1982
  (SI No 1786) 28, 162, 182
  r 3 ....28, 30
  r 10 47
Supreme Court Fees (Amendment)
  Order 1982 (SI No 1707)...........624
Attachment of Debt (Expenses) Order
  1983 (SI No 1621)................212
Judicial Trustee Rules 1983 (SI No 370)
  ....227, 491
  r 2(1) 492
  r 3(5)(6) 493
  r 4(1)-(4) 492
  r 5 493
  r 6 ....493, 510, 522
  rr 7, 8 493
  rr 9, 10 ....174, 493
  r 11 ....493, 522
     (11)(*a*) 174
  r 12 ....174, 493
     (5).......................509, 510
  r 13................174, 493, 510
     (2).........................509
  rr 14, 16 494
  r 17 495
     (1) 228
Insolvency Rules 1986 (SI No 1925)
  ....603, 605
  r 2.2(1)........................591-2
  r 2.4............................606
  r 2.10(1)(4) 592
  rr 4.14, 4.25 606
  r 4.27 601
     (1).........................600
  r 6.4 603

Insolvency Rules 1986—*contd*
  r 6.5(4)..........................603
  r 6.11............................603
  rr 6.67-6.72 603
  Pt 4 605
  Form 2.1.........................606
  Form 2.4A 592
  Form 4.1.........................605
  Form 4.2......................605-6
  Form 4.3.........................605
  Form 4.15........................601
  Forms 6.1-6.3 603
  Forms 6.7-6.10 604
Landlord and Tenant Act 1954, Part II
  (Assured Tenancies) (Notices)
  Regulations 1986 (SI No 2181)
  Forms 1, 8 387
Court Fund Rules 1987 (SI No 821)—
  r 7 187
  rr 15, 16 186
Insolvency (Amendment) Regulations
  1987 (SI No 1959) 603
Insolvency (Amendment) Rules 1987
  (SI No 1919)......................605
Insolvent Companies (Disqualification
  of Unfit Directors) Proceedings Rules
  1987 (SI No 2023)—
  r 9 590
Civil Legal Aid (General) Regulations
  1989 (SI No 339)—
  r 145 282
Insolvency (Amendment) Rules 1989
  (SI No 397).......................603
Rules of the Supreme Court
  (Amendment No 4) 1989 (SI No 2427)—
  rr 19, 20 16
  r 24 16
  Ord 5, r 4 15
County Court (Amendment No 3) Rules
  1990 (SI No 1764)—
  r 12(3) 264
Local Government Finance (Repeals,
  Savings and Consequential
  Amendments) Order 1990
  (SI No 776).......................373

Abbreviations

AP	The Annual Practice 1991
Atkin	Atkin's Encyclopaedia of Court Forms (2nd edn)
Halsbury	Halsbury's Laws of England (4th edn unless 3rd is indicated)
Ord	Order made under the Rules of the Supreme Court
RSC	Rules of the Supreme Court
RCJ	Royal Courts of Justice, Strand, WC2.
Chancery chambers	The offices of the Chancery Division
Chancery district registries	The district registries of Birmingham, Bristol, Cardiff, Leeds, Liverpool, Manchester, Newcastle-upon-Tyne and Preston.

Part I

Chancery Practice Generally

Chapter One

Chancery Chambers— Introduction

1. Breadth of jurisdiction

The Chancery Division derives its powers from Lord Chancellors throughout the ages and they, having an interest in the executive and the legislature as well as the judiciary, gave the court very extensive jurisdiction. Moreover, with the Queen's Bench Division in the earlier years restricting itself to money judgments, this left a considerable gap in the requirements of the public for suitable relief from the courts. The Chancery Division filled the gap, providing specialised orders, declaratory judgments, and other forms of relief. It also formed new and specialised procedures to fit the relief sought. Practitioners today should make the best use of the flexible procedures now available in the division. Through these procedures has grown up a court of unusual breadth, and used with knowledge and wisdom, the Chancery practitioner can find an effective answer to peculiar and unusual problems. Its procedures can even be used with effect in single debt cases to force recalcitrant debtors to address questions prior to the trial reducing the cost of recovery.

The numbers of judges and masters in the division has changed from time to time but presently consists of 12 judges and five masters. The division is situated on the 5th, 6th and 7th floors in Thomas More Building (a name appropriate to the Chancery court), at the Royal Courts of Justice and is serviced by a principal officer, senior and higher executive officers and numerous clerical staff. The division has statutory jurisdiction relating to the Law of Property Act 1925, The Settled Land Act 1925, the Trustee Act 1925, the Landlord and Tenant Act 1927 Part I and the Landlord and Tenant Act 1954 Part II, the Leasehold Property (Repairs) Act 1938, the Leasehold Reform Act 1967 and the Inheritance (Provision for Family and Dependants) Act 1975, the Patents Acts 1949-1988, and the Land Registration Acts 1925-1988. There is also specifically assigned to the Chancery Division by the Supreme Court Act 1981, Sched 1, all causes and matters relating to:

(1) the sale, exchange or partition of land, or the raising of charges on land,

(2) the redemption or foreclosure of mortgages,
  (3) the execution of trusts,
  (4) the administration of the estates of deceased persons,
  (5) bankruptcy,
  (6) the dissolution of partnerships or the taking of partnership or other accounts,
  (7) the rectification, setting aside or cancellation of deeds or other instruments in writing,
  (8) probate business, other than non-contentious or common form business,
  (9) patents, trademarks, registered designs or copyright,
  (10) the appointment of a guardian of a minor's estate

and all causes and matters involving the exercise of the High Court's jurisdiction under the enactments relating to companies.

Its jurisdiction also includes actions for summary possession (Ord 113) and actions by mortgagees for possession (Ord 88).

It is also concerned with enforcement, including charging orders, garnishee orders, equitable enforcement by appointment of a receiver and orders for sale.

The functions of the division are not only judicial but, for some matters peculiar to the Chancery Division, supervisory and protective.

2. The structure of Chancery chambers

Four sections have been established to deal with the transaction of business in Chancery chambers, namely:

  (1) The Chancery chambers (registry), which deals with court files (ie those which are maintained in the Chancery Division), master's summonses and the issue of process.
  (2) The drafting section, which deals with the drafting of orders. Officers of this section sitting in court are known as associates.
  (3) The listing section, which deals with setting down all cases except motions and listing all cases except motions and patent actions.
  (4) The accounts section, which deals with the examination of accounts and any certificates arising from the accounts.

The Schedule to Practice Direction (Chancery Chambers) [1982] 1 WLR 1189, sets out a full list of the various types of business and the appropriate room for inquiries or the lodging of papers. These are as follows:

Chancery Chambers—Introduction

The Chancery registry

The address of the registry is: Rooms 307/308, 3rd Floor, Thomas More Building, Royal Courts of Justice, Strand, London WC2.
The registry deals with:

(1) Issue of all originating process.
(2) Amendment of process.
(3) Payment of fees.
(4) Filing affidavits.
(5) Issue of masters' summonses.
(6) Inquiries regarding masters' summonses.
(7) Bespeaking files for *ex parte* applications to masters.
(8) Applications to serve out jurisdiction.
(9) Filing stop notices (RSC, Ord 50, r 11).
(10) Filing testamentary documents in contested probate cases.
(11) Filing grants lodged under RSC, Ord 99, r 7.
(12) Filing acknowledgments of service.
(13) Certification of documents for use abroad.
(14) Applications for office copy documents, including orders.
(15) Judgments by default.
(16) Filing affidavits relating to funds paid into court under the Trustee Act 1925.
(17) Compulsory Purchase Act 1965 and the Lands Clauses Consolidation Act 1845.
(18) Notices of appeal from decisions of masters.
(19) All pre-paid court fees and stamped documents.
(20) The lodging or filing of any documents or papers to be included in the court file, not listed above.

The drafting/associates section

The address of the drafting section is: Rooms 504-514, 5th Floor, Thomas More Building, Royal Courts of Justice, Strand, London WC2.
The drafting section deals with:

(1) Masters' orders drawn by solicitors.
(2) Agreed minutes of order.
(3) Questions arising on orders made after September 30, 1989.
(4) Allocation of masters' appointments dates and all queries relating to the work of the masters, and requests for *ex parte* hearings, and applications to serve out of the jurisdiction—in rooms 709/710. The section is headed by a senior civil service lawyer and staffed by the associates, who attend the judges in court.

The listing section

The address of the listing section is: Rooms 412-414, 4th Floor, Thomas More Building, Royal Courts of Justice, Strand, London WC2.

The listing section is in the charge of the clerk of the lists, who is responsible for most of the listing in the Chancery Division. Under him is the cause clerk, who is the proper officer to receive and enter all documents received on setting down an action for trial. In the case of an originating summons or ordinary summons, the original originating summons of summons is handed to the master.

While the clerk of the lists is in charge of listing, he carries out his work under the direction of the judge in charge of the lists, to whom all parties have a right to apply in any dispute or if any problem on listing arises. The clerk of the lists deals with the listing of patent business and the revenue paper, but not motions or companies business (except when the clerk to the motions judge is not available).

The accounts section

The address of the accounts section is: Rooms 415/416, 4th Floor, Thomas More Building, Royal Courts of Justice, Strand, London WC2.

The accounts section deals with:

(1) Bills of costs for assessment.
(2) Small payments (Ord 92).
(3) Sales by private treaty or auction.
(4) Settlement of advertisements.
(5) Settlement of payment and lodgment schedules (otherwise than part of order).
(6) Accounts of receivers, judicial trustees, guardians and administrators.
(7) Applications relating to security set by the court.
(8) References to taxing masters.
(9) Matters arising out of accounts and inquiries ordered by the court.

The court file

A court file is maintained in the registry for each case. The documents relevant to a particular case will be kept on the file, including the originating process, copies of civil aid certificates, acknowledgments of service, notices of change of solicitors, summonses, affidavits, pleadings and orders. The master will make his notes on the file and the associate in court will complete a case note, which will also be filed in respect of each hearing including motions. The court file will be sent to the master when required by him. It will also be available in court on the trial of any action or interlocutory application, and it will be used by the drafting section when drawing up any order of a judge or master.

On any *ex parte* application it is necessary for the practitioner to bespeak the file from Chancery chambers. The application should be made before 12 noon the previous day unless there is an emergency, in which case, the court has always been found to be very helpful.

3. Masters and judges—general

The broad demarcation in years past between the jurisdiction of the masters and the judges was that while masters were empowered to make nearly any order which might be made by a judge in chambers (Ord 32, r 14(3) formerly 14(4)), the masters' orders were mostly administrative and the judges' orders mostly judicial; but for many years the judges have indicated by way of practice directions the widely differing types of orders comprised in which are many for judicial decisions which they consider it proper to be made by the masters. Certain orders are directed not to be made by the master without authority; there are other orders which it is not the practice for the master to make.

The matters which are dealt with by a judge and those which are normally dealt with by a master or district registrar are set out in the Supreme Court Practice 1982, para 32/14/2. The following can be taken as a fair guide.

4. Judges

The judge may reserve any matter to himself, authorise any matter to be decided by a master, or rule on any matter which a master could have ruled upon.

Judgments and orders only for the judge in court

(1) All final judgments in contested hearings for trial in open court in writ actions.
(2) All orders on contested hearings in actions commenced by originating summons if that summons expressly requires a judicial decision on law (Ord 32, r 14(3)).
(3) All orders for injunctions, except injunctions ancillary to an order for appointment of a receiver by way of equitable execution and injunctions by consent.
(4) Orders for specific performance (except summary orders under Ord 86 for which the plaintiff does not rely on part performance).
(5) Orders for summary possession of land in trespass cases (Ord 113).

(6) Final orders under the Variation of Trusts Act 1958 except when the only relief sought is for removal of a protective trust.
(7) Orders on an originating summons expressly requesting determination of questions of construction (Ord 32, r 14(3)).
(8) Orders for a new lease under the Landlord and Tenant Act 1954 Part II (ss 23–46).
(9) Orders comprising probate actions where (which may or may not be the case) the compromise involves an order pronouncing against a particular will.
(10) Orders for the dissolution or winding up of any partnership in cases where the area of dispute goes beyond 'accountancy'.

For the judge in chambers

(1) Orders for the appointment of trustees other than judicial trustees (not being cases where the appointment arises from disability), in which the trust fund or property is significantly in excess (as at present) of £30,000 and a trustee is to be superseded without his consent (Ord 32, r 14 and Practice Direction of 24 May 1976 [1976] 1 WLR 637).
(2) Orders approving purchases of property by trustees and personal representatives other than in clear cases.
(3) Orders vesting property or directing a conveyance whenever there is pending an application for a new trustee.
(4) Orders for kin inquiries when necessity for the order is not clear.
(5) Orders approving compromises on behalf of persons under disability when the value of the person's interest in the fund, or if there be no fund, the maximum amount of the claim as certified by counsel, significantly exceeds £30,000.
(6) Orders sanctioning any compromise or arrangement other than those which the master is empowered to make.
(7) Orders for payment out of funds in court where devolution of the trust fund has to be proved and it significantly exceeds £30,000.
(8) Orders binding persons on whom service of a judgment or order for accounts and inquiries has been dispensed with.
(9) Orders for the maintenance or advancement of an infant under a trust (if notwithstanding the wide powers in ss 31–32 of the Trustee Act 1925 an order should be necessary) if the case is not clear.

5. Masters

Historically a chancery master has not been an assistant judge like a district judge of county courts but the deputy of the judge pronouncing orders in the judge's name. In modern times, the functions and powers of chancery masters have been equated to those of Queen's Bench Masters and they are now recognised as having personal judicial powers inherently. Any 'cause or matter' may with the consent of the parties be tried by a master instead of an official referee (Ord 32, r 9); the conduct of such a trial may require a hearing in open court but with this uncommon exception all orders made by masters are in chambers.

Judgments and orders likely to be made by the master (in chambers)

(1) Appointing judicial trustees, or appointing a trustee or additional trustee when a trustee is under disability.
(2) Appointing trustees except where the trust fund or property is significantly in excess of £30,000 and a trustee is to be superseded without his consent.
(3) Under s 1(1) of the Variation of Trusts Act 1958 to the extent of removing protective trusts when the interest of the principal beneficiary has not failed or deteriorated.
(4) Orders under s 59 of the Trustee Act 1925 when a trustee cannot be found.
(5) Orders pursuant to s 27 of the Leasehold Reform Act 1967 when a landlord cannot be found.
(6) Orders on joint application under s 38(4) of the Landlord and Tenant Act 1954 to authorise an agreement excluding the provisions of ss 24-28 or for the surrender of a tenancy before its natural expiration unless there exists the possibility of oppression or coercion.
(7) For interim rent under s 54 of the Landlord and Tenant Act 1954 (though in practice the interim rent is usually assessed by the judge when he assesses the rent under the new tenancy).
(8) Vesting property or directing a conveyance, unless there is pending an application for a new trustee when it must be dealt with by a judge.
(9) Orders relating to straightforward kin inquiries.
(10) Orders approving compromise on behalf of persons under disability when the value of the person's interest in the fund, or if there be no fund, the maximum amount of the claim does not significantly exceed £30,000.
(11) Orders for payment out of funds (except where devolution of the trust fund must be proved and the part of the fund proposed to be dealt with significantly exceeds £30,000). The master if himself making the order must be satisfied that there is no real risk of the payment out prejudicing parties to any later application in respect of the remainder of the fund.
(12) Orders made summarily for specific performance except where part performance must be relied on.
(13) Authorising pursuant to s 57 of the Trustee Act 1925 and s 64 of the Settled Land Act 1925 in clear cases the purchase of trust property by trustees and personal representatives and

authorising the acquisition of property not authorised by the trust instrument.
(14) Authorising solicitor trustees and trust corporations to charge remuneration for acting as trustees (in the case of corporate trustees not to exceed their published rates).
(15) For the administration of estates and the execution of trusts.
(16) Orders under the Inheritance (Provision for Family and Dependants) Act 1975 including orders under s 2 of the Act for extending time and for interim maintenance unless likely to involve a long or complex issue of fact or law (see note 6 to Ord 99, r 8 in AP vol 1).
(17) Giving leave to trustees and personal representatives to bring or defend proceedings (a 'Re Beddoe Order').
(18) Under s 50(2) and (3) of the Law of Property Act 1925 where the court can declare property free of incumbrances on payment by the mortgagor of a sufficient sum into court.
(19) For leave to serve out of the jurisdiction.
(20) For substituted service.
(21) For leave to file any document out of time.
(22) Approving acts of receivers.
(23) To carry on proceedings, between the continuing parties where there has been a transmission of interest (Ord 15, r 7).
(24) In garnishee proceedings including orders absolute.
(25) Charging land by way of execution.
(26) Appointing a next friend or guardian *ad litem*.
(27) For leave to take proceedings to enforce any right of re-entry or forfeiture or covenant for repairs under the Leasehold Property (Repairs) Act 1938.
(28) For the foreclosure of any mortgage or for possession, or for enforcing any charge or lien (Ord 88).
(29) For the dissolution or winding up of any partnership.
(30) For summary judgment (other than for relief by way of injunction or prohibitory order).
(31) For summary possession of land other than trespass cases under Ord 113.
(32) For leave *ex parte* to issue a writ in a probate action (Ord 76, r 2).
(33) For the appointment of receivers, and injunctions ancillary to the appointment of a receiver by way of equitable execution when the parties are unwilling to consent to an undertaking.
(34) For directions in *inter partes* litigation including directions special to technical or specialised proceedings either on the hearing or adjourned hearing of an originating summons or on a master's summons issued after writ proceedings.
(35) Directing the steps to be taken to fulfil an order eg conveyancing directions consequent upon an order for specific performance.
(36) Declaring result of audit of receiver's accounts.
(37) Certifying an assessment of damages.

(Authorities: Ord 32, r 14 (AP vol 1 32/14/2); Practice Directions (Chancery: Masters' Powers) [1975] 1 WLR 129; (Chancery: Masters' Powers) (No 2) [1975] 1 WLR 405; (Chancery: Masters' Powers) (No 3) [1976] 1 WLR 637; (Chancery: Masters' Powers) (No 4) [1977] 1 WLR 1019); (Chancery: Procedure No 2 of 1982 [1983] 1 WLR 4 extending the masters' powers to cases in which the monetary amount does not exceed £30,000).

Provisos to the above are that where a party who is to appear before a master considers the matter to be one suitable to be referred to a judge under Ord 32, r 12 (as applied by Ord 32, r 14(3), he shall mention it to the master before the hearing and seek directions thereon. Where an application is likely to last more than two days, it will normally be referred to a judge.

The masters are not to deal with the following

Subject to para 2 the masters of the Chancery Division 'shall not deal' with the following matters and proceedings:

(1) making orders for specific performance of repairing covenants and where it is necessary for the plaintiff to rely on acts of part performance;
(2) making orders for an injunction;
(3) approvals of compromises (other than on applications under the Inheritance (Provision for Family and Dependants) Act 1975) (a) on behalf of a person under disability where that person's interest in a fund, or if there is no fund, the maximum amount of the claim, exceeds £30,000, and (b) on behalf of absent, unborn and unascertained persons;
(4) making declarations other than in plain cases;
(5) making orders under Part II of Sched 1 to the Solicitors Act 1974 except under paras 10 and 11 of that Sched;
(6) making final orders under s 1(1) of the Variation of Trusts Act 1958 save for the removal of protective trusts where the interest of the principal beneficiary has not failed or determined;
(7) giving leave to executors, administrators and trustees to bring or defend proceedings or to continue the prosecution or defence of proceedings, and granting an indemnity for costs out of the trust estate, other than in plain cases;
(8) granting an indemnity for costs out of the assets of a company on the application of a minority shareholder or minority shareholders bringing a derivative action, other than in plain cases;
(9) making orders for rectification, other than for rectification of the register under the Land Registration Act 1925 in plain cases;

(10) making orders to vacate entries in the register under the Land Charges Act 1972 other than in plain cases;
(11) making final orders on applications under s 19 of the Leasehold Reform Act 1967;
(12) making final orders under s 48 of the Administration of Justice Act 1985;
(13) making final orders on applications under ss 21 and 25, Law of Property Act 1969;
(14) making orders under the Landlord and Tenant Act 1972 and the Landlord and Tenant Act 1954 except (a) by consent, (b) orders for interim rents under s 24A of the Landlord and Tenant Act 1954 and (c) on applications to authorise agreements under s 38(4) of the Landlord and Tenant Act 1954;
(15) making orders in proceedings taken in the Patents Court pursuant to Ord 104, r 2(1) except (a) consent orders and (b) orders on summonses for extension of time.

With specific authority of a judge

Practice Direction (No 4 of 1989) issued by the Vice-Chancellor on December 5, 1989, para 2, provides that in a special case, with specific authority of a judge, the master may make an order which the judge has power to make in chambers, except one required by RSC to be made only by a judge.

The allocation of cases to masters

Cases are now allocated according to the last digit of the action number as follows:

Last digit	Name of master
8 or 9	Chief Master (Munrow)
6 or 7	Master Cholmondeley-Clarke
4 or 5	Master Dyson
2 or 3	Master Gowers
0 or 1	Master Barratt

The location of masters

The masters are located as follows:

Room no (6th floor)	Name of Master
607	Chief Master Munrow
609	Master Gowers
605	Master Barratt
611	Public waiting room
705	Deputy Master

Room no (7th floor)	Name of master and masters' appointment clerks
708	Master Cholmondeley-Clarke
706	Master Dyson
707	Public waiting room

Chapter Two

Commencement and Conduct of an Action

1. Introduction

The basic elements of civil proceedings of the type classified formerly as *'inter partes'* are some form of originating process accompanied or followed by a statement of the facts or allegations upon which the plaintiff bases his claim and by a prayer for the order or declaration which he seeks from the court. An opponent to such proceedings will in turn give his version of the facts and set out what he seeks by way of cross-prayer. He may deny the allegations of the plaintiff, that is, traverse them, or agree with them but put another explanation on them, ie plead confession and avoidance, or may say simply that he does not admit them, thereby putting the plaintiff to proof. The term *'inter partes'* used in much modern litigation may be equivocal in that the titles 'plaintiff' and 'defendant', although they continue in use, are often applied to parties who are not in conflict. Such parties may, for example, be merely asking the court to approve some dealing or arrangement which they both desire; in such a case the adversarial element implicit in an exchange of allegations will be absent. In other cases a party is simply producing a document to the court and asking for its construction as a matter of law and here again, once the proceedings have been initiated, the process will be one of putting undisputed material before the court. There are also matters dealt with in the Chancery Division which are only administrative, for example directing and considering accounts and inquiries.

Whilst the Rules of the Supreme Court apply equally to the Chancery and Queen's Bench Divisions, there are Orders which relate specifically to Chancery. Order 43 which relates to accounts and inquiries and Ord 86 relating to summary judgment in actions for specific performance, are examples which are specific to the division. Moreover, there are a considerable number of Practice Directions, although fortunately those which are no longer of practical use have recently been formally discarded.

So far as possible, all current Practice Directions have been incorporated into the text. They can be found in the Supreme Court Practice, vol 2, Part 3B. Some of them are relatively unchanging, and of long standing, whilst others are constant in principle, but have to be varied in detail to take account of changing circumstances—an example is those relating to procedures for trial out of London. A complete index was published in 1982 and this is given in an Appendix, and inserted therein are those commonly used Practice Directions which have been issued since the index was published. As and when Practice Directions are issued, they are reproduced in legal journals, and in particular in the Law Society's *Digest* which accompanies gratis *the Gazette* issued to all practising solicitors; the Digests are kept, separately, at the Law Society's Library, though they are not in any of the Inn Libraries. *Law Notes*, a magazine published monthly by the College of Law, also gives the Practice Directions, their yearly index showing them under 'Chancery Procedure', and the Practice Directions, as and when they are issued, being shown in their section of 'New Orders'. Most, if not all, Practice Directions will find themselves in due course in the All England Law Reports.

It is to be noted that the heading or entitlement of any particular Practice Direction often does not give an indication of its contents, which may comprise a proliferation of miscellaneous items besides the one given in the heading. For example, 'Practice Direction (Chancery Applications: Change of Name) (No 1 of 1984)' covers applications for summary judgment and Notices of Appeal.

2. Selection of originating process

Where the proceedings are *inter partes* in the adversarial sense, a decision has often to be made whether they should be commenced by writ of summons or originating summons. The latter will set out the prayer, often with a reference to a specific statute, and will be accompanied by an affidavit which presents the facts surrounding and supporting the plaintiff's case. If contested the affidavit will be followed by the defendant's affidavit and by the plaintiff's further affidavit in reply. Thus the evidence is on record in the form of affidavits prior to any substantial hearing; formal pleadings are eliminated and in many instances the matter is disposed of in chambers or else set down in the 'non-witness list' for trial. Because the originating summons procedure has a provision for discovery, it is often used with good effect to shorten the interlocutory aspects of the litigation and bring the matter to the court's attention the more quickly. If there are points of substance in dispute it is probable that pleadings and discovery are necessary and will be ordered.

Basically an action is more appropriate to be begun by originating summons where the matter is one of construction, or when there is no substantial dispute of fact (Ord 5, r 4 RSC (Amendment No 4) 1989 (SI 1989/2427) empowers the court, in proceedings begun by originating summons, to order affidavits or particulars of any claim to stand as informal pleadings, and enables the court to require 'points of claim' to be provided (r 24). A writ of summons, which is either accompanied by an indorsement or else followed by a statement of claim, is generally more appropriate when there is likely to be contention on the facts, as the court is then better enabled to contrast these and thus to identify the issues. A writ of summons may also be appropriate where the plaintiff anticipates that he/she may be able to have recourse to the summary procedure for judgment (Ord 14) available in actions for debt or in actions for specific performance under Ord 86. Subject to these considerations, there used to be the desirability of issuing a writ to achieve an element of surprise, especially in cases alleging fraud or duress (the oral considerations being disclosed in writ cases at the hearing); though new provisions as to exchange of witnesses' statements may have qualified this. An 'acid test' may be whether it is possible to discover from affidavits how a case is being put, in which case an originating summons is appropriate, if not, a writ is called for, but this old test again is now much attenuated by the introduction of exchange of witnesses' statements which was introduced by Ord 38, r 2A.

The court may give directions under Ord 28, r 4 concerning various matters including the filing of evidence in proceedings commenced by originating summons in the same way as it may give Directions under Ord 25 or otherwise in proceedings commenced by writ. Under Ord 28, r 4(5), the court may, at any stage, direct that any affidavit or any particulars stated in an affidavit shall stand.

There used to be a discretionary power to grant leave to administer interrogatories, and the principle followed was not to allow them if they were directed as to the evidence of the party interrogated, or where they were merely 'fishing'; the position is now changed by virtue of rr 19 and 20 of the Rules of the Supreme Court (Amendment No 4) 1989 (SI 1989/2427) which came into force as of February 1990. Interrogatories may now be administered, on not more than two occasions, without a court order.

In certain cases a plaintiff is required to issue either a petition or an originating motion, or an originating summons or a writ as the case may be. A full list of the proceedings which must be commenced by petition is given in Halsbury, vol 37, para 140. Examples of proceedings which must be commenced by notice of originating motion are given in AP, vol 1 8/1-5/2 and listed fully in Halsbury, vol 37, para 137.

Exchange of witnesses' statements (Ord 38, r 2A)

A far reaching change has been introduced for the simultaneous exchange of the witnesses' statements on an 'exchange date', thereby eliminating the 'surprise' elements, and whilst an order for such exchange can be made at any stage, it is likely to be made on a summons for directions. The statement of the witness which will include the plaintiff or defendant, must contain only facts within the witness's own knowledge, and no evidence may be lead from that witness the substance of which has not been included in the statement served, except if it is new matter, by consent, or with the leave of the court. The statements which represent the witness's evidence in chief should be in narrative form and in chronological order, and in the very language and words which the witness himself uses. The statements should be in book format, following continuously from page to page, both sides numbered at the bottom, in compliance with Practice Direction (Evidence: Documents), para 41/11/1 of the Supreme Court Practice. The statement will normally be directed to be signed. The statement itself is the witness's evidence in chief, and the witness is called for cross-examination.

Petitions

No specific form of petition is prescribed, but a petition must contain a concise statement of the nature of the claim made or the relief or remedy required. It should be entitled 'In the Chancery Division' and 'In the matter of the Act [under which the application is made]' and of the property, person or document to which it relates. It must conclude with the names of the persons to be served therewith or, if there is no such person, a statement to that effect (Ord 9, r 2). A petition may be presented in the district registry of Leeds, Liverpool, Manchester, Newcastle-upon-Tyne, Preston, Birmingham, Cardiff or Bristol: otherwise it must be presented in the chancery registry (rooms 307/308). Two copies must be left, the original being returned to the petitioner or his solicitor (Ord 9, r 3). On presentation, a day and time for the hearing of the petition will be fixed, allowing, unless the court otherwise directs, not less than seven clear days between service and hearing (Ord 9, r 4). Any affidavit in support must be filed and a copy supplied to each party to be served.

Originating motions

These are oral applications heard in open court. They may be *ex parte* in case of urgency but otherwise are preceded by a notice of motion allowing not less than two clear days between service of the notice and the date of the hearing unless the court, upon an *ex parte* application, gives leave for 'short notice' (Ord 8, r 2). The procedure for the issue and hearing of originating motions is contained in Practice Direction (Chancery: Originating Notice of Motion: case stated and similar proceedings) [1984] 1 WLR 1216. The notice of motion (AP, vol 2, Appendix A, Form 13) must include a concise statement of the nature of the claim or the relief or remedy sought. It is issued and served in the same manner (with any necessary modifications) as a writ or originating summons. Any supporting affidavit must be filed and a copy supplied to each party to be served. In a simple case the hearing of the motion may, by agreement between the parties, be treated as a trial of the action in which case the court may hear oral evidence on both sides. The notice may be issued out of the Royal Courts of Justice or out of the district registry of Leeds, Liverpool, Manchester, Newcastle-upon-Tyne, Preston, Birmingham, Cardiff or Bristol. If relief is not sought under an originating motion, it may if appropriate be sought by a motion in the action which may be served at any stage after appearance has been entered or time has elapsed for appearance. Evidence on motion is always by affidavit.

Proceedings which must be commenced by writ of summons

These include actions for relief or remedy of any tort, other than trespass upon land (Ord 5, r 2(*a*)); actions based upon allegations of fraud (Ord 5, r 2(*b*)); actions for damages for breach of duty resulting in death, personal injury or damage to property (Ord 5, r 2(*c*)); contentious probate actions (Ord 76, r 2(1)); actions for infringement of a patent (Ord 104, r 5(11)); and (in practice) actions for specific performance.

Originating summonses

An originating summons must be used in applications to the High Court or to a judge thereof (other than applications in pending proceedings) under any Act except where, by the rules of the court or by or under any Act, the application in question is expressly required or authorised to be made by some other means (Ord 5, r 3). Acts under which applications are made include: Supreme Court Act 1981, s 33 (Ord 29, r 7A); Mental Health Act 1983, s 139 (Ord 32, r 9); Finance Act 1975, s 19 (Ord 91, r 2); Electricity (Supply) Act 1919 (Ord 93, r 3); Variation of Trusts Act 1958 (Ord 93, r 6); Landlord and Tenant Acts 1927 Part I and 1954 Part II (Ord 97, r 3); Leasehold Property (Repairs) Act 1938; Inheritance (Provision for Family and Dependants) Act 1975 (Ord 99, r 3); Companies Act 1985 (Ord 102, rr 2, 3, 5); Patents Act 1977, s 40 (Ord 104, r 13); Solicitors Act 1974, s 35 (Ord 106, r 5); and Charities Act 1960 (Ord 108, r 1). For a list of non-statutory applications which are to be commenced by originating summons and not writ see Halsbury, vol 37, para 128. There are nearly 40 such proceedings, and they include applications for discovery before action commenced, applications with respect to funds in court (unless in a pending matter) for the variation of trusts, proceedings relating to business tenancies, applications under the Inheritance (Provision for Family and Dependants) Act 1975, many applications relating to companies, charity proceedings and summary proceedings under RSC, Ord 113 against wrongful occupiers.

Proceedings which should have been brought by writ and have been brought by originating summons may proceed on an order that the proceedings continue as if the action had been commenced by

COMMENCEMENT AND CONDUCT OF AN ACTION 19

writ. Such an order will often provide that the affidavits filed should stand as the pleadings (Ord 28, r 8). A similar order may also be made in those cases where the originating summons has been correctly issued, for example in a claim under a statute, but the statement of the issues is more appropriate to be dealt with by pleadings. Similarly, wheresoever a writ has been issued, an order may be made that there be trial without pleadings if it is a case which might better have been commenced by originating summons, but while such orders are made in the commercial court, they are not made within the Chancery Division and such proceedings, if they have been commenced by writ, will invariably so proceed.

Forms for originating process

Order 6, r 1 as amended by RSC (Writ and Appearance) 1979 (SI 1979 No 1716) provides a single form of writ of summons which can be adapted for use in district registries, for indorsement of statement of claim or for probate actions. Law stationers supply forms with or without flysheet. RSC Appendix A contains the following forms of originating summons, notice of motion and acknowledgments of services:

No 8 Originating Summons	(General Form)
No 9 Originating Summons	(District Registry)
No 10 Originating Summons	(Expedited Form)
No 11 Originating Summons	(Ex parte Form)
No 11A Originating Summons	(For use only in proceedings for recovery of land under Ord 113)
No 13 Notice of Motion	
No 14 Acknowledgment of Service	(To accompany Service of Writ)
No 15 Acknowledgment of Service	(To accompany Service of Originating Summons Nos 8, 9 and 10)

Form No 8 is an originating summons between parties to which an acknowledgment of service is required. This is the usual form of originating summons and is used in all applications for relief where the inherent jurisdiction of the court needs to be applied and all cases of construction of documents, administration actions and kin enquiries, mortgage actions under Ord 88 and applications under statutes. Form No 10 (Expedited Form) is *inter partes* and an acknowledgment of service is required. It should be used in applications for relief by way of interpleader (Ord 17, r 3); applications for withdrawal of stop order on transfer of securities (Ord 50, r 14(4)); applications for order prohibiting transfer of securities (Ord 50, r 15) and applications for approval of settlement or compromise on behalf of person under disability (Ord 80, r 10). Form No 10 can be regarded as a more specialised form covering the kind of cases where matters are to be placed before the court, very often the master, for an expeditious decision where no other originating process is specifically applicable. Form No 11 is an *ex parte* originating summons which is to be used when there is no other party to be served initially. An example would be an application under Ord 92, r 5 relating to funds in court where perhaps a minor on attaining his majority might be applying for transfer of funds into his own name. Form No 11A is a specialised summons prescribed for one purpose only, ie an application under Ord 113 for possession against trespassers.

Completion of forms

In completing forms of writ or originating summons the following must be given:

(1) The capacity (if any) in which each party sues or is sued, eg executor or trustee.
(2) If the plaintiff is suing in person, his name, address and description and any separate address for service and if he is represented, the name and address of his solicitors and of any firm for which they are acting as agents.
(3) A writ, if not indorsed with a statement of claim, must contain a concise statement of the nature of the plaintiff's claim or the relief or remedy required (Ord 6, r 2).
(4) An originating summons must include a statement of the questions on which the plaintiff seeks the determination or direction of the court or, as the case may be, a concise statement of the relief or remedy claimed with sufficient particulars to identify the cause or causes of action in respect of which the plaintiff claims that relief or remedy (Ord 7, r 3). Where a statute is invoked the section or sections on which the plaintiff's claim is founded should be specified in the body, eg 'This application is made under section 30 of the Law of Property Act 1925' (Practice Direction (Chancery Chambers) No 2 of 1982 [1983] 1 WLR 4).
(5) Dates and sums should be expressed in figures. (See generally AP vol 2, 1033 Practice Direction (Title of Proceedings) [1959] 1 WLR 743; Practice Direction (Central Office: Description of Parties) [1969] 1 WLR 1259).

Leave to issue

In the Chancery Division leave to issue a writ or originating summons is required in the following cases:

(1) Where the sole defendant or all of several defendants is/are out of the jurisdiction and it is desired to serve the process abroad (Ord 11, r 1).

(2) Where it is desired to join two or more causes of action (Ord 15, r 1).
(3) Where application is sought to bring proceedings under s 139 of the Mental Health Act 1983 (Ord 32, r 9).
(4) Where the issue of a writ is sought by a vexatious litigant (Supreme Court of Judicature (Consolidation) Act 1925, s 51).
(5) Where it is sought to institute a probate action (Ord 76, r 2). The writ and a copy should be left at Room 307/308, and if satisfied the master will indorse the top copy of the writ of summons with a memorandum to denote that leave has been granted.

3. General provisions relating to writs and originating summonses

The procedure in a writ action in the Chancery Division is governed by the same rules as in the Queen's Bench Division. Pleadings are served within the same time limits, and discovery follows the usual course of events. The difference in Chancery is in the obligation of the plaintiff to the action to lodge copies of all pleadings and certain other relevant documents with the court to keep the court file up-to-date. These can either be lodged in rooms 307/8 (Chancery registry) or sent by post, clearly marking that destination on the letter and envelope. Failure to do so might result in adjournments or penalties as to costs.

A writ, if not indorsed with a statement of claim, must contain a concise statement of the nature of the plaintiff's claim or the relief or remedy required (Ord 6, r 2).

An originating summons must include a statement of the questions on which the plaintiff seeks the determination or direction of the court and a concise statement of the relief or remedy claimed with sufficient particulars to identify the cause or causes of action in respect of which the plaintiff claims that relief or remedy (Ord 7, r 3). Where a statute is invoked the section or sections on which the plaintiff's claim is founded should be specified in the body eg 'This application is made under s 30 of the Law of Property Act 1925' (Practice Direction (Chancery Chambers) No 2 of 1982 [1983] 1 WLR 4).

Dates and sums should be expressed in figures. (See generally AP, Vol 2, 1033 Practice Direction (Title of Proceedings) [1959] 1 WLR 743; Practice Direction (Description of Parties) [1969] 1 WLR 1259).

Originating summons procedure is governed by Ord 28. Affidavits take the place of pleadings, and are lodged and served as such. Exhibits are lodged with the affidavits and must be separately bound and correctly marked.

Directions are required at an early stage, and the issue of the First Appointment (the form of summons in the procedure) is advisable at an early stage. Directions will be given for evidence to be lodged and served together with any other appropriate order, and the appointment adjourned. When directions have been complied with, the matter becomes the subject of a master's note on the file and is formally referred to the judge for trial. Directions as to witnesses and mode of trial are also given.

Supporting documents

In an action commenced by writ the statement of claim must set out (in numbered paragraphs) the facts and allegations upon which the plaintiff's claim is based. The legal consequences of those facts need not be stated, nor should evidence. If not indorsed on the writ, a copy must be served on each defendant within 14 days after he has acknowledged service of the writ (Ord 18, r 1). If settled by counsel, the top copy will be signed by him, otherwise it must be signed by the plaintiff (if suing in person) or by his solicitor.

An originating summons must be supported by an affidavit by the plaintiff setting out the evidence to be adduced by him in support of his claim or application (Ord 28, r 2). It must be drawn in the first person and confined to facts within the deponent's knowledge.

Issuing

The Chancery Division has its own 'central office' in room 307/308 for the issue of originating processes and the filing and lodging of all pleadings and affidavits and other documents and papers. In the case of writs and originating summonses the applicant must present:

(1) A copy of the writ or originating summons for each defendant and two additional copies, one (the top copy) for retention by the plaintiff and the other for the court file.
(2) With each copy for service (excepting Forms 11 and 11A) a form of acknowledgment of service.
(3) Consent of next friend if plaintiff under disability, with certificate by solicitor (Form No PF 164).
(4) With Form 11A (and, if the plaintiff so wishes with Forms 8, 9 and 10) the plaintiff's supporting affidavit with a copy thereof (including a copy of any exhibit thereto) for each copy of the originating summons and a copy for the court file; but with Forms 8, 9 and 10 the plaintiff may elect to defer the presentation of his supporting affidavit and the filing and service thereof until after the issue of the originating summons (Ord 28, r 1A).
(5) A copy of the plaintiff's civil aid certificate (if any).
(6) Solicitor's cheque, money order or cash for the appropriate fee (£60) made payable to HM Paymaster-General.

The registry (room 307/8) will mark each copy of the writ or originating summons with a reference number prefixed by the year of issue and the initial letter of the plaintiff's surname, thus: Ch 1990-A-No. Cases are assigned to masters according to the last digit of the action number (*see the allocation of cases to masters in Chapter 1*) and not on an alphabetical basis as was previously the case. In the case of an originating summons on Form 10 or Form 11A application must then be made to the registry to fix a hearing date which will be entered in the appropriate space. The registry will then seal each copy of the writ or originating summons. The copy of the writ or originating summons retained in the court file will be stamped to denote payment of the fee.

Application for the issue of a writ or originating summons (but not for an originating summons in expedited form) may be made by post by sending the above documents with a covering letter and a stamped addressed envelope for reply—for detail see Chancery: Applications by Post or Telephone: Practice Direction (No 2 of 1983) (*see Chapter 14*).

A concurrent writ or originating summons may at the request of the plaintiff be issued at the same time as or subsequent to the issue of the original, and for service within or, subject to the leave of the master, outside of the jurisdiction (Ord 6, r 6; Ord 7, r 4).

It is not necessary to use the printed forms but it is important to ensure that the Royal Coat of Arms is impressed on the document. Room 307 provides a seal which can be used if the printed form is not used.

Service

Once an originating summons or writ is issued sealed copies should be served. Except where substituted service is directed by the court, all forms of originating process must be served personally or by post (Ord 10, rr 1 and 5). The practice whereby a defendant's solicitor, if authorised to accept service, would indorse the writ or summons to that effect, is now largely discontinued since his signature on the acknowledgment of service is sufficient evidence. On service the following rules must be observed:

(1) All writs and all originating summonses except Forms 11 and 11A must be accompanied by a form of acknowledgment of service.
(2) A copy of the plaintiff's statement of claim, unless indorsed on or served with the writ, must be served on the defendant within 14 days after his acknowledgment of service (Ord 18, r 1).
(3) A copy of the plaintiff's affidavit in support of an originating summons on Forms 8 or 9 must be served with the summons or within 14 days after the defendant has acknowledged service thereof (Ord 28, r 1A(1)).

(4) A copy of the plaintiff's affidavit in support of an originating summons on Form 11A must be served with the summons (Ord 28, r 1A(2)).
(5) When proceedings are taken for the recovery of possession of land under Ord 113 and the defendants, or some of them, cannot be identified, then unless the court directs some other means of service, the originating summons on Form 11A and the accompanying copy of the plaintiff's affidavit should be affixed to the main door or other conspicuous part of the property and copies, in an envelope addressed to 'The Occupiers', must be placed in the letter box (if any) (Ord 10, r 5; Ord 113, r 4).
(6) When leave is given for service out of the jurisdiction or substituted service and in consequence the time for acknowledgment of service is extended, the form of acknowledgment of service should be amended accordingly.
(7) Writs, originating summonses and all originating processes including third party notices must be served within four months from the date of issue (Ord 6, r 8; Ord 7, r 6) unless renewed.

If it can be shown to be impracticable to serve an originating process personally or by post, the court may make an order for substituted service by advertisement or such other means as may be expected to bring the process to the defendant's notice (Ord 65, r 4). Application is made *ex parte* to the master supported by an affidavit showing what attempts have been made to effect service and what method of substituted service is proposed. An order for substituted service out of the jurisdiction may be made if the writ or summons was issued with leave for that purpose, but not if it was issued for service in England, unless it can be shown that the defendant was in England when the process was issued and left the country with knowledge of its issue (*Jay v Budd* [1898] 1 QBD 12). If that cannot be established, the plaintiff must obtain leave to issue a concurrent writ or summons for service abroad.

4. The sequence of proceedings

Whether commenced by writ or originating summons an action continues by the parties taking certain steps at stages in sequence. First, and unless he wishes to allow the plaintiff to take judgment in default, the defendant completes and delivers to room 307/308 within 14 days after service the form of acknowledgment which will have been served accompanied by guidance instructions with the writ or originating summons. On receipt of the acknowledgment, the court itself will make a photocopy and post it to the plaintiff.

Commencement by originating summons

If the proceedings are brought by originating summons, while there is no requirement to use any particular wording, this must include the questions on which the plaintiff seeks the determination or direction of the court, or else a concise statement of the relief sought or remedy claimed with sufficient particulars to identify the cause or causes of action (Ord 7, r 3). The material facts upon which each party relies are set out in affidavits.

With Forms 10 and 11A a first appointment does not have to be obtained because a hearing date is given and inserted in the originating summons upon issue; with the other forms, a first appointment is obtainable after the plaintiff has filed his affidavit, and this effectively assigns the proceedings to a particular master. Pursuant to Ord 12, r 9 (as now amended) each defendant named in and served with an originating summons (other than an *ex parte* summons or an originating summons under Ord 113) must acknowledge service of the summons as if it were a writ. This acknowledgment of service is required in all cases (except *ex parte*) commenced by originating summons if the defendant intends to participate in the proceedings and is an essential step in the timetable (Ord 28, r 1A). The plaintiff must file his supporting affidavit within 14 days after acknowledgment (Ord 28, r 1A(1, 2)).

After the hearing on the first appointment it is the master's function to consider all aspects of the case. The master must, at as early a stage of the proceedings as appears to him to be practicable, consider whether there is or may be a dispute as to fact, and whether the summons should be heard on oral evidence or partly so and particularly whether all interested persons are joined as parties or are sufficiently represented. If, in the master's judgment, the plaintiff is entitled to his order and there are no grounds for considering that there could be a defence, the master can make the order asked for on the first appointment but if, as is more usual, the summons is not then disposed of or is ordered to be transferred to a county court or some other court or ordered to be continued as if begun by writ (with affidavits filed to be treated as pleadings), the master must give such directions as to the further conduct of the proceedings as he thinks best adapted to secure 'the just, expeditious and economical disposal thereof' (Ord 29, r 4). This will involve considering whether further affidavits should be filed by one side or the other, whether the evidence should be limited, and whether any other order or direction is required. If a final order has not been made on the first appointment, the master will either fix the date of the next appointment or direct that the summons be restored, usually when certain evidence is complete, within a given time (Practice Direction (Chancery Chambers: Expedition) [1970] 1 WLR 95). Where the originating summons is restored, two clear days notice must be given to all parties (Ord 32, r 4(2)), but if it has been adjourned to a fixed date, no notice of the restored hearing is required.

Where a defendant fails to attend, the court may proceed in his absence but may require to be satisfied that the summons or notice has been served (Ord 28, r 1; Ord 32, r 5). Where the court makes an order in the absence of a defendant, the order may be later varied or revoked by a subsequent order (Ord 28, r 4(1)).

The timetable in originating summons proceedings is possibly simpler than in writ actions since there are no pleadings, no automatic discovery and usually no oral evidence in chief. Application for a first appointment for the hearing of an originating summons where forms other than 10 and 11A have been used may be made by the plaintiff at any time after he files his first affidavit. It is at the party's discretion as to when application for the first appointment should be applied for, and this will depend very much upon what the plaintiff and other parties consider may be the particular directions required to be given at any given time in the course of the matter proceeding. There may be occasions when the matters in issue are complicated or not clearly defined, or where one party is being unco-operative, or dilatory to his own ends, or where it becomes clear, perhaps at an early stage, that additional parties need to be added. On all of these occasions discretion may be particularly required as to when application for an appointment should be made for the master to give directions for trial. Not infrequently final directions for adjournment into court or chambers are not in practice given until several adjourned hearings of the originating summons before the master.

If a party does wish to call oral evidence on the hearing of an originating summons whether in chambers or in open court then when setting down, a certificate signed by counsel of the estimated length must be annexed to the summons (Practice Direction [1963] 1 WLR 326). If a party wishes at the hearing to cross-examine a deponent to an affidavit then before the originating summons is adjourned to the judge he should apply to the master furnishing the master with the names of deponents to affidavits required to attend the trial. The court will draw up the requisite order and a copy can be served in the usual way, or notice given to the person concerned. It is important to obtain such an order which limits evidence at any trial and it is possible to obtain an order at any stage. The order may inhibit the reading of an affidavit without leave unless the deponents are produced (Practice Direction (Affidavits: Cross-Examination) [1969] 1 WLR 983).

Discovery is not generally required as the relevant documents should have been exhibited to the affidavits so that the only undiscovered documents are likely to be those referred to in an affidavit but not exhibited, an omission that can be rectified by a solicitor's letters requesting a copy. Nonetheless, every party in proceedings commenced by originating summons is entitled to ask any other party to disclose all documents in his possession, custody or power regarded as relevant, and save for those documents which a party claims are privileged, opportunity for inspection must be given. 'Inspection' is in practice given by one party or the other asking for photographic copies on payment. There is nothing to prevent a litigant in proceedings commenced by originating summons from applying to the master by issuing a general summons, but this would generally be unnecessary because the litigant can appear before the master on successive appointments obtained on the originating summons itself, and at any such appointment an application for discovery or inspection if it should be required can be made, and if shown to be necessary, will be made.

Timetable for originating summons procedure

Originating Summons Form 8 (General Form)	Originating Summons Form 10 (Expedited Form)	Originating Summons Form 11 (Ex Parte Form)	New Rules effective from 1.1.83
Within 14 days after acknowledgment of service	Within 14 days after acknowledgment of service	4 clear days before day fixed for hearing	Plaintiff files supporting affidavit (Ord 28, r 1A(1, 2))
Within 14 days after acknowledgment of service	Within 14 days after acknowledgment of service	No service required	Plaintiff serves copy affidavit on defendant (ibid r 1A(3))
Within 28 days after service of plaintiff's affidavit	Within 28 days after service of plaintiff's affidavit		Defendant files if he wishes affidavit and serves copy on plaintiff (ibid r 1A(4))
Within 14 days after service of defendant's affidavit	Within 14 days after service of defendant's affidavit		Plaintiff may file affidavit in reply and serves copy on defendant (ibid r 1A(5))

Notes:

(1) The originating summons general form sets out the questions on which the plaintiff seeks the court's determination,

requiring the defendant to return the acknowledgment of service. The expedited form also requires acknowledgment of service, but gives an appointment. The short rules which apply to both are in RSC, Ord 7.

(2) The plaintiff may apply for an appointment for the hearing of the originating summons at any time after filing his supporting affidavit.

(3) After the plaintiff's affidavit in reply, no further affidavits can be filed without leave.

(4) On 12 October 1982 the Supreme Court Rule Committee produced draft amendments to Ords 7 and 28 designed to implement the Review Body's recommendations. These required (*inter alia*) that a party issuing an originating summons should lodge his supporting affidavit at the time of issue and that in the case of an expedited originating summons (Form 10) a copy of the affidavit should accompany the service of the summons on the defendant. The amended Rules (RSC (Amendment No 3) 1982 (SI 1982 No 1786)) published by the Rules Committee on 29 November 1982 and effective from 1 January 1983 omitted the draft amendment to Ord 7 and departed somewhat from the draft amendments to Ord 28. Although it was still open to the parties to conform with the timetable proposed by the draft amendments, the effect of the rules as published was to extend the time within which a plaintiff must lodge his affidavit and (in an 'expedited' case) the time within which he must serve a copy on the defendant.

(5) These times may be abridged so as to expire, respectively, on the fifth day before, and the next day but one before, the day fixed for the hearing (ibid, r 2(2)).

(6) The periods run during the month of August (Ord 3, r 3 as amended by r 3 of RSC (Amendment No 3) 1982), which excludes August applies only to service of pleadings).

(7) Rule 2(2) of Ord 28 incorrectly refers to r 1A(2) and (3) and the reference should be to r 1A(4) and (5).

Commencement by writ

If the proceedings are commenced by writ the facts are set out in documents called pleadings, first by the plaintiff in a 'statement of claim', which may either be indorsed on the writ or served as a separate document within 14 days after the acknowledgment of service, and then by the defendant in his defence which should be served within 14 days after service of the statement of claim or after the time limited for acknowledgment of service whichever is the later, unless time is extended by order or agreement. The defence may traverse the facts alleged in the statement of claim, admit facts in it, putting on them a different interpretation, or may allege a different set of facts: but whichever, the issue or issues in the defence should be made immediately apparent both to the plaintiff and to the court ultimately to try the case. The defence will usually be met by the plaintiff serving a reply. The defendant on his part may have served a counterclaim accompanying his defence and to meet this the plaintiff will serve a defence to counterclaim. Conduct of an action commenced by writ of summons in the Chancery Division as governed by Ord 25 is the same as in the Queen's Bench Division. Pleadings being exchanged between the parties do not usually reach the court file.

Hence, if any summons or other interlocutory application is issued in a writ action, the applicant should ensure that a copy of the pleadings is available for the hearing by lodging them at the time the summons or application is issued. Rule 9 of Ord 2 provides for 'Standard Directions by Consent in Chancery Actions'. Where in any action in the Chancery Division the parties agree, not more than one month after the pleadings are deemed to be closed, that the only directions required are as to the mode of trial and the time for setting down, the provisions of 8(1)(*e*) (that the action shall be tried in London if proceeding in London or if at a district registry at the trial centre for the time being designated for that registry) and (*g*) (that the court shall be notified on setting down of estimated length) shall apply and the action shall be tried by a judge alone and shall be set down within six months (r 9(1)). Nonetheless, any party to an action may take out a summons for directions at any time after a defendant has given notice of intention to defend (r 1(7)). The court may give such further directions or orders, whether on application by a party or of its own motion, as may, in the circumstances, be appropriate (r 9(3)) and pursuant to Practice Direction (Chancery: Exchange of Witness Statements and the Lodging of Pleadings) No 1 of 1989, on the hearing of a summons for directions the master will normally make an order under Ord 38, r 2A for the exchange of witness statements specifying an exchange date. On issue of the summons, there must be lodged a complete set of pleadings to date.

Failure to comply with a direction given under Ord 38, r 2A may have a stultifying influence on that party's case since then no evidence relating to the matters to which the direction referred may be given without the leave of the court.

Order 38, r 2A applies to any cause or matter in the Chancery court although it is likely to be applied mainly to writ actions.

An application by a party for such directions would be by way of a summons and might well be for directions for further discovery or for further and better particulars of a pleading. On an application by a party for directions, any other party to the application may himself ask for directions but should have given prior notice to the applicant and other interested parties.

Discovery in writ actions is intended to be automatic (Ord 24, r 2);

the pleadings are deemed to end with the plaintiff's 'Reply and Defence to Counterclaim' or with the defendant's 'Reply to Defence to Counterclaim' (Ord 15, r 20) and within 14 days of such close of pleadings each side should serve his list of documents.

Timetable for writ procedure

(1) Plaintiff prepares writ and issues it in room 307/308.
(2) Plaintiff serves writ on defendant.
(3) Defendant acknowledges service within 14 days (Ord 12, r 3).
(4) Unless statement of claim indorsed on writ, plaintiff serves statement of claim on defendant within 14 days after acknowledgment.
(5) Defendant serves defence on plaintiff within 14 days of service of statement of claim.
(6) Plaintiff may serve reply on defendant within 14 days of service of defence.
(7) Within 14 days of pleadings being closed automatic discovery of documents, and inspection within seven days thereafter.
(8) Within one month of pleadings being closed plaintiff may issue summons for directions, and this is more likely in Chancery writ actions than to rely on the automatic directions (Ord 25, r 8) to set down in London or trial centre within six months of close of pleadings.

Note: The time for service of pleadings does not now run during the month of August: Ord 3, r 3 as amended by r 3 of RSC (Amendment No 3) 1982 (SI 1982 No 1786).

Interlocutory applications

The procedure for making interlocutory applications, and whether they should be by way of summons, on notice of motion, or by lodging an affidavit, is given in Chapter 4.

Place of trial

This will usually be at the trial centre for the place in which the action is proceeding but may be at such other trial centre as the parties agree or the court may direct, the practitioners having in mind the conveyance of witnesses and parties.

Third party notice

Where a defendant to an action claims against any person *not* already a party, some contribution or indemnity, or some other relief or remedy, or settlement of an issue connected with the subject matter of the action, then he must proceed by way of a Third Party Notice. The procedure which applies is under RSC, Ord 16, and the Notice is in Form No 20 or 21 in Appendix A, this containing a statement of the nature of the claim.

The claim raised against the third party should be for a remedy similar to the remedy which the plaintiff claims, or a question arising out of the plaintiff's claim and should be decided not only as between the plaintiff and the defendant, but also as between either or both of them and the third party (RSC, Ord 16, r 1).

If served after defence, which is probably more often the case, then leave must be obtained (Ord 16, r 1(1)(2)), though in the case it is issued before defence, then no leave is required. The third party having given notice of intention to defend, the defendant issuing the third party notice then issues a summons for third party directions, the summons being in Queen's Bench Masters Forms No 20 and Ord 16, r 4(1) applying. The court may direct that the third party notice stands as a third party statement of claim, or alternatively may direct a statement of claim to be served in a specified period, and give further directions for pleadings and discovery. It will of course be open to the court to give summary judgment against the third party, or direct an issue to be tried, or of course to dismiss the application. The third party directions are given on the summons for the same issued by the defendant who issued the third party notice, or hopefully to be returnable on the same day as the plaintiff's summons for directions in the main action. The third party directions will usually contain a provision which gives leave to the third party to appear at the trial of the action, and to be bound by the result of the trial (specimen order given in Queen's Bench Masters Practice Form No 21).

It may well be that the plaintiff wishes to obtain judgment against the third party, in which case he must apply to add the third party as a defendant (Ord 15, r 6); if a third party wishes to counterclaim against the plaintiff, he must himself apply to be added as a defendant.

The issues as between the defendant and the third party will usually be sufficiently identified in the third party notice and the defence. Where the defendant succeeds against the third party, but the plaintiff succeeds against the defendant, the order will be that the defendant pay the plaintiff costs, and the third party the costs that the defendant is called upon to pay, and also the costs of defending the action and the costs of the third party proceedings.

A defendant may also make a third party claim against any other defendant, in which case leave to issue is not required, but notice should be given to a co-defendant that contribution will be sought in the event that damages are awarded.

Third parties may apply for leave to issue a fourth party notice, and so on. The application for leave to issue a third party notice, made in the first instance by a defendant, may be made *ex parte* with an affidavit setting out the circumstances, as specified in Ord 16, r 2(2), the summons and affidavit being lodged at the Registry, room 307/308 (Ord 16, r 2(2)). If a third party does not appear at the hearing of the action, he is deemed to admit the notice and is bound by the judgment, even if that judgment is by consent. After judgment, execution may not be issued against the third party, without leave of the court, until the defendant has satisfied the judgment against him. A party brought in, or who has a notice served by way of contribution notice, may make an offer of contribution. There are cases where the defendant makes a claim against someone who is already a party in the same action, and in that case he simply serves on such party a notice making such a claim. A specimen of the form which a third party notice might take follows this text.

Specimen third party notice

IN THE LULLINGTON COUNTY COURT   Case No 9150049

BETWEEN

SAPRICIUS PROPERTIES PLC

Plaintiffs

-and-

(1) VERONA BIANCO
(2) JOHN CALYBITES

Defendants

To the First Defendant Verona Bianco of 82, Constant Street, Collington Town, London E9.

TAKE NOTICE that this action has been brought by the Plaintiffs against you the First Defendant and against the Second Defendant. In it the Plaintiffs claim against you the First Defendant possession of the premises in the Statement of Claim herein referred to, and against each of the Defendants rent mesne profits damages costs and interest (in the case of the claim against the Second Defendant limited to a maximum of £111,250) as appears from the Writ of Summons and Statement of Claim herein copies thereof are served herewith.

THE SECOND DEFENDANT CLAIMS AGAINST YOU to be indemnified against all sums it may be found liable to pay to the Plaintiff in these proceedings whether by way of rent mesne profits damages interest or costs

ON THE GROUNDS following that is to say

(a) by the lease in the Statement of Claim herein referred to the Plaintiff demised to you the property therein mentioned at the rent and on the terms and conditions therein set out;

(b) by clause 7 of and the Sixth Schedule to the said lease the Second Defendant as guarantor covenanted with the Plaintiff as set out in paragraph 12 of the Statement of Claim herein;

(c) the principal liability for the sums claimed by the Plaintiff in these proceedings is that of you, the First Defendant, the Second Defendant's liability (if any) being as surety of your liability only.

Dated the 30th day of August 199 .

Worples & Co, 182 Lewis High Road, Lowton BN4 XYZ
....   Solicitors for the Second Defendant

To the District Judge

And to the First Defendant
and to his solicitors

Interpleader

Where a person is under a liability for debt, money, or goods, in respect of which he is sued, or expects to be sued, by two or more, persons, who will be making adverse claims thereto, he may apply to the court for relief by way of 'interpleader' (RSC, Ord 17, r 1 1(1)(A)).

The application is made by originating summons, unless during an action which is already pending, when the application is simply made by a summons within the action. In any case, a supporting affidavit must be given setting out that the applicant claims no interest in the subject matter other than for charges and costs, that he does not collude with any of the claimants, and that he is willing to pay the subject matter into court or dispose of it as the court may direct; a form of affidavit is given in Queen's Bench Masters Practice Forms No 27.

Procedure on first hearing of the originating summons is that, if there is an obvious issue, an order that an issue be stated and tried is made, which will direct which claimant is to be plaintiff and which defendant. There is a distinction as to hearing the issue summarily, which is usual, or adjourning into court trial of the issue. The issue will be heard summarily where the facts are not in issue and the question turns on law. Commonly, they are heard in the Master's Chambers, with the person who has issued the interpleader proceedings giving evidence, following his and any claimants' affidavits being read; the claimants are then heard.

Whilst the above relates to what is called a stakeholder's interpleader, perhaps the more common form is where the sheriff interpleads, and this occurs, for example, where a person's goods have been seized in execution and he claims their ownership and that they should not be seized to satisfy some execution creditor's debt. The notice making claim (which must be given to the sheriff) is important here. This is often given in writing by solicitors, and must provide an address for service. On receipt of the notice, the sheriff office solicitors give notice to the execution creditor, in Queen's Bench Masters Form No 23, who should state within seven days whether he admits or disputes the claim (RSC Ord 17, r 2(2)). Whensoever the execution creditor disputes the claim, or fails to admit it, then the sheriff officer solicitors apply to the court for interpleader relief, which they do by way of summons within the proceedings; no affidavit or any other evidence is generally supplied by the sheriff office solicitors.

Should the claimant in a sheriff's interpleader fail, then the costs, including possession monies, will be payable by him, whereas if he succeeds, the sheriff is entitled to costs from the execution creditor. In any event, the sheriff can look to the execution creditor for his costs.

See orders at the end of Chapter 4, Atkin, Vol 22 (1980 Issue) and SCP, Vol 2.

Notes to orders in interpleader proceedings Where a person is under a liability in respect of a debt or any other money, goods or chattels and he expects to be sued by two separate claimants he may apply to the court for relief by way of interpleader under Ord 17, r 1. There are two types of interpleader, a stakeholder's interpleader and a sheriff's interpleader. Application is made by originating summons in the expedited form (Form No 10 in Appendix A) or by summons in a pending action.

Any person making a claim must give notice of his claim to the sheriff giving his name and address (Ord 17, r 2). Where the claimant in a sheriff's interpleader fails the sheriff is usually entitled to his costs (including possession money) from the time of the notice of claim or from the sale, whichever is earlier. Where the claimant succeeds the sheriff is entitled as against the execution creditor to costs from the time the latter authorised interpleader proceedings. In either case the sheriff gets his costs from the execution creditor who, if successful, has a remedy against the plaintiff. See Orders, Chapter 4; Atkin, vol 22 (1980 Issue) and SCP vol 2.

Security for costs

Security may be ordered when a plaintiff is ordinarily resident out of the jurisdiction (Ord 23, r 1(1)(*a*)) or when the plaintiff is a nominal plaintiff and there is reason to believe that he will be unable to pay the costs if ordered to do so (Ord 23, r 1(19)(B)), or else under s 726(1) of the Companies Act 1985, where the plaintiff is a limited company and there is reason to believe that the defendant will be unable to recover his costs—if it is in liquidation this is *prima facie* evidence. There is complete discretion, depending on the justice of matter, and there is no longer a rigid rule that a plaintiff resident abroad must provide security. Principles to be considered will be whether or not the plaintiff is *bona fide*, whether the company has a reasonably good prospect of success, whether there is any admission, or payment into court, or open offer, whether the application is in fact used oppressively to stifle a claim, and lastly whether the plaintiff's lack of means has been brought about by any conduct of the defendants.

Application for security may be made on the summons for directions, or separate application, and a common order is that there be a payment into court, or, more conveniently, into joint names of solicitors. Proceedings are likely to be stayed until the security is given. The court looks at a sum which is about two thirds of the estimated party and party costs up to the stay. Applicants are expected to provide a skeleton bill, referred to in the affidavit which supports the application. Security may also be ordered as a term of prosecuting an appeal, if it has not been pursued with due diligence.

The court has power to impose a condition of payment as a condition of setting aside a judgment, even where there is a good arguable defence, not to punish the defendant, but to encourage the proper future conduct of the action and to provide a measure of security for the plaintiff. The amount should be fixed in accordance with the defendant's means. See *City Construction Contracts (London) Ltd v Adam*, (CA) [1988] *The Times*, 4 January.

Claims for interest

For directions as to the manner in which claims for interest should be pleaded and what conditions must be fulfilled before a default judgment for interest can be obtained, see Practice Note (Claims for Interest) (No 2) [1983] 1 WLR 377. The following is a full proforma:

And the Plaintiff claims the said sum of [£250.00] together with interest pursuant to ... at the rate of 15 per cent per annum from the [the date upon which payment became due] to the date hereof [£3.70] and continuing hereafter at the daily rate of [£0.1027] until the date of judgment or sooner payment.

The Plaintiff therefore claims the said sum of [£253.70] continuing interest and costs. However, pleaders usually say 'interest pursuant to s 35A of the Supreme Court Act 1981'; if contractual interest is payable, that only can be claimed.

Contractual interest This is the interest which one person agrees to pay to another and principal and interest thereon calculated up to the date of judgment should be claimed thereafter judgment interest is paid on the total sum.

Judgment interest This is interest payable on a judgment debt by virtue of s 17 of the Judgments Act 1838. The interest runs from the date of judgment until payment but, where costs have to be taxed or damages assessed, the interest runs from the date of the taxing master's certificate or the date of the order assessing damages. The amount of interest is prescribed from time to time by statutory instrument. The judgment always bears interest at the rate prescribed when the judgment is entered, eg, if the rate is 12 per cent when judgment is entered it will continue at that rate until payment, even though subsequent statutory instruments may increase or decrease the rate of interest on judgments.

Interest may be claimed under s 35A of the Supreme Court Act 1981 inserted by s 15 of the Administration of Justice Act 1982 and set out in Sched I to that Act.

It is important to note:

(1) The amount on which interest is to be paid is within the discretion of the court.

(2) The rate of interest is also discretionary.
(3) The period in respect of which interest is to be paid is discretionary but it cannot start earlier than when the cause of action arose and it cannot continue later than judgment.

Pleading of interest   Order 18, r 8(4) states that a party must plead specifically any claim for interest under s 3A of the Supreme Court Act 1981 and this is amplified in Practice Note (Claims for Interest (No 2)) [1983] 1 WLR 377. In other words, interest must be claimed both in the body of the pleadings and in the prayer.

Default judgments   To obtain a judgment under Ord 13, r 1(2) the writ must not claim a higher rate of interest than that payable under a judgment debt at the time the judgment is entered. If the plaintiff seeks a higher rate then he must enter judgment for interest to be assessed.

Inactivity   Where a year or more has elapsed since the last proceeding in a cause or matter, the party who desires to proceed must give the other parties one month's notice of his intention. A summons on which no order was made is not a proceeding for this purpose (Ord 3, r 6). Service is normally effected by post on the solicitors or party on the record. The rule does not apply to a summons to dismiss for want of prosecution.

A notice given before the year has expired is invalid (*Suedeclub Co Ltd v Occasions Textiles Ltd* [1981] 3 All ER 671).

5. Service

The Companies Act 1985 provides special rules for method of service on limited companies (*see below*). For service on any person a distinction is drawn between method of service of originating process and service of other documents.

Service of originating process (Ord 10) on persons

The originating process may be served personally on the person who is a party to it, or be left in his presence and service is deemed to have taken place as at that moment. If the action is against a partnership or firm, then the originating process may be served in similar manner on any partner or any person appearing to have control at the place of business.

A sealed copy of the writ and acknowledgment of service and guidance instructions may be put in the letterbox of the address of the party to be served or may be posted by first class letter post to the last known address. If the originating process is against a partnership, then the originating process is to be sent by first class post to the principal place of business. Service is deemed to have been effective on the seventh day from posting, or as on the day when the originating process was put in the letterbox.

The sealed copy of the writ together with acknowledgment of service and guidance instructions may be sent by post and provided the solicitors can say that they are instructed to accept service, service will be deemed to have taken place on the date which they acknowledge service (Ord 10, r 1(4)).

For all writs, originating summonses or other originating processes, the address to which the process should be sent by post is 'the proper address' of the person to be served; in the case of originating processes this is the usual or last known address of the defendant, but if the defendant gives an address other than that stated in the writ in his acknowledgment of service then that address will become his address for service (Ord 12, r 3).

Service of documents other than originating process (Ord 65) on persons

Personal service is to be made at the address or place of residence of the person to be served.

Postal service may be elected. The document should be posted to the 'proper address' (*see above*) of the person to be served and service will be deemed effected if the document was sent by first class prepaid letter post, one day after the date on which the document was posted, or if sent by second class prepaid letter post, two days later, provided in such case that the posting was not later than the latest prescribed time for posting (Master's Practice Direction (Central Office: 1st and 2nd class mail) No 26A [1968] 1 WLR 1489).

Such documents may be served on solicitors instructed to accept service, at the business address of the solicitor.

Service of originating process or other documents on companies

A process or document may be served on a limited company by leaving it at or sending it by post to the registered office pursuant to s 725 of the Companies Act 1985.

The fact that the limited company has vacated its registered office and/or made no arrangements for forwarding post does not affect the validity of service though in such a case it may be necessary to show that the address to which the document was sent was the registered office.

General rules relating to postal service

All documents sent by post for service whether originating process or otherwise and whether to companies or to other persons should be sent by prepaid letter post, not registered or recorded. Originating process must be sent by first class post only, if service is to be deemed effected; only documents other than originating process can be sent by second class post. By s 7 of the Interpretation Act 1978 proof of prepaid posting to the proper address raises a statutory presumption of delivery (provided that the document has not been returned through the Post Office as undelivered). According to Practice Direction (1985) 1 WLR 489, if a document (other than originating process) is sent by first class post, it is presumed to arrive on the second working day after posting—working days being Monday to Friday, excluding Bank Holidays.

Personal service necessary or desirable

Service by post is obviously quicker, more convenient and the least costly. However, in some instances personal service may be necessary or desirable.

Where there is an order requiring a person to do or refrain from doing an act it may be enforced under Ord 45, r 5 once an indorsed copy has been served pursuant to Ord 45, r 7 and there is default. 'Served' means generally that a copy of the order has been served personally on the person required by or within a specified time to do or abstain from doing the act in question; to be enforceable the copy order must have been served before the expiration of the time specified in the order. Where an order has been made against a body corporate, Ord 45, r 7(3) provides that it cannot be enforced unless a copy of the order has been served personally on the officer against whom an order of committal is sought.

For the order to be enforceable a penal notice pursuant to r 7(4) must have been indorsed on the copy of the orders.

Substituted service may be ordered for service of orders requiring a person to do or refrain from doing an act but a committal order will not be readily made except where service has been effected personally unless the court is satisfied that he had notice of the order, either because he was present in court or was otherwise notified.

Personal service may also be effected on all writs and originating summonses in lieu of service by post (Ord 10, r 1(11)); this obviates the possibility of a defendant applying for a summary judgment to be set aside on grounds that he did not receive the originating process.

Crown and government departments

Service must be effected on one of the persons acting or deemed to be acting as solicitor for the department and a list of authorised departments and their solicitors and addresses is published by the Treasury for the Civil Service and is reproduced in AP, Vol 2, para 2979 and at p 1089 of the County Court Practice 1982.

Minors and mental patients (Ord 80)

If a defendant is a minor and not also a mental patient process should be served on his parent or guardian, or if he has no parent or guardian then on the person with whom he resides or in whose care he is. If, however, the defendant is a mental patient, then the summons must be served on the person, if any, who is authorised under the Mental Health Act 1983 to conduct proceedings on the defendant's behalf or if there is no such person, then on the person with whom he resides or in whose care he is.

Members of the armed forces

Reference should be made to the Memorandum issued by the Lord Chancellor's office on 26 July 1979 entitled 'Memorandum on service of legal process on members of HM Forces' published in *Service of Documents* by Anthony Radevsky, Oyez Longman, 1982, pp 40-43. This requires a letter of inquiry to be addressed to the Ministry of Defence, for example.

Partners

Where partners are sued in their firm name the process may be served on an individual partner personally or at the principal place of business of the firm by delivering it to the person having, or appearing to have, control or management there. If a firm has been dissolved, the process must be served on every person sought to be made liable.

Corporations aggregate

Service may be effected on the mayor or other head officer or on the chief executive, clerk, treasurer or secretary in the absence of any other statutory provision.

Substituted service

There may be circumstances when there is no means of contact except through third parties, or where, in the case of service, the party evades attempted personal service. In such circumstances an affidavit in support of an application for an order for substituted service can be made and if satisfied that the party is attempting to evade service or that it is impracticable to serve in the prescribed way, the court will usually order that service be by prepaid first class letter post addressed to his address or the address of a person with whom he has been shown as likely to be in communication or that service be effected by advertisement or by other means (Ord 65, r 4). Applications for substituted service are made *ex parte* to the master, supported by affidavit.

Subpoenas

Subpoenas must be served personally and four days notice (unless the court otherwise orders) is required.

Notices of motion to commit

An application by motion to the judge for a committal under Ord 52, r 1(3) must be served personally on the person sought to be committed though substituted service may be ordered.

Affidavit of service

Affidavit of service of originating process is only necessary (*a*) if a defendant fails to acknowledge service and the plaintiff wishes to obtain judgment in default or proceed with the action (*b*) in proceedings under Ord 113 (squatters) and Ord 88 (mortgagee possession) cases.

Service outside the jurisdiction

Leave must be sought pursuant to Ord 11 when the plaintiff must show on affidavit that the English courts are the most convenient and that he has a good cause of action, and must give the place or country where the defendant is or possibly may be found, and finally must satisfy the master that one or other of the grounds specified in Ord 11 apply, namely that (*a*) the subject matter of the action is land situated within the jurisdiction, (*b*) an act, will, deed, contract, obligation or liability affecting land within the jurisdiction is to be construed or rectification setting aside or enforcement relating to it is to be prayed for, (*c*) the defendant is domiciled or ordinarily resident within the jurisdiction, (*d*) the action concerns the administration of the estate of a person who died domiciled within the jurisdiction, (*e*) the action is for execution in relation to property within the jurisdiction of trusts which ought to be executed according to English law and the person to be served is a trustee, (*f*) the action is for breach of a contract either made within the jurisdiction or made by an agent trading or resident within the jurisdiction on behalf of a principal outside the jurisdiction, or is a contract governed by English law (this provision does not apply to defendants domiciled or ordinarily resident in Scotland), (*g*) the action is for a breach committed within the jurisdiction or a contract made within or out of the jurisdiction (this provision does not apply to defendants domiciled or ordinarily resident in Scotland or Northern Ireland), (*h*) the action is in respect of a tort committed within the jurisdiction, (*i*) the action is in respect of an injunction to affect the defendant's actions within the jurisdiction, (*j*) a person outside the jurisdiction is a proper or necessary party to an action brought against a person properly served within the jurisdiction, (*k*) the action is by a mortgagee or mortgagor of property other than land situated within the jurisdiction—this does not cover orders for payment of moneys due under a mortgage or a personal judgment, (*l*) the action is a probate action, or (*m*) the action is in respect of a claim by the commissioners of inland revenue for estate duty or capital transfer tax, the defendants not being domiciled or ordinarily resident in Scotland or Northern Ireland.

A specimen of an affidavit for an order for service out of the jurisdiction follows.

Forms and precedents

Atkin, Vol 35 (1991 issue).

6. Amendments

Writs

Before service, amendments can relate to causes of action or parties and leave is not required. After service and if before close of pleadings, leave is not required for the first amendment, unless it relates to causes of action or parties, but is required otherwise under Ord 20, r 5(1) when it may be granted on terms including as to costs.

Originating summons

Leave is always required prior to any amendments.

Acknowledgment of service

The defendant can amend his acknowledgment to remove notice of intention to defend and also, provided he does so before judgment, to include a notice of intention to defend (Ord 20, r 2; a fresh acknowledgment must be lodged in the court office).

Any party may amend his pleading once without leave, provided this is before close of pleadings, ie before the expiry of 14 days after last pleading served, this does not enable change of parties, for which leave is required (RSC Ord 20, r 3(a)—unless the amendment is made before service). There is opportunity for the other party to apply within 14 days for the court to order the amendment to be disallowed, and it can be disallowed if leave to amend would have been refused had it been a case where leave to amend had been necessary.

Pleadings

In any cause or matter, any pleading may be amended at any stage by written agreement between the parties (Ord 20, r 12(1)) as amended. The rule says nothing as to costs and in practice there may be instances where a party may be found only too willing to agree to an amendment at the cost of the party proposing it (see Ord 62, r 3(3)). Order 20, r 12(1) does not apply to amendments to counterclaims which would consist of the addition, omission or

Affidavit for an order of service out of jurisdiction

FILED on behalf of the Plaintiff
AFFIDAVIT No 1 Deponent: ANTHONY BODKIN
Date Sworn: 31 August 1991

IN THE HIGH COURT OF JUSTICE   CH1991 B No 99
CHANCERY DIVISION

[In the Matter of the Supreme Court Act 1981

And in the Matter of an intended action]

BETWEEN

      ANTHONY BODKIN Intended Plaintiff
        -and-
      CHARLES DARWIN Intended Defendant

I, ANTHONY BODKIN, of 8 Lammas Street, Harmsworth, Wessex, publisher, MAKE OATH and say as follows:

1. I am the intended Plaintiff in this intended action.

2. I am entitled to the reversion in premises known as Tyglas Farm, Benaford, West Wales.

3. By a lease dated 3rd September 1983 and made between (1) me, this deponent, and (2) Gwilym Jones, the said premises were demised to Gwilym Jones who on 6th June 1988 assigned his interest in the lease to the above-named intended Defendant, who is now entitled to the term demised by the lease.

4. The lease contained a covenant by which the tenant undertook to keep the premises in good repair and condition.

5. The premises are not in good repair and condition in accordance with the said covenant, and the above-named intended Defendant has refused and still refuses to carry out the said repairs. The following are short particulars of the said want of repair and refusal: The main timbers are collapsing and the premises require to be re-roofed.

Affidavit for an order of service out of jurisdiction

6. The intended Defendant is at present residing at 17 Rue de la Palace, Chemins de Fer, Brittany, in France outside the jurisdiction of this Honourable Court.

7. I am advised and verily believe that I have a good cause of action against the intended Defendant in respect of the matters set out in paragraphs 2-5 hereof.

8. In the circumstances I respectfully crave leave to issue a Writ for service out of the jurisdiction against the said Charles Darwin for damages for breach of covenant in respect of the said lease and to serve the Writ out of the jurisdiction on the intended Defendant. I submit that this application falls within Order 11 rule 1(a) of the Rules of the Supreme Court.

Note:

Care will have to be taken to ensure that the case in question falls within one of the several categories listed in RSC Ord 11 r 1.

Sworn at
Lawless, Sussex
this 30th day of August
1991

   Before me

      M LEWIS

      Solicitor

         Filed on behalf of the Intended Plaintiff

substitution of a party (r 12(2)). Without written agreement leave must be obtained and will be granted on the basis that a party has a right to amend his pleading and that there is no injustice if other parties can be compensated by costs.

However, leave to amend will not be granted without consent to raise a cause of action (unless within Ord 20, r 5(5)) which accrued to the plaintiff only after the action commenced, to raise causes of action after the expiry of limitation periods, or to withdraw an admissions consciously made (*Hollis v Burton* [1982] 3 Ch 226). Leave to amend is sometimes but only reluctantly given at the trial—for the general principles for grant of leave, see AP, Vol 1, 20/5-8/6.

Method of making amendments

Room 307/308 will require two top copies of the amended writ (or originating summons) and additional copies for each defendant to be served and a copy of the amended pleading. The customary sequence of colour for the written or typewritten amendment is red followed by green followed by violet, and then yellow (Masters' Practice Direction No 15 (AP, Vol 2, 916). Superseded words must remain legible but struck out in the appropriate colour and counsel's name must be retyped again in the appropriate colour. Re-service will be required unless dispensed with and the amended document must be indorsed 'amended -/- '91 under RSC Ord 20, r 3' or 'amended -/- '91 pursuant to Order dated -/- '91'.

7. Default judgments

The plaintiff may apply to the court for judgment in default of a notice of intention to defend or in default of defence. It is essential in cases where no response has been received from the defendant to prove that the writ was served on the defendant. A judgment in default is not a judgment on the merits of the case but simply the result of failure to answer the claim. Such a judgment is available only for claims to money, goods or land (but not in a mortgage action or in relation to a dwelling house). It is not possible by this means to obtain an injunction, an order for specific performance or other equitable relief, or judgment on a counterclaim. In such cases an application by way of motion for judgment may be appropriate.

Pleadings

Under Ord 18, r 19, a court has power to strike out part or the whole of a pleading or a writ of summons or originating summons which discloses no reasonable course of action or is frivolous, vexatious or scandalous, or is in any other way an abuse of court procedure. The court will consider an application to strike out only where there is a plain and obvious case to do so, as judgment should never be given without a party having every reasonable opportunity to put forward his case. Since affidavits under the originating summons procedure in many ways equate with pleadings, the court will treat the contents of affidavits with regard to striking out in the same way as they might do a pleading.

Discovery

Disobedience in respect of an order to make discovery or produce documents for the purpose of inspection, or for any other purpose, may be penalised under Ord 24, r 16 by the claim or defence being struck out in an extreme case, and judgment given for the other party, and in some cases by committal. Under Ord 45, r 5 the court reserves to itself powers to commit to prison a party who has failed to comply with an order restraining him from acting or defaulting in a positive order to take action. In all such cases, it is necessary to serve the party or at least to be able to say that he has been made aware of the terms of the order (see Ord 24, r 16(3)) be it only through his solicitors. A solicitor whose client has failed to comply with such an order and who himself has not discharged his duties to the court, may also be the subject of a committal. In the Chancery Division such an order can be invoked by the other party, or by the court of its own motion, if production of information for the drawing up of accounts, or for inquiries, or investigations have not been forthcoming and the court is not provided with an adequate explanation. Such orders give the court the necessary sanctions to ensure that an investigation is properly and completely exhausted. A party, however, seeking to enforce any order must strictly comply with the rules of court. If no overt action has been taken in any matter for a period of 12 months by any party, it is necessary to give (usually by letter) one month's notice setting out intention to proceed (Ord 3, r 6).

'Four-day' orders

Under Ord 42, r 2 any party required to take a positive action by reason of a judgment or order of the court must do so within the time specified in the order. That time is normally given in the order but if it is not given and is an order to pay money or give possession of a property forthwith, the court will construe the time as one in which, taking into consideration all the circumstances of the case, a party could be expected to comply. In the Chancery Division, it became common practice to make an order without fixing a time, and if the party against whom the order was made did not comply with it a further application was made to enforce the order which invariably required the party within four days of taking the supplemental order to comply with the original order within four days. The court nowadays does not keep strictly to this 'four-day' rule and will give a party a reasonable time to comply with the order. In this order, still commonly called a 'four-day' order, will be given not only the time within which the original order must be complied with, but also exactly how the party is to comply, for example a specific statement as to the place where accounts or answers to inquiries are to be given.

Discontinuance

Under Ord 21, in an action, whether commenced by writ or originating summons, the plaintiff may discontinue not later than 14 days after defence but otherwise, except in certain circumstances, the plaintiff cannot discontinue, without the leave of the court. The court will give consideration to the possibility that the action should be struck out and what should be determined as to costs. If on application for leave to discontinue, the action is dismissed, the plaintiff cannot commence a fresh action. If the plaintiff can bring a fresh action, it could be stayed until the defendant's costs of the prior action were paid.

It is possible without the leave of the court for the plaintiff to withdraw his claim or any part of it or to discontinue an action commenced by writ or to withdraw any question or claim in an originating summons (Ord 21, r 2(3A) as inserted by r 10 or RSC (Amendment No 3) 1982)) provided he does so not later than 14 days after service of defence or defendant's affidavit by the last defendant served. Notice should be served. A defendant may withdraw his defence or any part of it at any time or discontinue any counterclaim up to 14 days after the defence has been served, unless an interim payment has been ordered. There may also be discontinuance or withdrawal of proceedings commenced by originating summons at any time not later than 14 days after service of the defendant's affidavit, or the last affidavit if there are two or more defendants. In all other instances, save by agreement, leave must be applied for on summons. Parties may always agree to the discontinuance of an action and for an order on their own terms. A party may withdraw an interlocutory summons only by consent or with leave of the court (Ord 21, r 6).

In the County Court, County Court Order 18, r 1 does allow a plaintiff to discontinue without the necessity of leave, and on notice only.

8. Time

A defendant has to return the form of acknowledgment of service by handing it in at or by posting it to the court office, and if posted the date of acknowledgment is the date of receipt by the court office and not the date of posting (Ord 12, r 1(5) as amended). The period within which the defendant may acknowledge service is 14 days after the service of the writ and inclusive of the day of service.

The writ itself remains valid for the purpose of service for 12 months beginning with the date of its issue. The duration of the writ for the purpose of service and the time within which acknowledgment of service must be given are inclusive as compared with nearly all other periods of time fixed by the rules or by order of the court which are exclusive, that is, so many days after a specified date or so many clear days before a specified date.

The rules relating to time are set out in Ord 3.

(1) The word 'month' in any judgment and order means a calendar month unless the context otherwise requires (Ord 3, r 1).

(2) Where an act is required to be done within a specified period after or from a specified date, the period begins immediately after that date, eg, if the act is to be done within one month from 15 January the last date for doing the act is 15 February, if the act is to be done within one month after 31 March the last day is 30 April (Ord 3, r 2(2), (3)).

(3) Where the period in question is seven days or less, Saturdays, Sundays, and bank holidays are excluded (Ord 3, r 2(5)).

(4) If the expression 'clear days' is used, the date from which the period commences and the day when the act is done are excluded from the computation (Ord 3, r 2(5)).

(5) Time for serving, filing and amending pleadings does not run in the long vacation, ie August unless the court otherwise directs (Ord 3, r 3). This does not cover the service of an affidavit nor a notice of appeal. Time continues to run during the short vacations.

(6) Where the time for doing an act at an office of the Supreme Court expires on a Sunday or other day when the offices are closed, the act may be done on the next day on which the office is open (Ord 3, r 4).

(7) The court may on such terms as it thinks fit, extend or abridge any period for doing any act which is fixed by the rules of court or by any judgment or order (Ord 3, r 5(1)). Such extension may be made even if application is not made until after the time has expired (Ord 3, r 5(2)).

(8) An extension of the time of any pleading can be made in writing between the parties without any order of the court (Ord 3, r 5(3)).

(9) Sometimes the court will make an order that unless a party does a certain act by a certain time, eg, serve further particulars of the defence in 14 days, the action will be dismissed with costs. The court has power to extend that time in an appropriate case (*Samuels v Linzi Dresses Ltd* [1981] QB 115). The court will very rarely make a peremptory order or attach a default clause on a first application (*Siebe Gorman & Co Ltd v Pneupac Ltd* [1982] 1 WLR 185 at 190).

Commencement and Conduct of an Action—Orders

1. ORDERS FOR DIRECTIONS ON ORIGINATING SUMMONS: VARIOUS EXAMPLES

IT IS ORDERED

1 that ... be added as a plaintiff/defendant in this Action and that the Originating Summons be amended accordingly

2 that the plaintiff be at liberty to amend the said Originating Summons in the manner indicated in red on the copy annexed hereto initialled by the Master

3 that the plaintiff be at liberty to amend the said Originating Summons by adding/deleting the words '...'

4 that the defendant be at liberty to serve a Counterclaim to the said Originating Summons [in accordance with the copy annexed hereto]

5 that the plaintiff shall on or before ... file at Room 307/308 Thomas More Building Chancery Chambers Royal Courts of Justice Strand London WC2A 2LL his/her/its/their Affidavit evidence [as to .../as to the matters set forth in the schedule hereto] and do at the same time serve copies of the same on the defendant

6 that the defendant shall within ... days after service upon him/her/it/them/of the plaintiff's said Affidavit/evidence file at the said Chancery Chambers his/her/its/their/Affidavit evidence in answer and do at the same time serve copies of the same on the plaintiff

7 that the plaintiff shall within ... days after service upon him/her/it/them/of the defendant's affidavit evidence in answer file at the said Chancery Chambers his/her/its/their/Affidavit/evidence in reply and do at the same time serve copies of the same on the defendant

8 that the plaintiff be at liberty to cross-examine the deponents named in the first schedule hereto upon their respective affidavits or affirmations sworn or affirmed in this Action

9 that the defendants be at liberty to cross-examine the deponents named in the second schedule hereto upon their respective affidavits or affirmations sworn or affirmed in this Action

10 that such cross-examination be taken before the court at the hearing in court of the said Originating Summons

11 that the defendant shall produce the deponents named in the first schedule hereto for cross-examination accordingly and that the plaintiff do produce the deponents named in the second schedule hereto and that if any of the said deponents be not produced for cross-examination the party failing to produce such deponent is not to be at liberty to read or use the evidence of such deponent without the leave of the court

12 that the plaintiff and/or the defendant are to be at liberty to adduce oral evidence at the hearing in court of the said Originating Summons

13 that lists of documents be served on or before ... and that there be inspection within ... days thereafter

14 that the plaintiff and the defendant respectively shall on or before ... or subsequently within ... days after service of this Order make and serve on the other of them a list duly verified by affidavit of the documents which are or have been in their possession custody or power relating to the matters in question in this Action [and Counterclaim] and accounting therefor and serve on the other of them a copy of the said Affidavit and shall at the same time serve on the other of them a Notice stating a time within ... days thereof when the documents may be inspected at a place specified in the said Notice

15 that the parties shall on or before ... exchange lists of the comparable properties to which they may wish to refer

16 that the costs of this application are to be costs in the cause

17 that the further hearing of the said Originating Summons shall stand adjourned to ...

18 that the further hearing of the said Originating Summons shall stand adjourned generally with liberty to restore the same

19 that the further hearing of the said Originating Summons is adjourned to be heard in Court and be set down in Part ... of the Witness List for hearing in London before a judge alone the estimated duration of the hearing being ... days ... AND the parties are to be at liberty to apply.

Notes

1 An originating summons is one of the four possible ways in which a plaintiff may commence proceedings in the High Court (the others being writ of summons, originating notice of motion and petition). For the provisions as to issue and as to the form of the originating summons see RSC Ord 7 and Vol 29 Atkins Court Forms Title 'Originating Summons'.

2 The procedure governing an originating summons is contained in Ord 28 unless there are other provisions either in the Rules of the Supreme Court or under any Act relating to any particular type of originating summons (Ord 28, r 1).

3 Unless the master disposes of the originating summons at the first appointment (Ord 28, r 4(1)), or transfers it to some other court or directs that the originating summons should continue as if it had been begun by writ of summons under Ord 28, r 8, the master will give such directions for the further conduct of the proceedings as he thinks best adapted to serve the just expeditious and economical disposal thereof (Ord 28, r 4(2)).

4 By Ord 20, rr 5 and 7 the originating summons may be amended at any stage of the proceedings with the leave of the court. This may be done by summons or *ex parte* in an appropriate case.

5 The defendant may counterclaim instead of having a separate action but he must inform the court at the first or any resumed hearing of the nature of his counterclaim and obtain the leave of the court (Ord 28, r 7).

6 Except in such applications where there are special rules affidavit evidence is filed in accordance with a time-table fixed by the Rules of Court (Ord 28, r 1A).

7 The court may order the attendance of deponents for cross-examination at the trial or that the parties may adduce oral evidence at the hearing (Ord 28, r 4(3)).

8 The court may also give any further directions for discovery or otherwise as may be given under a summons for directions in a writ action (Ord 28, r 4(4)).

9 The court may adjourn the originating summons from time to time but it is the usual practice to stand over the hearing to another fixed date (Ord 28, r 5).

10 Where the matter has to be determined by a judge the master will adjourn the originating summons into the appropriate list. The plaintiff's solicitors will hand to the master the original originating summons and no further action by them is required (Ord 28, r 9). No fee is payable.

2. ORDER TO CONVERT TO WRIT

IT IS ORDERED

1 that these proceedings shall continue as if this Action had been begun by Writ of Summons

2 [that the Affidavit of ... sworn ... shall stand as the Statement of Claim] [the plaintiffs do serve a Statement of Claim on or before ...]

3 that the defendants shall serve a Defence and Counterclaim (if any) within ... days after the service of the said Statement of Claim

4 that the plaintiffs may serve a Reply and Defence to Counterclaim (if any) within ... days after the service of the said Defence and Counterclaim (if any)

5 that the costs of the hearing this day of the said application are to be costs in the cause
AND the further hearing of the said Originating Summons (standing pursuant to Order 28 Rule 8(2) as a Summons for directions) is to stand over generally with liberty to restore.

3. DIRECTIONS IN WRIT ACTIONS: VARIOUS EXAMPLES

IT IS ORDERED

1 that ... be added as a plaintiff/defendant in this Action and that the Writ of Summons be amended accordingly

2 that the plaintiff be at liberty to amend the Writ of Summons by adding ... as a defendant/plaintiff in this Action and by making consequential amendments

3 that the plaintiff shall serve a Statement of Claim on or before ...

4 that the defendant shall serve a Defence and any Counterclaim on or before ... [within ... days after service of the Statement of Claim]

5 that the plaintiff be at liberty to serve a Reply and Defence to Counterclaim on or before ... [within ... days after service of the Defence and Counterclaim]

6 that the time for service of the Statement of Claim/Defence/Reply be extended so as to expire on . . .

7 that the plaintiff be at liberty without re-serving the same to amend the Statement of Claim in the manner indicated in red on the copy annexed hereto initialled by the Master by . . .

8 that the plaintiff be at liberty on or before . . . to serve an amended Statement of Claim

9 that the defendant be at liberty to serve an amended Defence and Counterclaim within . . . days after service of the amended Statement of Claim

10 that the plaintiff be at liberty to serve an amended Reply and Defence to Counterclaim within . . . days after service of the amended Defence and Counterclaim.

11 that the plaintiff/defendant shall on or before . . . serve on the plaintiff/defendant the further and better particulars of the Statement of Claim/Defence and Counterclaim/Reply and Defence to Counterclaim in accordance with the Request therefore served . . . a copy of which is annexed hereto specified in the schedule hereto

12 that lists of documents be served on or before . . . [within . . . days after the close of Pleadings] and that there be inspection within . . . days thereafter

13 that the plaintiff and the defendant respectively shall on or before . . . or subsequently within . . . days after service of this order . . . make and serve on the other of them a list duly verified by affidavit of the documents which are or have been in their possession custody or power relating to the matters in question in this Action/Counterclaim and accounting therefor and serve on the other of them a copy of the said affidavit and shall at the same time serve on the other of them a Notice stating a time within . . . days thereof when the documents may be inspected at a place specified in the said Notice

14 that the plaintiff and the defendant respectively shall on or before . . . or subsequently within . . . days after service of this Order make and file and serve on the other of them copies of full and sufficient affidavits stating whether they respectively have or have had in their possession or power any and (if any) what documents relating to the matters in question in this Action and Counterclaim and accounting therefor

15 that the plaintiff and the defendant respectively shall within ... days after such affidavits shall have been filed at all reasonable times upon reasonable notice produce at the offices of their respective solicitors the documents which by such affidavits shall appear to be in their possession or power except such of the said documents (if any) as they may by such affidavits respectively object to produce

16 that the defendant and plaintiff respectively or their respective solicitors and agents are to be at liberty to inspect and peruse the documents so produced and to make notes of their contents and are to be entitled to be supplied with copies thereof and extracts therefrom as they respectively shall be advised upon payment therefor at the prescribed rate

17 that the plaintiff and the defendant respectively shall produce such documents upon any examination of witnesses in this Action and Counterclaim and at the trial thereof as the defendant and the plaintiff respectively shall require

18 that experts' reports be agreed if possible and that in default of agreement the expert evidence at the trial be limited ... witnesses for the plaintiff and ... for the defendant being witnesses whose reports have been disclosed on or before ...

19 that the plaintiff and the defendant respectively shall on or before ... not later than ... days after this Action and Counterclaim is set down for trial before the commencement of the trial of this Action and Counterclaim disclose to each other in the form of a written report or reports the substance of any expert evidence by which is to be adduced by them at the trial.
[That if either/any of the parties intends to place reliance at the trial on expert evidence he shall on or before the ... disclose the substance of that evidence to the other party/parties in the form of a written report which shall be agreed if possible]
[That unless such reports are agreed the parties shall be at liberty to call as expert witnesses those witnesses the substance of whose evidence has been disclosed as aforesaid but not more than ... expert witnesses shall be called for each party]
[That at the trial of the Action and Counterclaim the plaintiff ... and the defendant be each at liberty to adduce the expert evidence of one Chartered Accountant/Surveyor being a Witness whose report has been disclosed to the other party as aforesaid on or before ... [not later than ... days after their Action and Counterclaim is set down for trial] before the commencement of the trial of this Action and Counterclaim]

20 that the plaintiff shall on or before ... 199.. set down this Action and Counterclaim in Part ... of the Witness List for the trial

COMMENCEMENT AND CONDUCT OF AN ACTION 55

in London before a Judge alone the estimated duration of the trial being ... days

21 that the costs of the said Application are to be costs in the cause.

Note

This is a composite form and paragraphs not required should be deleted.

4. ORDERS FOR SUBSTITUTED SERVICE

(1) By post

IT IS ORDERED that service of the said writ of summons/originating summons by sending not later than one month from the date of this order [or not later than ... 199 ..] a sealed copy of such summons accompanied by the prescribed form of Acknowledgment of Service together with a copy of this order through the Post Office by prepaid ordinary first class letter post in an envelope addressed to ... [state full name of defendant and address for service] at ... be deemed good service of the said writ/originating summons upon the defendant.

(2) By advertisement

IT IS ORDERED that service of the said writ of summons/originating summons, on the defendant AB be effected by inserting and publishing not later than ... 199 .. once the ... newspaper and the ... newspaper a proper advertisement to the above named defendant AB of the institution of and claim in this action and of this order and of the requirement to acknowledge service and that such advertisement so published shall be deemed to be good and sufficient service of the said writ/originating summons on the defendant.

(3) By fixing to property

AND it appearing from the affidavit of AB that no person appears to be in possession of the property the subject matter of the action and that the plaintiff has served the said writ/originating summons by causing a copy thereof to be affixed to a conspicuous part of the said property that is to say on the front door thereof and that service of the said writ/originating summons could not otherwise have been effected on the defendant.

IT IS ORDERED that such affixing of the said writ of summons/originating summons be treated as good service on the defendant.

5. ORDER FOR SERVICE OUT OF JURISDICTION (ON MOTION)

IT IS ORDERED

1 that the plaintiffs be at liberty to issue a concurrent Writ of Summons [Originating Summons] and to serve
(1)   the said Writ of Summons [Originating Summons] with the prescribed form of acknowledgment of service.
(2) Notice of Motion for...
(3) this Order upon the defendant out of the jurisdiction of this Court at... or elsewhere in the... of...

2 that the time within which the defendant is to acknowledge service is to be within... days after service

3 [that service of the said document by sending a copy of the said Writ of Summons [Originating Summons] duly sealed with the seal of the Court office copies of the other documents together with the prescribed form of Acknowledgment of Service through the Post Office by prepaid airmail letter post in an envelope addressed to... be deemed good service of the said documents upon the defendant]

4 [that the said documents be deemed to be duly served on the defendant at the expiration of... days from the date of the posting of the said copies].

Notes

1 If a writ has already been issued it will probably be endorsed 'Not for service out of the jurisdiction' and the leave will be to issue a concurrent writ.

2 The time for acknowledging service is found in the Extra Jurisdiction Tables in para 941, p 226 of the SCP Vol 2.

3 Order 11, r 5 deals with the manner of service. A writ need not be served personally if it is served in accordance with the law of the country in which service is effected. Order 10, r 1(2) and (3) do not apply and postal service is not necessarily sufficient. Sometimes an order for substituted service is combined with an order for service out of the jurisdiction. When this happens paras 3 and 4 of the precedent should be included.

6. ORDER SETTING ASIDE SERVICE ABROAD

IT IS ORDERED

1 that the Order dated ... (which is endorsed on the Writ of Summons in this Action) the said Writ of Summons the service of the same on the Defendant and all subsequent proceedings in this Action be set aside

2 that the Plaintiff shall pay to the Defendant £ ... costs of this Action to be taxed if not agreed

7. EXAMPLES OF FORMS OF ORDER GIVING LEAVE TO AMEND PLEADINGS

1 IT IS ORDERED that A B be added as a defendant and the writ of summons be amended accordingly.

2 IT IS ORDERED that the defendant be at liberty on or before ... to serve an amended defence.

3 IT IS ORDERED that the defendant be at liberty to amend his defence without reserving the same by ...

4 IT IS ORDERED that the plaintiff be at liberty to amend his statement of claim by substituting the words ... for the words ...

5 IT IS ORDERED that the plaintiff be at liberty to amend his statement of claim as shown in red on the amended statement of claim initialled by the master.

Note

1 By Ord 42, r 4 orders giving leave to amend need not be drawn up unless the court otherwise directs. An order is usually drawn up when there are other directions which require drawing up.

8. DEFAULT JUDGMENT IN ACTION FOR LIQUIDATED DAMAGES (Ord 13, r 1; Ord 19, r 2; Ord 42, r 1)

The ... day of ... 199 ...
No notice of intention to defend having been given [or no defence having been served] by the defendant herein, it is this day adjudged that the defendant do pay the plaintiff £ ... and £ ... costs [or costs to be taxed].

9. DEFAULT JUDGMENT IN ACTION FOR UNLIQUIDATED DAMAGES (Ord 13, r 2; Ord 19, r 3; Ord 42, r 1)

The ... day of ... 199 ..
No notice of intention to defend having been given [or no defence having been served] by the defendant herein, it is this day adjudged that the defendant do pay the plaintiff damages to be assessed

10. DEFAULT JUDGMENT IN ACTION RELATING TO DETENTION OF GOODS (Ord 13, r 3; Ord 19, r 4; Ord 42, r 1)

The ... day of ... 199 ...
No notice of intention to defend having been given [or no defence having been served] by the defendant herein.

It is this day adjudged that the defendant deliver to the plaintiff the goods described in the writ of summons [or statement of claim] as [description of goods] or pay the plaintiff the value of the said goods to be assessed [and also damages for their detention to be assessed]

or

It is this day adjudged that the defendant pay the plaintiff the value of the goods described in the writ of summons [or statement of claim] to be assessed [and also damages for their detention to be assessed]

11. DEFAULT JUDGMENT IN ACTION FOR POSSESSION OF LAND (Ord 13, r 4; Ord 19, r 5; Ord 42, r 1)

The ... day of ... 199 ..
No notice of intention to defend having been given [or no defence having been served] by the defendant herein, it is this day adjudged that the defendant give the plaintiff possession of the land described in the writ of summons [or statement of claim] as ... and pay the plaintiff £ ... costs [or costs to be taxed]

[and that the defendant pay to the plaintiff £ ... for mesne profits at the rate of £ ... per ... from (the date when mesne profits begin to run) up to the date hereof and further mesne profits at the same rate up to the time of obtaining possession] [mesne profits to be assessed].

Notes

1 Sometimes a plaintiff wishes to obtain judgment for part of his claim and abandon the rest (eg injunctive relief). There should be a recital 'No defence having been served [No notice of intention to defend having been given] and the plaintiff abandoning his other claims in the action'.

2 A liquidated demand is in the nature of a debt and its amount must be already ascertained or capable of being ascertained by arithmetic. A default judgment cannot be entered in a mortgage action when Ord 88, r 6 applies.

3 A plaintiff may enter judgment for less than he claims, eg, if something has been paid since the issue of the writ.

4 If judgment is being claimed for possession of land a certificate must be endorsed on the original judgment (1) that the plaintiff is not claiming any relief in a mortgage action under Ord 88 and (2) the claim does not relate to a dwelling house of which the rateable value comes within the provisions of the Rent Act 1977.

5 Any claim for interest should be specifically pleaded as required by Ord 18, r 8(4). Contractual interest if properly pleaded can result in a liquidated claim. So does any interest under Ord 13, r 1(2). In other cases judgment is for interest to be assessed.

Chapter Three

Intitulement and Parties

1. Intitulement

Statutes

If proceedings are under a statute it is not now to be mentioned in the title; but it should be referred to in the body of the writ or originating summons (para 2 Practice Directions (Chancery Procedure) No 2 1982) [1983] 1 WLR 4).

Probate actions/administration of estates

Above the names of the parties and below 'Chancery Division'— 'In the Estate of AB deceased' (ibid).

Construction of wills, deeds and document

The terms of a will or contents of a deed or instrument are often put before the court for construction or implementation when the will, deed or instrument must be included in the heading thus— 'In the matter of the Trusts declared by a conveyance dated   and made between the   and   of 67, St. Lukes Hill, Battersea, SW11.' (ibid).

When naming the parties to deeds or instruments in a heading, the initials only and not the full names should precede the surnames; if there are numerous parties 'between AB and others' will usually suffice. The exhibits may be even further shortened, eg *'in re Luke deceased Smith v Brown'*. Where an action is intituled 'In the matter of   and in the matter of', the intitulement to the affidavit should read: 'In the matter of   and other matters'.

The description of the property in the heading should be the postal address; if this is inapplicable, then the description should be a short concise one. The tenure, eg freehold, leasehold, need not be given in titles. Where there are several documents or instruments only the main or first document need be referred to. Where a specific property is referred to, its postal address suffices without mention of its tenure or area or the type of any building thereon.

Parties suing or sued in representative capacities

Any representative capacity in which a plaintiff sues or a defendant is sued should not be stated in the title. Thus, 'AB (Executor of the estate of the late John Avery deceased)' is wrong, and the correct heading in the title is simply the full name of the executor or trustee; it is in the body of the originating process that should be stated the representative capacity in which the plaintiff sues or the defendant is sued together with particulars of the deceased.

Numerous defendants

There may be numerous defendants; each name should then be prefixed by a number or letter in brackets (Practice Note [1981] 1 WLR 1561).

Parties added

Not infrequently parties, whether plaintiffs or defendants, have to be added and the procedure is that application must be made either on a hearing of the originating summons, or on the hearing of a summons taken out for that purpose, for leave to add a party and to amend the proceedings. The court may at any time allow or direct the addition of striking out or substituting any person as a party (Ord 15, r 6; Ord 20, rr 5, 8; Ord 15, r 1(1)). Application is made on summons. Plaintiffs cannot be added without their consent in writing which may be given by their solicitor having authority to do so and in the case of a person under disability not without consent in writing of the next friend. Following an order, the additional or substituted names will appear in the title and in all court documents by inserting after the name of the party added '(added ... / ... / ... 91)'. If proceedings are stayed against any party then after that party's name in the title and in all subsequent documents should be added: '(proceedings stayed ... / ... / ... 91)'. Where proceedings are stayed against any particular party, then subsequent documents will show his name and after his name the words '(proceedings stayed ... / ... / ...)'. Where a party has by order been added the writ or originating summons should be amended (Ord 15, r 8(1)).

Transmission of interest

If because of death or bankruptcy the interest of a party is assigned or transmitted to a personal representative, trustee, or other person, application must be made by summons to the master for an order to carry on proceedings (Ord 15, r 7) and all subsequent documents will be headed, if there has been a trustee in bankruptcy appointed 'The trustee of the property of AB, a bankrupt' or in the case of a grant having been issued in respect of the estate of a deceased, 'AB and CD, executors of the will of the late AB deceased'. The name of the individual appointed as trustee in bankruptcy is not given.

Change of name

If there is a change of name by a party after proceedings have been commenced (as on the marriage of a woman), that party must promptly file a written notice of the change of name in Chancery Chambers or the appropriate Chancery district registry, and serve a copy on every other party. When the notice has been filed, the new name must be substituted in the title of the proceedings, followed by the former name (prefaced by the word 'formerly') in brackets. The action number, including the letter will remain unchanged (para 4 Practice Direction (Chancery Applications: Change of Name) No 1 of 1984).

Substituted names

Whensoever a party changes his, her or its name during the currency of proceedings which he may do without order, he files written notice (see Masters' Practice Directions 13(3) and (4) in AP, Vol 2 para 914)) and the new name is substituted thenceforth, the former name being mentioned in brackets after it. This applies to both individuals and to limited companies. There is maintained in chancery masters' chambers 'The Chancery Book', in which each of the masters retains notes sent round relating to practice directions referable to those litigants who have a substantial amount of work in the department and who have changed their names. In the main these are building societies and banks who may be always taking action in the Chancery Division. To obviate unnecessary expenditure the direction which enables the alteration when first applied for becomes an internal practice direction referable to all other cases which are then current.

Minors

If a plaintiff is an infant, that is under 18 years of age, at the time the action is commenced, he will be shown in the title as 'AB (a minor)'. In the body of the originating summons or writ but not in the heading, the name of the minor's next friend must be given eg 'AB sues by CD his next friend'. The term minor should be used throughout in lieu of infant, the description minor having been introduced by the Family Law Reform Act 1969. The minor may attain full age during the course of proceedings and the title of all subsequent documents will then be amended by the addition of the words after the minor's name '(... late a minor)'. The originating summons or writ will not be amended (Ord 6, r 3).

Mentally disordered persons

Where the plaintiff is a mentally disordered person, the name of his next friend must be set out in the title, thus: 'AB by CD his next friend'.

Companies in liquidation

If the company is in liquidation the words 'in liquidation' should follow the name and after the registered office of the company should be added 'by the liquidator AB of his address and description to be given'. It will be noted that in the case of bankruptcy, actions are headed: 'Trustee of the property of AB a bankrupt' and the name of the trustee is not given.

Description of females

The description of females within documents should be 'Mrs' or 'Miss' (and not descriptions such as 'spinster', 'married woman' or 'feme sole'). The names only should be given in the heading.

2. Parties

Plaintiff residing out of England and Wales

When it appears that the plaintiff is ordinarily resident out of England and Wales on the defendant's application the court may order the plaintiff to give security for costs (Ord 23, r 1(1)). Plaintiffs may make similar applications against defendants who counterclaim (Ord 23, r 1(3)). The court may say on what terms security is to be ordered, and has discretion as to the manner in which it is to be given.

Plaintiff limited company

Where it appears that a plaintiff limited company wheresoever registered may be unable to pay a successful defendant's costs, security may be ordered by a judge (s 726 of the Companies Act 1985).

Members' clubs

One or more persons may sue or be sued on their own behalf and on behalf of the club if they have a common interest with all the other persons (Ord 15, r 12). A judgment in such represented proceedings may not be enforced against a non-party without leave of the court (Ord 15, r 12(3)). Proprietary clubs are often limited companies and if so they sue and are sued in their corporate name.

Limited companies

The registered office must be given on all documents and no other address need be stated unless it is for the purpose of showing a business address within England and Wales or to show at what address notices for a plaintiff company should be sent. A corporation resides where it carries on business and it can reside in more places than one (*Davies v British Geon Ltd* [1957] 1 QB 1).

Partnerships

Any one of two or more partners carrying on business in England or Wales may sue and be sued in the name of the firm in which he was a partner when the cause of action arose (Ord 81, r 1) subject to his obligations to account and his rights of indemnity against other partners. This is the situation even if one of the partners is under a disability, such as minority. However, a defendant has the right to know the full names of all the partners of a plaintiff firm (Ord 81, r 2) and may obtain an order staying the actions until his request for particulars has been complied with. Judgment cannot be enforced against unnamed individuals who are partners without the leave of the court.

Business firms

A person carrying on business in other than his own name may be sued in his own name followed by the words 'Trading as XYZ', or may be sued in his business name followed by the words 'A Trading name' (Ord 81, r 1). He may not, however, sue in his business name. If he sues in his own name, his business name may properly be cited in the body of the statement of a claim.

The Crown

The title of the department suing or being sued must be precisely stated in accordance with the list of Crown Departments published under s 17 of the Crown Proceedings Act 1947. This list appears in AP, Vol 2 para 3979 and at p 1089 of The County Court Practice 1982. The statement of claim in actions against the Crown must specify the circumstances in which the Crown's liability is said to have arisen and as to the Government Department and Officers of the Crown concerned. No default judgment can be entered against the Crown save by leave of the court on application on seven days' notice, nor can summary judgment be given against the Crown (Ord 77, r 9).

Trustees in bankruptcy

Such a trustee should sue or be sued as 'trustee of the property of AB a bankrupt' without adding his own name (s 76 of the

Insolvency Act 1986; *Pooley's Trustee v Whetham* (1884) 28 Ch D 38). A trustee to a bankrupt mortgagor may be in possession actually or constructively and should be made a party.

Transmission of interest

If an interest is transmitted by death or bankruptcy for example or by a person coming into existence after commencement of the proceedings, then the trustee or executor must apply for 'an order to carry on' the proceedings (Ord 15, r 7).

Representation orders where all desire to be represented

Where numerous persons have the same interest application may be made by summons (or by notice under Ord 25) for the court to make a representation order for one or more persons to be a party on behalf of himself and all others who have the same interest but the order will be made only if the persons to be represented are numerous, or their interests are small, and the court is satisfied that all desire to be so represented.

Representation orders where persons cannot be readily ascertained in cases of trust property, administration and construction

Pursuant to Ord 15, r 13 in any proceedings concerning property subject to a trust, administration of estates or construction the court may appoint one or more persons to represent any person (including an unborn person) or class who is or may be interested (whether presently or for any future contingent or unascertained interest) provided it is satisfied that it is expedient to do so and that one or more of the following conditions are satisfied:

(1) The person, class or some member of the class cannot be ascertained or cannot be readily ascertained.
(2) The person, class or some member of the class, though ascertained, cannot be found.
(3) Though the person or the class and the member of it can be ascertained and found, it appears to the court expedient (regard being had to all the circumstances, including the amount at stake and the degree of difficulty of the point to be determined) to exercise the power for the purpose of saving expense.

Judgment and orders given under Ord 15, r 12 or r 13 provided the person or persons appointed are before the court, are generally binding on all the persons represented, with exceptions in case of fraud or non-disclosure or on the grounds that the judgment should not be enforced.

Persons under a disability

The rules relating to litigants under a disability, that is, minors and mentally disordered persons are contained in Ord 80.

A minor is defined as a person who has not attained the age of 18 years (Family Law Reform Act 1969) and a mentally disordered person as a person who by reason of 'mental disorder' within the meaning of the Mental Health Act 1983 is incapable of managing and administering his property and affairs. A mentally disordered person is referred to as 'a patient' whether or not he is within the jurisdiction of the Court of Protection. A minor or patient must sue by his 'next friend' and be sued through his 'guardian *ad litem*', and his next friend or guardian *ad litem* must be represented by a solicitor (Ord 80, r 2(3)).

When a minor or patient is a plaintiff the writ or originating summons will not be issued until his solicitor has lodged the following documents in room 157:

(1) The written consent of the next friend (see AP, Vol 2 394 for form).
(2) (In the case of a minor) a certificate by the solicitor that he knows or believes that the plaintiff is a minor and (unless the Official Solicitor has been appointed) that the next friend is a fit and proper person and has no interest in the matter adverse to the plaintiff (Form PF 164).
(3) (In the case of a patient) an office copy of the order of the Court of Protection authorising the next friend to conduct the proceedings (Ord 81, r 3(6) and (8)) or (if the patient is not within the jurisdiction of the Court of Protection) a certificate by the solicitor that he knows or believes that the patient is a mentally disordered person (giving grounds for his knowledge or belief); that there is no person authorised by the Court of Protection to take proceedings on behalf of the plaintiff; and (unless the Official Solicitor has been appointed) that the next friend is a fit and proper person and has no interest in the matter adverse to the plaintiff or defendant as the case may be.

When a minor or patient is a defendant the same documents (mutatis mutandis) must be lodged by the solicitor upon or prior to his acknowledging service of the writ or originating summons.

Save when the Court of Protection has nominated a person to conduct proceedings on behalf of a patient any person may be appointed next friend or guardian *ad litem* without an order of the court, unless, (a) the appointment is required to replace an appointee who has died or been discharged, (b) one of the parties has become a patient after the commencement of proceedings or (c) a minor or patient has been served with a writ or originating summons or (not being already a party to the action) with a counterclaim or third party notice and (no acknowledgment of service having been made on his behalf) the plaintiff or claimant requires the appointment of a guardian *ad litem* in order that the action may proceed.

Except when the appointment is required to replace a deceased appointee (when an *ex parte* application suffices) the application must be made by summons supported by affidavit and notice of the application, unless the master sees fit to dispense with it, must be served on the minor or patient at least seven days before the hearing.

A next friend in proceedings in the High Court (unlike in the county court) is *not* required to file an attested statement to be responsible for costs. Any writ or originating summons issued against a person under a disability should be served (in the case of a minor) on his father or guardian or the person with whom he resides or in whose care he is, or (in the case of a patient) on the person authorised by the Court of Protection to conduct proceedings on his behalf or (if there is no such person) on the person with whom he resides or in whose care he is; but the court may direct that any document served upon the minor or patient personally shall be deemed to have been duly served. Thereafter all documents in the case should be served on the solicitor acting for the next friend or guardian *ad litem*, excepting orders requiring the minor or patient to do or refrain from doing any act which should be served on him personally, unless the court otherwise orders.

If a guardian *ad litem* fails to enter a defence, the plaintiff, instead of applying for judgment by default must set the action down for trial on the assumption that the defendant denies all the allegations on which the plaintiff's claim is founded.

If, in the course of an action, a minor attains his majority or a patient recovers his mental faculties, he must file a notice to that effect, a copy of which must be served on the other party or parties, together with an application by summons for the discharge of his next friend or guardian *ad litem* (as the case may be). The notice (see Masters' Practice Direction 31 in AP, Vol 2 para 932) should state whether he intends to continue (ie adopt) or discontinue the proceedings and in either case he assumes liability for costs as from the commencement of the action, but until his discharge a next friend or guardian *ad litem* is personally liable for costs awarded against him, subject to his right of indemnity from the minor's or patient's property (if any) provided he has acted in good faith and with reasonable prudence.

Any settlements or compromises or payment or acceptance of money into court must receive the approval of the court where money is claimed by, or on behalf of, a person under disability (Ord 80, r 10). In many such cases the settlement has been agreed upon between the respective solicitors, and in such cases the application for approval is by originating summons, and this may be issued either at Chancery chambers or out of any at all of the district registries (Ord 80, r 3). The summons should be supported by affidavit

(Practice Form PF 166 or PF 170-AP, Vol 2, 306, 309). The amount of the settlement should not be inserted in the summons. The affidavit is commonly made by the solicitor for the plaintiff who will set out particulars of the minor, and, unless they are succinctly set out in an originating process, will set out the facts, the present stage of the action, the issues, the offer to settle, and the opinion of the solicitor that it would be in the best interests of the plaintiff for the offer made to be accepted and if applicable, that this is supported by the opinion of counsel. It will state that the costs will be paid by the defendant or from a trust fund and that no deduction will be made from the sum to be paid in settlement, and conclude if appropriate, that the father and next friend of the minor is desirous of accepting the proposed settlement. These applications are heard by the judge unless the amount involved does not significantly exceed £30,000 (AP, Vol 1 80/10-11/4 and 32/14/2). If the proceedings have been begun by writ, then a summons is issued for the approval of the settlement, and if begun by originating summons, then they may be dealt with on the hearing of an appointment, due notice having been given to the defendants. In all such applications the next friend and minor should attend at the hearing of the application. The costs (unless the court otherwise directs) must be taxed (Ord 62, r 30 and notes to AP, Vol 1 80/12/10 and 11). The costs will be taxed on a solicitor and own client basis (AP, Vol 1 62/30/2).

Forms and precedents

Atkin, Vol 30 (1990 issue).

Intitulement and Parties—Orders

1. SOLICITOR CEASING TO ACT

UPON THE APPLICATION of Messrs... the solicitors on the record for the plaintiff/defendant
AND UPON HEARING
AND UPON READING the documents recorded on the court file as having been read
IT IS ORDERED that the applicants (and Messrs... their London Agents) have ceased to act as the solicitors and their London Agents respectively for the plaintiff/defendant in this action
AND IT IS ORDERED that the plaintiff/defendant shall pay the applicant £... their assessed costs of the application.

2. ORDER FOR DISCHARGE AND APPOINTMENT OF NEXT FRIEND

IT IS ORDERED

1 that... be discharged from his office as the Next Friend of the... of the plaintiff

2 that... be appointed Next Friend of the... plaintiff by whom... may continue the prosecution of this Action jointly with the other plaintiff

3 that the costs of the said Application be costs in the cause.

Notes

1 Where a new next friend is required in the place of an existing next friend, or where a next friend is required when a plaintiff in existing proceedings becomes a patient, an order is required and a summons must be issued (Ord 80, rr 3-5).

2 No summons is required on the death of a next friend. In such a case application is made to the master *ex parte* on affidavit.

3 See Atkin, Vol 30 (1990 Issue).

3. ORDER APPOINTING GUARDIAN *AD LITEM*

IT IS ORDERED that... be assigned guardian *ad litem* of the... defendant (a minor) by whom he/she/may acknowledge service and defend this action

AND the further hearing of the said Originating Summons is to stand over generally until...

Note

1 See Ord 80 for occasions on which an order of the court is required.

4. THIRD PARTY DIRECTIONS

IT IS ORDERED

1 that the Third Party Notice shall stand as the Statement of Claim in the Third Party proceedings

2 [that the defendant... shall on or before... serve a statement of his/her/its/their/claim upon the Third Party who shall plead thereto within... days after such service]

3 that the Third Party shall on/or before serve his/her/its/their/ Defence in the Third Party proceedings

4 that the defendant... and the Third Party shall exchange lists of documents within... days after the Pleadings in the Third Party proceedings are closed and that there be inspection of documents within... days thereafter

5 that the Third Party be at liberty to appear at the trial of this Action and take such part therein as the judge shall direct and be bound by the result of the trial

6 that the question of the liability of the Third Party to indemnify the defendant... be tried at the trial of this Action but subsequent thereto

7 that the costs of the said application be costs in the Action and in the Third Party proceedings.

Notes

1 The order for third party directions is normally drawn up and attached to the pleadings in the third party proceedings.

2 For setting down the defendant in the action supplies the plaintiff in the action with two copies of the pleadings and orders for third party directions and these are lodged with the court by the plaintiff's solicitors at the same time as the main action is set down or subsequently if this has already been done. No setting-down fee is required unless the

main action has been settled and the third party proceedings are being tried as a separate action.

3 See Atkin, Vol 37 (1990 Issue).

5. ORDER TO CARRY ON

1 IT IS ORDERED that the proceedings in this Action be carried on by the plaintiff against AB (the executor of the will of the deceased defendant CD) as defendant.
(It is desirable to show in brackets whether or not the new party is an executor or administrator because of the chain of executorship whereby the executor of A's executor is A's executor. See s 7 AEA 1925.)

2 IT IS ORDERED that the proceedings in this action be carried on by the plaintiff against the second third fourth and fifth defendants and AB (the administrator of the estate of the deceased first defendant) as defendants.
(In the title to the next order after the order to carry on AB will appear as the sixth defendant. The name of the first defendant will remain in the title with the words '(since deceased)' after the name.)

3 IT IS ORDERED that the proceedings in this action be carried on by Brand New Building Society as plaintiffs against the defendants.
(This presupposes that the building society which was formerly the plaintiff has been amalgamated with another and that its interest has been transmitted to 'Brand New Building Society'.)

4 IT IS ORDERED that AB (a bankrupt) cease to be the plaintiff in this action.
... the proceedings in this action be carried on by the trustee of the property of AB (a bankrupt) against the defendants.
(Here AB is the plaintiff, he has become bankrupt, he is no longer a necessary party and his trustee is carrying on the proceedings.)

5 IT IS ORDERED that the proceedings in this action be carried on by AB and the trustee of the property of the said AB (a bankrupt) against the defendant.
(Here the original plaintiff remains a plaintiff. His trustee joins him as second plaintiff.)

6 IT IS ORDERED that the proceedings in this action be carried on

by the second and third plaintiffs and AB (a new trustee of the will of CD) as plaintiffs against the defendants.
(Here the plaintiffs are trustees. There has been a change in the trustees. The first plaintiff is no longer a trustee and AB has become a trustee.)

7 IT IS ORDERED that the proceedings in this action be carried on by AB (to whom the former applicant EF has assigned the lease in the originating summons mentioned) and CD as applicants.
(Something like this could be used where there is *ex parte* originating process and there are no plaintiffs or defendants. Before the coming into force of the Supreme Court Act 1981 the word 'matter' would have been used instead of 'action' but s 151 of that Act defines 'action' as 'any civil proceedings commenced by writ or in any other manner prescribed by rules of court' so it seems permissible to use the word 'action' here.)

8 THE COURT APPOINTS AB to represent for the purposes of this action the estate of CD deceased.
AND IT IS ORDERED that the proceedings in this action be carried on by the plaintiff against AB (the person so appointed) as defendant.
(This can be used when the Order is made under Order 15, r 6A or Order 15, r 15.)

9 IT IS ORDERED
   (1) that the proceedings in this action be carried on by AB (the administrator of the estate of the deceased plaintiff) as plaintiff against the defendants.
   (2) that the proceedings in the counterclaim be carried on by ... against CD and EF and AB (the said administrator) as defendants
(The order should make it clear whether the proceedings in the counterclaim as well as in the action are to be carried on.)

10 IT IS ORDERED that the proceedings in this action be carried on by the plaintiff against the defendant CD (both in his personal capacity and as one of the executors of the Will of the deceased defendant EF) and GH and KL (the other executors of the said Will) as defendants.
(Here one of the defendants has died. He has three executors one of whom is already a defendant in his personal capacity. It may well be that if CD were the only executor of EF no order to carry on would be required although the probate would have to be proved at the appropriate moment in the proceedings.)

Notes

1 An order to carry on proceedings between the continuing parties and the new parties has to be obtained in the following circumstances:
   (1) the death of the party;
   (2) the bankruptcy;
   (3) the assignment of the interest or liability;
   (4) the transmission of the interest or liability;
   (5) the devolution of the interest or liability.

2 An *ex parte* application is made by the plaintiff or party having the conduct of the proceedings under Ord 15 r 7 but the rule does not apply to any change arising by reason of marriage or a mere change of name, nor to a change in the capacity of a party, for example a party becoming a patient or minor attaining majority. For change of name see Practice Direction (Chancery: Applications: and Change of Name) [1984] 1 WLR 447.

3 Order 15, r 7(4) provides that the order must be noted at the Chancery Registry and after it has been noted it must be served on the continuing party or parties or their solicitors and upon any new party. Any new party may acknowledge service and new parties must be served personally or by substituted service by post if permissible. A copy of the order should be endorsed with a memorandum informing a new party that he will be bound by the proceedings and that he may acknowledge service. The form of memorandum is as follows:

Take notice that from the time of the service of the within order upon you, you will be bound by the proceedings in the above action. You may within 14 days of the service of the within order upon you acknowledge service in the said action either personally or by solicitor in Chancery Chambers, Thomas More Building, Royal Courts of Justice, Strand, London WC2; and in default of your so doing the plaintiff may proceed in the said action in your absence.

4 No order is necessary where a female party has married after the commencement of the proceedings unless there has been a transmission of interest or liability.

5 If the interest of a deceased plaintiff survives to the others, no order is necessary; but if it does not, his personal representative should be joined. The consent in writing of the plaintiff to be substituted must be produced. If the defendants are jointly liable the liability continues in the survivors.

6 If a sole plaintiff becomes bankrupt the right of action in most cases passes to his trustee, who alone can continue the action, and he must obtain an order to carry on. The main exceptions are injuries to the person or character which have no immediate reference to the property. A receiving order does not in itself cause any 'transmission of interest'.

7 Where an order is made to carry on proceedings the writ or originating

process is not amended and the order to carry on appears in the title to any subsequent order.

8   Sometimes an assignor remains a party so that costs prior to the assignment can be sought against him.

9   A distinction must be drawn between r 6 and r 7 of Ord 15. By r 6 if a party has been joined or not joined by mistake then he may be struck out or added. Rule 7 only applies where a party has been properly joined and subsequently there has been a transmission of his interest.

Chapter Four

Interlocutory and Enforcement Applications

From the issue of the originating process until trial of the action or until its settlement, discontinuance or abandonment, there is a preparatory stage during which applications may be made to the court. 'The court' for the purpose of such interlocutory applications is defined by Ord 1, r 4(2) as the High Court or any one or more judges thereof whether sitting in court or chambers or any master or any registrar (district judge) of a district registry. In the Chancery Division, interlocutory applications are made either by summons to the master when they are heard by the master in chambers or *ex parte* without a hearing supported by an affidavit or by motion that is an application before a judge in open court.

1. Application by summons

A summons may be issued before a master supported where appropriate by an affidavit in the following cases:

  (1) For directions in writ actions (although direction as to the exchange of lists of all relevant documents and inspection, and for setting down 28 days after close of pleadings, may be automatic: Ord 24, r 1(2)), or for discovery of particular documents, but on a summons for such directions, no evidence will be required.
  (2) For directions (an instance of where the summons may be referred by the master to the judge) as to carrying out an order or judgment in administration or other actions.
  (3) For leave to examine witnesses before trial or for cross-examination of deponents on their affidavits, for the addition of parties, for consolidation, or for dismissal for want of prosecution. These may be by separate application, but such orders are usually made on the summonses for directions when a trial date is sought.
  (4) For an order for withdrawal of a solicitor's name from the

record; an affidavit needed to explain the circumstances (limited powers).
(5) For an order for transfer to the County Court—this is considered on directions.
(6) For an Ord 86 for specific performance the master either gives a final order, or directions on trial before judge.

2. Applications *ex parte* by affidavit

Applications which can be made by lodging an affidavit (Ord 11, r 4 and Ord 65, r 4) and (unless the master otherwise directs) without a summons may be for:

(1) leave to serve a writ or originating summons out of the jurisdiction (Ord 11, r 4),
(2) leave to issue concurrent writs or originating summonses (Ord 7, r 4),
(3) substituted service (Ord 65, r 4),
(4) leave to issue a third party notice (Ord 16, r 2),
(5) garnishee orders nisi (Ord 49, r 2),
(6) the appointment of a next friend or a guardian *ad litem* to replace one who has died (Ord 80, r 3) (if otherwise the appointment may be without order),
(7) payment out of funds in court not exceeding £50,000 if straightforward (Ord 92, r 5),
(8) leave to renew a writ (Ord 6, r 8) or originating summons (Ord 7, r 6),
(9) leave when required to file any document,
(10) leave to extend any period within which compliance is required under any rule or order,
(11) the determination (*see below*) of procedural questions,
(12) for an order to carry on proceedings.

If the master is prepared to make the order he will so mark the backing sheet of the affidavit, which may be collected, or will be returned to the applicant, to enable him to draw up the order if necessary, and to proceed. If the master declines to make the order he will usually give his reasons and may require the applicant to appear before him to give further explanation or require the issue of a summons.

An application for leave to file an affidavit notwithstanding formal defects is made by the lodging of the affidavit itself for scrutiny by a senior executive officer. A senior executive officer will also scrutinise and mark affidavits lodged for garnishee orders nisi and for substituted service (Practice Direction: Principal Clerk's Functions [1974] 1 WLR 461).

Application to amend

Any party may amend his pleading once without leave, provided this is before close of pleadings, ie before the expiry of 14 days after the last pleading served, but this does not enable change of parties, for which leave is required. There is opportunity for the other party to apply within 14 days for the court to order the amendment to be disallowed, and it can be disallowed if leave to amend would have been refused had it been a case where leave to amend had been necessary.

3. Applications on motion

The hearing of motions

A full code for the hearing of motions is set out in Practice Direction (Chancery Division: Motions Procedure) [1980] 1 WLR 751 and Practice Direction (Chancery Division: Motions Procedure) No 2 [1985] 1 WLR 244.

Applications by 'interlocutory' motion may be for

(1) an interlocutory injunction,
(2) an Anton Piller order in a trademark, copyright or breach of confidence action,
(3) summary judgment rescinding contract where the defendant fails to obey an order for specific performance,
(4) directions on technical aspects, or to amend specifications, in patent actions,
(5) immediate and urgent matters, and
(6) summary judgment.

All interlocutory procedural applications should be made by summons to the master, and not by motion, unless for good reason.

Applications made by motion to the judge are speedy and this is therefore the procedure utilised in the Chancery Division whenever a party seeks urgent relief. A hearing is obtained by the issue of a notice of motion, usually after the issue of the originating process. The equivalent procedure usual in the Queen's Bench Division is a summons to the judge. Both procedures are supported by affidavit evidence only (Ord 38, r 2(3)).

If any motion is likely to exceed three hours, the judge will order it to be put over to a date to be fixed. Any motion, other than a motion for an interlocutory injunction, may be stood over by consent.

A judge before whom is any application in open court, including any motion, may, if he does not then hear and decide upon it, direct a speedy trial. This will usually require the issue of a pro forma summons for directions expressed to be returnable for the date the directions were actually given. Every day is a motions day and the motions judge is appointed for a term. The Vice-Chancellor usually takes one or more of the heavier notices of motion referred to him by the motions judge. Motions are now issued and are called by the motions judge in the order on the list, although it is up to the motions judge which case is heard in which order and by whom.

The listing of motions

The listing and hearing of interlocutory motions is governed by the Practice Direction (Chancery Division: Motions Procedure) [1980] 1 WLR 751.

The procedure applies to ordinary interlocutory motions, including *ex parte* motions, and applications for directions made in respect of originating motions.

Basically, for interlocutory motions the procedure is that a judge called 'the motions judge' is appointed to sit to hear all motions, and there is a standby if business requires.

As far as possible, all motions are to be listed and entered into a book maintained for the purpose, called 'the motions book'. Entry is by lodging with Clerks of the Lists (rooms 412, 413 and 414), not later than 12.00 noon on the day before the date for which the notice of motion has been given, or on the preceding Friday if a notice has been given for a Monday, two copies of the writ and two copies of the notice of motion and an estimate of time signed by counsel.

Ex parte applications on motion

These may be made if the matter is urgent and a delay might cause harm. In exceptional urgency the plaintiff may produce a writ in draft only at the *ex parte* hearing, with an affidavit headed 'In the matter of an intended action'. The draft writ will be retained by the court and the applicant will be required to give an undertaking to issue his writ the same day or within 24 hours. Similarly an unsworn affidavit may be tendered with an undertaking to swear and file it, though if the deponent is in the court building, he could attend before one of the court staff authorised to administer oaths.

'Motions by order'; by consent as trial of action and 'saving motions'

The judge may direct a motion to be set down and heard without witnesses, (or with leave, to supplement affidavit evidence by oral testimony) and if such a motion is, by consent, to be treated as a trial, points of claim and defence may be ordered.

A motion for judgment may be made where an action is ordered to be set down without pleadings as a short cause on motion for judgment. This includes applications for judgment in default of defence, when writ and statement of claim should be served. Such motions are not heard as interlocutory motions, but can be marked short, on certificate of counsel, and will then be placed in the list of short causes on the first available day. Certificate of counsel should not be given unless the hearing will occupy less than ten minutes; if longer, they will come into the 'general paper' (Supreme Court Practice paras 8/1 to 5/8).

The expression 'saving motions' used in the Chancery Division refers to the discretion of the court to allow the parties to mention, see *Yap v Williams* (1901) WN 91 and *Arthur v Consolidated Collieries* (1905) 49 SJ 403.

Procedure

Motions entered in the motions book will be listed in the daily list. There is no warned list and information must be sought from the clerk to the motions judge. Should it become apparent that a motion will take less than five minutes, it will be marked, on request, as 'short', when it will be taken before the more lengthy motions with the proviso that the judge exercises his discretion as to the order of applications. Motions which it has not been possible to list, that is unlisted motions, will be heard last, motion likely to last more than three hours will normally be made motions by order.

Applications may be heard in chambers, where in the exercise of his discretion, the judge considers it may be unjust to the defendants if the application is heard in public.

Applications which are very urgent, and for which the motions judge is unavailable to hear promptly, may be heard by any judge. A request for this purpose must be made to the clerk to the motion judge, or in default, to the clerk of the lists. The notice of motion and other documents have to be lodged with the clerk of the lists.

Evidence

The likely sequence of evidence is the affidavit in support, affidavit in answer, and affidavit in reply. The court directs filing of evidence and adjourns motions until completed, maintaining the status quo by extracting undertakings or granting interim injunctions. When satisfied, the court will stand over for trial (motion by order).

Attitude of the court

Firstly the court will wish to be satisfied that the party moving the motion is ready to proceed: as the initial hearing continues it will become apparent how long will be needed to hear the motion and, if an order is not made at the first hearing, the court may stand it over. Applications to stand over may be opposed on the grounds that the application should not have to be made and consequently that there should be an order discharging it with costs.

It is usually only if the matter is short (ie, unlikely to exceed ten minutes) and counsel has given his certificate to that effect, that the motion will be heard immediately. Among such short motions are commonly motions for judgment in default of acknowledgment of service or defence or on admission. It would be very unusual to hear all of the evidence on the first hearing of an application for an interim injunction, but the court may be asked on such evidence as may be before it to make such interim orders or injunctions as may be appropriate to maintain the status quo until further evidence is filed and a final decision can be made. When an order for an interim injunction has been made *ex parte* and it comes back before the court for the order to be continued (whether or not the person injuncted attends), the court has inherent jurisdiction to discharge its own order.

Agreed adjournment of motions

If all parties to a motion agree to do so, a motion can be adjourned for not more than 14 days if necessary by counsel or solicitors attending before the clerk of the lists (room 412/413/414) at any time before 4.30 pm on the day before the hearing of the motion and producing a consent or consents signed by counsel or solicitors representing all parties agreeing to the adjournment but more usually by clerks attending or by post. In addition an agreed timetable for the swearing of any evidence must be produced to the clerk of the lists (Practice Direction (Chancery Division: Agreed adjournment of Chancery motions) No 2 of 1988).

Applications for agreed directions to be given pursuant to para 9 of Practice Direction (Motions Procedure) of 1980 ([1980] 1 WLR 751; [1980] 2 All ER 750) and Practice Direction (Application for rectification of the register of patents or designs agreed directions) [1985] 1 All ER 192 must be made to the clerk of the lists.

On all applications for the adjournment of motions or the giving of directions, the court file must first be bespoken from room 307/308.

The above procedure shall apply to motions the parties agree should stand over to be heard as motions by order. Parties who wish to take advantage of the procedure for the agreed adjournment of motions must bespeak the court file before making their application in room 412/414.

Adjournments in which an undertaking to the court is to be varied, or a new undertaking given, must be dealt with by the court. As a matter of practice, a motion cannot be adjourned to the last of the two motion days of any sittings. If a motion is not to be adjourned by consent then it must be mentioned to the court or it will be treated as abandoned.

Hazards and pitfalls

Where opposing parties both attend before the court, undertakings may be offered in lieu of an injunction which, if acceptable to the parties, will generally be accepted by the court. As there is no means of re-opening a claim for an interlocutory injunction other than by seeking an order for discharge of an undertaking and applying afresh for an injunction, a party offering to accept an undertaking which proves inadequate may be in difficulties: accordingly, particular care should be exercised in their wording.

An applicant should ensure that the order he is requesting in a notice of motion is the entire order necessary in wording which is exact. The court does have power to amend wording but will not often do so in favour of the party moving the motion. Counsel's advice on evidence is usually sought before a motion is formulated and the motion itself and the draft order should be settled by him.

Interim injunction

The copy of the interim order to be served must be indorsed with a penal notice and good office practice might indicate the indorsing also of the original, in the following words: 'TAKE NOTICE THAT UNLESS YOU OBEY THE DIRECTIONS CONTAINED IN THIS ORDER YOU WILL BE GUILTY OF CONTEMPT OF COURT AND WILL BE LIABLE TO BE COMMITTED TO PRISON'. This wording should be in block capitals on the front of the copy order (Ord 45, r 7(4)). All mandatory injunctions must give a time within which they are to be carried out, though 'forthwith' or 'forthwith on service' is sufficient where proper.

Undertaking as to damages

An undertaking as to damages will be required to be given.

Undertakings in lieu of injunctions

Where in the Chancery Division a defendant agrees to give an undertaking in lieu of an injunction, a cross-undertaking as to damages is automatically inserted. This practice is peculiar to the Chancery Division and derives from Practice Note (1904) WN 203 at p 208, and should be noted because of the possible consequences. For example, if the plaintiff seeks and is granted leave to discontinue, the response may be a claim under his cross-undertaking, which would not be the case in other divisions.

Furthermore, undertakings may not be subject to applications by the party in whose favour they are made to vary, as would be the case with an injunction.

Procedure for obtaining hearings or appointments for interlocutory applications

Any party may make an interlocutory application though if for an injunction the party applying will usually be the plaintiff. The procedure for obtaining appointments and hearings is according to the nature of the application and is given in Chapter 7.

Fees

The fee payable is currently £15.

4. Summary judgment

The possibility of making use of Ord 14, enabling a plaintiff on his claim or a defendant on his counterclaim to apply for a summary judgment in any action commenced by writ of summons, should not be overlooked. Any application for judgment under Ord 14 must, by r 2(1), be made by summons; and the same applies to applications for judgment under Ord 86 (see r 2(1)). Such applications will not be heard on motion save in exceptional circumstances.

The procedure for Ord 14 summonses in the Chancery Division is the same as in the Queen's Bench Division: a formal summons under Ord 14 is issued supported by an affidavit. Printed forms can be used. It is necessary to expand upon the facts of the case or the reasons for applying for summary judgment, as the court in practice is less disposed to grant summary judgment. The time to issue such a summons is left open to the litigant and it can be at any time after the acknowledgment of service is filed until up to the time of trial. The plaintiff may in some cases be wise to wait until time has expired for service of a defence to see whether the defendant does have a defence before embarking peremptorily on Ord 14 proceedings, which could otherwise delay the final outcome and add to the costs. Moreover, where there is a danger that a summons under Ord 14 could be dismissed, such procedure may disadvantage the plaintiff tactically.

The summons is issued in room 307/308 and assigned to a master. An estimate of time for the return date will be required along with indication as to whether counsel will represent the plaintiff. If another specific order applies, for example Ord 86 in specific performance proceedings, then Ord 14 is not available.

Where an application includes an application for an injunction, it has to be adjourned to a judge because in no case can a master grant an injunction. It is better in such cases that the summons should be made returnable directly before the judge in Chambers instead of the master (Practice Direction (Chancery Applications: Change of Name) [1984] 1 WLR 447, para 1).

The return date to be inserted in the summons will be on a motion day which (i) for Ord 14 is at least ten clear days (r 2(3)) after the date when the summons will be served, and (ii) for Ord 86 is at least four clear days (r 2(3)) after the date when the summons will be served.

The summons should be issued in Chancery chambers, and the following documents must be lodged: two copies of the summons; the affidavit in support, together with any exhibits; and a certificate of counsel as to the estimated length of the hearing.

5. Applications to determine procedural questions

So that applications relating to procedural matters may be brought before the court quickly many such matters wil be heard *ex parte*. The master has general jurisdiction but in some cases he will refer the application to the judge, consideration being given individually on each occasion as to what course should be taken. Matters which may be submitted *ex parte* to the master on affidavit without the necessity either of the issue of a summons or an attendance include renewal of a writ, joinder of causes of action, the filing of defective affidavits, and leave for short notice of service of notice of motion (and see also Applications *ex parte* by affidavit above). For such matters, an affidavit giving an explanation of the position and the reasons why the order is requested is left in room 307/308, and is available for collection or may be sent back to the applicant with the master's observations usually the following day.

Where applications in procedural matters are made on summons with notice to other parties and are short, a decision is likely to be given forthwith by the master, but if it is apparent that the application may take some time he may appoint another date. Alternatively, he may refer it to the judge, either in chambers or open court. If it is heard in chambers it will usually be heard with the master present. The file will have meanwhile been passed to the judge with a detailed note prepared by the master both as to the case itself and the point in issue. The judge may be able to give a decision at once on most of such summonses, but it may be adjourned to a fresh date for consideration of any lengthy issues. The date will then be given by the clerk of the lists.

6. Treating as trial

There is a long standing practice whereby ordinary interlocutory motions are treated as motions for judgment or as the trial of the action.

Where a motion is not contested and an agreed order is sought the motion may be treated as a motion for judgment and the setting down fee is paid. In such a case a statement of claim need not be served (*Re Cadogan and Hans Place Estate (No 2) Ltd* (1906) WN 112).

Where the motion is contested the consent of the parties is required that the motion should be treated as the trial of the action. If the judge is satisfied with the affidavit evidence then he is at liberty to give judgment on the evidence filed. In such a case the motion is treated as the trial of the action and the setting down fee must be paid.

As a rule of thumb a consent order should be by motion for judgment and a contested motion may be treated as a trial of the action if the parties consent to this course. The fees must be paid before the order is entered.

For forms and precedents, see Atkin, Vol 22 (1980 issue), Vol 28 (1986 issue) and Vol 32 (1985 issue).

Interlocutory and Enforcement Applications—Orders

1. ORDER FOR FURTHER AND BETTER PARTICULARS

IT IS ORDERED

1 that the... do on or before... or subsequently within... days after service of this order serve on the... the Further and Better Particulars of... specified in the request [dated...] [annexed hereto]

2. ORDER FOR INTERROGATORIES

IT IS ORDERED

1 that the defendants by ... or other their proper officer do on or before ... or subsequently within 4 days after service of this Order make and file an Affidavit in answer to the Interrogatories for their examination set forth in the schedule hereto.
[that the plaintiffs be at liberty to serve on the defendants the Interrogatories set forth in the schedule hereto]
[4 days after service upon them of this Order and the said Interrogatories make and file an Affidavit in answer to the said Interrogatories].

Notes

1 Order 26 deals with interrogatories. See too Atkin, Vol 22 (1980 issue).

2 It is important to note that whereas previously an order was required before interrogatories could be administered it is now open to a party to serve interrogatories without any order in most cases (Ord 26, r 1), up to a limit of two occasions (r 3).

3 Since failure to comply with an order may lead to an application to commit it is important that the order should be clear and precise. Normally the words 'or subsequently within 4 days after service...' are inserted.

4 These orders can take two forms. The first is a direct order to answer the interrogatories and nothing needs to be served apart from the order. The other form gives leave to serve interrogatories which then have

3. ORDER FOR DISCOVERY

IT IS ORDERED

1 that lists of documents be served within ... days and that there be an inspection within ... days thereafter

2 that this action [and counterclaim] be tried in London before a Judge alone and be set down by the plaintiffs in the List Part ... on or before ...

4. UNLESS ORDER

(1) AGAINST PLAINTIFF

IT IS ORDERED

1 that unless the plaintiff shall on or before ... or subsequently within 4 days after service of this Order make and serve upon the defendant a list of documents as required by Order 24, r 2 of the Rules of the Supreme Court the action be dismissed and that the defendant's costs be taxed and paid by the plaintiff.

2 that the costs of the said application are to be borne by the plaintiff in any event.

(2) AGAINST DEFENDANT

IT IS ORDERED

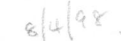

1 that unless the defendant shall on or before ... or subsequently within [4] days after service of the order make and serve on the plaintiff a list of documents as required by Order 24, r 2 of the Rules of the Supreme Court the defence be struck out [and the defendant shall pay to the plaintiff damages to be assessed and his costs of the action to be taxed]

2 that the costs of the said application are to be borne by the defendant in any event.

Notes

1 An 'unless order' is a convenient method of making a party in the action take some necessary step.

2 Such an order may be made against a defendant that the defence be struck out. Sometimes a further order may be made, eg, that the defendant pays damages to be assessed.

5. ORDER FOR EXAMINATION OF WITNESSES

(1) Before an examiner

IT IS ORDERED

1 that ... a witness on behalf of the plaintiff/defendant be examined viva voce on oath or affirmation before one of the examiners of the Court [an Examiner to be agreed by the Parties or in default of agreement appointed by the Court].

2 that solicitors for the plaintiff/defendant shall give the solicitors for the defendant/plaintiff ... days' notice in writing of the time and place where such examination is to take place

3 that the deposition taken at the examination be filed in the Central Office of the Supreme Court and that office copies thereof may be read and given in evidence at the trial of this action saving all just exceptions without any further proof of the absence of the said witness that the affidavit of the solicitor or agent of the party using the same as to his belief

4 that the costs of the said application and of the examination are to be costs in the cause.

Note

See Ord 39, r 1, Ord 38, r 9, Form No 32 in Appendix A in SCP, Vol 2 and Atkin, Vol 37 (1990 issue).

(2) Before judicial authority abroad

IT IS ORDERED

1 that a letter of request shall issue directed to the proper judicial authority for the examination of the following witnesses namely ... of ... and ... of ...

2 that the deposition taken pursuant thereto when received be filed in the Central Office of the Supreme Court

3 that office copies thereof may be read and given in evidence at the trial of this action saving all just exceptions without any further proof of the absence of the said witnesses than the affidavit of the solicitor or agent of the party using the same as to his belief

4 that the trial of this action be stayed until the said depositions have been filed

5 that the costs of and incidental to the application for this order and the said letter of request and examination be costs in the cause.

Note

See Form 34 in Appendix A in SCP Vol 2, Ord 39, r 2(a) and Atkin, Vol 37 (1990 Issue).

(3) Before an examiner abroad

IT IS ORDERED

1 that the British Consul or his deputy at ... or ... be appointed as special examiner for the purpose of taking the examination cross-examination and re-examination viva voce on oath or affirmation of ... witnesses on the part of ... at ... in ...

2 that the examiner be at liberty to invite the attendance of the witnesses and the production of documents but shall not exercise any compulsory powers

3 that otherwise such examination shall be taken in accordance with the English procedure

4 that the solicitors for ... give the solicitors for the ... days' notice in writing of the date on which they propose to send out this order to ... for execution.

5 that ... days after the service of such notice the solicitors for the plaintiff and defendant respectively do exchange the names of their agents at ... to whom notice relating to the examination of the said witnesses may be sent

6 that ... days (exclusive of Sunday) before the examination of any witness hereunder notice of such examination shall be given by the agent of the other party unless such notice be dispensed with

7 that the deposition when taken together with any documents referred to therein or certified copies of such documents or of extracts therefrom be sent by the examiner under seal to the Senior Master of the Supreme Court of Judicature Royal Courts of Justice London WC2A 2LL on or before the ... day of ... next

or such further or other day as may be ordered there to be filed in the proper office

8 that either party be at liberty to read and give such depositions in evidence on the trial of this action saving all just exceptions

9 that the trial of this action be stayed until the filing of such depositions

10 that the costs of and incidental to the application for this order and such examination be costs in the cause.

6. ORDER FOR EXCHANGE OF WITNESS STATEMENTS

IT IS ORDERED

that (a) signed written statements of the oral evidence which each party intends to lead on any issue of fact to be decided at the trial be exchanged by... [and (b) any party be at liberty to serve a supplemental statement within... days thereafter dealing with any matters raised in any statement of their opponent(s)]

Note

It is now common practice to exchange witness statements, with a view to narrowing the issues, before the action is set down for trial.

7. ORDER FOR CROSS-EXAMINATION OF DEPONENTS

(1) Of one party

IT IS ORDERED

1 that the [plaintiff] [defendant] be at liberty to cross-examine the deponents named in the schedule hereto upon their respective affidavits sworn in this action

2 that such cross-examination be taken before the Court at the hearing in Court of the action/originating summons

3 that the [plaintiff] [defendant] shall produce the said deponents for cross-examination accordingly and that unless the said

deponents are so produced the [plaintiff] [defendant] is not to be at liberty to read or use the said affidavits as evidence in this action without the leave of the Court.

The Schedule

(2) Of both parties

IT IS ORDERED

1 that the plaintiff be at liberty to cross-examine the deponents named in the First Schedule hereto upon their respective affidavits or affirmations sworn or affirmed in this action

2 that the defendant be at liberty to cross-examine the deponents named in the Second Schedule hereto upon their respective affidavits or affirmations sworn or affirmed in this action

3 that such cross-examination be taken before the Court at the hearing in Court of the action/originating summons

4 that the defendant shall produce the deponents named in the First Schedule hereto for cross-examination accordingly and that the plaintiff shall produce the deponents named in the Second Schedule hereto and that if any of the said deponents are not produced for cross-examination the party failing to produce such deponent is not to be at liberty to read or use the evidence of such deponent without the leave of the Court.

The First Schedule
(The defendant's deponents)

The Second Schedule
(The plaintiff's deponents)

Notes

1 Evidence at the hearing of an originating summons is normally by affidavit—see Ord 38, r 2(3), but the court may order the attendance for cross-examination of any deponent.

2 No summons is required for the order and even if the order is in fact made at the hearing of the OS it is permissible to treat it as separate and begin simply 'Upon the application of the plaintiff'. If however a number of directions are given which have to be drawn up, the order for cross-examination can be included among them.

3 If the solicitors for both parties were present when the order was made this should be shown.

INTERLOCUTORY AND ENFORCEMENT APPLICATIONS 91

4 The words 'at the hearing in court of the originating summons' are suitable when the originating summons is to be heard in court. This is the usual case. In other cases these words may have to be altered.

5 Where a party has affirmed the word 'affirmation' will be substituted for the word affidavit.

6 The schedule will contain the full names of the deponents.

8. ORDER FOR EXPERT EVIDENCE

IT IS ORDERED

1 that if either/any of the parties intends to place reliance at the trial on expert evidence he shall on or before ... disclose the substance of that evidence to the other party/parties in the form of a written report which shall be agreed if possible

2 that unless such reports are agreed the parties shall be at liberty to call as expert witnesses those witnesses the substance of whose evidence has been disclosed as aforesaid [but not more than ... expert witness shall be called for each party]

3 that the costs of the said Application are to be costs in the cause

9. ORDER FOR TRIAL BEFORE MASTER

IT IS by consent ORDERED

1 pursuant to Order 36, Rule 11 of the Rules of the Supreme Court that this Action be tried before a Master

2 that this Action be tried before ... one of the Masters of the Supreme Court accordingly

3 that the plaintiff shall on or before ... set down this Action in Part ... of the ... Witness List for trial in London before the Master the estimated duration of the trial being ...

4 that this Action shall come on for trial on ...

5 that the costs of the said application are to be costs in the cause.

Notes

1 By Ord 36, r 11 the parties may consent to trial of the action by a master and the master must agree. The order for trial is drawn up.

2 The action must be set down in the usual way and in the case of a writ action the setting down fee of £20 must be paid.

10. ORDER ON TRIAL BEFORE MASTER

THIS ACTION by the Order dated ... having been directed to be tried before a Master and the Master having tried this Action and (upon hearing Counsel for the plaintiff and for the defendant and hearing oral evidence and reading the documents recorded on the court file as having been read) directed that judgment as hereinafter provided be entered for the plaintiff

IT IS ORDERED that the defendant shall pay to the plaintiff

1 £... by way of damages and

2 ... costs of this Action to be taxed if not agreed.

ORDERS IN INTERPLEADER PROCEEDINGS

11. SHERIFF'S CLAIM BARRED

UPON THE APPLICATION of the Sheriff of ... for interpleader relief by Summons dated ...

AND UPON HEARING counsel/the solicitors for the said Sheriff for the plaintiff/for the ... defendant ...

AND UPON READING the documents recorded on the court file as having been read

IT IS DECLARED (but not so as to affect the rights of the Claimants as between themselves) that the Claimant and all persons claiming under him are for ever barred from prosecuting against the said Sheriff and all persons claiming under him the claim notice of which was given to the said Sheriff by the Claimant on ...

AND IT IS ORDERED

1 that the plaintiff/defendant (who is the Execution creditor) shall pay to the said Sheriff his costs of these interpleader proceedings (including therein his possession money caused by the said claim) to be taxed if not agreed

2   that the Claiment shall pay to the plaintiff/defendant (a) his costs of these interpleader proceedings to be taxed if not agreed (b) the amount of the costs paid by the plaintiff/defendant to the said Sheriff as hereinbefore directed.

12. SHERIFF TO WITHDRAW

IT IS ORDERED

1   that the said Sheriff shall withdraw from possession of the goods seized by him under the Writ of fieri facias herein

2   that the Claimant be restrained from bringing an Action against the said Sheriff for or in respect of his having taken possession of the said goods

3   that the plaintiff (who is the judgment creditor) do pay to the said Sheriff his costs of these interpleader proceedings (including therein his possession money) to be taxed if not agreed

4   that the plaintiff do pay to the claimant his costs of these interpleader proceedings to be taxed if not agreed

Note

See Ord 17, r 2(4).

13. SHERIFF, CONDITIONAL ORDER TO WITHDRAW (1)

IT IS ORDERED

1   that upon the Claimant (1) on or before ... or subsequently within 4 days after service of this Order either (a) lodge in court as directed in the lodgment schedule I hereto the sum of £... or (b) give security to the satisfaction of the master for the payment of the said sum in accordance with any Order hereafter to be made in these proceedings the said Sheriff shall upon payment to him of his possession money from the date of this Order withdraw from possession of the goods seized by him under the Writ of fieri facias herein which are claimed by the Claimant.

2   that unless such lodgment in court be made or security given within the time aforesaid the said Sheriff shall sell the goods seized by him under the Writ of fieri facias herein which are

claimed by the Claimant and do lodge in Court as directed in the lodgment schedule II hereto the net proceeds of sale after deducting the expenses thereof.

Note

Lodgment Schedules to be attached.

14. SHERIFF, CONDITIONAL ORDER TO WITHDRAW (2)

IT IS ORDERED

1 that upon the Claimant either (a) lodging in court as directed in the lodgment schedule I hereto the sum of £... or (b) giving security to the satisfaction of the master for the payment of the said sum in accordance with any Order hereafter to be made in these proceedings the said Sheriff shall withdraw from possession of the goods seized by him under the Writ of fieri facias herein which are claimed by the defendant

2 that in the meantime the said Sheriff shall continue in possession of the said goods

3 that the Claimant shall pay to the Sheriff possession money for the time the said Sheriff continues in possession of the said goods as aforesaid

4 that if the Claimant desires the said goods to be sold and gives Notice in writing to the said Sheriff of such desire the said Sheriff shall sell the goods and lodge in court as directed in the lodgment schedule II hereto the net proceeds of sale after deducting the expenses thereof and any possession money due to him as from the date of this Order.

Note

Lodgment Schedules to be attached.

15. SHERIFF, SALE AND TRIAL OF ISSUE

IT IS ORDERED

1 that the said Sheriff shall sell the goods seized by him under the Writ of fieri facias herein which are claimed by the Claimant

and do lodge in court as directed in the lodgment schedule hereto the net proceeds of sale after deducting the expenses thereof

2 that the following issue be tried that is to say WHETHER at the time of the seizure by the said Sheriff the said goods were the property of the Claimant as against the plaintiff (who is the execution creditor)

3 that the Claimant be the plaintiff in the said Issue and that the plaintiff in this Action be the defendant in the said Issue

4 that the plaintiff in the said Issue shall on or before ... serve a Statement of Claim therein that the defendant in the said Issue do within ... days after service of the said Statement of Claim serve a Defence and Counterclaim and that the plaintiff in the said Issue shall within ... days after service of the said Defence and Counterclaim serve a Reply and Defence to Counterclaim

5 that lists of documents be exchanged within ... days after the close of the Pleadings in the said Issue and that there be inspection within ... days thereafter

6 that the plaintiff in the said Issue shall on or before ... set down the said Issue in Part ... of the ... Witness List for trial in London before a judge alone the estimated duration of the trial being ... days

7 that the costs of these interpleader proceedings and all other questions arising therein be reserved to be dealt with after the trial of the said Issue

8 that the further hearing of the said Summons be accordingly adjourned generally with liberty to restore.

16. SHERIFF, SALE (1)

IT IS ORDERED

1 that the said Sheriff shall sell enough of the goods seized by him under the Writ of fieri facias in this Action to satisfy (a) the expenses of the sale (b) the rent if any due and required to be paid thereout (c) £ ... being the amount of the claim of the Claimant and (d) the amount of the execution

2 that out of the proceeds of sale (after deducting the said expenses and rent if any) the said Sheriff shall pay (a) to the Claimant

the said sum of £... (b) to the plaintiff (who is the execution creditor) the amount of his execution and (c) the residue if any to the defendant

3 that the Claimant be restrained from bringing an Action against the said Sheriff for or in respect of his having taken possession of the said goods

4 that the plaintiff shall pay to the Claimant his costs of these interpleader proceedings to be taxed if not agreed.

17. SHERIFF, SALE (2)

AND the plaintiff (who is the execution creditor) by his solicitors/counsel undertaking to secure the Claimant against any deficiency or loss by reason of the sale hereinafter directed

IT IS ORDERED

1 that the said Sheriff shall proceed to sell sufficient of the goods (other than those specified in the ... schedule hereto) seized under the writ of fieri facias issued in this Action to satisfy:
   (1) the expenses of and incidental to the sale;
   (2) the rent (if any) duly claimed by the landlord of the premises on which the goods were seized;
   (3) the taxes (if any) charged upon the defendant (the execution debtor) and in arrear or payable for the year in which the goods were seized not exceeding the taxes for one year;
   (4) £... being the amount due to the Claimant with interest and costs to be agreed or settled by the master;
   (5) the costs of the execution;
   (6) the amount which by the said Writ of fieri facias he is directed to levy.

2 that out of the proceeds of the sale the said Sheriff (after deducting the expenses thereof and the costs of the execution and the rent and taxes if any) shall pay to the Claimant the amount of his claim and to the plaintiff the amount which by the Writ of fieri facias he is directed to levy and the residue (if any) to the defendant

3 that if the proceeds of the sale shall be insufficient to pay any of the sums herein directed to be paid in priority to the claim of the plaintiff then the plaintiff shall pay so much of the sums as such proceeds shall be insufficient to pay to the several parties entitled thereto respectively

4 that the plaintiff shall pay to the said Sheriff and to the Claimant their respective costs of these interpleader proceedings to be agreed or taxed and possession money from the date of the Claimant's claim

5 that no action be brought against the said Sheriff in respect of the seizure and sale of the said goods

6 that the parties are to be at liberty to apply.

The Schedule
(Goods not to be sold)

18. STAKEHOLDERS—SUMMARY DETERMINATION

[AND the defendants consenting to the summary determination of the issue between them pursuant to Order 17, Rule 5(2) of the Rules of the Supreme Court]

IT IS DECLARED that the debt referred to in the Originating Summons has been validly assigned by the first defendant and that the second defendant is entitled to give a good receipt therefor to the plaintiff

AND IT IS ORDERED that the first defendant shall pay to the plaintiff and to the second defendant their respective costs of this Action to be taxed if not agreed.

Note

See Ord 17, r 5(2).

PRELIMINARY ISSUES

19. ORDER FOR TRIAL OF ISSUE

IT IS ORDERED

1 that the following question be tried as a Preliminary Issue in this Action that is to say WHETHER...

2 that until the said Issue has been determined all further proceedings in this Action except for the purpose of the determination of the said Issue be stayed

3   that the plaintiff/defendant in this Action is/are to be the plaintiff/ defendant in the Issue and that the plaintiff/defendant in this Action is to be ... the plaintiff/defendant in the Issue

4   that the plaintiff in the Issue shall on or before ... set down the said Issue in Part ... of the Witness List for trial in London before a judge alone the estimated duration of the trial being ... days

5   that the costs of the said Application are to be costs in the Issue.

Note

Sometimes directions are also given for pleadings and discovery.

20. ORDER ON TRIAL OF ISSUE

UPON THE TRIAL of the Preliminary Issue directed by the Order dated ... THE COURT DECLARES ...

[WHEREAS by the Order dated ... it was ordered that the following questions be tried as a preliminary issue that is to say 'Whether ...'
NOW UPON THE TRIAL of the said Preliminary Issue ...].

Notes

1   A preliminary issue is set down for trial in the same way as an action.

2   In the case of an originating summons it is better done by directing a summons in the proceedings specifying the issue to be tried and adjourning that summons into court with the appropriate supporting affidavits. Alternatively the originating summons may be amended to include the preliminary issue and that paragraph of the originating summons adjourned into court for hearing.

3   By Ord 33, r 7 if it appears to the court that the decision on the preliminary issue renders the trial of the action unnecessary it may dismiss the action or give judgment in the action as may be just.

4   The court may direct any party to be plaintiff or defendant in the issue as may be most convenient.

Chapter Five

Injunctions

1. Injunctions—general

Injunctions are the speedy procedure, provided by way of motion, which enable a party to apply urgently for an order to preserve the status quo until the hearing of the main action in which they are involved. A party may apply either *ex parte* or on notice. In a proper case, as where there is clearly no defence or where the defendant is clearly acting in breach of covenant or statute, the court will forthwith grant an interim injunction, even though to do so would be to grant the plaintiff much or even all of the remedy or relief which he claims in the action; an application so dealt with will in effect have originated the action itself without other process. More often, however, a writ is issued claiming both damages and an injunction and the motion arises out of that action.

Orders likely to be made on an interlocutory motion for an injunction include:

(1) standing over the motion to a date to be fixed on terms which may include an interim injunction (for which the applicant should have ready a draft (Ord 42, r 7)),
(2) an order as asked for example, the grant of an interim injunction (when the judge should have before him the applicant's draft) (ibid),
(3) an order that on the plaintiff/defendant's undertaking to the court in the terms set out in the order, no order save costs in the cause,
(4) staying the proceedings in the form of a Tomlin order,
(5) adjourning the hearing on terms (Ord 8, r 5),
(6) a Mareva injunction and
(7) an Anton Piller order.

2. Mareva injunctions

A Mareva injunction restrains a defendant from moving any of his or her assets and as such has the effect of ensuring that the trial judgment of the court cannot be floated by a recalcitrant defendant removing assets out of the court's jurisdiction. As they are issued *ex parte* without notice to the defendant, he or she can be taken off guard (*Mareva Compania Naveria SA v International Bulk Carriers SA* [1975] 2 Lloyds Rep 509 CA). Mareva injunctions may be made, and are commonly needed, after judgment. Notification of the injunction will be necessary to those holding assets.

3. Anton Piller orders

An Anton Piller order compels a defendant to permit the plaintiff to enter his premises and search for, and in some cases take away, documents or property (*Anton Piller v Manufacturing Processes Ltd* [1976] Ch 55 CA). Such an order is commonly used in claims for the infringement of intellectual property rights.

As with Mareva injunctions, applications are made *ex parte*. The applicant granted an order will be required to give the usual undertaking as to damages. If something out of the ordinary is shown, the hearing of an Anton Piller appeal may be *in camera* so as to preserve confidentiality (announcement of the Master of the Rolls sitting in the Court of Appeal, 5 November 1982 (1982), *The Times*, 9 November). Anton Piller orders should not be used as a 'fishing' exercise, to put a competitor out of business, or as a means of finding out what charges can be made and the plaintiff should serve his statement of claim within the time specified in the rules (unless the court otherwise orders) (*Hytrac Conveyors Ltd v Conveyors International Ltd* [1982] 3 All ER 415 CA).

The initial application for an Anton Piller order, as mentioned above, is necessarily *ex parte* and where as is common, a defendant is outside the jurisdiction, leave to serve out of the jurisdiction must be obtained on the application. Draft writ (unless writ itself has been issued), the affidavit in support, and a draft of the injunction must be available when making the application. Frankness is required on the part of the plaintiff with an indication of the defence (if any) being made available to the defendant against whom the injunction is sought.

The successful plaintiff will be required to undertake to inform the defendant forthwith of the order, of the writ and the affidavit in support, and so far as third parties may be affected, the plaintiff must also undertake to inform them of their right to apply for a variation of the order or directions, undertaking also to pay the costs incurred by the third parties in complying with the court's order. The order will usually specify the maximum amount of assets to which the injunction applies. The injunction will usually express to run as usual, until judgment or further order; applications should be sought to continue the order therefore, if a default judgment is applied for and granted.

Specimen interim injunction

Writ of Summons (O.6, r.1)

IN THE HIGH COURT OF JUSTICE   19 91 .— B .—No. 3421
Chancery Division
[**District Registry**]

Between

           BLOCKERS & CO LTD.   Plaintiff

AND

           DATA COMPUTATION LTD   Defendant

(1) Insert name.   **To the Defendant** ($\frac{1}{s}$) DATA COMPUTATION LTD

(2) Insert address.   of (^{2})   Unit D Industrial Centre Loftus Road   Southleate Wessex.

This Writ of Summons has been issued against you by the above-named Plaintiff in respect of the claim set out overleaf.

Within 14 days after the service of this Writ on you, counting the day of service, you must either satisfy the claim or return to the Court Office mentioned below the accompanying **Acknowledgment of Service** stating therein whether you intend to contest these proceedings.

If you fail to satisfy the claim or to return the Acknowledgment within the time stated, or if you return the Acknowledgment without stating therein an intention to contest the proceedings, the Plaintiff may proceed with the action and judgment may be entered against you forthwith without further notice.

(3) Complete and delete as necessary.   Issued from the (^{3}) [Chancery Chambers] [District Registry]
of the High Court this   24th   day of   September   1991 .

NOTE:—This Writ may not be served later than 4 calendar months *(or, if leave is required to effect service out of the jurisdiction, 6 months)* beginning with that date unless renewed by order of the Court.

IMPORTANT

Directions for Acknowledgment of Service are given with the accompanying form.

Specimen interim injuction

(1) Delete if inapplicable.

(¹) **Statement of Claim**

The Plaintiffs' claim is for

1. A Declaration that all Data Cards supplied by the Plaintiffs to the Defendants and identified in the Plaintiffs' invoices numbered 400.06, 400.10, 400.20 and 400.30 are, with one exception of those data cards sold by the Defendants prior to 1st July 1991, the property of the Plaintiffs.

2. An Order that the Defendants do deliver up to the Plaintiffs forthwith the data cards referred to in the preceding paragraph hereof.

3. Damages

4. Interest on such damages to be assessed pursuant to Section 35A of the Supreme Court Act 1981.

MUNGO KENTGERA

Mandatory and prohibitive injunction

IN THE HIGH COURT OF JUSTICE　　　　　　1991 B No. 3421
CHANCERY DIVISION

BETWEEN

BLOCKERS & CO. LTD.　　　Plaintiff

-and-

DATA COMPUTATION LTD　　　Defendant

CONSENT ORDER

[Mandatory and Prohibitive Injunction]

UPON HEARING COUNSEL for the Plaintiff AND BY CONSENT:

IT IS ORDERED THAT:

1. The Defendants do deliver up to the Plaintiffs the Data Cards supplied by the Plaintiffs to the Defendants and referred to in the Plaintiffs' invoices numbered 400.00, 400.10, 400.20 and 400.30 and stored in 6 pallets at premises at Unit D, Industrial Centre, Loftas Road, Southall, Wessex, by no later than Saturday, 29th September, 1991.

2. The Defendants whether by its officers, its servants or agents or otherwise howsoever be restrained until delivery up of the Data Cards referred to in paragraph 1 above from removing from the jurisdiction, selling, charging, disposing of or otherwise dealing with any of the said cards.

3. The Plaintiffs' costs be paid by the Defendants to be taxed if not agreed between the parties.

DATED this 24th day of September, 1991.

....　　　　..

Signed for and on
behalf of　　　　　　　　　　Signed for and on
　　　　　　　　　　　　　　behalf of
the Plaintiffs　　　　　　　　the Defendants

[Note: Where the Injunction (or Undertaking) is not by consent, the Court will require an Undertaking as to Damages to preface the Order.]

4. Preservation orders

A specimen of a summons, with accompanying writ, follows. The summons could be heard and an order made on the plaintiff's undertaking by their counsel to forthwith issue a writ of summons in the form of the draft initialled by the court.

For detailed treatment and precedents on injunctions, see David Bean, *Injunctions*, 5th edn (Longman, 1991).

Specimen preservation order

IN THE HIGH COURT OF JUSTICE   1991. B. No. 820
QUEEN'S BENCH DIVISION

BETWEEN

WILLIAM BISCOP & CO LTD

Plaintiffs

-and-

CASSETTE PRODUCTS LTD

Defendants

SUMMONS

LET ALL PARTIES concerned attend the Judge in Chambers on Tuesday, 3rd June, 1991 at not before 2 in the afternoon on the hearing of an application on the part of the Plaintiff for the following orders:

1. Delivery up forthwith to the Plaintiff of the cassettes supplied by the Plaintiff to the Defendant and referred to in the Plaintiff's invoices numbered 213.609, 213.798, 213.852, 213.853, 213.854, 213.855, 213.856, 213.857, 213.885, 213.982 and 214.060, and without prejudice to the generality of the foregoing, this Order shall apply to cassettes supplied by the Plaintiff to the Defendant and stored in 47 pallets at Premises at Unit C, Harbour Centre, Lamp Road, Industrial Estate, Westhall, Essex.

2. That the Defendant, whether by its officers, its servants or agents or otherwise however be restrained until final or further order from removing from the jurisdiction, selling, charging, disposing of or otherwise dealing with any of the said envelopes otherwise than in accordance with the Order at 1 above.

3. That the Defendant by its duly authorised officer do disclose the whereabouts of a number of cassettes supplied by the Plaintiff to the Defendant and referred to in the invoices identified in paragraph 1 above with the exception (a) of those cassettes which at the date hereof have already been sold by the Defendant and (b) of those cassettes stored at Unit C, aforesaid such disclosure to be in writing and verified by affidavit by the said officer of the Defendant and served on the Plaintiff's solicitors within seven days of service of this Order.

4. Plaintiff's costs of this application to be paid by the Defendant in any event.

To: Cassette Products Limited,
       Unit C,
       Harbour Centre,
       Lamp Road,
       Industrial Estate,
       Westhall,
       ESSEX

Dated this 1st day of June, 1991.

THIS SUMMONS was issued by Snooks & Co, 32 Langley Street, London, E8; Solicitors for the PLaintiff.

Injunctions—Orders

1. NO ORDER ON MOTION (DEFENDANTS GIVING UNDERTAKING)

AND the Plaintiffs by his/her/its their Counsel undertaking to obey any Order this Court may make as to damages if it shall consider that the Defendants shall have sustained any damages by reason of the undertaking hereinafter mentioned which the Plaintiffs ought to pay

AND the Defendants by his/her/its their Counsel undertaking... until after... Judgment in this Action or until further Order in the meantime that he/she/it they will not do (as regards the Defendant whether by its directors or by its servants or agents or any of them or otherwise howsoever and as regards the ... and ... Defendants whether by themselves or by their servants or agents or any of them or otherwise howsoever) the following acts or any of them that is to say

IT IS ORDERED that the said Motion be dismissed

THE COURT DOES NOT THINK FIT to make any Order on the said Motion

THE costs of the said Motion are reserved

AND the parties are to be at liberty to apply.

2. ORDER TO STAND OVER MOTION (UNDERTAKING AS TO EVIDENCE)

UPON MOTION for an Injunction made by Counsel for the Plaintiff
  AND UPON HEARING Counsel for the Defendant
  AND UPON READING the Court file
  AND the Plaintiff by Counsel undertaking

1 to use ... best endeavours to serve/file the rest of ... evidence on the said Motion on or before ... by ... and

2 to obey any Order this Court may make as to damages if it shall consider that the Defendant shall have sustained any damages by reason of the first undertaking on the part of the Defendant hereinafter contained which the Plaintiff ought to pay

   AND the Defendant by ... Counsel undertaking

1 until after... or until further Order in the meantime that... will not do (as regards the ... Defendant whether by its directors

or by its servants or agents or any of them or otherwise howsoever and as regards the ... and ... Defendants whether by ... or by ... servants or agents or any of them or otherwise howsoever) the following acts or any of them that is to say

2 to use ... best endeavours to serve file ... evidence on the said Motion on or before ... by ...

IT IS ORDERED

1 that the further hearing of the said Motion shall stand to ... over to a date to be fixed

2 that the Plaintiff shall use ... best endeavours to serve/file ... evidence on the said Motion on or before ... by ...

3 that the Defendant shall use ... best endeavours to serve/file ... evidence in answer on the said Motion on or before ... by ... within ... days after service of the Plaintiff's evidence

4 that the Plaintiff shall use ... best endeavours to serve/file ... evidence in reply on or before by ... within ... days after service of the Defendant's evidence.

3. INTERLOCUTORY MOTION TREATED AS MOTION FOR JUDGMENT

AND the Plaintiffs and the Defendants by their Counsel

1 agreeing that the said Motion be treated as a Motion for Judgment

2 ... stating that they have agreed to the terms set forth in the Schedule hereto and consenting to this Order

[*or, if the defendant's consent is in writing.*]

AND the Plaintiffs by their Counsel

1 requesting that the said Motion should be treated as a Motion for Judgment

2 stating that the Plaintiffs and the Defendants have agreed to the terms set forth in the Schedule hereto and

3 consenting to this Order

AND the Defendants by their Solicitors having consented in writing to this Order

IT IS ORDERED [include stay provisions if Order is in Tomlin form]

4. INTERIM INJUNCTION (INTENDED ACTION)

IN THE MATTER of an Intended Action

BETWEEN

             Intended Plaintiff

    and

             Intended Defendant

UPON MOTION made by Counsel for the Intended Plaintiff(s) (hereinafter called the Plaintiff(s))

AND UPON READING the draft Writ of Summons/the Draft Affidavit of ... [the documents specified in the Schedule hereto]

AND the Plaintiff by his/her/its/their/Counsel undertaking

1 [forthwith] [on or before ...] to issue a Writ of Summons claiming relief similar to or connected with that hereinafter granted

2 [to make and file] [to cause to be sworn] an Affidavit [substantially] [verifying what was alleged by Counsel] [in the terms of the draft Affidavit of ...]

3 to serve upon the Intended Defendant(s) (hereinafter called the Defendant(s)) a copy of the said Affidavit and Notice of Motion for ...

4 to obey any Order this Court may make as to damages if it shall consider that the Defendant(s) shall have sustained any damages by reason of this Order which the Plaintiff(s) ought to pay

IT IS ORDERED

1 that the Defendant(s) [and each of them] be restrained until after ... or further Order in the meantime from doing (as regards the Defendant [Company] whether by its directors or by its servants or agents or any of them or otherwise howsoever/and regards the Defendant(s) [individual or partnerships] by his/her/its/their/ servants or agents or any of them or otherwise howsoever) the following acts or any of them that is to say ...

AND the Plaintiff(s) ... is/are at liberty to serve short notice of Motion for ...

AND the Defendant(s) ... is/are to be at liberty to move to discharge or vary this Order upon giving to the Plaintiff(s) ... hours/days Notice of his/her/its/their intention so to do.

5. INTERIM INJUNCTION

AND the Plaintiffs by his/her/its/their Counsel undertaking to obey any Order this Court may make as to damages if it shall consider that the Defendants shall have sustained any damages by reason of this Order which the Plaintiffs ought to pay

IT IS ORDERED

1 that the Defendants be restrained until after Judgment in this Action or until further Order in the meantime from doing (as regards the ... Defendant whether by its directors servants or agents or any of them or otherwise howsoever and as regards the ... Defendants whether by themselves or by their servants or agents or any of them or otherwise howsoever) the following acts or any of them that is to say ...

6. ANTON PILLER ORDER

IN THE MATTER of an Intended Action

BETWEEN

Intended Plaintiff

and

Intended Defendant

UPON MOTION made by Counsel for the intended plaintiff(s) (hereinafter called the plaintiff(s))

AND UPON READING the documents specified in the schedule hereto
AND the plaintiff(s) by his/her/its/their/counsel undertaking

1 forthwith/on or before ... to issue a Writ of Summons claiming relief similar to or connected with that hereafter granted

2 to make and file an Affidavit verifying what was alleged by Counsel in the terms of the draft Affidavit of ...

3 to serve upon the intended defendant(s) (hereinafter called the

defendant(s)) a copy of the said Affidavit and Notice of Motion for ...

4   to pay the reasonable costs incurred by any person other than the defendant(s) to whom notice of this Order may be given in ascertaining whether any assets to which this Order applies are within their power possession custody or control and in complying with this Order and to indemnify any such person against all liabilities which may flow from such compliance

5   to obey any Order this court may make as to damages if it shall consider that the defendant(s) shall have sustained any damages by reason of this Order which the plaintiff(s) ought to pay

IT IS ORDERED

1   that the defendant(s) [and each of them] be restrained until after ... or until further Order in the meantime from doing (as regards the ... defendant(s) whether by ... directors or by ... servants or agents or any of them or otherwise howsoever and as regards the defendant(s) whether by ... or by ... servants or agents or any of them or otherwise howsoever) the following acts or any of them that is to say removing from the jurisdiction of this court or otherwise disposing of or dealing with his/her/its their [respective or joint] assets within the jurisdiction of this court including and in particular
   (i)   the freehold property known as ... or (if the same has been sold) the net proceeds of sale thereof after discharge of any subsisting mortgage or charge
   (ii) the property and assets of the business known as ... carried on by the defendant(s) from premises at ... or (if and insofar as the same have been sold) the proceeds of sale thereof
   (iii) any moneys in [any] account(s) [numbered ...] at ... at ... and without prejudice to the foregoing pledging charging or otherwise parting with title to or possession of SUCH ASSETS
      (a) SAVE and in so far as the said assets of [each of] the defendant(s) exceeds £ ...
      (b) SAVE that the defendant(s) [and each of them] is/are to be at liberty to expend a sum not exceeding £ ... [each] per week/month for ordinary living expenses
      (c) AND a sum of £ ... for ordinary and proper business expenses
         AND (not otherwise in each case upon informing the plaintiff's solicitors of the source or accounts from which such sums are to be drawn) and
      (d) THAT the defendant(s) [and each of them] may expend

[a sum not exceeding £ ... [each]] [such reasonable sum] on Legal Advice and representation as may be requisite

(e) PROVIDED nothing in this injunction shall prevent any bank from exercising any rights of set off it may have in respect of facilities afforded by any such bank to the defendant(s) or any of them prior to the date of this order

2   that the defendant(s) [and each of them] shall forthwith disclose the full value of his/her/its/their/ [respective and joint] assets within and without the jurisdiction of this Court identifying with full particularity the nature of all such assets and their whereabouts and whether the same be held in his/her/its/their own names or by nominees or otherwise on his/her/its/their behalf and the sums standing in such accounts such disclosures to be verified by affidavit(s) to be made by the defendant(s) [and in the case of defendants by its/their proper officer] and served on the plaintiffs' solicitors within ... days of service of this Order or notice thereof being given

3   that the defendant(s) [and each of them] shall forthwith upon the service of this Order deliver up or cause to be delivered up into the custody of the plaintiffs' solicitors the ... specified in the schedule hereto

AND the plaintiff ... is/are at liberty to serve Short Notice of Motion for ...

AND the defendant(s) ... is/are at liberty to move to discharge or vary this Order upon giving to the plaintiff ... days Notice of ... intention so to do.

The Schedule
(documents read)

Notes

1   By Ord 29, r 2 the court has power to order the detention, custody or preservation of any property which is the subject matter of the action and also has an inherent jurisdiction to make such order.

2   Where the plaintiff can show a strong *prima facie* case that he will suffer potential or actual damage he may apply *ex parte* by motion for an Anton Piller order. Such an order is made if the defendant has in his possession documents or articles and there is a real possibility that he might destroy such material before an *inter partes* application can be made. The order enables the plaintiff to enter the defendant's premises for the purpose of inspecting and taking away such documents and articles. The order also usually provides that the defendant must disclose

the whereabouts of all articles, eg, pirate films and plates in his possession and records relating to them.

3 Applications for such orders are normally heard in camera in the Chancery Division. Counsel for the plaintiff must apply for this to be done.

4 The plaintiff is required to give certain undertakings set out in the order.

5 Such an order will always give liberty to the defendant to apply to discharge the order after giving notice to the plaintiff or the plaintiff's solicitors.

7. ORDER FOR DIRECTIONS

UPON MOTION for an Injunction made by Counsel for the plaintiffs
AND UPON HEARING Counsel for the defendants
AND UPON READING the court file
THIS COURT DOES NOT THINK FIT to make any Order on the said Motion save that the costs thereof be costs in the cause
AND the Court treating the Summons for directions as now before it

IT IS ORDERED

1 that the plaintiffs shall serve his/her/its/their/Statement of Claim on or before ... 199 ...

2 that the defendants shall serve his/her/its/their Defence and any Counterclaim within ... days after the service of the said Statement of Claim

3 that the plaintiffs shall serve his/her/its/their Reply and Defence to any Counterclaim within ... days after the service of the said Defence and any Counterclaim

4 that the plaintiffs and the defendants respectively shall within ... days after service of the Reply and Defence to Counterclaim (if any) or if there is no Reply or Defence to Counterclaim then within ... days after service of the Defence and Counterclaim (if any) within ... days after the close of the Pleadings or subsequently within 4 days after service of this Order make and serve on the other of them a list (duly verified by Affidavit) of the documents which are or have been in their possession custody or power relating to the matters in question in this Action and Counterclaim (if any) and accounting therefor and serve on the

other of them a copy of the said Affidavit and do at the same time serve on the other of them a Notice in conformity with Order 24 Rule 9 of the Rules of the Supreme Court

5 that the rest of the said Summons be heard in Chambers before Master ... at Room ... The Royal Courts of Justice, Strand, London WC2A 2LL at ... am/pm on ... 199 ... when the Master may direct that this Action and any Counterclaim be set down on or before ... for trial

AND the parties are to be at liberty to apply
(a) to the court (after setting down) to fix an early date for the trial of this Action and any Counterclaim and
(b) generally.

8. DISCHARGE OF CAUTION

IT IS ORDERED

1 that the Caution in favour of the defendant registered on ... in the ... register of Title Number ... at Her Majesty's Land Registry (being the Title relating to the property) ... be vacated.

9. DISCHARGE OF LAND CHARGE

IT IS ORDERED

1 that the registration of the alleged land charge registered in the register of land charges kept at Her Majesty's Land Registry on ... 199 ... in the name of the plaintiff as estate owner and numbered ... be vacated [that the registration of the pending land action registered in the register of pending actions kept at Her Majesty's Land Registry on ... 199 ... in the name of the plaintiff as estate owner and numbered ... be vacated]

2 that the defendant do pay to the plaintiff his/her/its/their costs of the said Motion such costs to be taxed if not agreed.

Notes

1 The 'register of land charges' is one of the five registers mentioned in s 1 of The Land Charges Act 1972. The 'register of pending actions' is another. Section 1(6) says that 'registration may be vacated pursuant to an order of the court'. Section 3(1) says that a land charge shall be registered in the name of the estate owner whose estate is intended

to be affected. There is a similar provision in s 5(4) with regard to pending actions.

2 Section 5(10) says that the court when making an order vacating a registration in the register of pending actions may 'direct the party on whose behalf it was made to pay all or any of the costs and expenses occasioned by the registration and by its vacation'.

3 Although it is convenient to have a precedent, any form of words which satisfactorily identifies the land charge can be adopted by the draftsman. He may therefore follow the wording of the notice of motion if this is unobjectionable.

4 Undertakings in damages are not usually included in these orders as the order is in the nature of a final not an interlocutory order pending trial.

10. MAREVA ORDER

IN THE MATTER of an Intended Action

BETWEEN...

                                      Intended Plaintiff

and

                                   Intended Defendant

UPON MOTION made by Counsel for the intended plaintiff(s) (hereinafter called the plaintiff(s))

AND UPON READING the documents specified in the schedule hereto

AND the plaintiff(s) by his/her/its/their Counsel undertaking

1 forthwith on or before... to issue a Writ of Summons claiming relief similar to or connected with that hereafter granted

2 to make and file an Affidavit verifying what was alleged by Counsel in the terms of the draft Affidavit of...

3 to serve upon the intended defendant(s) (hereinafter called the defendant(s)) a copy of the said Affidavit and Notice of Motion for...

4 to pay the reasonable costs incurred by any person other than the defendant(s) to whom notice of this Order may be given in ascertaining whether any assets to which this Order applies are within their power possession custody or control and in complying with this Order and to indemnify any such person against all liabilities which may flow from such compliance

5 to obey any Order this court may make as to damages if it shall consider that the defendant(s) shall have sustained any damages by reason of this Order which the plaintiff(s) ought to pay

IT IS ORDERED

1 that the defendant(s) [and each of them] be restrained until after ... or until further Order in the meantime from doing (as regards the ... defendant(s) whether by ... directors or by ... servants or agents of any of them or otherwise howsoever and as regards the defendant(s) whether by ... or by ... servants or agents or any of them or otherwise howsoever) the following acts or any of them that is to say removing from the jurisdiction of this court or otherwise disposing of or dealing with his/her/its/their/ [respective or joint] assets within the jurisdiction of this court including and in particular
  (i) the freehold property known as ... or (if the same has been sold) the net proceeds of sale thereof after discharge of any subsisting mortgage or charge
  (ii) the property and assets of the business known as ... carried on by the defendant(s) from premises at ... or (if and in so far as the same have been sold) the proceeds of sale thereof
  (iii) any moneys in [any] account(s) [numbered ...] at ... at ... and without prejudice to the foregoing pledging charging or otherwise parting with title to or possession of SUCH ASSETS
     (a) SAVE and in so far as the said assets of [each of] the defendant(s) exceeds £ ...
     (b) SAVE that the defendant(s) [and each of them] is/are to be at liberty to expend a sum not exceeding £ ... [each] per week/month for ordinary living expenses
     (c) AND a sum of £ ... for ordinary and proper business expenses
         AND not otherwise in each case upon informing the plaintiffs' solicitors of the source or accounts from which such sums are to be drawn and
     (d) THAT the defendant(s) [and each of them] may expend [a sum not exceeding £ ... [each]] [such reasonable sum] on legal advice and representation as may be requisite
     (e) PROVIDED nothing in this injunction shall prevent any bank from exercising any rights of set off it may have in respect of facilities afforded by any such bank to the defendant(s) or any of them prior to the date of this Order

2 that the defendant(s) [and each of them] shall forthwith disclose the full value of his/her/its/their/ [respective and joint] assets within and without the jurisdiction of this Court identifying with

full particularity the nature of all such assets and their whereabouts and whether the same be held in his/her/its/their own names or by nominees or otherwise on his/her/its/their behalf and the sums standing in such accounts such disclosures to be verified by affidavit(s) to be made by the defendant(s) [and in the case of defendants by its/their proper officer] and served on the plaintiffs' solicitors within ... days of service of this Order or notice thereof being given

3 that the defendant(s) [and each of them] shall forthwith upon the service of this Order deliver up or cause to be delivered up into the custody of the plaintiffs' solicitors the ... specified in the schedule hereto

AND the plaintiff ... is/are at liberty to serve Short Notice of Motion for ...
AND the defendant(s) ... is/are at liberty to move to discharge or vary this Order upon giving to the plaintiff ... days Notice of intention so to do.

The Schedule
(Documents specified as being read).

Notes

1 A Mareva injunction restrains a defendant whether or not domiciled or resident in the United Kingdom from removing from the jurisdiction or disposing or dealing with his assets within the jurisdiction in order to defeat the plaintiff's claim. This power is now statutory by Supreme Court Act 1981, s 37(3).

2 A Mareva injunction operates *in rem* and takes effect from the moment it is pronounced on every asset of the defendant including those specified in the order.

3 The plaintiff should normally provide minutes of order including all the usual undertakings.

4 Mareva injunctions are usually granted *ex parte* and save in exceptional circumstances any early return date for the hearing of the motion *inter partes* is fixed.

5 The defendant will always be given liberty to apply to discharge the injunction after giving notice to the plaintiff or his solicitor.

6 One some occasions the court will order the defendant to deliver up certain or all his chattels into the custody of a receiver appointed by the court where there is clear evidence that the defendant is likely to dispose of his chattels. Normally no order would be made to hand over his ordinary household effects or tools of trade.

Chapter Six

Orders and their Issue

1. Orders—general

In the main, the court will take on the responsibility of drawing up orders but particularly in the case of interlocutory orders will consider first whether it is necessary for an order to be drawn up at all. Orders may not be necessary in many instances and in particular are not required in applications for:

(1) leave to issue an originating summons or writ other than one for service out of the jurisdiction;
(2) leave to amend a writ, originating summons or pleading (Ord 20, r 5);
(3) leave to renew a writ (Ord 6, r 8) or originating summons (Ord 7, r 6);
(4) leave to file a document;
(5) leave to extend the period within which the applicant must comply with a rule or order; and
(6) directions sought by judicial trustees, receivers, administrators, *pendente lite* or other officers (except solicitors) of the court.

Orders made by the master

In the case of all interlocutory orders by masters, the master having heard the parties directs whether or not the order is to be drawn up and if so, whether it is to be drawn up by the court or by the solicitors if the master agrees (Practice Direction (Chancery Chambers) (1982) 1 WLR 1189, para 13).

Masters' orders drawn up by solicitors

If the solicitors fail to draw up their own order, the master having agreed that they should do so, then the solicitors must accept that the matter will take its own course through the court with any consequences that follow. If the order is to be drawn up by the court it will be sealed and entered and a sealed copy will be sent to the party having the carriage of it. Similarly, when the master makes a final order the court will draw it up, and again a sealed copy will be sent out.

If because of emergency, or for other reasons, the solicitors wish themselves to draw up a final order whether made by the master or the judge, special arrangements must be made with the order department.

If a solicitor has been given leave to draw up an interlocutory order himself, two engrossments of the order proposed are required, and these may be lodged at room 508, or sent by post to: Drafting Section, Chancery Chambers, Thomas More Building, Royal Courts of Justice, Strand, WC2A 2LL (Practice Direction (Chancery: by Post or Telephone Applications) No 2 of 1983, para 10) (*see Chapter 14*).

Sound practice would be to lodge, or post the engrossments as quickly as possible and certainly well within the seven days allowed.

The party having the carriage of the order has the duty to serve a copy on all interested parties, within three days.

Orders made by the judge

Orders made by the judge on motion will not be drawn up by the court unless it is requested to do so. For all other orders, the court will draw up the order and send it out to the party having carriage of the order unless the court directs that no order need be drawn up, or that minutes of the order be produced. It is very desirable for minutes of the order to be prepared before an application is issued or at least to be ready before the hearing, as for example in summary procedure in specific performance actions (Ord 86) and in such cases they will usually be settled by counsel. If minutes are to be produced they should be agreed and signed by counsel and either handed to the associate or else lodged in room 508.

When a judgment order or declaration is made *by the judge*, it will only be necessary occasionally and when the contents of the order are likely to be particularly complicated, for a party to submit additional documents such as indorsed counsel's briefs, or exhibits to affidavits, in order to assist in the drafting of an order. Whilst additional documents need not usually be lodged, the associate can always ask parties to assist in drafting the order or to furnish documents needed. If a party fails to lodge them, any other party affected may apply to the master for an order requiring the offending party to lodge such documents. Even without such application, the court may well have inherent jurisdiction to make such further orders or directions as it deems fit.

If the drafting section does not agree with minutes settled by counsel they should be referred back to counsel through the solicitors (Practice Direction (Minutes of Order) [1960] 1 WLR 1168 para 1).

Lodging of documents when order drawn up by court

The court might not in some circumstances be able to draw up the order without the original summons or other documents and if a party fails to lodge them, any other party affected may apply to the master for an order requiring the offending party to lodge such documents. Even without such application, the court may well have inherent jurisdiction to make such further orders or directions as it deems fit.

If a party who has carriage of the order fails to comply with any direction given by the order after a limited period of time, possibly as short as 14 days, the Chancery file will be returned from the order room into the central filing system in room 307/308 and will have to be retrieved if further action is to be taken on it.

In the taking of accounts, certificates will no longer be given and such directions as the court makes will be in the form of an order (Ord 44, r 11). The Chancery file will be retained for a limited period of time in the accounts section (room 415/416) until the matter has been disposed of. Delays in dealing with matters by the parties would cause the file to be returned to room 307/308 with consequent delays, or the order itself might be affected.

Wording of orders

A modern form of wording should be used, and archaic expressions and recitals discarded. See notes on drawing up orders below.

Agreed orders

Where the terms of an order are agreed by all parties, the party having the carriage of the order may send either the summons with the date of hearing left blank (if the order is to be made in the terms of the summons), or the minutes of order, in each case indorsed with the consent of the solicitors for each of the parties. The consent of a party in person must be signed by that party personally. The master may make technical or minor adjustments to the draft order, or, if he considers that there should be a hearing, he will notify the parties accordingly.

In legal aid cases, copies of the civil aid certificate should be lodged if the originals were filed at the Central Office prior to 1 October 1982 (para 4 of Chancery: Applications by Post or Telephone: Practice Direction (No 2 of 1983)).

Copies of orders

Copies may be obtained from room 508 upon payment of the appropriate fee (Practice Direction (Chancery Chambers) [1982] 1 WLR 1189, para 16).

Amendments to orders

Any party dissatisfied with the form of the order must notify room 508. If the differences cannot be resolved the objecting party may apply by motion or summons for the order to be amended (Practice Direction (Chancery Chambers) [1982] 1 WLR 1189, para 15).

Orders on motions by agreement

For procedure for solicitors to draw up orders made on motion by agreement see Practice Direction (Chancery Motions: Drawing up of orders) [1970] 1 WLR 249.

Consent orders in the absence of a party

The normal conditions for the making of a consent order in court, in the absence of a party are set out in Practice Direction (Chancery: Consent orders in Court) [1985] 1 WLR 593.

2. The drawing up of orders

Orders are drawn up by the court or the solicitors. Those drawn up by the court are drawn by the drafting section in Chancery Chambers.

Orders made on motion are not drawn up unless one of the parties asks the judge or associate in court that this should be done. This is necessary to ensure that the court does not draw up orders which are not required by the parties (Practice Direction (Chancery Chambers) [1982] 1 WLR 1189, para 14(c)).

Where a master makes an interlocutory order he will ask the parties whether or not they want the order to be drawn up. If an order is to be drawn up the master will ask the party seeking the order whether he wishes to draw it. If the parties so desire and the master agrees he marks his file 'S' and the order is drawn up by the solicitors and must be lodged in room 508 within seven days. (Practice Direction (Chancery Chambers) [1982] 1 WLR 1189, para 13(a)).

By Ord 42, r 4 certain orders need not be drawn up unless the court otherwise directs:

(1) Extending the time for doing an act required by the rules or under any order of the court.
(2) Giving leave to issue a writ other than a writ for service out of the jurisdiction.
(3) Giving leave to amend any writ or pleading.
(4) For a defendant to issue a notice of appointment to hear an originating summons where the plaintiff has failed to do so (Ord 28, r 2(3)).
(5) Giving leave to file any documents.

(6) Giving leave for the doing of any act by a receiver or other officer of the court other than a solicitor.

Orders when passed and entered by the drafting section are filed in the court file held by the Chancery registry (Ord 42, r 6(1)).

The duties of the draftsman

The following are the basic duties of the draftsman to be undertaken in Chancery chambers:

(1) To check the parties and their representatives and acknowledgments of service or affidavits of service.
(2) To check the documents on the court file recorded as read.
(3) To make sure that any order made by a master is within the master's jurisdiction.
(4) To ensure that notice of intention to proceed has been given if more than one year has elapsed since the last proceedings (Ord 3, r 6).
(5) To see that a minor or patient is represented by a properly constituted next friend in the case of a plaintiff or by a guardian *ad litem* in the case of a defendant.
(6) Where the proceeding is under some statute see that the statute is mentioned in the body of the writ or originating summons but not in the title.
(7) Check whether any recitals or undertakings are necessary but avoid unnecessary recitals.

Correction or alteration of an order

Before entry An order pronounced by a judge, whether in open court or in chambers, can always be withdrawn, altered, or modified by him, either on his own initiative, or on the application of a party, at any time before the order has been passed and entered. The oral order is in the meanwhile provisionally effective, and it can be treated as a subsisting order when the justice of the case requires it and the right of withdrawal would not thereby be prevented or prejudiced (*Re Harrison's Share under a Settlement, Harrison v Harrison* [1955] Ch 260 [1955] All ER 185).

After entry Clerical errors. By virtue of 'the slip rule' (Ord 20, r 11) clerical mistakes in judgments or orders or errors arising from any accidental slip or omission may at any time be corrected by the court or a judge on motion or summons without an appeal. Any party may apply to correct a slip (*Re Marly Laboratory Ltd's Application* [1952] 1 All ER 1057). The application should be made to the judge or court, or by restoring the summons upon which the order was made to the master's list, if made in chambers.

Inherent jurisdiction. The court has an inherent power to vary its own orders so as to carry out its meaning and to make its meaning plain. In *Re Swire, Mellor v Swire* (1885) 30 Ch D 239 to 243, Cotton LJ said:

It is only in special circumstances that the court will interfere with an order which has been passed and entered except in cases of a mere slip or verbal inaccuracy; yet in my opinion the court has jurisdiction over its own records and if it finds that the order as passed and entered contains an adjudication upon that which the court in fact has never adjudicated upon, then in my opinion it has jurisdiction which it will in a proper case exercise to correct its record that it may be in accordance with the order really pronounced.

The correction should be made upon motion and is not a matter for appeal or rehearing (per Lord Watson in *Hatton v Harris* [1892] AC 547 at 650).

If the order as drawn correctly expressed the intention of the court, it cannot be corrected under either the slip rule or the inherent jurisdiction even if the decision of the court has been obtained by fraud or misrepresentation (*Preston Banking Co v William Allsup & Sons* [1895] 1 Ch 141). In such case a new action must be commenced to rescind the judgment on the ground of the discovery of new evidence which would have had a material effect upon the decision of the court, eg, fraud or misrepresentation.

The drafting section has power, where the order has not been correctly entered, to correct the order by consent (Practice Direction (Chancery Chambers) [1982] 1 WLR 1189, para 15).

If the differences *can* be resolved and the associate decides to amend the order he must remember Ord 42, r 7(3).

A judgment shall not be amended except on production of the duplicate thereof last issued, and if the judgment is amended the duplicate so issued shall be similarly amended, and the amendment sealed, under the direction of the proper officer.

If the differences *cannot* be resolved then the application to the court mentioned in the Practice Direction will be under Ord 20, r 11 (commonly called 'the slip rule'). This says:

Clerical mistakes in judgments or orders, or errors arising therein, may at any time be corrected by the court on motion or summons without an appeal.

The contents of an order

Heading (title and parties) This shows that the action is in the High Court in the Chancery Division, the number, the date and the parties. It also gives the name of the judge or master concerned and in some cases indicates what the action is about; eg, 'In the Estate of AB deceased'.

Upon application The application paragraph states by whom the application is made and by what method, eg, by summons or motion.

Upon hearing This paragraph indicates whether the plaintiff and defendant respectively are represented by counsel or solicitor or in person and shows who has been heard.

Upon reading The court file indicates the documents read by the court before giving judgment or making an order. Each document on the court file has a number and the court file is marked, eg, Read 1, 2, 3, 5.

Recitals In some cases it is necessary to have recitals to explain the purpose of the order and to include undertakings.

Operative part This consists of the actual order made by the court which may be divided into numbered paragraphs for the purpose of clarity.

Backsheet This includes the information that the action is in the High Court, Chancery Division, the short title, the word 'order' and the name and address of the solicitors having carriage of the order.

The carriage of orders

The successful party or the applicant normally has the carriage of the order unless the court otherwise directs.

The duplicate order is sent out to the party having the carriage of the order without any fee (Ord 47, r 7(1)). It is the duty of such party to serve a copy of the order on every other party affected by the order.

A party desiring to enforce an order should serve it on the other party endorsing a copy with a penal notice under Ord 45, r 7(4) if appropriate.

Action number

Since 1 January 1983, the letters CH have been placed before the action number of proceedings issued in Chancery chambers to distinguish Chancery actions from Queen's Bench actions. Otherwise there would be actions in two divisions of the High Court with the same action number.

In the Chancery Division numbers are given chronologically whatever the letter of the alphabet, eg, 1984 A 1, and 1984 C 2. While in the Queen's Bench Division, each letter has its own series of numbers.

In the case of a clearing bank or a building society the governing factor will be the first letter of the defendant's name.

Title and parties

Title to writ or originating process

(1) The general rule is that the title should contain only the parties to the proceedings but there are two exceptions:
    (a) where the proceedings relate to the administration of an estate or a probate action they should be entitled 'In the estate of AB deceased';
    (b) where they relate to the construction of a document they should be entitled 'In the matter [describe document with parties and date]'. If there is more than one deed only the main or first deed need be referred to.

       If proceedings are under some Act of Parliament the Act need not be mentioned in the title but should be referred to in the body of the writ or originating summons (Practice Direction (Chancery: Procedure [1983] 1 All ER 131)). There is an exception in certain *ex parte* proceedings.

(2) The capacity in which persons are sued, eg, as executors should be omitted from the title. The representative capacity should be endorsed on the writ as provided by Ord 6, r 3.

(3) A party who is a minor should be so described.

(4) When a minor is a party the name of the next friend if a plaintiff and the name of the guardian *ad litem* if a defendant should not appear in the title but in the body of the writ. (Practice Direction (1946) WN 154).

(5) In the case of a mentally disordered person who is a party the name of the next friend if a plaintiff and the name of the guardian *ad litem* if a defendant is set out in the title.

(6) Where AB is the trustee in bankruptcy of CD AB's name is not mentioned in the title, but only 'the trustee of the property of CD a bankrupt' (Bankruptcy Act 1914, s 76).

(7) Where a bankrupt is a trustee or a mortgagor in possession he should be made a party *(Re Solomon (A Bankrupt) ex parte The Trustee of the Property of the Bankrupt v Solomon* [1967] Ch 573).

(7A) Where a person sues as attorney for another, the principal should be named as plaintiff.

(8) Where it is necessary to sue an unincorporated charity for the purpose of determining a question of the right of the charity to a legacy or any similar question a responsible officer such as the treasurer or secretary should be sued on behalf of the charity *(Re Pritt, Morton v National Church League* (1915) 85 LJ Ch 166).

(9) A female party need not be described as spinster, married woman or widow, but if there is likely to be any doubt she may be so described or described as 'Mrs' or 'Miss'. The term 'feme sole' should not be used (Ord 6, r 1, note 4).

(9A) It is a helpful practice when the name of a party is unfamiliar to place the word 'male' or 'female' in brackets after it to indicate gender.

(10) If the true legal description of a corporate or other body is not apparent from its name the description should be stated, eg, a company limited by guarantee (Practice Direction (Central Office: Description of Parties) [1969] 2 All ER 1130).

(11) The title in a relator action should be 'Her Majesty's Attorney General at the relation of AB plaintiff'. It sometimes happens that the relator as well as the Attorney General is a plaintiff.

(12) Where the plaintiffs or defendants are numerous the name of each plaintiff or defendant is prefixed by a number in brackets. The names of the plaintiffs should be listed each one on a separate line with an appropriate numeral in brackets before each name, and when all have been set out they should be described by the single word 'plaintiffs'.

Then, and only then, should there be an 'and' separating all the plaintiffs from all the defendants and the defendants should be similarly listed and numbered (Practice Note (Chancery: Deposition) [1981] 1 WLR 1560).

Title to future proceedings The title to the originating process will not be amended except where the Rules of Court require, eg, Ord 15, r 8; but the title to any subsequent orders and process will record the changes made.

(1) If by reason of any event causing a transmission of interest or liability, eg, death, bankruptcy or the assignment of the interest of any party, then an order to carry on is required (Ord 15, r 7). In subsequent summonses and orders the title will show that the new parties have come in in the place of the old.

(2) Where an action has been reconstituted on more than one occasion the title should set out no more than the original title and the one constituted by the last order to carry on.
(3) Where a minor attains his or her majority during the course of proceedings the title will be amended and he or she will be described in the title as 'AB (late a minor)'.
(4) Where a person has by order been added as a party insert after his name '(added.../.../9   )'.
(5) Where a defendant has become a plaintiff or vice versa insert after his name his former capacity and the date of the order effecting the change, eg, '(AB former defendant.../.../9   )'.
(6) Where after the completion of proceedings by or against a limited company the name of the company is changed the new name should be substituted and the former name mentioned in brackets in all future proceedings (Practice Direction (Limited Companies' Change of Name) [1965] 1 All ER 43).
(7) Where a party changes his or her surname during the course of proceedings or a female party has married his or her surname shall be substituted and the former surname mentioned in brackets in all future proceedings (Practice Direction (Change of Surname) [1965] 1 All ER 928 and MPD No 13 and Practice Direction (Chancery: Applications; and Change of Name) [1984] 1 WLR 447).

The party who has changed his or her name must promptly file a written notice of change in the Chancery registry and serve a copy on every other party.
(8) Where a party dies and no order to carry on is sought evidence of death such as the death certificate or grant of representation should be filed and the words (since deceased) will be added after his name.
(9) In all orders subsequent to acknowledgment of service it is the practice after the name of the minor to add 'a minor by his guardian *ad litem* AB'.
(10) Where it is clear that a company is in liquidation the words 'in liquidation' may be added after the name of such a party.
(11) Where proceedings against a party are stayed or discontinued this is shown: 'AB (proceedings stayed by order dated...)' or 'CD (proceedings discontinued by notice dated...)'.
(12) When parties are added this is shown: 'AB (added by order to carry on dated...)' or 'CD (added by the order dated...)'. Where no order is drawn up and leave is given to add a party 'EF (added...)'.
(13) By Ord 81, r 4(1) where persons are sued as partners in the name of their firm service may not be acknowledged in the name of the firm but only by the partners thereof in their own name, but the action nevertheless continues in the name of the firm.
(14) By Ord 81, r 9 an individual carrying on business in a name

and style other than his own name may be sued in that name as if it were the name of a firm. An individual served in this name must acknowledge service in his own name.

3. Representation orders

By Ord 15, r 13, in any proceedings (including probate proceedings) concerning an estate or property subject to a trust or the construction of a written instrument the court may in certain specified circumstances appoint one or more persons to represent any person (including an unborn person) or class who is or may be interested, and such persons will be bound by the order. Before such an order can be made the following conditions must be fulfilled: (a) that a person or class cannot be ascertained or cannot readily be ascertained, or, though ascertained, cannot be found, and (b) that the court is satisfied that it is expedient that an order should be made. The order is normally made by the judge at the hearing of the action.

By Ord 15, r 14, trustees, executors and administrators may sue and be sued on behalf of or as representing the property of the estate without joining any of the beneficiaries. They are considered as representing such persons, but the court may at any stage order any beneficiary or beneficiaries to be made parties. When the beneficiaries are neither parties nor represented, the trustees *prima facie* represent them, whether they are ascertained or not, and it is the duty of the trustees' counsel to put before the court any considerations which may affect the interest of any of them (*Re Brown's Will* (1884) 27 Ch D 179).

By Ord 15, r 12, where there are numerous persons having the same interests, one or more persons may sue or be sued, or may be authorised by the court to defend, on behalf of all persons so interested.

An order is required for authority to defend, and this may be obtained on summons or notice under Ord 25 where applicable. An order should not be made where there are only a few such parties, eg, five residuary legatees, unless the amount is very small and the court is satisfied that it is the wish of all persons interested that the representation desired should be ordered (*Re Braybrook, Braybrook v Wright* [1916] WN 74).

By Ord 15, r 13(4), where a compromise is proposed in any proceedings concerning the estate of a deceased person, or property subject to a trust or the construction of a written instrument, and some of the persons who are interested or may be affected are not parties (including unborn or unascertained persons) but there is some other person in the same interest who assents, or the absent parties are represented by a person appointed under Ord 15, r 13 who assents, the court may approve the compromise if satisfied that the compromise will be for the benefit of the absent parties, and that it is expedient to exercise the power, and the absent persons will be bound.

By Ord 15, r 15, where any deceased person interested in proceedings has no legal personal representative the court may proceed in the absence of the personal representative or may appoint some person to represent the estate for the purpose of the action.

Application is normally made at the hearing. The consent of the party to be appointed must be obtained, but the court may select any person for the appointment, including the official solicitor.

Under the Inheritance (Provision for Family and Dependants) Act 1975, where a defendant has been added and there are other persons having the same or similar interest the court may order that such defendant be authorised to defend on behalf of all persons having the same interest. There should be a special paragraph in the originating summons asking for a representation order. By Ord 15, r 6A(1), where any person against whom an action would have lain has died but the cause of action survives the action may, if no grant of probate or administration has been made, be brought against the estate of the deceased.

4. Declarations

A declaration is a judicial act and ought not to be made on admissions of the parties, or by consent, but only if the court is satisfied by evidence (*Wallersteiner v Moir* [1974] 1 WLR 991 at 1029). Consequently declarations are not usually made on motions for judgment since no evidence is read but only the pleadings. In modern practice the decision of the court is frequently a declaration of the rights of the parties. Such declaration can only be made by a judge and *not* a master (except in plain cases).

There is however another kind of declaration relating to certain facts which have been found by the court, eg, a master, having taken account, will declare that £X is due to A and £Y due to B. Such declarations are often made by the master as they are not declarations of law but findings of fact ascertained in chambers. For examples of declaratory judgments, see Atkin, Vol 14 (1991 issue).

Orders and their Issue—Orders

1. HEADINGS

IN THE HIGH COURT OF JUSTICE   CH1991S No 1234
CHANCERY DIVISION

MR JUSTICE [at chambers] [sitting at Bristol] [sitting with assessors]

[MASTER]

    Dated the .... day of 199

    IN THE ESTATE of A deceased

    IN THE MATTER of a SETTLEMENT ... and made between (1) John Doe (2) Richard Roe

BETWEEN
       1   JOHN SMITH
       2   Michael Jones
            and
       1   GEORGE ROBINSON
       2   William Brown

UPON THE APPLICATION ...

UPON READING ...

UPON HEARING ...

Note

The practice is to put the names of the first plaintiff and the first defendant in capitals. Note also the positioning of the numerals.

2. PROCEEDINGS AGAINST ESTATES

By Ord 15, r 6A a plaintiff may issue proceedings against 'the Personal Representatives of AB deceased'.
    The plaintiff must subsequently apply to the court for an order appointing a person to represent the estate. After such appointment the title will be read.

BETWEEN
     A   Plaintiff
    and
  The personal representatives of
    B deceased Defendants
    (by original action)

AND BETWEEN
     A   Plaintiff
    and
  C (appointed by order dated ... to represent the estate of B deceased)

3. EXAMPLES OF TITLES

(1) Third Party Proceedings

An example of third party and fourth party proceedings is

BETWEEN

	A	Plaintiff
	and	
1	B	
2	C	
3	D	Defendants
	and	
1	E	
2	F	
3	G	
		Third Parties
	and	
1	H	
2	J	Fourth Parties

Fourth Parties are brought in by Third Parties and Fifth Parties by Fourth Parties.

In a complicated case it may be useful to add explanatory words at the foot of the title, eg, (by original Action and Counterclaim by the Third Defendant against the Plaintiff. Third Party proceedings by the Second Defendant against all the Third Parties and Fourth Party Proceedings by the first Third Party against all the Fourth Parties).

(2) Proceedings between Defendants

Title to an action

BETWEEN

	A	Plaintiff
	and	
1	B	
2	C	
3	D	Defendants

Where there are proceedings between C and D there are two courses open. The following words can be added to the title. (Action and proceedings by the Second Defendant against the Third Defendant).

Alternatively the title can be set out:

BETWEEN

	A	Plaintiff
	and	
1	B	
2	C	
3	D	Defendants

(Action)

AND BETWEEN

	C	Plaintiff
	and	
	D	
		Defendants

(proceedings pursuant to Notice under Ord 16, r 8)

(3) Counterclaims

Where all the defendants together counterclaim against all the plaintiffs it is only necessary to add at the bottom of the title (Action and Counterclaim).

Where not all the defendants counterclaim the practice is to set out the counterclaim separately.

eg, BETWEEN

1	A	
2	B	
3	C	Plaintiffs
	and	
1	D	
2	E	
3	F	Defendants

(by original action)

AND BETWEEN

1	D	
2	E	Plaintiffs
	and	
1	A	
2	B	Defendants
(by counterclaim)		

Alternatively after the title in the main action is set out the following words could be added (by original ACtion and by Counterclaim of the first and second defendants against the first and second plaintiffs).

4. EXAMPLES OF TITLES TO *EX PARTE* ORIGINATING SUMMONSES

(1) Funds in Court

IN THE MATTER of an application by AB with regard to funds in court under ledger credit No...

(2) Joint Applications under the Landlord and Tenant Act 1954

IN THE MATTER of a joint application by AB and Another with regard to [short description of property].

(3) Taxation of Costs

IN THE MATTER of AB (A solicitor) and the Taxation of Costs.

(4) Leasehold Reform Act 1967

IN THE MATTER of an application by AB under the Leasehold Reform Act 1967 in respect of [short description of property].

(5) Trade Marks

IN THE MATTER of Trade Mark Number... in the name of AB. IN THE MATTER of an application by AB for the registration of a Trade Mark.

(6) Patents

IN THE MATTER of Letters Patent No... granted to AB.

IN THE MATTER of an application by AB under the Patents Act 1977.

(7) Order 113

IN THE MATTER of (short description of property) (where, as is usual, the application is *inter partes* the names of the plaintiffs and defendants should be set out in the usual way).

(8) Commons

IN THE MATTER of ... and the COMMONS REGISTRATION ACT 1965.

(9) Guardianship of Estate of Minor

IN THE MATTER of AB (A Minor).

(10) Other Cases

IN THE MATTER of an application by AB and Another ... (very brief indication of nature of application).

5. EXAMPLES OF 'UPON APPLICATION' PARAGRAPHS

1 UPON THE APPLICATION of the plaintiff
This is used where there is no summons and the matter is not brought before the court by motion or in some other way indicated below. For example, it is used on *ex parte* applications to a master. Order 32, r 1 says that 'except as provided by Ord 25, r 7 every application in chambers not made *ex parte* must be made by summons'.

2 UPON THE APPLICATION of the plaintiff by summons dated ...

3 UPON THE APPLICATION of the plaintiff for judgment by summons dated ...

4 UPON THE SEVERAL APPLICATIONS of the plaintiff (1) by summons dated ... and (2) by summons dated ...

5 UPON THE APPLICATION of the plaintiff for directions by notice dated ... [This is a notice under Ord 25, r 7 referred to above].

6 UPON THE SEVERAL APPLICATIONS for the directions (1) of the

plaintiff by summons dated ... and (2) of the defendant by notice dated ...

7 UPON THE APPLICATION of the plaintiff by originating summons
As there is only one originating summons in an action it is unnecessary to give the date. This formula should be used whether the originating summons is before the master or before the judge.

8 UPON THE SEVERAL APPLICATIONS by originating summons (1) of the plaintiff in the above mentioned action 1980 A 1 and (2) of the plaintiff in the above mentioned action 1980 B 1.

9 UPON THE TRIAL of this action and counterclaim and the third and fourth party proceedings and the proceedings by the ... defendants against the ... defendants against the ... defendants.

10 THIS ACTION AND COUNTERCLAIM being mentioned to this court
This should be used only (1) when the case is listed 'To be Mentioned' or (2) the case is not listed at all but is in fact mentioned. Thus it should be used if the case is listed for hearing and counsel briefly 'mention' it as having been settled.
   Where an action is mentioned on the minutes of order the order should begin as in 9 above.

11 UPON MOTION made by counsel for the plaintiff
A motion is an oral application made to a judge in open court. Whenever counsel makes an application to a judge in open court the application can be described as a motion unless there is some good reason for describing it as something else.

12 UPON THE SEVERAL MOTIONS made by counsel (1) for the plaintiff and (2) for the defendant.

13 UPON THE SEVERAL MOTIONS made by counsel for the plaintiff (1) pursuant to notice of motion dated ... (2) pursuant to notice of motion dated ...

14 UPON THE SEVERAL MOTIONS made by counsel for the plaintiff (1) for an injunction and (2) for the appointment of a receiver.

15 UPON MOTION made by counsel for ... pursuant to notice of originating motion.

16 UPON MOTION made by counsel for the plaintiff by way of appeal from the order dated ...

17 UPON MOTION for judgment on the default of the defendant in serving a defence made by counsel for the plaintiff.

18 UPON MOTION made by counsel for the plaintiff for judgment on admissions.

19 UPON THE APPEAL of the plaintiff from the order of the master dated ...

20 UPON A CASE stated by way of appeal from the decision dated ... of ...

21 UPON A CASE STATED pursuant to s 56 of the Taxes Management Act 1970 by the Commissioners for the Special Purposes of the Income Tax Acts.

22 UPON THE APPEAL under s ... of ... of the appellant from the decision of ... on ...

23 UPON THE APPEAL under para 7 of sched 4 of the Finance Act 1975 of the appellant from the determination of the defendants referred to in the originating summons.

24 UPON A CASE STATED by the respondents pursuant to s 13 of the Stamp Act 1891.

25 UPON THE PETITION of ...

26 UPON THE ASSESSMENT of damages pursuant to the order dated ...

27 UPON THE ACCOUNT AND INQUIRIES directed by the order dated ...

28 UPON THE EXAMINATION of the items numbered ... in the account from ... to ... (both days inclusive) of ... (hereinafter called the receiver) the receiver and manager appointed by the order dated ...

29 UPON THE ACCOUNT from ... to ... (both days inclusive) of ... (hereinafter called the receiver) the receiver and manager appointed by the order dated ...

30 UPON THE TRIAL of the preliminary issue directed by the order dated ...

31 WHEREAS (1) by the order dated ...
(2)
NOW UPON MOTION ...

32 UPON THE APPLICATION by originating summons of the plaintiff who sues by AB his next friend.

Where the plaintiff is a minor the name of his next friend should be shown in the body of the order.

33 UPON THE APPLICATION by summons dated ... of the plaintiffs of whom the third plaintiff sues by AB his next friend.

Notes

1 Now that most statutes no longer appear in the title it is necessary to insert the statute in the body of the order, eg, an order under The Inheritance (Provision for Family and Dependants) Act 1975 to indicate the nature of the proceedings.

2 When a summons or motion is dismissed it is good practice to indicate briefly what relief was sought by the applicant.

6. EXAMPLES OF 'UPON HEARING' PARAGRAPHS

1 UPON HEARING the solicitors for the plaintiff [no one appearing for the defendant].

2 UPON HEARING the solicitors for the plaintiff and for the defendant.

3 UPON HEARING the solicitors for the plaintiff and the defendant in person.

4 UPON HEARING the solicitors for the plaintiff and for the [first two] defendants and the [third] defendant in person.

5 UPON HEARING counsel for the plaintiff.

6 UPON HEARING counsel for the plaintiff and for the defendant.

7 UPON HEARING counsel for the plaintiff and for the [first and third] defendants and the solicitors for the second defendant.

8 UPON HEARING counsel for the plaintiff and the solicitors for the defendant.

9 UPON HEARING counsel for the plaintiff and the defendant in person.

10 UPON HEARING counsel for the plaintiff and the solicitors for the [first and third] defendant and the [third] defendant in person.

11 UPON HEARING the solicitors for ... (hereinafter called the applicant) and for the plaintiff and the defendant.

12 UPON HEARING the solicitors for ... being a person served with notice of the order dated ...

7. EXAMPLES OF 'UPON READING' PARAGRAPHS

UPON READING the documents recorded on the court file as having been read [the affidavit of A sworn the ... day of ... 199 ..] [the documents set out in the schedule hereto].

Each document on the court file has a number but the judge or master does not read every item in the court file. When an application is before the judge or on the trial of the action the associate will note on the file all the documents that the judge has read to come to his conclusion. Where the application is before the master the master will himself record the numbers of the documents he has read.

8. RECITALS

Occasionally it is necessary to explain why the order has been made or that there has been some agreement between the parties which will be recited before the operative part is reached.

Frequently undertakings are given to the court which are recorded in the order and sometimes liberty to apply is given to enforce the undertakings.

AND IT APPEARING from the evidence that the defendant has not paid the balance of the purchase money and costs as ordered on ..., 199 ...

AND the plaintiff by his counsel undertaking that he will not sell mortgage or part with possession of Blackacre pending the determination of this action.

9. EXAMPLES OF OPENINGS TO OPERATIVE PARTS

IT IS ORDERED ...

IT IS DECLARED ...

IT IS by consent ORDERED

IT IS with the consent of the plaintiff and the third defendant ORDERED

IT IS notwithstanding the ORDER dated...ORDERED.

IT IS pursuant to the ORDER dated... ORDERED.

THE COURT DOES NOT THINK FIT to make any order on the said application/motion save that...

10. FORM OF BACKSHEET

IN THE HIGH COURT OF JUSTICE

.... CHANCERY DIVISION

....

....

MR JUSTICE

[MASTER]

[DATE]

Re A deceased

B

v

C

ORDER

[Solicitor's name]

[address]

11. EXAMPLES OF OPERATIVE PARTS

(1) General order for account and inquiry

IT IS ORDERED

1 that the following Account and Inquiry be taken and made that is to say
    (1) An Account
    (2) An Inquiry

2 that the defendant shall on or before ...
or subsequently within 4 days after service of this order lodge at Room 508, Chancery Chambers, Thomas More Building, the Royal Courts of Justice, Strand, London WC2A 2LL the said Account duly verified by being exhibited to an Affidavit together with such Affidavit and an Affidavit (which may be the same Affidavit) in answer to the said Inquiry and do within the same time serve on the Plaintiff copies of such account and Affidavit or Affidavits.

[2 that the Defendant shall on or before ...
lodge the said Account duly verified by being exhibited to an Affidavit and an Affidavit in answer to the said Inquiry and do within the same time serve copies of the same on the Plaintiff]

[2 that the Plaintiff shall on or before ... lodge/serve his evidence on the said Account and Inquiry]

3 that the Plaintiff/Defendant be at liberty within ... days after the service of the said Account and Affidavit evidence to lodge evidence in answer

4 that the Plaintiff/Defendant be at liberty to lodge evidence in reply within ... days after service of the said evidence in answer

5 that the costs of the said Application be costs in the Account and Inquiry.

Notes

1 Sometimes the order merely says that the account is to be taken and gives no direction as to evidence. When this is the case paras (2), (3) and (4) in the precedent will not be wanted.

2 The accounts and inquiries should be numbered (Ord 43, r 2(2)) even if there is only one and so that all the accounts and inquiries in an action are numbered successively. Thus one order may direct inquiries Nos 1 and 2 and another order may direct inquiry No 3.

3 Para (2) in Form No 1 should only be used when it is clear that this was the judge's or master's intention. A four-day order is not usually made until there has been an initial failure to comply.

4 It should be borne in mind that there are two types of case. In one the plaintiff needs the defendant's account and unless he has it he may not be able to obtain what he is entitled to in the action. In such cases the court may eventually compel the defendant to put in his account.

In other cases a defendant's affidavit may be required more for the defendant's own sake than for the plaintiff's and if the defendant fails to put in his evidence the plaintiff will be able to obtain what he wants on his own evidence. In this second type of case there is unlikely to be a 'four-day order'. Equally, it is unlikely that the court would make a 'four-day order' against the party who sought the account!

5   It will sometimes be the plaintiff or person who sought the inquiry who will be directed to lodge evidence first. In such cases the third form '2' in the rider may be appropriate.

(2) Partnership account

IT IS ORDERED

1   that the following Account and Inquiry be taken and made that is to say
    (1)   An Account all dealings and transactions between the Plaintiff and Defendant as partners from . . .
    (2)   An account of the assets and liabilities of the partnership as at . . .
    (3)   An Inquiry of what the property now belonging to the said partnership consists.

2   that the costs of the said Application be costs in the said Account and Inquiry.

Notes

This is the usual order see Atkin, Vol 30 (1979 issue) and that volume contains other forms of account and inquiry which may be needed in different circumstances.

(3) Declaration on partnership accounts

IT IS DECLARED

1   that as a result of the dealings and transactions between the Plaintiff and the Defendant as partners from . . . there is due to the Plaintiff from the Defendant the sum of £ . . . there is due to the Plaintiff £ . . . and to the Defendant £ . . . from the property of the partnership and that after payment of the two said sums the balance if any of the said property after payment of all proper costs and expenses belongs to the Plaintiff and to the Defendant in equal shares . . .

[2   that there is now no property belonging to the partnership]

[2 that the credits properly belonging to the partnership consist of the items specified in the Schedule thereto.]

The Schedule

1 The leasehold property (valued at £...) known as ... and held under a lease dated ... and made between ... 1 and ...2

2 The goodwill (valued at £...) of the business of ... carried on by the partners at ...

3 The chattels (valued at £...) listed in exhibit ... to the Affidavit of ... sworn

4 The debts amounting to valued at £... due to the partnership listed in exhibit ... to the Affidavit of ...

5 The sum of £... or thereabouts on current account with ... Bank plc at their branch at ... in the name of ... the Receiver and Manager appointed by the Order dated ...]

(4) Declaration on trustees' or agents' accounts

IT IS DECLARED

1 that the money received by the Defendant and by other persons on behalf of the Defendant as trustee or agent of the Plaintiff in or about the year 19... amounted to the sum £... and that of this sum the Defendant expended £... in proper disbursements on behalf of the Plaintiff and retained the balance of £...

2 that the balance due to the Plaintiff on ... was accordingly £... that interest on the said sum at the rate of ... per cent per annum from that date to the date of this Order is £... and that accordingly the total now due from the Defendant to the Plaintiff is £...

AND IT IS ORDERED

1 that the Defendant shall pay to the Plaintiff the said sum of £...

2 that the Defendant shall pay to the Plaintiff ... costs of the said Account and Inquiry to be taxed if not agreed.

(5) Against personal representative

IT IS ORDERED

1 that the following Account be taken [on the basis of wilful default] that is to say
   1 the Account of the property not specifically devised or bequeathed by the above named deceased in the hands of the Defendant the Executor of his Will/Administrator of his estate or either of them or in the hands of any other person or persons by the Order or for the use of them
   2 that the Defendant shall on or before ... lodge the said Account duly verified by being exhibited to an Affidavit and shall within the same time serve copies of the same on the Plaintiff
   3 that the Defendant shall out of his own monies pay to the Plaintiff his costs of this Action down to and including this Order to be taxed if not agreed
   4 that the further consideration of this Action be adjourned
   5 that the parties be at liberty to apply.

Notes

1 Sometimes an account is ordered on the basis of wilful default. An account on this footing charges the accounting party with what he should have received but for his wilful neglect or default.

2 Wilful default consists of a deliberate failure by a person to do what he legally ought to do.

(6) Order for an account—('four day' order)

IT IS ORDERED

1 that the defendant shall on or before ... or subsequently within 4 days after service of this order lodge at Room 307/308, Chancery Chambers, Thomas More Building, The Royal Courts of Justice, Strand, London WC2 2LL the following Account duly verified by being exhibited to an affidavit together with such affidavit and an affidavit (which may be the same affidavit) in answer to the following Inquiry that is to say
   (1) An Account ...
   (2) An Inquiry ...

2 that the defendant shall within the same time serve upon the plaintiff copies of the said Account and the said affidavit or affidavits

3 that the costs of the said application are to be borne by the defendant in any event.

Notes

1 Order 42, r 2(1) states that a judgment or order which requires a person to do an act must specify the time after service of the judgment order or some other time within which the act is to be done. Rule 2(2) states that this does not apply where the order is
    (a) to pay money to some other person
    (b) to give possession of any land
    (c) to deliver any goods.

2 Where a time is fixed by the court to do any act (not being an order to do an act within x days of service of the order), under the above rule the draftsman should insert the order 'or subsequently within 4 days after service'. *Re Tuck-Murch v Loosemore* 1906 1 Ch 693 at p 696.

3 Such words are not included in orders unless directed by the court
    (a) to pay money to a person
    (b) to give possession of land
    (c) to deliver goods
    (d) to serve pleadings, including particulars
    (e) to serve evidence
    (f) for discovery and inspection.

4 Where it is contemplated that a committal or sequestration would be the sanction for disobedience, the words should be included but not where the order only relates to routine directions in interlocutory matters.

12. COMPROMISE

AND the plaintiffs and defendants other than the defendants who are minors by their Counsel agreeing to the terms set forth in the Schedule hereto

THE COURT HEREBY APPROVES the said terms on behalf of the defendants who are minors

AND IT IS ORDERED that the ... are to be at liberty to carry the said terms into effect.

Notes

1 Compromises on behalf of persons under a disability must be approved by the court. Where an action is pending a summons is issued in the proceedings setting out the terms of the proposed compromise. Where

there is no pending action an originating summons should be issued under Ord 85.

2 An affidavit must be filed by the next friend or guardian *ad litem* of the minor or patient exhibiting the case to counsel and counsel's opinion advising that the compromise is for the benefit of the minor and stating that he personally approves the compromise (*Re Birchall decd Wilson v Birchall* (1980) 16 Ch D 41). The minor or patient should be separately represented by counsel before the court.

3 Where an action is brought or is defended under the sanction of the Court of Protection no compromise should be effected without the sanction of the master of the Court of Protection.

4 The master may approve the compromise if the value of the minor's or patient's share does not significantly exceed £30,000 (Practice Direction (Chancery: Masters' Powers) [1975] 1 All ER 255, para 11, as amended by Practice Direction (Chancery: Procedure) [1983] 1All ER 131, para 3).

13. ORDER FOR STAY OF PROCEEDINGS

(1) By consent

UPON THE APPLICATION of the ... by Summons dated ...
AND UPON READING the documents recorded on the Court File as having been read
AND the Plaintiff and the Defendant by their Solicitors having consented in writing to this Order and to there being no Order as to costs
IT IS ORDERED that this Action and Counterclaim be discontinued.

(2) Tomlin form

AND the Parties having agreed to the terms set forth in the schedule annexed hereto

IT IS BY CONSENT ORDERED

1 [that the costs of the plaintiff/defendant be taxed pursuant to the Legal Aid and Advice Act 1974]

2 that all further proceedings in this Action and Counterclaim except for the purpose of carrying the said terms into effect be stayed

AND for that purpose the parties are to be at liberty to apply.

Notes

1 A 'Tomlin' order is an order which the court makes staying the proceedings upon terms which the parties have agreed themselves. The court is not concerned with the scheduled terms which are a new agreement made by the parties which may be enforced in the same action. The court is only concerned that the terms should not be nonsensical.

2 Where the following provisions are required they must be inserted in the body of the order and not in the schedule
   (a)   a provision for the taxation of costs
   (b)   a direction for payment out of court
   (c)   a release from an undertaking given to the court
   (d)   a variation or discharge of some previous orders.

3 The schedule is normally typed at the end of the order but it can be annexed. Sometimes the agreed terms are contained in a deed and then a copy of the deed can be annexed to the order. The draftsman will not alter the schedule.

4 If it is necessary to have a 'schedule' to a Tomlin schedule it is normally called an appendix.

5 See Atkin, Vol 12 (1990 issue) and Vol 37 (1990 issue).

(3) Terms not stated

IT IS BY CONSENT ORDERED that all further proceedings in this Action [and Counterclaim] be stayed.

14. ORDER FOR DISMISSAL OF ACTION

(1) At trial

UPON THE TRIAL of this action
[UPON THE APPLICATION of the plaintiff by originating summons]
AND UPON HEARING counsel for the plaintiffs and for the defendants
AND UPON HEARING oral evidence
AND UPON READING the documents recorded on the court file as having been read
   IT IS ORDERED that the action [originating summons] shall stand dismissed with costs to be taxed and paid by the plaintiffs to the defendants.

(2) At trial (alternative form)

UPON THE TRIAL of this action and counterclaim and the Third and Fourth Party proceedings and the proceedings by the ...

                                                                    Defendants
against the...
                                                                    Defendants
AND UPON HEARING Counsel for the plaintiff for the defendants and for the Third and Fourth Parties
AND UPON HEARING oral evidence
AND UPON READING the documents recorded on the Court File as having been read
  IT IS by consent ORDERED

1 that this action and counterclaim and the Third and Fourth Party proceedings and the said proceedings between the defendants do stand dismissed with no order as to costs

2 that the plaintiff do pay the... defendants his/her/its/their/costs of this action and counterclaim such costs to be taxed if not agreed

   [that the... defendant do pay to the Third Party his/her/its/their costs of the Third Party proceedings such costs to be taxed if not agreed]

   [that the Third Party do pay to the Fourth Party his/her/its/their costs of the Fourth Party proceedings such costs to be taxed if not agreed]

   [that the ... defendant do pay to the ... defendant his/her/its/their costs of the said proceedings between the defendants such costs to be taxed if not agreed]

   [that the costs of the plaintiff.../defendant/Third Party/Fourth Party be taxed pursuant to the Legal Aid Act 1974]

   AND save as aforesaid THE COURT MAKES NO ORDER as to the costs of this action and counterclaim or the Third Party proceedings or the Fourth Party proceedings or the said proceedings between defendants.

(3) In chambers

UPON THE APPLICATION of the defendants by [originating summons] [summons dated...]
  AND UPON HEARING [counsel] [solicitors] for the plaintiff and for the defendants
  AND UPON READING the documents recorded on the court file as having been read
  IT IS ORDERED that the action [originating summons] be dismissed with costs to be taxed and paid by the plaintiffs to the defendants.

15. 'SLIP RULE'

IT IS ORDERED

1 that so much of the Order dated ... as is set out in the first schedule hereto be corrected so as to read as set out in the second schedule hereto

2 that the plaintiff/defendant shall pay to the plaintiff/defendant ... costs of the said Motion to be taxed if not agreed

3 that the costs of the said Motion [Summons] are to be borne by ... in any event.

The First Schedule

The Second Schedule

Notes

1 By Ord 20, r 11 any clerical mistakes in orders may at any time be corrected by the court on motion or summons—see Atkin, Vol 23 (1978 Issue) p 310, Form 48.

2 A distinction must be drawn between (a) the correction of an order under the slip rule and (b) a subsequent variation of an order which was drawn up correctly. The precedent only applies to (a). The words 'be corrected' should be used.

3 By Ord 42, r 9(b) a judgment cannot be amended except on production of the duplicate first issued. The original and duplicate are both amended and sealed by the proper officer.

4 An error made in the drafting section may be corrected by consent by the drafting section (Practice Direction (Chancery Chambers) [1984] 1 WLR 1189, para 15).

16. ORDER VARYING PREVIOUS ORDER

IT IS ORDERED

1 that notwithstanding the Order dated ...

2 that the Order dated ... shall have effect as if .../subject to the variations set out in the schedule hereto

3 that the Order dated ... be varied and be as follows ...

4 that in lieu of the Accounts and Inquiries directed by the Order ... the following Accounts and Inquiries be taken and made that is to say ...

5 that the Injunction contained in the Order dated ... shall cease to have effect/be discharged.

The Schedule

1 For the words '...' in Paragraph ... of the Order there shall be substituted the words '...'

2 All the words after '...' in Paragraph ... of the Order shall be omitted

3 Paragraph ... shall be amended by adding at the end of it the following words '...'

4 After the word '...' in Paragraph ... there shall be inserted the words '...'

5 Paragraph ... shall be amended by substituting for the full stop at the end of it a colon and by adding at the end the words '...'

Notes

1 This form is intended for use when a properly drafted and entered order is varied by a later order.

2 Often there will be various ways in which the amending order can be drafted and what is the best way will depend on the circumstances.

3 The formula 'notwithstanding the order dated ...' is often helpful.
   Two examples
   (a) that notwithstanding the order dated ... the defendant do pay the sum of £ ... therein mentioned into an account in the joint names of ... instead of lodging it in court as thereby directed
   (b) that notwithstanding the order dated ... upon the plaintiff paying for the defendant the sum of £ ... being ... at ... the defendant do thereupon ...

4 Paragraph (3) is from Seton, p 1979.

5 Paragraph (4) is from Chancery Masters' Practice Form No 25 on p 137 of SCP, Vol II.

6 Where it is ordered that an injunction shall 'cease to have effect' the words contain no implication that it ought not to have been granted in the first place whereas the word 'discharged' may have that implication.

7   There are two useful precedents in Atkin, Vol 23 (1978 Issue). Form 46 (p 308) is a variation of an order to pay money into court. It is essential that there be a new lodgment schedule as shown in this Form so that the Funds Office are properly informed. Form 47 (p 309) varies an order but confirms acts done prior to variation.

Chapter Seven

Listing, Obtaining Appointments, Setting Down and Place of Trial

1. General

As litigation increases, the importance of interlocutory procedure and knowledge of listing procedures becomes more important. In general, the attitude of the courts and the Lord Chancellor's department is to transfer as many trials to the County Court as possible and it is only the ability of the practitioner to establish the specialist nature of the litigation or some other good reason which will enable retention in the High Court.

Chancery practitioners are fortunate in that the work covered by the division is normally of a specialised nature and with the increase in jurisdiction of the chancery masters there are distinct advantages to the issue and retaining of proceedings in the division where judges and staff alike have the specialist knowledge to enable litigation within the division to be conducted efficiently and expeditiously.

Like the other divisions, an effort is being made to increase the speed at which cases come on for trial and unnecessary delays will not be permitted and are likely to be penalised. The practitioner is warned to comply with time limits so far as he can for questions will be raised and embarrassing situations will have to be faced if delays cannot be explained or properly excused.

It is therefore axiomatic that preparation for a trial should take place at the earliest possible moment. It is important to submit a list of documents well before any matter is entered into the warned list to give sufficient time to prepare an agreed bundle of documents and it cannot be too strongly emphasised that the court is now endeavouring to insist that cases listed should be ready for trial. If they are not ready when they should be or if there is delay (or worse, delaying tactics), solicitors should be aware that explanations will have to be given for the judge in charge of the lists, and they can be personally penalised in costs, and other sanctions and penalties imposed.

The lists themselves are dealt with by the clerk of the lists who in effect organises the judges' time. There are no fixed times or appointments for making arrangements, which, in most cases, are made by agreement over the telephone. Basically, all documents have to be lodged with the clerk of the lists, or the motions clerk in the case of a motion, and in accordance with the Practice Directions. Further detail is given later in the text.

2. Lists

Practice Direction (Chancery Lists) (No 1 of 1983) (1 WLR 436) has consolidated former directions relating to the chancery lists. The three lists, namely the non-witness list, the witness list Part 1 and the witness list Part 2 will function according to the very clear and straightforward directions now contained in the 1983 Practice Direction and accordingly this is given in full at the end of these notes.

Listing categories

(Practice Direction (Assessment of case: substance) [1972] 1 WLR 3 and AP, Vol 1 25/3/6.) applies only to Queen's Bench Division and there are no listing categories in the Chancery Division.

The witness lists

In all cases where witnesses are to give evidence the action appears in the witness list Part 1 unless the certificate from counsel shows that there is agreement that the trial is not likely to last longer than three days when the case will be listed in Part 2. Such actions are likely to appear in the warned list the term after they are set down for trial. There are no fixtures as such for these short actions but the cause clerk co-operates as far as possible with counsels' clerks in providing a date suitable to them for the trial. In the longer cases, that is those in the witness list Part 2, application can be made for the case to be fixed. Any decision made by the clerk of the lists is subject to appeal to the judge in charge of lists, on one clear day's notice, but any such appeal should be made within seven days of any ruling by the clerk of the lists.

The certificate from counsel (*see* 'setting down' *below*) should be lodged within ten days of setting a case down for trial and all causes or matters to be placed in Part 2 of the witness list will then appear in that list 28 days after setting down.

The non-witness list

This contains appeals from masters and witness actions given only a day or part day, and matters referred to the judge for trial where the facts are agreed but there is an issue as to either the law or the consequences.

The warned list

This is published each Friday, is available in room 412, and is posted in RCJ main hallway. The next day's cause list is posted outside rooms 412, 413 and 414 each afternoon.

The short probate list

Matters in this list come before the judge in open court for hearing on affidavit evidence only, and are usually listed for a Monday morning. They consist of matters referred to the judge for confirmation of compromise which have been ordered to be tried on affidavit evidence either following a compromise, or on default by the defendant.

Withdrawal of cases from the list

If an action is to be withdrawn from the list a consent for the case to be withdrawn signed by all parties should be given to the clerk of the lists (Ord 21, r 2). All parties are under a duty to provide any information to the clerk of the lists which affect the lists as soon as possible, or which might affect the estimated length of a hearing especially if the hearing is likely to fall short. Thus, notification of possible withdrawal or settlement should be given to the clerk of the lists immediately.

Practical observations

Every endeavour is made by the clerk of the lists to ensure that all parties are satisfied with the listing. When fixtures are given, it should be understood that it is not possible for the court to say with certainty that the action will be commenced on the date fixed, and precisely when a case will be taken must always be dependent on the progress of other cases in the list. Cases put into the lists which have not been fixed can, at the outset at least, be given only very approximate estimates of when they might be called on. Cases which appear in the warned list can be called on with very short notice, and consequently parties should keep in the closest contact with the clerk of the lists once such actions have appeared in the warned list. If a transfer from one list to another is required, application can be made to the clerk of the lists.

In general, so long as all parties co-operate with the clerk of the lists, matters will proceed satisfactorily; if the clerk of the lists should consider that he is not receiving proper co-operation from the parties, he can always refer any case under his jurisdiction to the judge in charge of the lists, who may make orders penalising any party. What is essentially required is that contact should be maintained with the clerk of the lists, all due co-operation given, and all formalities complied with.

Practice Direction (Chancery Lists) (No 1 of 1983), 1 WLR 436

The purpose of this Direction is to consolidate all the former Directions relating to the Chancery Lists, with minor revisions to indicate the present practice.

1. The Lists

There are three main lists in the Chancery Division: the Witness List Part 1; the Witness List Part 2; and the Non-Witness List. Witness actions are allocated to Part 1 if the master's provisional estimate of duration exceeds three days; otherwise they are allocated to Part 2. Each list is in the charge of the judge named in the Cause List.

2. Responsibility for listing

The clerk of the lists (room 412/414, Royal Courts of Justice) is in general responsible for listing. All applications relating to listing should in the first instance be made to him. Any party dissatisfied with any decision of his may, on one clear day's notice to all other parties, apply to the judge in charge of the list, at a date and time to be fixed with the judge's clerk. Any such application should be made within seven days of the decision of the clerk of the lists.

3. List of Witness Actions set down and warned

(1) By the beginning of each term the clerk of the lists will publish a list showing under separate headings the actions set down for hearing in each Part of the Witness List, with the dates (if any) fixed for hearing.

(2) By the beginning of each term, and subsequently on each Friday of term (and on such other days as may be appropriate), the clerk of the lists will publish a Warned List, showing the actions in each Part of the Witness List that are liable to be heard during the following week (or weeks in the case of Part 2), and showing the dates, if any, fixed for hearing. Any action for which no date has been fixed is liable to appear in the List for hearing with no warning save that given by the next day's Cause List posted each afternoon outside room 163.

(3) With the written consent of all parties, the clerk of the lists may postpone a trial if an application to him is made within 3 days of the action first appearing in the Warned List. Any other application for a postponement must, after consultation with the clerk of the lists, be made to the judge in charge of the list as soon as possible after the action has appeared in the Warned List.

(4) If an action is not ready for hearing when it is called on for trial it will be put at the bottom of the list unless the judge otherwise directs.

4. *Witness actions: fixed and 'floating' dates*
   (1) Within 28 days after an action has been set down in Part 1 any party may give one clear day's notice to all other parties and to the clerk of the lists of his intention to apply for a fixed date for trial. Fixed dates are not normally given for actions set down in Part 2, but any party who claims that there are special circumstances which justify a fixed date being given may apply for one in the same way as for a case in Part 1.
   (2) On an application for a fixed date, the clerk of the lists will consider the wishes of the parties, the circumstances of the case, and the state of Part 1 and Part 2 of the List. He may then either fix a date for the trial, or else direct that the case shall be in the List for trial on or shortly after some specified date, depending on the state of the list then (a 'floater'). If he does neither, the action will be liable to appear in the Warned List for hearing at any time after 28 days from setting down, although it may appear earlier if this is agreed by the parties or directed by the court.
   (3) The clerk of the lists may alter or vacate a date, whether fixed or 'floating'—
      (a) on an application made by any party after giving one clear day's notice to all other parties; or
      (b) of his own motion, if a revised estimate of duration or the state of the lists makes this necessary, or if circumstances arise which make it unlikely that there could be an effective hearing on the fixed or 'floating' date.

5. *Estimates of duration*
   (1) Within ten days of an action being set down, the solicitor for each party separately represented must lodge with the cause clerk (room 412/414) a certificate signed by counsel stating the estimated length of the trial. A single certificate signed by all counsel should if possible be lodged. Certificates may be sent by post. Any undue delay in lodging the certificate may result in the hearing of the action being delayed.
   (2) If the estimated length of trial is varied, or the action is settled, withdrawn or discontinued, the solicitors for the parties must forthwith inform the clerk of the lists in writing. If the action is settled but the parties wish the master to make a consent order, the solicitors must notify the clerk of the lists in writing, whereupon he will take the case out of the list and notify the master. The master may then make the consent order.

(3) Seven days before the date for trial, whether fixed or 'floating' (or if there is no such date, within seven days after the action appears in the Warned List), the plaintiff's solicitor must inform the clerk of the lists whether there is any variation in the estimate of duration, and in particular whether the case is likely to be disposed of in some summary way. If the plaintiff is in person, this must be done by the solicitor for the first named defendant who has instructed a solicitor. If a summary disposal is likely, the solicitor must keep the clerk of the lists informed of any developments as soon as they occur.

6. *The Non-Witness List*

(1) By the beginning of each term, and subsequently on each Friday of term (and also on such other days as may be appropriate), the clerk of the lists will publish a Warned List, showing the matters liable to be heard during the following week, and the dates (if any) fixed for hearing. Any matter for which no fixed date appears is liable to appear in the List for hearing with no warning save that given by the next day's Cause List posted each afternoon outside room 412/414.

(2) Appeals from masters will appear in the Non-Witness List and will be heard in chambers. Such appeals (stamped £5) must be lodged in Room 307/308. On being notified that the case has been set down, the solicitors should forthwith inform the clerk of the lists whether they intend to instruct counsel, and, if so, the names of counsel.

(3) An originating summons which is adjourned into court with witnesses will be put into the appropriate Part of the Witness List, save that if the master considers that the hearing can be concluded within one day he may put the case into the Non-Witness List.

3. Obtaining appointments and directions for hearing

The manner of obtaining an appointment or hearing, and the time or date given, will depend on the nature of the proceedings to be dealt with or heard.

Proceedings before the master

	Nature of proceedings	Date/Time
(1)	First appointment on originating summons often for directions only, but final orders (eg in mortgage possession actions see Ord 28, r 4(1)) are also frequently made.	An appointment will be given with time allotted as required: ten to 30 minutes can be considered usual.

(2) With counsel. An appointment at a time from 12 noon onwards.

Note: An appointment is obtainable on the plaintiff's applying for it in room 308 after he has filed his affidavit, except where Form 10 (expedited form) or Form 11A (recovery of land under Ord 113) is used when a hearing date must be given at the time of issue. Where an appointment is obtained after issue, within four days of application for the appointment the party applying should put in a pro forma at room 308 giving the names, addresses and telephone numbers of the solicitors. The plaintiff's affidavit in support should be filed within 14 days after acknowledgment of service (Ord 28, r 1A(1)). At the first hearing the master will consider whether all proper parties are before the court and may require further evidence to be filed. A copy of the affidavit in support should have been served as early as possible, so as to avoid any application for an adjournment on the part of the parties served. If it is intended to instruct counsel, room 308 should be informed and other parties should be advised.

(3) The hearing of an originating summons for an order for the summary possession of land under Ord 113. In open court in the non-witness special list.

Note: There must be a minimum of five clear days from the date of service to the date of hearing. The date of hearing before the master will be given at the time of issue of the originating summons. If urgent less than five days can be given.

(4) Subsequent appointments on originating summonses and on master's summonses. At such fixed time as may be appointed by the master when he adjourns the hearing.

Note: If the summons has not been adjourned by the master to a fixed date he may have directed the summons to be restored within a given time (Practice Direction (Chancery Chambers: Expedition) [1970] 1 WLR 95) when a further appointment can be obtained in room 308; neither the originating summons nor the acknowledgment of service is required (Practice Direction (Chancery Chambers) No 1 of 1982); on requesting a further appointment the applicant will give estimate of time, particularly required if the master is likely to be asked himself to adjudicate on the matter, and indicate whether counsel will be instructed; a minimum of two clear days' notice (and often advisedly much longer) should be given of the restored hearing

(Ord 32, r 4(2)). If a lengthy adjudication by the master is anticipated the appointment is likely to be in the afternoon.

(5) *Inter-partes* masters' summons (the usual form of application in writ matters). — As at 1 and 2 above.

(6) Short summonses—solicitors who wish a summons to be heard in the short summons list should mark the back sheet 'short summons list' and draw the summons clerk's attention to this marking.

The copy for service on the other parties should be similarly marked. This applies to summonses unlikely to last for more than five minutes. These summonses are heard between 10.30 and 11.30 am.

Solicitors should make sure that all documents that will be needed at the hearing are lodged beforehand, including copy pleadings.

(7) Application for orders by consent for agreed directions for trial, or consent orders to stay on terms or orders for agreed directions in patent actions. — These orders may be made without a hearing and on the lodging of the signed summons or else a signed minute.

Note: When directions for setting down are applied for, the parties must certify that the case is ready for hearing and give an estimate of time.

(8) *Ex parte* applications for leave to serve out of the jurisdiction, to file any documents where leave is required, for approval of any act by receivers, for orders to carry on proceedings, garnishee orders, appointments of next friend or guardian *ad litem*, for substituted service, charging orders, and applications for payment out of funds. — Many *ex parte* orders are made on the perusal of an affidavit only without any attendance. If attendance is necessary, the applicant attends at a time between 2.15 pm and 2.45 pm before the master dealing with the matter, or if no such master, such master as may be available.

Note: Notice should be given to the summons clerk (room 308) by noon on the day the application is to be made so that the file may be bespoken. This can be done personally or by telex or telephone (071-405 7641 extension 3148) to room 308. For genuinely urgent applications, notice may be given at any time (Practice Direction (Chancery Chambers) No 1 of 1982 [1982] 1 WLR 1189).

Vacation of appointments

Adjournment of appointments listed for a time exceeding one hour will not normally be permitted, even by consent, unless an application to adjourn is made to the master concerned on a day not less than five clear working days prior to the appointment to be vacated.

The application should be made at 2.15 pm, the court file having been bespoken, and unless made on notice to all other parties their consents should be produced. A very strong case would have to be made out for any opposed application to succeed. This only applies to adjournments, not to cases where appointments are vacated because the application has been settled.

Proceedings before the judge

(1) Masters' summonses referred or adjourned to the judge (Ord 32, r 12).

Possibly a Monday fixed by the master at 10.30 am in the judge's chambers, or in open court, or before the judge in chambers for a date to be fixed.

Note: There is no judge's summons as such in the Chancery Division but any master's summons may always be referred by the master to the judge (Ord 32, r 12). When the hearing is expected to last more than 15 minutes, the master will either put it at the end of the Monday morning list or adjourn it to a day to be fixed by the clerk of the lists (Practice Direction (Chancery Lists) No 1 of 1983).

(2) Short causes (where counsel certifies less than four hours).

Any day in court.

(3) Summons to compromise in a contentious probate action if complicated.

On the same day as referred by the master to the judge, and in chambers.

(4) The same where a pronouncement is sought against a particular will.

Open court.

Note: The master will refer such a summons and order the hearing to be set down in the short probate list, which is normally taken on Mondays.

(5) Motions for judgment.	Any day in court in the 'short cause list'.
(6) Motions other than short motions for judgment, but including motions for interlocutory injunctions.	These motions are not listed but counsel rise to apply before the judge taking the non-witness list any weekday on the day of issue.

Note: The clerk of the lists will arrange for any necessary assistance to be given by any judge available (para 2 of Practice Direction (Chancery Division: Motions Procedure) [1980] 1 WLR 751 as varied by Practice Direction (Chancery Chambers No 1 of 1982). When counsel certifies that a motion is not likely to exceed ten minutes it can be marked 'short' and be put into the 'short cause list'; otherwise it must be entered in the non-witness list. The solicitor for the party who wishes to apply on motion should prepare and sign a notice of motion which accords with Form No 38 given in SCP, Vol 2, p 22. Two copies of the notice together with the original affidavit in support are required for issue and are to be taken to room 301/308 where the notice will be issued. An affidavit of service should be made ready for the return date where the application is *inter partes*. An *ex parte* motion can be heard on any day of the week without any return day being given; if *inter partes*, a return date is given and service effected. On the day given or on any day of the week for an *ex parte* motion, counsel will make his application. Before he does so, and unless it has been impossible to do so before the court sits, a copy of the notice of motion together with a copy of the writ and the affidavit should have been handed to the judge's clerk (Practice Direction [1950] WN 279). In the event that the court cannot then hear it (it is not likely to hear any motion if the hearing will exceed two hours) an order should be asked for that the motion be stood over to a day and a time to be fixed. Solicitors will then apply to the clerk of the lists for a fixed or 'floating' day and it will then subsequently appear in the court list under 'motions by order'.

(7) Appeals from masters to the judge (Ord 58, r 1 as amended).	Before the judge taking the non-witness list.

Note: Two copies (one stamped £15) of the notice of appeal against the decision of the master must be lodged in room 307/308 within five days after the judgment, order or decision appealed against. The notice of appeal will be in the Queen's Bench Masters' Practice Form No PF 114, save that in place of a fixed date the words 'on a date to be notified' should be inserted. The names, addresses, references and telephone numbers of all solicitors should be shown. Appeals will be entered in the non-witness list and shown in the warned list as for hearings in chambers. When set down solicitors should give the clerk of the lists the name of any counsel to be instructed (Practice Direction (Chancery Chambers) No 1 of 1982 as read with Practice Direction (Chancery Lists) No 1 of 1983).

(8) The hearing of the originating summons.   Any day before the judge in chambers, alternatively on a fixed date if in Pt I of the witness list or during a week for which the action is warned if in Part II of the witness list or in the non-witness list before the judge in open court (Practice Direction (Chancery Chambers) No 1 of 1982).

Note: The relief sought will determine whether the originating summons is to be heard in chambers or in court. It is likely to be adjourned for hearing in court except where the relief is of an administrative nature. If of an administrative nature with a hearing estimated at not more than 15 minutes it may be heard among the cases first listed for a Monday morning before the judge.

(9) The hearing of the originating summons where the judge will be making a declaration or judicial decision on the law as applied to the facts of the case, but where no cross-examination is required.   The master will have adjourned such an originating summons for hearing into court in the non-witness list.

(10) The hearing of the originating summons where the judge is acting in a judicial capacity and witnesses are to be cross-examined.   Open court.

Note: The master will have directed the originating summons to be adjourned to the witness list Pt I or Pt II according to the current estimate; if more than three days then Pt I otherwise Pt II. Final estimates are those of counsel. For setting down see below.

(11) The hearing of a writ action.	Open court in Pt I or II of the witness list.
(12) The hearing of patent actions.	Application for a date of hearing following directions, is to be made direct to one of the clerks to the two judges hearing patent actions.

4. Setting down

A chancery case may be set down for trial or hearing in general when the master or judge considers it ready. He must then (Ord 33, r 1) fix the place of trial, the mode of trial (invariably to 'a judge alone'), and where the trial is in London, must (Ord 34, r 3(3)) specify the list in which the case is to be entered. Leave of the court or the consent of the other parties is not required for setting down for trial out of time, provided Ord 3, r 6 is complied with. One month's notice of intention to proceed is required where a year has elapsed since the last proceeding.

Directions for setting down writ actions

On the hearing or final hearing of the summons for directions, the master must (Ord 34, r 2(1)) fix a period within which the plaintiff is to set down the action. Subject to the requirement that notice of intention to proceed after a year's delay must be given (Ord 3, r 6) a plaintiff need not obtain the leave of the court, or the consent of the defendant, before setting an action down for trial after the period fixed by an order made under Ord 34, r 2(1). However, the plaintiff's failure to set down may result either in the defendant doing so, or in his applying for the action to be dismissed for want of prosecution under Ord 34, r 2(2) (Practice Direction (Chancery: Setting down for Trial) (No 1 of 1981) [1981] 1 WLR 322).

In some cases a hearing of the summons for directions may be omitted altogether by reliance on the automatic directions contained in Ord 25, r 8 which now cover chancery actions (RSC (Amendment No 3) 1982), or by the parties lodging either personally or by post a summons for directions by consent. This practice is implicitly approved but should only be adopted and will only be accepted in very straightforward cases. The court may, on the application of any interested party, or of its own volition, give such further or additional directions at any time as it thinks fit. This practice is not infrequently implemented when the master gives on the hearing of a summons, or of any application which may be before him appropriate directions as may be found to be required, thus pre-empting the summons for directions. If a party defaults in complying with any direction and there has been an order for speedy trial (Ord 25, r 2(4)), the master may nonetheless order that an action be set down (Practice Direction (Chancery: Speedy Trial) [1979] 1 WLR 204).

Setting down (adjournment to the judge) originating summonses

New Ord 28, one of its objects being to reduce the number of occasions that parties are obliged to appear before the master, provides a fixed timetable. The affidavits which will have been consecutively filed by plaintiff and defendant will be, unlike pleadings in writ actions, on the court file. If the issues after the last affidavit (which is usually the plaintiff's in reply to the affidavit filed by the defendant) have been clearly defined, then the hearing on the first appointment should result in full directions for adjourning the summons into court or to the judge in chambers. If not, further directions will be given, and ultimately the master will direct that the summons be adjourned into court or in chambers with appropriate directions as to listing. Application for a first appointment may be made at any time after the plaintiff's first affidavit is required, but as to when might be the proper time see Chapter 2.

Cases in which setting down or adjournment to the judge is obviated

In many cases, such as in claims for specific performance of a contract under Ord 86, or in claims for possession by mortgagees under Ord 88, and in all of those cases listed in Chapter 1 the master in chambers has himself jurisdiction to make the order. It follows that in cases where the master has jurisdiction and is likely to make the order, the parties should, at the appointment before him, be prepared to present their case and to argue all such issues as are likely to arise.

'Squatters' actions

The procedure under Ord 113 makes the Chancery Division a useful adjunct to the litigation armoury, whereby a peremptory order can be obtained against squatters. Directions for trial are not given but a date for hearing before the master will be given on issue of the originating summons. If the case is presented correctly, there is no reason why an order should not be made at the first appointment. If a problem does exist, then the master may adjourn it to a fresh date.

Procedure on setting down

Writ actions The parties setting down must provide two identical bundles (one for the judge and the other as the official court record) on judicature paper (A4 ISO size) and complying with Ord 66, rr 1 and 2 (which specify margins and methods of printing) containing the writ, the pleadings (including further and better particulars and any voluntary particulars), the order for directions, notice of issue of any legal aid certificate and any amendments thereto, and any third party notice (the defendant being obliged to supply the plaintiff with copies of any third party notice) (AP, Vol 1, 34/3/3. The second copy of the bundle can be a photographic copy but not a carbon copy.

The two bundles are handed in to the summons clerk in rooms 412/413/414 accompanied by a copy of the writ of summons stamped with the setting down fee of £30. The summons clerk will check and indorse the papers with a note that an order has been duly made authorising setting down. The papers should then be taken to the listing section in rooms 412/413/414. A blank form of certificate as to the length of trial will be handed to or sent through the post to the party setting down and this must be completed, by counsel for each of the parties, giving estimate of the length of the trial; the certificate is then lodged with the causes clerk who will then enter the action in the appropriate list.

Originating summons actions

Where the master adjourns the originating summons to *judge in chambers*: the originating summons is handed in to the master.

The file will be sent to the judge accompanied by a note from the master (para 7 of Chambers Summonses, Practice Direction (Chancery Lists) (No 1 of 1982)) where the master adjourns the originating summons to be set down within a given number of days.

Within that period, or such period as may be extended, the originating summons stamped with the fee of £30 together with an additional top copy of the originating summons, are to be handed to the summons clerk in room 412/413/414 (Ord 28, r 9).

The file will then be sent to the listing office in room 412/413. This will contain all the affidavit evidence, so no bundle of these is required to set down an originating summons for hearing. The originating summons may be put into the witness or non-witness list, but if a case adjourned into court with witnesses can, in the opinion of the master, be concluded in a day, the master may instead of putting it in the witness list put it into the non-witness list (para 6 of Practice Direction Chancery Lists (No 1 of 1982)).

5. Place of trial

Whilst in the Queen's Bench Division there is an overriding requirement that the court should have regard to the convenience of the parties and their witnesses in determining the place of trial, the date at which the trial can take place, and the locality of any object to be viewed (AP, Vol 1, 33/4/2), these considerations can only be fulfilled to a limited extent in chancery actions because of their specialised nature and the comparatively small number of chancery judges available.

However, sittings do take place at such towns as are authorised (Ord 33, r 1). There were previously five such towns or cities, namely Leeds, Liverpool, Manchester, Newcastle-upon-Tyne and Preston (Practice Direction (Chancery: Proceedings outside London) (Chancery Division) [1972] 1 WLR 1), but to these five have been added three more, namely Birmingham, Bristol and Cardiff (Practice Direction (Chancery Chambers) No 1 of 1982 [1982] 1 WLR 1189). The district registries of the High Court at these cities are called 'chancery district registries'. The Practice Directions says that it is 'expected' that a cause or matter proceeding in any one of the eight provincial chancery registries will be ordered to be heard in those cities or 'trial centres'. If the cause or matter is proceeding at RCJ in London, or in any district registry other than in one of these eight provincial chancery registries, the proceedings must (unless special arrangements are made) be ordered to take place in London or in one of the eight trial centres.

Practice Direction (Chancery: Proceedings outside London) (No 4 of 1971) [1971] 1 WLR 5 'appointed' a chancery High Court judge to sit in the five, (as it then was) specified towns outside London for chancery court and chambers hearings; such a judge is still appointed and additionally the current practice is to request circuit judges to sit as deputy judges of the High Court for the purpose of trying cases at trial centres, with two nominated chancery High Court judges in London looking at the papers beforehand to decide whether the case should be heard by such a circuit judge sitting as deputy, or only by a chancery judge of the High Court. When a cause or matter was proceeding in one of the five (now eight) specified district registries, it was required that any application for hearing by the appointed judge should be made to that judge and not to a judge in London, unless the parties otherwise agreed or the court otherwise directed.

The present arrangements are:

Birmingham

A circuit judge exercising the powers of a judge of the Chancery Division sits at Birmingham for cases proceeding in the Birmingham District Registry.

South Wales and Bristol

His Honour Judge Hywell Moseley QC currently exercises chancery jurisdiction in South Wales and Bristol.

Hearings will be listed after consultation with the parties and all enquiries should be directed to Cardiff County Court (Telephone: 0222 395631). Motion days are listed below.

Northern Area

Mr Justice Scott sits in the north; applications in one of the district registries of Leeds, Liverpool, Manchester, Newcastle-upon-Tyne or Preston should be made either to Mr Justice Scott or (unless an excepted matter within para 2 of the 1972 Practice Direction), to an authorised Circuit Judge. Applications may nonetheless be heard in London if the parties agree, or the court directs.

The Lord Chancellor's office is empowered to authorise the sitting of the High Court at any proposed place of trial for the hearing of a particular case, or cases of a particular class, but this is unlikely to be possible except in special circumstances, eg where it would be difficult for the witnesses to come to London. In such a case, inquiries should be made of the appropriate circuit administrator before the master or district registrar is asked to fix a local venue.

Excepted matters: some matters will only be heard in London. These are revenue, bankruptcy, and patents matters; certain statutory jurisdictions, namely proceedings under Part VII of the Mental Health Act 1983, or under the Defence Contracts Act 1958 or the Registered Design Acts 1949-61; appeals to a divisional court of the Chancery Division; and appeals cases stated and questions referred for the opinion of the court which fall within Ord 93, r 10(2).

Motion days outside London

Motion days are published, by way of press notes, as an illustration of what the practitioner is looking for, the list is published in the following format:

Civil Procedure.
Chancery business in the northern area. Motion days.
Hilary and Trinity sittings 1990

	June	July
Manchester	8, 15, 25	9, 20, 30
Leeds	11	2, 23
Liverpool	29	
Newcastle	22	27
Birmingham	4, 11, 18, 25	2, 9, 16, 23, 30
Bristol	7, 14, 21, 28	5, 12, 19, 26
Cardiff	1, 8, 15, 22, 29	6, 13, 20, 27

The paper required for case in court must reach the cause clerk (Chancery Division) of the particular provincial chancery registry two days previous to the day on which the application is to be made, accompanied by a certificate of counsel that the case requires to be immediately or promptly heard giving reasons, and also accompanied by a copy of the notice of motion bearing the district registry's seal, a copy of the writ and of the pleadings (if any), and if called for, extra copies of affidavits. In a case which has proceeded in a district registry other than one of the eight chancery district registries, the papers may be required to be lodged at the district registry at least one day prior to the date when they are to reach the cause clerk of the chancery district registry.

Adjournment to the non-witness list is appropriate where it is a question of a final hearing of some contested matter, but there is to be no cross-examination or the district registrar is satisfied that cross-examination will not subsequently extend the length of the hearing and will not lead to applications to call witnesses. Adjournment to the witness list part 2 is appropriate where it is a final hearing of a contested matter with substantial cross-examination, unless the hearing is estimated to last significantly more than three days. In the latter event the adjournment should be to the witness list part 1. If the matter is adjourned to be heard in the witness list a certificate as to estimated length of the hearing, signed by counsel for all parties, must be lodged.

A party on whom a notice of motion has been served shall not serve a cross notice for hearing elsewhere than at the place of hearing of the first motion, and basically if the plaintiff has instituted his proceedings in one of the district registries in the north, then his notice of motion and any other shall be heard by the judge appointed to sit there.

Appeals from district judges

Details of arrangements for the hearing by a judge of appeals arising from decisions made by district judges must in each case be obtained from the relevant court. If the appeal is to be heard in London the papers are sent, with a district judge's note to the judge, to the secretary to the Chief Chancery Master, Chancery Division, RCJ, but there may be local arrangements for the hearing of such appeals and if so details will be given by the district registry (Practice Direction (Chancery Chambers) No 1 of 1982 [1982] 1 WLR 1189 and RSC (Amendment No 2) 1982 (SI 1982 No 1111).

The Crown

The place of trial for proceedings in the High Court by or against the Crown shall be at RCJ except with the Crown's consent (Ord 77, r 13).

The circuit administration, and practice procedure

The circuit administrators from whom inquiry may be made are the Administrator of the Northern Circuit, Aldine House, New Bailey Street, Salford M3 5EU and the Administrator of the North Eastern Circuit, West Riding House, Albion Street, Leeds LS1 5AA (Tel: 0532 441841).

There are no instructions issued by the circuit administrators and reliance must be placed on the Practice Directions, press notices published information in the Legal Journals and direct enquiries. A convenient sources are:

(1) The Law Society's *Gazette Digest*, issued quarterly and accompanying the Law Society's *Gazette* issued without charge to all solicitors holding current practising certificates.
   They are in the Law Society's library in Chancery Lane, but not in the Inn libraries.
(2) *Law Notes* magazine, published monthly by the College of Law.

Listing, Obtaining Appointments, Setting Down and Place of Trial—Orders

1. ORDER FOR SETTING DOWN

IT IS ORDERED that the plaintiff shall on or before... set down this Action in Part... of the... Witness List for trial in London before a Judge alone the estimated duration of the trial being... days
  AND the costs of the said application are to be costs in the cause.

2. ALTERNATIVE FORM

IT IS ORDERED

1 that lists of documents be served within... days and that there be an inspection within... days thereafter

2 that this Action [and Counterclaim] be tried in London before a Judge alone and be set down by the Plaintiffs in the... List Part... on or before...

Chapter Eight

Proceedings under Orders and Judgments

1. The 'accounts and inquiries section'

Because of the type and style of work assigned to the Chancery Division, a department has grown up within the division known as the 'accounts and inquiries section'. This now plays a very useful part in the work of the division and is considered as giving the orders in the division 'teeth' which the other divisions do not possess.

Hitherto it was intended that the accounts side of that section would consider accounts drawn up by the receivers appointed by the court and the inquiries restricted to the kind of investigation arising out of 'kith and kin' actions. However, as with so much of the useful procedure we now have as part of the armoury of the litigator, the accounts and inquiries section has expanded its work to cover all types and kinds of action in the division and, if the professional litigator is aware of his procedure, this is one area which can be used to great effect to defeat tactics designed to delay or enlarge expense to the point where prosecuting a claim becomes unwise.

2. The enforcement of orders and judgments

There are two aspects to the enforcement of orders and judgments; one relating to those orders made during the course of proceedings; and the other to the enforcement of judgments and orders after trial or final judgment where different considerations will be given with that in mind. Also, because the procedure is elastic, the court has in its power the opportunity of giving directions which are relevant to each case and which are designed to produce the desired result quickly and cheaply.

Order 43 governs the procedure which is to be adopted in all interlocutory matters and Ord 44 lays down the rules governing enforcement of judgments and final orders. Because the procedure can become complicated, a considerable knowledge is essential in designing the most useful method of prosecuting the claim and defeating any tactics of the defendant. For example, in the case of a commercial debt action where a defendant seeks to produce a large number of exaggerated allegations in a pleading, to provide an ostensible defence forcing a plaintiff to a full blown trial with all the attendant expense and risk, it might be possible under Ord 43 to obtain an order that there should be an inquiry on each separate point thereby forcing the defendant to place his evidence on affidavit incurring expense for him and testing the validity of his allegations. Particularly in cases where the debt is comparatively small, and a lengthy trial therefore unwarranted, this kind of procedure is a useful addition to the practitioner's armoury. In such a case, even if a trial had to take place, the procedure under Ord 43 would have reduced the length of the trial to manageable proportions. It also gives both parties a clear indication early in the procedure of the strengths and weaknesses on each side and might also give a clearer indication to the practitioner as to the possibilities of resolving issues by settlement.

There are many cases where there will be an automatic reference to the accounts and inquiries section which should be considered by the practitioner as part of the investigation procedure used by the chancery master to provide information which will enable the court to give an order with the best available knowledge of the facts. Where one of the parties issues a summons requesting the taking of an account or an inquiry, the chancery master will choose one of the parties to lodge evidence on affidavit relating to that aspect of the matter. Directions will then be given as to further evidence. Where either no evidence exists or a party defaults in carrying out the directions, the court can appoint any other interested party failing which the official solicitor can carry out an investigation. This gives the chancery master powers of investigation which might well be needed in the case of 'kith and kin' actions or disputed probate actions but which can be used elsewhere to great effect.

In any Chancery action it is part of the duty of the chancery master to ensure that all individuals having an interest in the matters in question have been added as parties in the litigation so that when a final judgment is given it will be after all representation on matters in dispute is before the court, thereby reducing the possibility of further litigation. However, it should be appreciated that such final judgment is effective against anyone who will be bound as if he had been originally a party to the action. Such an individual, however, may, within one month after service upon him, apply to the court to discharge, vary or add to the judgment and in such circumstances such a party would formally acknowledge service of the notice of the judgment and make application on summons.

3. Procedures

The proceedings relating to such investigations as accounts and inquiries will be in chambers if before the master but in open court if before the judge and directions at the time of judgment or during the proceedings will almost certainly be required as to the manner in which they are to be conducted.

It is envisaged (Ord 44, r 3(1)) that the court may give these further directions when giving judgment or making the order, but they may also be given at any time 'during proceedings under judgment' (ibid). The method of applying for further directions if they are not given when judgment is given is not specified, though 'liberty to apply' is to be inferred (*Fritz v Hobson* (1880) 14 Ch D 542) in all judgments and orders requiring further direction if such directions are not given at the time of making the judgment or order; otherwise a summons to proceed may still be necessary.

Order 44, r 3(1) by providing that the further directions may, in particular, include (*a*) the manner in which any account or inquiry is to be presented, (*b*) the evidence in support thereof (*see* '**Accounts and inquiries**' *below*), (*c*) the preparation and service of the draft of any deed or other instrument which is directed to be settled by the court and the service of any objections to the draft, (*d*) the parties required to attend all or any part of the proceedings, (*e*) representation of a class by the same solicitor, or by different solicitors of parties who ought to be separately represented and (*f*) the time within which each proceeding is to be taken and the fixing of days for further attendance.

Rule 3(2) provides that the court may rewrite or vary any directions it has given. In actions for the administration of the estate of a deceased person, the execution of a trust, or the sale of any property when giving judgment or making a direction affecting persons not party to the action, the court may when giving the judgment or making the direction, or at any stage in the proceedings under the judgment, direct that notice of the judgment or direction shall be served on any such person, and any person so served shall be bound by the judgment as if he had been originally a party to the action, provided that he may within one month after service apply to the court to discharge, vary or add to the judgment. Acknowledgment of service of such notice is necessary if the person served wishes to attend the proceedings under judgment (Ord 44 as substituted by r 53 of RSC (Amendment No 2) 1982).

4. Accounts and inquiries

Accounts and inquiries can be ordered by the court at any time during the course of the proceedings, at judgment or after judgment. Such orders become necessary in those chancery matters which concern full or part administration of the estate of a deceased, the execution of trusts, partnerships, and sales of a property. While orders for accounts and inquiries can be made in any division, it is the Chancery Division which has the greater expertise in the taking of accounts and its practices are recognised as being the better for detailed inquiries when these are required.

Order

Order 43 covers those cases where an account or inquiry is ordered during the course of the proceedings and Ord 44, which now omits outdated practices, lays down the ground rules for accounts and inquiries on judgments.

The objective of the plaintiff

The plaintiff's intention is to ascertain the true facts surrounding circumstances which might be speculative or unknown or as yet unspecified by his opponent. He will be looking to ensure that any investigation is as complete as possible and that nothing is concealed.

Sequence

(1) An account or inquiry may have been ordered at the time of giving judgment in which case all consequential directions (such as are listed in Ord 44, r 3(1) *ante*) should desirably have been included in the judgment or final order. If it is during the course of proceedings that an order for accounts and inquiries is required a general form of summons should be issued. Order 43 permits this to be done following even a generally indorsed writ, once time for acknowledgment of service has expired. If the summons is for directions and reasonable in all the circumstances, it will not be required to be supported by an affidavit because the contents of the summons will speak for itself and it may well be that the application will have the consent or active support of the other party, or at least will not be opposed. If the summons for an account is opposed, then an affidavit will have to be produced by the applicant setting out the reasons why he considers that for example an account should be taken or an inquiry made. At the first appointment of an opposed summons the master should be asked for directions for further evidence, normally restricted as is usual to three affidavits in all, and when such evidence is complete, he will give his decision as to whether the account should be taken or inquiry made. If accounts and inquiries should be ordered the master will give directions as to the taking of the accounts and the making of the inquiries and as to how each step should be verified and whether by affidavit or otherwise.

(2) If there is delay in prosecuting an account or inquiry, under Ord 43, rr 7, 8 and 9 the court reserves to itself powers to complete the investigation and in certain circumstances can call upon individuals to carry out an investigation and report and even to employ the official solicitor if that need should arise.

(3) When an order for an account is made it is drawn up by the court and the party receiving the sealed order should serve copies on interested parties or as may have been directed. The person charged with the preparation of the account or the making of the inquiry will then have an order specifying exactly what he should do. When that party has fulfilled the terms of the order and supplied other interested parties with copies he will only need to present the account and/or details of investigation (usually verified by affidavit) to the registry (room 307/308) if there are matters in dispute which have not by then been resolved and restore the summons before the master. Any questions or comments can then be raised by the other parties. On the appointment before the master he will give directions if necessary as to what further information, accounts or verification should be lodged. He may well direct cross-examination before him on disputed items and facts. There may always be a direction that no settled account may be reopened.

A party who is dissatisfied with the accounts may give to the receiver and the court a notice specifying the item or items to which objection is taken and requiring the accounts to be lodged with the court within 14 days. Both the accounts and the copy notice must be lodged at room 415/416. (Practice Direction (Chancery Chambers) No 1 of 1982). The items to which objection is taken having been examined, the result will be certified by a master (Ord 30, r 5).

A receiver may apply to the court informally for any directions he may require.

A judicial trustee who is not a corporate trustee must (unless the court otherwise orders) make up his accounts annually in such form as the court requires and must submit them to the court (rr 9, 10, 12 and 13 of the Judicial Trustee Rules 1983 (SI 1983 No 370 and s 57 of the Administration of Justice Act 1982). The accounts will be accepted in any reasonable form but should always include a cash account, and no further action need be taken unless some objection is raised when the accounts department will do its best to ascertain the points in issue and refer them to the master. If the trustee is a corporation the accounts need only be submitted to interested parties (or as the court directs) and the court reserves its powers to penalise or if necessary to bring in the official solicitor as a last resort. Remuneration can now be authorised on reasonable terms (r 11(11)(*a*) ibid).

Plaintiff's/defendant's considerations

There may be occasions in the course of many proceedings when it is wise to ascertain how much is involved before the action goes too far and substantial sums are incurred in costs; for example sometimes a plaintiff, from whatever sources, believes his claim on an estate to be large, whereas the realities may be different; there may however be cause for deferring an application for accounts and inquiries or even to await the result of a trial, for reasons of tactics. The defendant without acting to his own disadvantage should co-operate in any investigation as best he can, because otherwise its length and its expense could be augmented with a subsequent bearing on costs.

Attitude of the court

The procedure involves adversarial litigation in any argument as to why an account should be taken or is needed, administrative work in the detailed taking of the account or in the making of the investigation, and the supervisory function of the division in ensuring that the investigation is full and complete, that the parties are satisfied at the conclusion of the investigation, and that this has not been more extensive than was absolutely necessary. The procedure therefore covers the whole ambit of the varied functions of the Chancery Division.

Hazards and pitfalls

When an account or investigation is ordered it is wise to consider employing professional assistance because producing inadequate material will result in further applications and directions causing costs to be thrown away as well as delay. Other parties and the court itself are unlikely to be satisfied until the accounts or investigation are correct and complete.

Costs

Costs as always are in the discretion of the court. On the application for an account or investigation invariably costs will be left to the discretion of the master or judge giving the final order which as always will depend very much on the facts. The court can however take into consideration the attitude of the parties in relation to what may have been a very expensive investigation or preparation of accounts when making its decision on costs.

5. Receivers

Under s 37 of the Supreme Court Act 1981, replacing s 45 of the Judicature Act 1925, the High Court has jurisdiction (formerly assigned to Chancery but now extended to all divisions) to appoint a receiver by interlocutory or final order in all cases in which it appears to the court to be just and convenient to do so. This jurisdiction is commonly invoked in actions by mortgagees, debenture holders, claimants to the assets or profits of a partnership, beneficiaries of an estate or trust, and judgment creditors seeking equitable execution, but the court's general purpose being the protection and preservation of property for the benefit of all those entitled, an application may be made in any case in which there are grounds for apprehension that without the appointment of a receiver the property or its income may be wasted, misused or unaccounted for.

Application may be made by motion in open court or by summons in chambers (Ord 30, r 1) and will not be heard unless there are proceedings current but in cases of urgency an application by motion or summons may be made *ex parte* or notice of motion may be served with the writ or originating summons (Ord 29, r 1). A plaintiff may indorse his writ with a request for the appointment of a receiver as incidental to his claim, but a writ should not be preferred to an originating summons merely on that account.

When the application is made by summons in chambers the master has power to make the order (Practice Direction (Chancery: Masters' Powers) [1975] 1 WLR 129).

Any application must be supported by an affidavit stating the nature of the property and the grounds upon which the appointment is required and (where a proposed appointee is named) an affidavit of his fitness, preferably by a solicitor or bank manager who has known him for not less than five years. If no appointee is named by the applicant or if his nominee is not approved by the court or is opposed by other parties, the order, if made upon motion, will usually leave the nomination to be determined by the master when the cause is adjourned into chambers.

An order appointing a receiver of a company or firm may include his appointment as manager, though usually for a limited period with a view to a sale or winding up.

The order will usually provide that the appointment shall take effect upon the appointee giving security or that the appointee be at liberty to act forthwith, subject to his giving security by a specified date in which case the applicant may be required to give an undertaking to be responsible for his acts and defaults until the security is given.

Before the return of the summons the applicant should file an affidavit by a deponent having possession or knowledge of the property to pass into the hands of the receiver showing the capital value and the income thereof. Upon the return of the summons the master will give directions as to:

(1) the nominaton of the receiver (if none has been named in the order),
(2) the amount of security to be given,
(3) the receiver's remuneration, and
(4) the accounts to be rendered by the receiver.

Unless the court otherwise directs, the security will be by guarantee (see AP, Vol 2, 379 for form) if the amount exceeds £1,000 and otherwise by an undertaking with two sureties (ibid 380). The guarantee or undertaking will be filed in rooms 307/308 and a certificate of the completion of the security and of the dates and periods set for the receiver's accounts will be indorsed on the duplicate order, signed by the master and sealed. Should circumstances require, the amount of the security may be increased or reduced and the form of guarantee makes provision for any such change to be indorsed thereon.

The receiver's accounts are no longer lodged and certified by the master (Ord 30, r 5 as amended).

When interlocutory orders or directions are required regarding the exercise of the receiver's duties, the application to the master should be made by the party having the conduct of the proceedings and not by the receiver, unless such party declines to act, when the receiver may issue a summons for such orders or directions, addressed to all parties.

The court will not discharge a receiver upon his own application unless he shows reasonable cause or unless all parties consent, nor upon the application of the party at whose instance he was appointed if other parties oppose the application for good cause; but any person whose interests are adversely affected by the receiver's continuance in office, though not a party to the action, may apply by summons for his discharge.

The receiver's duties and obligations will terminate when he has complied with the master's final order which will refer to the passing of final accounts (unless all parties agree that they be dispensed with), payment into court or to the party entitled of any cash balance certified to be outstanding, delivery up of all property and documents in the receiver's possession, and vacation of the receiver's guarantee (if any). The master's order will conclude by providing for the discharge of the receiver.

Detailed guidance will be found in Atkin, Vol 33, pp 135 et seq; Procedural Table pp 177 et seq; Forms pp 189 et seq.

6. Sales by order of the court

The court may order the sale of land under s 30 of the Law of Property Act 1925 or Ord 85, r 2(3) or Ord 31, r 1.

Section 30 of the Law of Property Act 1925

Section 30 provides that where trustees for sale refuse to sell or are unable to obtain a requisite consent, 'any person interested may apply to the court for a vesting or other order under section 44 of the Trustee Act 1925 for giving effect to the proposed transaction or for an order directing the trustees for sale to give effect thereto and the court may make such order as it thinks fit'. Excepting the means (considered below) by which the absence of a requisite consent can be overcome or by which a 'proposed transaction' can be effected by a 'vesting or other order', the substance of this section is that a refusal by the trustees can be met with an order directing them to sell.

Order 85, r 2(3)

Rule 2(3) provides that any interested party may apply to the court for an order directing a person to do or abstain from doing any particular act in his capacity as personal representative or trustee. In appropriate circumstances, such an order could include an order for the sale of any property held on the trusts.

Order 31, r 1

Rule 1 provides that where in any cause or matter in the Chancery Division relating to land (not confined to land held upon trust for sale) it appears necessary or expedient for the purposes of the cause or matter that the land or any part thereof should be sold, the court may order that land or part to be sold. The rules contained in Ord 31 are procedural only and give the court no substantive power to order a sale where no statutory or inherent jurisdiction exists. Thus for example a tenant for life will not be ordered to sell land which is an authorised investment and to which he is legally entitled.

The entitlement of an interested party to obtain an order for sale is subject to the qualification that the court's powers are discretionary and the court will have regard to the considerations expressed by Devlin LJ in *Jones v Challenger* [1961] 1 QB 176 (and see *Re Evers' Trusts* [1980] 1 WLR 1327 for recent developments of the law).

Evidence of a secondary or collateral object may be found where a settlor has created a trust for sale in preference to the complexities of a settlement, but with the intention that the trust property shall provide a residence for the beneficiaries for the period of a life or lives, if they should so desire, and as a safeguard against a premature sale by the trustees, has included the requirement that the consent of a named person or persons be obtained. If, in such a case, consent is refused, the court will not order a sale unless it is satisfied that the refusal is unreasonable and that a sale would be in the best interests of the beneficiaries. A secondary or collateral object may also be found where, as is commonly the case with husband and wife, a house is conveyed to purchasers as joint tenants in law and equity and becomes their home. Although the provisions of the Matrimonial Homes Act 1967 do not preclude a sale by order of the court against the wishes of a spouse who is in occupation, the court will not readily make such an order so long as the marriage is subsisting (*Bedson v Bedson* [1965] 2 QB 666 CA).

Even if a sale is ordered, contention may arise as to the apportionment of the proceeds and the court's decision may be sought as to the intention of the parties at the time of the purchase, whether the equitable ownership was to be divided equally or made commensurate with the financial contributions of the respective parties towards the purchase price, the mortgage repayments (if any) and the cost of repairs and improvements. In such a case the summons should include an application for a direction that the net proceeds of sale be paid into court or into a joint account of the parties' solicitors and additionally 'that the parties be at liberty to apply for directions (such application to be made within one month of the completion of the sale) as to the division of the proceeds of sale and generally'.

Assuming that the applicant has sufficient cause to seek an order for sale, then whichever mode of procedure he adopts, he must consider to what extent he wishes the conduct of the sale to be taken out of the hands of the trustees, or other person or persons in whom the property is presently vested, and brought under the direction of the court. This will normally be a matter for agreement between the parties but if no agreement can be reached, it may be necessary to ask on the order for sale for detailed directions as to how the sale should be effected, for example by private treaty or tender or auction. Only if entirely necessary should an order be sought in terms which will assign full control to the court. Such an order may entail the following sequence:

(1) Appointment of party to have conduct of the sale.
(2) Mode of sale (if by auction, security (if any) to be given by auctioneer, and liberty of parties to bid).
(3) Valuation.
(4) Inquiry into incumbrances.
(5) Settling particulars and conditions of sale and (if so required) abstract of title and draft conveyance.
(6) Settling advertisements.
(7) Payment of proceeds of sale into court or otherwise.

As some of these directions will have to be formulated successively as the sale proceeds, the master will fix dates for further attendances and name the parties who will be required to attend. During that period the solicitor for the party having conduct of the sale will lodge (as the case requires):

(1) Valuer's report.
(2) Affidavit as to incumbrances.
(3) Affidavit of fitness of auctioneer.
(4) Auctioneer's guarantee or undertaking.
(5) Draft particulars and conditions of sale, abstract of title and conveyance for settlement by the master who may refer them to conveyancing counsel.
(6) Draft advertisements.

After the sale the following documents must be lodged in chambers:

(7) Auctioneer's or vendor's certificate of the result of the sale, verified by affidavit, if required.
(8) Completion statement with vouchers.
(9) Engrossment of conveyance with affidavit certifying its conformity with the draft.
(10) If proceeds to be paid into court, the lodgment schedule.

The solicitor acting obtains the discharge of the auctioneer's guarantee or undertaking. It will be appreciated that if all of these procedures have to be directed and followed, there will be considerable expense and delay, with consequential orders for costs.

Mortgage actions

Although the court is empowered upon the application of a mortgagee under Ord 88, r 1(1)(*b*), to order a sale of the mortgaged property, the more usual procedure is for the mortgagee to apply for an order for possession which will enable him to make his own sale out of court. Subject to any prior rights, an equitable mortgagee can achieve the same end by first applying for a vesting order under s 90 of the Law of Property Act 1925.

Binding effect of judgments and orders for sale

When making a judgment or order in respect of the sale of any property the court may direct that notice of the judgment be served on any person not a party, and such person shall, subject to his right to make application within one month of such service, be bound by the judgment (Ord 44).

Other procedures

Where trustees for sale desire to sell but are unable to obtain a requisite consent, application may be made to the court for an order under s 57 of the Trustee Act 1925 enlarging the powers of the trustees in a manner which will enable them to effect a sale without such consent.

Where a sale has progressed to a stage at which the purchaser is contractually entitled to require the property to be vested in him (but not before) the court may make a vesting order to that effect under s 44 of the Trustee Act 1925. Alternatively, if a conveyance or other instrument has been drawn of which execution has been refused by the trustees or a dissenting trustee, the court may appoint a person authorised to execute the document under s 50 of the same Act or s 39 of the Supreme Court Act 1981.

The removal and replacement of a dissenting trustee with a consequential vesting order is a procedure rarely adopted as a means of enforcing a sale.

Forms and precedents

Atkin, Vol 35, Form No 1 *et seq*.

7. Funds

The Chancery Division often has monies available for distribution where trustees or beneficiaries cannot be found or where a class of beneficiaries cannot be yet ascertained and so frequent use is made of procedures for bringing into and retaining funds in court. While the procedures are the same within all the divisions, arising from its supervisory and protective attitude, the Chancery Division has come to apply the procedures with its own particular finesse and applications to remove or dispose of funds or assets must often be presented for consideration on their merits. Applications are made to the master who usually has control of the funds or assets. The Chancery Division does not relinquish its responsibility even if there is an order from some other division; such an order, if it bears on the removal or disposal of funds, is not of itself operative until there has been a subsequent application and supporting order from the master or judge of the Chancery Division.

The purpose of the Chancery Division's supervisory attitude over funds or assets, whether or not administered by the court, is to protect those who have an interest in them. In handling funds, especially payment out, investigations may ensue and these may extend to, for example, inquiries as to charges on land representing a fund or devolution of title.

Statutes

Apart from 'payment in' in *inter partes* litigation, payment into court can, (in some cases should) be made under a variety of statutes, for example, the Lands Clauses Consolidation Act 1845, and the Trustee Act 1925.

There is also statutory provision enabling a trustee to obtain a discharge contained in s 63(1) and (2) of the Trustee Act 1925:

(1) Trustees or the majority of trustees having in their hands or under their control money or securities belonging to a trust may pay the same into court; (2) the receipt or certificate of the proper officer shall be a sufficient discharge to trustees for the money or securities so paid into court.

To justify payment into court by trustees under s 63 the trustees must be able to show that otherwise they would be unable to obtain a discharge.

Order 92, r 2 gives the material which must be included in an affidavit in support of an application for an order for payment into court under s 63, as well as for payment into court under other particular statutes.

As well as payment in under statute, payments in may be ordered on various occasions, upon the termination of a receivership for example when one of the partners can no longer be traced, and in many other situations of a similar nature.

Orders

Order 92 and Ord 22, r 4 govern payment into and out of court, and both of these orders make reference to the Chancery Division.

Payments into and out of court

Where the fund is small (£5,000—Ord 92, r 5(3) as amended by RSC (Amendment No 3) 1982) the procedure for dealing with the fund is made as simple as possible. Where there have already been any proceedings before the court which can be regarded as current, an *ex parte* application by affidavit to the Chief Master is all that is required to seek an order to deal with the funds or remove the assets. The object of the affidavit is to prove the applicant's title or the circumstances. The master may direct persons further to the applicant to be joined. Should a summons *inter partes* be issued an affidavit will be necessary and the summons together with the supporting affidavit must be served on all other interested parties. Where there have been no proceedings which can be regarded as current before the court, the application must be made by way of an originating summons again supported by an affidavit. In the course of *inter partes* litigation a party may accept funds paid into court in settlement of the whole or any part of a claim in the action and may do so without an order; otherwise, unless the court makes an order of its own volition, it will always be necessary to make application to the court for an order for payment out; this will be on summons supported by an affidavit setting out the reasons and facts as to why payment out should be made.

Originating process

The originating process is a general summons and, if *inter partes*, supported by an affidavit establishing title, or an originating summons supported by a similar affidavit if there is no current action.

Parties and intitulement

The heading of any originating application for payment out must refer to the fund in court by its ledger number and give particulars and refer to any relevant trust deed; unless the originating application is *ex parte* all parties having any interest in the fund or trust must be joined.

Requirements and sequence

The applicant's title to any claim on the funds must unless obvious be strictly proved and the court will want to consider very carefully all the evidence including wills or probates, how the funds came to be in court in the first place, and who if anyone might have opposing claims. A certificate of funds must be lodged, together with a draft payment schedule. If the matter is reasonably straightforward and the funds are not substantial (not significantly in excess of £30,000) then the master may make an order himself and if the funds are not in excess of £5,000, in order to minimise costs, only the bare minimum will be expected in the conduct of the application. If the funds are substantial the master is likely to adjourn the application together with all the evidence when complete to the judge for hearing in the non-witness list.

In *inter partes* litigation notice of acceptance of monies paid into court together with notice of payment in is all that is initially required to obtain payment from the Supreme Court Pay Office (room 60) but if the payment in has been made under an order it will be necessary also to produce that order. Before making any such order the master will require a certificate of funds which has to be bespoken from the Pay Office. In order to obtain payment at the Supreme Court Pay Office an application for payment and an accompanying schedule showing where payment is to be made or reciting events to accord with the order must be completed and handed in.

Attitude of the court

The main concern of the court is to protect all persons who might have any possible claim to the fund and this includes unborn beneficiaries; however, the court will endeavour to see that persons are not kept away from monies to which they have entitlement because of interests which will never vest, on behalf of children, for example, who may never attain a required age, or who because a predecessor is beyond child bearing age will never be born. Nonetheless, the Chancery Division does adopt a protective attitude towards all, and will ensure not only that any payments out are made only to those entitled but that those who have contingent interests or who are unable to safeguard themselves are not disadvantaged. Thus it is that often funds will be retained sometimes for many years to protect possible unborn children or those who by reason of age or mental health are unable to look after their own interests.

The court will scrutinise the applicant's title in applications under Ord 92 as if the court were a purchaser and accordingly the applicant must prove his title in his affidavit as if he and the court bore that relationship.

Costs

If an application is made for payment out of a fund in court and it is found that the application was in all the circumstances a suitable one to be made, the applicant's costs would usually be ordered to be paid out of the fund. The court however will always maintain discretion as to the order for costs it might make, weighing the penalty to the party against the loss to the fund.

Hazards and pitfalls

If a mortgagor in an action for redemption (Ord 88, r 1(1)(e)) pays into court redemption monies which the mortgagee for some reason cannot or will not accept, the payment must include a reasonable sum to cover the costs of applying for payment out.

Where an applicant seeks payment out of compulsory purchase monies, the correlation of the land as shown in the compulsory purchase order and in any deeds produced by the applicant must be clear before any order will be made.

Payments

A payment in must be accompanied by what is called a 'request for lodgment form' (Court Funds Office Form 100) setting out the funds or assets coming under the protection of the court and a copy of the order for payment in will be required whenever payment in is made under an order. Payment into court of funds or the lodging of assets in court always requires an order, save where money is paid in in the course of *inter partes* proceedings in full or partial satisfaction of the claim.

On the sealing of the order, the order section (room 503) will submit the lodgment schedule to room 60 (basement) and on receipt of the schedule the clerk in room 60 will submit a direction to the party wishing to pay or bring assets into court. That party may attend in room 60 or may send the fund to the court by post, and he will receive a receipt for the payment or the lodgment of assets.

A copy of that receipt should be sent to other interested parties

Proceedings under Orders and Judgments

to show that the party paying in has complied with the court's orders and directions.

In case of urgency if a party needs to make a payment in or hand over an asset immediately, it will be possible to expedite the procedure with the leave of the master and his appropriate directions.

To obtain payment from the Supreme Court Pay Office requires production of an order for such payment or notice of acceptance of payment in and completion of a Payment Schedule (Court Funds Office Form No 200). Under normal circumstances, payments out can be made through the post and it can be expected that this will be done within seven days of an application being accepted, but if collection of assets is required special arrangements may have to be made.

The accounts are kept on computer and it is possible without any difficulty to obtain details of them at any time.

Interest will be added to the funds in court automatically under the new rules. Forms relating to payment into court follow.

Request for lodgment

Request for Lodgment	In the _CHANCERY_ **Division of the High Court**
Please use BLOCK CAPITALS	~~District Registry~~

Full Account Title: JOHN BLACK and WILLIAM GREEN

Action or Case Number: 1991 B. 8900

Location Code:

We request the Accountant General to receive into Court for lodgment to the above account

£ 5000 00 which is paid in *(Complete relevant section below)*

A on behalf of the Defendant
in satisfaction of the claim of
subject to RSC O.22, r.1   Has the hearing begun?   Yes ☐ No ☐ *(Please tick)*

B on behalf of
against the claim of
with defence setting up tender subject to RSC O.22, r.1
(Delete as appropriate)

C under Order dated   copy attached/I do not have a copy because

D for the following reason   payment into Court with denial of liability

Has a Certificate of Total Benefit been issued under Section 22 of the Social Security Act 1989? YES/NO. If YES, then a copy of the Certificate **shall** accompany this Request for Payment into Court.

And if any subsequent deductions have been made from the sum to be lodged then a Certificate of Deduction **shall** accompany this Request.

Has a previous lodgment in this action been made? Yes ☐ No ☐ *(Please tick)*

Signed _____

Name and address of other side's solicitors

Firm's name	Spooks & Co	Lookout & Co
Address	90 Champneys Street	51 South Street
	Northold N4Y 32A	London W2A 6AZ
Solicitor for the	Defendant	Plaintiff
Ref.	AB/SA	Dated 20/8/91 Ref. LA/SB

Note. Payments into Court made to the Court Funds Office, 22 Kingsway, London WC2B 6LE, may be made by cheque, bankers draft, or in cash *(payments in cash should not be made by post)*. Cheques and drafts must be made payable to the **Accountant General of the Supreme Court** and crossed.

Date Stamp/Seal

For CFO use
Restraint
A/c No
Placed B now/+21 days
Date investment schedule requested
Bank Date / Receipt Number
Date input
Lodgment approved

Court Funds Office — Form 100
(Court Funds Rules 15 & 16)

OYEZ The Solicitors' Law Stationery Society Ltd., Oyez House, 27 Crimscott Street, London SE1 5TS
High Court E33

1991 Edition
1.91 F19060
5050076

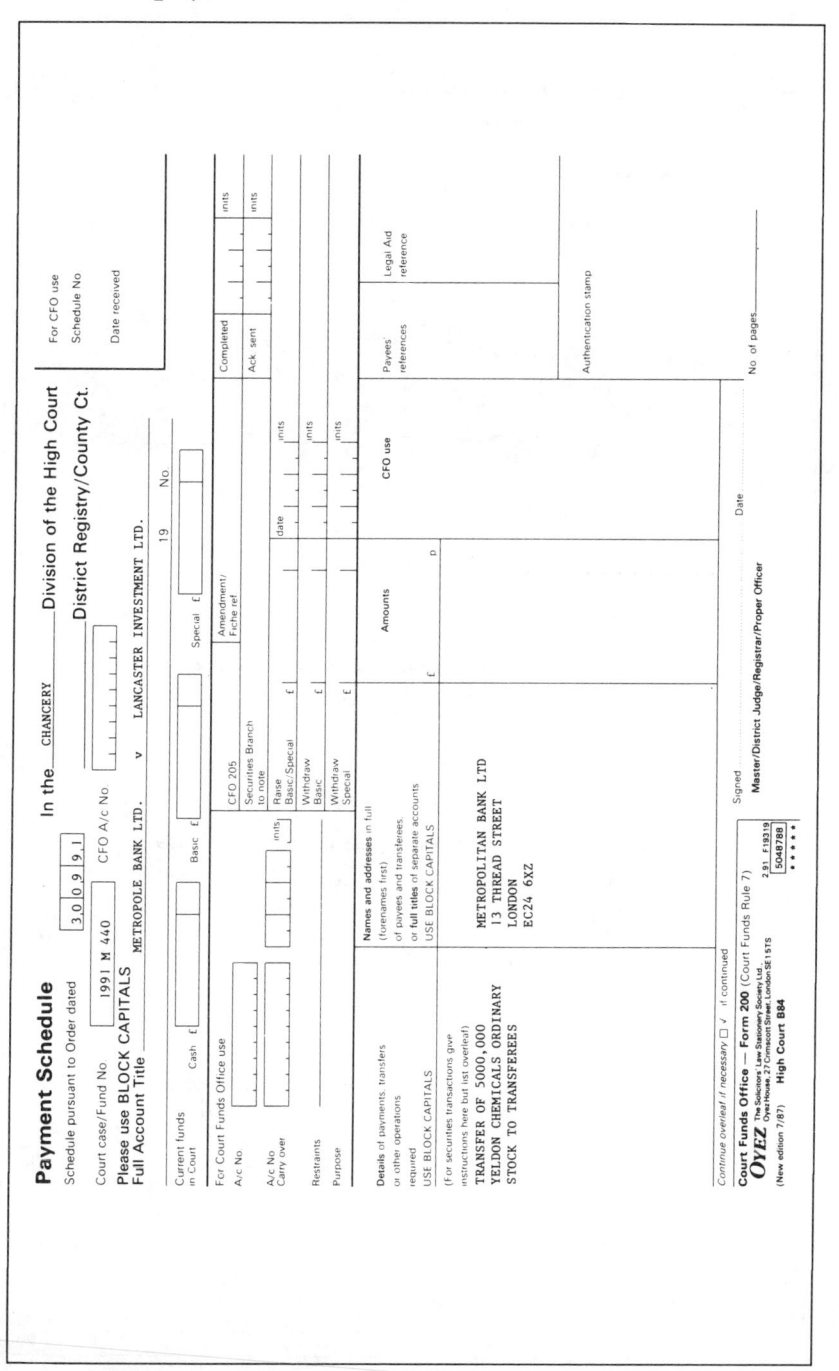

Form for payment into court

Payment Schedule

Schedule pursuant to Order dated: 3.0.0.9.91

Court case/Fund No: 1991 M 440 CFO A/c No:
Please use BLOCK CAPITALS
Full Account Title: METROPOLE BANK LTD. v LANCASTER INVESTMENT LTD.

In the CHANCERY Division of the High Court
District Registry/County Ct.

Current funds in Court: Cash £ Basic £ Special £

For Court Funds Office use
A/c No:
A/c No Carry over:
Restraints:
Purpose:

CFO 205
Securities Branch to note
Raise Basic/Special
Withdraw Basic
Withdraw Special

Details of payments, transfers or other operations required
USE BLOCK CAPITALS

(For securities transactions give instructions here but list overleaf)
TRANSFER OF 5000,000 YELDON CHEMICALS ORDINARY STOCK TO TRANSFEREES

Names and addresses in full (forenames first) of payees and transferees, or full titles of separate accounts
USE BLOCK CAPITALS

METROPOLITAN BANK LTD
13 THREAD STREET
LONDON
EC24 6XZ

Amounts
£   p

CFO use
Amendment/Fiche ref
date   ints
              ints

Completed
Ack. sent

Payees references
Legal Aid reference

Authentication stamp

For CFO use
Schedule No
Date received

Continue overleaf if necessary ☐ ✓ if continued

Signed .... Date ....
Master/District Judge/Registrar/Proper Officer

Court Funds Office — Form 200 (Court Funds Rule 7)
OYEZ The Solicitors' Law Stationery Society Ltd.
Oyez House, 27 Crimscott Street, London SE1 5TS
(New edition 7/87) High Court B84

2·91 F19319
5048788
* * * * *

No. of pages

Form for payment into court

Notice of Acceptance of Money Paid into Court (O. 22, r.3)

IN THE HIGH COURT OF JUSTICE　　　1991.—B.—No. 8900
CHANCERY **Division**

Between

JOHN BLACK　　　Plaintiff

AND

WILLIAM GREEN　　　Defendant

Take Notice that—

The Plaintiff accepts the sum of £5000.00 paid in by the Defendant in satisfaction of the cause[s] of action in respect of which it was paid in and in respect of which the Plaintiff claims [against the Defendant] [and abandon the other cause[s] of action in respect of which he claim in this action].

Dated the　27th　day of　August　1991

To　Spooks & Co　　　　　　Lookout & Co
　　　90 Champneys Street　　　of 51 South Street
　　　Northold　　　　　　　　　London W2A 6AZ
　　　NY4 32A

Solicitor for the Defendant　　　[Agent for

[and to　　　　　　　　　　　　of

　　　　　　　　　　　　　　　　　　　　　　　　　　　　　　　　　　　]

Solicitor for the Defendant]　　Solicitors for the Plaintiff

Form for payment into court

Notice of Payment into Court (O.22,rr.1,2)

IN THE HIGH COURT OF JUSTICE 19 91 .—B .—No. 8900

CHANCERY **Division**

Between

JOHN BLACK — Plaintiff

AND

WILLIAM GREEN — Defendant

Take Notice that—

(1) If by a particular Defendant insert name.

The Defendant (¹)

has paid £5000.00 into Court.
The said £5000.00 is in satisfaction of [the cause of action] [~~all the causes of action~~] in respect of which the Plaintiff claim [~~and after taking into account and satisfying the above-named Defendant's cause of action for~~

~~in respect of which he counterclaim~~]

or

~~The said £_____ is in satisfaction of the following causes of action in respect of which the Plaintiff claim , namely,~~

~~[and after taking into account and satisfying the above-named Defendant's cause of action for~~

~~in respect of which he counterclaim]~~

or

~~Of the said £_____ , £_____ is in satisfaction of the Plaintiff's cause[s] of action for~~

~~[and after taking into account and satisfying the above-named Defendant's cause of action for~~

~~in respect of which he counterclaim]~~
~~and £_____ is in satisfaction of the Plaintiff's cause[s] of action for~~

~~[and after taking into account and satisfying the above-named Defendant's cause of action for~~

~~in respect of which he counterclaim].~~

[~~The Defendant has withheld from this payment into court the sum of £_____ in accordance with paragraph 12(2)(a)(i) of Schedule 4 to the Social Security Act 1989].~~

Dated the 20th day of August 19 91 .

To Lookout & Co
51 South Street
London W2A 6AZ
[ ]
The Plaintiff's Solicitor

(2) If there are co-Defendants a copy of the notice must also be served upon their Solicitors.

or Agent
[and to [
]
~~Solicitor for the Defendant~~ (²) [ ]
[ ]]

of Spooks & Co
90 Champneys Street
Northold
N4Y 32A

[~~Agent for~~

of

]

Solicitors for the Defendant

Persons under disability

Order 80, r 12 provides for the control of money recovered for the benefit of a person under disability (see notes in AP, Vol 1, p 1294). An order may be made for the money in court to be transferred to a county court, or for payment to be made to a county court (County Courts Act 1959, s 174 and 174A). Funds in the county court are administered by the county court and the next friend is able to apply on completing a form of application attending before the registrar with the minimum of formality. If the monies are not paid or transferred to the county court, they are paid to the Special Account (Court Funds Rules 1987).

Monies recovered on behalf of a patient are normally administered by the Court of Protection. The order will provide for the investment of the monies pending the appointment of a receiver (AP, Vol 1, 80/12/9).

Interest on payments into court in satisfaction

While such payments were formerly placed to a short-term investment account on the application of a party, they will now automatically be placed on deposit after the time for acceptance has elapsed (Court Fund Rules 1987). The special, formerly the short-term investment account is now confined to funds held in court for the benefit of persons under disability (r 34 ibid).

Forms and precedents

See Atkin, Vol 31 (1987 issue).

Notes for guidance on completion of payment schedules

In addition to the requirements in the column headings the following details should also be included where appropriate:

(1) Except in the case of a firm or company the address given should be the actual residential address of the payee or transferee.
(2) Where the payee or transferee is entitled otherwise than in his own right the reason for his entitlement should be stated.
(3) Where the order directs dealings with a fund during the minority of the beneficiary the date of birth of the minor should be stated.

8. After judgment

Garnishee proceedings

RSC Ord 49 applies and reference should be made to s 40 of the Supreme Court Act 1981. Any person who obtains a judgment or order for payment of money may endeavour to obtain payment of any debt owing or accruing to the judgment debtor from any other person, called the 'garnishee' provided he is in England or Wales, and for so much of such debt as may be sufficient to satisfy his own judgment or order and the costs of the garnishee proceedings.

The judgment order must be for at least £50 (Ord 49, r 1(1)). Where the debt is due from a partnership carrying on business in England or Wales, the debt may be attached even though one of the partners is resident outside of England or Wales. Monies in current and deposit bank accounts with any clearing bank in National Savings Bank accounts, and in building society accounts, may be attached with a proviso for the benefit of the garnishee that the balance on any building society or Credit Union account must not be reduced below £1.

There are some types of debt which may not be attached, and these are a legacy in the hands of an executor, unless there has been an account from the executor which would constitute the legacy as a legal debt. This includes:

(1) Money paid into court in an administration action.
(2) Money in court under a judgment.
(3) A dividend distributable amongst creditors in the hands of the officer receivers.
(4) Debts which are due to a judgment debtor coupled with another party.
(5) Money which the judgment debtor and his wife have in a joint bank account, even though only one has the authority to draw money.
(6) Officers' pay and pensions.
(7) Money in a wife's bank account (possibly house-keeping).
(8) Money held by a trustee under a settlement.

In case of any doubt, reference should be made to SCP RSC Ord 49 and r 1 and the notes thereunder.

Procedure

Order 49 and r 2 requires a supporting affidavit giving the name and address of the judgment debtor, identifying the judgment to be in force, stating the amount remaining unpaid, and also stating that the garnishee is within the jurisdiction and is indebted to the judgment debtor, giving the sources of information and grounds for belief. Finally, the affidavit should state the branch concerned and the account number, where the garnishee is a deposit taking institution, or alternatively that this information is not known to the deponent. A specimen affidavit is given in Queen's Bench Master Practice Forms No 103.

Charging orders

The Charging Orders Act 1979, s 2 provides that a charge may be imposed on the debtor's beneficial interest under a trust. This occurs where the debtor has an interest in land held upon trust for sale, where such interest may be charged (*National Westminster Bank Ltd v Stockman* (1981) 1 All ER 800). This also applies to land, securities which consist of Government stock, other stock being not that of a building society, unit trusts, and on funds in court—the precise descriptions of stock as given in the section should be referred to.

Charging orders may also be made under s 23 of the Partnership Act 1890, for the procedure on which notes are given to RSC Order 81, r 10. They may also be made under s 73 of the Solicitors Act 1974, upon property recovered or preserved through the instrumentality of the solicitor, though such charges orders are very rare.

Receivership

Security by the person appointed may be directed by the court (RSC Ord 30, r 2(1)); alternatively, an undertaking may be accepted by the applicant to answer for what the receiver receives, or becomes liable to pay. Where security is directed, unless otherwise ordered, it is to be given by guarantee (Ord 30, r 2(3)), and a form of security is given in Chancery Masters Practice Forms No 30.

Receivers' accounts, to be submitted as and when the court directs, are verified by affidavit, unless otherwise directed. A form of receivers' account, which is pursuant to Ord 30, r 4(1), is usefully provided in Heward on Chancery Practice, (Butterworth, 1990) at p 105.

Assessment of damage by master

A summons to proceed is issued on the appointment for which all necessary directions are obtained or RSC Ord 44 applies.

Proceedings under Orders and Judgments—Orders

1. ORDER ON ACCOUNTS AND INQUIRIES

IT IS as the result of the said Account and Inquiries directed by the said Order dated...

DECLARED

 (1) that there is due to the plaintiffs
   (a) under and by virtue of the Charging Order £...
   (b) for their costs assessed in Chambers pursuant to the said Order £...

 (2) ...

 (3) ...

[AND THE COURT APPOINTS

on ... at the offices of ... at ... as the time date and place for payment by the defendant of the sum of £... (being the total of the two said amounts) to the plaintiff as provided in the said Order.]

Notes

1 It will be noted that the numbering of the declarations corresponds with the numbering in the main order.

2 It is not necessary to set out the calculations which lead to the figure shown to be due to the plaintiff under the charging order.

3 An example of possible declarations in (2) and (3) is:
   (2) 'that the defendant is the sole beneficial owner of the property
   (3) that there is one incumbrance on the said property namely a mortgage made ... between the defendant and the building society'.

2. ORDER ON ASSESSMENT OF DAMAGES

UPON THE ASSESSMENT of damages pursuant to the order dated...

AND UPON READING the documents recorded on the Court File as having been read

IT IS CERTIFIED that the amount of the damages assessed pursuant to the said Order is £...

AND IT IS ORDERED

(1) (so as to carry into effect the said Order) that the Defendant shall pay to the plaintiff the said sum of £... and

(2) that the defendant shall pay to the Plaintiff £... being assessed costs of the assessment of the said damages this Action to be taxed if not agreed.

Notes

1 Order 37 deals with the assessment of damages. Rule 2 of this order says that 'Where in pursuance of this order or otherwise damages are assessed by a master, he shall certify the amount of the damages...' This is why the order contains a certificate.

2 Under Ord 58, r 2(b) an appeal 'on an assessment of damages under Ord 37 or otherwise' lies straight from the master to the Court of Appeal.

3 (a) Sometimes the court gives directions at the time the order is made but if not a summons to proceed under the order should be issued.
   (b) Insert the date of the order or judgment which directed payment or assessment of the damages.
   (c) Delete the words '(so as to carry into effect the said Order)' if the previous order did *not* direct payment.
   (d) The order for costs may relate to the whole action or merely to the costs of assessment of damages.

3. ASSESSMENT OF INTEREST OF MESNE PROFITS

UPON THE ASSESSMENT OF [Mesne Profits] [Interest] pursuant to the Order [Judgment] dated...

AND UPON HEARING Counsel/the Solicitors for the Plaintiff and Counsel/the solicitors for the Defendant

AND UPON READING the documents recorded on the court file as having been read

THE COURT ASSESSES the [Mesne Profits] [Interest] payable by the Defendant to the Plaintiff under the said Order/Judgment at £...[made up as set out in the Schedule hereto]

AND IT IS ORDERED that the Defendant shall pay to the Plaintiff £...being the assessed costs of the assessment of the said [Mesne Profits] [Interest] this Action.

[The Schedule]

Note

It is not usually necessary to show how the total payable is made up since this will be shown on the court file.

4. ORDER FOR PAYMENT

(1) IT IS ORDERED that the defendants shall pay to the plaintiffs the sum of £... [by way of damages]

[(2) the sum of £... for their costs of this Action]

[(2) their costs of this Action to be taxed].

5. CHARGING ORDER

(1) Order Nisi

AND IT APPEARING that by the Order dated ... it was ordered that the defendant/plaintiff do pay to the plaintiff/defendant the sum of £... of which £... the whole of which remains due and unpaid and that the defendant/plaintiff has a beneficial interest in the asset specified in the Schedule hereto.

IT IS ORDERED that unless sufficient cause to the contrary be shown before Master ... at Room ... Chancery Chambers, Thomas More Building, the Royal Courts of Justice Strand London WC2A 2LL on ... day the ... day of ... 199.. at ... am/... pm the Plaintiff's/ Defendant's interest in the said asset shall (and it is ordered that in the meantime it shall) stand charged with payment of the said sum of £... due on the said Order and the interest due thereunder by virtue of Section 17 of the Judgments Act 1838 together with the costs of this Application

The Schedule

(2) Order absolute

IT IS ORDERED that the interest of the defendant/plaintiff in the asset specified in the Schedule hereto shall stand charged with the payment of £...the amount due from the plaintiff/defendant under the Order dated...the interest due thereunder by virtue of Section 17 of the Judgment Act 1838 and £...being the costs of this Application the said costs to be added to the Judgment debt.

The Schedule

6. ORDER ENFORCING CHARGING ORDER

(1) Land

AND IT APPEARING that the plaintiff is by virtue of the Charging Order specified in the Final Schedule hereto entitled to an equitable charge upon the interest of the defendant in the property specified in the Second Schedule hereto.

IT IS ORDERED

1 that the costs of the plaintiff of this Action be assessed in chambers and paid by the defendant

2 that the said property be sold within further reference to the Court [at a price of not less than £...] save that the sale price or reserve be fixed by the court

3 pursuant to Section 90 of the Law of Property Act 1925 and for the purpose of enabling the plaintiff to carry out the sale that there be created and vested in the plaintiff a legal term of 3000 years in the said property as if the mortgage had been created by deed by way of legal term pursuant to the said Act

[3 pursuant to Section 90 of the Law of Property Act 1925 and for the purpose of enabling the plaintiff to carry out the sale of the said property that there be created and vested in the plaintiff a legal term of years for the remainder of the term granted by the lease under which such property is held by the defendant less the last day thereof]

[4 that the following Account and Inquiries be taken and made that is to say

PROCEEDINGS UNDER ORDERS AND JUDGMENTS 197

   (i) An Account of what is due to the plaintiff
      (a) under and by virtue of the said Charging Order and
      (b) for his said costs
   (ii) An Inquiry as to what interest the Defendant has in the said property
   (iii) An Inquiry whether there are any and if any what other liens charges or incumbrances upon the said property or upon any and if any what parts thereof respectively and what are their priorities and what is due on account thereof respectively]

[5 that the defendant shall within 14 days after personal service upon him of this Order file in Chancery Chambers Thomas More Building The Royal Courts of Justice Strand London WC2A 2LL an affidavit stating what (if any) deeds and other documents relating to the title of the said property are in his possession or power and whether any deeds or other documents relating to the said title are known by him to be in the possession or power of any person or persons and if so stating the name and address of every such person and that he do within the same time lodge at the said Room 156 all (if any) such deeds and documents as are stated by him to be in his own possession or power]

[6 that the defendant shall within 28 days after personal service upon him of this Order deliver to the plaintiff possession of the said property]

7 that unless otherwise agreed by the parties interested therein the proceeds of sale of the said property after payment thereout of (a) what shall be due to any incumbrancers other than the plaintiff and (b) all proper costs charges and expenses incurred in connection with the said sale be lodged in Court to the credit of this Action

                    ...v...

19...Proceeds of sale of Freehold/Leasehold property subject to further order

8 that the parties are at liberty to apply for possession and generally.

The First Schedule

The Order dated...of the...made in the Action...

[AND THE COURT APPOINTS

on ... at the offices of ... at ... as the time date and place for payment by the defendant of the sum of £... (being the total of the two said amounts) to the plaintiff as provided in the said Order.)

Notes

1 It will be noted that the numbering of the declarations corresponds with the numbering in the main order.

2 It is not necessary to set out the calculations which lead to the figure shown to be due to the plaintiff under the charging order.

3 An example of possible declarations in (2) and (3) is:
 (a) 'that the defendant is the sole beneficial owner of the property, or
 (b) that there is one incumbrance on the said property namely a mortgage made ... between the defendant and the building society'.

(2) Shares

AND IT APPEARING that the plaintiff is by virtue of the Charging Order specified in the First Schedule hereto entitled to an equitable charge upon the interest of the defendant in the Shares specified in the Second Schedule hereto

IT IS DECLARED that the defendant is a Trustee of the said Shares for the plaintiff within the meaning of Section 51(1) of the Trustees Act 1925

AND IT IS ORDERED

1 that the right to transfer the said Shares and to receive the dividends now due or to accrue due thereon vest in the plaintiff

2 that as many of the said Shares as shall be required to repay the plaintiff the amount due to him be sold by the plaintiff

3 that the plaintiff be at liberty to discharge out of the moneys to arise on such sale and any dividends received by him (a) what shall be due to him under and by virtue of the said Charging Order and (b) £ ... being his assessed costs of this Action

4 that the parties be at liberty to apply.

The First Schedule

The order dated ... of the ... made in the Action.

The Second Schedule

... Ordinary Shares of £... each in ... PLC (the Share Certificate number of the said Shares being ...)

7. ORDER GIVING LEAVE TO ISSUE WRIT OF POSSESSION

IT IS ORDERED

1 that the plaintiff be at liberty to issue a Writ of Possession in respect of the property known as ... to enforce the Order dated ...

2 that the defendant do pay to the plaintiff ... costs of the said application ... assessed costs of the said application.

Notes

1 By Ord 45, r 3(2) a writ of possession is not issued without the leave of the court except where an order for possession under Ord 88 (mortgage actions) has been made. The court has to be satisfied that every person in actual occupation has been given notice of the proceedings.

2 Usually a summons is required and served on all persons in actual possession but sometimes in particular circumstances an *ex parte* application may be made to the master on affidavit.

3 Very often the order is not drawn up but the master writes 'Leave to issue' on the original order.

8. RESULT OF ACCOUNT FOR MONEY DUE

IT IS DECLARED

1 that the money received by the Defendant and by other persons on behalf of the Defendant as trustee or spent by the Plaintiff in or about the year 19... amounted to the sum of £... and that of this sum the Defendant expended £... in proper disbursements on behalf of the Plaintiff and retained the balance of £...
2 that the balance due to the Plaintiff on ... was accordingly £... that interest on the said sum at the rate of ... per cent per annum from that date to the date of this Order is £... and that accordingly the total now due from the Defendant to the Plaintiff is £...

AND IT IS ORDERED

1 that the Defendant shall pay to the Plaintiff the said sum of £...
2 that the Defendant shall pay to the Plaintiff £... costs of the said Account and Inquiry to be taxed if not agreed.

9. ORDER FOR EXAMINATION OF JUDGMENT DEBTOR

IT IS ORDERED

1 that the Defendant shall attend before one of the officers of the High Court of Justice at such time and place as such officer may appoint and be orally examined as to whether any and if any what debts are owing to him and whether he has any and if so what other means of satisfying the Order dated ...

2 that the defendant shall produce to the said officer at the time of the examination any books and papers in the defendant's possession or power relating to the matters aforesaid

3 that the costs of the said application and of the examination be reserved.

Note

See Ord 48. The examination is usually taken by an officer of the Queen's Bench Division.

10. APPOINTMENT OF GUARDIAN OF MINOR'S ESTATE

(1) Where legacy to be paid into court

[AND the said guardian having given security to the satisfaction of the court]

THE COURT APPOINTS AB of ... guardian of the estate of the said minor during minority or until further order

AND IT IS ORDERED

1 that the guardian be authorised to receive on behalf of the said minor from CD the present trustees of the Will of XY deceased the legacy payable under the said will (hereinafter called the Fund) and to give a good receipt and discharge therefor

2 that the costs of the applicant and the guardian be taxed on the indemnity basis [assessed in chambers] and paid out of the Fund

3 that the guardian shall upon receipt by him of the said legacy of £... deduct the [assessed] taxed costs and lodge in court to the credit of the action the residue of the said legacy in accordance with the lodgment schedule attached hereto and thereupon the guardian be discharged from his office of guardian and his guarantee be discharged

4 The parties are at liberty to apply.

Notes

1 This is the simplest form when the legacy is simply paid into court and invested by the court and paid out when the minor comes of age.

2 Security is normally required but an affidavit of fitness is not usually required as the guardian's duty is only to receive the money and pay it into court.

(2) Where damages to be paid into court

[AND the said guardian by ... solicitors/counsel undertaking to expend the sums directed to be paid to ... by the payment part of the lodgment and payment schedule hereto for the maintenance and education of the said minor and to account for all moneys to be received by ... as Guardian when required to do so]

AND the said guardian having given security to the satisfaction of the Court

THE COURT APPOINTS AB of ... Guardian of the estate of the said Minor during ... minority or until further Order

AND IT IS ORDERED

1 that the said guardian be authorised to accept on behalf of the said Minor in settlement of claims made on ... behalf in an action which is before ... the sum of ... [state currency] [hereinafter called the Fund] and to execute and do or concur in executing and doing on behalf of the said minor all instruments acts and things necessary or proper to accept such sum and to give a discharge therefor to ...

2 that the costs of the said minor and the said guardian of the said Application be taxed on a common fund basis [be assessed in chambers]

3 that the said guardian shall retain and pay such costs when taxed [assessed] out of any monies coming into ... hands as such guardian as aforesaid in respect of the said sum of [currency]

4 that the said guardian shall lodge in Court as directed in the lodgment part of the lodgment and payment schedule hereto the balance of such monies remaining after paying such taxed costs and any other costs properly incurred by her as such guardian as aforesaid

5 that upon such lodgment the said security be discharged

6 that the funds so lodged in Court be dealt with as directed in the payment part of the said lodgment and payment schedule

7 that the parties are to be at liberty to apply.

(3) Where legacy to be paid to trustees

[AND the said guardians having given security to the satisfaction of the Court]

THE COURT APPOINTS A B of ... and C D of ... guardians of the estate of the said minor during minority or until further order

AND IT IS ORDERED

1 that the said guardians be authorised to accept on behalf of the said minor the monies to which the minor has become entitled under the Will of ... (which said monies are hereinafter referred to as 'the Fund') and give a good receipt and discharge therefor

2 that the said guardians shall hold the Fund upon trust to invest the same in investments authorised by law and to use the income thereof for the maintenance of the said minor and to pay the capital to the said minor on his/her attaining the age of 18 years

3 that the said ... as one of the said guardians shall receive such remuneration as may be determined from time to time by the Court and that he be at liberty to act as solicitor to the Trust and subject to the approval of the Court be allowed as part of his remuneration all proper costs in respect of professional work done by him as such solicitor as though he were not a Trustee

4 that the costs of the Applicant of this application and of the guardians [be assessed in chambers] be taxed on the indemnity basis and paid out of the Fund

5 that the parties be at liberty to apply.

Notes

1 An affidavit of fitness of the proposed guardians is usually required; also consents to act.

2 The order may attract stamp duty.

(4) Appointment of official solicitor in case of compensation from Criminal Injuries Compensation Board

IN THE MATTER OF ... (A Minor)

UPON THE APPLICATION by Originating Summons of ... the secretary and solicitor of the Criminal Injuries Compensation Board ...

AND UPON HEARING the solicitor for the Applicant

AND UPON READING the documents recorded on the court file as having been read

THE COURT APPOINTS the Official Solicitor of the Supreme Court without giving security and during the minority of the above named minor (who was born on ... 19...) or until further Order in the meantime guardian of the minor for the purpose only of receiving the money which have been awarded to the said minor by the Criminal Injuries Compensation Board (hereinafter called the Fund)

AND IT IS ORDERED

1 that the Official Solicitor be at liberty to receive the Fund from the Applicant and to give a valid receipt therefor

2 that the Official Solicitor be at liberty to invest the Fund for the benefit of the minor in such investments as are or may be authorised by law for investment by trustees

3 that the Official Solicitor be at liberty to apply the whole or part of the income of the Fund for the maintenance of the minor or to accumulate the same as he may think fit

4 that the Official Solicitor be at liberty if he thinks fit to advance not more than one half of the Fund for the advancement or benefit of the minor

5 that the Official Solicitor be at liberty to retain from time to time out of the estate of the minor his proper costs, charges and expenses in respect of work done by him as guardian of the estate of the minor

6 that the parties are to be at liberty to apply.

11. FUNDS IN COURT: EXAMPLES OF FORMS FOR USE IN PAYMENT AND LODGMENT SCHEDULES

(1) Payment schedule

1 NOTWITHSTANDING the Order dated ...
SELL the Stock
OUT of the proceeds of such sale Money on Deposit and any Interest
PAY Income Tax (if any)
DIVIDE the residue into halves

PAY one half	The plaintiff A B of
OUT of the other half	Messrs ... of ...
PAY the costs of the plaintiff to be taxed under this Order	The Solicitors for the plaintiff AB Messrs ...
PAY the residue of such half	of ... the solicitors for the defendant CD who is an assisted person

(2) Lodgment schedule

2 £ ... together with Interest thereon at the rate of £ ... per centum per annum from ... to the date of lodgment

3 CASH (the amount to be verified by affidavit) in the current account of AB with ... Bank plc at ... branch

4 CASH to be hereafter declared due from AB of ... (the receiver appointed by the Order) dated ... on his final account

5 CASH on account of the funds due from the receiver on his first account £ ...

6 CASH being proceeds of sale of 50 tonnes of ... potatoes detained by ... as officers of the Court pursuant to the Order dated ... after deducting expenses of sale (Amount to be verified by affidavit of solicitor).

(3) Restraints

THE RESTRAINT dated ... is hereby discharged for the purpose of this Order only [If the words 'for the purpose of this Order only' are not included the Restraint will be taken as having been discharged permanently]

7 NOTWITHSTANDING the directions contained in the payment schedule to the Order dated ... in respect of payment of interest and in lieu thereof.

(4) Out of specific funds

8 OUT of residue of cash and (so far as necessary) out of Short Term Investment Account

9 OUT of Money on Deposit Cash and any Interest

10 OUT of Money on Deposit and any Interest

11 GIVE Notice to repay £... of the ...
OUT of the proceeds of such repayment
PAY Income Tax (if any) ...

(5) Recitals

12 IF residue is sufficient ... IF residue is not sufficient ...

13 UPON production of an affidavit by a solicitor deposing that ...

14 FOR the purpose of computation add to the balance of the funds £... DIVIDE the total so ascertained into 3 equal parts

15 WITHDRAW from Money on Deposit sufficient together with any Interest to make the following payments

16 DEDUCT the amount which bears the same proportion to £A as £B bears to £C.

(6) Investment

17 INVEST AND ACCUMULATE funds to be lodged in [state investment] ... pending appointment of Receiver by Court of Protection
ON such appointment CARRY OVER fund to Court of Protection for the credit of [full names of patient] ...

18 AFTER providing for the payment of £... under the Order dated ... INVEST residue of Money on Deposit and Cash to be received as above in ...

19 INVEST and ACCUMULATE Cash to be lodged as above by placing in a Short Term Investment Account

20 INVEST above Money on Deposit and any Interest in ... without deducting applicable charges [the order would contain an undertaking to pay the charges]

21 INVEST balance of Cash in High Yield Fund Units [Provision should be made for the payment of the income]

22 INVEST as near as possible the following amounts of cash in the following securities
(1) £... cash in ...
(2) £... cash in ...
INVEST the residue of cash in ... [Presumably a direction as to the payment of interest will follow].

(7) Sale

23 SELL the Stock...

24 SELL the...

25 SELL all the above Stocks

26 SELL ... [in Securities Column] [here not all is being sold—the amount to be sold is stated in the Securities Column]

27 SELL (if necessary) sufficient ... to raise with cash the amount required to make the payments in respect of Income Tax and costs hereinafter directed

28 SELL the Gross Income Fund Units
OUT of proceeds thereof...

29 SELL the Common Investment Fund High Yield Units.

(8) Transfer

30 TRANSFER the Stock   The plaintiff
                                         [Full names and address]

31 TRANSFER the Consols [if need be specify which kind of Consols].

(9) Particulars of payments

32 PAY the plaintiff [Full names and address] £... (being the equivalent in sterling at the rate of exchange on the ... day of ... Dollars United States Currency) [The figure has to be worked out by the solicitors before the schedule is signed]

33 PAY the sums set out in this column together with interest without deducting tax on such of them as are described as debts at the

rate of ... per cent per annum from ... to the date of payment.
Debt £15   The defendant ...
                                                                     AB ...
                                                                     of ...
Costs £10.
After 'interest' state either 'less tax' or 'without deducting tax'

34 PAY (on account of their entitlement as beneficiaries under the Will of the Testator)
£...   The defendant ...
                                                     AB ...

35 PAY (1) £... plus (2) the Interest less tax earned up to the date of payment by £... since the lodgment of the funds in Court
                                       Messrs ... of ...
                                                (Ref...)
                                        the solicitors
                                        for the plaintiff
                                                   AB

36 PAY one half of the Interest as it accrues

37 PAY (amount due being £... proportion of annuity to the date of death of AB on ...

38 PAY balance of fund for distribution to the creditors of ...
                                                    Messrs ...

39 PAY Interest as it accrues on both above stocks

40 PAY the amounts to be verified by affidavit remaining due to the legatees named in the second column respectively in respect of ...

41 PAY dividends received until further Order.
                               The defendant [Full names]
                                                   of ...

42 PAY funeral expenses of the testator ... converted at rate of exchange at the date of death ... ie, £... together with interest thereon at the rate of £... per centum per annum from ... to the date of payment less Income Tax

43 PAY the creditors named in the second column the amounts set opposite their names in this column together with Interest less tax on such amounts...

44 PAY the balance due to the receiver as declared
by the Order dated   A B of ... £...
                                 the Receiver appointed
                                 by the Order dated ...

45 PAY remuneration allowed to receiver by the Order dated ...
                                                          £...

46 PAY costs allowed by this Order of passing the receiver's 5th
Account   £...

47 DIVIDE the Interest on Short Term Investment Account due ...
[or ...] and any further Interest into 4 equal parts
PAY one such part without deduction of tax...

(10) Costs

48 PAY Assessed Costs of the defendants AB   Messrs ... £...
                                                 the solicitors for ...

49 PAY (on account of agreed costs)   £...

50 PAY taxed costs of the plaintiff under the Order dated...
                                                             £...

51 PAY costs to be taxed under this Order and the Order dated
...   Messrs ...

52 PAY (on account of plaintiff's costs to be taxed under this Order)
                                                             £...

[There will have to be another direction as to the balance of the costs, presumably in a later Payment schedule]

53 PAY assessed costs of solicitors for the receiver and manager
                                                             £...

54 PAY balance of the costs of the receiver
                                                             £...

55 PAY costs to be taxed or agreed under this Order (the amount of the agreed costs in the event of agreement to be verified by an affidavit of the solicitor for the defendant AB) or £... whichever is the less.

(11) Carry over

56 DIVIDE the residue into fifths and carry over as under
    One fifth...   This Action
                                        'The Account of AB deceased'
    One fifth...   This Action
                                        'The Account of CD deceased'

57 CARRY OVER residue of funds to the general credit of this Action

58 THE BALANCE of the fund to remain in Court pending further Order [If funds remain in court the formula should be used].

(12) Payee

59 The personal representatives when constituted of AB

60 The plaintiff AB Ltd (a Company in Liquidation) by its Liquidator CD...of...

61 AB of Messrs. CB of ... the trustee of the property of EF (A Bankrupt)

62 The plaintiff AB as Treasurer of the Synod of ... of [address]

63 The person or persons to be hereafter declared as entitled to receive the said sum

64 The plaintiffs AB and CD the executors of the Will of EF deceased of ... [make clear whether they are executors or administrators].

12. GARNISHEE ORDERS

A Garnishee Order is an effective method of enforcing judgment against a person, eg an employee (the judgment debtor) who is owed money by a third person, eg the employer (the garnishee), by obtaining an order for payment of the judgment debt (or part of it) by the garnishee direct to the judgment creditor. See Ord 49.

(1) Nisi

UPON THE APPLICATION of the judgment creditor
AND UPON HEARING the solicitors for the judgment creditor
AND UPON READING the documents recorded on the Court File as having been read

AND IT APPEARING that the name and address of the branch of the garnishee Bank at which the judgment debtor's account is believed to be held is...

IT IS ORDERED

1 that all debts due or accruing due from the garnishee to the judgment debtor ... be attached to answer the Order dated ... (whereby it was ordered that the judgment debtor do pay to the judgment creditor £... and costs to be taxed and whereon the sum of £... remains due and unpaid) together with the costs of these garnishee proceedings
2 that the garnishee attend Master ... at Room ... Thomas More Building The Royal Courts of Justice Strand London WC2A 2LL on ... day the ... day of ... 199 ... at ...am/...pm on an application by the judgment creditor that the garnishee pay to the judgment creditor the debt due from the garnishee to the judgment debtor or so much thereof as is sufficient to satisfy the said Order together with the costs of these garnishee proceedings.

(2) Absolute where garnishee owes more than judgment debt

UPON THE APPLICATION of the judgment creditor
AND UPON HEARING the solicitors for the judgment creditor the judgment debtor and the garnishee
AND UPON READING the court file including the Order to show cause dated ... whereby it was ordered that all debts due or accruing due from the garnishee to the judgment debtor be attached to answer the Order dated ... (whereby it was ordered that the judgment debtor do pay to the judgment creditor £... and costs to be taxed and whereon the sum of £... remained due and unpaid) together with the costs of these garnishee proceedings
IT IS ORDERED that the garnishee shall forthwith pay to the judgment creditor £... being so much of the debt due from the garnishee to the judgment debtor as is sufficient to satisfy the said Order dated ... together with £... the costs of these garnishee proceedings and that the garnishee be at liberty to retain £... for the garnishee's costs of this Application [and £... towards the clerical and administrative expenses of complying with the order] out of the balance of the debt due from the garnishee to the judgment debtor.

(3) Absolute where garnishee owes less than judgment debt

UPON THE APPLICATION of the judgment creditor

AND UPON HEARING the solicitors for the judgment creditor the judgment debtor and the garnishee

AND UPON READING the documents recorded on the court file as having been read including the Order to show cause dated... whereby it was ordered that all debts due or accruing due from the garnishee to the judgment debtor be attached to answer the Order dated ... (whereby it was ordered that the judgment debtor pay to the judgment creditor £... and costs to be taxed and whereon the sum of £... remained due and unpaid) together with the costs of these garnishee proceedings

IT IS ORDERED

1. that the garnishee (after deducting therefrom £... for the garnishee's costs of this application [and £... towards the clerical and administration costs of complying with the order] shall forthwith pay to the judgment creditor £... of the debt due from the garnishee to the judgment debtor

2. that the sum of £... the costs of the judgment creditor of this application be added to the judgment debt and be retained out of the money recovered by the judgment creditor under this Order and in priority to the amount of the judgment debt.

Notes

1. Garnishee orders are dealt with in Ord 49; Atkin, Vol 1; and Nos 72, 73 and 74 of Appendix A SCP, Vol 2.

2. Order 49, r 3 provides that an order must unless the court otherwise directs be served (a) on the garnishee personally at least 15 days before the time appointed for further consideration and on the judgment debtor at least seven days before the date so fixed.

3. A separate order should be drawn up for each garnishee if there is more than one, save where garnishees are a firm when one order will suffice.

4. For the practice where judgment is expressed in foreign currency see SCP, Vol 1, 49/1/17.

5   Order 49, r 10 provides that unless the court otherwise directs the judgment creditor shall retain his costs out of the money recovered by him in priority to the judgment debt. The fixed costs are prescribed in Appendix 3 to Ord 62. Fixed costs are also prescribed for the garnishee who may deduct these costs from the debt due from him.

6   Section 40A of the Supreme Court Act 1981 (inserted by s 55 of the Administration of Justice Act 1982) enables a sum to be prescribed which certain institutions may deduct towards their clerical and administrative expenses of complying with the order. By the Attachment of Debt (Expenses) Order 1983 SI. 1983/1621 a sum of £30 has been fixed. This sum is only deducted if ordered by the court and is not inserted as a matter of course.

7   Examples of recitals relating to the judgment debt:
  (a) whereby it was ordered that the judgment debtor shall pay to the judgment creditor £...and costs to be taxed which costs have been taxed in the sum of £...whereof the sum of £...(including the whole of the said costs) remains due and unpaid
  (b) shall pay to the judgment creditor damages to be assessed and costs to be taxed which damages have been assessed at £...and which costs have been taxed at £...whereof the sum of £...remains due and unpaid
  (c) ...ordered that the judgment debtor shall pay to the judgment creditor the amount which on taking the account thereby directed should be shown to be due to him and which amount was by the order dated...declared to be £...and remains due and unpaid.

8   If the judgment debt consists of more than one item, eg, a liquidated sum and costs and it is not clear whether sums already paid by the debtor are in satisfaction of the liquidated sum or the costs the garnishee order will obviously have to be silent as to this. Where it is clear what the position is, it is better to state it.

CONTEMPT OF COURT

Disobedience of a court order constitutes contempt of court and, unfortunately, it is necessary in many cases to initiate proceedings for contempt in order to receive compliance. Actual orders for committal to prison are rare. See Atkin, Vol 12 (1990 issue).

13.   ORDER FOR COMMITTAL

AND IN THE MATTER of an application on behalf of the plaintiff against the defendant for an Order for committal

UPON MOTION made by Counsel for the plaintiff
AND UPON HEARING Counsel for the defendant
AND UPON READING the documents set out in this Schedule hereto AND THIS COURT being satisfied that the defendant has been guilty of Contempt of Court in failing to comply with/the Order dated .../ paragraph(s) ... of the Order dated .../the Undertakings given to the court on ... and contained in the Order dated .../those parts of the Order dated ... set forth in the Schedule hereto/by ...

IT IS ORDERED

1 that the defendant shall stand committed to ... Prison for a period of ... from the date of his apprehension [PROVIDED that as soon as possible after his apprehension the defendant be brought before the Honourable Mr Justice ... if available or failing him another Judge of the High Court to enable the defendant to make such representations to the Court as he may think fit]

2 that the defendant shall pay to the plaintiff his costs of this motion such costs to be taxed on a common fund basis if not agreed.

The Schedule
[Specify documents recorded]

Notes

1 In the recital where the court finds the defendant guilty of contempt:
   (a) delete the inappropriate words, but
   (b) add after the word 'by' at the end of the recital the acts of the defendant found to be contempts by the court. These will probably be set out in the notice of motion.

2 Insert in the order for committal (a the name of the appropriate prison (Pentonville for men over 21 years of age, Chelmsford for men over 17 but under 21 years of age and Holloway for women) and (b) the period of imprisonment. This must not exceed two years (s 14(19) of the Contempt of Court Act 1981).

3 Whenever an *ex parte* order for committal is made the court must dispense with service of the Notice of Motion (see Ord 52, r 4(3)) and the order should recite this. In addition, the proviso in the square brackets after the order for committal must be included.

4 If on an *inter partes* motion the judge dispenses with the service of the Notice of Motion, the order should recite this.

5 The most common forms of costs orders on committal motions are for taxation on a common fund basis or on solicitors and own client and indemnity basis.

6 The associate must not forget to send the governor of the prison to which the contemnor is being committed a copy of the order and the appropriate letter.

7 Section 14(3) of the Contempt of Court Act 1981 (applying section 19(1) of the Powers of the Criminal Courts Act 1973) provides that a person under 17 years of age cannot be imprisoned for contempt but s 9 of the Criminal Justice Act 1982 gives the court power if no other method of dealing with him is available to commit a prison a person aged 17 years or more but under 21 years for default in payment of a fine for contempt.

14. ORDER REFUSING COMMITTAL AND ACCEPTING AN APOLOGY

AND IN THE MATTER of an application on behalf of the plaintiff against the defendant for an Order for committal
   UPON MOTION made by Counsel for the plaintiff
   AND UPON HEARING Counsel for the defendant
   AND UPON READING the documents recorded on the Court file as having been read
   AND THE COURT being satisfied that the defendant has been guilty of Contempt of Court in failing to comply with/the Order dated .../paragraph(s) ... of the Order dated .../the Undertaking(s) in the Order dated ... contained/those parts of the Order dated ... set forth in the Schedule hereto/by ...
   AND the defendant by his Counsel apologising and expressing his regret for such contempt
   THE COURT DOES NOT THINK FIT to make any order on this Motion save that the defendant shall pay to the plaintiff his costs of this Motion such costs to be taxed on a common fund basis if not agreed.

Notes

1 In the recital where the court finds the defendant guilty of contempt:
   (a) delete the inappropriate words, but
   (b) add after the word 'by' at the end of the recital the acts of the defendant found to be contempts by the court. These will probably be set out in the notice of motion.
2 Where the court finds the defendant guilty of contempt but declines to make any order on the motion save as to costs without an apology being given by the defendant the recital concerning the apology should be deleted.

15. ORDER REFUSING APPLICATION FOR COMMITTAL

AND IN THE MATTER of an Application on behalf of the plaintiff against the defendant for an Order for Committal
UPON MOTION for the committal of the defendant made by Counsel for the plaintiff
AND UPON HEARING Counsel for the defendant
AND UPON READING the documents recorded on the Court File as having been read
THE COURT DOES NOT THINK FIT to make any Order on the said Motion save that [add provisions as to costs].

16. ORDER FOR RELEASE OF CONTEMNOR

UPON MOTION made by Counsel for the defendant
AND UPON HEARING Counsel for the plaintiff
AND UPON READING the documents recorded on the Court Files as having been read

IT IS ORDERED

1 that the defendant be released from the custody of the Governor of ... Prison in respect of his committal by the Order dated ...

2 [add provision as to costs].

Notes

1 Add the name of the prison where the contemnor was held and the date of the order committing him to prison.

2 The associate must not forget (a) to send to the governor of the prison a copy of the order for release and (b) to hand to the prison warder, tipstaff or solicitors for the contemnor the appropriate letter.

17. ORDER FOR PAYMENT OF A FINE AND ENFORCEMENT UNDER s 16(1)(a) OF THE CONTEMPT OF COURT ACT 1981

AND IN THE MATTER of an application on behalf of the plaintiff against the defendant for an order for committal
UPON MOTION made by Counsel for the plaintiff
AND UPON HEARING Counsel for the defendant

AND UPON READING the documents recorded on the Court File as having been read

AND THE COURT being satisfied that the defendant has been guilty of Contempt of Court in failing to comply with/the Order dated .../paragraph(s) ... of the ... Order dated .../the Undertaking(s) in the Order dated ... contained/those parts of the Order dated ... set forth in the Schedule hereto/by ...

IT IS ORDERED

1 that the defendant shall on or before ... pay to her Majesty the Queen a fine of £...

2 that the said fine be enforced in like manner as a judgment of the High Court for the payment of money

3 that the defendant shall pay to the plaintiff his costs of this Motion such costs to be taxed on a common fund basis if not agreed.

Notes

1 In the recital where the court finds the defendant guilty of contempt
   (a) delete the inappropriate words, and
   (b) add after the word 'by' at the end of the recital the acts of the defendant found to be contempts by the court. These will probably be set out in the notice of motion.

2 The judge should specify a date within which the fine should be paid. If not add the word 'forthwith'. In practice this means the fine will not be enforced for 30 days.

3 The associate must not forget to send the appropriate letters.

18. PAYMENT OF A FINE AND ENFORCEMENT UNDER s 16(1)(b) OF THE CONTEMPT OF COURT ACT 1981

AND IN THE MATTER of an application on behalf of the plaintiff against the defendant for an Order for committal
   UPON MOTION made by Counsel for the plaintiff
   AND UPON HEARING Counsel for the defendant
   AND UPON READING the documents specified in the schedule hereto
   AND THE COURT being satisfied that the defendant has been guilty of Contempt of Court in failing to comply with/the Order dated .../the paragraph(s) ... of the Order dated .../the Undertaking(s) in the Order dated ... contained/those parts of the Order dated ... set forth in the schedule hereto/by ...

IT IS ORDERED

1 that the defendant shall on or before ... pay to Her Majesty the Queen a fine of £...

2 that the Clerk to the Justices of ... at ... shall collect for and on behalf of Her Majesty the Queen the said fine from the defendant

3 that in default of the defendant paying the said fine within the time aforesaid (a) the ... Magistrates Court shall enforce the payment of the said fine and (b) the defendant shall stand committed to Prison for a period of ...

4 that the defendant shall pay to the plaintiff his costs of this Motion such costs to be taxed on a common fund basis if not agreed.

The Schedule
[Specify documents read]

Notes

1 In the recital where the court finds the defendant guilty of contempt
   (a) delete the inappropriate words, but
   (b) add after the word 'by' at the end of the recital the acts of the defendant found to be contempts by the court. These will probably be set out in the notice of motion.

2 The judge must indicate a time within which payment of a fine should be made (s 31(1) of the Powers of the Criminal Courts Act 1973).

3 The appropriate magistrates' court and its address must be entered into the order. The Criminal Appeals office has maps showing the catchment areas of the magistrates' courts and these should be referred to if there is any difficulty nominating a magistrates' court. Alternatively, the associate could suggest to the judge that he request the solicitors for the party who has brought the committal motion to inform the associate of the name and address of the appropriate magistrates' court.

4 The term of imprisonment which the person is to undergo if the fine is not paid must not exceed 12 months (s 31(3) of the Powers of the Criminal Courts Act 1973). Enforcement under s 16(1)(6) is inappropriate if the contemnor is under 17 years of age because a court cannot impose a sentence of imprisonment on such a person (s 19(1) of the Powers of the Criminal Courts Act 1973).

5 The associate must not forget to send to the magistrates' court a copy of the order and the appropriate letter.

19. ORDER FOR SUSPENDED COMMITTAL UPON PAYMENT OF A FINE

AND IN THE MATTER of an application on behalf of the plaintiff against the defendant for an order for committal
   UPON MOTION made by Counsel for the plaintiff
   AND UPON HEARING Counsel for the defendant
   AND UPON READING the documents specified in the schedule hereto
   AND THIS COURT being satisfied that the defendant has been guilty of Contempt of Court in failing to comply with/the Order dated .../paragraph(s) ... of the Order dated .../the Undertaking(s) in the Order dated ... contained/those parts of the Order dated ... set forth in the schedule hereto/by ...

IT IS ORDERED

1 that the defendant shall stand committed to ... Prison for a period of ... beginning with the date of his apprehension

2 that the Order for Committal shall not have effect provided the defendant do on or before ... pay to Her Majesty the Queen a fine of £...

3 that the defendant shall pay to the plaintiff his costs of his Motion such costs to be taxed on a common fund basis if not agreed.

The Schedule
[Specify documents read]

Notes

1 In the recital where the court finds the defendant guilty of contempt
   (a) delete the inappropriate words, but
   (b) add after the word 'by' at the end of the recital the acts of the defendant found to be contempts by the court. These will probably be set out in the notice of motion.

2 Insert in the order for committal (a) the name of the appropriate prison (Pentonville for men over 21 years of age, Chelmsford for men over 17

but under 21 years of age and Holloway for women) and (b) the period of imprisonment. This must not exceed two years (s 14(1) of the Contempt of Court Act 1981).

3   A person under 17 years of age cannot be imprisoned for Contempt (s 14(3) of the Contempt of Court Act 1981 applying s 19(1) of the Powers of the Criminal Courts Act 1973).

4   The court must specify a date on or before which the fine should be paid.

5   The associate must not forget to send the appropriate letters.

6   The court may instead order committal but suspend it upon the contemnor doing or refraining from doing some act or acts. This form may be used as the basis for such an order.

20. ORDER FOR THE ISSUE OF A WRIT OF SEQUESTRATION

UPON MOTION made by Counsel for the plaintiff
　AND UPON HEARING Counsel for the defendant
　AND UPON READING the documents specified in the schedule hereto
　AND THE COURT being satisfied that the defendant has been guilty of Contempt of Court in failing to comply with/the Order dated .../ paragraph(s) ... of the Order dated .../the Undertaking(s) in the Order dated ... contained/those parts of the Order dated ... set forth in the schedule hereto/by ...

IT IS ORDERED

1   that the plaintiff be at liberty to issue a Writ of Sequestration directed to the Commissioners named therein to sequester all the real and personal property of the defendant for his said contempt of this Court and the said Writ of Sequestration shall remain in full force and operation until the defendant shall purge his contempt [or until further order in the meantime]

2   that the defendant shall pay to the plaintiff his costs of this Motion and of the issue and execution of the said Writ of Sequestration such costs to be taxed on the indemnity basis if not agreed.

The Schedule
[Specify documents read]

Notes

1 In the recital
   (a) delete the inappropriate words, but
   (b) add after the word 'by' at the end of the recital the acts of the defendant found to be contempts of the court. These will probably be set out in the notice of motion.

2 Sequestration is usually directed against public or private companies or their directors, or against unincorporated associations (eg trades unions). For the duties of sequestrators see *Inland Revenue Commissioners v Hoogstraten* [1984] 3 WLR 939.

3 The court usually includes the costs of the issue and execution of the writ of sequestration in its order for costs.

21. DIRECTIONS TO SEQUESTRATORS (SALE OF SEQUESTRATED ASSETS AND PAYMENT BY SEQUESTRATORS OF FINE)

AND IT APPEARING

1 that the real and personal property of the Defendant set forth in the schedule hereto is in the possession of the said Commissioners
2 that the funds in the sum of £... plus any accrued interest held to the order of the Commissioners in an account entitled '...' maintained at ... have been seized by the said Commissioners pursuant to the said Writ of Sequestration

IT IS ORDERED

1 that the said Commissioners be at liberty to sell at the best price obtainable the said property set forth in the Second Schedule hereto or so much of the said property as is equal to the fine of £... directed to be paid to Her Majesty the Queen in the order dated ... contained together with the Plaintiff's costs in that said Order directed to be paid by the Defendant and the costs hereinafter directed to be paid

2 that the said Commissioners shall out of the proceeds of sale pay the said fine and the Plaintiff's said costs and the said costs hereinafter directed to be paid

3 that the fine of £. . . directed to be paid to Her Majesty the Queen in the Order dated . . . contained together with the Plaintiff's costs in that said Order directed to be paid by the Defendant be paid out of the said funds held by the said Commissioners in the said Account

4 that the costs of the said Commissioners of this Motion be taxed on a common fund basis and paid forthwith out of the proceeds of sale of the said property [the said funds held by the said Commissioners in the said Account] or [are to be costs in the sequestration]

5 that the said Commissioners ascertain so far as they are able the costs (if any) which any third parties have incurred by reason of the sequestration of the said property of the Defendant and that such costs be taxed on the indemnity basis and paid forthwith by the said Commissioners to such third parties out of the proceeds of sale of the said property [the said funds held by the said Commissioners in the said Account]

6 that the said Motion shall stand adjourned to . . .

Notes

1 Sequestrators have only the right to detain and hold the property of the contemnor. They must apply to the court for any orders necessary to complete their seizure of the property and for orders of management and sale. It should be noted that the court has no power to order the sale of land except possibly leaseholds although even this is unclear.

2 The form is concerned with sale of assets or payment out of the proceeds of sale or from a fund in order that a fine imposed by the court on the contemnor can be paid. It is for guidance only—the associate should remember that the orders will vary according to each action.

3 The court may, in respect of the order for sale, order the sale of specific assets in which case the order should specify which assets are to be sold. The following is a precedent for this purpose:

( ) that the said Commissioners be at liberty to sell at the best price obtainable [the following property] [the property set forth in the second schedule]

4 The court may make other orders for the seizure or management of the sequestrated assets. The associate must follow the directions of the judge. It should be remembered that the Notice of Motion may be assistance in framing these orders. See also *Seton's Judgments and Orders*, Vol 1, pp 440-454 and *Daniell's Chancery Forms* (7th Edn), pp 337-346.

5   The common form of costs orders is for taxation on the indemnity basis.

6   Third parties who have been affected by the sequestration should be able to recover their costs from the sequestrated assets. This provision is similar to the 'Seatrain undertaking' given by the plaintiff in Mareva injunction orders. If the judge does not make such an order then the associate should mention to him the possibility that such an order can be made.

7   If the court wishes to retain control over the sale of sequestrated assets it will direct that the motion be adjourned to a specific day.

22. DISCHARGE OF A WRIT OF SEQUESTRATION

UPON MOTION made by Counsel for the Commissioners for Sequestration in the Writ of Sequestration ordered by the Order dated ... to be issued
  AND UPON HEARING Counsel for the Plaintiff and for the Defendant
  AND UPON READING the documents recorded on the Court file as having been read and the Affidavits [and Affirmations] specified in the First Schedule hereto

IT IS ORDERED

1   that the said Writ of Sequestration shall stand dissolved

2   that the said Commissioners shall on or before ... lodge in room 165 Chancery Chambers the Royal Courts of Justice Strand London WC2A 2LL their final amounts

3   that the costs charges and expenses of the said Commissioners of the said sequestration including all usual and proper allowances to the said sequestrators in respect of their office including the costs of this motion be taxed on a common fund basis and paid forthwith out of the proceeds of sale of the property of the Defendant by the Order dated ... directed to be sold [the funds held to the order of the said Commissioners in an account entitled '...' maintained at ...]

4   that the said Commissioners ascertain so far as they are able the costs (if any) which any third parties have incurred by reason of the Sequestration of the said property of the Defendant and

Proceedings under Orders and Judgments   223

that such costs be taxed on a common fund basis and paid forthwith by the said Commissioners to such third parties out of the proceeds of sale of the said property [the said funds held by the said Commissioners in the said Account]

5   that the said Commissioners shall withdraw from possession of the property [as specified in the Second Schedule hereto] of the Defendant seized by the said Commissioners pursuant to the said Writ of Sequestration

6   that the said Commissioners shall pay forthwith after the payment of the costs hereinbefore directed to be paid to the Defendant any balances held in their hands and the said funds held by the said Commissioners in the said Account

7   that upon lodging the said Accounts and paying the costs and balances hereinbefore directed to be paid the said Commissioners be released and discharged from all liability in respect of their said office.

Notes

1   Once the contempt has been cleared or once the fine has been paid in the case of sequestration to enforce payment of a fine the sequestrators must apply on motion for their discharge.

2   The form is the normal order which should be made. The court must direct that the sequestrators pass their accounts in Chancery chambers and that the sequestrators pay over any balances remaining after the payment of costs to the contemnor.

3   The common forms of costs orders are for taxation on a common fund basis or the indemnity basis.

4   Third parties who have been affected by the sequestration should be able to recover their costs from the sequestrated assets. This provision is similar to the 'Seatrain undertaking' in Mareva injunction orders. If the judge does not make such an order then the associate should mention to him the possibility that such an order can be made.

23. RELEASE ON BAIL ON GIVING A RECOGNISANCE BY THE COURT OF APPEAL

UPON MOTION for bail to be granted to the defendant pending the hearing of the Appeal made by Counsel for the defendant
   AND UPON HEARING Counsel fot the plaintiff

AND UPON READING the documents recorded on the Court File as having been read

AND IT APPEARING that the defendant (a) was committed by the Order dated ... to ... Prison for his contempt in the said Order mentioned for a period of ... from the date of his apprehension and (b) is in the custody of the Governor of the said Prison and desires to Appeal from the said Order

IT IS ORDERED that the defendant after complying with the conditions specified in the first schedule hereto be released on bail subject to the conditions specified in the second schedule hereto with a duty to surrender to the custody of the tipstaff before the Honourable Mr Justice ... at ... Court Royal Courts of Justice Strand London WC2A 2LL.

The First Schedule
[Conditions to be complied with before release on bail].

The Second Schedule
[Conditions to be complied with after release on bail].

Notes

1 The powers of the Court of Appeal to grant bail may be exercised by a single judge (Ord 59, r 20(8) RSC).

2 The defendant must surrender his bail before the judge who originally committed him unless the order for committal is reversed by the Court of Appeal (Ord 59, r 20(2) RSC).

3 Details of the recognisance and any other conditions to be complied with before the defendant can be released on bail must be entered in the first schedule to the order.

4 If the court imposes conditions to be complied with after release on bail, eg, reporting to a court officer these should be entered into the second schedule. If no such conditions are imposed by the court all reference to the second schedule must be deleted from the order.

24. ENFORCEMENT OF A FORFEITED RECOGNISANCE UNDER S 140(1)(a) OF THE SUPREME COURT ACT 1981

UPON THE COURT'S OWN MOTION
AND UPON HEARING
AND UPON READING the documents recorded in the Court File as having been read

AND IT APPEARING that the defendant (a) was released on bail by the Order of the Court of Appeal dated ... with a duty to surrender to the custody of the tipstaff on this day before this court and (b) has failed to so surrender

IT IS ORDERED

1 that the Recognisance entered into by the defendant details of which are set forth in the first schedule to the said order dated ... be forfeited

2 that ... [as Surety for the defendant] shall pay to Her Majesty the Queen the sum of £. . . being the amount due under the said forfeited Recognisance

3 that the said sum be enforced in like manner as a judgment of the High Court for the payment of money.

Notes

1 The order directing forfeiture may be made by the Court of Appeal (s 140(1) of the Supreme Court Act 1981).

2 The court will move by its own motion to order forfeiture of the recognisance.

3 In the Second Order
   (a) add 'the defendant' if the defendant stood his own recognisance or the name of the person who stood as surety for the defendant and
   (b) enter the sum due under the forfeited recognisance.

4 The Associate must send letters to the following:
   (a) The Exchequer and Audit Department
   (b) The Court Funds Office
   (c) The solicitors for the defendant
   (d) The defendant and any surety who is required to pay the sum due.

5 If the court wishes the sum due under a forfeited recognisance to be enforced under s 140(1)(b) of the Supreme Court Act 1981 the following precedent should be used:
   (a) the recognisance entered into by the defendant details of which are set forth in the first schedule to the said order dated. . .be forfeited
   (b) that. . .[as surety for the defendant] do pay to Her Majesty the Queen the sum of £. . .being the amount due under the said forfeited recognisance

(c) that clerk to the justices of...at...do collect for and on behalf of Her Majesty the Queen the sum due under the said forfeited recognisance from the...

(d) that in default of the...paying the said sum due under the said forfeited recognisance (a) the...magistrates' court do enforce the payment of the said sum and (b) the...do stand committed to prison for a period of...

6 (a) In the Second Order:
(i) add the 'defendant' if the defendant stood his own recognisance *or* the name of the person who stood as surety for the defendant and
(ii) enter the sum due under the forefeited recognisance. The term of imprisonment must not exceed 12 months (s 31(3) of the Powers of Criminal Courts Act 1973) and the surety can be committed to prison for non-payment of the sum due under the forfeited recognisance.
(iii) A copy of the order and the appropriate letter must be sent to the Clerk of the Justices.

Chapter Nine

District Registries

1. District registries

Unrestricted jurisdiction

The eight district registries, referred to (RSC (Amendment No 2) 1982) as Chancery District Registries, of Leeds, Liverpool, Manchester, Newcastle-upon-Tyne, Preston and (added by RSC (Amendment No 2) 1982) of Birmingham, Bristol and Cardiff have almost unlimited Chancery jurisdiction, (but not for probate actions—Ord 76, r 2(1); Ord 4, r 5(4)), that is, they have the same jurisdiction as applies in Chancery chambers at the RCJ in London.

Restricted jurisdiction

There are over 130 district registries of the High Court and these are listed in the District Registries Order 1980 (SI 1980 No 1216) as now read with RSC (Amendment No 2) 1982 (SI 1982 No 1111) and Practice Direction (Chancery Chambers) No 1 of 1982 [1982] 1 WLR 1189. These district registries have restricted Chancery jurisdiction in that while any writ (except a writ in a probate action) may be issued, any originating summons may only be issued where there is specific provision (Ord 7, r 5(2)), or under the Companies Acts. There is specific provision for the following originating summonses to issue:

(1) mortgagees' actions (Ord 88)—the mortgaged property must be within the district of the district registry;
(2) applications under the Landlord and Tenant Acts 1927-1954 (Ord 97, r 3) if the premises are within the district of the registry;
(3) settlements of claims by persons under disability (Ord 80, r 11(3));
(4) applications under the Judicial Trustees Rules 1983 (SI 1983 No 3700);
(5) applications under the Leasehold Property (Repairs) Act 1938, s 1 (Ord 32, r 9(2)); and

(6) applications under the Inheritance (Provision for Family and Dependants) Act 1975 (Ord 99, r 3(1)).

Notices of originating motion (Ord 8, r 35) and petitions (Ord 9, r 3(1)) may only be issued in one of the eight Chancery district registries, unless under the Companies Acts.

If an excepted action is wrongly commenced in a district registry it must (Ord 86, r 3; Ord 4, r 5(4)) be transferred by the district registrar to the RCJ in London.

Rule 17(1) of the Judicial Trustee Rules 1983 (SI 1983 No 370) states that 'notwithstanding any provision contained in the Rules of the Supreme Court an originating summons may be issued out of a district registry for the purpose of an application to appoint a judicial trustee'.

Applications in Chancery Division except the eight provincial Chancery registries

There are numerous practice directions (see Supreme Court Practice 1982, paras 1031 to 1040 AF and Practice Direction, 29 July 1982 [1982] 3 All ER 124).

Jurisdiction of the district registrar

The general jurisdiction of district registrars is contained in Ord 32, rr 23–26. A district registrar has in general the same powers as a master in the High Court in London subject, in the case of the Chancery Division, to any direction given by the Chancery judges to the contrary (Ord 1, r 4(2); Ord 32, rr 14 and 23). No such directions to the contrary have been given, and thus the district registrar has the same powers in his district registry as the Chancery master in London.

Practice and procedure

The practice of the central office in London must be followed in district registries (Ord 63, r 11), but with such variations as the circumstances may render necessary. Whenever any originating or other application or a writ action is to be adjourned or set down for hearing in court, or whenever any application is referred or adjourned (Ord 32, r 12) to the judge in chambers, district registrars must forward to Chancery chambers at RCJ, Strand, London the original sealed copy of the originating process (plus a copy), all the affidavits (and exhibits if with the court) and a schedule of such documents. It follows that as there is no judge except in London or as may be available at a trial centre, usually no orders for summary judgment in actions for specific performance (Ord 86), for new tenancies which are required to be determined by the judge under the Landlord and Tenant Act 1954, or for orders for summary possession of land (Ord 113) can be made at any district registry other than at one of the eight Chancery district registries.

Where the adjournment is to the judge in chambers, the papers are sent, with the district registrar's note to the judge, to the Chief Chancery Master, Secretary to the Chief Master, Chancery Division, Royal Courts of Justice, London WC2A 2LL, who sends them to the appropriate master of the group concerned. Where the adjournment is into court, the papers should be sent to the Chief Chancery Registrar. No fee is payable.

Where a district registrar adjourns a summons (originating or interlocutory) of his own motion to the judge, he may adjourn:

(a) to the judge in chambers;
(b) into court to the non-witness list;
(c) into court to the witness list, part 1 or part 2; or
(d) into court as a procedure summons.

He may refer any matter to a judge under Ord 32, r 12, if he thinks that it should properly be decided by a judge (Ord 32, r 14(2)). Adjournments to the judge in chambers are appropriate where it is a question of some non-controversial matter or almost non-controversial matter which is not expected to last over 15 minutes.

When a summons for summary judgment in an action for specific performance etc under Ord 86 is issued in a district registry, other than at the eight provincial Chancery registries, the district registrar must transfer the action to London of his own motion (Ord 86, r 3).

Adjournment is to the non-witness list where it is a question of a final hearing of some contested matter, but there is to be no cross-examination or the district registrar is satisfied that cross-examination will not subsequently extend the length of the hearing and will not lead to applications to call witnesses.

Adjournment to the witness list, part 2 is appropriate where it is a final hearing of a contested matter with substantial cross-examination, unless the hearing is estimated to last significantly more than three days. In the latter event the adjournment should be to the witness list, part 1. If the matter is adjourned to be heard in the witness list, a certificate as to estimated length of the hearing, signed by counsel for all parties, must be lodged.

There is now no right for a party to have a summons adjourned to a judge. This has been replaced by a right to appeal to a judge in chambers (SI 82/1111) and Practice Direction, 29 July 1982 [1982] 3 All ER 124.

Where the adjournment is to the judge in chambers, the papers are sent with the district registrar's note to the judge, to the Chief Chancery Master, Secretary to the Chief Master, Chancery Division, Thomas More Building, Royal Courts of Justice, London WC2A 2LL, who sends them to the appropriate master of the group concerned.

Where the adjournment is into court, the papers should be sent to the Chief Chancery Registrar. No fee is payable.

Except in the case of the eight provincial Chancery registries, district registrars have no power to take accounts or answer inquiries in actions in the Chancery Division unless the order expressly directs them to do so (see Supreme Court Practice 1982, para 32/23-26/12).

Chapter Ten

County Court Jurisdiction and Transfer of Actions

1. County court jurisdiction

Under the heading 'equity jurisdiction', s 23 of the County Court Act 1984 provides that the county court has all the jurisdiction of the High Court in proceedings for the administration of the estates of deceased persons where the estate does not exceed £30,000 in amount or value—the limit would appear to be the value of the deceased's net estate (see s 22(1) of the Inheritance (Provision for Family and Dependants) Act 1975), for the execution of any trust, for a declaration that a trust subsists, for variation under the Variation of Trusts Act 1958 where the estate or fund subject or alleged to be subject to the trust does not exceed £30,000, for the foreclosure or redemption of any mortgage, for enforcing any charge or lien where the amount owing in respect of the mortgage charge or lien does not exceed £30,000, for specific performance, rectification, delivery up or cancellation of any agreement for the sale, purchase or lease of any property where in the case of a sale or purchase, the purchase money or in the case of a lease, the value of the property, does not exceed £30,000, for the dissolution or winding up of any partnership where the whole assets of the partnership do not exceed in amount or value £30,000, for relief against fraud or mistake where the damage sustained or the estate or fund in respect of which the relief is sought does not exceed £30,000. Section 24 of the Act lists a variety of enactments including the Trustee Act 1925, the Law of Property Act 1925, the Settled Land Act 1925, the Administration of Estates Act 1925, the Leasehold Property (Repairs) Act 1938, the Landlord and Tenant Act 1954, and the Land Charges Act 1972, wherein the parties may agree in writing that the county court shall have jurisdiction.

Besides their general jurisdiction under the 1984 Act, the county courts have special jurisdiction under the Inheritance (Provision for Family and Dependants) Act 1975 and the Landlord and Tenant Act 1954. The county court also has jurisdiction in contentious probate matters where the value of the estate is less than £30,000 exclusive of property or assets vested in the deceased as a bare trustee and after deduction of funeral expenses, debts and encumbrances (s 32 of the 1984 Act).

County court limits now means the limits for the time being as specified by an Order under s 192 of the County Courts Act 1959 as the county court limits for the purpose of the particular enactment.

By s 105(1) of the County Courts Act 1984, a judgment or order of the High Court is enforceable in the county court without an application having to be made to the county court by the party prosecuting the judgment. High Court judgments or amounts exceeding £5,000 may be enforced by charging orders either in the High Court or a county court (County Court Rules, Ord 25, r 11).

The county court may grant injunctions, or make declarations, without any other claim being added, in certain excepted cases, which, for the purpose of 'Chancery' work are (*a*) injunctions or declarations relating to land (when the net annual value for rating is within the county court's jurisdiction) and (*b*) declarations under Part II of the Landlord and Tenant Act 1954. In cases outside these exceptions unless some enactment specifically empowers the granting of an injunction or the making of a declaration, declarations or injunctions may only be claimed or applied for as ancillary to another claim which is within the county court's jurisdiction. The ancillary claim is sometimes founded on damages for trespass to goods, and the ancillary claim may be for an amount which is nominal (see *Hatt & Co (Bath) v Pearce* [1978] 1 WLR 885).

The County Court Rules 1981 (SI 1981 No 1687) as amended which replaced the County Court Rules 1936, are intended to assimilate the rules of procedure in the county court with those of the High Court but there are necessarily many variances in the detailed procedure.

A useful textbook on this subject is: Robert Blackford, *County Court Practice Handbook*, 9th edn, Longman, 1989.

2. Transfer

From county court to High Court—by order of High Court

Whether the proceedings have been commenced in or transferred to a county court the High Court may at any stage, on application or its own motion, order their transfer to the High Court (County Courts Act 1984, s 40). Applications for transfer from a county court can be made by originating summons (Ord 107).

From county court to High Court—by order of county court

When the county court considers that some important question of law or fact is likely to arise or that a counterclaim is beyond the jurisdiction of the county court or a party is 'likely to be entitled' in respect of a claim or counterclaim to an amount exceeding the amount recoverable in the county court then the county court may at any stage, either on its own motion or on applications, transfer the whole or any part of them to the High Court.

The county court may also transfer a county court action to any district registry (Ord 107, r 1(4)).

Applications to the county court to transfer to the High Court or to a district registry may be made at the pre-trial review or by completing a general form of application (County Court Rules, Ord 13, r 1).

Transfer of Chancery business by High Court to county court

In a Practice Direction issued by the Vice-Chancellor on 26 May 1988 (Practice Direction (Chancery) Transfer of Business (1988) 1 WLR p 741), he referred to cases being heard at the right level, and directed that on the summons for directions, the masters would consider whether or not a case was suitable for transfer to a county court under s 40 of the County Courts Act 1984, and unless they raise an important issue of law or fact, the following, among others, are likely to be transferred, namely, applications under s 30 of the Law of Property Act 1925 for new tenancies of business premises under Part II of the Landlord and Tenant Act 1954, under the Inheritance (Provision for Family and Dependants) Act 1975, for the appointment of a judicial trustee, for replacement of personal representatives under s 50 of the Administration of Justice Act 1985, and boundary disputes. When orders are made by the Chancery masters—or indeed by the judge, under s 40, the court will, unless there is a specific request otherwise by the parties, be the Mayor's and City of London Court (where Chancery expertise is concentrated), and on making his order the master will give directions, obviating the necessity of a pre-trial review and the Chancery Registry pre-trial review, and the Chancery Registry will send to the Mayor's and City of London Court, the court file, except when there have been unusually extensive documents, when the sending of the file will have to be initiated by the parties (side subs (7) and (8) of s 40).

When the case is transferred, the parties should send to the Mayor's and City of London Court, or to such other court as the proceedings are transferred to, any further documents not already filed which will be needed for the trial together with information to assist in listing.

The Crown

There is no longer any restriction on making an order for the transfer to a county court of proceedings against the Crown in the High Court without the consent of the Crown (Crown Proceedings Act 1947, s 20(2) as amended by the Supreme Court Act 1981, s 152(4) and Sched 7).

Transfer to district registry; or from registry to London

The place where the cause of action arose or where the defendant resides or carries on business, while relevant to whether any particular process can be issued in the county court, is irrelevant in the district registry. However, when a defendant completes his acknowledgment of service he may thereon apply for a transfer either to London or to a district registry, by completing the relevant section of the acknowledgment (Ord 4, r 5(2)). If he wants to transfer out of London, an order will have to be obtained on the summons for directions. Besides this, any party to a cause or matter proceeding in a district registry (or proceeding at RCJ in London) may apply to the court to transfer such cause or matter, or to transfer any summons or other application therein, to some other district registry or, if not already in RCJ, to the RCJ in London (Ord 4, r 5(1)). Applications to transfer are often made on a summons for directions under Ord 25 or on a summons under Ord 14, but may be made by a general summons issued for that purpose giving at least two clear days notice.

An action issued and pending in a county court may be transferred to any district registry by order (Ord 107, r 1(4)). The application is made by originating summons in the district registry, or by general form of application if in the county court, supported by affidavit.

A district registrar may transfer proceedings in a county court to the High Court, but only if the district for which the county court is held is contained in the district of the registry of which he is registrar (Ord 107, r 1).

Whensoever there is an order transferring an action or matter to a district registry, when the documents are received in the district registry they are filed and the district registrar gives notice to all parties that the action is proceeding in the High Court in the named district registry and that the defendant is required to acknowledge service (Ord 78, r 2).

The district registrar may refer any matter to a judge under Ord 32, r 12 if he thinks that it should properly be decided by a judge (Ord 32, r 14(2)).

Where the adjournment is of a summons to the judge in chambers, the district registrar's note to the judge will accompany the file which will be sent if not to the judge sitting at a trial centre, to the secretary to the chief chancery master, RCJ, London. No fee is payable.

Transfers between one district registry and another, or to and from district registry and the chancery chambers

A master or the district registrar is empowered to order transfer on such terms as he thinks fit.

When a defendant, as he may, applies for an order to transfer when completing his acknowledgment of service, the plaintiff has eight days in which to object to the making of such an order and if no such objection is made, the district registrar or master is likely to make an order in accordance with the defendant's application. On any objection being made by the plaintiff, in district registries, notification of a time and place for the hearing of the application will be sent out (Ord 4, r 5, as amended).

Transfers from one division to another

The court is empowered, pursuant to the Supreme Court Act 1981, s 65 to transfer any cause from one division to another, with, or without, application. Should a party wish to apply, he applies to the division in which the cause is at the time proceeding (Ord 4, r 3). The application is on summons with notice to other parties. It may be supported by affidavit.

Business is allowed to be conducted by post at the district registries accommodated in the same offices as the local county courts where postal facilities are permitted under the County Court Rules. Consent orders, including uncontested orders for directions may be made by post, but the district registrar may decline to make an order for directions without requiring the attendance of the parties.

County Court Jurisdiction and Transfer of Actions—Orders

1. TRANSFER TO HIGH COURT

IT IS ORDERED

1 pursuant to Section 41 of the County Courts Act 1984 that the proceedings commenced in the... County Court the short title and reference to the record whereof is... v... Case No... be transferred from the said County Court to the Chancery Division of this Court

2 that the costs of the said application are to be costs in the said proceedings.

2. TRANSFER TO COUNTY COURT

IT IS BY CONSENT ORDERED

1 that this Action be transferred to the... County Court

2 that the costs incurred in this action in this Court be [costs in the action] [in the discretion of the said County Court].

3. TRANSFER TO OFFICIAL REFEREE

IT IS by consent ORDERED

1 that this Action be tried by an Official Referee

2 that the costs of the said Application are to be costs in the cause.

4. TRIAL BY OFFICIAL REFEREE

THIS ACTION by the Order dated... having been ordered to be tried before an Official Referee and His Honour Judge... being one of the Circuit Judges nominated to deal with official referees' business having tried this Action and having by his Certificate dated... directed that judgment as hereinafter provided be entered for the plaintiff

IT IS ORDERED that the defendant shall pay to the plaintiff £... and his costs of this Action to be taxed if not agreed.

Notes

1 Section 25 of the Courts Act 1971 says that no-one should be appointed to the office of official referee and that such of the circuit judges as the Lord Chancellor may from time to time determine shall discharge the functions conferred on official referees. However Ord 1, r 4(1) of the RSC says that 'Official Referee' means a person nominated under s 68 of the Supreme Court Act 1981 to deal with official referees' business and Ord 36, r 3(2) refers to trial 'by an Official Referee'; hence it is correct to use the expression 'an Official Referee'.

2 By Ord 36, r 3(2) if the court considers that a matter may more appropriately be dealt with by an official referee it may on its own motion order the cause to be tried by an official referee. There is no need to transfer a Chancery action to the Queen's Bench Division but the action is heard in the Chancery Division. By Ord 36, r 3(4) no order for transfer shall be made unless the parties have had an opportunity to be heard on the issue or consented to such an order.

3 A certificate of order is received in Chancery chambers from the official referees' department and this certificate is incorporated in an order of the Chancery Division to enable execution to be effected.

4 Precedent No 2 follows Form No 47 Appendix A Supreme Court Practice.

5. CONSOLIDATION

IT IS ORDERED

1 that the above mentioned Action... be consolidated with the above mentioned Action... and that the two said Actions do proceed as one Action and Counterclaim under the title set forth in the schedule hereto
[that the said Action... do stand as a Counterclaim in the consolidated action]
[that the Counterclaim in the said Action... shall stand as a Counterclaim in the consolidated Action]
[that the plaintiffs in the said Action be the plaintiffs in the consolidated Action and that the plaintiffs in the said Action be the defendants in the consolidated Action which is to be prosecuted under the title set forth in the Schedule hereto]
[that the Statement of Claim served in the said Action... shall stand as the Statement of Claim in the consolidated Action]
that the costs of the said Application be costs in the consolidated Action.

The Schedule

IN THE HIGH COURT OF JUSTICE

1991A
and
1991B

CHANCERY DIVISION

BETWEEN

                                                Plaintiffs

and

                                                Defendants

(Actions consolidated by Order dated . . .)

Notes

1. Order 4, r 9 governs consolidation.
   Two actions cannot be consolidated where the plaintiff in one action is the same person as the defendant in another action unless one action can be ordered to stand as a counterclaim in the consolidated proceedings. All the plaintiffs must be represented by the same solicitor.

2. There is a form of order including various directions on p 41 of Atkin, Vol 39 (1982 issue) and there are notes beginning on p 13.

3. In drafting the order both the full titles of the two or more actions which are being consolidated are set out. The earlier is normally shown first.

4. In drafting the body of the order it is helpful to set out the new title in the schedule.

5. For example in the case of two actions. In one A and B sue M N and O. In the other A and C sue M P and Q. On consolidation the new title would show A B and C as plaintiffs and M N O P and Q as defendants (in that sequence).

6. In one action A B and C sue M. In another M sues A and D. The new title would show the second action as a counterclaim to the first. D would not become a plaintiff but would be a defendant to the counterclaim. Thus

BETWEEN

                                  A, B, C

                                                    Plaintiffs

                                    and

                                     M

                                                        Defendant

(by original Action 1991 . . .)

and BETWEEN

M
Plaintiff
and

A
D
Defendants

(by original Action 1991 ... standing as Counterclaim)
(Actions consolidated by order dated ...)

7 If there is to be a schedule setting out the parties to the consolidated action it is really unnecessary to say in the body of the order who is to be plaintiff and defendant.

6. DE-CONSOLIDATION

IT IS ORDERED that this Consolidated Action be de-consolidated and that the two above mentioned Actions do henceforth proceed as separate Actions [that the Order dated ... shall cease to have effect in so far only as it was thereby directed that the two above mentioned Actions be consolidated and proceed as one Action].

Notes

1 The two forms in the precedent are alternatives.

2 By virtue of Ord 15, r 5 the court has power to de-consolidate actions which have previously been consolidated. See *Lewis & Anr. v Daily Telegraph Ltd* [1964] 2 QB 601.

Chapter Eleven

Appeals

1. Appeals—general

Initially, the Chancery Division was so constituted that all decisions were in effect made by the judge, even though pronounced by the master. Until October 1982, the parties had the right to require the master to adjourn the summons before him to the judge even if a full hearing had taken place. This right was sometimes used to gain tactical advantage, and in any case was often wasteful of time. The rules now equate procedure with that of the Queen's Bench Division, abrogating the right to an adjournment to the judge and providing for an appeal to the judge from the Chancery master.

2. Appeals from the master

Appeals on interlocutory and final orders

There is a right of appeal from the master to a judge in chambers under Ord 58, r 1 as amended (RSC (Amendment No 2) 1982 (SI 1982 No 1111)). The appeal is brought by a notice of appeal, and this is issued out of room 307/308. The appellant opens the appeal, but even if the appeal is against only part of the master's order, the whole of the summons is treated as being before the judge, who will make such order on it as he thinks fit (para 7 of Practice Direction (Chancery: Procedure) No 2 of 1982 [1983] 1 WLR 4). Leave is required to introduce new evidence. This equates with the Queen's Bench Division. Leave, if granted, may be subject to the master ordering that the party applying to introduce the new evidence be ordered to pay costs.

While it may be thought undesirable that an appellant should be allowed to raise entirely new points on his appeal before the judge in chambers, thus putting his case on different grounds, there have already been instances where a judge has so allowed. It could be that a direction will in due course be issued defining the practice.

In a notice of appeal from a decision of a master it is no longer necessary to state the grounds of appeal (para 7 of Practice Direction

No 2 of 1982). Practice Direction (Chancery: Procedure) [1983] 1 WLR 4 is varied accordingly.

Appeals from the master on post-trial orders

Formerly the master gave his 'certificate' when, for example, inquiring into damages and making his assessment, his function being to decide evidence on the facts. It might therefore have been anticipated that under new Ord 44, the judge, on an appeal from the master's order, would have been confined to considering the same evidence, but apparently new evidence may be introduced before him. This situation may not have been anticipated when the new order was framed, and it is possible that a practice note or direction may in due course be issued.

Time within which to appeal from the master

An appeal from the master's decision to the judge in chambers must be issued within five days of the decision (not the service of the order), otherwise leave to appeal must be obtained.

Appeals from the master (or district judge) in proceedings tried by the master or district registrar

The appeal lies direct to the Court of Appeal (ord 58, rr 2 and 3).

3. Appeals from the judge

Order 59 (and the Practice Direction issued by the Master of the Rolls on 18 May 1983) contain the full provisions for all appeals to the court of appeal. If a final judgment is given in open court, no leave to appeal is required, but if an interlocutory order is made, leave either from the judge or the court of appeal must first be obtained.

Whether an order is interlocutory or final depends on the nature of the application, and where in doubt, reference should be made to SCP at 51/1/25 (*see below*). The leave of the judge or Court of Appeal to the bringing of an appeal from an interlocutory order, expressly excepts (*inter alia*) cases of granting or refusing an injunction. When an injunction is granted the court will sometimes suspend its operation pending an appeal. An appellant given leave where leave is required will not necessarily be required to act upon it if subsequently advised not to. Applications can be made after judgment has been given, but apart from other considerations, this will encroach further upon the limited time available in which to lodge an appeal; hence if there is any possibility at all that an appeal might be made, leave should be sought at the time where it is required. Moreover, and as a matter of practical expediency, where leave to appeal is required from the judge and leave is requested immediately following the conclusion of his judgment, the matter will be fresh in the judge's mind, and all the parties will be present. If the judge refuses necessary leave it may be sought from the Court of Appeal. Such leave is applied for by a notice of motion supported by affidavit, which must exhibit the intended notice of appeal.

The appellant has four weeks in which to appeal from the date on which the judgment or order was signed, entered or otherwise 'perfected' if it is an appeal from the final decision of the judge in open court. If the order is made in chambers, and this would include orders made under Ords 14 and 86, the party has 14 days only, commencing from the date when the order (unless this time is abridged or extended by order of the court below, the registrar, the single judge of the Court of Appeal or the Court of Appeal) is 'perfected'—in the Chancery Division this is the date when the order is entered, that is sealed by the court.

Procedure on appeal from the judge

The notice of appeal is to be served on the solicitors for the respondents to the appeal within the time allowed. It may be sent by post, remembering that first class post is deemed to have arrived two days after posting.

The notice of appeal from the judge should comply with Ord 59, r 3 and if it does so, it will both define and confine the area of controversy on the hearing of the appeal, thus saving both time and expense to the parties. It is intended that wherever possible the members of the court will have read the notice of appeal, any respondent's notice and the reasons for the judgment under appeal before the appeal is called on. A properly drawn notice of appeal will enable counsel to come at once to the central issues without any prolonged opening. Failure to give the court this essential assistance by means of a carefully drawn notice of appeal may well lead to special orders being made in relation to time wasted and additional costs incurred (Practice Note 4 October 1982).

The notice of appeal requires the appellant to specify whether he proposes to set down in the final or interlocutory Chancery Division list.

If the appellant is out of time in serving notice of appeal, under Ord 59, r 15 the parties themselves can agree to extend the time, otherwise application for leave must be made to the registrar—'it will only be in exceptional cases that such leave will be granted' (Practice Note of 4 October 1982).

Within 21 days after service of the notice of appeal, the appellant must apply to set it down, and for this purpose the notice of appeal must be lodged either personally, or by post, with the Registrar of Civil Appeals, Court of Appeal accompanied by the following: (*a*) A copy of the order appealed from, (*b*) Two copies of the notice of appeal (on one of these must be certified the date on which the notice of appeal was served; the other copy of the notice will be used for the fee stamp) (Ord 59, r 5).

Having set down within 21 days of service of the notice, then a letter must be sent to the respondent to the appeal stating that the appeal has been set down, within four days of setting down.

Practice direction appearing at 41/11/1 in the Supreme Court Practice requires that within 14 days after the appeal is in the list of forthcoming appeals, three copies of 'core bundles', ie the documents on which the Court of Appeal is going to be asked to hear the case, must be lodged, although there need be only one copy of what is termed the 'main bundle', which is for the judges for reference only. Bundles will have to be made for counsel's use, and for the solicitors and opponents. For requirements as to bundles it is best to use stationery firms who prepare them professionally, unless the solicitors have good facilities themselves. The bundles must contain the notice of appeal, the respondent's notice if any, the order of the court below, the pleadings, and transcripts of the shorthand note or recording of the evidence and a copy of the sealed judgment or order appealed from.

Order 59, r 6(1) enables a respondent, if he so chooses, to contend that the decision of the court below should be affirmed on grounds other than those relied upon, or to contend by way of cross appeal that the decision of the court below was wrong in whole or in part. It must specify the grounds of the contention and the form of the order which it is proposed to ask the Court of Appeal to make. This notice should be served within 21 days of service of the notice of appeal (or seven days if there is an appeal form and interlocutory order) and the respondent is required to lodge two copies of this notice with the Civil Appeals Office, within four days after service.

Forms and precedents

Atkin, Vol 5 (1984 issue).

Skeleton arguments

Where there is a full court application, and in every case of an appeal, four copies of counsel's skeleton argument have to be lodged with the Civil Appeals Office not later than 14 days before the date on which the hearing is due to commence. Furthermore, a copy has to be sent to the opposing counsel at the same time, or before the skeleton argument is lodged.

If the case is assigned to the short warned list, the time is also 14 days which will run from the date when the parties solicitors are notified, which they are by letter, by the Civil Appeals Office that the case has been assigned to the short warned list. Solicitors must therefore be very careful to inform their counsel straight away when they are notified the case has been so assigned.

The sanctions for failure to lodge skeleton arguments in time will be listed in 'the daily cause list'. Any appeal will come before the Master of the Rolls Court for counsel to give an explanation, when the court may make such order or directions as it considers appropriate. This is an automatic listing, on which no notification aside from listing will be given to the defaulting counsel, or for that matter to the solicitors.

A skeleton argument should state points and not argue them—the Court of Appeal is 'wedded to oral argument' (see further Practice Direction issued by the Master of the Rolls on 16 May, 1990).

Distinguishing between final and interlocutory orders

The order is final if it has ultimately determined the proceedings, otherwise it is interlocutory: the test is given in *Salter Rex & Co v Ghose* (1971) 2 AG ER 865 CA. Reference should be made to the SCP at 51/1/25 if there is any query.

4. Leave to appeal

Restrictions on appeals are governed by the Supreme Court Act 1981, s 18 and Ord 59.

No appeal lies:

(1) From any order of the High Court allowing an extension of time for an appeal.
(2) Where the High Court is by statute the final court of appeal.

No appeal lies without the leave of the court:

(1) Against an order for costs.
(2) From a consent order.
(3) From any interlocutory order save:
    (i) where the liberty of the subject or welfare of a minor is concerned.
    (ii) all access to a minor refused.
    (iii) an injunction or the appointment of a receiver is granted or refused.
    (iv) claim of any creditor or liability of any contributory under company law.
(4) From an order of a judge made in chambers (Ord 58, r 6).
(5) From judgment in interpleader proceedings (Ord 58, r 7).
(6) From appeals on cases stated under certain Acts set out in Ord 93, r 10(2).
(7) From an appeal from the Commons Commissioners under s 8 of the Commons Registration Act 1965.

Form of notice of appeal follows below. It should be noted that a certificate as to service upon the respondent's solicitors should be given on the back of the notice.

Form of notice of appeal

Notice of Appeal to Court of Appeal (O. 59, r. 13)

IN THE COURT OF APPEAL   19 . — . — No.
On Appeal from the Buryside County Court

[No. 9123148]

Between

JESSIE SMITH   Plaintiff /Petitioner

AND

MICHAEL MYERS

Defendant /Respondent

NOTICE OF APPEAL

Take Notice that the Court of Appeal will be moved so soon as Counsel can be heard on behalf of the above-named

(1) Insert "decree," "judgment" or "order" as the case may be

on appeal from [the] [so much of the](1)   herein of

His Honour Judge S Ewan, QC

[given] [made] at the trial of this   on the **30th** day

(2) Insert "pronounced" "adjudged" or "ordered" or as the case may be

(3) Set out the decree, judgment or order or that part which is appealed against

of **August**, 1991 [whereby it was] [as](2) Ordered that(3)

(1) There be judgment for the Plaintiff for £17,000

(2) The plaintiff's costs be taxed on scale 3 and paid by the Defendant

(4) State the precise form of order for which the appellant proposes to ask

For an order that(4)   Appeal be allowed and the Plaintiff's claim be held dismissed with costs

(5) Specify the grounds of appeal

And further take notice that the grounds of this appeal are: —(5)

That in holding that the Defendant was within the meaning of Section 27(9)(c) of the Housing Act 1988, entitled to possession, the learned Judge erred in law

Form of notice of appeal

And further take notice that the **Defendant** proposes to apply to set down this Appeal in the County Court Final and New Trials List.

Dated the 30th day of August 1991.

(Signed) Lewis & Co

of 30 Horne St, London SW1

Agent for

of

Solicitor for the Defendant

To the above-named Plaintiffs and to Green & Co of 60 Parkside, London W1

Solicitor or agent.

for the Plaintiff

No notice as to the date on which this Appeal will be in the list for hearing will be given: it is the duty of solicitors to keep themselves informed as to the state of the lists. A respondent intending to appear in person should inform the office of the Registrar of Civil Appeals, Royal Courts of Justice, London WC2A 2LL, of that fact and give his address; if he does so he will be notified by telemessage to the address he has given of the date when the Appeal is expected to be heard.

Appeals—Orders

1. STAY PENDING APPEAL

(1) From judge

IT IS ORDERED

1 that this Order shall not have effect until the expiration of the time for serving Notice from this Order

2 that if such Notice of Appeal is served within that time and the Appeal is prosecuted with all due diligence then this Order shall not have effect until after the said Appeal is disposed of.

(2) From master

IT IS ORDERED

1 that this Order shall not have effect until the expiration of the time for issuing the Notice referred to in Order 58 Rule 1 of the Rules of the Supreme Court

2 that if such a Notice in respect of this Order is issued within that time and the Appeal thereby instituted is prosecuted with all due diligence then this Order shall not have effect until after the said Appeal is disposed of.

Notes

1 There is no standard formula for directing a stay pending appeal and, as always, the draftsman must be careful to draw up the order actually made by the court. Sometimes an undertaking is given to prosecute any appeal with all due diligence. When this happens this goes in the order as an undertaking and should not be made a condition of the stay. Formulas that have been used include 'no steps be taken to carry this order into effect', 'the operation of this order be suspended', 'no steps be taken to enforce this order' and 'execution of this order be stayed'. There is also a form in Atkin, Vol 5 at p 275. There may be subtle differences between these different forms and in *Berliner Industrie bank AG v Jost* [1971] 2 QB 463; [1971] 2 All ER 1519d and [1971] 3 WLR 68H. The Court of Appeal said that it thought that the form directing a stay of execution should receive some attention as it would not prevent garnishee proceedings.

   This Rider has been drafted to meet this point.

2 Sometimes it is not the whole order which is to be 'stayed' and sometimes the order is 'stayed' as regards one party only eg 'the operation of the

said injunction and the said direction and the said inquiry so far as they affect the defendants so appealing...' and 'so far as it directs assessment of damages'.

3 One must remember that the first step in an appeal is the service of the notice of appeal which normally has to be served within four weeks from the date when the order is perfected (Ord 59, r 4(1)). The court can of course make it a condition of the stay that the notice of appeal is served earlier. In view of an amendment to Ord 59, r 15 it seems that the court below can now also abridge the time for appealing. The appellant has to lodge his papers for setting down within seven days after service of the notice of appeal (Ord 59, r 5(1)). Presumably if he failed to do this it could be argued that he was not prosecuting his appeal with all due diligence.

2. ORDER ON APPEAL FROM MASTERS

UPON THE APPEAL of the Plaintiff/Defendant from the Order of the Master dated... pronounced on

AND UPON HEARING Counsel/the Solicitors for the Plaintiff and Counsel/the Solicitors for the Defendant.

AND UPON READING the documents recorded on the Court File as having been read

IT IS ORDERED

1 that the said Order be discharged/affirmed save in so far as but so that the time for... as provided in the said Order be extended so as to expire on...

2 that the said Order be varied so as
or
[THIS COURT being of opinion that the directions in the said Order should in certain particulars be varied but otherwise confirmed IT IS ORDERED that the said Order be discharged [such an order should then set out the whole Order made by the judge]

3 that the Plaintiff/Defendant shall pay to the Defendant/Plaintiff his/her/its/their costs of the said Appeal and of the Application to the Master such costs to be taxed if not agreed
that the costs of the said Appeal and of the Application to the Master are to be borne by the Plaintiff/Defendant in any event
that the costs of the Plaintiff/Defendant of the said Appeal and of the Application to the Master are to be his/her/its/their costs in the cause.

Notes

1 The appeal is under Ord 58, r 1 to the judge in chambers. The notice of appeal is PF 114 and the information required in the form is set out in para 5 of Practice Direction (Chancery: Applications by Post and Telephone) [1983] 2 All ER 541; [1983] 1 WLR 791.

2 The master's order is usually drawn up and remains an effective order until actually discharged or varied on appeal. Any application for a stay of execution should be made to the master at the hearing or subsequently.

3 Sometimes when a judge affirms a master's order the time limits imposed by the master will have passed without those directions being complied with. The associate in court will then ask the judge what the new time limits are to be.

3. ORDER ON APPEAL FROM COMMONS COMMISSIONER

(1) Disputed registration

IT IS ORDERED

1 that the said decision be affirmed
that the said decision refusing to confirm/confirming the registration at Entry Number ... is the Land Section of Register Unit Number ... in the Register of Common Land/the Register of Town and Village Greens maintained by the County Council be discharged [and the said registration be confirmed] [AND THIS COURT DOES refuse to confirm the said registration]

2 that the Appellant/Respondent shall pay to the Appellant/Respondent ... costs of this Appeal to be taxed if not agreed

3 that the Appellant/Respondent be at liberty to appeal from this Order [that the Appellant/Respondent be refused leave to appeal from this Order].

Notes

1 Order 93, r 16 says that proceedings in the High Court under s 14 or 18 of the Commons Registration Act 1965 shall be assigned to the Chancery Division. The rule indicates the procedure under s 18.

2 Order 56 'Appeals etc to High Court by Case stated: General' is relevant to these appeals and particularly rr 7 and 10 of that order. Order 8, r 3(1) prescribes the form of the notice of an originating motion.

APPEALS

3   These notes are concerned with appeals under s 18—not with s 14 (rectification).

4   (a) A brief description of the land should go in the title.
    (b) The reference to the 'Chief Commons Commissioner' may have to be amended.
    (c) If there is more than one respondent it may be that only some of them will have to be referred to in (2) (costs) and (3) (leave to appeal).

5   The express refusal to confirm registration should be used only where a Chancery judge, on an appeal from confirmation of a registration, discharges the registration.

6   Generally, see Atkin, Vol 8 (1990 issue).

(2) Unclaimed land

IN THE MATTER of

and the COMMONS REGISTRATION ACT 1965

UPON A CASE stated by way of
Appeal from the decision dated ... of the
Chief Commons Commissioner
AND UPON HEARING Counsel for ... (hereinafter called the Appellant) and ... (hereinafter called the Respondent)
AND UPON READING the documents recorded on the Court File as having been read

IT IS ORDERED

1   that the said Decision be affirmed
    that the said Decision directing the ... County Council to register ... as the owner of the [above-mentioned] land [described in the Schedule hereto] at Entry Number ... in the Ownership Section of Register Unit Number ... in the Register of Common land maintained by the said County Council be discharged

2   that the said County Council shall register ... as the owner of the said land in the said Register

3   that the Appellant/Respondent shall pay to the Appellant Respondent ... costs of this Appeal to be taxed if not agreed

4   that the Appellant/Respondent be at liberty/be refused leave to appeal from this Order.

Notes

1 A brief description of the land should go in the title. If a conveyancing description is required this should go into a Schedule to the order.

2 The reference to the 'Chief Commons Commissioner' may have to be amended if the appeal is from a Commons Commissioner.

3 The associate must substitute 'The Register of Town and Village Greens' for 'The Register of Common Land' if the appeal relates to land registered in the Register of Town and Village Greens.

4 Paragraph 2 of the Rider is required if the Commons Commissioner's decision is discharged and the court directs another person or body to be registered as owner.

5 If there are more than one respondent it may be that only some of them will have to be referred to in 2 (costs) and 3 (leave to appeal).

4. MAKING ORDER OF HOUSE OF LORDS ON ORDER OF COURT

IT IS ORDERED

1 that the Order of the House of Lords a copy of which is annexed hereto be made an Order of this Court

2 that the defendant/plaintiff shall pay to the defendant/plaintiff costs of the said application to be taxed if not agreed [£ ... being ... assessed costs of the said application.]

Note

1 See Ord 32, r 10 and the note to it.

5. LEAPFROG ORDER

IT IS ORDERED that the said Originating Summons shall stand dismissed with costs to be taxed if not agreed and paid by the plaintiff to the defendant

AND THE COURT CERTIFIES (a) that a point of law of general public importance is involved in the decision of the Court in these proceedings [and that such point of law relates [wholly] [mainly] to the construction of an [enactment] [statutory instrument] and has been fully argued in the proceedings and fully considered in the judgment of the court] [and that such point of law is one in respect of which the judge is bound by a decision of the [Court of Appeal] [the House of Lords] in previous proceedings and was fully considered in the judgments given by the [Court of Appeal] [House of Lords] in those previous proceedings] (b) that a sufficient case for an appeal to the House of Lords under Part II of the Administration of Justice Act 1969 has been made out to justify an application for leave to bring such an appeal and (c) that all the parties to the proceedings consent to the grant of this Certificate.

Notes

1 This procedure is authorised by Administration of Justice Act 1969, s 12.

2 The precedent refers to an originating summons but the procedure is available in an action, originating motion or any other form of proceedings.

3 In drafting the certificate it is necessary to delete one of the two formulas set out in square brackets in clause (a) of the certificate.

4 In the first alternative either 'wholly' or 'mainly' is deleted and either 'enactment' or 'statutory instrument' is deleted.

5 In the second alternative either the words 'Court of Appeal' or 'House of Lords' are deleted.

6. APPEAL FROM MASTER—DISMISSED BY CONSENT

IT IS by consent ORDERED

1 that the Appeal of the Plaintiff/Defendant from the Order of the master dated ... be dismissed with no order as to costs

2 that the Plaintiff/Defendant pay to the Defendant/Plaintiff his/her/its/their costs of the said Appeal such costs to be taxed if not agreed

3 that the costs of the said Appeal are to be borne by the Plaintiff/Defendant in any event

4 that the costs of the Plaintiff/Defendant of the said Appeal are to be his/her/its/their costs in the cause.

Notes

1 On 14 November 1984, Sir Robert Megarry the Vice-Chancellor in the case of *Buckbod Investments Ltd v Nana Otchere* stated: 'It is often possible for an appeal from a Chancery master to be dismissed by consent, without

any hearing by a judge, the practice being for a document signed by the solicitors for all parties to be lodged with the clerk of the lists requesting dismissal of the appeal. After consideration by a judge, the appeal could thereupon be dismissed without any hearing.'

2   This form is designed for such an order.

7. REFERENCE TO EUROPEAN COURT

IT IS ORDERED

1   that the question set forth in the schedule hereto concerning the interpretation/validity of ... be referred to the Court of Justice of the European Communities for a preliminary ruling in accordance with Article 177 of the Treaty establishing the European Economic Community/Article 150 of the Treaty establishing the European Atomic/Energy/Community/ Article 41 of the Treaty establishing the European Coal and Steel Community

2   that all further proceedings in this action be stayed until the said Court of Justice shall have given its ruling on the said question or until further Order in the meantime

3   that the costs of the said Motion are to be costs in the cause.

THE SCHEDULE

REQUEST FOR PRELIMINARY RULING OF THE COURT OF JUSTICE OF THE EUROPEAN COMMUNITIES ... The preliminary ruling of the Court of Justice of the European Communities is accordingly requested on the following question ... Dated the ... day of ... 199 ...

Notes

1   See Ord 114 and notes thereunder and the form of order in para 109 of SCP, Vol II.

2   There will often be a minute of the order.

3   The reference will normally be in accordance with one of the three articles mentioned in the form and the reference to the other two will therefore have to be deleted.

APPEALS ON REVENUE MATTERS

8. ORDER ON CASE STATED BY INLAND REVENUE COMMISSIONERS

UPON A CASE STATED pursuant to Section 56 of the Taxes Management Act 1970 [Section 225 of the Capital Transfer Act 1984] by the Commissioners for the Special Purposes of the Income Tax Acts/ General Purposes of the Income Tax for the ... Division in the County of ...

AND UPON HEARING Counsel for the Appellant and for the Respondent

AND UPON READING the documents recorded on the Court File as having been read including Notices served by the Appellant and the Respondent of points which he/she/it/they intended to take at the hearing

IT IS DECLARED that

THE COURT being of opinion that the determination hereinafter mentioned is [erroneous] [correct]

IT IS ORDERED

1 that the determination of the said Commissioner in respect of which the said Case has been stated (that is to say the determination ... be [reversed] [affirmed] amended so that ... and that accordingly)

2 [that the matter be remitted to the said Commissioners for them to adjust in accordance with the judgment of this Court (a transcript of which is filed with this Order) the assessment made upon the Respondent/Appellant to Income Tax under schedule ... for the year]

3 [that the said Case be remitted to the said Commissioners for them to make further findings of fact as to the following matters that is to say]

4 that the Appellant/Respondent do pay to the Appellant/ Respondent his/her/its/their costs of this Appeal such costs to be taxed if not agreed.

9. ALTERNATIVE ORDERS

1 ... of opinion that the payments mentioned in paragraph ... of the said Case are capital payments

2 ... that the assessments under appeal be varied as follows:

3 ... that the said Case be remitted to the said Commissioners for further findings of fact with regard to the following matters ... unless the parties agree on a supplementary statement of facts in the meantime

4 ... affirms the assessment in the said Case mentioned for each of the years ... in the sums of ... respectively

5 that the assessment for the year ending ... be discharged

6 ... that the matter be remitted to the ... Commissioners ... for the additional assessment made upon the Respondent under schedule ... for the year ended ... in respect of his interest in a Pension Fund created by his employers to be confirmed in the sum of £ ...

7 ... the matter be remitted to the said Commissioners for them to amend the assessment made upon the Appellant under ... so that ...

8 ORDERED (1) that the determination of the ... Commissioners ... that the sum of £ ... in the said Case mentioned was not a premium in respect of a qualifying policy within the meaning of Section ... of the ... be reversed (2) that the assessment made upon the Appellant under schedule E of the said Act for the year ... be amended accordingly.

Notes

1 This precedent is for use where there is an appeal by case stated. The appeal may be from the special commissioners or the general commissioners. The draftsman must amend the opening paragraph accordingly. The general and the special commissioners must not be confused with the commissioners of Inland Revenue who are frequently a party to the appeal.

2 Various types of Revenue proceedings are referred to in Ord 91 (which is concerned with Revenue proceedings in the Chancery Division) but it is understood that perhaps 90 per cent of the Revenue list consists of cases stated under the two statutory provisions already mentioned.

3 Rule 4 of Ord 91 refers to the notices mentioned in the precedent. It is desirable that these notices be mentioned specifically in the order.

4 There are forms in Atkin, Vol 34 (1977 Issue) on p 187 et seq.

5 Section 56(6) says that the court 'shall hear and determine any question

or questions of law arising on the case and shall reverse affirm or amend the determination in respect of which the case has been stated or shall remit the matter to the commissioners with the opinion of the court thereon in relation to the matter as the court may think fit'. The provisions of the Finance Act 1975 are similar.

6   Section 56(7) says that the High Court may cause the case to be sent back for amendment and thereupon the case shall be amended accordingly, and judgment shall be delivered after it has been amended.

7   When the court directs that the case be amended or directs that it be remitted to the commissioners for further findings of fact the signed case is itself sent back to the commissioners and they amend the case or state a supplemental case. On the other hand at the end of the appeal the signed case is retained in the court file. It is usual to state in the order that 'the matter' be remitted.

8   Sometimes the court directs that the matter be remitted to the commissioners 'for them to adjust in accordance with the judgment of this court (a transcript of which is filed with this order) the assessment...' In these cases the practice is not to sign the order until a copy of the transcript is received. The transcript is not 'annexed' to the order and there is no copy to go with the duplicate. The Commissioners of Inland Revenue supply a copy to the commissioners from whose determination the appeal has been made.

9   It is the practice to draw up a separate order for each appeal and to indicate in the order that the appeal was heard contemporaneously with another appeal or appeals when this is the case. The other appeals are then specified in a schedule.

10. DISMISSAL

UPON THE APPLICATION of the Appellant for the dismissal of ... Appeal by case stated pursuant to Section 56 of the Taxes Management Act 1970 [section 225 of the Inheritance Tax Act 1984]

AND UPON READING the documents recorded on the court file as having been read

IT IS ORDERED

1   that the said Appeal shall stand dismissed

2   that the Appellant shall pay to the Respondent... costs of the said Appeal such costs to be taxed if not agreed.

Notes

1 Where an applicant is *sui juris* and does not desire to prosecute a revenue appeal he may lodge at Room 163, Royal Courts of Justice a request signed by his solicitor stating that he is *sui juris* and asking to have the appeal dismissed. The file will be sent to the appropriate judge to initial the order and the order will be drawn up by the drafting section.

2 The order will be for the appeal to be dismissed with costs to be taxed if not agreed and paid by the appellant.

11. DISMISSAL BY CONSENT

UPON THE JOINT APPLICATION of the Appellant and the Respondent for the dismissal of ... Appeal by case stated pursuant to Section 56 of the Taxes Management Act 1970

IT IS BY CONSENT ORDERED

1 that the said Appeal shall stand dismissed

2 that the Appellant shall pay the Respondent's costs of the said Appeal such costs to be taxed if not agreed.

12. APPEAL (S 222 OF INHERITANCE TAX ACT 1984)

UPON THE APPEAL under section 222 of the Inheritance Tax Act 1984 of the Appellant from the determination of the defendants referred to in the Originating Summons

UPON THE APPLICATION under section 222 of the Inheritance Tax Act 1984 of the plaintiff for leave to appeal to this Court from the determination of the defendants referred to in the Originating Summons

AND UPON HEARING Counsel for the plaintiff and for the defendants

AND UPON READING the documents recorded on the court file as having been read

IT IS ORDERED

1 that the plaintiff be refused leave to appeal to this Court from the said determination

2 that the plaintiff do pay to the defendants their costs of the said Application to be taxed if not agreed

THE COURT DECLARES (1) . . .

AND IT IS ORDERED

1 that the said determination be [confirmed] [quashed] [varied] so that

2 that the plaintiff/defendants do pay to the plaintiff/defendants . . . costs of the said Appeal (including the costs of the application for leave to appeal to this Court) to be taxed if not agreed.

Notes

1 Section 221 of the Inheritance Tax Act 1984 states that when the Board (the Commissioners of Inland Revenue) think that a person is liable to Inheritance Tax they may serve a notice on him stating that they have determined the matters specified in the notice.
    Section 222(1) states that he can then appeal 'against any determination specified in the Notice' by giving notice in writing to the Board.

2 Appeals are normally heard by the special commissioners but s 222(3) says 'where it is so agreed between the appellant and the Board, or the High Court, on an application made by the appellant, is satisfied that the matters to be decided on the appeal are likely to be substantially confined to questions of law and gives leave for that purpose, the appeal may be to the High Court'.

3 Order 91, r 2 lays down the procedure for an appeal to the High Court and states that 'the appeal must be brought by originating summons'.

4 See form of order in Atkin, Vol 34 (1977 Issue) at p 205 and there are notes on p 117.

5 Order 91, r 2(5) states 'the originating summons shall be in Form No 10 in Appendix A'. Form No 10 uses the words 'plaintiff' and 'defendant' and so these words are used in the precedent although they seem inappropriate to an appeal.

6 These appeals follow the normal originating summons procedure. They come before the master who, when he is satisfied that the evidence is complete, adjourns them into court for hearing by the judge.

7 The words 'confirmed' 'quashed' and 'varied' are to be found in para 9(5) of the schedule. The word 'quashed' is not often used in Chancery but it has been used in this type of order.

13. PENALTY APPEAL

UPON THE APPEAL under [Section 53] [100] of the Taxes Management Act 1970 [section 249(3) and section 251(2) of the Inheritance Tax Act 1984] of the Appellant from the decision on ... 199 ... of the First Respondents awarding a penalty in the sum of £ ...

UPON HEARING Counsel for the Appellant and for the Second Respondents the Court not requiring the First Respondents to be represented

AND UPON READING the documents recorded on the court file as having been read

IT IS ORDERED

1   that the decision of the said Commissioners be confirmed/reversed

2   that the said penalty be increased/reduced to ...

3   that the Appellant/Second Respondents do pay to the Appellant/ Second Respondents his/her/its/their costs of the said Appeal to be taxed if not agreed.

Notes

1   This precedent applies to appeals
    (1)   Under s 53 of the Taxes Management Act 1970.
    (2)   Under s 100 of that Act.
    (3)   Under s 249(3) of the Inheritance Tax Act 1984.
    (4)   Under s 251(2) of that Act.
    The necessary deletions must be made to the opening paragraph so that it is clear under which provision the appeal is made.

2   Order 91, r 5 applies to those appeals which have to be commenced by notice of originating motion.

3   The first respondents are the special or general commissioners who imposed the penalty and the order should contain the statement in the precedent 'the Court not requiring the First Respondents to be represented'.

4   Section 53(2) says '... on any such appeal the court may either confirm or reverse the decision of the Commissioners or reduce or increase the sum awarded'. Hence the use of the words 'confirmed' and 'reversed' in this precedent. The other provisions are similar.

14. STAMP DUTY APPEAL

UPON A CASE STATED by the Respondents pursuant to Section 13 of the Stamp Act 1981
AND UPON HEARING Counsel for the Appellant and for the Respondents
AND UPON READING the documents recorded on the Court File as having been read including a Notice served by the Appellant and the Respondents of points which ... intended to take at the hearing
THE COURT DECLARES that the instrument described in the schedule hereto is not chargeable with any stamp duty
AND THE COURT ASSESSES the duty with which the instrument described in the schedule hereto is chargeable with stamp duty at £ ...

IT IS ORDERED

1 that the excess of duty paid in conformity with the assessment of the Respondents together with the fine penalty paid in consequence thereof be repaid to the Appellant together with interest ...

2 that the Appellant/Respondents do pay to the Appellant/Respondents their costs of this Appeal to be taxed if not agreed.

The Schedule

Notes

1 This precedent is intended for use in connection with appeals under s 13 of the Stamp Act 1981. The procedure is very similar to that for the appeals by case stated under s 56 of the Taxes Management Act 1970 but there are some differences. The 'special' and 'general' Commissioners are not concerned and the Commissioners of Inland Revenue are always the respondents. There is a form of order on p 207 of Atkin, Vol 34 (1977 Issue), a table on p 165 and notes on pp 118 and 124 et seq.

2 Section 13 is as follows:
   (1) Any person who is dissatisfied with the assessment of the Commissioners may, within twenty-one days after the date of the assessment, and on payment of duty in conformity therewith, appeal against the assessment to the High Court of the part of the United Kingdom in which the case has arisen, and may for that purpose require the Commissioners to state and sign a case, setting forth the question upon which their opinion was required, and the assessment made by them.
   (2) The Commissioners shall thereupon state and sign a case and deliver the same to the person by whom it is required, and the

　　　　case may, within seven days thereafter, be set down by him for hearing.
　(3)　Upon the hearing of the case the court shall determine the question submitted, and, if the instrument in question is in the opinion of the court chargeable with any duty, shall assess the duty with which it is chargeable.
　(4)　If it is decided by the court that the assessment of the Commissioners is erroneous, any excess of duty which may have been paid in conformity with the erroneous assessment, together with any fine or penalty which may have been paid in consequence thereof, shall be ordered by the court to be repaid to the appellant...'

3　Section 91 of the Finance Act 1965 provides that where under s 13(4) of the Stamp Act 1981 the court orders any sum to be repaid by the Commissioners the court may order it to be repaid with such interest as the court may determine.

4　The instrument may be described in the schedule as 'A Conveyance made between AB of the one part and CD of the other part'.

Chapter Twelve

Bundles of Documents; Affidavits; Exhibits

1. Bundles

When bundles are required

The documents and correspondence intended to be read or referred to at any trial or appeal should be bundled and presented as follows. In appeals, the documents which are peripheral and intended only to be referred to in passing (which are often greater in quantity than the documents on which the case turns) may be bundled separately, so that the crucial documents will form a 'core bundle', of which three bundles are required for the Civil Appeals Office (or two only in the case of a two judge court), together, of course with copies for the other side, counsel and solicitors. One bundle of documents for reference only is sufficient. It seems no more than a guideline, but if there are more than 100 documents, the method of bundling the core bundles and a main bundle separately, should be adopted.

The presentation of bundles

Bundles must be firmly secured, in chronological order (earliest on top) and paged consecutively at the centre bottom. Pages which are not easily legible because they are in manuscript should be retyped and inserted under the illegible manuscript or document and renumbered 1A, 2A, 3A, etc. The bundle should be indexed at the beginning. The services of specialised stationery firms are best employed for binding, unless the solicitors have very good facilities themselves.

Transcripts of evidence and transcripts of judgments

These are not to be bound up with other documents but are to be kept separate. However, if it is an appeal from the county court, the ruling differs, and photocopies of the judge's notes of evidence and of his judgment *must* be included in the bundles—the Civil

Appeals Office's notes excepts notes of judgment where these were tape recorded, and it appears that strictly these should be separate, even though they are in the County Court, and not be put in the main Bundle.

When to lodge with the court

(a) On appeals Within 14 days of the appeal coming into the 'list of forthcoming appeals'. This could well be only about a month from setting down the appeal, giving only around six weeks from setting down; therefore preparation of these bundles should have been started well in advance.

(b) On trials The High Court requirement appears to be only two working days before the hearing, but obviously much longer is desirable for the judge to look at them, particularly when the case is going to be effective. In the county court, by virtue of the County Court (Amendment No 3) Rules 1990, r 12(3) it is now necessary to lodge an indexed bundle at least seven days before the hearing.

Indexes

In all cases, trials and appeals, a copy of the index should be sent to opponents. The Civil Appeals Office says that when bundles are ready for lodging, the appellant's solicitors 'must immediately' serve a photocopy of the index.

Agreed bundles

What the bundles are to contain is generally agreed; if not, there will be a plaintiff's or appellant's bundle and a defendant's or respondent's bundle; (in Family Division, it seems usual for there always to be separate petitioner's and respondent's bundles, as a matter of practice).

2. Affidavits

Marking

At the top right hand corner of the first page of every affidavit, and also on the back sheet, there must be written in clear permanent dark blue or black marking:

(1) the party on whose behalf it is filed;
(2) the initials and surname of the deponent;
(3) the number of the affidavit in relation to the deponent; and
(4) the date when sworn.

For example—Filed on behalf of the Plaintiff J Snooks, 3rd affidavit sworn: 5 December, 1990.

Binding

Affidavits must not be bound with thick plastic strips or anything else which would hamper filing.

Form

Rules as to form are given in Ord 41, r 1 paras 4–8. The first person must be used and the place of residence of the deponent and his occupation be given; if he is employed by a party, this must be stated. All affidavits should be in book form on A4 paper following continuously from page to page and, whether or not both sides of the paper are used, the typed or written pages must be numbered consecutively. Every affidavit must be divided into numbered paragraphs, each paragraph being as far as possible confined to a distinct part of the subject or covering a distinctive period in the narrative. The affidavit should be typed (or written) in black ink with double spacing between lines. Dates, sums, and other numbers must be expressed in figures and not words.

Every affidavit must be signed by the deponent or deponents. The jurat must not be on a separate page, it must be completed and the signature of the commissioner must be decipherable, whether by rubber stamp or otherwise. The affidavit may be made jointly by two or more deponents (Ord 41, r 2).

The expression 'and/or' must not be used in Chancery Division affidavits (Practice Note [1940] WN 155).

Where an affidavit is being used in interlocutory proceedings it may contain hearsay but, if so, must indicate what parts of it are statements of information or belief giving the sources of the information and the grounds for the belief. While affidavits may aver that the deponent has been advised of and verily believes the statement, they should not contain specific reference to opinions which the deponent may have been given.

Generally speaking, leave is required to file an affidavit containing any interlineation, erasure or alteration unless this has been initialled; leave may be given for the filing of an affidavit notwithstanding any irregularity in its form (Ord 41, r 4). Where all evidence is given by a witness who has been a deponent to an affidavit, it is common practice in cross-examination to put his affidavit to him, and to draw attention to inconsistencies.

Headings in affidavits

These are shortened so that if the action itself is entitled in more than one matter, it is sufficient to state in the title to the affidavit the first matter followed by the words 'and other matters', and similarly '*A, B and C v D, E and F*' may be shortened to '*A and others v B and others*'. The indorsement on the affidavit and the indorsement on its exhibits may be even further shortened, eg '*in re Luke deceased Smith v Brown*'. Where an action is intituled 'In the matter of ... and in the matter of ...' the intitulement to the affidavit should read: 'In the matter of ... and other matters'.

Office copies

'Office copies' of affidavits are admitted as if they were originals but office copies of affidavits are normally no longer required for use either in court or in chambers, and para 1 of Practice Direction (Affidavit Evidence) [1969] 1 WLR 974 (apart from the last sub-paragraph) has been revoked. If office copies of an affidavit are required, they may be obtained from room 307/308.

Reading of affidavits in court or chambers

In actions begun by originating summons, motion or petition, evidence may be given by affidavit unless the court or statute otherwise directs. If it is desired that deponents to affidavits should attend for cross-examination, application should be made for an order that the applicant be at liberty to cross-examine the deponents named (in a schedule to the order if necessary). The order may contain a term that the party do produce the deponent or otherwise be not at liberty to read his affidavit without leave.

In actions begun by writ if in the circumstances of the case the court, usually on application, thinks it reasonable to so order, it may order the affidavit of any witness to be read at the trial.

3. Exhibits

General rules

(1) Exhibit the **original** deeds and documents if they are available except in mortgage possession cases (Ord 86) when only a copy of the mortgage should be exhibited.
(2) However, clearly legible photographic copies of original documents may be exhibited instead of the originals, provided that the originals are made available for inspection by the other parties before the hearing and by the judge at the hearing.
(3) When original letters or original letters and copies of replies are exhibited as one bundle, the exhibit must have a front page attached stating that the bundle consists of so many original letters and so many copies. The letters and copies must be arranged in sequence and paged.
(4) Court documents, such as probates, letters of administration, orders, affidavits or pleadings should never be exhibited. Office copies of such documents prove themselves.

(5) In the case of births, deaths and marriage certificates, where these certificates merely prove the devolution of a fund in court or change of trusteeship, or where they are required to prove a claimant or to prove identity in order to carry on proceedings, then they can be merely produced. Only for other purposes is it necessary to exhibit them so as to become admissible in evidence.

(6) Any document which the court is being asked to construe or enforce, or the trusts of which it is being asked to vary, should be separately exhibited, and should not be included in a bundle with other documents. Any such documents should bear the exhibit mark directly, and not on a flysheet attached to it.

Marking; numbering

(1) Every exhibit should have indorsed on it the short title of the proceedings. They should be marked, if possible, as on the affidavit, with the words:

'This is the Exhibit marked "AB1" referred to in the Affidavit of AB sworn before me this ... day of ... 199 ..'

'A Solicitor/Commissioner for Oaths' should be written or typed on the original copy document unless this is impracticable, when a fly sheet may be used.

(2) Where a number of documents are contained in one exhibit, a front page must be attached setting out a list of the documents, with dates, which the exhibit contains, and the bundle must be securely fastened. The traditional method of securing is by tape, with the knot sealed (under the modern practice) by means of wafers; but any means of securing the bundle (except by staples) is acceptable, provided that it does not interfere with the perusal of the documents and it cannot readily be undone.

Exhibits must not be bound up with or otherwise attached to the affidavit itself.

(3) Any exhibit containing several pages must be paged consecutively at centre bottom.

Where a deponent deposes to more than one affidavit to which there are exhibits in any one matter, the numbering of such exhibits should run consecutively throughout, and not begin again with each affidavit.

(4) Where, by the time of the hearing, exhibits or affidavits have become numerous, they should be put in a consolidated bundle, file or files, and be paged consecutively throughout in the top right hand corner—affidavits and exhibits being in separate bundles of files.

Legibility

It is the responsibility of the solicitor by whom any affidavit is filed to ensure that every page of every exhibit is fully and easily legible. In many cases photocopies of documents, particularly of telex messages, are not. In all cases of difficulty, typed copies of the illegible document (paged with 'a' numbers) should be inserted.

Forms and precedents

Atkin, Vol 37 (1990 issue).

Chapter Thirteen

Costs

1. Liability

In determining where the costs shall lie, the court makes orders in one or other of the following standard forms:

Term	Effect
'Costs' (the party entitled is designated)	(1) Where this order is made in interlocutory proceedings, the party in whose favour it is made shall be entitled to his costs in respect of those proceedings whatever the outcome of the cause or matter in which the proceedings arise; and (2) where this order is made at the conclusion of a cause or matter, the party in whose favour it is made shall be entitled to have his costs taxed forthwith.
'Costs in any event' (the party entitled is designated)	The party required to pay is to do so whether he eventually wins or loses the actual case. The party who has the right to these costs will include them in his bill and is entitled to recover them even if he loses.
'Costs in the cause' or 'costs in application'	The party awarded such costs can recover these costs if he is successful and if he loses the case he will not have to pay his opponent's costs covered by the order.

'Plaintiff's costs in the cause' or 'Defendant's costs in the cause'	The plaintiff or defendant, as the case may be, shall be entitled to his costs of the proceedings in respect of which such an order is made if judgment is given in his favour in the cause or matter in which the proceedings arise, but he shall not be liable to pay the costs of any other party in respect of those proceedings if judgment is given in favour of any other party or parties in the cause or matter in question.
'Costs thrown away' (the party entitled is designated)	Where proceedings, or any part of them, have been ineffective, or have been subsequently set aside, the party in whose favour this order is made shall be entitled to his costs of those proceedings, or that part of the proceedings, in respect of which it is made (RSC Ord 62, r 3(6)).

Costs reserved

This is an order made before the final order so that the decision as to what order should be made is left until an order is applied for on any subsequent hearing. Unless applied for, the costs will be lost.

Plaintiff's/defendant's costs

The party who has been awarded such costs may recover them. An order in this form is usually made on a final hearing.

Plaintiff's/defendant's costs of the day

This order awards plaintiff's/defendant's costs in any event incurred by a hearing.

Costs on claim and counterclaim

Where the issues 'are very much interlocked' or wherever the counterclaim is a set off the court may be asked to give a single judgment for the balance between claim and counterclaim and may make a special order for costs (Ord 15, r 2(4)). If claim and counterclaim are both successful, the plaintiff may be given his costs on his judgment for his claim less the counterclaim but disallowed the costs of his defence to the counterclaim. In other cases, and where both claim and counterclaim are successful, or both fail, there should be two judgments and two orders for costs. The taxing officer then treats the claim as if it stood alone and allows as costs of the counterclaim only the amount by which the costs have been increased by reason of the counterclaim (see generally AP, Vol 1 62/9/9 and 62/9/13).

Plaintiff's/defendant's costs thrown away

This order is particularly applicable to orders setting aside judgments or other wasted applications. It has the effect of awarding plaintiff's/defendant's costs in any event for all items of work in and incidental to the application.

Order that unsuccessful defendant pay costs of successful co-defendant direct

A 'Sanderson order' (*Sanderson v Blyth Theatre Co* [1903] 2 KB 533 CA) may be made; alternatively, the court may order that the plaintiff pay the successful defendant's costs, and so add such costs to his own, all to be paid by the unsuccessful co-defendant in what is known as a 'Bullock order' (*Bullock v London General Omnibus Co* [1907] 1 KB 264 CA). Such orders are in the discretion of the court and only apply where the action has been founded in contract or in tort (AP, Vol 1 62/2/39).

No order as to costs

The court may expressly decline to make any order for costs, in which case each of the parties must bear their own costs.

Legal aid taxation

The court has no power to refuse to make an order for legal aid taxation as the costs payable out of the legal aid fund do not belong to the legally aided party but to his solicitor and counsel (Legal Aid Act 1988).

One or other of the above orders should be obtained on any hearing or appointment. If the order is for costs to be reserved, then those costs must be dealt with specifically either on or before any final order, as otherwise they will be disallowed on taxation against a paying party (AP, Vol 1 62/4/5).

Discretion

The court has an absolute discretion as to the award of costs (Supreme Court Act 1981, s 51(1)), but, except in the family division, the general rule is that costs should follow the event. If the court, in the exercise of its discretion sees fit to make any order as to the costs of any proceedings the court shall follow the event except where it appears to the court that some other order should be made as to the whole or any part of the costs (RSC Ord 62, r 3(2) and (3)).

The absolute nature of the discretion was explained in *Campbell (Donald) & Co v Pollock* [1027] AC 732 at 804:

> A successful defendant has a reasonable expectation of obtaining an order for payment of costs by the plaintiff; but he has no right to costs unless and until the court awards them to him, and the court has an absolute and unfettered discretion to award or not to award them. This discretion must of course be exercised judicially, and the judge ought not to exercise it against the successful party except for some reason connected with the case.

A successful plaintiff may similarly expect an order for costs against the defendant. The judicial process may amount to awarding costs in such way or in such proportions as the court thinks fair. Success is one factor in the exercise of the court's discretion but there are other factors, for example oppressive or vexatious conduct, conduct inducing proceedings, an unnecessary action or an excessive claim, as well as the nature of the proceedings themselves.

The court, in exercising its discretion as to costs, shall consider, or take into account:

(1) Any offer of contribution brought to its attention in accordance with Ord 12, r 7.
(2) Any payment of money into court and the amount of such payment.
(3) A written order, for example, to consent in specific terms to an injunction or declaration, provided that the court shall not take such an offer into account if, at the time it was made, the party making it could have protected his position as to costs by means of payment into court (RSC Ord 62, r 9(d)).
(4) In the case of an assisted person, the effect of s 8(1)(e) of the Legal Aid Act 1974. The discretion of the court to award costs against an assisted person is limited by the section to the amount (if any) which is reasonable for him to pay having regard to all the circumstances, including the means of all the parties, and of their conduct in connection with the dispute. Before the amount of any costs which might be awarded against an assisted person can be decided, his means must be determined (Legal Aid Regulations 1989). Regulations set out the criteria and procedure for determining means in such circumstances and provide protection in respect of costs for next friends or guardians of assisted minor or patient.
(5) The court may award a specific proportion of taxed costs from or up to a specified stage of the proceedings or a specified sum (RSC Ord 62, r 7(4)).

(6) The court has no power to refuse to make an order for legal aid taxation (Legal Aid Act 1974, s 10(1) and 2A).
(7) The costs rules contained in Ord 22, r 14 give statutory recognition to 'Calderbank' or *'Cutts v Head'* letters. It is to be noted that a 'Calderbank' letter does not apply against a party legally aided; in any case, any letter must be sent within 14 days of and a copy should be sent to the Supreme Court Taxing Office (Room 294), Royal Courts of Justice, Strand, London WC2A 2LL, or if the proceedings have been in the County Court, to the County Court Registrar.

2. Bases

There are two bases of costs:

The standard basis

On this basis, a reasonable amount is to be allowed in respect of all costs reasonably incurred, any doubt as to the reasonableness of incurrence or amount being resolved in favour of the payer.

The standard basis applies (unless otherwise ordered):

(1) where one party to a proceedings is ordered to pay another party's costs;
(2) where an order is made for payment of costs out of any fund (including the Legal Aid Fund); or
(3) where no order for costs is required—the court may order the indemnity basis in any of these cases (RSC Ord 62, r 3(3) and (4)). No order is required where a payment into court is accepted and in the other cases set out in RSC Ord 62, r 5.

The indemnity basis

On this basis all costs are allowed unless they are of an unreasonable amount or have been unreasonably incurred, any doubt being resolved in favour of the payee.

If neither basis is specified, costs are taxed on the standard basis (RSC Ord 62, r 12).

The indemnity basis applies (unless otherwise ordered):

(1) to the costs of a trustee or personal representative (RSC Ord 62, r 14(1));
(2) to a solicitor's bill to his own client (save for a Legal Aid taxation) (RSC Ord 62, r 15(1));
(3) to the costs of a minor or patient (RSC Ord 62, r 16).

Despite the rules of court limiting the bases on which orders for costs may be made, the court may in its discretion order costs on any basis (*EMI Records Ltd v Ian Cameron Wallace Ltd and Another* [1982] 3 WLR 245).

3. Costs on claim and counterclaim

(1) Where the claim succeeds and the counterclaim fails, or vice versa, judgment is entered for the plaintiff (or defendant) on both claim and counterclaim with a likely order for costs on claim and on counterclaim on the appropriate scale or scales;
(2) where the claim and the counterclaim are both wholly, or both partially, successful, or where both fail, there should generally be two judgments with, if appropriate, a final set-off as to damages and two orders for costs, with a final set-off after taxation. The registrar on taxation will then treat the claim as if it stood alone, and allow as costs of the counterclaim only the amount by which the costs have been increased by reason of the counterclaim.

Giving two separate judgments in favour of the plaintiff and the defendant respectively and making two orders for costs may, however, be unjust for cases where the issues on the claim and the counterclaim are substantially the same or 'are very much interlocked', or wherever the counterclaim is a set-off. For example, this might apply in a road collision case, where often the only different issues are the damages themselves as claimed by the respective parties. In these cases, the principles in *Medway Oil and Storage Co v Continental Contractors* [1929] AC 88 apply and the plaintiff will be allowed the full costs of proving the common issues as to liability, and as to his damages, whilst the defendant will be allowed only the costs of proving his damages. For instance, a defendant may be given a net judgment in his favour where he is awarded 50 per cent of, say, £6,000 on his counterclaim, and the plaintiff 50 per cent of, say £2,000 on his claim, which, on set-off, provides for a net judgment of £2,000 in favour of the defendant. In such a case it may be put to the court that it should exercise its discretion as to costs with consideration for the results of the order so as to avoid an incongruous outcome, and that an order might properly be made so that costs are awarded to the party who in effect succeeds after a set-off is made in respect of the damages. The scale applicable would then be the scale appropriate to the net balance recovered; in the example given above, costs for the defendant on scale 2 on his net judgment of £2,000.

An unsuccessful defendant may be ordered to pay the costs of a successful co-defendant direct (a 'Sanderson order' from the case *Sanderson v Blyth Theatre Co* [1903] 2 KB 533, CA). Again, the court may order that plaintiff to pay the successful defendant's costs, and to add such costs to his own, all to be paid by the unsuccessful co-defendant (a 'Bullock order' from *Bullock v London General Omnibus Co* [1907] 1 KB 264, CA). Such orders are in the discretion of the court.

4. Stage of proceedings at which costs to be taxed

Generally the costs of any proceedings shall not be taxed until the conclusion of the cause or matter in which the proceedings arise. However, if it appears to the court when making an order for costs that all or any part of the costs ought to be taxed at an earlier stage it may order accordingly unless the person against whom the order for costs is made is a legally aided person (Ord 13, r 1(9) and RSC Ord 62, r 8(1) and (3)).

In an action in which provisional damages are awarded under RSC Ord 29, Part II the conclusion of the cause or matter is construed as a reference to the conclusion of the proceedings in which the provisional damages are awarded, notwithstanding the possibility that the plaintiff may claim further damages at a future date.

Lastly, where it appears to a taxing officer on application that there is no likelihood of any further order being made in a cause or matter he may tax forthwith the costs of any interlocutory proceedings which have taken place (Ord 38, r 1(3) and RSC Ord 62, r 8).

Procedure on taxation in the Supreme Court Taxing Office

The procedure for taxation of a bill is set out in Ord 62, rr 21-27. The judgment, order or direction of the court or other document (Ord 62, Appendix 1) under which costs are to be taxed must be referred (by producing it or sending it by post), to the Supreme Court Taxing Office (room 294 on the second floor of the central block of RCJ). The Masters' Practice Notes 1979 (AP, Vol 1 62/A2/34-45E) contain detailed directions as to the form of the bill and a list of the relevant papers which must be lodged in support of the bill, setting out the order in which they should be arranged.

In district registries a preliminary inquiry should be made as to the practice to be followed in the particular registry.

The time limit for taking a reference is three months from the date of the judgment or order etc, except in the case of a taxation under the Solicitors Act 1974 when it is seven days from the date of the order. The bill and supporting papers must be lodged at the time when the reference is taken, unless it is impracticable to do so. If the party entitled to take the reference does not do so within the proper time then in order to prevent delay any other party to the proceedings may apply to take the reference using a copy of the judgment or order. (AP, Vol 1 62/21/1).

Delay in taking out a reference may mean that the costs of taxation (item 12(*a*)) may be disallowed or reduced and unreasonable or unconscionable delay in taxation which prejudices any other party may result in the whole bill being disallowed. It follows that as soon as possible after obtaining the judgment or order etc, on which a bill is to be taxed steps should be taken to put the necessary papers in order and to draw the bill. Many solicitors employ costs draftsmen, who are usually members of the Association of Law Costs Draftsmen, to prepare their bills and some also employ the draftsmen to attend taxations on their behalf. It should be borne in mind that solicitors remain fully responsible for the figures in their bills and particularly for statements of fact employed, as a draftsman is always treated by the Taxing Office as a member of the staff of the solicitor whose bill he draws and also when he attends the taxation. In cases where the bill is large or complicated or there are matters affecting the sums claimed which may require detailed explanation, it is always desirable that the partner or other fee-earner who had the actual conduct of the litigation should attend the taxation personally, whether or not he is accompanied by the draftsman.

The officer who issues the reference is called the rota clerk, who determines the identity of the taxing officer who will conduct the taxation, by ballot. In addition to being satisfied that everything is in order to enable the reference to be taken, the rota clerk will require to know which class of taxation is being applied for. Bills which do not exceed £100 in amount are classed as 'short and urgent' and are dealt with by a simplified procedure. Bills which do not exceed £2,000 in amount (excluding bills taxed under the Solicitors Act 1974) are taxed by Senior Executive Officers in the Taxing Office and are classed as 'SEO taxations' (Ord 62, r 13). All other bills are taxed by the taxing masters and are classed as 'masters' taxations'. A solicitor may object to his bill being taxed by an SEO, provided he does so before the taxation has begun, and may then require a masters' taxation.

Short and urgent taxations, in practice are referred to the Chief Clerk. SEO and masters' taxations are referred to the taxing officer to whom they have been allocated in the ballot. The rota clerk carries out separate ballots for masters and SEOs and it is the responsibility of the solicitor to ensure that he applies for the correct reference. If there has been a previous reference in the same matter within the past four years this fact must be disclosed by the solicitor, in which case there is no ballot but the bill is referred to the taxing officer who dealt with the previous reference or his designated successor.

In SEO taxations the bill and papers are processed by the SEO himself. In masters' taxations they are first processed by an Executive Officer (EO) or Higher Executive Officer (HEO), who will communicate with the solicitors if any queries arise at this stage. Some queries may simply be marked on the bill and must then be dealt with on the taxation. The bill is then normally returned to the solicitors with an appointment for the taxation indorsed on it.

Appointments can usually be varied if necessary to suit the convenience of the parties. In some cases, instead of the bill being returned, it is retained by the taxing officer and an appointment is given by letter in which attention will be drawn to any queries which will be required to be dealt with at the taxation.

Following the taxation, the bill must be completed, that is totalled, and there must be added as a disbursement a sum equivalent to VAT at the appropriate rate on the amount of the profit costs in so far as the tax is not deductible as input tax by the receiving party (AP, Vol 1 62/22/4). The taxing officer will sign a certificate of the total amount allowed, distinguishing between disbursements, counsel's fees, profit costs and VAT. Before such certificates can be issued, all disbursements including counsel's fees (except in legal aid cases) must be vouched for by producing receipts. Instead of receipts for disbursements which individually do not exceed £100 a certificate signed by the receiving party's solicitor to the effect that all such disbursements have been paid will normally be accepted.

In legal aid cases, the solicitor may lodge his bill for taxation either on an order for taxation, or on a notice of discharge or revocation under reg 84 of the Legal Aid (General) Regulations 1980 (SI 1980 No 1894). The area committee may on application to them direct, make payment on account of disbursements and counsel's fees, from time to time (para 25 of the Legal Aid Scheme 1980).

A judgment or order for costs when taxed is enforceable by execution on production of the judgment and the taxing officer's certificate (AP, Vol 1 45/1/1A).

Where costs are to be taxed after a payment into court, which has been accepted in full satisfaction of the successful party's claim, the successful party is entitled to his costs incurred at the time of receipt of the notice of payment into court and may sign judgment for his taxed costs 48 hours after the issue of the taxing officer's certificate.

In the Chancery Division, in every case where a master makes an interlocutory order the parties must inform the master if they want the order to be drawn up. No costs will be allowed in respect of counsel attending before the master unless the master so certifies in the order. Similarly in a case heard before a judge in chambers no costs will be allowed in respect of more than one counsel attending unless the judge so certifies in the order.

Where judgment is signed in a writ action in default, then fixed costs are allowed. VAT does not apply to fixed costs. Assessed costs may be awarded in the Chancery Division up to a limit of £1,500. If an order for specific performance, foreclosure or redemption, or for enforcement of judgments on orders on land, provides for the plaintiff's costs to be assessed in chambers then there is no monetary limit.

Any party dissatisfied with the taxation of his costs may apply for a review of the taxation within 14 days after the taxing officer's decision or such other period as the taxing officer may fix.

The application cannot be made after the taxing officer's certificate has been signed. In such a case an application has first to be made for the certificate to be set aside.

The application must be in writing specifying the individual items or parts of items to which objection is taken and the nature and grounds of the objection must be stated in respect of each item. This is referred to as bringing in 'objections', and a copy must also be served on the opposing party or parties who may bring in 'answers to objections', in similar form, within 14 days or such shorter period as may be fixed by the taxing officer. If a party who is entitled to lodge answers is also dissatisfied with the taxation he must bring in his own separate objections, and cannot combine them with his answers.

Objections to an SEO taxation must be heard by a master. After objections have been brought in and answers have also been lodged, or the time for answers has expired, the master will give an appointment to hear the objections. A party who has declined to lodge answers is still entitled to be heard on the appointment.

At the hearing of the objections the master will review his taxation of the items in question and if necessary will amend the taxed bill to give effect to his decisions on the review. The master may award costs of the objections which will normally follow the event.

Any party dissatisfied with the master's decision on objections may apply to a judge for an order to review the taxation provided that one of the parties has requested the master to state in writing his reasons for his decision on the review: such request must be made either at the review or within 14 days thereafter or such shorter time as the master may fix, but cannot be made after the master has signed his certificate. In such a case an application has first to be made for the master to set aside his certificate.

Application for a review before the judge is by summons issued in room 156 who pass the file to the Supreme Court Taxing Office who then make arrangements for a judge, and customarily for two assessors to sit in chambers with him. One of these is invariably a taxing master and the other normally a practising solicitor nominated by the president of the Law Society. The SCTO will give the date of hearing (para 5 of Practice Direction (Chancery: Procedure) No 2 of 1982 [1983] 1 WLR 4).

Assessment

The limit of costs which may be assessed or settled in chambers by a master is currently £2,500 (Chancery Division, Practice Direction (Chancery: costs: assessment in Chambers) No 3 of 1985, issued by the Chief Chancery Master by direction of the Vice-Chancellor on 1 July 1985; [1985] 1 WLR 968; [1985] 2 All ER 1024).

Personal liability of solicitor

RSC, Ord 62, r 11 provides that, aside from failure to conduct the proceedings with reasonable competence and expedition, there can be liability for failing to watch lists and for a totally inexcusable adjournment. Moreover, the solicitor seemingly does not abdicate all responsibility for relief sought, if it is obviously wrong, by having instructed counsel. The effect of the rule is given fully in SCP, para 61/11/1.

Costs—Orders

1. SECURITY FOR COSTS ON APPEAL

IT IS ORDERED

1 that the ... shall on or before ... 199 ... give security for the costs of his/her/its/their Appeal from the Order dated ... by making the lodgment in Court directed in the schedule hereto

2 that until such lodgment is made and notice thereof given to the Registrar of Civil Appeals and the solicitor for the ... (such notice to be given on the same day as the lodgment is made) all proceedings in the said Appeal are to be stayed

3 that in default of the ... making such lodgment as aforesaid within the time aforesaid or within such further time as the Court on application made with seven days after the said ... 199 ... may for special reasons allow the said Appeal shall (upon the solicitors for the ... certifying such default to the Registrar of Civil Appeals) stand dismissed out of this Court without further order

4 that in that case the ... shall pay to ... his/her/its/their/costs occasioned by the said Appeal such costs to be taxed

5 that if such lodgment be made and notice thereof given as aforesaid the said Appeal shall stand out of the list for hearing for 10 days from the date of such lodgment

6 that the costs of this Motion are to be borne by the ... in any event.

2. SECURITY FOR COSTS

IT IS ORDERED

1 that the plaintiff shall on or before ... or subsequently within 4 days after service upon him/her/it/them of this Order give security for costs in that sum of £ ... in case any costs shall be awarded to be paid by the plaintiff to the defendant by making the lodgment in Court directed in the schedule hereto or by procuring some sufficient person to give security by bond in the said sum to the satisfaction of the court in case the parties differ or by depositing the said sum in a bank to be selected by the

defendant in the joint names of the solicitors for the plaintiff and for the defendant or in such other manner as the solicitors for the parties may agree

2   that until such security shall have been given and notice thereof given to the defendant the plaintiff(s) is/are not to take any further proceedings in this Action against the defendant

3   that the costs of this Application are to be borne by the plaintiff in any event.

3. LEGAL AID COSTS

IT IS ORDERED

1   that this Action shall stand dismissed

2   that subject as hereinafter mentioned the plaintiff shall pay to the defendant ... costs of this Action to be taxed

3   that it be referred to the Taxing Master
    (a)   pursuant to Regulation 127(a) of the Legal Aid (General) Regulations 1989 to determine the amount of liability of the plaintiff (who is an assisted person) for the said costs
    (b)   pursuant to Regulation 143 of the said Regulations to hear and determine the application of the defendant this day made to the Court for payment of ... costs out of the legal aid fund and
    (c)   to tax the costs of the plaintiff pursuant to the Legal Aid Act 1974

[that the plaintiff shall pay to the defendant £ ... being the amount which the Court determines pursuant to Section 12 of the Legal Aid Act 1988 to be a reasonable amount for the plaintiff to pay in respect of the defendant's costs of this Action.]

[that the plaintiff shall pay to the defendant the amount of the said costs where taxed or £ ... whichever is the lesser the said sum being the amount which the Court determines pursuant to Section 8(1)(e) of the Legal Aid Act 1974 to be a reasonable amount for the plaintiff to pay in respect of the costs of this Action.]

[that the Taxing Master shall certify (a) the amount of the said costs incurred while the plaintiff was an assisted person and (b) the amount thereof incurred while the plaintiff was not an assisted person.]

[that payment of the said costs of the amount of the said costs incurred while the plaintiff was an assisted person shall not be enforced until the amount of the liability of the plaintiff (who is an assisted person) therefor has been determined pursuant to Section 12 of the Legal Aid Act 1988.]

[that the question what is a reasonable amount for the plaintiff (who is an assisted person) to pay in respect of the said costs shall stand over generally with liberty to restore.]

[pursuant to Regulation 127(b) of the Legal Aid (General) Regulations 1989 that the following question of fact be referred by the Taxing Master to the appropriate Master of the Chancery Division for investigation and report, that is to say]

[that the application by the defendant this day made to the Court for the payment of ... costs of this Action out of the legal aid fund shall stand adjourned.]

[pursuant to Regulation 145 of the Legal Aid (General) Regulations 1989 that the said application be referred to the Taxing Master for inquiry and report]

[that the application of the Defendant this day made to the court for payment of costs of this action out of the legal aid fund shall stand dismissed].

4. ORDERS FOR COSTS—SOME COMMON FORMS

Costs in cause

1   THE costs of the said Application are to be costs in the cause.
(This means that the party who is awarded his costs of the Action can include in those costs his costs of the Application. In the absence of such a direction he would probably have to bear them himself. The costs of a Summons, Motion or other Application are not normally included in the costs of the Action unless there is a specific direction to that effect.

However the last sentence does not apply where the Order on the Summons or Motion before the Court disposes of the Action. Thus a Judgment made under Order 14 will say 'that the Defendant do pay to the Plaintiff his costs of this Action' without adding '(including his costs of the said Summons)' and the principle is the same for Motions for Judgment, Summonses to dismiss for want of prosecution, Tomlin Orders etc.).

2 THE costs of the said Application are to be costs in the said Inquiry.

3 THE costs of the Plaintiff of the said Application are to be his costs in the cause.
(This means that if the Plaintiff is awarded his costs of the Action he can include in those costs his costs of the Application. If however the Defendant is awarded his costs of the Action he cannot include in them his costs of the Application.

4 THE costs of the said Application incurred down to and including 1 October 1991 are to be costs in the cause and the costs of the Plaintiff of the said Application incurred after 1 October 1991 are to be his costs in the cause.

In any event

5 THE costs of the said Application are to be borne by the Plaintiff in any event.
   (a) This means that the Plaintiff will eventually have to bear or pay the costs of the Application. There is to be no immediate taxation. If the Defendant is awarded his costs of the Action he can include in those costs his costs of the Application. If on the other hand he has to pay the Plaintiff's costs of the Action the Defendant can tax his costs of the Application and they will be deducted from the costs he has to pay to the Plaintiff.
   (b) 'In any event' usually means 'whatever happens at the trial of this Action' and reflect an unnecessary or improperly made interlocutory application. It follows that it is not usually satisfactory to make such an Order when there has already been Judgment in the Action.
   (c) The form 'borne and paid' is often found but it should not be used because it is usually not intended that there should be an immediate payment.
   (d) It will be noted that this Form does not say 'The costs of the *Defendant* of the said Application...' and in omitting these words it follows what is believed to have been the normal practice of the Registrars' Department. The Plaintiff must bear his own costs of the Application as well as the Defendant's. So far as the Plaintiff's costs are concerned the effect is the same as if there had been 'no order'.
   (e) The form on page 184 of Atkin is 'the costs of the [Plaintiff or Defendant] of the said Motion are to be the [Plaintiff's or Defendant's] costs in any event'. This says who is to receive the costs rather than, as has been usual in Chancery, who is to pay them but the effect is the same.

6 As between the Plaintiff and the first Defendant the costs of

the said Application are to be borne by the Plaintiff in any event but as between the Plaintiff and the other Defendants the costs of the said Application are to be costs in the cause.

Payment of costs

7 IT IS ORDERED that the Plaintiffs shall pay to the Defendant his costs of this Action to be taxed if not agreed
- (a) Generally costs should only be directed to be taxed on the making of the final Order in an Action (Ord 62, r 8).
- (b) A mistake beginners sometimes make is to omit to state what the costs are of ie the Action, Motion etc.
- (c) The words 'if not agreed' should not be inserted automatically. In certain cases relating to Minors, trusts etc they would be inappropriate.
- (d) If, exceptionally, costs are to be taxed and paid at an interlocutory stage the Taxing Office will only proceed on the following wording 'costs of the Motion be taxed forthwith and paid by X to Y'.
- (e) The liability of the Plaintiffs (or the Defendants as the case may be) to pay costs is joint and several unless the contrary is shown and there is no need to include words indicating this.

Reserved costs

8 THE costs of the said Application are reserved

9 THE costs of the said Application are reserved to be dealt with by the Judge at the trial of this Action

10 THE question how and by whom the costs of the said Application are to be borne and paid is reserved

11 THE costs of the said *ex parte* Motion are reserved to be dealt with at the hearing of the *inter partes* Motion

12 THE costs of the hearing this day of the said Motion are reserved to be dealt with at the further hearing thereof

13 THE costs of the said Application are reserved to be dealt with after the taking of the said Account
(Form 10 may seem more elegant than Form 8 but the effect of the two forms is the same. Normally reserved costs are dealt with at the trial but the draftsman should not say when they are to be dealt with unless the Court says when. As the Forms show, it is sometimes directed that the reserved costs be dealt with on some other occasion. If a party is successful at the trial

he does not get reserved costs unless he asks for them and they are actually awarded by the Court. See the Forms which follow)

14 ... shall pay to the Plaintiff his costs of this Action (including the costs of the Motion made to the Court on ...)

15 (including the costs reserved by the Order dated ...)

16 (including all reserved costs).

No order

17 THE COURT MAKES NO Order as to the costs of the said Application

18 ... with no Order as to costs ...

19 ... stating that they agree that there shall be no Order as to costs ...
    If the Order is silent as to costs the effect is normally the same. The parties have to bear their own.
    Two suggestions are made.
(a) If nothing is said about costs the Order should be silent too.
To put in 'no Order' or something to the same effect is to suggest that there was a conscious decision that there should be no Order as to costs when in fact the matter may have been overlooked.
(b) In Tomlin and other consent Orders one should so far as possible follow what the parties actually say. For example, if a Tomlin Schedule says 'the parties shall bear their own costs of these proceedings' one should leave these words as they are and not cross them out in order to put 'no Order as to costs' in the body of the Order.

Occasioned by

20 THE costs of and occasioned by the said amendment are to be borne by the Plaintiff in any event

21 that the Defendant do pay to the Plaintiff his costs occasioned by the adjournment into Court of the said Summons to be taxed if not agreed

22 THE costs of the said Application incurred in Chambers are to be costs in the cause but the costs occasioned by the adjournment thereof into Court are to be borne by the Defendant in any event (where it is ordered that one party pay to the other his costs of an Application and the Application is an Originating or other

Summons the Order will carry the costs of the Application both in Chambers and in Court. Sometimes however the costs incurred in Chambers will be dealt with differently from the costs occasioned by the adjournment of the Application into Court. These Forms may be helpful when this happens).

23 that the Defendant do pay to the Plaintiff his costs of and incidental to and thrown away by reason of the adjournment ... (See Atkin, p 187 Form 36 where this is said to be a Chancery Form).

Down to and including

24 do pay to the Plaintiff his costs of this Action down to and including this Order to be taxed forthwith
THE costs of the said Inquiry are reserved
AND the parties are to be at liberty to apply
(The phrase 'down to and including this Order' is used when costs are to be paid but the proceedings are to be dealt with later. A common example is an Order made on Motion for Judgment directing Inquiries. The Plaintiff gets his costs of the Action 'down to and including this Order' but the costs of the Inquiries are reserved.)

25 THE costs of this Action incurred down to and including are to be borne by the Defendant in any event.

From the foot

26 ORDERED that there be taxed from the foot of the taxation directed by the Order dated ... the costs of the Plaintiff of this Action
(There will have been a previous Order directing payment of the Plaintiff's costs of this Action. The new Order directs taxation of the Plaintiff's costs of the Action not dealt with on the previous taxation. The following form which produces the same result was used when one did not know whether or not there had been a previous Order directing taxation).

27 ... that there be taxed in so far as not already taxed the costs of the Plaintiff of this Action.

'Personally'

28 that the Plaintiff do out of his own moneys pay to the Defendant his costs ...
(This is used where for example the Plaintiff is a Trustee and he is told to pay the costs 'out of his own moneys' and not out of the trust funds which he might otherwise consider himself

entitled to do. It is better to say 'out of his own moneys' than 'personally').

Set-off

29 that there be taxed if not agreed
    (a)   the costs of the Plaintiff of this Action incurred down to and including 30 September 1991
    (b)   the costs of the Defendant of this Action incurred after 30 September 1991 and his costs of the Counterclaim
AND the Taxing Master is to set off the said costs of the Plaintiff and of the Defendant and to certify to the balance upon which such set off is due
AND IT IS ORDERED that the said balance be paid by the party from whom the same shall be certified to be due
(This Form serves to remind us that the costs of an Action do not include the costs of a Counterclaim. Both the Action and the Counterclaim must be mentioned when dealing with costs.)

A particular claim or issue

30 that there be taxed if not agreed
    (a)   the costs of the Plaintiff of this Action except so much thereof as relates to the issue raised by paragraph 5 of the Statement of Claim and paragraph 2 of the Defence
    (b)   the costs of the Defendant of so much of this Action as relates to the said issue (A direction for a set-off would follow. Note that the 'issue' here is not a 'preliminary issue' but one of the issues arising on the Pleadings at the trial).

31 that the Defendant do pay to the Plaintiff his costs of this Action except so far as such costs have been increased by the Plaintiff's claim for an Injunction . . .

Usual directions in trustee cases

32 (1)   that there be taxed if not agreed
        (a)   on the indemnity basis the costs of and incidental to the said Application of the . . . Defendants as Personal Representatives/Trustees of the deceased
        (b)   on the standard basis the costs of and incidental to the said Application of the Plaintiff and the Defendant
        (c)   the costs of the Plaintiff . . . Defendant pursuant to the Legal Aid Act 1988
   (2)   that the costs specified in (a) and (b) above be paid out of the estate of the deceased in a due course of administration out of the funds subject to the trusts of the said Will

(costs of Trustees and executors are taxed on the indemnity basis. However, it is important to identify the capacity of the parties since there is a presumption that any costs incurred outside the duty of a trustee were unreasonably incurred.

As if a trustee

33 that the Defendant shall pay to the Plaintiff his costs of this Action such costs to be taxed as if he were a Trustee
(This is the usual form but 'on the trustee basis' would achieve the same result).

Add to security

34 AND the Plaintiffs are not to add to their security any costs
  (a) in respect of the affidavit ... sworn on ...
  (b) thrown away by reason of the adjournment of the hearing on ...
  (c) in respect of the hearing before the Master on ...
(Building Societies and other Mortgagees often do not ask for an Order for taxation and payment of costs because they are entitled to add their proper costs to their security and take them out of the proceeds of sale of the mortgaged property. The purpose of the above form is to make it clear that the mortgagees must not take the costs referred to out of the proceeds of sale because they were not properly incurred.)

Including and excluding

35 that there be taxed if not agreed the costs of this Action of the second and third Defendants (including therein the like costs of the deceased first Defendant) ...
(An example of a situation in which such an Order might be made is where the first Defendant has died and an Order to carry on has been made joining the second and third Defendants as his personal representatives.)

36 his costs of this Action (including therein the costs of the Summons dated ... but excluding therefrom the costs of the evidence of John Smith at the trial.)

Pay a proportion

37 that the Defendant shall pay to the Plaintiff four fifths of his costs of this Action to be taxed if not agreed.

'As a contribution'

38 that the Defendant shall pay to the Plaintiff £... by way of damages and £... as a contribution to his costs of this Action
(A form like this would be found in a consent Order. In drafting consent Orders one should follow the language used by the parties unless there is a good reason for not doing so.)

Assessed and fixed

39 pay to the Plaintiff £... being his assessed costs of the said Application

40 ...£... for his assessed costs of the said Application

41 ...£... being his fixed costs of the said Application
(*Fixed costs* are those laid down in Appendix 3 to Order 62 and are usually encountered in garnishee and charged order proceedings and applications under Order 14)
'*Assessed*' *costs* up to £2,500 may be assessed in Chambers but in cases relating to land such as specific performance there is no limit (see Ord 62, r 13 note 1).

Standard indemnity and solicitor and own client

Order 62 was extensively revised in 1986. The old basis of taxation was scrapped and the new one has the general intent of being more generous to a successful party. The overall test is one of reasonableness. Unless otherwise directed all costs are taxed on the standard basis under which a reasonable amount of costs reasonably incurred is allowed. Any uncertainty as to what is reasonable is decided in favour of the paying party. Silence in an Order as to the basis of taxation indicates that it is to be on the standard basis.

42 '... such costs be taxed on the indemnity basis'
This basis allows all costs save any unreasonably incurred. In doubtful cases the recipient is favoured by the Taxing Office

43 '... such costs be taxed as between solicitor and own client'. The costs are taxed on the indemnity basis but there are the additional presumptions that all costs are reasonable if expressly or impliedly approved by the Client and are unreasonable only if they are of a wholly unusual nature.

Disallow

44 AND in taxing the said costs the Taxing Master is not to allow any more than would have been allowed if this Order had been made by the Master on an application by summons

45 AND in Taxing the said costs the Taxing Master is to look into the Affidavit of the Plaintiff and the exhibits thereto and to disallow so much of the Plaintiff's costs thereof as he shall find to be unnecessary for enabling the Court to determine the true construction of the Will.

5. ORDER ON ASSESSMENT OF COSTS BY MASTER

UPON THE ASSESSMENT of costs pursuant to the Order dated ...
AND UPON HEARING ...
AND UPON READING the documents recorded on the Court file as having been read
IT IS DECLARED that the amount in which the said costs are assessed pursuant to the said Order is £ ...
AND IT IS ORDERED so as to give effect to the said Order that ... shall pay to ... the said sum of £ ...

6. ORDER TO DELIVER BILL

UPON THE PETITION of ...
                    or
UPON THE APPLICATION of the Plaintiff by Originating Summons
AND UPON HEARING

IT IS ORDERED

1 that the above named Solicitors shall within ... days after service of this Order deliver to the Petitioner/Plaintiff a bill of costs in respect of all matters in which they have been employed as the Solicitors for the Petitioner/Plaintiff

2 that it be referred to the Taxing Master to tax and settle the said bill and that the Petitioner/Plaintiff and also the said Solicitors do produce before the said Master upon oath as he shall direct all books papers and writings in their custody or power respectively relating to the said same and that they be examined touching the same as the said Master shall direct

3 that the said Solicitors shall give credit for all sums of money received of or on account of the Petitioner/Plaintiff and be at liberty to charge all sums of money paid to or on account of the Petitioner/Plaintiff

4 that the said Master shall certify to whom having regard to Section 70 of the Solicitors Act 1974 the costs of this reference are payable and do tax such costs accordingly and certify the amount payable by and the amount due from the Petitioner to the said Solicitors or from the Solicitors to the Petitioner/Plaintiff as the case may be having regard to the costs of this reference so to be taxed as aforesaid and any sum or sums of money which may have been so received or paid as aforesaid

5 that the amount so certified as payable be paid within 21 days after service of this Order and of the Taxing Master's Certificate made in pursuance thereof by the party from whom to the party to whom the same shall be certified to be due, unless the Court shall (upon special circumstances to be certified by the said Master) otherwise order upon application to be made within one week after the date of the said Master's Certificate by the party liable to pay such amount

6 that upon payment by the Petitioner/Plaintiff to the said Solicitors of what may be certified to be due to the Solicitors as aforesaid or in case it shall appear that there is nothing due the said Solicitors shall deliver to the Petitioner/Plaintiff upon oath all deeds books papers and writings in their custody or power belonging to the Petitioner/Plaintiff

7 that no proceedings be commenced against the Petitioner/Plaintiff in respect of the said bill until after completion of the taxation.

7. SOLICITOR'S APPLICATION FOR TAXATION

UPON THE PETITION OF . . .
UPON THE APPLICATION of the Plaintiffs by Originating Summons
AND UPON HEARING . . .

IT IS ORDERED

1 that it be referred to the Taxing Master to tax and settle the bill specified in the Schedule hereto and that the Petitioners/Plaintiffs and also the Client named in the said Schedule do produce before the said Master upon oath as he shall direct all books papers and writings in their custody or power respectively relating to this matter and that they be examined touching the same as the said Master shall direct

2 that the Petitioners/Plaintiffs shall give credit for all sums of money received of or on account of the Client and be at liberty to charge all sums of money paid to or on account of the Client

3 (in case the Client shall attend upon such taxation) that the said Master shall certify to whom having regard to Section 70 of the Solicitors Act 1974 the costs of this reference are payable and do tax such costs accordingly and certify the amount payable by and the amount due from the Client to the Petitioners/Plaintiffs ... or ... from ... the Petitioners/Plaintiffs to the Client as the case may be having regard to the costs of this reference (so to be taxed as aforesaid) and any sum or sums of money which may have been so received or paid as aforesaid

4 that the amount (if any) so certified as payable be paid within 21 days after service of this Order and of the Taxing Master's Certificate to be made in pursuance thereof by the party from whom to the party to whom the same shall be certified to be payable unless the Court shall upon special circumstances to be certified by the said Master otherwise order upon application to be made within one week after the date of the Master's said Certificate by the party liable to pay such amount

5 in case the Client shall pay to the Petitioners/Plaintiffs such sum as may be certified to be due without further Order or in case the said Master shall certify that there is nothing due to the Petitioners/Plaintiffs or that they have been overpaid that the Petitioners shall deliver to the Client upon oath all deeds books and writings in the Petitioners' custody or power belonging to the Client

6 that no proceedings be taken by the Petitioners/Plaintiffs against the Client in respect of the said bill until after completion of taxation

7 that a copy of this Order be personally served on the Client one week at the least before any appointment is taken out for the taxation of the said bill

The Schedule

The bill of costs dated ... delivered on or about ... by the Petitioners/Plaintiffs to ... (in this Order referred to as the Client) relating to ...

Notes

1 The application may be by petition or originating summons.

2 An order for taxation may not be made within one month from or after one year from the delivery of the bill.

3 The solicitor must lodge a certificate that the requirements of the Solicitors Act 1974 have been met.

8. ORDER ON CLIENT'S APPLICATION FOR TAXATION

UPON THE PETITION of ...
or
UPON THE APPLICATION of the Plaintiff by Originating Summons who submits to pay what shall be certified as payable to the above named [Defendant] Solicitors on the taxation of the bill hereinafter mentioned
AND UPON HEARING ...

IT IS ORDERED

1 that it be referred to the Taxing Master to tax and settle the bill specified in the Schedule hereto and that the Petitioner/Plaintiff and also the said Solicitors shall produce before the said Master upon oath as he shall direct all books papers and writings in their custody or power respectively relating to this matter and that they be examined touching the same as the said Master shall direct

2 that the said Solicitors shall give credit for all sums of money received of or on account of the Petitioner/Plaintiff and be at liberty to charge all sums of money paid to or on account of the Petitioner

3 that the said Master shall certify to whom having regard to Section 70 of the Solicitors Act 1974 the costs of this reference are payable and do tax such costs accordingly and certify the amount payable by and the amount due from the Petitioner/Plaintiff to the said Solicitors or from the said Solicitors to the Petitioner/Plaintiff as the case may be having regard to the costs of this reference so to be taxed as aforesaid and any sum or sums of money which may have been so received or paid as aforesaid

[4 that the amount so to be certified as payable be paid within 21 days after service of this Order and of the Taxing Master's Certificate to be made in pursuance thereof by the party from whom to the party to whom the same shall be certified to be payable unless the Court shall upon special circumstances to be certified by the said Master otherwise order upon application to be made within one week after the date of the said Master's Certificate by the party liable to pay such amount

5 that upon payment by the Plaintiff to the said Solicitors of what is certified to be due as aforesaid or in case it shall appear that there is nothing due the said Solicitors shall deliver to the Plaintiff upon oath all deeds books papers and writings in the Solicitors' custody or power belonging to the Plaintiff]

6 that (i) no proceedings be commenced against the Petitioner/Plaintiff in respect of the said bill and (ii) any existing proceedings as aforesaid be stayed until after completion of the taxation

The Schedule

The bill of costs dated ... delivered to the Petitioner/Plaintiff on or about ... relating to ...

Notes

1 A Client has an absolute right to require the taxation of a bill of costs provided the application is made within a month of receipt of the bill. Such an application is currently made by way of petition although this is under review by the Supreme Court Rules Committee. The order is immediate on presentation of the petition and the matter is not referred to a master. The order is made in the name of the Chief Master. Since the order is made as of right there is no fetter placed on the client where the application is made within the time limit. In these cases the submission to pay and paras 4 and 5 *must not be included in the order.*

2 The court has a discretion to direct the taxation of a client's bill if the application is made between one month and a year after receipt. No orders can be made after a year has passed. Formerly the court could exercise a discretion under its inherent jurisdiction to discipline solicitors. However the House of Lords has decided that the discretion has been displaced by the Solicitors Act 1974 [*Harrison & anr v Tew* 1990 2 WLR 210]. The application is made by the expedited form of originating summons with the solicitors as defendants. The order is conditional on the client submitting to pay what shall be certified due and accordingly paras 4 and 5 should be included.

3 Under para 3 the solicitors pay the costs of the taxation if more than a fifth is taxed off otherwise the costs are borne by the Petitioner/Plaintiff.

9. ORDER ON APPLICATION BY PERSONS LIABLE TO PAY BILL (THOUGH NOT CHARGEABLE)

UPON THE PETITION of ...
[who submits to pay what shall be certified as payable to the above named Solicitors on the taxation of the bill hereinafter mentioned]

or

UPON THE APPLICATION of the Plaintiff by Originating Summons
AND UPON HEARING

IT IS ORDERED

1   that it be referred to the Taxing Master to tax and settle the bill specified in the Schedule hereto and that the Petitioner/Plaintiff and also the said Solicitors shall produce before the said Master upon oath as he shall direct all books papers and writings in their custody or power respectively relating to this matter and that they be examined touching the same as the said Master shall direct

2   that the said Master shall certify to whom having regard to Section 70 of the Solicitors Act 1974 the costs of this reference are payable and shall tax such costs accordingly and certify the amount payable by the Petitioner/Plaintiff to the said Solicitors or from the said Solicitors to the Petitioner/Plaintiff as the case may be having regard to the costs of this reference so as to be taxed as aforesaid

3   that the amount so to be certified be paid within 21 days after service of this Order and of the Taxing Master's Certificate to be made in pursuance thereof by the party from whom to the party to whom the same shall be certified to be payable unless the Court shall upon special circumstances to be certified by the said Master otherwise order upon application to be made within one week after the date of the said Master's Certificate by the party liable to pay such amount

4   that no proceedings be commenced against the Petitioner/Plaintiff in respect of the said bill pending this reference but the said Master is to make his Certificate in a month (unless the said Master shall extend the time to enable him to make his Certificate) or this Order to be of no effect

The Schedule

The bill of costs dated ... delivered to ... on or about ... relating to ...

Notes

1   These applications most usually arise on the instance of a mortgagor who is liable to pay a mortgagee's legal fees or a lessee who is liable to pay the costs of a lessor on the assignment of the lease.

2 The application may be made by petition or originating summons. If made more than a month but less than a year after delivery of the bill the order will include the same submission to pay and other conditions that apply to an application by a client.

10. ORDER ON APPLICATION BY PERSON INTERESTED IN FUNDS (FROM WHICH BILL IS TO BE PAID)

IT IS ORDERED

1 that it be referred to the Taxing Master to tax and settle the bill of costs specified in the Schedule hereto and delivered by the Defendants to ... as the Executors/Administrators of the estate of ... which bill has been [*or* is to be] paid out of property in which the Plaintiff has an interest

2 that the Taxing Master certify the amount payable out of the said property

3 that the costs of the said Application and the taxation are reserved

4 that the parties are to be at liberty to apply

The Schedule

The bill of costs dated ... delivered to ... and enlarged on or about ... relating to ...

Notes

1 The application is made by originating summons.

2 The court may, if the circumstances demand it, impose conditions on the parties similar to those imposed on a solicitor or client applying for taxation under s 70 of the Solicitors Act 1974.

11. ORDER FOR REVIEW OF TAXATION

IT IS ORDERED

1 that the objections to the Taxation directed by the Order dated ... specified in the [First] Schedule hereto be allowed and it be referred back to the Taxing Master to vary his Certificate accordingly

2 that the objections specified in the [Second] Schedule hereto be referred back to the said Taxing Master for review in the light of the principles contained in the Judgment of this Court

3 that ... do pay to ... his/her/their costs of this Application such costs to be taxed if not agreed.

The [First] Schedule

[The Second Schedule]

Notes

1 An application for a review of taxation by a judge is made by ordinary summons issued in the proceedings in which the taxation was directed. The judge will usually sit with two assessors.

2 If any objections are allowed the judge will refer the taxation back to the taxing master for the amendment of the taxing certificate. Exceptionally, the judge may refer items of a bill back for further taxation on the basis of the judgment of the court (*Reed v Gray* [1952] Ch 337).

12. ORDER BY CONSENT ON CLIENT'S APPLICATION

IT IS by consent ORDERED

1 That it be referred to the taxing master to tax and settle the bill of costs delivered to the petitioner and specified in the schedule hereto and that the said solicitors do give credit for all sums of money received by them from or on account of the said petitioner/plaintiff and that they refund what (if anything) they may on such taxation appear to have overpaid

2 That the taxing master tax the costs of the reference and certify what shall be found due to or from either party in respect of the bill and of the costs of the reference to be paid according to the event of the taxation pursuant to the statute

3 That no proceedings be commenced against the petitioner in respect of the said bill until taxation is completed.

The Schedule

The bill of costs dated ... delivered to the petitioner on or about ... relating to ...

Chapter Fourteen

Post and Telephone

If an acknowledgment of the receipt of papers is required the papers should be accompanied by a list either written on a stamped addressed postcard or else sent with a stamped and addressed open envelope. The court will not accept responsibility for documents alleged to have been sent unless an acknowledgment is produced. If there is any deficiency in the papers lodged they will be returned to the sender.

The following are the applications which may be made by post:

1. Issue of writ or originating process

(1) The following documents should be posted in a prepaid envelope properly addressed to:
            Chancery Chambers Registry
            Royal Courts of Justice
            Strand
            London
            WC2A 2LL

    (a) An application by letter duly signed by or on behalf of the solicitor requesting the issue of the writ or originating process (hereinafter called the writ).

    (b) The original and one copy of the writ together with a further copy for service on every defendant to be served. Each copy of the writ must comply with the provisions of Ord 6 and in the case of an originating summons Ord 7. The copy of the writ intended to be stamped with the fee must be signed by or on behalf of the solicitors. The signature to a statement of claim endorsed on the writ is not sufficient for this purpose.

    (c) A cheque, postal order or money order for the proper fee (which is now £60), crossed and made payable to HM Paymaster-General. In the case of a litigant in person, cash, a postal order or a banker's draft must be sent.

    (d) A stamped addressed envelope for the return of the relevant documents to the solicitors.

(2) An application for the issue of a writ will be treated as having been made at the date and time of the actual receipt and acceptance of the requisite documents at Chancery chambers (on a day when Chancery chambers is open), and for this purpose the date and time of despatch of the requisite documents will be wholly disregarded.
(3) On receiving the requisite documents and proper fee the officer in Chancery chambers will affix to the application an official stamp showing the date and time of receipt. If it is in order, he will seal the writ and copies for service and return these to the solicitors by post in the stamped addressed envelope provided. If it is not in order, he will not issue the writ but will return all documents by post to the solicitors making the application.
(4) No responsibility will be accepted for non-delivery to the solicitors of any documents sent by post to the court. The use of these facilities is at the risk of the solicitors concerned, and particular care should be taken when any period of limitation may be involved.
(5) This direction does not apply to an originating summons in the expedited form.

2. Acknowledgment of service

An acknowledgment of service as provided in Ord 12, r 3, may be sent to Chancery chambers by post. Particular care should be exercised in completing the form by inserting the action number, inserting the full names of the defendants, ticking the appropriate box and signing the form.

3. Issue of summons

The following documents must be lodged:

(1) The proposed summons or notice of appointment to hear the originating summons, or notice under Ord 25, in duplicate, with the hearing date left blank.
(2) Affidavit of service, if the writ was issued on or after 1 October 1982, and there has been no acknowledgment of service. If the writ was issued before 1 October 1982, there must be an acknowledgment of service, certificate of no acknowledgment of service (if obtained prior to 1 October 1982), or an affidavit of service.
(3) Minutes of any proposed order if the case is complex.
(4) Complete set of pleadings up to date, if required.

(5) The original Grant of Probate or Letters of Administration if required.
(6) Any affidavits not already filed, together with any exhibits.
(7) Copy of any writ issued prior to 1 January 1982.
(8) An estimate of the length of appointment, stating whether counsel will attend.
(9) Stamped addressed envelope for reply.

4. Agreed orders

See chapter 8—Orders and Judgments.

5. Appeals from masters

See chapter 11—Appeals.

6. Adjournment by consent

Where all parties require the adjournment of the hearing of a summons, a letter of consent signed by all parties is required. If the master agrees, the summons will be taken out of the list. Such an application should be made as soon as possible so that the appointment vacated can be used for another hearing.

7. Legal aid taxation

Where an assisted person's civil aid certificate has been discharged or revoked and an order for taxation is required, no summons is required but an application may be made *ex parte* to the master or by letter.

8. Filing documents by post

The following documents may be filed by sending them by prepaid post to Chancery chambers:

(1) Affidavits. Affidavits for use at a hearing must be filed either personally or by post at least two days before the hearing.
(2) Civil Aid Certificates.
(3) Notices of change of solicitors.

9. Office copies

A party wishing to obtain an office copy of an affidavit, order or other filed document may apply by post. The Registry will reply by post or telephone, indicating the fee required, and on receipt of the fee will send the office copy to the party by post.

10. Drawing up of orders

See Chapter 8—Orders and Judgments.

11. Telephone

The telephone number of the Royal Courts of Justice is: 071-936 6000 and the exchange will connect with all rooms including room 307/308 for inquiries. Notice of intention to make an *ex parte* application to the master, to be given by noon on the day the application is to be made, may be given by telephoning 071-936 6000 ext 3148 (Practice Direction (Chancery Chambers) No 1 of 1982). The Chancery registry is also on direct lines 071-936 6167/6148. Telephone calls should preferably be made between 10.00 am to 11.00 am and 4.00 pm to 4.30 pm, but in genuinely urgent applications, notice may be given at any time (ibid). Application may be made by telephone to restore a summons which has been adjourned generally. Information concerning the issue of process (ext 3642) or concerning master's appointments (ext 3148) may be obtained by telephone, and solicitors may telephone to *bespeak* files required for *ex parte* applications, (heading lettered B of Chancery: Applications by Post or Telephone: Practice Direction (No 2 of 1983)).

12. Telex

There are now two telex machines at the Royal Courts of Justice, one specifically for use of the commercial court, and the other for use of all courts, situated in the post room which is on the right hand side of the main hall as entered through the main entrance in the Strand, about half way along. Courts and court officers can be communicated with through use of this machine at any time on telex no 296933. Solicitors and others having a telex machine will know that the special facility that it provides is that the message is given in writing. There may be many occasions when it would be to the convenience of the court and court officers to receive messages on the telex in preference to telephone, particularly in emergencies arising through illness or absence of witnesses or other inextricable difficulties. The notice in room 412/414 (the newly numbered room of the clerk of the lists) in the chancery corridor explains that the telex can be used to communicate with the court but requests that it should be made absolutely clear to whom the message is to be referred, and if it is for the clerk of the lists, his room number should be mentioned in the message. The telex machine in the court cannot be used by litigants or their advisers to send out messages and the use of the machines for sending out messages is confined to use by the court or its officers only.

13. Fax

The listing section, rooms 412/414 on the fourth floor has a fax machine (Fax no 071 936 7345). This is the only section with a fax.

Part II
Particular Chancery Actions

Chapter Fifteen

Intellectual Property

1. Copyright

The law of copyright has recently been revised and simplified by the Copyright, Designs and Patents Act 1988, but many of the concepts and principles of the previous law have survived, even where the wording of the new Act differs slightly from that of the Copyright Act 1956, so much of the existing case law is still applicable.

Copyright is a property right derived entirely from statute which consists of the copyright owner's exclusive right to reproduce literary, dramatic, musical or artistic works, sound recordings, films, computer programs, broadcasts, cable programmes or typographical works. It does not protect either ideas or speeches as such. Basically, its duration is the author's life (if an identifiable individual) plus 50 years for literary, dramatic, musical or artistic works, and 50 years for works in the other categories except for typographical arrangements and designs which have been commercially exploited (both 25 years).

In addition to redefining a copyright owner's rights the 1988 Act established new, so-called moral rights, which are vested in the author and are not assignable (though they are transmissible on death), and will normally be protected by injunctive relief. Moral rights consist of the right to have the work attributed and for the work not to be treated in a derogatory fashion, and the right not to have a work falsely attributed to one. The subjects of privately commissioned photographs and films also have rights of privacy. The duration of these rights is the same as the relevant copyright, except that in the case of the right not to have a work falsely attributed the duration is the life of the person so injured plus 20 years.

Statute

The Copyright, Designs and Patents Act 1988, which in relation to copyright took effect on 1 August 1989; the Copyright Act 1956 (for infringements occurring before the 1988 Act took effect).

Order

There is no particular order dealing with copyright.

Parties

In most cases the plaintiff will be the copyright owner and the defendant an alleged infringer of copyright.

Intitulement

There is no special intitulement for copyright actions.

The objective of the plaintiff

The plaintiff's objective will be to establish that his rights have been infringed in one of the ways specified in the 1988 Act (which may be either primary or secondary infringement) and to obtain relief in the form of an injunction to prevent future infringement, and/or an account of profits, and/or damages for infringement, with the possibility of additional damages where the infringement has been flagrant or particularly beneficial to the infringer, and/or an order at the discretion of the court for the delivery up or disposal of infringing copies.

Required/have ready/on issue

Writ and statement of claim.

Sequence

(1) Preliminary. To avoid giving the defendant the opportunity to rely on the statutory defence to a claim for damages that he did not know and had no reason to believe that that copyright subsisted in the relevant work it may be worth while to ensure that he has been given notice of the copyright.

(2) Preliminary. Rather than applying to the court for a roving Anton Piller Order as was previously necessary, the copyright owner may now consider it advisable to exercise the right to seize and detain infringing copies found exposed or otherwise available for sale or hire, after giving notice of the time and place of the proposed seizure to a local police station. This can be useful where the infringing copies are being sold by an itinerant trader. It is not however permissible to enter private or business premises or to use force (see 1988 Act, s 100).

(3) Application to court *ex parte* for interim injunction.

(4) Application *ex parte* for an Anton Piller order to inspect and/or remove all infringing articles and relevant documentation with an undertaking by the plaintiff for their safe custody, and to give (under penalty) the answers to specific questions.

Affidavit evidence must be produced to show that there is a strong case of infringement and a likelihood that the articles or evidence will otherwise be destroyed. A Mareva injunction may also be sought if there is a risk of removing articles or assets representing them from the jurisdiction, see *CBS United Kingdom Ltd v Lambert* [1982] 3 WLR 746.
(5) Directions.
(6) Hearing.
(7) Assessment of damages for infringement, which unless nominal will be assessed by the master on inquiry. The inquiry should be applied for and ordered at the hearing (Ord 43).

Hazards and pitfalls

The statutory presumptions should be studied. Apart from the necessity to establish title to the copyright (including the need to demonstrate that the plaintiff is qualified for protection under the Act), the plaintiff will need to be sure that the acts complained of do not fall within the various statutory exceptions. Some technical knowledge or advice may be required when dealing with a case concerning computer-generated material. Care is needed in establishing in an individual case whether the 1988 Act is applicable or whether the Act of 1956, which confers an additional remedy in the form of damages for notional conversion, is still relevant. There are special transitional arrangements regarding designs (see s 51 and Sched 1, para 19 of the 1988 Act.

Costs

The usual principles apply.

Alternative jurisdiction

Previously all civil proceedings concerning copyright were brought in the Chancery Division of the High Court. Provision is made in ss 115 and 205 of the 1988 Act for the county court to exercise jurisdiction in proceedings for the delivery up or disposal of infringing copies or recordings and for certain other purposes where the value of the articles or recordings concerned does not exceed the county court limit in tort.

Copyright tribunal

The 1988 Act constituted the Copyright Tribunal in place of the former Performing Rights Tribunal to govern licensing schemes and the grant of certain licences. An appeal on a point of law lies to the High Court under s 152 of the 1988 Act.

Textbooks

P Stone, *Copyright Law in the United Kingdom and the European Community*, (The Athlone Press Ltd 1990).
C Tootal, *The Law of Industrial Design*, (CCH Editions Ltd 1990).
E P Skone James, J F Mummery, J E Rayner James, A Latman and S Silman, *Copinger and Skone James on Copyright*, 12th edn (Sweet & Maxwell).

Forms and precedents

Atkin, Vol 12 (1990 issue).

2. Patents and registered designs

Patents relate to inventions. It is not mandatory to obtain a patent for an invention, but in return for disclosure of his invention by patenting it, the inventor is given for a period of 20 years a monopoly in its use.

If the invention does not involve an inventive step, the process, specification, or mode of operation may be unpatentable. Nonetheless, if the novelty is merely in the design as opposed to the function, it may be possible to protect such a design as a registered design or in copyright (*see above*). If the inventor has a registered patent and his monopoly is infringed, then he may want an injunction or damages or both.

Statutes

The Patents Act 1977 and the Patents Rules 1978 (SI No 216) for patents sealed after 11 June 1978. For patents sealed prior to 1978, the Patents Act 1949. Procedure has not been changed substantially under the 1977 Act, but pleadings under each Act will have their variations.

For designs, the Registered Designs Acts 1949–61 and the Designs Rules 1949 (SI No 2368) and various Amendment Rules 1955–81. The Copyright Designs and Patents Act 1988 confers a new design right. The register of designs is kept at the Patent Office (designs branch) and only designs which are new are registrable. The registered proprietor has the monopoly to make use of the design. Innocent infringers are not liable in damages but may be injuncted and ordered to deliver up infringing articles.

Orders

Proceedings are before the patents court in which sit two nominated judges. Orders 103 and 104 apply. Notes to Ord 104 in AP, Vol 1 cite many cases decided since *American Cyanamid Co v Ethicon*

Limited [1975] AC 396 relating specifically to injunctions in patent infringement actions.

Parties

Normally the registered proprietor of the patent is the plaintiff and the party who has infringed the patent is the defendant.

Intitulement

All writs, summonses and affidavits are to state: 'PATENTS COURT' below 'CHANCERY DIVISION'.

The objective of the plaintiff

The plaintiff will usually seek an injunction for infringement additionally where appropriate, an order for delivery up or destruction additionally, judgment for damages or an account of profits and/ or a declaration of validity and infringement. Damages may only be recovered where there has been a deliberate as opposed to an innocent infringement. Infringement since the 1977 Act includes keeping a patented article or product as well as making use of it.

Required/have ready/on issue

Writ and statement of claim in readiness for service and facsimile copies of the specification of the letters patent for use at all hearings.

Sequence

(1) After writ and service, the master may on summons extend time or make orders on agreed matters. He may also give specific directions on a summons for directions which in all proceedings for infringement or revocation should be taken out within 28 days of reply or answer and which is returnable within 21 days. Directions will always be sought as to place and mode of trial and if other specific directions are given they are likely to include discovery and inspection; opportunity to inspect apparatus or photographs may be particularly important to a defendant who intends to set up the defence of prior use.

(2) Practice Direction (Patent Actions: Directions) [1973] 1 WLR 1425 has been revoked by Practice Direction (Chancery: Applications by Post or Telephone) dated 24 May 1983 and replaced in more expanded form so that agreed minutes of an order for directions made (seemingly with or without attendance) on a summons for directions, *or any other interlocutory order*, (also seemingly with or without attendance) may all be sent by post, para 4(2) of the new Practice Direction providing that:

agreed minutes of order on a summons for directions or any other interlocutory order, must be signed by counsel for all parties. If the parties are not agreed, an application must be made by motion to one of the assigned judges.

Hitherto application has also been made by motion to one of the assigned judges on technical questions.

While the new Practice Direction does not explicitly so state, it would be necessary to forward to the summons clerk, together with the agreed and signed minutes of order, the original summons and the original writ.

There is a detailed and compendious specimen of an order for directions in a patent action given in AP, Vol 1 104/10/1.

If on a petition for an extension of the term of an unexpired patent under s 23 of the Patents Act 1949 the petitioner wishes to apply for the dismissal of his petition his summons must be indorsed with an undertaking by the petitioner not to present a further petition on that patent,

(para 4(2) of Practice Direction (Chancery: Applications by Post or Telephone) above).
(3) Applications for a date for the hearing of the motion are made to the clerk to one of the two nominated judges.
(4) An order may be made to hear an issue on validity of the patent as a preliminary issue. In simple, but not complex, amendments (*see below*) leave to amend the specification may also be heard as a preliminary issue.
(5) By Practice Direction [1970] 1 WLR 94 where the parties agree that the specialised knowledge of the patent judge is likely to be involved and that the application is likely to be adjourned into court in any event, then the preliminary hearing before the master should be eliminated. The summons in such instances should be issued by the summons clerk in room 307/308 without a hearing date being inserted. The summons at the time of issue should be accompanied by two copies, two sets of pleadings, and affidavits, and a certificate of both solicitors that the summons is suitable for hearing by a judge. The summons will then be set down for hearing without any further action by the parties.

Plaintiff's considerations

The statement of claim will aver infringement by reference to accompanying particulars which will include particulars of knowledge and circumstances. To restrain threatened infringement, the plaintiff may ask for an interlocutory injunction.

The plaintiff may after commencing his action for injunction of a patent wish to amend the specification (which concerns the scope and validity of his patent) and having entered an advertisement to this effect in the official journal (patents) he may seek leave to do so as a preliminary issue (*see above*) on motion prior to the hearing or at the hearing (Ord 104, r 3).

Plaintiffs will want to prepare expert evidence so as to assist the court in coming to a conclusion that the invention is new and capable of industrial application. Experts will be inhibited from giving their opinion as to what the specification means, or as to whether any step is or is not obvious, as those matters are for the court (the provisions of the Civil Evidence Act 1972 as to expert witnesses seeking to give statements of opinion in evidence appears not to have yet been fully considered in patent cases).

Defendant's considerations

Since the 1977 Act, proceedings may be brought against a defendant who is not a user but only a carrier.

A defendant may plead denial of any infringement, and whilst it is not essential to accompany a mere denial with particulars, it is advisable to do so.

A patent to be valid must be of an invention which is new, not obvious, and capable of industrial application; hence these averments are made by implication by every plaintiff with the consequence that a defendant may traverse all or any of such averments in his pleadings. Additionally or by way of alternatives, a defendant may plead that the patentee has exhausted his rights or plead want of novelty or prior use. If other than a mere denial, all grounds of defence must be set out with strictness.

Attitude of the court

The judge will anticipate hearing expert evidence.

Hazards and pitfalls

Order 14 proceedings are very rarely applicable. No damages are available for the plaintiff if the defendant has infringed innocently; the onus is on the defendant to establish innocence and he should do so on the basis of an objective test of reasonableness.

Costs

The normal rules as to giving of security will apply. Costs may be apportioned where only some claims are infringed and the patent is only partially valid or where the successful defendant fails on counterclaim for revocation.

Alternative jurisdiction to the patents court

The Comptroller has limited jurisdiction. Under the Copyright, Designs and Patents Act 1988 the Lord Chancellor may designate particular county courts to hear patent matters. Only Edmonton County Court has so far been designated.

Appeals

The intitulement is 'In matters originating from the Comptroller (see Ord 59, r 17) and in other matters the Supreme Court Act 1981' (s 54 and Ord 59).

Textbooks

WR Cornish, *Intellectual Property, Patents, Copyright, Trade Marks and Allied Rights*, (Sweet & Maxwell, 1980).
W Aldous, D Young, A Watson & S Thorley, *Terrell on The Law of Patents*, 13th edn, (Sweet & Maxwell 1982).

Forms and precedents

Atkin, Vol 30 (1990 issue).

3. Trademarks

A trademark may give the exclusive right to attach to goods a particular mark. The plaintiff may proceed against a party who uses a mark so as to induce purchasers to believe that the goods he is selling are the manufacture of the plaintiff or connected with the plaintiff in course of trade. If the plaintiff has a registered trademark his exclusive right derives from the registration. The register consists of Parts A and B, Part B covering marks which are not sufficiently distinctive for registration in Part A and consequently are more limited in respect of the rights conferred. The duration of registration is seven years and there are 34 classes. No-one has the right to represent his goods as the goods of someone else but if the plaintiff's trademark is not registered he can only bring a 'passing off' action (*see below*) with the evidential burden of establishing his reputation in the mark.

Statute

The Trade Marks Act 1938 and Trade Marks Rules 1938 (SR & O 1938 661) and a number of Amendment Rules, and the Trade Marks (Amendment) Act 1984 for the registration of marks in relation to services.

Order

Ord 100, r 3 says that a defendant may in proceedings for infringement challenge validity and counterclaim for cancellation or rectification of the entry in the register and that all proceedings are assigned to the Chancery Division.

Parties

The plaintiff in an action for infringement will generally be the proprietor of the registered trademark. A registered user may institute proceedings in his own name making the proprietor a defendant if that proprietor fails to take proceedings within two months of being called upon so to do. Defendants may include innocent carriers or those in temporary possession.

Intitulement

There is no special intitulement but the relevant Trade Marks Act must be mentioned in the body of the statement of claim.

The objective of the plaintiff

The plaintiff will seek an injunction, a declaration as to damages or an account of profits for wrongful use or imitation and, if required, an order for delivery up of offending material.

Required/have ready/on issue

(a) Writ—the general indorsement will be for an injunction to restrain, etc, the defendant, his servants or agents from infringing the plaintiff's trademark and secondly, the obliteration upon oath of all marks the use of which would be an infringement of the injunction prayed for and thirdly, an inquiry as to damages alternatively an account of profits. (b) Statement of claim in readiness for service. This should identify the infringement adapting the identification to one or other of those cited in the statute, eg that the other mark is used in trade and is identical or so nearly resembles as to deceive or cause confusion and is used in relation to goods in respect of which the plaintiff's mark is registered. (c) As proof of the original, a sealed copy of the trademark as certified by the registrar of the patent office.

Sequence

There may be:

(1) An *ex parte* application for an 'Anton Piller' order (*Anton Piller KG v Manufacturing Processes Ltd* [1976] Ch 55 CA) by interlocutory motion before or after the issue of the writ.
(2) An *ex parte* or *inter partes* application by interlocutory motion

for an injunction if he is confident that he can prove entitlement and one act of infringement. If the defendant has a concurrent right to have his mark registered this relief will either not be granted or will be granted subject to a proviso that the defendant should pursue his application for registration. Relief by way of injunction is unlikely to be given where the infringement is trivial or inadvertent but the plaintiff may obtain a declaration.
(3) An order for discovery to include an order for inspection of premises.
(4) At the trial the order made should contain directions for an inquiry as to assessment of damages or for an account to be taken of profits coupled with an order to pay the sums certified.

Plaintiff's considerations

A plaintiff in a trademark action need only assert his registered trademark and allege infringement. While the proprietor of a registered trademark is thus seemingly obviated from proving anything else 'passing off' is usually alleged in the alternative and this being so the plaintiff will in practice have to be ready to carry the evidential burden of establishing reputation and likelihood of confusion in addition to proving the infringement. The ingredients for infringement are identity or near resemblance with the registered mark, its use in trade, and its use in relation to goods in respect of which the trademark is registered.

In trademark actions including applications therein for interlocutory injunctions the court must consider the balance of convenience (see thereon *American Cyanamid Co v Ethicon Ltd* [1975] AC 396) and are likely to do so on the basis of the degree of deceptive resemblance of the two marks.

While evidence as to the manner in which a trade is carried out and evidence from the public that they have in fact been deceived may be admissible, evidence by members in the trade as to whether there is likely to be deception in the trade, is not.

Notice of intent to bring a trademark action need not be given.

Defendant's considerations

Particulars of objections must accompany a plea of invalidity of registration with a copy of the counterclaim served on the comptroller of trade marks (address: Trademarks Branch, Patent Office (Department of Trade), State House, High Holborn, London WC1).

A defendant may aver that all the ingredients to establish infringement are not satisfied and, more frequently, that there is no sufficiently deceptive resemblance between the registered mark and his mark, that is, that the plaintiff's claim to the exclusive use of the mark cannot be made out, further or alternatively, that the registration does not extend to the defendant's particular use of the mark. Where the defendant has vested rights such as his continuous use of his mark from before the first use or registration of the plaintiff's mark, he may have registered his mark which may then afford him a statutory defence.

It is no defence that the defendant was ignorant of the plaintiff's right. A defendant may where appropriate claim laches or acquiescence.

Attitude of the court

Exemplary damages (*Cassell & Co Ltd v Broome* [1972] AC 1027) may be awarded where appropriate.

Hazards and pitfalls

The plaintiff must be the registered owner of the trademark but provided application has been made for registration at the date of issue of the writ, leave may be given on his application for an injunction for him to continue with his application.

Alternative jurisdiction

There is no jurisdiction outside the Chancery Division.

Textbook

TA Blanco White & R Jacob, *Kerly's Law of Trade Marks and Trade Names*, 12th edn, (Sweet & Maxwell, 1986).

4. Passing off

Passing off is an action at common law between traders, one alleging against the other the use of a name or get up calculated to cause confusion with his own name or get up. A cognate tort is unlawful competition. Both such torts are considered injuries to a right to property in protection of which the courts will interfere. The onus on the plaintiff in a passing off action is to establish the existence of the business reputation which he seeks to protect and that the public have been and would be deceived.

Parties and intitulement

There are no special requirements.

The objective of the plaintiff

The remedies and relief are as for an action for infringement of a registered trademark namely for an injunction and damages or an account.

Required/have ready/on issue

Writ—the general indorsement will be for an injunction to restrain the defendant from passing off the defendant's product as and for the plaintiff's product and for damages or an account.

Sequence

(1) The normal procedure which accompanies a writ action.
(2) Discovery or interrogatories cannot be resisted merely because they might disclose information as to the defendant's customers. Particulars of confusion, deception and passing off are not generally ordered before the defence is served.

Plaintiff's/defendant's considerations

As for infringement in trademark actions.

Alternative jurisdiction

There is no alternative tribunal.

Textbooks

D Young, *Passing Off*, 2nd edn, (Longman, 1989).
J Drysdale & M Silverleaf, *Passing Off Law and Practice*, (Butterworths, 1986).

5. Breach of confidence

Breach of confidence is a tort which has affinities with conversion. The wrong is unauthorised use of information given in confidence to another. When such unauthorised use additionally constitutes a breach of some specific contract it may be sufficient simply to bring an action for breach of that contract instead of bringing an action for breach of confidence. In litigation concerning breach of confidence there may be a conflict between public interest and private interest. For example, the court may consider that public interest in some medical drug outweighs any private interest of the makers in preventing discussion of it. However, a conflicting view taken by some judges is that information which is regarded by the giver and recognised by the recipient as confidential and the nature of which has connection with the commercial interests of the party confiding it, necessarily imposes on the recipient a fiduciary obligation to maintain its confidentiality (see for example the conflicting judgments of Denning MR and Shaw LJ in *Schering Chemicals Ltd v Falkman Ltd* [1981] 2 WLR 848 at 851 and 868).

The present law does not apply where information is taken from another by telephone-tapping, theft, or deception; and on the grounds that the present law is too limited in scope, conceptually uncertain, and inadequate as to remedies the Law Commission's Report of 1981 (Law Com No 110 Cmnd 8388) recommends that it should be replaced by statute.

Statute/order

There is as yet no statute and no specific order.

Parties

The plaintiff will be the party who has divulged the information and the defendant the party who has made unauthorised use of it.

Intitulement

There is no special intitulement.

The objective of the plaintiff

The plaintiff's objective will be to obtain a declaration as to the confidentiality of the information and that the defendant is not entitled to use it. He is likely to seek an injunction to restrain future use of the information and also if appropriate a mandatory injunction to compel disclosure of the use which has been made of it already. The plaintiff may also ask for an order for delivery up of material containing the information. There may also be claimed as relief, damages or an account and, if appropriate, the appointment of a receiver to take possession of profits made.

Required/have ready/on issue

In simple cases an originating summons could be used but otherwise in order to show how the case is put, a writ and pleadings will be necessary. In any case, an originating summons should not be used if it would be unwise to divulge evidence in chief before the trial.

The statement of claim should be precise as to the information or communication alleged to be confidential, failing which an interim injunction is likely to be refused. The confidential information may be contained in exhibits to affidavits used in support of a motion to obtain an interlocutory injunction, including an *ex parte* motion before issue of writ. In such cases, the statement of claim should refer to the exhibits without setting out their contents and should plead that the confidential information should not be read out in open court.

Sequence

(1) If particulars of confidentiality are ordered, this may be on terms that they be not filed with the pleadings and that they

be used by the defendant only for the action and that their disclosure be limited to the defendant and his legal advisers.

(2) The action if commenced by writ will pursue the normal course of a writ action; if not it will proceed as is usual with an originating summons.

Plaintiff's considerations

The plaintiff will need to plead (*a*) the precise content of the information, (*b*) the origin of its confidentiality, (*c*) the circumstances in which the defendant obtained it, (*d*) the identity of any relevant contract, when how and by whom made and its relevant terms, (*e*) full particulars of the alleged unauthorised use and/or disclosure of the information and, finally, (*f*) the nature of the loss suffered and if applicable the loss anticipated.

Defendant's considerations

The defendant may be in a position to deny the plaintiff's title or plead a denial of any confidentiality. In some cases he may be able to deny that any process was secret in respect of which he obtained the information. Additionally, he may be able to assert that the information is in the public domain and was not obtained from the plaintiff or his predecessor under an obligation of confidence. The defendant may also simply aver that the information is not of a kind which the court protects, putting the onus on the plaintiff to advance legal argument.

Alternative jurisdiction

The county court's jurisdiction would be limited to those cases in which the damages claimed did not exceed £5,000. However, judges and registrars of county courts are not likely to have had familiarity with this type of action which rarely if at all appear in county court lists.

Textbook

A E Turner, *The Law of Trade Secrets*, (Sweet & Maxwell, 1962).

Forms and precedents

For writ see Form 45 in Atkin, Vol 31. For Affidavit see Form 49 in Atkin, Vol 31. For injunction see Form 22 in Atkin, Vol 22.

Intellectual Property—Orders

1. ORDER APPOINTING SCIENTIFIC ADVISER

UPON MOTION made by Counsel for the Plaintiff .../Defendant ...
AND UPON HEARING Counsel for the Defendant .../Plaintiff ...
AND UPON READING the documents recorded on the Court file as having been read

IT IS ORDERED

1 that ... of ... ((hereinafter called the Scientific Adviser) be appointed under Order 104, Rule 11 of the Rules of the Supreme Court to

2 sit with the Judge at the trial of this Action [and Counterclaim] ... inquire and report on the following questions of fact [or of opinion] that is to say ...

3 that the Scientific Adviser shall conduct his first examination in the presence of the duly authorised expert and representatives of the Plaintiff ... and of the Defendant ... respectively

4 that the report of the Scientific Adviser be made to the Court and be accompanied by ... photographic copies for the use of the Plaintiff ... and Defendant ... respectively

5 that the Plaintiff ... and the Defendant ... be at liberty to cross-examine the Scientific Adviser at the trial of this Action [and Counterclaim]

6 that the costs of the said Application be costs in the Action [and Counterclaim]

2. EXAMPLES OF DIRECTIONS

IT IS ORDERED [by consent] that

1 The official printers' copies or legible facsimile copies of the specification of the Patent in suit [and of the specifications of the Patent cited in the Particulars of Objections together with legible facsimile copies of any other documents cited therein] may be used at the trial without further proof thereof of their contents

2 The plaintiff ... and the defendant ... respectively shall on or before ... make and serve on the other of them a list of the documents which are or have been in their possession custody or power relating to the matters in question in the Action [and Counterclaim] and on request file an affidavit verifying such list. If either party wishes to inspect the documents it shall give notice in writing that it wishes to do so and such inspection shall be allowed at all reasonable times upon reasonable notice

3 The plaintiff ... be at liberty [without re-serving the same] to amend the Writ of Summons [in the manner indicated on the draft amended Writ of Summons retained on the court file] and that the costs of and occasioned by the said amendment be the defendant's costs in any event

4 The plaintiff ... be at liberty to amend the Statement of Claim [and Particulars of Infringements] as shown in red in the proposed amended Statement of Claim [and Particulars of Infringements] as signed by the solicitors for the parties [and retained on the court file] and to reserve the amended Statement of Claim [and Particulars of Infringements] on or before ... and that the defendant ... be at liberty to re-serve an amended Defence (if so advised) within ... days thereafter (and that the plaintiff be at liberty to re-serve an amended Reply (if so advised) within ... days thereafter) and that the costs of and occasioned by the amendments be the defendant's costs in any event

5 (1) The defendant ... be at liberty to amend the Defence [and Counterclaim and Particulars of Objections] as shown in red in the proposed amended Defence [and Counterclaim and Particulars of Objections] as signed by the solicitors for the parties hereto [and retained on the court file] and to re-serve the amended Defence [and Counterclaim and Particulars of Objections] on or before ... 199 ... with liberty to the plaintiff to re-serve an amended Reply [and Defence to Counterclaim] (if so advised) within ... days thereafter] and that the costs of and occasioned by the amendments be the plaintiff's in any event

(2) The plaintiff ... shall on or before ... 199 ... elect whether they will discontinue this Action and withdraw their Defence to the Counterclaim and consent to an Order for the revocation of Patent No ... and if the plaintiff ... shall give notice thereof to the defendant ... within the time aforesaid it is ordered that Patent No ... be revoked and that it be referred to the Taxing Master to tax the costs of the defendant ... of this Action up to and including the date of the delivery of the Particulars of Objections and the Counterclaim except in so far as the same have been increased by reason of the failure

of the defendant ... originally to deliver the Particulars of Objections in their amended form and to tax the costs of the plaintiff ... of this Action subsequent to the date of delivery of the Particulars of Objections to the date of this order and of the Counterclaim in so far as they have been increased by reason of the failure of the defendant ... aforesaid AND it is ordered that the Taxing Master is to set off the said costs of the defendant ... and of the plaintiff ... when so taxed as aforesaid and to certify to which of them the balance after such set-off is due AND it is ordered that such balance be paid by the party from whom to the party to whom the same shall be certified to be due

6 The plaintiff ... shall give security for the defendant's costs in the sum of £ ... by [paying the said sum into court and giving notice of such payment in to the defendant] [paying the said sum into an account at ... Bank of ... in the joint name of solicitors for the parties] [giving to the defendant a bond securing the said sum] on or before ... and that in the meantime all further proceedings be stayed

7 The plaintiff ... shall serve on the defendant ... on or before ... 199 ... the further and better Particulars of the Statement of Claim [and the Particulars of Infringement] specified in the defendant's request for further and better Particulars served on ... 199 ...

8 The defendant ... shall serve on the plaintiff ... on or before ... 199 ... the further and better Particulars of the Defence [and Counterclaim and the Particulars of Objection] specified in the plaintiff's request for further and better Particulars served ... 199 ...

9 The plaintiff ... shall serve on the defendant ... on or before ... 199 ... the further and better Particulars of the Reply [and Defence to Counterclaim] specified in the defendant's Request for further and better Particulars served ... 199 ...

10 The plaintiff ... shall state in writing on or before ... 199 ... whether or not it makes the admissions requested in the defendant's Request for Admissions served ... 199 ...

11 The defendant ... shall state in writing on or before ... 199 ... whether or not it makes the admissions requested in the plaintiff's Request for Admissions served ... 199 ...

12 (1) (a) If either party shall desire to rely at the trial of this Action [and Counterclaim] upon any model apparatus drawing

photograph or cinematograph film that party shall on or before ... 199 ... give notice thereof to the other shall afford the other party an opportunity within ... days of the service of such notice of inspecting the same and shall if so requested furnish the other party with copies of any such drawing or photograph and a sufficient drawing photograph or other illustration of any model or apparatus

(b) If either party shall wish to rely upon any experiment that party shall within the like period give notice thereof to the other accompanied by full and precise details of the same and shall afford the other party an opportunity if so requested of inspecting a performance of such experiment. Any such inspection shall be requested within 14 days after delivery of the notice to which it relates and shall take place within ... days of the date of such request

(2) If either party shall wish to rely upon any model apparatus drawing photograph cinematograph film or experiment in reply to any matter of which notice was given under sub-paragraph (1) of this paragraph that party shall within ... days after the last inspection to be made in pursuance of the said sub-paragraph (1) give to the other party a like notice accompanied in the case of an experiment with details to that to be given under the said sub-paragraph (1) if so requested within 14 days of delivery of such notice and shall afford like opportunities of inspection which shall take place within ... days of such request and shall in like manner furnish copies of any drawing or photograph and illustration of any such model or apparatus

(3) A party offering inspection under the foregoing provisions of this paragraph of the performance of any experiment shall (unless and to the extent that he shall have been given exemption by consent or by order of the court) secure to the party inspecting the experiment an opportunity to obtain drawings or photographs or other sufficient illustrations or data as may be requested by that party of any apparatus on or in connection with which such experiment was performed and provide any samples as may be reasonably requested. A party making any such drawings or photographs or other illustrations within ... days after such inspection give notice to the other party of any of them upon which he desires to rely at the trial and shall if so requested furnish copies thereof

(4) No further or other model apparatus drawing photograph cinematograph film or experiment shall be relied upon in evidence by either party save with mutual consent or by leave of the court

13 Any of the times herein mentioned may be enlarged by mutual consent for a period not exceeding one month or otherwise by leave of the court

14 The trial of these proceedings shall be before an Assigned Judge alone in London

15 Any party may set down this Action [and Counterclaim] for trial within 21 days after the expiry of all times provided for in this Order

16 The costs of this application [save for those hereinbefore referred to] are to be costs in the cause

17 The parties are to be at liberty on 2 days' notice to apply for further directions and generally.

Notes

1 This is a composite form to include all the likely orders required in a patent action and is the specimen form of order for directions approved by the patent judges.

2 In patent actions agreed minutes of order on a summons for directions, or on any interlocutory order, must be signed by counsel for all parties and lodged at room 156 so that the order can be made by the master without an attendance. If the parties are not agreed, an application must be made by motion to one of the assigned judges. Practice Direction (Patent Actions: Directions) [1973] 1 WLR 1425 and Practice Directions (Chancery: Applications by Post or Telephone) [1983] 1 WLR 791.

3. DECLARATION THAT PATENT IS VALID BUT NO INFRINGEMENT

IT IS DECLARED that the plaintiff's Patent numbered ... is valid but that such Patent has not been infringed by the defendant ...

AND IT IS ORDERED

1 that this Action shall stand dismissed out of this court

AND THIS COURT CERTIFIES that upon the trial of this Action the validity of the Patent was contested

AND IT IS ORDERED

2 that the following costs be taxed that is to say
   (i) the costs of the plaintiff ... in so far as the same relate to the issue of validity
   (ii) the costs of the defendant ... in so far as the same relate to the issue of infringement
   AND the general costs of this Action are to be apportioned between these two issues as the Taxing Master shall think fit.
   (iii) the costs of the defendant ... of the Counterclaim except in so far as such costs have been increased by the claim for revocation in such costs to be the plaintiff's costs
   AND the Taxing Master is to set off the respective costs of the plaintiff ... and of the defendant ... and to certify to which of them the balance after such set off is due

IT IS ORDERED

3 that such balance be paid by the party from whom to the party to whom the same shall be certified to be due.

4. EXAMPLES OF ORDERS ON APPEAL FROM THE COMPTROLLER GENERAL OF PATENTS

1 THIS COURT DOES NOT THINK FIT to grant leave to the Appellant to adduce further evidence

2 IT IS ORDERED
   that the Appellant be at liberty to adduce further evidence [being the ... of ...] [specified in the schedule hereto] and the exhibits therein referred to

3 that the said Appeal be allowed and that the said Decision dated ... be discharged

4 that the said Decision dated ... be affirmed and that the Appeal of the Appellant therefrom be dismissed

5 THIS COURT remits the above mentioned application of the Appellant to the Comptroller-General [for him to take such further steps as may be necessary in the light of the judgment of this Court] [to enable the Appellant to file evidence in support of the above mentioned application to amend [Letters] Patent numbered ... and for the said application to be reconsidered by the Comptroller-General in the light of the judgment of this Court] [to enable the same to be proceeded with]

6 IT IS DECLARED that pursuant to Section 5(2) of the Patents Act 1977 Application No ... in suit be allowed to proceed with the declared priority date of ... for the Appellant's United Kingdom Application based on its/their ... Application No ...

7 THE COURT DETERMINES that the patent in suit do stand with the claim amended in the form of amended Claim numbered ...

8 THIS COURT FINDS ... in respect of Claims numbered ... of the Specification in suit

9 AND THIS COURT decides that no opportunity be given to the Appellant to submit proposals for amendment of the Application in suit

10 AND THIS COURT refuses the grant of a Patent in pursuance of the application in suit

11 THIS COURT grants the Appellant a period of ... from the date of this Order in which to submit proposals for amendment to the Comptroller-General to consider in the light of the judgment of this court

12 THIS COURT decides that in the event of the Appellant appealing from this Order and such appeal being allowed then the times limited by Section ... of the Patents Act 199 ... for putting the application for a Patent in order for acceptance shall be extended for a period of ... after the determination of such appeal

13 IT IS DECLARED that the Appellant's time under Section ... of the Patents Act 199 ... for putting the application in order for acceptance be extended for a period of 4 weeks from the date of entry of this Order and if an appeal to the Court of Appeal be lodged within such period and be prosecuted with diligence then the time under the said Section ... shall be further extended for a period of ... after the determination of such appeal but if no appeal be lodged within such period then the time under Section ... be extended for ... after the expiry of the said period

14 THIS COURT [sets aside the Order for costs before the said Officer and] awards the ... the sum of £ ... as a contribution towards its/their costs of the said Appeal and ORDERS that this sum be paid to them by the ...

15 THIS COURT DOES NOT THINK FIT to grant leave to the ... to appeal from this Order

16 AND IT IS ORDERED that the ... be at liberty to appeal from this Order to the Court of Appeal.

5. LEAVE TO AMEND SPECIFICATION

[AND the plaintiff ... by its/their Counsel having requested in the presence of Counsel for the defendant ... that in addition to the amendments to the Specification indicated in red on the copy annexed hereto the plaintiff ... be at liberty to make the further amendments as indicated in green ink on the said copy Specification
THE COURT DISPENSES with the advertisement pursuant to Order 104 Rule 3 of the Rules of the Supreme Court of the said further amendments]
[THIS COURT DOES NOT THINK FIT to give leave to the plaintiff ... to amend the Specification of Patent numbered ...]

IT IS ORDERED

1 that the plaintiff ... be at liberty to amend the Specification of Patent numbered ... in the manner indicated in red (and green) ink in the copy of the Specification annexed hereto

2 that the plaintiff ... and the defendant ... are to be at liberty to make any consequential amendments to the Pleadings

3 that the costs of the said Motion [including therein the costs reserved by the Order dated ...] and of and occasioned by the amendments to the Pleadings be borne by the plaintiff ... in any event

AND the defendants are to be at liberty to appeal from this Order.

6. INTERIM ORDER: LEAVE TO AMEND SPECIFICATION

And the plaintiff by his counsel undertakes to obey any Order this court may make as to terms which this court may hereafter think fit to impose as to the matters mentioned in Order 104 Rule 3 of the Rules of the Supreme Court including terms as to the costs of the said Motion and not in the meantime to threaten to bring or proceed with any pending actions for infringement of the said Patent

IT IS ORDERED

1 that the plaintiff ... be at liberty to proceed with this Motion for leave to amend the Specification upon which Patent numbered ... was granted as indicated in red ink on the copy of the said

specification certified by Her Majesty's Comptroller-General of Patents Designs and Trade Marks on the court file

2 that the plaintiff ... shall on or before ... 199 ... serve a statement of the reasons relied upon in support of the said Motion and that the defendant ... do serve an Answer thereto on or before ...

3 that the evidence to be adduced at the hearing of the said Motion be adduced by affidavit

4 that the plaintiff ... shall on or before ... 199 ... file evidence in support of the said Motion including an affidavit of documents

5 that the defendant ... shall file evidence in answer within ... weeks after the filing of the said evidence of the plaintiff ...

6 that the plaintiff ... shall within ... weeks after receipt of copies of the defendant ... evidence (filed as aforesaid) file evidence in reply

7 that the said Motion be heard before the trial of the Action and Counterclaim

8 that the parties are to be at liberty within ... days after [service of the Answer] [the expiry of the time limited for filing evidence in reply by the defendant ...] to set down the said Motion for hearing in the Non-Witness List

9 that the said Motion be made on oral evidence and shall come on with the trial of this Action and Counterclaim and for that purpose the said Motion is to stand over accordingly

10 the costs of this hearing of the said Motion are [to be costs in the said Motion] [to be costs in the Action and Counterclaim] [reserved to be dealt with by the judge upon the determination of the said Motion]

AND the parties are to be at liberty to apply [(a) for further directions including discovery and (b) generally].

7. ORDER DISMISSING APPEAL BY CONSENT

UPON READING the Notice of Appeal dated ... of the Appellant from the Decision of the Officer acting for the Comptroller-General of

Patents [Designs and Trade Marks] dated ... and the documents recorded on the court file as having been read

IT IS BY CONSENT ORDERED

1 that the said Appeal be dismissed and struck out of the list of appeals for hearing

2 that the ... shall pay to the Comptroller-General his costs of and occasioned by the said Appeal such costs to be taxed if not agreed

[AND THIS COURT awards the Comptroller-General the sum of £ ... as an agreed contribution towards his costs and by consent ORDERS that the said sum be paid to him by the Appellant].

8. ORDER ON TRIAL OF INFRINGEMENT ACTION WITH COUNTERCLAIM FOR REVOCATION OF PATENT ETC—INFRINGEMENT CLAIM SUCCEEDS

IT IS ORDERED

1 that the Defendant ... be restrained (whether acting by [...] directors officers servants or agents or any of them or otherwise howsoever) from infringing the Plaintiff's Patent numbered ...

2 that the Defendant ... do [forthwith] deliver up to the Plaintiff ... or destroy upon oath all [articles] in the Defendant's possession custody or power which infringe the Plaintiff's Patent numbered ...

3 that the following Inquiry be made that is to say
An Inquiry as to what damages (if any) the Plaintiff ... has/have sustained by reason of the infringement of its/their Patent numbered ... by the Defendant

4 AND THIS COURT CERTIFIES that upon the trial of this Action and Counterclaim the validity of claims ... of the specification of the Plaintiff's Patent numbered ... was contested

AND IT IS ORDERED

that the Counterclaim shall stand dismissed
that the Defendant ...shall pay to the Plaintiff ... its/their costs

of this Action and Counterclaim down to and including this Order such costs to be taxed if not agreed
    that the costs of the Inquiry be reserved
    AND the parties are to be at liberty to apply.

Notes

1. This form is a composite of typical orders which may be made at the end of a patent infringement action and revocation counterclaim. With slight differences noted below it is equally applicable to a trademark, registered design or passing off actions and demonstrates the similarity in purpose of actions dealing with intellectual property.

2. Injunction against infringement. In a common type of trademark case the act restrained could be 'from infringing the Plaintiff's Registered Trademark No ...;'
   Similarly in a passing off action the act restrained could be 'from passing off ... not of the Plaintiff's as and for ...of the Plaintiff';
   In a copyright case the prohibited act could be 'infringing the Plaintiff's copyright by [causing to be heard in public the sound recording... during the subsistence of the Plaintiff's copyright in the said sound recording]';
   In a registered design case the prohibited act could be 'from infringing the Plaintiff's Registered Design No ...'

3. Delivery up. Such an order is not appropriate in trademark cases as the Plaintiff is only entitled to destruction of the mark not the article bearing such mark. In these cases the court may order the obliteration of the mark.
   In passing off actions orders for delivery up are more commonly made if the infringing act is in the passing off of a design 'get up' rather than by a confusingly similar mark as in trademark cases where obliteration of the mark would more appropriately be ordered.
   In registered design cases the equivalent order might be 'that the Defendants do at the Defendants' option either deliver up or destroy on oath all articles in their possession custody or control which infringe the Plaintiff's Registered Design No ...'

4. Inquiry. With minor changes in terminology inquiries as to damages may also be ordered in trademarks, registered design, passing off.

5. Certificate of contested validity. In registered design cases the certificate would be that upon the trial of this action the validity of the registration of the said design was contested.

9. ORDER WHERE INFRINGEMENT ACTION FAILS, REVOCATION COUNTERCLAIM SUCCEEDS

IT IS ORDERED

1. that this Action shall stand dismissed

2 that upon the Counterclaim that the Patent numbered ... be revoked save that the said Order for revocation shall lie in the Patent Office for four weeks from the date on which this Order is entered and if during the said four weeks the Plaintiff ... shall serve upon the Defendant ... a Notice of Appeal from this Order [or do give notice of intention to apply under Section *[ ] of the Patents Act 19 for leave to amend the Specification of the said Patent] the said Order for revocation shall continue to lie in the pending determination of the said appeal [or pending the determination of the said application to amend]

AND THIS COURT CERTIFIES

1 paragraphs ... of the ... Particulars of Objections [in so far as they allege ...] to have been proven

2 paragraphs ... of the ... Particulars of Objections to have been reasonable and proper

3 If on any Appeal the Defendant ... are allowed to amend paragraphs ... of the ... Particulars of Objections that the said Particulars have been reasonable and proper

AND IT IS ORDERED

(...) that the Plaintiff ... shall pay to the Defendant ... its/their costs of this Action and Counterclaim save for the costs of the issues raised by the ... Particulars of Objections which have not been certified by this Court as proven or as reasonable and proper such costs to be taxed if not agreed (...)

AND THIS COURT makes no Order as to the costs of [the Plaintiff's Experiments in Reply].

Notes

1 The form may be adapted for proceedings commenced by petition for revocation of a patent. However, the issue more frequently comes before the court by way of a counterclaim in an infringement action which fails.

2 In either case there will be particulars of objection filed which the associate should refer to, particularly when the judge is dealing with certifying proven and reasonable or proper objections. As objections are frequently re-amended, be sure to obtain the most up to date copy from the parties.

3 Petitions as well as counterclaims for revocation are tried on oral evidence.

4 Section 30 of the Patents Act 1949 and s 75 of the Patents Act 1977 apply to petitions for revocation as well as to actions for infringement and a patentee may be allowed to amend his specification after the legal proceedings have commenced.

5 If the court decides that the patent is invalid (as in this form) it may allow the specification to be amended instead of revoking the patent.

6 It is usual to stay the order for revocation pending an appeal. The associate should seek clarification if the judge leaves the point unclear after the issue of leave to appeal has been referred to.

7 The successful petitioner/counterclaimant will ask for a certificate regarding the various particulars of objection. Usually the objections are identified in the order by their number for this purpose. The importance of the certificate is that no costs are allowable on taxation of any particulars of breaches or objections not certified by the court to have been proved or to have been reasonable and proper.

8 If any claim in a patent whose validity is contested is found to be valid the court may so certify. This is the 'certificate of contested validity'.

9 The revocation proceedings may also come before the court by way of appeal from the decision of the comptroller.

10 Procedure for an appeal is prescribed by Ord 104, r 14. The appellant issues a notice of appeal by originating motion. The evidence at the hearing is the same as that used before the comptroller unless leave to adduce further evidence is obtained.

11 Further appeal lies to the Court of Appeal from the Patents Court acting in its appellate capacity when considering revocation.

12 An appeal lies from any decision of the comptroller on infringement or invalidity to the Patents Court and thereafter, with leave of the Patents Court or the Court of Appeal, to the Court of Appeal.

10. REGISTERED DESIGN ORDER ON TRIAL OF INFRINGEMENT ACTION

IT IS ORDERED

that the Defendant ... be restrained (whether acting by its/their directors servants agents or any of them or otherwise howsoever) from infringing the Plaintiff's Registered Design No ...

that the Defendant ... do either deliver up or at the Defendant's option destroy on oath all articles in its/their possession custody or control which infringe the said Registered Design that the following Inquiry be made that is to say an Inquiry as to what damages the Plaintiff ... has sustained by reason of the Defendant's infringement of the said Registered Design

[that the Counterclaim shall stand dismissed]

that the Defendant shall pay to the Plaintiff its cost of this Action [and Counterclaim] incurred down to and including this Order such costs to be taxed if not agreed

that the costs of the Inquiry be reserved

that the parties be at liberty to apply

AND THIS COURT CERTIFIES that the validity of the registration of the said Design was contested in these proceedings

11. REGISTERED DESIGN—EXAMPLES OF APPEAL ORDERS

REGISTERED DESIGNS APPEAL TRIBUNAL [IN BANC] ... 19...

MR JUSTICE

[and]

MR JUSTICE

... DAY the ... day of ... 19...

IN THE MATTER of the APPLICATION No ...

by ...

for ...

UPON THE APPEAL of ... (hereinafter called the Appellant) from the Decision of the Registrar of Designs dated ...

AND UPON HEARING ... for the Appellant and ... for ... (hereinafter called the Respondent)

AND UPON READING the documents recorded on the Court file as having been read

THIS TRIBUNAL affirms the said Decision and dismisses the Appeal of the Appellant

THIS TRIBUNAL reverses the said Decision and allows the Appeal of the Appellant therefrom

AND THIS TRIBUNAL remits the above mentioned Application to the Registrar [for the Application to proceed to Registration]

AND THIS TRIBUNAL FINDS that the Appellant is entitled to the priority date of ... in respect of its/their above mentioned Application

IT IS ORDERED

that the Register of Designs be rectified by expunging therefrom the Designs Nos ...
   that due notice of this Order be given to the Registrar
   AND THIS TRIBUNAL makes no Order as to costs
   AND THIS TRIBUNAL awards the ... the sum of £ ... as a contribution towards ... costs of the said Appeal and ORDERS that the said sum be paid to ... by the ...

12. TRADEMARKS—ORDERS ON APPEAL FROM THE REGISTRAR OF TRADEMARKS

IN THE MATTER of APPLICATION Number ... by ... to register a TRADEMARK

[IN THE MATTER of OPPOSITION Number ... by ... thereto]
   UPON MOTION pursuant to Originating Notice of Motion made by Counsel for the Appellants ... by way of Appeal from the Decision dated ... of the Registrar of Trademarks whereby ...
   AND UPON HEARING Counsel for the Respondents to the said Motion the above named ...
   AND UPON READING the documents recorded on the Court File as having been read

IT IS ORDERED

1   that the said [Motion do stand dismissed] [Decision be reversed]

2   that the Registrar do proceed with the Registration of Trade Mark No ... as modified by ...

THIS COURT DECLARES that for the purpose of the above-mentioned Application to the Registrar the Mark applied for by the Application is to be deemed to be a distinctive one within the meaning of Section 9 of the Trade Marks Act 1938

AND IT IS ORDERED

1   that the Registrar shall accept the said Application No ... by ... to register a Trademark and shall proceed with the same accordingly

2   that the said Decision be reversed and that the Registrar do not proceed with the Trademark Application No ...

3 that the Appellant/Respondent/Registrar shall pay to the Respondent/Appellant/and to the Registrar (a) their costs of the same Motion such costs to be taxed if not agreed and (b) their costs of the proceedings before the Registrar on the Registrar's official scale

4 that the Appellant/Respondent shall pay to the Registrar the sum of £ ... for his costs of the said Appeal

5 that an office copy of this Order be duly served by the ... upon the Registrar

13. TRADEMARKS—EXAMPLES OF ORDERS FOR RECTIFICATION OF THE REGISTER OF TRADEMARKS

1 IN THE MATTER of REGISTERED TRADEMARK NO ... registered in the name of ... in Class ...

2 UPON MOTION made by Counsel for ... (hereinafter called the Applicant) pursuant to Originating Notice of Motion
    AND UPON HEARING Counsel for ... the Respondent
    AND UPON READING the documents recorded on the Court File as having been read

IT IS ORDERED

3 that the Register of Trade Marks be rectified by the removal of the Mark therein registered in Class ... for [...] included in that Class and numbered ...

4 that the Register of Trade Marks be rectified by removing therefrom the name of ... as proprietors of the above-mentioned Trademark No ... and substituting therefor the name of ... as the registered proprietors

5 that the entry of Trademark No ... in the Register of Trade Marks be varied by adding a note that ...

6 that the Register of Trade Marks be rectified by limiting the claim in respect of Trademark No ... registered in Class ... to

7 that the [Applicant] [Respondent] shall pay to the [Respondent] [Appellant] [and the Registrar] their costs of the said Motion such costs to be taxed if not agreed

8 that the Decision of the Registrar (whereby he awarded the [Applicant] [Opponent] ... the sum of £ ... for costs in the above mentioned [Application] [Opposition] and directed that the said sum be paid by the said [Applicant] [Opponent]) be made an Order of this Court

9 that the [Applicant] [Opponent] shall pay to the Respondent £ ... their costs of the said Motion to be taxed if not agreed

10 that an office copy of this Order be duly served upon the Registrar.

Chapter Sixteen

Land and Other Specific Property

1. Joint property

Introduction

When there is no express trust, the contributions or mortgage repayments of a husband, wife or cohabitee, or particular circumstances, may raise an equity and a trust may be implied. Contention as to whether an equity has been raised is frequently litigated (see *Snell's Principles of Equity* (28th edn) 180-183). Apart from proceedings where husbands, wives, cohabitees and other joint tenants cannot agree, a court order may be required whenever trustees are not in accord as to the exercise of their power of sale, where beneficiaries desire a sale which is refused by trustees, or where trustees require an enlargement of their powers of sale, for example, where a consent requisite under the terms of the trust is withheld. Whether a trust be created by the same instrument which creates rights, or whether the trust be created collaterally, neither statute nor common law gives a court power to adjust property rights by redrafting the terms of a trust. For example, if there is a trust to provide a home for parties and/or their children for the indefinite future if the court considers a sale would 'redraft' the terms of the trust, the court may refuse an immediate sale or any sale. Always it is the terms and the intention of the trust, and the evidence thereof, that are paramount.

Statutes

The Law of Property Act 1925, s 30 provides that if trustees for sale or any one of them refuse to sell, or if a requisite consent cannot be obtained, then a person interested may apply to the court for an order directing the trustees to give effect to the proposed transaction and the court may then make such order as it thinks fit.

The Trustee Act 1925, s 57 gives the court power to authorise dealings with trust property. Section 12(1) of the Law of Property Act 1925 gives a general power to trustees to sell subject to such conditions respecting title as they think fit. Ord 31, r 1 empowers the Chancery Division to order possession and sale of land where it appears necessary or expedient for the purposes of the cause or matter.

Order

Ord 93, r 4 contains rules relating to applications under a variety of statutes which include the Trustee Act 1925 but not the Law of Property Act 1925 and there is no order specific to the enforcing of a trust for sale. Order 44 enables the court where the action is (*inter alia*) for the execution of a trust or the sale of any property to direct notice of any judgment (or order) or direction to be served on any person who although not a party is affected by the judgment or direction, and such person, subject to opportunity to apply, shall be bound by the judgment, order, or direction.

Parties

The plaintiff will be a person beneficially entitled to a share in the proceeds of sale or a trustee who is not himself a defendant and the defendants will be all of the other trustees if they themselves are not plaintiffs and any person who refuses his requisite consent.

Intitulement

Example 'In the matter of the Trusts Deed/Conveyance between AB of the one part and CD of the other part'.

The objective of the plaintiff

The plaintiff will seek an order for sale of the joint property, a declaration as to the division of the proceeds, an inquiry as to the ownership of shares in the proceeds, and for such directions as may be required.

Originating process

The action is usually commenced by originating summons. Action may be taken under Ord 93 when the plaintiff requires an order for the sale of the trust property or for the concurrence of a dissenting trustee leaving the conduct of the sale in the hands of the trustees unless it is considered preferable to apply for an order for a sale under the control of the court (Ord 31) when the court may be asked to give directions on any of the following matters:

(1) appointment of solicitors to have conduct of the sale,
(2) manner of sale and whether by auction, private treaty or otherwise,
(3) obtaining a valuation and fixing a reserve price,
(4) approval by the court of the contract and conditions of sale,

(5) reference to conveyancing counsel,
(6) scale of fees and security (if any) of auctioneer,
(7) payment into court of the proceeds of the sale, and
(8) liberty to apply.

If the parties can obtain it by prior negotiation the order the most convenient and expeditious and the least expensive to them would be 'that the conduct of the sale be with Messrs XY the plaintiff's/defendant's solicitors with liberty to apply'.

Required/have ready/on issue

(1) Originating summons quoting therein s 30 of the Law of Property Act 1925.
(2) An affidavit establishing facts from which it may be adduced that the trust has ended and exhibiting the trust deed or office copies and any other supporting documents.
(3) The trust deed or conveyance or office copy entries and if separate, the vesting deed or assent. (Specimen originating summons, affidavits and orders are given below.)

Sequence

(1) On the first appointment the evidence should be complete and when the only resistance must be weak and the master can be so persuaded, the master will make the order but if he considers evidence should be filed in answer and reply, he will so direct. If he considers there is no evidence or doubtful or arguable evidence he will generally adjourn the summons into court in the non-witness list so that the evidence and argument may be considered. There will be cases where it will be necessary to have more than one appointment and the master may continue to give directions until he is satisfied that the evidence is complete at which time he will consider, but only if there are strong grounds, any application for oral evidence of deponents; if such evidence is to be given, he will direct that the action be set down in the witness list.
(2) When the application is made under Ord 31, the consequential directions may be expected to be included in the order for sale, but if not directions are deferred and if they are still required then after the order has been passed and entered application should be made for the order; necessary directions to be given by the master. In this instance a summons in the form of a 'summons to proceed' may be the only appropriate procedure.
(3) When the directions require the payment of the proceeds into court the party having the conduct of the sale should obtain from the auctioneer or if the sale is by private treaty from the vendor's solicitors, a certificate of the result of the sale which should be lodged in chambers together with an affidavit

in verification and a lodgment schedule for approval by an executive officer and for signature by the master. After lodgment the certificate and affidavit must be filed in room 157.

Plaintiff's/defendant's considerations

The terms of the trust may entirely inhibit the court from interfering and the court will always have regard to the considerations as expressed by Devlin LJ in *Jones v Challenger* ([1961] 1 QB 176 at 181):

This simple principle [that a trust for sale is enforceable unless all the trustees agree in exercising their power of postponement] cannot prevail where the trust itself or the circumstances in which it was made show that there was a secondary or collateral object besides that of a sale.

Evidence of a secondary or collateral object is commonly found where a settlor has created a trust for sale in preference to the complexities of a settlement but with the intention that the trust property shall provide a residence for the beneficiaries for the period of a life or lives. In such a case and as a safeguard against a premature sale by the trustees, the terms of the trust may call for the consent of a named person or persons and if such consent is refused, the court will not order a sale unless it is satisfied that the refusal is unreasonable and that a sale would be in the interests of the beneficiaries. Evidence of a secondary or collateral object may well be found where, as is often the case with husband and wife, a house is conveyed to purchasers as joint tenants in law and in equity and becomes their home. Although the provision of the Matrimonial Homes Act 1967 does not preclude a sale by order of the court against the wishes of a spouse who is in occupation, the court will not readily make such an order so long as the marriage is subsisting: (*Bedson v Bedson* [1965] 2 QB 666 CA). Even if a sale is ordered, contention may arise as to the apportionment of the proceeds. The court's determination may then be sought as to the intention of the parties at the time of the purchase or subsequently and as to whether the equitable ownership was to be divided equally or as to whether it was to be made commensurate with the financial contributions of the respective parties towards the purchase price, mortgage repayments and cost of repairs and improvements. In such cases, the summons should include an application for a direction (*a*) that the proceeds of sale be paid into court unless, as would be more desirable, the parties have agreed that solicitors hold it on joint or other deposit, (*b*) that the parties have liberty to apply, (*c*) that the division of the proceeds of sale be provided for, and (*d*) that such further or other order may be made as shall be just. The application for such directions should be made within one month from the completion of the sale.

Attitude of the court

See introduction and plaintiff's/defendant's considerations.

Hazards and pitfalls

A legally aided litigant should be advised on the effect of the Law Society's charge pursuant to s 9(*b*) of the Legal Aid Act 1974 for costs under any order or agreement for costs made in the assisted person's favour and for any deficiency between costs recovered and the legal aid costs of the assisted person. The Law Society's practice is to agree to postponement of enforcement of the charge 'in appropriate cases'. The charge is on property 'recovered' or 'preserved' and this has a wide meaning (see Jessel MR in *Foxon v Gascoigne* (1874) LR 9 Ch App 654 at 657 followed by *Till v Till* [1974] QB 558).

Alternative jurisdiction

The county court has jurisdiction if the value of the equity does not exceed £30,000 (this remains notwithstanding the High Court and County Courts Jurisdiction Order 1991).

Textbooks

Sir R Goff & G Jones, *The Law of Restitution*, 3rd edn, (Sweet & Maxwell, 1986).
Sir R Megarry & HWR Wade, *Manual of the Law of Real Property*, 6th edn, (Sweet & Maxwell, 1982).

Forms and precedents

Atkin, Vol 35, pp 6 et seq; Forms Nos 1 et seq: Vol 41, pp 153-4, 166-7.

Originating summons with indorsement

IN THE HIGH COURT OF JUSTICE   1991 L. No. 6582
CHANCERY DIVISION

IN THE MATTER of the Trust declared by a Deed of
              Transfer dated 3rd February 1977
              and made between John Smith (1) and
              Jack Locket and Lucy Locket (2)

B E T W E E N

LUCY LOCKET

                                                    Plaintiff

- and -

JACK LOCKET

                                                    Defendant

TO JACK LOCKET of 57, Inner Lane, Brighton, Sussex, BN4 6AL, one of the Trustees of the above mentioned trusts.

LET the Defendant, within fourteen days after service of this Summons on him, counting the day of service, return the accompanying Acknowledgment of Service to the appropriate Court Office.

BY THIS SUMMONS, which is issued on the application of the Plaintiff LUCY LOCKET of 7, Cavendish Gardens, Spalding-on-Sea, Sussex SU4 6YN, the other Trustee of the above mentioned trusts the Plaintiff seeks the following relief namely:-

1. That the Plaintiff and the Defendant the present Trustees of the trusts declared by the above named transfer may be ordered to sell the property set forth in the Schedule hereto, being property held by them as such Trustees upon trust for sale, notwithstanding that the Defendant refuses to consent to the sale.

Originating summons with indorsement

2. Alternatively, that the property be sold by order of this Honourable Court.
3. If necessary, that the trusts may be carried into execution by this Honourable Court.
4. That the Defendant may be ordered to pay the costs of this application personally.
5. Further or other relief.

This application is made under Section 30 and 203(5) of the Law of Property Act 1925 and Section 57 of the Trustee Act 1925.

SCHEDULE

The property 57, Inner Lane, Brighton, Sussex as is registered at H.M. Land Registry under Title Number 53218 with Absolute Title.

If the Defendant does not acknowledge service, such judgment may be given or order made against or in relation to him as the Court may think just and expedient.

DATED the 17th day of August 1991

NOTE: This Summons may not be served later than four calendar months beginning with the above date unless renewed by order of the Court

---

THIS SUMMONS was taken out by Messrs. Layton & Dwyer of 1045, Bedford Gardens, London WC1B 7DS
Solicitor for the said Plaintiff whose address is as stated above.

IMPORTANT

Directions for Acknowledgment of Service are given with the accompanying form.

Affidavit

FILED on behalf of the Plaintiff
AFFIDAVIT No 1 Deponent: LUCY LOCKET
Date sworn: 21 August 1991

<u>IN THE HIGH COURT OF JUSTICE</u>   1991 L. No. 6582
<u>CHANCERY DIVISION</u>

IN THE MATTER of the Trust declared by a Deed of Transfer dated 3rd February 1977 and made between John Smith (1) and Jack Locket and Lucy Locket (2)

B E T W E E N

LUCY LOCKET

<u>Plaintiff</u>

- and -

JACK LOCKET

<u>Defendant</u>

I, LUCY LOCKET of 7, Cavendish Gardens, Spalding-on-Sea, Sussex SU4 6YN Housewife MAKE OATH AND SAY as follows:-

1. I am the Plaintiff herein. I make this affidavit from the facts within my own knowledge.

2. On 18th August 1985 I was married to Jack Locket the Defendant herein, ("Jack"). I was 20 years old and working as a secretary and Jack was 27 and working as an Equipment Salesman.

3. Six months before the wedding we had bought a flat at Clapham Park, London, for £10,000 the conveyance of which was to ourselves as joint tenants at law and in equity. I provided the deposit of £1,000 and the balance of £9,000 was borrowed on mortgage from the Seagreen Building Society.

4. We moved into the flat after the wedding. I paid the telephone bills and bought all our food and housekeeping items out of my income as a secretary, as Jack never gave me any housekeeping money. I did not directly pay any mortgage instalments.

Affidavit

5. After 18 months we sold the flat for £17,000 and on 3rd February 1987 we bought the above-named property 57, Inner Lane, Brighton, Sussex for £20,000. A true copy of the transfer thereof is now produced and shown to me marked "LL 1". The purchase price was provided as to £5,000 from the net proceeds of sale of the flat and £15,000 was borrowed on mortgage from the Seagreen Building Society. With most of the profit realised on the sale of the flat we carpeted the house and had central heating installed. The financial arrangements continued as before save that when the mortgage repayments were increased by the building society in May 1989 I paid Jack £25.00 per month towards them.

6. At this time Jack began neglecting me spending all his spare time with his friends.

7. Lack of communication and separate lives resulted in my having a nervous breakdown and I found that I could not cope with my job properly and decided to give it up in March 1990.

8. On or about 20th April 1990 I went back to live with my parents.

9. Jack is now in sole occupation of 57, Inner Lane, Brighton, which consists of a 3 bedroomed family home the value of which I estimate at £28,000. The amount outstanding on mortgage is about £13,000 so that if the property were sold we would have some £7,750 each. Jack, whose income as an Equipment Salesman is about £10,000 a year, would be perfectly able to buy a smaller property for himself with a mortgage. My own income is now about £4,000 from a part-time job and with the help of my parents and with my share of the proceeds I would be able to buy a small place of my own.

Affidavit

10. There are now produced and shown to me marked "LL 2" a true copy of a letter from my solicitors to Jack's solicitors dated 20th June 1991 and the reply thereto dated 4th July 1991 from which it appears that Jack will not agree to a sale of the property because he cannot accept that our marriage is at an end and that I have no intention whatsoever of returning to live with him. In view of his attitude however I have decided not to petition for divorce at the present time.

11. In the above circumstances I request this Honourable Court to grant the relief prayed for in the Summons herein.

SWORN at 28 High Street)
Spalding-on-Sea, Sussex)
this 21st day of August 1991)

    Before me

        LEWIS BROWN

           Solicitor

           <u>Filed on behalf of the Plaintiff</u>

Order for sale

IN THE HIGH COURT OF JUSTICE   CH 1991 M. No. 17831

CHANCERY DIVISION

        The Hon. Mr. Justice Smith

        Dated the 10th day of September 1991

BETWEEN

        MANSION LIMITED

                                      Plaintiff

        - and -

        LEWIS COLE

                                      Defendant

UPON THE APPLICATION of the Plaintiff by summons dated the 31st day of August 1991 AND UPON HEARING Counsel for the Plaintiff and the Defendant.

IT IS ORDERED that the Freehold property situate at and known as Laura Villas, Edgcombe Street, Lewes belonging to the Plaintiff be sold by public auction.

AND IT IS ORDERED that reserve prices for the said Freehold property and the remuneration of the auctioneer be fixed by the Court.

AND IT IS ORDERED that any party to this Action is to be at liberty to bid at the said sale.

AND IT IS ORDERED that the net proceeds of such sale after payment of what shall be due to any incumbrancer or incumbrancers according to their priorities and of all other proper costs charges and expenses of such sale be lodged in Court to the credit of this Action "Proceeds of sale of property" subject to further order.

Order for sale

AND IT IS ORDERED that the Defendant do pay to the Plaintiff his costs of this action down to and including this Order such costs unless agreed to be taxed by the Taxing Master on party and party basis.

Dated the 20th day of September 1991.

2. Specific performance

The grant of an order for specific performance being an equitable remedy is discretionary. In substitution for or in addition to an injunction or an order for specific performance the court in its discretion may award damages. As an example, damages are likely to be available in addition to specific performance where there has been delay in completion. Any damages awarded will be on the principles of the common law. Damages are likely to be assessed as at the date of the breach or date the wrong was committed, and not as at the date of judgment, though not necessarily (*Johnson v Agnew* [1980] AC 367).

Statute

None specifically applicable.

Order

Order 86 which applies to writ actions empowers the plaintiff to make application for summary judgment for specific performance in actions brought on contracts relating to sales, purchases, or exchanges of any property real or personal and whether the defendant has entered acknowledgment of service or not so that the summons can be issued concurrently with the writ. Order 86 does not permit a summary application for specific performance to be made in respect of a contract for the sale of landed property in which a portion of the purchase price is to be left outstanding on mortgage to the vendor.

Parties

The parties to the contract or their personal representatives or their assigns.

Intitulement

In the heading 'In the matter of a contract made the   day of   between AB and CD'.

Required/have ready/on issue

Originating summons in a simple case, for example, where it is known that there can be no defence, otherwise writ. The general indorsement in a simple action is for specific performance of an identified agreement further or alternatively, damages for breach of a specific contract, in the alternative for rescission and for forfeiture (or return) of the deposit. While under Ord 86 (unlike Ord 14) it is not a condition precedent for a statement of claim to have been served it is preferable for the statement of claim to be indorsed on the writ of summons. The statement of claim (whether or not indorsed on the writ) should set out the agreement and give particulars of its making. The plaintiff should in addition aver the performance of all conditions precedent to the relief and say that he is ready, willing and able to perform his part of the agreement and that the defendant is in breach, giving particulars of that breach.

Sequence

If the contract relates to land and whether or not an intention to defend is notified, service acknowledged, or defence served, the plaintiff is nonetheless entitled to seek summary judgment under Ord 86. The following is the procedure.

(1) Issue of a summons for an order for specific performance. Minutes of the order sought are to accompany the summons (Ord 86, r 2).
(2) The summons is to be supported by an affidavit which, if he deposes to being duly authorised, may be made by the plaintiff's solicitor and will in any case verify the facts on which the claim is based and depose to the belief that there is no defence (Ord 86, r 2). Oral evidence will not be accepted. The affidavit in support of the summons should be filed in room 156 at least four clear days before the return day.
(3) The minimum notice for service of the summons and copy affidavit is four clear days before the hearing but it is advisable to serve the summons and copy affidavit as early as possible before the return day so that a defendant will have difficulty in justifying asking for a deferment; in the event that he has been given ample notice and still serves his evidence late, the plaintiff if the summons is adjourned may seek an order for his costs of the wasted hearing.
(4) For an appointment to be obtained the summons with a copy together with the writ and a copy and the affidavit if ready together also with the acknowledgment of service, should be taken or posted to room 156.
(5) On the hearing of the summons, the master is likely to make the order if the claimant is clearly entitled (except in cases where part performance must be established). The master's powers extend similarly to claims for recission or for forfeiture of deposit. If the defendant satisfies the master that he is entitled to defend, the master will give leave with or without conditions, and then give directions. The directions would be as to further pleadings and discovery.
(6) Where title is in dispute and an order is obtained on the Ord 86 summons, or judgment obtained at trial, an inquiry as to title with all consequential directions may be ordered. The inquiry will be as to whether the vendor can show a good title. Upon the hearing of the inquiry before the master the plaintiff must provide the abstract and documents of titles

in evidence by way of exhibits to an affidavit unless the documents (for example, office copy, land registry entries and certificates of search) prove themselves. The master may but very rarely does, refer the evidence to conveyancing counsel to advise and to settle an appropriate deed or transfer. If the documents are not in the custody or control of the claimant he could consider using examined copies and give notice to produce, or use the machinery of discovery and production against a party to the suit. Where a third party, for example a mortgagee, has the documents, orders can be obtained for their production (Ord 38, r 13).

(7) Where the plaintiff is the vendor and the defendant has failed to complete in compliance with the decree of specific performance, the plaintiff may apply by motion or by summons for an order rescinding the contract and declaring plaintiff and defendant discharged from further performance, for forfeiture of deposit, and for an inquiry as to damages (*Johnson v Agnew* [1980 367 AC]). Plaintiffs who are purchasers will apply for return of deposit. The order declaring the parties to be discharged is essential if the plaintiff wishes to pursue an inquiry as to damages, otherwise the defendant could complain that he is in double jeopardy at the same time under the decree, and under the order for an inquiry; substantive damages cannot be had so long as a defendant continues to be bound by a decree. The minutes of the order where a defendant purchaser has been let into possession before completion should provide that the defendant do lodge in court the balance of the purchase monies and in default deliver up possession.

(8) Where a decree of specific performance is made by the master or the judge, the successful party will be given the usual consequential directions if title is in dispute or if after discharge of the decree there is to be an inquiry as to damages. On the hearing of the summons in a case in which the decree has not been discharged, if necessary, directions may be given as to the form of the conveyance, but in any case, the master will order the amount of the sum due on completion, the plaintiff's costs, and the time and place appointed for completion. For the preparation of the order, the plaintiff attends the accounts section and takes an appointment for the assessment of his costs and lodges a draft bill, enabling settlement of the sum due on completion which together with the time (and place) of completion will in due course be inserted in the order. Having lodged his draft bill and taken the appointment, he serves notice of the appointment with a copy of the bill. It is not necessary to take out a summons to proceed if the decree or any subsequent order did not direct the holding of an inquiry as to damages and the decree merely refers, by

way of damages or contractual addition to the price, to interest payable on completion. The decree in favour of a purchaser will describe as the amount payable on completion the sum representing the balance of the purchase price less the amount of the purchaser's assessed costs as certified, and in the decree in favour of a vendor, such balance plus contractual interest plus vendor's certified assessed costs. If the decree of specific performance is one which has not given a figure for damages, interest, or assessed costs, or if any step remains to be fulfilled, or if the decree or any subsequent order directed the holding of an inquiry, then it will be necessary to take out a summons to proceed or otherwise seek directions.
(9) When the draft conveyance or transfer has been settled, the master makes an order or declaration as to the plaintiff's title; this order will be drafted by the drafting section (room 180).

Costs

The costs may be taxed on the order for specific performance; however, in the interests of speedy completion costs of actions disposed of by summary applications are usually directed to be assessed in chambers. Costs may be ordered to be paid forthwith by a plaintiff whose application for specific performance is dismissed. Costs in specific performance applications may be assessed in chambers without monetary limits (Practice Direction, Costs: Assessment of Costs in Chambers [1975] 1 WLR 1202).

Alternative jurisdiction

The county court has jurisdiction if the value of the property does not exceed £30,000. All district registries have jurisdiction in these actions.

Textbook

ICF Spry, *The Principles of Equitable Remedies, Injunctions, Specific Performance and Equitable Damages*, 3rd edn, (Sweet & Maxwell, 1984).

Specimen action

In the action documented below the purchaser Miss Celia House has agreed orally to purchase the property owned by Miss Lorna Garden who has decided that despite taking a deposit the written receipt for which contained the terms of the agreement she would not sell the property to her. She issues a writ for specific performance. The statement of claim which appears could be indorsed on the writ of summons and indeed this may be a more expeditious way of proceeding. There may be good reasons for a short indorsement on the writ of summons with a separate statement of claim but it should be noted that if the summary procedure is to be used effectively there must be no difference of substance between the two documents. For example, the identification of the contract in both the writ and the statement of claim must strictly coincide.

As in proceedings under Ord 14 it is possible under Ord 86 to apply for summary judgment. The following is a summons for summary judgment or alternatively directions to lead to a trial of the action. This summons is issued as in Ord 14 procedure after service of the statement of claim although on some occasions it can be issued after service of the defence. It must be accompanied by the document 'minutes of order'. A summary judgment will only be given at this stage in the proceedings if there are clearly no points in issue. The evidence by affidavit therefore must be conclusive.

It is assumed that the court has decided after considering the application for summary judgment that there is a sufficient point in issue for this matter to proceed to trial and now gives an order giving leave to defend.

There may be occasions when the plaintiff purchaser may be satisfied with the return of his deposit. Very often a vendor purchaser is satisfied to retain the deposit in settlement of his claim for damages thereby reducing the cost of the action and obviating the necessity of an expensive inquiry as to damages. If however the plaintiff requires damages then specific liberty to apply for an inquiry as to damages must be inserted before any general liberty to apply otherwise the plaintiff may find difficulty in prosecuting the action for damages.

Writ of summons (specific performance)

IN THE HIGH COURT OF JUSTICE   CH 1991 H. No. 26582
CHANCERY DIVISION

BETWEEN

CELIA HOUSE

Plaintiff

- and -

LORNA GARDEN

Defendant

TO THE DEFENDANT Lorna Garden of 44, Briars Drive, London, SW7 4ND.

THIS WRIT OF SUMMONS has been issued against you by the above named Plaintiff in respect of the claim set out on the back.

Within fourteen days after the service of this Writ on you, counting the day of service, you must either satisfy the claim or return to the Court Office mentioned below the accompanying Acknowledgment of Service stating therein whether you intend to contest these proceedings.

If you fail to satisfy the claim or to return the Acknowledgment within the time stated, or if you return the Acknowledgment without stating therein an intention to contest the proceedings, the Plaintiff may proceed with the action and judgment may be entered against you forthwith without further notice.

Issued from the Central Office of the High Court this 16th day of April 1991.

NOTE: This Writ may not be served later than four calendar months beginning with that date unless renewed by order of the Court.

IMPORTANT
Directions for Acknowledgment of Service are given with the accompanying form.

Writ of summons (specific performance)

The Plaintiff's claim is for:-

1. Specific performance of an oral agreement between the Plaintiff and the Defendant dated 17th November 1990 for the sale by the Defendant to the Plaintiff of certain freehold property situate at and known as 44, Briars Drive aforesaid.

2. Further or alternatively, damages for breach of contract.

3. Alternatively, a declaration that by reason of the repudiation of the said agreement by the Defendant the Plaintiff is relieved of all liability for the further performance of his obligation thereunder.

4. Repayment to the Plaintiff of the deposit of £7,300 paid thereunder with interest under Section 35A of the Supreme Court Act 1981 from the 24th November 1990.

5. A declaration that the Plaintiff is entitled to a lien on the said property for his deposit (together with interest thereon) and any damages and costs awarded in this action.

6. Further or other relief.

7. Costs.

WILLIAM SNOOKS
Leyton & Dwyer

(Signed by Solicitors) . ...

THIS WRIT was issued by Messrs. Leyton & Dwyer of 1045, Bedford Gardens, London WC1B 7DS Solicitor for the Plaintiff whose address is 35, Plant Crescent, Bedford, Bedfordshire.

Statement of claim (specific performance)

IN THE HIGH COURT OF JUSTICE   CH 1991 H. No. 26582
CHANCERY DIVISION

Writ issued the 14th day of January 1983

BETWEEN

CELIA HOUSE

Plaintiff

- and -

LORNA GARDEN

Defendant

STATEMENT OF CLAIM

1. By an oral agreement made between the Plaintiff and the Defendant on or about the 17th November 1990 at 29, Acacia Road, West Kensington, London W17, the Defendant agreed to sell and the Plaintiff agreed to buy certain freehold property situate at 44, Briars Drive, London SW17 and known as Loveacre at the price of £73,000.

2. It was further provided by the said agreement that the Plaintiff should pay a deposit of £7,300 in respect of the said purchase price. The Plaintiff duly paid the said sum to the Defendant on the 24th November 1990 and a receipt therefor containing particulars of the said agreement was given by the Defendant to the Plaintiff to which the Plaintiff will at the trial refer for its full terms and effect.

3. Notwithstanding repeated requests by the Plaintiff the Defendant has neglected and refused and continues to neglect and refuse to take any steps towards the completion of the said agreement for sale.

4. The Plaintiff has at all material times been and is now ready and willing to fulfil all her obligations under the said agreement.

Statement of claim (specific performance)

AND the Plaintiff claims:

(1) Specific performance of the said agreement.

(2) Further or alternatively, damages for breach of contract.

(3) Alternatively, a declaration that by reason of the repudiation of the said agreement by the Defendant the Plaintiff is relieved of all liability for the further performance of her obligation thereunder.

(4) Repayment to the Plaintiff of the deposit of £7,300, paid thereunder with interest from the 24th November 1990 at the rate of   (such rate may be claimed as does not exceed the rate of interest on judgment debts current at the date of issue of the Writ), total of such interest from 24th November 1990 to   (date of issue of this Writ) being £   , and further interest from the said   (date of issue) to judgment or sooner payment at the daily rate of £   under Section 35A of the Supreme Court Act 1981.

(5) A declaration that the Plaintiff is entitled to a lien on the said property for his deposit (together with interest thereon) and any damages and costs awarded in this action.

(6) Further or other relief.

(7) Costs.

WILLIAM SNOOKS

Served the 20th day of April 1990 by Leyton & Dwyer of 27, Pimlico Road, London SW17 7NZ Solicitor for the Plaintiff.

Summons for summary judgment

IN THE HIGH COURT OF JUSTICE   CH 1991 H. No. 26582
CHANCERY DIVISION

BETWEEN

CELIA HOUSE

Plaintiff

- and -

LORNA GARDEN

Defendant

LET ALL PARTIES attend before Master Rattle in Room number 10X, Royal Courts of Justice, Strand, London WC2A 2LL on Wednesday the 4th day of June 1991 at 11.45 o'clock in the forenoon on the hearing of an application on the part of the Plaintiff for the following relief:-

1. An Order pursuant to Order 86 of the Rules of the Supreme Court for specific performance of the agreement dated 17th November 1990 in the Writ in this action mentioned in the terms of the minutes hereunto annexed, or alternatively.

2. Directions as to the pleadings in and further conduct of this action.

Dated the 15th day of May 1991

This Summons was taken out by Leyton & Dwyer of 27, Pimlico Road, London SW17 7NZ Solicitor for the Plaintiff

Plaintiff's affidavit (specific performance)

Filed on behalf of the Plaintiff
Affidavit No 1 Deponent: CELIA HOUSE
Date Sworn: 15th May 1991

<u>IN THE HIGH COURT OF JUSTICE</u> CH 1991 H. No. 26582
<u>CHANCERY DIVISION</u>

B E T W E E N

CELIA HOUSE

<u>Plaintiff</u>

- and -

LORNA GARDEN

<u>Defendant</u>

AFFIDAVIT OF CELIA HOUSE

I, CELIA HOUSE of 35, Plant Crescent, Bedford, Bedfordshire a Sales Manager MAKE OATH and say as follows:-

1. I have known the Defendant a number of years as an acquaintance and from time to time she has mentioned to me that she would be wanting to sell the house. At or about the beginning of November 1989 she telephoned me to say that she had made up her mind to sell the property and that if I would visit her it might be possible to negotiate a sale to me.

2. I arranged to go to her house at 44, Briars Drive, London SW7 on the 17th November 1989, when we discussed and agreed upon all the details for my purchase of the property in the sum of £73,000. I told her that before handing over the deposit I would need to have the house properly surveyed and she agreed to allow my surveyor access for that purpose.

Plaintiff's affidavit (specific performance)

3. Having received a satisfactory report from my Surveyor, I was invited by the Defendant to return to the house on the 24th November 1990 when I handed to her my cheque in the sum of £7,300 being a ten per cent deposit of the purchase price and I then drew up a form of receipt which she signed and which is now produced to me and exhibited hereto marked "CH.1".

4. Despite many requests and reminders from me the Defendant has failed or neglected to proceed with the purchase of the property despite the fact that I am now, and have since the 24th November 1990, been ready and willing to perform my part of the agreement and that I am able to provide the balance of the purchase price on completion.

5. I am advised and believe that there is no defence to this action and humbly request the Court to grant me an order for specific performance of the contract to enable me to complete my purchase of the said property.

SWORN at 82, Pimlico Street)
London, SW17 5QZ.   )
this 15th day of May 1991   )

before me,

    ARNOLD LEWIS

        Solicitor

Filed on behalf of the Plaintiffs

Defendant's affidavit (specific performance)

FILED on behalf of the Defendants
AFFIDAVIT No 1 Deponent LORNA GARDEN
Date Sworn: 30th May 1991

<u>IN THE HIGH COURT OF JUSTICE</u>   CH 1991 H. No. 26582
<u>CHANCERY DIVISION</u>

B E T W E E N

CELIA HOUSE

<u>Plaintiff</u>

- and -

LORNA GARDEN

<u>Defendant</u>

<u>AFFIDAVIT OF LORNA GARDEN</u>

I, LORNA GARDEN of 44, Briars Drive, London SW7 4ND housewife **MAKE OATH** and say as follows:-

1. I am the Defendant in this action and I have read what purports to be a copy of an Affidavit sworn by the Plaintiff on the 15th May 1991.

2. I do not accept that there was any final agreement or arrangement between the Plaintiff and myself made either on the 17th November 1990 or on the 24th November 1990 or indeed at any time. It is true that the Plaintiff came to visit me at my house to discuss the possible purchase of the property. On the 17th November 1990 she offered me £70,000 for my property which I refused. She further offered to pay a deposit of £7,000 to me immediately which I again refused. I did agree to allow her surveyor to have access to the property to provide her with a survey and said that I would meet her again on the 24th November 1990 when the survey would be complete.

Defendant's affidavit (specific performance)

3. At the meeting on the 24th November 1990 the Defendant raised her offer to £73,000 but I said I would have to think about the offer which I was not prepared to accept at that time. She then asked me if I would not sell the house to anyone else whilst I was considering her offer and handed me a cheque for £7,300 in case I should accept. I signed a receipt for that sum but do not accept that this signified any final arrangement between us. I still hold the sum of £7,300 which I am prepared to return to her because I have received a better offer for the house.

SWORN at 84, Rosebush Road,)
London SW3 8YP. This 30th   )
day of May 1991   )

before me,

    WILLIAM FLOOD

       Solicitor

               Filed by the Defendant

Order giving leave to defend (specific performance)

IN THE HIGH COURT OF JUSTICE　　　　CH 1991 H. No. 26582
CHANCERY DIVISION
MASTER WILSON MASTER IN CHAMBERS

BETWEEN

CELIA HOUSE

Plaintiff

- and -

LORNA GARDEN

Defendant

ON THE APPLICATION of the Plaintiff by Summons dated 15th May 1991 for specific performance of the agreement dated 17th November 1990 in the Writ of Summons mentioned in the terms of the minutes annexed thereto or for directions as to pleadings.

IT IS ORDERED that the Defendant be at liberty to defend this action.

AND IT IS ORDERED that the Defendant do serve her defence within fourteen days.

The costs of the said application are to be costs in the action.

Dated the 4th day of June 1991

Defence

IN THE HIGH COURT OF JUSTICE   CH 1991 H. No. 26582
CHANCERY DIVISION

BETWEEN

      CELIA HOUSE

                 Plaintiff

      - and -

      LORNA GARDEN

                 Defendant

1. The Defendant denies that any such agreement as is alleged in paragraph 1 of the Statement of Claim herein or any other agreement relating to the property therein mentioned was ever made between the Plaintiff and the Defendant on 17th November 1990 or at all.

2. The Defendant will rely upon the provisions of Section 40 of the Law of Property Act 1925, and if, contrary to the Defendant's contention, the receipt mentioned in paragraph 2 of the Statement of Claim contains or constitutes a memorandum of any of the terms of any contract or agreement between the Plaintiff and the Defendant, the Defendant will say that it does not contain the whole of such terms, and is in consequence not a sufficient memorandum to satisfy the said Section.

PARTICULARS

The omitted terms related to:-

(1) Date for completion.
(2) Full names of parties.
(3) Details as to whether part and if so what part of the purchase price related to furniture and effects.

Defence

3. The Defendant admits the receipt of the sum of £7,300 from the Plaintiff wrongly alleged in the Statement of Claim herein to have been paid by way of deposit, but in fact paid by way of loan, and is and has since the 14th December 1982 when she tendered the same to the Plaintiff with interest at 10 per cent per annum down to the said date, been ready and willing to repay the same to the Plaintiff.

4. Each and every allegation of fact in the Statement of Claim contained and not herein expressly admitted is denied as if the same had been specifically set forth herein and expressly traversed.

   Served the 20th day of June 1991 by Miss Lorna Garden of 44, Briars Drive, London SW7 4ND the Defendant in person.

Minutes of order

IN THE HIGH COURT OF JUSTICE   CH 1991 H. No. 26582
CHANCERY DIVISION

BETWEEN

        CELIA HOUSE

                                            Plaintiff

        - and -

        LORNA GARDEN

                                            Defendant

ORDER that the agreement dated 17th November 1990 in the Writ of Summons mentioned be specifically performed and carried into execution.

Let the following accounts be taken that is to say:-

1. An inquiry as to damages and/or loss of interest suffered by the Plaintiff by reason of the Defendant's breach of contract.

2. Leave to the Plaintiff to lodge evidence within 21 days.

3. Leave to the Defendant to lodge evidence in reply 21 days thereafter.

4. Leave to the Plaintiff to reply, if so advised, within 14 days thereafter.

Alternatively,

2. Liberty to apply for an inquiry as to damage and/or generally.

3. That the costs hereof and in connection with or incidental to these proceedings be paid by the Defendant to the Plaintiff such costs to be taxed on a party and party basis if not agreed.

                      Dated the 30th day of August 1991

3. Boundary disputes

Disputes as to boundaries may be relevant to trespass or nuisance, and may be between vendor and purchaser, landlord and tenant, or adjoining owners. If claims are based on title deeds, the familiar case as between adjoining owners, and there is a clear definition in the deeds, then such definition might well be conclusive. Evidence in some cases may be adduced by reference to the positioning of hedges, walls, banks and streams. Whatever the nature of the evidence, boundary disputes are arguments on facts. There are some presumptions which are rebuttable, and these are set out in Chapter 3 of *Boundaries and Fences* (2nd edn) by Powell-Smith (*see below*).

Statute

By virtue of s 58(1) of the Law of Property Act 1925 mutual rights of support are given in respect of joint party walls; otherwise there is no statutory reference.

Order

Order 15, r 16 enables declarations to be made without other relief.

Parties

A vendor or purchaser, or neighbours.

Intitulement

There is no special intitulement except that where there is a question of construction the heading will be 'In the matter of the conveyance/transfer made etc, between AB of the one part and CD of the other part'.

The objective of the plaintiff

To obtain a declaration and injunction and where appropriate damages for trespass and/or nuisance.

Required/have ready/on issue

Originating summons or writ which may claim a declaration and damages for trespass and/or nuisance.

Sequence

As appropriate to an originating summons or writ action with an order for directions for discovery of all deeds.

Plaintiff's/defendant's considerations

The plaintiff's primary evidence may be acceptable maps or plans or evidence of use or conduct. Records if derived at least indirectly from personal knowledge compiled by recorders under a duty to record may subject to Rules of Court be admissible under the Civil Evidence Act 1968, s 2. The weight to be attached to such records is to be estimated according to the considerations given in s 6(3)(*a*). Documents available for public inspection are admissible ostensibly only if produced from proper custody.

Reliance may be made on an ordnance survey map. If it is copied, an acknowledgment should be given on the copy of its source (and the solicitors should have either paid the annual fee in accordance with the arrangement outlined in the Law Society's *Gazette*, Vol 54 (1957) p 83, or the standard royalty charge).

Statutory admissibility of evidence of reputation is provided for in the Civil Evidence Act 1968, s 9(3) but is confined by s 9(4) to three isolated instances; if these do not assist, it is doubtful if reliance can still be made on the common law. In any event evidence of reputation will only be admitted at all in the case of private boundary disputes if general or public interest is concerned, or where private boundaries are defined by reference to public boundaries.

Where it may be given, evidence of acts of ownership and evidence of the boundaries as they were is the evidence most commonly given albeit evidence of reputation is not the strongest evidence.

Hazards and pitfalls

Declarations can only be entertained if there has been an assertion by the defendant and the case is contested. Evidence is excluded to vary clear descriptions, but may be admitted to explain ambiguities.

Costs

The usual provisions will apply.

Alternative jurisdiction

The county court where the net annual value for rating is within the court's jurisdiction (County Courts Act 1959, s 51A).

Textbooks

Halsbury, Vol 5, para 83.
T Aldridge, *Boundaries, Walls and Fences*, 6th edn, (Longman, 1986).

4. Easements

Since every piece of land is necessarily annexed to some other piece of land, the exercise by any landowner of all those rights called ownership may include rights over the land of another. Such rights can be acquired by prescription as well as grant and are good against all successive owners of the land, notice or no notice. On the other hand, many rights which might be the subject of a licence or a lease cannot be granted as freehold estates unless they are within the category of a legal easement, that is, where there is a dominant and a servient tenement in separate ownership and separate occupation, the easement is calculated to benefit the dominant tenement as a tenement, and is capable of being granted by deed. Easements impose negative burdens upon the owner of the servient tenement in that they either compel him to allow his neighbouring landowner to do something on the servient tenement which would otherwise be a trespass (for example to walk across it, or discharge his drains over it) or by preventing him from doing something on the servient tenement which he otherwise might do (for example, not to build so as to obstruct his neighbour's light). Easements thus include rights of way, rights to the unimpeded access of light to a building, rights to impede the flow of water in a defined channel or to pollute it, rights to have one's building supported by a neighbour's land, to discharge drains upon a neighbouring close, or to inflict what would otherwise constitute an actionable nuisance by noise or fumes. Much of the law on the subject, with the exception of the Prescription Act 1832, is judge made law of the last century. Easements may be claimed under the doctrine of implied grant or reservation on the basis that 'a man may not derogate from his own grant which is construed strongly against him' so that he is deemed to pass ways of necessity and all quasi-easements over the land retained by him which have been continuously and apparently exercised in the past. Easements may also be claimed under express grant or by prescription.

Parties

The plaintiff may be the owner of the dominant tenement and/or a reversioner if the interference be of a permanent nature; the party creating the disturbance will then be the defendant. Alternatively, the plaintiff may be the owner of the servient tenement seeking an injunction and/or declaration against a dominant owner who is claiming or exercising rights in excess of his entitlement.

The objective of the plaintiff

An injunction and a declaration.

Land and Other Specific Property

Required/have ready/on issue

Writ indorsed for an injunction, damages or declaration in specific terms, the statement of claim pleading specifically the plaintiff's claim to title. Where the question at issue is one of construction of documents only an originating summons, and supporting affidavit.

Sequence

(1) An interim injunction may be sought by motion upon notice or if urgent *ex parte* supported by an affidavit showing a *prima facie* case. The defendant may file an affidavit in opposition alleging triviality, no good claim, delay or acquiescence, or that the balance of convenience is against the grant of an injunction.
(2) On directions, particulars may be ordered and the master may be asked to record the agreement of plans or facts or the refusal so to agree. A point of law may be ordered to be tried as a preliminary issue.
(3) On the final order, if a declaration as to an easement is made and if evidence of interference is before the court an injunction to give effect to the declaration should be sought concurrently. If there is an interlocutory injunction to restrain an obstruction the plaintiff may have leave reserved to apply within a fixed time for relief by way of mandatory injunction.

Plaintiff's considerations

The plaintiff should be ready to prove his title unless his action is in respect of natural rights where a possessory title will suffice. The plaintiff must be able to show that the defendant is responsible for the interference.

Defendant's considerations

The defendant may himself be able to assert an easement.

Hazards and pitfalls

The possible liability of the plaintiff having to pay damages if the injunction is discharged.

Alternative jurisdictions

The county court is available if the net annual value of the hereditament does not exceed £30,000.

Textbook

S G Maurice, *Gale on Easements*, 15th edn, (Sweet & Maxwell, 1986).

5. Summary applications for possession: trespass cases

Order

Ord 113, rr 1-4 and see the comprehensive detailed notes in AP, Vol 1 thereunder. Rule 1 states:

Where a person claims possession of land which he alleges is occupied solely by a person or persons (not being a tenant or tenants holding over after the termination of the tenancy) who entered into or remained in occupation without his licence or consent or that of any predecessor in title of his, the proceedings may be brought by originating summons in accordance with the provisions of this Order.

Parties

The person with the right to possession is plaintiff; he may be the legal owner, a landlord, or a legal mortgagee. The unauthorised occupiers are the defendants. If any of the occupiers is unidentified he will be described as 'person unknown' in the proceedings.

Intitulement

Parties only.

The objective of the plaintiff

To obtain an order that the defendant do give the plaintiff possession of the land described in the writ or originating summons as '54, The Avenue, etc' and to pay the plaintiff £ fixed costs, or alternatively, costs to be taxed.

Required/have ready/on issue

The proceedings cannot be commenced by writ (Ord 113, rr 1 and 2) but only by an originating summons in the prescribed Form 11A (AP, VOL 2) which after formal parts should continue 'On the hearing of an application by AB for an order that he do recover possession of (54, The Avenue, Chiswick, London W14) on the grounds that he is entitled to possession and that the person in occupation is in occupation without licence or consent'.

The originating summons must have at the end of it the following note: 'Any person occupying the premises who is not named as a defendant by this summons may apply to the court personally or by solicitor or counsel to be joined as a defendant. If a person occupying the premises does not attend personally or by counsel or solicitor at the time and place above mentioned such order would be made as the court may think just and expedient.'

Sequence

(1) The plaintiff should stamp and issue the originating summons in room 307/308, and the date for hearing before a judge in chambers will be inserted in the body of the summons, giving at least five clear days between the date of issue and the date of hearing. The affidavit in support of the originating summons is filed in room 307/308. It is not necessary to take an appointment before the master prior to the judge (Practice Direction (Chancery: Procedure) No 2 of 1982 [1983] 1 WLR 4). The plaintiff's affidavit shall state (*a*) his interest in the land, (*b*) the circumstances in which the land has been occupied without licence or consent and in which his claim to possession arises and if so (*c*) that he does not know the name of any person occupying the land who is not named in the summons (Ord 113, r 3). A time of less than five days may be given in an emergency, but an adjournment will follow if the plaintiff fails to show good reason at the hearing.

(2) Where any person in occupation of the land is named in the originating summons, the summons together with a copy of the affidavit in support shall be served on him (*a*) personally or in accordance with Ord 10, r 5 or (*b*) by leaving a copy of the summons and of the affidavit or sending them to him, at the premises or (*c*) in such other manner as the court may direct. The summons shall, in addition to being served on the named defendants, if any, in accordance with the above provisions be served, unless the court otherwise directs, by (*a*) affixing a copy of the summons and a copy of the affidavit to the main door or other conspicuous part of the premises, and (*b*) if practicable, inserting through the letter-box at the premises a copy of the summons and a copy of the affidavit enclosed in a sealed envelope addressed to 'the occupiers' (Ord 10, r 4). An affidavit of service in all cases is mandatory. See the note prefacing the originating summons below.

(3) The plaintiff, though not required to take steps to identify occupiers, must state in his affidavit in support, if such be the case, that he does not know the names of occupiers not named in his proceedings. His affidavit must also prove his entitlement to possession and must refer to the defendant's occupation as being without his licence and consent.

(4) Defendants who do not need to acknowledge service need not hand in their affidavits to the judge until the hearing but will then be at risk on costs if the plaintiff asks for an adjournment. No cross-examination at this first hearing is permissible. Once the case is before the court if there should have been short service, the judge may be asked to abridge the time; if he declines, the summons will be stood over probably to the following Wednesday.

(5) On the hearing in addition to the original affidavit in support the plaintiff should have ready for handing in to the judge an affidavit verifying service as at in 2 above. The judge will need to be satisfied that service has been properly effected and whether the case really falls within Ord 113, r 1. If a *prima facie* defence is shown, leave to file evidence will be given and if so, the summons will be adjourned. If there is no *prima facie* defence, or if at the hearing the defendant fails to attend, or if no defence is shown, a forthwith order is normally made then and there.

Plaintiff's considerations

These proceedings are available to a legal mortgagee against a trespasser and to a head landlord against unlawful sub-tenants and against former licencees whose licences have expired, as well as those who have simply entered without licence or consent. They are not available against a formerly lawful tenant holding over. Order 113 indicates that irregularities as to service will not necessarily invalidate but irregularities may cause delay if further service has to be effected.

The owner of residential property, unlet, may find that he is given assistance by the police thus obviating the necessity of recourse to the courts.

Order 113 does not prevent the court from ordering possession at a specified date if it could have done so if the action had been commenced by writ.

No leave is required to issue a writ of possession to enforce an order made under Ord 113 and such writs of possession can be executed against all persons in possession whether or not they were parties to the proceedings (*R v Wandsworth County Court ex parte Wandsworth London Borough Council* [1975] 1 WLR 1314).

Defendant's considerations

Persons not named may apply at any stage to be joined.

Attitude of the court

The procedure does not extend to proceedings for possession where consent or licence may be an issue; if an issue appears the court will use its discretion as to whether the proceedings be dismissed, adjourned or transferred.

Hazards and pitfalls

The order provides a specific remedy and requires exact fulfilment of all its terms, if a possession order will be made. The claim must be limited to possession; hence, no claim to rent or mesne profits can be included.

Costs

Orders for costs against trespassers and squatters are likely to be of little value.

Appeals

As well as the usual right of appeal to the court of appeal, if an order has been made in the absence of a defendant the judge may be asked to set aside or vary a summary order for possession though he is likely to do so only where there is fresh material.

Alternative jurisdiction

Summary proceedings for the possession of land where the net annual value for rating does not exceed £1,000 are governed by Ord 24, rr 1-11 of the County Court Rules 1981 (SI 1981 No 1687). The net annual value is treated as that shown in the valuation list in force on 31 March 1990, or if that value is not available, the yearly value when the proceedings are commenced (reg 4 of the Local Government Finance Repeals, Savings and Consequential Amendments) Order 1990 (SI No 776).

Specimen action

In addition to the evidence in support it will be necessary to prove service of the originating summons by showing that every effort has been made to bring the proceedings to the notice of the occupiers of the property. Service is normally effected in practice by handing a copy of the originating summons to each individual met by the process server and in addition attaching a copy of it to the front door of the property and to some convenient place inside the property.

Additional to an order for possession costs can be claimed but in this specimen as the defendants were persons who were unknown it was thought advisable not to waste the time and effort involved in a taxation where it was considered unlikely that there could be any recovery, and so a prayer for costs was not included.

6. Summary applications for possession: Ord 113 not applicable

Order

Whilst Ord 113 provides for obtaining possession without financial claims, Ord 13, r 4 enables a plaintiff to indorse on a writ of summons a claim for possession of land coupled with claims for rent/mesne profits or damages for use or occupation (but no other relief) and in default the plaintiff may enter summary judgment for possession provided the solicitor has certified on the writ that the proceedings do not relate to a dwelling protected by the Rent Acts and do not relate to a mortgage transaction.

If Ord 13, r 7, Ord 45, r 3 applies there can be no enforcement without leave for which an affidavit setting out the facts should be lodged in room 307/308, to be collected with the master's indorsement the following day.

Alternative jurisdiction

There is no summary procedure in the county court for obtaining possession in non-trespass cases to which the Rent Acts apply; where they do not apply, such as where the rateable value exceeds £5,000 or where consent or licence may have been given, proceeding under Ord 13, r 4 (supra) in the Chancery Division is likely to offer the speediest remedy.

Originating summons (possession)

IN THE HIGH COURT OF JUSTICE CH 1991 M. No. 4389
CHANCERY DIVISION
IN THE MATTER of

BETWEEN

MANSION LIMITED

Plaintiffs

- and -

PERSONS UNKNOWN

Defendants

TO ALL persons in occupation of Flat 3, 34 Glynn Close, Copley, East Ham, London E84 7DX

LET all persons concerned attend before Judge in Chambers, Royal Courts of Justice, Strand, London WC2A 2LL, on the 30th day of September 1991 at 10.30 o'clock on the hearing of an application by Mansion Limited for an Order that they do recover possession of Flat 3, 34 Glynn Close, Copley, East Ham, London E84 7DX

on the ground that they are entitled to possession and that the persons in occupation are in occupation without licence or consent.

DATED the 31st day of August 1991

This summons was taken out by Patel & Co
Solicitors for the Plaintiffs, whose address is 9 The Parade, Kings Cross, London NW11 6LD

NOTE: Any person occupying the premises who is not named as a Defendant by this Summons may apply to the Court personally or by Counsel or Solicitor to be joined as a Defendant. If a person occupying the premises does not attend personally, or by Counsel or Solicitor at the time and place above mentioned, such Order will be made as the Court may think just and expedient.

Plaintiff's affidavit (possession)

FILED on behalf of the Plaintiffs
AFFIDAVIT No 1 Deponent: ROBERT BLUE
Date Served: 31 August 1991

IN THE HIGH COURT OF JUSTICE   CH 1991 M. No. 4389
CHANCERY DIVISION
IN THE MATTER of

BETWEEN

MANSION LIMITED

Plaintiffs

- and -

PERSONS UNKNOWN

Defendants

I, Robert Blue of 90 Aberdeen Road, Newcastle, Company Director

MAKE OATH AND SAY as follows:-

1. I am a Director of the Plaintiff Company herein and make this Affidavit from my own knowledge of the facts.

2. The Plaintiffs are the owners of the freehold land and premises known as 34 Glynn Close, Copley, East Ham, London E84 7DX which were purchased by the Company on the 10th August 1991.

3. An Inspection of the property on the 12th August 1991 showed that certain individuals were in occupation without licence or consent and, on my approach to them as to their right to be there, they refused to answer or leave the property or co-operate any other way.

4. The property was inspected by me late on the day of the Company's purchase of the property on 10th August 1991 and was found to be vacant.

Plaintiff's affidavit (possession)

5. The Plaintiff company is anxious to commence building works as soon as possible and request an Order for possession forthwith.

6. The Plaintiffs do not know the name of any person occupying the said premises who is not named in the Summons.

SWORN at 90 High Street, East Ham E8)
)
this 31st day of August 1991)

Before me,

      LOUIS DEAN

          Solicitor

Filed for and on behalf of the Plaintiffs

7. Landlord and Tenant Act 1954, Part II

By s 25 of the Landlord and Tenant Act 1954, the landlord of business premises may serve notice on the tenant to terminate the tenancy of the premises on a date not being earlier than the date when apart from the Act it would have determined. Not less than six months' prior notice must be given, but more than 12 months' prior notice is invalid. The notice is prescribed in Form 1 of the Landlord and Tenant Act 1954, Part II (Notices) Regulations 1983. On being served with the notice the tenant if he wishes to make an application to the court for a new tenancy must, within two months of receipt of the notice, notify the landlord that he is unwilling to give up possession, such counter-notice being a condition precedent to his right to apply to the court. Alternatively a tenant, although not served with a landlord's notice to terminate, may himself under s 26, make a request for a new tenancy on Form 8, observing the same time limits as in the landlord's notice to determine.

Statute

The Landlord and Tenant Act 1954, Part II.

Order

Order 97, r 2 assigns all proceedings in the High Court under Part II of the 1954 Act to the Chancery Division. Proceedings for a new tenancy must be commenced within four calendar months of the date of the original notice or the tenant will lose his rights under the Act. This limitation of time is absolute. To protect his rights a landlord should file his answer by way of affidavit even if negotiations are in progress, to comply with the rules. A landlord may also issue a summons under s 24(*a*) of the 1954 Act seeking an order from the court for an interim rent from the date when the lease expires or from when the tenant's notice under s 26 expires or such application is made, whichever is the later. Where as may be in the case of long leases, the landlords may not have full and accurate particulars as to who are the occupiers and the terms upon which they occupy, they would be well advised before serving Form 1 to make inquiries in an effort to obtain such particulars.

Parties

The plaintiff will be the tenant and the landlord the defendant but if head lessees or mortgagees are likely to be affected they should be added as defendants and served, or else notice should be given to them that they may apply to be joined if desired. Mortgagees in possession must be joined as defendants.

Land and Other Specific Property

Intitulement

In the matter of '50, Chiswick Avenue, London W4' (address of the property).

The objective of the plaintiff

To obtain an order that the defendant execute a new lease upon the same terms as in the current lease or at such rent and on such terms as the court may order.

Required/have ready/on issue

Originating summons which must describe the premises and the business carried on thereat, and must give particulars of the plaintiff's current tenancy and of all notices and requests, and of the plaintiff's proposed terms for the new tenancy, including its proposed length and proposed rental. If a question of validity of notices arises it can be raised in the originating summons. If this has not been done a summons should be issued subsequently setting out this issue. The originating summons may be issued in the district registry for the district in which the premises are situated.

Where the tenant on receipt of notice to determine the tenancy wishes to make application to the court for a new tenancy, he must, within two months of receipt of the landlord's notice, notify the landlord that he is unwilling to give up possession, and this counter notice—for which there is no prescribed form, is a condition precedent to his right to apply to the court. It is a fatality if the counter notice is not given in time.

The grounds on which a landlord may oppose a tenant's application are limited to those set out in s 30(1) of the Act, eg tenant's failure to comply with obligations, alternative accommodation offered, landlord's intention to reconstruct. The section should be referred to.

Sequence

(1) On issue of the originating summons the plaintiff files in chambers a short affidavit verifying the facts and exhibiting his lease and the notices which have been given, therein raising the invalidity of notices if this is intended to be an issue. To avoid the circumstances of a possible unjustified extension of security subject to renewal under Ord 6, r 8 service of the originating summons must be within two months of issue. No acknowledgment of service to the originating summons is required by defendants. Practice Direction (Chancery: Originating Summons) [1974] 1 WLR 708 must be followed, viz before issuing the date of hearing (alternatively if the parties are negotiating 'a day to be fixed') must be inserted in room

156 by the master's summons clerk. He will then seal the originating summons.

(2) Not less than four days before the first appointment the defendant should file an affidavit stating (*a*) whether or not he opposes a new tenancy and if so his grounds, (*b*) whether should a new tenancy be granted he objects to the plaintiff's proposed terms or any of them and what terms he would substitute for them and (*c*) whether he has a lease with less than 14 years to run and if so giving the name and address of his immediate landlord. On the first appointment the master will check all the notices and requests and their dating. The tenant's application for a new tenancy must have been made not less than two or more than four months after service of his own notice, or counter notice, as the case may be. The irregularity of a premature application may however be waived by the landlord. A certificate of service of a copy of the summons and copy of the affidavit should be indorsed on the original affidavit. It is sometimes useful for a landlord to exhibit a draft of the new lease that he proposes should be accepted by the tenant. This helps to ascertain the points in issue.

(3) On the first appointment directions are likely to file further evidence and for surveyors' reports (which should contain comparables) to be exchanged. The oral evidence of surveyors may be directed wherever there is a difference of fact or opinion or where the parties require it. When the master is satisfied that the affidavit evidence is complete and that the reports have been exchanged and filed, he will adjourn the summons into court usually with liberty to call oral evidence.

If the grounds of the landlord's objection to a new tenancy is ground (*f*) in s 30 of the 1954 Act ie intention to demolish or reconstruct and that he could not reasonably do so without obtaining possession, and this is contested and in issue, then the originating summons may be adjourned into court for this issue to be determined as a preliminary issue. Similarly, there may be preliminary issues relating to validity of notices or other matters.

(4) Sometimes a defendant landlord will have separate claims against a tenant applying for a new lease; these could include a claim for possession for breaches of contract. Ord 28, r 7 ('Counterclaims by defendant') provides for the possibility of including such claims as counterclaims in the same proceedings and if so included the court has power to give such directions or orders as may be expedient. It may be appropriate for such counterclaims to be tried separately or else as preliminary issues. If there is a fear that the tenant will withdraw the originating summons, landlord could include a claim under s 24(*a*).

(5) The court may make an order by consent for possession, or

any other order appropriate to the proceedings. By virtue of s 34 of the 1954 Act, the court may in the absence of agreement designate the property comprised in the holding 'by reference to the circumstances existing at the date of the order'.

Plaintiff's/defendant's considerations

The 1954 Act provides for the continuation of business tenancies indefinitely after they would otherwise have expired and thus the onus is always on the landlord to show that a new tenancy should not be granted; if he does not discharge this burden then subject to the giving of the necessary notices the court must make an order for the grant of a new tenancy mandatorily.

The only grounds on which the landlord may oppose the tenant's application are those set out in s 30. The landlord must either in his notice to terminate or in the notice given by him to the tenant within two months of a tenant's request set out those grounds on which he relies. If the landlord establishes any ground on which he is entitled to oppose an application, the court cannot make an order for the grant of a new tenancy. For a detailed summation of authorities under the various headings in s 30 reference can usefully be made to the notes given under the section in Part II of The County Court Practice.

Proposals made by a tenant as to a new lease or tenancy will be considered judicially by the judge irrespective of whether the landlord participates in the proceedings, and plaintiffs must prepare themselves with evidence accordingly.

Attitude of the court

As an unjustified extension of security could be obtained by delay in service, if a respondent has not been served by the first appointment explanation will be expected. Additionally, the court will inquire on the first appointment as to whether head lessees or mortgagees may be affected and if so and not served, whether notice has been given to them; the court may require them to be added as defendants and to be served.

Experts may give opinions and views based on matters on which they have no first hand knowledge but subject to this exception, only admissible evidence may be given. Experts are expected if possible to agree the facts (*English Exporters (London) Ltd v Eldonwall* [1973] Ch 415). Even without an order to do so, evidence as to rents charged for similar premises or 'comparable ones' are expected by the court to have been obtained, exchanged and as far as possible agreed. Where evidence of comparables is given the evidential value of the comparables will depend on their criteria.

Hazards and pitfalls

It is a fatality to the plaintiff tenant's application if notice has not been given in time. All the notices must be in accordance with the prescribed forms except the tenant's request for a new tenancy which can be in any form (for example by letter) provided it is in writing.

If the wrong person is made defendant by the plaintiff tenant then unless application is made to amend within four months of the issue of proceedings, the proceedings will be abortive. For a landlord, it is unwise to allow the tenant to serve his notice under s 26 prior to his notice because an application for a revised rental is thereby postponed for twelve months.

Costs

Older decisions implied that the only order was 'no order as to costs' but recent decisions have said that there can be such an order depending on the behaviour of the parties and on how near the final figure is to the proposals made by the landlord in his affidavit and the response thereto of the tenant.

Alternative jurisdiction

Proceedings are to be brought in the county court when the net annual value does not exceed £5,000 per annum and if such proceedings have been wrongly commenced in the High Court or county court then they will be transferred and the proceedings are not invalidated (Landlord and Tenant Act 1954, s 63(4)). If the proceedings are transferred from a county court to the High Court they shall be as if commenced in the central office in London (Ord 97, r 11(2)).

Interim rents

The earliest date from which interim increase of rent can be payable is the date of determination of the landlord's notice under the Act (or alternatively, the tenant's notice if that originated the procedure), or the date of commencement of proceedings for determination of the interim rent whichever may be the later, but orders may be made dating from the date of the tenant's originating application to the court. The landlord must concede it to be less than a full rent, the question being what would be the rent of a hypothetical periodic yearly tenancy on the terms of the old lease.

Unless, which is unlikely, an application for interim rent has been included in the originating summons, the defendant landlord must issue a summons for interim rent. The summons is generally issued with inserted therein 'date to be fixed' and heard at the same time as the originating application; as the same evidence will be given on both summonses it is possible for the defendant landlord to ask the master to direct that his summons for interim rent shall stand

Land and Other Specific Property

as a counterclaim in the event that the originating summons is dismissed or discontinued; though strictly it may be otiose since the tenant's notice even if not substantiated still holds good by virtue of s 64 to enable the landlord to pursue his rights. While the summons is more usually adjourned with the main application to the judge (Ord 97, r 9A) the making of an order for interim rent is within a master's powers, and a separate hearing on this is sometimes beneficial, tactically.

Exclusion of the provisions of the Landlord and Tenant Act 1954

Applications under s 38 of the Landlord and Tenant Act 1954 as amended by s 5 of the Law of Property Act 1969 for approval of the court to an agreement excluding the provisions of the Landlord and Tenant Act 1954 are made on joint application of the landlord and the tenant on an *ex parte* originating summons (a precedent is given at p 737 of *McCleary's County Court Precedents* (4th edn)), one party issuing on behalf of both. An affidavit should be prepared setting out the reasons why both parties do not wish the provisions to apply (AP, Vol 1 97/6A/1). An example would be where the lessor has accommodation available temporarily only, and will require it again for his own business. The affidavit is produced at the hearing in support of the application. An early appointment may be obtained (Practice Note (Business Tenancies) Joint Application [1973] 1 WLR 299). The order may be made by the master on his being satisfied that there is no suggestion of oppression or coercion (Practice Direction [1971] 2 All ER 215). If he is not so satisfied the order must be made by the judge. The note in AP at para 97/6A/1 suggests that a representative of the tenant should attend in case any queries arise; the application is not a mere formality.

Textbooks

T M Aldridge, *Leasehold Law and Service*, (Longman, 1982).
M Barnes, *Hill and Redman's Law of Landlord and Tenant*, 18th edn, (Butterworths, 1988).
VG Wellings, *Woodfall's Law of Landlord and Tenant*, (Sweet & Maxwell).
County Court Practice, (Butterworths, 1989), (*see* Part II for notes giving summation of authorities).

Specimens of completed forms of landlord's notice to terminate, tenant's counter notice by way of solicitor's letter and landlord's notice under s 40(1) are set out below.

Landlord's notice to terminate

LANDLORD AND TENANT ACT 1954
Section 25
Landlord's Notice to Terminate Business Tenancy*

(1) Name of Tenant. To(^{1}) Alan Casey and Frank Murray (t/a Summerfields)

(2) Address of Tenant. of(^{2}) First Floor Offices, 40/41 Lordship Green, London E8

> IMPORTANT—This notice is intended to bring your tenancy to an end. If you want to continue to occupy your property you must act quickly. Read the notice and all the notes carefully. If you are in any doubt about the action you should take, get advice immediately e.g. from a solicitor or surveyor or a citizens advice bureau.

1. This notice is given under section 25 of the Landlord and Tenant Act 1954.

(3) Description of property. 2. It relates to(^{3}), First Floor Offices at 40/41 Lordship Green, London, E8 of which you are the tenant.

(4) See notes 1 and 8. (^{4})3. We give you notice terminating your tenancy on the 24th day of June 1988.

(5) See notes 2 and 3. (^{5})4. If you are not willing to give up possession of the property comprised in the tenancy on the date stated in paragraph 3, you must notify us in writing within two months after the giving of this notice.

(6) The landlord must cross out one version of paragraph 5. If the second version is used the paragraph letters must be filled in. (^{6})5. If you apply to the court under Part II of the Landlord and Tenant Act 1954 for the grant of a new tenancy, we will not oppose your application

(7) See notes 4 and 5. 6. All correspondence about this notice should be sent to (^{8}) [the landlord's agent] at the address given below

(8) Cross out words in square brackets if they do not apply.

Date 23 June 1991

Signature of (^{8}) landlord's agent

Name of landlord WESSEX BANK PLC
Address of landlord 54 Lamberton Street
London EC3P 3AH

(^{8})Address of agent MESSRS DORRINGTON
73 Littleside
London EC2V 6ER

---

*This form must *NOT* be used if—
  (a) no previous notice terminating the tenancy has been given under section 25 of the Act, and
  (b) the tenancy is the tenancy of a house (as defined for the purposes of Part 1 of the Leasehold Reform Act 1967), and
    (c) the tenancy is a long tenancy at a low rent (within the meaning of that Act of 1967), and
    (d) the tenant is not a company or other artificial person.
If the above apply, use form number 13 [Oyez No. L&T 24] instead of this form.

Tenant's counter notice by solicitor's letter

Messrs Dorringtons
Solicitors

DX 138 LONDON/CITY

Your Ref: MM/LP
Our Ref: DR/KP   27th June 1991

Dear Sirs,
RE: 40-41 LORDSHIP GREEN, LONDON N16
    YOUR CLIENTS: WESSEX BANK PLC
    OUR CLIENTS: ALAN CASEY AND FRANK MURRAY (t/a SUMMERFIELDS)

Our clients have passed to us your letter of 23rd June 1991, together with the enclosed Notice under Section 25 of the Landlord and Tenant Act.

Would you please treat this letter as Counter Notice to the effect that our clients are not prepared to give up possession of the premises upon the expiry of their Lease.

Yours faithfully,

HENDERSONS & SMITH

Landlord's notice under s 40

LANDLORD AND TENANT ACT 1954

Notice by Landlord requiring information about occupation and sub-tenancies of business premises

(Landlord and Tenant Act 1954, Section 40(1))

TO: LINDEN INVESTMENTS LIMITED

OF: 155-157a WARRINGTON HIGH STREET, LONDON

IMPORTANT—THIS NOTICE REQUIRES YOU TO GIVE YOUR LANDLORD CERTAIN INFORMATION. YOU MUST ACT QUICKLY. READ THE NOTICE AND ALL THE NOTES CAREFULLY. IF YOU ARE IN ANY DOUBT ABOUT THE ACTION YOU SHOULD TAKE, GET ADVICE IMMEDIATELY eg FROM A SOLICITOR OR SURVEYOR OR A CITIZENS ADVICE BUREAU

1. This notice is given under Section 40(1) of the Landlord and Tenant Act 1954.

2. It relates to 212 Whithouse Road, London NW8 of which you are the Tenant.

3. We require you to notify us in writing, within one month of the service of this notice on you:—
   (a) whether you occupy the premises or any part of them wholly or partly for business purposes; and
   (b) whether you have a sub-Tenant.

4. If you have a sub-Tenant we also require you to state:—
   (a) what premises are comprised in the sub-tenancy;
   (b) if the sub-tenancy is for a fixed term, what the term is, or if the sub-tenancy is terminable by notice, by what notice it can be terminated;
   (c) what rent the sub-Tenant pays;
   (d) whether, to the best of your knowledge and belief, the sub-Tenant occupies either the whole or part of the premises sub-let to him and, if not, what is his address.

5. All correspondence about this notice should be sent to the Landlord's Agent at the address given below.

DATED this 18th day of July 1991.

Signature of Landlord's agent

Name of Landlord: Eastern Estates Limited

Address of Landlord: 116 Littlehampton Street, Glasgow, G2 4EG

Address of agent: Pauline House, 74 Great Bond Street, London, W1Y 9DG

Landlord's notice under s 40

> ### NOTES
>
> Purpose of this notice
>
> 1. Your Landlord (or if he is a Tenant himself) has served this notice on you to obtain the information he needed in order to find out his position under Part II of the Landlord and Tenant Act 1954 in relation to your tenancy. He will then know, for example, whether when your tenancy expires, you will be entitled to apply to the Court for a new tenancy of the whole of the premises comprised in your present tenancy; you may not be entitled to a new tenancy of any part of the premises which you have sub-let. (In certain circumstances, a sub-Tenant may become a direct Tenant of the Landlord.)
>
> Replying to this notice
>
> 2. Section 40 of the 1954 Act says that you must answer the questions asked in the notice and you must let the Landlord have your answers in writing within one month of the service of the notice. You do not need a special form for this. If you don't answer these questions or give the Landlord incorrect information he might suffer a loss for which, in certain circumstances, you could be held liable.
>
> 3. If you have let to more than one sub-Tenant you should give the information required in respect of each sub-letting.
>
> Validity of this notice
>
> 4. The Landlord who has given this notice may not be the Landlord to whom you pay your rent. "Business" is given a wide meaning in the 1954 Act and is used in the same sense in this notice. The Landlord cannot ask for this information earlier than two years before your tenancy is due to expire or could be brought to an end by notice given by him. If you have any doubts about whether this notice is valid get immediate advice.
>
> Explanatory booklet
>
> 5. The Department of the Environment and Welsh Office booklet "Business Leases and Security of Tenure" explains the main provisions of Part II of the 1954 Act. It is available from the Department of the Environment Publications Store, Building Number 3, Victoria Road, South Ruislip, Middlesex.

8. Leasehold enfranchisement

The Leasehold Reform Act 1967, s 27, as read with ss 140, 141 and 142 of the Housing Act 1980 provides that a lessee of a lease exceeding 21 years at a rental not exceeding two thirds of the rental value who has actually occupied for the past three years or periods amounting to three years in the last ten may give notice in the prescribed form of his desire to acquire the freehold at a price to be determined by a leasehold valuation tribunal or to acquire an extended lease. Save for determining the principal issues, that is the right to acquire the freehold or to an extended lease or as to whether obligations consequent on the notice have been performed or as to what inquiries have been made to find an absent landlord, all other matters go to the land valuation tribunal including the price, the rent, the landlord's compensation, and the provisions in the conveyance, except that the provisions in the conveyance may be determined by the court where the court is otherwise seized of the matter and determination of those provisions is required.

It is the county court which has exclusive original jurisdiction to determine all the principal issues excepting those relating to s 19 (management schemes) and s 27 (landlord cannot be found) of the 1967 Act both of which are assigned to the Chancery Division. The county court's exclusive original jurisdiction notwithstanding, s 27 provides that if, after application has been made to the Chancery Court but before the freehold has been vested in the lessee, the missing lessor is located, then that will not remove the case from the jurisdiction of the High Court to that of the county court and the High Court may give such directions as it thinks fit as to the steps to be taken to give effect to the rights and obligations of the parties. These may include directions modifying or dispensing with any of the requirements of the Act or regulations made under the Act (also see s 49 of the Supreme Court Act 1981). When notice to enfranchise is given, the landlord is bound to convey. Similarly, when a tenant gives notice claiming an extended lease, his landlord is bound to grant it.

The notes below deal only with the situation where the tenant who wishes to enfranchise cannot find or cannot ascertain his landlord.

Order

Order 93, r 15 assigns proceedings under s 27 viz enfranchisement where the landlord cannot be found and also management schemes under s 19 to the Chancery Division.

Land and Other Specific Property

Required/have ready/on issue

Originating summons. Affidavit supporting claim to the freehold or to an extended lease setting out the history and establishing the applicant's rights and where applicable, the steps which have been taken to ascertain the landlord.

Sequence

(1) At the first hearing of the originating summons if the landlord should have been served, then the matter will proceed as at 5, 6 and 7 below.
(2) If the landlord cannot be found or his identity cannot be ascertained so that notice by the tenant cannot be given, then under s 27 the court has power to vest the premises in the tenant as if notice had been given. The plaintiff tenant will proceed by way of an *ex parte* originating summons accompanied by an affidavit in support exhibiting the lease and establishing his right and setting out what inquiries have been made. The master will have to be satisfied that all proper inquiries have been made; he will direct such further inquiries as he may consider necessary and if he does so direct, he will adjourn the summons to a later date. When the inquiries have been made, if still the landlord cannot be found or his identity ascertained, the master will direct advertisements in a form such as:

'Re the Leasehold Reform Act 1967'
'Re 50 Chiswick Avenue, W4' (The address of the property)
'Any person claiming to be the Freeholder or Successor in title to AB should communicate with CD at ...'

The draft advertisement will be settled by a Senior Executive Officer and inserted in such newspapers as may be directed by the master.
(3) If the landlord is traced, directions will be given and the application will proceed as if the tenant had duly given notice as at the date of his application.
(4) Suppose the landlord cannot be traced, then the matter will proceed as 5, 6, and 7 below.
(5) Prior to the first appointment or prior to the adjourned hearing the tenant should obtain the certificate of the president of the land tribunals as to a fair price, and after the first appointment will put this before the master. The master may himself make the order. The order will include a direction that a draft of the proposed conveyance should be lodged (in room 156) to be approved by the master or conveyancing counsel. The draft conveyance should follow the precedent settled by Megarry V-C in *Re Robertson's Application* [1969] 1 WLR 109 as is set

out in full in *Guide to Chancery Practice* (5th edn) by E Heward, Appendix III Form No 2.
(6) The order will also direct lodgment into court of the amount of the fair price and will provide that upon such lodgment the master do execute the conveyance and deliver the same to the applicant. Part II of the order will contain a lodgment and payment schedule which must be completed by the applicant and handed into room 180.
(7) The applicant after he has fulfilled the directions in the order may expect to hear from the court by post with the completed conveyance after he has satisfied the directions in the order.

Alternative jurisdiction

It is the county court and not the Chancery Division which has exclusive original jurisdiction.

Textbooks

T M Aldridge, *Leasehold Law and Service*, (Longman, 1982).
M Barnes, *Hill and Redman's Law of Landlord and Tenant*, 18th edn, (Butterworths, 1988).
V G Wellings, *Woodfall's Law of Landlord and Tenant*, (Sweet & Maxwell).
County Court Practice, (Butterworths, 1989), (*see* Part II for notes giving summation of authorities).

9. Mortgages

As against defaulting mortgagors in occupation of the mortgaged premises, mortgagees including building societies almost invariably seek orders for possession. Section 36 of the Administration of Justice Act 1970 gives the court power to make orders adjourning, suspending or postponing the date of delivery for possession but firstly, the court has no jurisdiction to order a stay or suspension without defining the period (*Royal Trust Company of Canada v Markham* [1975] 1 WLR 1416), and secondly, the court will only make a suspended order if it appears that the defendant is likely to clear all of the sums due within a reasonable time, six months being in practice treated as a maximum, and is able at the same time as clearing off all sums due, to pay all current instalments; thirdly, where there is an impending sale, the court may stay an order for possession to enable the property to be sold; and lastly where there is a claim for a money judgment the court is empowered to give judgment on the money claim and adjourn the claim for possession.

Statute

By s 37(1) of the Administration of Justice Act 1970, as amended by the Administration of Justice Act 1973, s 8 and Sched 2, exclusive jurisdiction is given to the county court in respect of mortgagee possession actions if the net annual value for rating does not exceed £1,000 outside of the Greater London area. The Chancery Division thus has jurisdiction if the dwelling house is within the Greater London area, and otherwise only if the net annual value exceeds £1,000. While generally writs may be issued in any district registry (Ord 6, r 7) in the case of a mortgage claim, the mortgaged property must be within the district of the district registry, except in the case of the district registries of Liverpool and Manchester (Ord 88, r 3).

Order

Order 88, (this is a lengthy order but reference to all of it may not be necessary in the usual action).

Parties

The mortgagee is the plaintiff and the mortgagor is the defendant. A mortgagor's trustee in bankruptcy should be joined as a defendant where there has been a receiving order in bankruptcy against a defendant. It seems clear since the decision in *Williams & Glyn's Bank Ltd v Boland* [1981] AC 487 that there are only two categories of occupiers which would concern a plaintiff mortgagee; those who have an interest in the property or equity of redemption, and those who are tenants, licencees or other occupiers. It is safest to join the first category as defendants, and to advise all in the second category making them aware of the proceedings by sending each a copy of the originating summons together with notice of first appointment, inviting them to be joined as defendants should they so desire, advising them that they may attend the hearing before the master, (giving the place, date and time) and warning them that if they do not attend an order may be made in their absence which would be effective against them. Such warning effectively putting them on notice, having been given by letter addressed to each, a copy of the letter or letters should be lodged for the court file or alternatively, they might well be exhibited to the plaintiff's affidavit. Where there are occupants whose identity is not known, the letter can be addressed: 'To Occupier', and a copy annexed to a suitable part of the property. Discretion should be exercised as to who is actually joined in the proceedings particularly when considering the first category, that is those who have an interest in the equity of redemption; examples of those who would obviously wish to be joined are spouses or close members of the family. A sensible approach at an early stage will avoid unnecessary delay in the plaintiff obtaining an order.

Intitulement

'In the matter of the property comprised in the Deed of Mortgage dated made between AB and CD'.

The objective of the plaintiff

To obtain payment of his mortgage which can often be achieved by his obtaining an order for possession so as to enable him advantageously to exercise his power of sale under s 87 of the Law of Property Act 1925. To obtain the order his right to it must be established and the court must be satisfied in all cases that possession is sought bona fide and reasonably for enforcing the security. Whilst the plaintiff may be entitled to a money judgment, the amount of which would depend on the terms of his mortgage and party and party costs, he may well have a right to deduct from the gross proceeds of a sale, after discharge of prior encumbrances, the whole of the amount of the principal and interest required to redeem together with costs which under the terms of the mortgage deed are likely to give him full indemnity. Hence the plaintiff may not wish to ask for a money judgment, attracting only party and party costs, albeit it may have been prayed for.

Required/have ready/on issue

(a) The originating summons should claim delivery of possession, such money claim as may be appropriate to the particular mortgage, foreclosure, sale, and such further or other relief as the court deems fit, and costs. At the foot of the originating summons must be added: 'The said premises are situate at [address] and [if the property is outside of the Greater London area] the rateable value is £— [in excess of £1,000 if the Chancery Court is to have jurisdiction].'

(b) An affidavit in support should set out the advance, the repayments, the instalments, particulars of the instalments in arrears as at the date of issue and also as at the date of the affidavit (so as to show whether they are being reduced or falling further into arrears), and the total amount due under the mortgage. If the plaintiff is seeking possession (and not repayment only) particulars are to be given of every person in possession of the property to the plaintiff's knowledge. Copy letters sent to occupants (see above) could then at this part of the affidavit, be exhibited. If interest to date of judgment is claimed, the affidavit must give the daily rate of interest. Finally, the affidavit must exhibit a copy of the mortgage, and must set out where the property is situated and the rateable value so as to establish jurisdiction, and should recite the title to the property; the latter may often be conveniently done by exhibiting a copy of the charge certificate.

Sequence

(1) Following service, an appointment will be taken out and the matter will follow the usual procedure for an originating summons. The plaintiff should have given notice to all non-occupiers who have an interest. If he has not, the master may decide to order such notice to be given.

(2) If there is default of appearance then the plaintiff should take out an appointment serving notice of appointment not less than four clear days before the return day. He should indorse on the outside fold of the affidavit a form of notice as follows: 'You the defendant having failed to enter an appearance to the originating summons an affidavit of which the within is a true copy has been sworn, and the plaintiff will on   at   apply to the Master at room No   Royal Courts of Justice for an order that you deliver up to the plaintiff possession of 50, Chiswick Avenue, W4 (address of the property)'. Copies of the exhibits of the affidavit need not be served when giving this notice. The affidavit should be indorsed with the plaintiff's solicitor's certificate (see AP, Vol 1 88/2-8/11) that notice of appointment and a copy of the affidavit were duly served. Where a suspended order is made, if it is subsequently sought to enforce it, then the plaintiff should issue a summons and serve this on the defendant together with a copy of any affidavit in support, and although the minimum period of notice is two clear days before the return day, in order to avoid the likelihood of an adjournment, longer notice and a minimum of four days, should be given. A certificate of service of a copy of the summons and copy of affidavit should be indorsed on the original affidavit.

(3) Should the summons have been adjourned generally with liberty to restore, such as in those cases where the master has been satisfied that the defendant(s) are likely to pay, then if restoration becomes necessary, the plaintiff should give four clear days notice to all defendant(s) by prepaid letter post at their last address. Again, a certificate of service should be indorsed on the affidavit, or a separate certificate of service should be available.

Considerations for the defendant or any prospective defendant

The powers of the court are limited, but the court will consider protection for a defendant against, for example, usurious rates of interest and charges. The court would also consider, if such were the case, any claims defendants may have to share in the equity of redemption, and whether a defendant could establish a lawful tenancy (if such were alleged) as against the mortgagee. If such rights are established then any sale ordered may be subject to them.

Costs

An order for costs is not sought by building societies nor generally by other mortgagees because their mortgage deeds invariably provide for their full costs of and incidental to enforcement to be added to the security and on an indemnity basis. The obligation to pay such costs as so provided in a mortgage deed overrides what would otherwise be a mortgagor's right to taxation. An aggrieved mortgagor's recourse is only under the Solicitors Act 1974, Part III.

Alternative jurisdiction

The county court has exclusive jurisdiction if the dwellinghouse is outside of the Greater London area and the rateable value does not exceed £1,000.

Textbook

ELG Tyler, *Fisher and Lightwood's Law of Mortgage*, 10th edn, (Butterworths, 1988).

Forms and precedents

Atkin, Vol 18 (1985 issue).

Power of sale and foreclosure

Foreclosure puts an end to the equity of redemption and leaves the property freed from it in the mortgagee. However, the remedy is inferior in many respects to the power of sale which was conferred on mortgagees by the Conveyancing Act 1881 re-enacted with modifications by the Law of Property Act 1925. A mortgagee by virtue of the Law of Property Act 1925, when the mortgage is made by deed, has a power when the mortgage money has become due, ie the contractual date for redemption is passed, to sell, but he may only exercise this power if either notice requiring the payment of the mortgage money has been served on the mortgagor and default has been made in payment for three months after such service, or some interest under the mortgage is in arrear and unpaid for two months after becoming due, or there has been a breach of some provision contained in the mortgage deed other than breach of the covenant to pay the mortgage money and interest. The legal mortgagee is thus empowered to sell and give title without the intervention of the court but brings proceedings because he needs a court order for possession.

Order
Order 88.

Parties
The mortgagee is the plaintiff and the defendants are the mortgagor and all incumbrancers subsequent to the plaintiff.

Intitulement
There is no special intitulement.

The objective of the plaintiff
To obtain an order nisi requiring the mortgagor to pay to the mortgagee on a given date normally six months ahead, the principal, interest, and costs then due and on failure to obey the order nisi, an order absolute putting an end to the equity of redemption. A mortgagee who forecloses becomes entitled to the mortgage property whether or not it exceeds in value the amount due to him subject only to prior encumbrances. Thus a mortgagee who forecloses and finds the property insufficient in value to satisfy the amount due to him can only sue the mortgagor on the covenant to pay upon terms of re-opening the foreclosure.

Required/have ready/on issue
Originating summons giving all particulars relevant to the mortgage debt and the amount due and stating if such be the case, that the mortgagee is in possession and is ready to account. The prayer is for payment or in default, foreclosure or sale.

Sequence
(1) On the hearing, the master may make a foreclosure order nisi ordering payment to the plaintiff of the balance of the principal sum and interest (from which income tax is deductible at the standard rate if the plaintiff is a company or resident abroad) or ordering an account to be taken of what is due and for the plaintiff's costs to be assessed in chambers, and in addition, if claimed, in the originating summons, an order for possession.
(2) Where an account is taken, the master would certify the amount due and the order will require payment within six months of the master's certificate.
(3) If the defendant defaults and thus fails to redeem, the plaintiff issues a summons for foreclosure absolute supported by affidavit; the order nisi should then be made absolute and the mortgage is thereby determined and foreclosed free of all equities of redemption.

10. Registered land

Parties in dispute may apply directly to the Chancery Division for removal of a caution entered after a contract or alleged contract or for removal of a Class F charge, and the chief land registrar (hereafter called 'the registrar') may refer disputes or appeal by way of case stated.

Statutes

Land Registration Acts 1925 to 1971.

Order

Order 93, r 10(2). Appeals under The Land Registration Act 1925 are to a single judge of the Chancery Division.

Objectives

The reversal or correction of a decision of the registrar on appeal by any person thereby aggrieved or a ruling on any question of law or fact referred to the court or by the registrar or rectification of the register by order of the court the removal of a Class F Land charge and any consequential orders or directions.

Parties

(*a*) The parties heard by the registrar (*b*) such parties as the registrar directs and (*c*) the plaintiff and any parties whose titles or interests may be affected.

Originating process

Originating motion if an appeal, originating summons if not an appeal, a writ if pleadings are called for.

Intitulement

'In the matter of (address or description of property) Title No ...'

Sequence

Hearing before a single judge of the Chancery Division (if by motion) whose decision will be final unless leave is given for appeal to the Court of Appeal. On an appeal from the registrar, the appeal must be lodged within 28 days from the notification to the appellant of the registrar's decision. Notice of intention to appeal should be delivered to the registrar as soon as possible. Any dealing for valuable consideration registered before delivery of such notice will not be affected. Appeal will be by way of rehearing, but the court may allow the introduction of new evidence, either oral or by affidavit.

When the facts are not materially in dispute an agreed statement of facts should be prepared and produced at the hearing. If rectification of the register is one of several grounds of relief (eg removal of a caution in an action for damages for repudiation of a contract for the sale of land), it may be included on a writ or an originating summons and normal procedure will follow.

Plaintiff's/defendant's considerations

The general right of appeal contained in r 299 of the Land Registration Rules 1925 (SR & O 1925, No 1093) augments and consolidates the specific cases mentioned in the Land Registration Act 1925 ss 15(2), 17(1), 56(1) and 57(3). It was decided in *Dennis v Malcolm* [1934] Ch 244 that no appeal lies to the court from the registrar's refusal to register as absolute a title about which he is not satisfied. Although this decision does not appear to have statutory authority, it has not been overruled.

Any person seeking rectification of the register has the option of applying to the registrar with right of appeal, or applying directly to the court within the terms of the Land Registration Act 1925, s 82. In the latter case he may first, by written application, seek the consent of the registrar. Without such consent the indemnity against costs provided by s 83(8) of the Act may be withheld. Orders for rectification may also be made by the court without a specific application but in consequence of a judgment affecting land where the fact that the title was registered is incidental to the cause of action.

Section 57 of the Act follows an application to the court for an order for the entry of an inhibition in the register, but as this is available by application to the registrar, there appears to be little purpose in seeking an order of the court except by way of appeal or as consequential to other relief.

Alternative jurisdiction

The jurisdiction provisionally assigned to county courts by s 138(3) of the Land Registration Act 1925 has not yet been brought into effect.

Textbooks

Halsbury, Vol 26, paras 901 et seq.
TBF Ruoff and RB Roper, *Ruoff and Roper on the Law and Practice of Registered Conveyancing*, 4th edn, (Stevens, 1979).

Forms and precedents

Atkin, Vol 23.
TBF Ruoff, *Land Registration Forms*, 2nd edn, (Sweet & Maxwell, 1987).

Originating summons (mortgagee's possession)

IN THE HIGH COURT OF JUSTICE   CH 1991 No.
CHANCERY DIVISION
IN THE MATTER of (address of property)

91 Cheam Road, East Ham E15 6TZ

BETWEEN

MARTIN MORTGAGES LTD

<u>Plaintiffs</u>

- and -

EDWARD TAKLETON

<u>Defendant</u>

TO EDWARD TAKLETON

of 91 Cheam Road, East Ham, London E15 6TZ

the Mortgagor under a Mortgage dated the 3rd day of June 1989 and made between the Plaintiff (a limited company holding Licence under Section 25 of the Consumer Credit Act 1974) of the one part and the Defendant (referred to in the said Mortgage as "the Lender") of the other part

LET the Defendant within fourteen days after service of this Summons on him inclusive of the day of service cause an Acknowledgment of Service to be filed to this Summons which is issued on the application of the Plaintiff Martin Mortgages Limited, whose registered office is situate at

under the Mortgage hereinafter mentioned.

BY THIS SUMMONS the Plaintiff seeks the determination of the Court on the following questions under Order 88 of the Rules of the Supreme Court namely:-

Originating summons (mortgagee's possession)

1. Delivery by the Defendant to the Plaintiff of possession of the above mentioned Mortgaged property at

2. Foreclosure or sale of the property comprised in the said Mortgage.

3. Further or other relief.

4. Costs.

If the Defendant does not cause an Acknowledgment of Service to be filed such Judgment may be given or Order made against or in relation to him as the Court may think just and expedient.

DATED the 30th day of August 1991

NOTE: This Summons may not be served later than twelve calendar months beginning with the above date unless renewed by Order of the Court.

This Summons was taken out by Lipson & Co of 96 Marlborough St, London ERO 6BD

Solicitors for the said Plaintiff
whose registered office is situate at 34 Marlborough St, London ERO 7BD

DIRECTIONS FOR ACKNOWLEDGEMENT OF SERVICE

Plaintiff's affidavit (possession)

FILED on behalf of the Plaintiffs
AFFIDAVIT No 1 Deponent: WILLIAM CHUZZLEWIT
Date Sworn: 30th August 1991

IN THE HIGH COURT OF JUSTICE   CH 1991. No. 43
CHANCERY DIVISION
IN THE MATTER OF (address of property)

91 Cheam Road, East Ham E15 6TZ

BETWEEN

MARTIN MORTGAGES LIMITED

Plaintiffs

- and -

EDWARD TAKLETON

Defendant

I, WILLIAM CHUZZLEWIT
of 23 Dickens Square, London W1Y 6DT
Collection Manager with the Plaintiff Bank, MAKE OATH AND SAY as follows:-

1. I am duly authorised by the Plaintiffs to make this Affidavit on its behalf. Save insofar as herein otherwise appears I am able to depose to the truth of the matters herein stated either from my own knowledge or from information supplied by the Plaintiffs' Solicitors Messrs.

2. The Plaintiffs hold a current Licence under Section 25 of the Consumer Credit Act 1974 enabling them to conduct the business of lending. The said Licence is now produced to me and exhibited hereto marked "A.1".

Plaintiff's affidavit (possession)

3. By a Legal Charge (hereinafter called "the Legal Charge") dated the 3rd day of June 1989 and made between the Plaintiffs Martin Mortgages Limited (therein and hereinafter called "the Lender") of the one part and the Defendant of the other part, the Lender advanced to the Plaintiffs the sum of £45,000 repayable together with interest as therein mentioned. The Legal Charge together with the office copy entries on the Register of the property the subject of the said Legal Charge is now produced and shown to me marked "A.2".

4. By Clause 1 of the Legal Charge it was provided that in consideration of the sum of £45,000 advanced by the Plaintiffs to the Defendant being as to £45,000 principal (the receipt of which principal sum the Defendant thereby acknowledged) the Defendant covenanted with the Plaintiffs to pay to the Plaintiffs the sum of £45,000 together with agreed interest thereon by 180 equal monthly instalments of £45,000 and that the first of such monthly instalments should be made on the 3rd day of July 1989 and the subsequent instalments paid on the 3rd day of each succeeding calendar month.

5. By Clause 4(8) of the Legal Charge should the Defendant default in payment of any one instalment due under the terms of the Mortgage he covenanted on demand to repay to the Lender the whole balance due under the terms of the Legal Charge credit being given as set out in the Second Schedule thereof together with all costs charges and expenses properly incurred thereunder by the Lender and that until so repaid such costs charges and expenses should be charged upon the premises for the time being subject to the security of the Legal Charge.

Plaintiff's affidavit (possession)

6. On or about the 3rd day of April 1991 the Defendant failed to pay the instalment of £5,000 due and has failed to pay any further instalments and the Plaintiffs have incurred and continue to incur legal fees of its Solicitors, Messrs Lipson & Co.

7. There is accordingly due from the Defendant at the date hereof pursuant to Clause 4(8) of the Legal Charge the sum of £25,000 being 5 instalments.

8. There is accordingly due to the Plaintiffs on the security of the Legal Charge the sum of £30,000 for the principal and interest and the costs charges and expenses properly incurred as Mortgagee as aforesaid in addition to the costs of this action under the terms of the Second Schedule to the Legal Charge amounting in all (but excluding costs of this action) to the sum of £450.

9. The Plaintiffs have not nor to my knowledge has any other person or persons by the Plaintiffs' order or for the Plaintiffs' use received the sums due on the security of the Legal Charge or any part of such sum or any security or securities, other than the said Legal Charge, or value in or towards satisfaction of any of them.

10. So far as the Plaintiffs are aware the Defendant and his family are the only occupants of the said mortgaged property. A Class F Land Charge has not been registered against the property.

Sworn at 90 Oxford Circus
this 30th day of August 1991

Before me

   EDWARD SMITH

     Solicitor

   Filed on behalf of the Plaintiffs

Land and Other Specific Property—Orders

LANDLORD AND TENANT

1. ORDER FOR POSSESSION, RENT, MESNE PROFITS

IT IS ORDERED

1 that the defendant shall give the plaintiff possession of the property known as ...

2 that the defendant shall pay to the plaintiff
   (a) £ ... being the balance of rent due on
   (b) £ ... being mesne profits at the rate of £ ... per annum in respect of the period beginning on ... and ending on ...
   (c) further mesne profits at the same rate in respect of the period beginning on ... and ending on ... the date on which possession of the said property is given to the plaintiff
   (d) his/her/its/their/costs of this Action to be taxed if not agreed.

Notes

1 This form can be used where a lease or tenancy has been forfeited for breach of covenant or where a tenant has remained in possession after his right to do so has expired.

2 A writ of possession cannot be issued to enforce this Order without the leave of the court—see Ord 45, r 3(2).

3 'Rent' implies the existence of a tenancy; 'mesne profits' are in the nature of damages for trespass. See para 22 on p 35 of Atkin, Vol 24 (1981 Issue). They cannot both be due in respect of the same period.

4 The words 'beginning on' and 'ending on' have been used because it is thought that they do not have the ambiguity which often adheres to 'from' and 'to'. The draftsman will however often find it more convenient to use the words used in the statement of claim.

2. ORDER FOR RELIEF FROM FORFEITURE

IT IS ORDERED

1 that the defendant having paid to the plaintiff the arrears of rent due ... and his/her/its/their costs of this Action and having remedied the dilapidations specified in the schedule of dilapidations annexed to the breaches of covenant specified in the Notice dated ... mentioned in the Statement of Claim that upon the defendant
 (a) ...
 (b) ...
 (c) ...
that upon the defendant complying with the conditions set forth in the schedule hereto the defendant be relieved from forfeiture and shall hold the premises mentioned in the Statement of Claim according to the Lease therein mentioned without any new lease

2 that the defendant shall pay to the plaintiff his/her/its/their costs of the said Application to be taxed if not agreed.

The Schedule

Notes

1 This form is drafted on the assumption that the tenant's application for relief from forfeiture is heard separately from the landlord's application for possession, rent, mesne profits etc., but often they will be heard together. The court may then give the landlord the relief he seeks but also give the tenant relief from forfeiture. The order may say that provided the tenant complies with certain conditions he be relieved from forfeiture and that the orders pronounced in favour of the landlord or some of them shall then not have effect. For example:

That the operation of the orders contained in (1) (2) and (3) above be suspended until after ... and that upon the plaintiff paying to the defendant on or before ... (a) the said sum of £ .. being arrears of rent and (b) the further sum of £ ... in respect of the rent falling due on ... next he be relieved from forfeiture and shall hold the said premises according to the Lease mentioned in the Statement of Claim without any new lease and the orders contained in (1) (2) and (3) above shall not have effect

2 Paragraph (1) of this precedent has to be adapted to the circumstances. The tenant may already have done enough to obtain relief. Alternatively, he may be granted relief on complying with conditions set out either in the body of the order or in a schedule.

3 There are forms in Atkin, Vol 24.

3. DECLARATION THAT CONSENT TO ASSIGNMENT UNREASONABLY WITHHELD

IT IS DECLARED

1 that the defendant has unreasonably withheld... consent to the assignment of the above mentioned Lease the Lease described in the schedule hereto by the plaintiff to... and

2 that the planitiff is entitled to assign the said Lease to the said... without the consent of the defendant

AND IT IS ORDERED that the defendant shall pay to the plaintiff... costs of the said Application to be taxed if not agreed.

The Schedule
A Lease made... between... (1) and... (2)

4. COMPENSATION FOR IMPROVEMENTS

IT IS ORDERED

1 pursuant to Section 1 of the Landlord and Tenant Act 1927 that the defendant shall pay to the plaintiff £... as compensation for an improvement carried out by the plaintiff/plaintiff's predecessors in title

2 that (the Court being of opinion that on account of the intention to [demolish] [alter] [change the use of] the premises mentioned in the said Originating Summons no compensation [reduced compensation] should be paid) the plaintiff be at liberty to make a further application for compensation if effect is not given to such intention on or before...

3 that such further application be made by Summons in this Action

4 that the defendant shall pay to the plaintiff... costs of the said application to be taxed if not agreed.

Note

1 See Ord 97, rr 3, 4 and 5 and Atkin, Vol 24 (1981 Issue) pp 75 et seq (notes) and 344, Form 248.

5. CERTIFICATE THAT IMPROVEMENT IS PROPER

THE COURT CERTIFIES pursuant to Section 3(1) of the Landlord and Tenant Act 1927 that (the plaintiff having failed to carry out... undertaking to execute the improvement hereinafter mentioned) subject to the modifications set out in the first schedule hereto and subject to compliance with the conditions set out in the second schedule hereto the improvement referred to in the Notice dated... served by the plaintiff on the defendant and shown in the specification and plan served therewith (copies of which specification and plan are annexed hereto) is a proper improvement

AND IT IS ORDERED that the defendant shall pay to the plaintiff costs of the said application to be taxed if not agreed.

The First Schedule
Modifications in Specification and Plan

The Second Schedule
Conditions

Notes

1 See Ord 97, r 3 and Atkin, Vol 24.

2 It may be desirable to amend copies of the specification but this is not essential if it would be inconvenient to do so.

6. CERTIFICATE THAT WORKS DULY EXECUTED

THE COURT CERTIFIES pursuant to Section 3(6) of the Landlord and Tenant Act 1927 that the improvement referred to in the Order dated... referred to in the Notice dated... served by the plaintiff on the defendant and shown in the specification and plan served therewith (copies of which specification and plan are annexed hereto) has been duly executed

THE COURT CERTIFIES pursuant to Section 3(6) of the Landlord and Tenant Act 1927 that £... is the amount of the reasonable expenses incurred by the plaintiff for the purpose of furnishing a certificate pursuant to the said Section 3(6)

AND IT IS ORDERED that the defendant shall pay to the plaintiff... costs of the said application to be taxed if not agreed.

7. ORDER GIVING LEAVE TO TAKE PROCEEDINGS

IT IS ORDERED

1 pursuant to the Leasehold Property (Repairs) Act 1938 that the plaintiff be at liberty to take proceedings against the defendant (a) for the enforcement of his/her/its/their right of re-entry by reason of breaches of the covenants to repair contained in the lease specified in the schedule hereto and (b) for damages for breaches of the said covenants

[2 that the plaintiff shall have the benefit of Section 146(3) of the Law of Property Act 1925 in relation to the costs and expenses incurred in reference to the said breaches]

3 that the defendant shall pay to the plaintiff his/her/its/their costs of the said application to be taxed if not agreed.

The Schedule
A lease dated... and made between... of the one part and... of the other part.

Notes

1 By virtue of Leasehold Property (Repairs) Act 1938 a landlord wishing to enforce his right of re-entry by reason of breaches of covenants in a lease may in certain circumstances have to obtain the leave of the court.

2 Paragraph (2) is inserted only when appropriate.

8. ORDER FOR NEW TENANCY

IT IS ORDERED

1 that the defendant shall on or before... or subsequently within 4 days after service of this Order execute and deliver to the plaintiff a new lease of the premises demised by the current lease mentioned in the Originating Summons (a brief description of which premises is set out in the first schedule hereto) in accordance with the provisions of the second schedule hereto but in other respects on the terms of the said current lease

2 that the plaintiff shall within the same time deliver to the plaintiff a counterpart of such new lease

3   that this Order be without prejudice to the right of the plaintiff within 14 days after the making of this Order to apply pursuant to Section 36(2) of the Landlord and Tenant Act 1954 for revocation of this Order

4   that the plaintiff be at liberty to make such application in these proceedings

5   that the defendant shall pay to the plaintiff his/her/its/their costs of this Action to be taxed if not agreed.

The First Schedule
The premises at ... demised by a lease made ... between the defendant of the one part and the plaintiff of the other part

The Second Schedule
Provisions of New Lease
The term is to be ... years from ... the termination of the current tenancy at a rent of £ ... per annum payable quarterly in advance on the usual quarter days instead of the rent of £ ... mentioned in the current lease.

Notes

1   The form in Atkin does not specify a time within which the new lease is to be delivered but in view of Ord 42, r 2 a time should be specified. It should not be earlier than 14 days from the making of the order.

2   This form assumes that the whole of the premises demised by the current lease are to be demised by the new lease. If this is not so, it will have to be amended. Only a brief description of the premises need be inserted in the first schedule.

3   It is assumed that the only differences between the current lease and the new lease will be as regards rent and term. This will not always be the case. Occasionally the order will be for a new lease 'in the form of the draft annexed hereto'. In these cases the draftsman should check that there are no gaps in the draft lease which need filling.

4   In the first schedule the words 'the termination of the current tenancy' should be deleted if a date is inserted.

9. ORDER REVOKING ORDER FOR NEW TENANCY

IT IS ORDERED

1 pursuant to Section 36(2) of the Landlord and Tenant Act 1954 that the Order dated ... be revoked save as to costs

2 that the plaintiff shall pay to the defendant his/her/its/their costs of this Action and the said Motion to be taxed if not agreed.

Note

See Atkin, Vol 24.

10. ORDER REFUSING NEW TENANCY
(Section 30(1) Landlord and Tenant Act 1954)

AND the defendant having established to the satisfaction of this court that on the termination of the current tenancy it intends to occupy the property demised by the lease mentioned in the Originating Summons for the purpose of a business to be carried on by it therein

IT IS ORDERED

1 that the said Originating Summons shall stand dismissed

2 that the plaintiff shall pay to the defendant his/her/its/their/ costs of this Action to be taxed if not agreed

AND IT IS CERTIFIED that this court is precluded by Section 31 of the Landlord and Tenant Act 1954 from making an Order under Part II of that Act for the grant to the plaintiff of a new tenancy of the said property on the ground that it has in accordance with Section 30(1)(g) of the said Act established to the satisfaction of this court that on the termination of the tenancy created by the said lease it intends to occupy the property for the purposes of a business to be carried on by it therein and not by reason of the existence of any ground specified in any other paragraph of the said Section 30(1).

Notes

1 This form may be compared with Form 213 on p 321 of Atkin, Vol 24 (1981 Issue).

2 The grounds on which a landlord may oppose a tenant's application for a new lease are set out in s 30(1) of the Landlord and Tenant Act 1954. Order 97, r 9 says that where the court is precluded by s 31 of the Act from making an order for the grant of a new tenancy the order shall state all the grounds by reason of which the court is so precluded. Hence the recital in this order. The recital is appropriate where ground (g) in s 30(1) is established. If some other ground is established the draftsman will have to draft the appropriate recital, following so far as possible the wording of the appropriate paragraph in s 30(1).

3 The certificate is included in the order because of s 37(4) of the Act which says that where the court is precluded from making an order by reason of one of the grounds specified in paragraphs (e) (f) or (g) and not any other ground it shall on the application of the tenant certify the fact. (The tenant is entitled to compensation in these circumstances.) The certificate in the precedent is appropriate where (g) is established and so where the landlord establishes (e) or (f) the draftsman will have to prepare the appropriate certificate following so far as possible the wording of paragraphs (e) or (f).

11. ORDER REFUSING NEW TENANCY
(Section 31(2) Landlord and Tenant Act 1954)

IT IS ORDERED

1 that the said Originating Summons shall stand dismissed

2 that the plaintiff shall pay to the defendant ... costs of this Action to be taxed if not agreed

AND IT IS DECLARED pursuant to Section 31(2) of the Landlord and Tenant Act 1954 that it would have been satisfied of the ground specified in paragraph (d) (e) (f) of Section 30(1) of the said Act in relation to the said application if the date of termination specified in the defendant's notice under Section 25 the plaintiff's request for a new tenancy as the date from which the new tenancy is to begin had been ...

Notes

1 This form relates to the unusual circumstances specified in s 31(2) of the Landlord and Tenant Act 1954. The landlord fails to establish any of the grounds specified in s 30(1) but if the relevant date had been different he would have succeeded on ground (d) (e) or (f). When this happens the court is to make a declaration to that effect 'but shall not make an order for the grant of a new tenancy'.

2 Section 31(2)(*b*) says:

If within fourteen days after the making of the declaration, the tenant so requires... the court shall make an order substituting the date specified in the previous order for the date in the landlord's notice or tenant's request and thereupon that notice or request shall have effect accordingly.

12. ORDER SUBSTITUTING DATE

IT IS pursuant to Section 31(2)(b) of the Landlord and Tenant Act 1954 ORDERED that in the defendant's notice under Section 25 of the said Act in the plaintiff's request under Section 26 of the said Act for a new tenancy for the date... specified therein there shall be substituted the following date that is to say...

Notes

1 This form is for use when the court makes an order under s 31(2)(*b*) of the Landlord and Tenant Act 1954. An order under s 31(2)(*a*) will previously have been made. See form 11 above.

2 Order 97, r 10(1) says that the application must be made *ex parte* in chambers.

3 The wording 'in the defendant's notice under Section 25 of the said Act' and 'in the plaintiff's request under Section 26 of the said Act for a new tenancy' are alternatives. It is assumed that the tenant is the plaintiff and the landlord the defendant.

4 The second date to go in (1) is the date mentioned in the previous Order (Form 11).

13. ORDER DETERMINING INTERIM RENT

THE COURT DETERMINES pursuant to Section 24A of the Landlord and Tenant Act 1954 that the rent which it would be reasonable for the plaintiff to pay while the lease in the Originating Summons continues by virtue of Section 24 of the said Act be at the rate of £... per annum.

14. ORDER PERMITTING DISCONTINUANCE OF APPLICATION

IT IS by Consent ORDERED

1 that the Summons seeking the determination of a rent which

it would be reasonable for the plaintiff to pay while the tenancy mentioned in the Originating Summons continues shall stand as a Counterclaim in this Action

2 that the plaintiff be at liberty to withdraw the claim for a new tenancy and that accordingly without prejudice to the Counterclaim this Action be forthwith discontinued with no Order as to the costs thereof.

Notes

1 The court has no power to backdate an order for discontinuance (*Covell Matthews v French Wools Ltd* [1978] 1 WLR 1477).

2 It often happens that the claim for interim rent has not been settled although the plaintiff does not wish to proceed with the originating summons for a new lease. It is to make clear that the summons for interim rent is not dismissed, that is continues as a counterclaim. Even if this is not done the application for interim rent is a wholly distinct claim which survives the discontinuances of the originating summons (*Artoc Ltd v Prudential Ltd* [1984] 1 WLR 1181).

15. ORDER ON JOINT APPLICATION TO EXCLUDE PROVISIONS OF ss 24-28 OF LANDLORD AND TENANT ACT 1954

[AND the Applicants by their solicitors having agreed in writing that the said Application should be dealt with by this court notwithstanding the rateable value of the above mentioned premises]

IT IS ORDERED

1 that the Applicants be at liberty to enter into an agreement excluding the provisions of Section 24 to 28 of the said Landlord and Tenant Act 1954 in relation to the [sub-underlease] of the above mentioned premises proposed to be granted by ... to ...

2 that the said agreement be [endorsed on] [contained in] the said sub-underlease when executed.

16. ORDER AUTHORISING AGREEMENT FOR SURRENDER OF TENANCY: (s 38 OF LANDLORD AND TENANT ACT 1954)

IT IS pursuant to Section 38 of the Landlord and Tenant Act 1954 (as amended by the Law of Property Act 1969) ORDERED that the Applicants be at liberty to enter into an agreement for the surrender of the tenancy of the above mentioned premises such agreement to be in the terms of an intended Agreement to be made between ... and ...

17. ORDER TO CONFER RIGHT OF FIRST REFUSAL ON TENANTS (LANDLORD AND TENANT ACT 1987)

IT IS ORDERED

1 that the Defendant shall on or before ... serve on the Plaintiffs [and all other tenants qualified in accordance with the provisions of the above mentioned Act] notice conferring the right of first refusal on the disposal by Defendant of the premises specified in the Schedule hereto

2 that the Defendant be restrained from disposing on or before ... (whether by its directors officers servants or agents or any of them or otherwise howsoever) of the property specified in the Schedule hereto other than to the Plaintiffs [or ... the person nominated by the tenants of the said property]

3 that the Defendant shall on or before ... serve on the Plaintiffs particulars of the terms on which it purchased the premises specified in the Schedule hereto from ... the former landlord of the Plaintiffs

4 that the Plaintiffs be at liberty to make the lodgment in Court directed in the Lodgment Schedule hereto being [the whole of the purchase price of the property specified in the Schedule hereto after payment thereout of all proper costs and charges incurred in the sale of the said premises] *or* [the principal and interest due under a Legal Charge dated ... and made between the Defendant and ...]

5 and upon the Plaintiffs making such Lodgment as aforesaid

IT IS DECLARED that the Transfer [conveyance] of the said property from the Defendant to the Plaintiffs operates to discharge the said property from the said Charge

1 that the Defendant shall pay to the Plaintiffs ... costs of the said Application such costs to be taxed on County Court scale [1, 2 *or* 3] if not agreed.

The Schedule
The Leasehold premises known as ...

Notes

1 The obligations imposed on a landlord by the Act are enforceable through the courts if disobeyed. The times are those prescribed by the Act; hence the wording of the injunction.

2 Tenants may assert their right to first refusal even if the original landlord has sold to a third party. Details of the sale can be demanded and a purchase effected by the tenants on like terms.

3 When purchasing from a third party tenants must discharge charges created on the property by the third party. The whole of the purchase price may be lodged if the charges cannot be found or the redemption figures are not readily available.

4 NB, The limitations of the taxation order.

5 In this case the order should be made 'in the matter of the Landlord and Tenant Act 1987'.

18. ORDER APPOINTING MANAGER (LANDLORD AND TENANT ACT 1987)

[AND THE COURT dispensing with service on the Defendant of a notice pursuant to Section 22 of the Landlord and Tenant Act 1987]

AND the Plaintiff by ... Counsel undertaking to be answerable for what the Manager hereinafter appointed shall become liable to pay until he shall have given security as hereinafter directed

THE COURT HEREBY APPOINTS ... of ... [without giving security] to manage [until further Order] the premises known as ... in accordance with the terms of the Lease specified in the Schedule hereto

AND IT IS ORDERED

1 that the said Manager shall on or before ... give security as such manager to the satisfaction of the Court

2 that if the said Manager shall not have given such security as aforesaid by the time aforesaid or within such further time as the Court may allow his appointment as such Manager is forthwith upon the expiration of such time to determine

[3 that all rights and liabilities of the Defendant in respect of contracts made by the Defendant in respect of the said premises become the rights and liabilities of the Manager

4 that the Manager be at liberty to prosecute all choses of action accruing to the Defendant in respect of the said premises

5 that the Manager be allowed such remuneration as the Court may from time to time direct such remuneration to be paid by the Defendant to the Manager]

6 that the Defendant shall pay to the Plaintiff... costs of the said Application such costs to be taxed on County Court scale [1 2 or 3] if not agreed

The Schedule
A lease made... between... of the one part and... of the other part

Note

1 In this case the order should be made 'in the matter of the Landlord and Tenant Act 1987'.

19. ORDER FOR COMPULSORY ACQUISITION OF LANDLORD'S INTEREST (LANDLORD AND TENANT ACT 1987)

[AND THE COURT dispensing with service on the Defendant of a notice pursuant to Section 27 of the Landlord and Tenant Act 1987]
  AND the Court being satisfied

1 that the Defendant is in breach of obligation to repair/maintain/insure/manage the premises comprised in the Lease specified in the Schedule hereto

2 that such breach is likely to continue

3 that the appointment of a manager would not be an appropriate remedy *or* [that... has been a manager pursuant to Part II of the above mentioned Act of the premises comprised in the Lease specified in the Schedule hereto for at least three years]

IT IS DECLARED that the Plaintiff is entitled to acquire the Defendant's interest in the said premises on such terms as may be agreed between the Plaintiff and the Defendant or in default thereof by a Rent Assessment Committee [PROVIDED that if the

Defendant shall on or before ... rectify the said breaches of obligation and thereafter comply with all such obligations the said right to acquisition be suspended until further Order]

AND IT IS ORDERED

1 that the Defendant shall pay to the Plaintiff ... costs of the said Application such costs to be taxed on County Court Scale [1 2 *or* 3] if not agreed

2 the parties be at liberty to apply

The Schedule
A Lease dated ... and made between ... of the one part and ... of the other part

Notes

1 It will be necessary to provide liberty for the parties to apply if the acquisition order is suspended or there is the likelihood of a subsequent application to discharge a charge on the premises.

2 In this case the order should be made 'in the matter of the Landlord and Tenant Act 1987'.

20. ORDER UNDER LEASEHOLD REFORM ACT 1967, s 27

IT IS pursuant to Section 27 of the Leasehold Reform Act 1967 ORDERED

1 that a proper conveyance pursuant to the said Section of the property described in Part I of the Order schedule hereto be settled by the Master

2 that the Master of the Supreme Court who is named in Part II of the said schedule be designated to execute the said conveyance

3 that the Applicant be at liberty to lodge in Court as directed in the lodgment part of the lodgment and payment schedule hereto the sum specified therein the said sum being made up as shown in Part III of the said Order schedule

4 that the funds in court when so lodged as aforesaid be dealt with as directed in the payment part of the said lodgment and payment schedule

5 that upon the said sum being lodged in court as aforesaid the said Master shall execute the said conveyance and deliver the same to the Applicant

6 that the parties are to be at liberty to apply

The Order Schedule
Part I
Short Description of Property.

Part II
Name of Master designated to execute conveyance

Part III
The amount certified to be a fair valuation in accordance with Section 9 of the Act £ . . .

Rent remaining payable in respect of period up to the date of the conveyance £ . . .

Sum to be lodged in court £ . . .

Note

1 This form of order applies where the freeholder cannot be found.

MORTGAGES

21. DECLARATION OF FREEDOM FROM INCUMBRANCES—FIRST ORDER

IT IS ORDERED

1 that the plaintiff be at liberty to lodge in court as directed in the lodgment schedule hereto the amount therein directed being the balance of the principal and interest due in respect of a Mortgage made . . . between the plaintiff of the one part and the defendant of the other part together with £ . . . for costs

2 that when such lodgment has been made the plaintiff is to be at liberty to apply for a declaration that the property described in the Order schedule hereto is freed from the said Mortgage.

The Order Schedule
The . . . hold property known as . . . and registered at Her Majesty's

Land Registry under Title Number ... [There is a lodgment schedule]

22. DECLARATION OF FREEDOM FROM INCUMBRANCES—SECOND ORDER

IT IS DECLARED that (funds having been lodged in court) the property described in the schedule hereto is freed from the incumbrance of a Mortgage thereon made ... between the plaintiff of the one part and the defendant of the other part

AND IT IS ORDERED that the plaintiff shall pay to the defendant his ... costs of this Action to be taxed if not agreed

The Schedule
The ... hold property known as ... and registered at Her Majesty's Land Registry under Title Number ...

23. ENFORCEMENT OF EQUITABLE MORTGAGE

AND the court being satisfied that the title deeds [Land Certificate] relating to the property described in the schedule hereto have/has been deposited by the defendant with the plaintiff as security and that the plaintiff is entitled to be considered as a mortgagee of the said property

IT IS ORDERED

1 that the said property be sold

2 pursuant to Section 90 of the Law of Property Act 1925 and for the purpose of enabling the plaintiff to carry out the sale that there be created and vested in the plaintiff a legal term of 3000 years in the said property as if the mortgage had been created by way of legal mortgage pursuant to the said Act
[pursuant to Section 90 of the Law of Property Act 1925 and for the purpose of enabling the plaintiff to carry out the sale of the said property that there be created and vested in the plaintiff a legal term of years for the remainder of the term granted by the lease under which such property is held by the defendant less the last day thereof]

3 that the conduct of the sale be committed to Messrs ... the solicitors for the plaintiff

4 that the price be hereafter fixed by the court but that subject

thereto the plaintiff be at liberty to proceed with the sale without further directions from the Court

5 [that the following Account be taken that is to say

(1) An Account of what is due to the plaintiff by virtue of the said deposit and of the memorandum of agreement relating to the same mentioned in the Originating Summons and for ... costs of this Action to be assessed in Chambers]

6 [that the amount which shall hereafter be declared on taking the said Account to be due to the plaintiff be considered a charge on the said property]

7 [that unless otherwise agreed between the parties the proceeds of sale after payment thereout of (*a*) the said amount declared to be due to the plaintiff (*b*) what shall be due to any incumbrancers to their priorities and (*c*) all proper costs charges and expenses incurred in connection with the said sale be lodged in Court to the credit of this Action ... v ... 199 ... Proceeds of Sale of Freehold/Leasehold Property subject to further Order]

[8 that the defendant shall deliver up possession to the plaintiff in 28 days of personal service of this order.]

9 that the parties are to be at liberty to apply.

The Schedule
The freehold/leasehold property known as ... and registered at Her Majesty's Land Registry under Title Number ...

Notes

1 Under the Law of Property Act 1925, ss 85 and 86 a legal mortgage can be created either by a demise for a term of years absolute subject to a provision for cesser on redemption or by a charge by deed expressed to be by way of legal mortgage. Any other mortgage of unregistered land is equitable. Under the Land Registration Act 1925 a charge has to be registered and if not registered can have effect in equity only.

2 The two most common forms of equitable mortgage are (1) a deposit of title deeds (or land certificate) with intent to pledge the property (2) a written agreement to execute a mortgage. A deposit is often accompanied by a memorandum signed by the borrower. If there is no deposit it may be appropriate to say 'satisfied that the Defendant has agreed to execute a legal mortgage of the property'.

3 Unless the mortgage is made by deed an equitable mortgagee has no power of sale. The plaintiff therefore asks the Court to order a sale of

the mortgaged property. Even when the order for sale has been made an equitable mortgagee cannot convey the property to the purchaser unless the Court exercises its power under s 90 of the Law of Property Act 1925 to vest in the mortgagee a legal term of years absolute to enable him to carry out the sale or its power to appoint a person to convey the property.

4 An account is not always ordered.

5 In an appropriate case an order for possession may be given on the first appointment if all necessary parties are before the court.

6 Sometimes the court will order that the plaintiffs be at liberty to sell the property without further reference to the court.

24. ORDER FOR FORECLOSURE NISI

1 IT IS ORDERED that the following Account be taken that is to say
   (1) An Account of what is due to the plaintiff under and by virtue of the Mortgage described in the first schedule hereto and for ... costs of this Action to be assessed in Chambers

2 that the amount due to the plaintiff on such Account be declared by further Order and that a date and time being not less than six months after the date of such further Order and the place for payment be thereby appointed

3 that unless the defendant shall give notice in writing to the solicitors for the plaintiff not less than 7 days before the date so appointed of intention to redeem the said Mortgage on the said date attendance at such date time and place to redeem the said Mortgage be treated (if the plaintiff shall so elect) as notice of intention so to attend 7 days thereafter at the same time and place and that the time for redemption of the said Mortgage be enlarged accordingly

4 that upon the defendant duly paying to the plaintiff what shall by such further Order be declared to be due to the plaintiff as aforesaid the plaintiff shall give a receipt pursuant to Section 115 of the Law of Property Act 1925 or otherwise duly discharge or transfer the said Mortgage and do deliver (upon oath if required) all deeds and writings in the custody or power of the plaintiff relating to the property comprised in the said Mortgage to the defendant or to whom the defendant shall appoint

5 that in default of the defendant paying to the plaintiff as hereinbefore provided what shall be declared to be due to the

plaintiff as aforesaid the defendant shall thenceforth stand absolutely debarred and foreclosed of and from all right title interest and equity of redemption of in and to the said property

6 that thereupon the defendant shall forthwith deliver to the plaintiffs possession of the said property which is described in the second schedule hereto

7 that in case the defendant or any/either of them shall so redeem the said property the defendant or defendants so redeeming is/are to be at liberty to apply without giving the plaintiff notice thereof

8 that this Order is made without prejudice to any question which may arise as to the rights or interests of the defendants as between themselves in or to the said property AND the parties are to be at liberty to apply.

The First Schedule
A Mortgage dated ... and made between ... (1) and ... (2)

The Second Schedule
The ... hold property known as ... and registered at Her Majesty's Land Registry under Title Number ...

Note

1 Where the mortgage in question is described as a legal charge that expression should be used throughout in place of the term 'mortgage'.

25. ORDER FOR FORECLOSURE ABSOLUTE

AND the Court being satisfied that the transaction hereby effected does not form part of a larger transaction or of a series of transactions in respect of which the amount or value or the aggregate amount or value of the consideration exceeds £ ...

IT IS ORDERED

1 that the defendant shall henceforth stand absolutely debarred and foreclosed of and from all right title interest and equity of redemption of in and to the property specified in the schedule hereto

2 that the defendant shall forthwith deliver to the plaintiff possession of the said property.

The Schedule
The... hold property known as... and registered at Her Majesty's Land Registry under Title Number...

Note

1 An order of foreclosure absolute attracts stamp duty and hence the insertion of a certificate of value. The duty is charged on the total amount owing for principal interest and costs on the mortgage foreclosed. See SCP, Vol 2, 719A and Finance Act 1898, s 6. This recital should not be used where the total amount due under the mortgage is £30,000 or more.

26. ORDER FOR POSSESSION

IT IS ORDERED

[that each of the defendants shall within... days after personal service of this Order upon that defendant deliver to the plaintiffs possession of the property comprised in the said Mortgage and known as...] [that each of the defendants do within... days after personal service of this order upon each of them deliver to the plaintiffs possession of... the property known as... being part of the property comprised in the said Mortgage]

BUT this Order is not to be enforced without the leave of the court provided the defendant shall pay to the plaintiffs [the sum of £... on or before... the monthly sum of £... in every calendar month in respect of both the monthly instalments payable under the said Mortgage and the arrears thereof until such arrears shall have been fully paid the first such payment to be made in/on... [the arrears now due under the said Mortgage by equal sums of £... on the... day of every calendar month commencing on... until such arrears shall have been fully paid and all sums hereafter to become payable by way of capital or interest or otherwise under the said Mortgage when such sums shall become due or would had there been no default have become due]

AND the parties are to be at liberty to apply.

Notes

1 When solicitors are present for the defendant but they are not on the record for him the precedent may read 'Solicitors acting for defendant although not on the record for him'.

2 Normally the description of the property should follow the description in the mortgage but long descriptions are not required. Occasionally a plan may have to be attached to the order. The order might then say

'the property on the north side of... Road... comprised in the said Mortgage and shown edged red on the plan annexed hereto'.

3 When service on one defendant only is personal a useful form of words is:

IT IS ORDERED that the first defendant shall within 28 days after personal service upon him of this Order and that the second defendant shall within 28 days after service upon her...

4 Sometimes, particularly when the defendant has solicitors, possession is ordered within so many days after service of the order. In these cases the word 'personal' must not be used.

5 The court frequently makes a suspended order. Two alternative forms are included in the precedent but there can be many variations depending on the circumstances.

27. ORDER FOR PAYMENT

IT IS ORDERED

1 that the defendant shall pay to the plaintiff £... (being as to £... the principal sum due under the said mortgage and as to £... interest due thereunder down to and including the date hereof)

2 Further interest on the said sum of £... at the rate of... % per annum from... until payment

3 Plaintiff's costs to be taxed and paid by the defendant

4 Liberty to apply generally.

28. ORDER FOR DISCLOSURE OF TITLE

IT IS ORDERED

1 that the Defendant shall within... days after personal service of this Order upon him file in Chancery Chambers room 156 The Royal Courts of Justice Strand London WC2A 2LL an affidavit stating what (if any) deeds and other documents relating to the title of the property described in the Schedule hereto are in his possession or power and whether any deeds or other documents relating to the said title are known by him to be in the possession

or power of any person or persons and if so stating the name and address of every such person

2 that the Defendant shall within the same time lodge in Chancery Chambers room 156 the Royal Courts of Justice Strand London WC2A 2LL all (if any) such deeds and documents as are stated by him to be in his own possession or power

The Schedule

The freehold/leasehold property known as...

29. SALE OF SHARES ('MUSGRAVE')

AND IT APPEARING that the Plaintiff is by virtue of the Charging Order specified in the First Schedule hereto entitled to an equitable charge upon the interest of the Defendant in the shares specified in the Second Schedule hereto

THE COURT DECLARES that the Defendant is a Trustee of the said Shares for the Plaintiff within the meaning of Section 51(1) of the Trustee Act 1925

AND IT IS ORDERED

1 that the right to transfer so many of the said shares as shall suffice to discharge the debt and to receive the dividends now due or to accrue thereon vest in the Plaintiff

2 that the said shares be sold by the Plaintiff

3 that the Plaintiff be at liberty to discharge out of the moneys to arise on such sale and any dividends received by him (a) what shall be due to him under and by virtue of the said Charging Order and (b) £... being his assessed costs of this Action

4 that the Parties be at liberty to apply

The First Schedule
The Order dated... of the... made in the Action

30. MUSGRAVE ORDER (NO ACCOUNT)

AND IT APPEARING that the Plaintiff is by virtue of the Charging Order specified in the First Schedule hereto entitled to an equitable charge upon the interest of the Defendant in the property specified in the Second Schedule hereto

IT IS ORDERED

1 that upon the Defendant duly paying to the Plaintiff £ ... (the said sum being made up as set out in the Third Schedule hereto) between the hours of ... on ... day 199 ... at the offices of the Solicitors for the Plaintiff Messrs ... at ... the Plaintiff shall forthwith

   (i) give a receipt therefor
   (ii) deliver (upon oath if required) to the Defendant or to whom the Defendant may direct all deeds or writings in his custody or power relating to the said property
   (iii) apply for satisfaction to be entered on the Judgment in respect of which the said Charging Order was made
   (iv) apply for cancellation of any registration of the said Charging Order under the Land Registration Act 1925 or the Land Charges Act 1972 and
   (v) apply for an Order that the said Charging Order be discharged

2 that in default of the Defendant paying to the Plaintiff the said sum as hereinbefore provided the Plaintiff be at liberty to restore the said Originating Summons to ask for an Order for the sale of the said property and for directions in relation thereto
AND the parties are to be at liberty to apply generally

The First Schedule
The order dated ... of the ... made in the Action

The Second Schedule
The ... hold property known as ... and registered at Her Majesty's Land Registry under Title Number ...

The Third Schedule
The judgment debt mentioned
in the Charging Order   £

The costs mentioned therein   £

Interest pursuant to the
Judgments Act 1838 on the
judgment debt and said costs
down to and including the date
mentioned in Paragraph 1 of
this Order   £

The assessed costs of the
Plaintiff of this Action   £

31. MUSGRAVE ORDER (COMPOSITE FORM)

AND IT APPEARING that the Plaintiff is by virtue of the Charging Order specified in the First Schedule hereto entitled to an equitable charge upon the interest of the Defendant in the property specified in the Second Schedule hereto

IT IS ORDERED

1   that the costs of the Plaintiff of this Action be assessed in Chambers and paid by the Defendant

2   that the said property be sold without further reference to the Court at a price of not less than £... save that the sale price or reserve be fixed by the Court

3   pursuant to Section 90 of the Law of Property Act 1925 and for the purpose of enabling the Plaintiff to carry out the sale that there be created and vested in the Plaintiff a legal term of 3,000 years in the said property as if the mortgage had been created by deed by way of legal mortgage pursuant to the said Act

4   pursuant to Section 90 of the Law of Property Act and for the purpose of enabling the Plaintiff to carry out the sale of the said property that there be created and vested in the Plaintiff a legal term of years for the remainder of the term granted by the lease under which such property is held by the Defendant less the last day thereof

5   that the following Account and Inquiries be taken and made that is to say
    (i) An Account of what is due to the Plaintiff
        (a) under and by virtue of the said Charging Order and
        (b) for his said costs
    (ii) An Inquiry as to what interest the Defendant has in the said property

(iii) An Inquiry whether there are any and if any what other liens charges or incumbrances upon the said property or upon any and if any what part or parts thereof respectively and what are their priorities and what is due on account thereof respectively

6 that the Defendant shall within 14 days after personal service upon him of this Order file in Chancery Chambers room 156 The Royal Courts of Justice Strand London WC2A 2LL an affidavit stating what (if any) deeds and other documents relating to the title of the said property are in his possession or power and whether any deeds or other documents relating to the said title are known by him to be in the possession or power of any person or persons and if so stating the name and address of every such person and that he shall within the same time lodge at the said room 156 all (if any) such deeds and documents as are stated by him to be in his own possession or power

7 that the Defendant shall within 28 days after personal service upon him of this order deliver to the Plaintiff possession of the said property

8 that unless otherwise agreed by the parties interested therein the proceeds of sale of the said property after payment thereout of (*a*) what shall be due to any incumbrancers other than the Plaintiff (*b*) what shall be due to the Plaintiff and (*c*) all proper costs charges and expenses incurred in connection with the said sale be lodged in Court to the credit of this Action
v
199... Proceeds of sale of Freehold/Leasehold Property subject to further Order

9 that in the event of the Defendant redeeming the said charge and paying the Plaintiff's costs of obtaining and executing this Order (including what is due to auctioneers and solicitors) this Order shall cease to have effect but without prejudice to the validity of any contract made prior to or without notice of such redemption and payment

10 that the parties are at liberty to apply for possession and generally

The First Schedule
The Order dated ... of the ... made in the Action

The Second Schedule
The ... hold property known as ... and registered at Her Majesty's Land Registry under Title Number ...

Notes

1 This is a composite form of order and those paragraphs in square brackets which are not required should be struck out.

2 An order for possession is not normally made on the first appointment but only if all the evidence required under s 88 is before the court.

3 Associates should not include in the order any of the paragraphs which are not stipulated by the master.

32. RESULT OF 'MUSGRAVE' INQUIRIES

UPON THE ACCOUNT AND INQUIRIES directed by the Order dated...
UPON THE APPLICATION of the Plaintiff by... Summons dated...
AND UPON HEARING the Solicitors for the Plaintiff and for the Defendant
AND UPON READING the Court file
IT IS as the result of the said Account and Inquiries directed by the said Order dated... DECLARED

1 that there is due to the Plaintiff
   (a) Under and by virtue of the Charging Order £...
   (b) for their costs assessed in Chambers pursuant to the said Order £...

2 ...

3 ...

AND THE COURT APPOINTS... on... at the offices of... at... as the time date and place for payment by the Defendant of the sum of £... (being the total of the two said amounts) to the Plaintiff as provided in the said Order

Note

1 An example of possible declarations in paragraphs 2 and 3 is:

   '2 that the defendant is the sole beneficial owner of the property

   3 that there is one incumbrance on the said property namely a Mortgage made... between the Defendant and the Building Society.'

SALE OF LAND

33. ORDER ON SALE AT AUCTION

THE AUCTION directed by the Order dated... being held this day in the presence of the Solicitors for...

AND... having at the said Auction become the purchaser of the property described in the said Order at the price of £...

IT IS accordingly ORDERED

1 that the said property be sold to the... at the price of £...

2 that the conduct of the said sale be committed to Messrs... the Solicitors for the...

3 that the balance of the purchase money after payment thereout of... be paid to Messrs... who shall be entitled to deduct therefrom their proper costs of acting in the sale and the abortive sale directed by the Order dated...

4 that unless otherwise mutually agreed the balance of the purchase money remaining after the aforesaid deductions be lodged by Messrs... in Court to the credit of this Action... subject to further Order

5 that the costs of all parties of the Auction and of this Order and the costs reserved by the Order dated... be taxed if not agreed and paid out of the proceeds of sale.

34. COMMON FORM ORDER

IT IS ORDERED

1 that the property described in the schedule hereto be sold at such time and in such manner as the parties may agree or as in default of agreement the Court may direct

2 that the conduct of the sale be committed to Messrs... the solicitors for the plaintiff

3 that each of the parties be at liberty to bid for or become the purchaser of the said property at the said sale

4 that unless otherwise agreed between the parties the proceeds

of sale after payment thereout of what shall be due to any incumbrancers according to their priorities and of all proper costs charges and expenses incurred in connection with the said sale be lodged in Court to the credit of this Action ... v ... 199 ... 'Proceeds of Sale of Freehold Property' subject to further order

5 that the following Inquiry be made that is to say
   (1) An Inquiry for what estates and interest and in what shares and proportions the plaintiff and the defendant respectively are interested in the said property or the net proceeds of sale thereof taking into account the mutual dealings of the plaintiff and the defendant in respect of the said property in relation to rents and profits or otherwise and the values of their respective occupations of the said property

6 that the costs of the plaintiff of this Action down to and including this Order be taxed if not agreed and charged against the defendant's share of the said proceeds of sale

7 that the costs of the plaintiff and of the defendant be taxed pursuant to the Legal Aid Act 1974

AND the parties are to be at liberty to apply (a) for further directions with regard to the said sale and (b) generally

The Schedule
The freehold property known as ... and registered at Her Majesty's Land Registry under Title Number ...

Notes

1 This precedent sets out a common form of order for sale and has to be adapted to the particular circumstances and the various forms of directions usually given are set out in Ord 31, r 2(2). The expressions 'sale out of court' and 'sale by approbation of the court' are no longer used and the order for sale is usually made without further reference to the court save for fixing the price or reserve.

2 The degree of control which the court exercises over sales varies according to the circumstances. Sometimes it is made clear that if the parties cannot agree they will have to come back for further directions. In other cases the party conducting the sale can proceed without the consent of the other party and without coming back for further directions except perhaps directions on particular matters (eg, reserve price) specified in the order.

3 When the court orders that the conduct of the sale is committed to the plaintiff's solicitors without naming them it is usually right to assume that the country solicitors and not their London agents are intended.

4 If the order provides for lodgment in court of the proceeds of sale the more usual course is not to annex a lodgment schedule but to leave this to be signed later by the master. It is often better for the proceeds of sale to be held in a joint deposit account at a specified bank in the names of the plaintiff's solicitors and the defendant's solicitors.

35. EXAMPLES OF OTHER CLAUSES

1 IT IS DECLARED that the defendant holds the property described in the schedule hereto on trust for the plaintiff and the defendant as tenants in common in equal shares

2 ... ORDERED that the statutory trusts affecting the property described in the schedule hereto be carried into execution

3 that the plaintiff be at liberty to proceed with the said sale without seeking further directions from the Court

4 ... that the property described in the schedule hereto be sold at such price as the Court shall approve and in such manner as the parties may on or before... agree or in default of such agreement by public auction on or before...

5 ... that the property described in the schedule hereto be sold by public auction subject to a reserve price and the auctioneers' remuneration being fixed by the Court

6 ... that the property described in the schedule hereto be sold free from the incumbrances (if any) of such of the incumbrancers as shall consent to the sale and subject to the incumbrances of such of them as shall not consent

7 ... be sold subject to and with the benefit of the tenancy of one... of the first floor thereof...

8 that the plaintiff be at liberty to sell the said property by private treaty for not less than...

9 that the defendant shall concur with the plaintiff in selling the said property to...

10 ... that the defendant shall concur with the plaintiff in effecting the sale of the property described in the schedule hereto pursuant to the statutory trusts affecting the same and that the defendant take all such steps and do and execute all such things and

instruments as may be necessary or convenient to implement such sale as aforesaid

11 that the defendant shall concur with the plaintiff in offering for sale by public auction the said property with vacant possession

12 that the reserve price be hereafter fixed and the auctioneers be hereafter appointed by the Court

13 ... that the property be sold for not less than £...

14 ... that the reserve price at the auction be £...

15 that the plaintiff shall on or before ... lodge in room 156 Chancery Chambers an Affidavit exhibiting thereto a valuation of the said properties and nominating auctioneers for the said sale
AND the defendant is to be at liberty within ... days after service on them of a copy of the last mentioned Affidavit to lodge an Affidavit in answer thereto

16 that in default of Agreement on or before ... as to the reserve price and the appointment of the auctioneers evidence directed to these matters be lodged on or before ...

17 that if the said property be sold by public auction then the remuneration of the auctioneers be at the rate of £...

18 that the remuneration of the auctioneers be as set out in the letter dated ... contained in the bundle being exhibit to the Affidavit of ... sworn

19 that the conditional contract dated ... and made between ... of the one part and ... of the other part for the sale of the said ... of the property ... be carried into effect

20 that the Conditional Agreement dated ... and made between ... be varied in the manner set forth in the schedule hereto and that as so varied it be carried into effect

The Schedule
Place where

        Words to be   Words to be
           deleted   inserted

the variation is
to be made

21 that the defendant shall within ... days after personal service on him of this Order make and file an Affidavit stating what (if any) deeds and other documents relating to the title of the property known as ... are in his possession and power and whether any deeds or other documents relating to the said title are known by him to be in the possession or power of any other person or persons and if so stating the name and address of every such person ... that the defendant do within the same time lodge at room 156 Chancery Chambers The Royal Courts of Justice Strand London WC2A 2LL all (if any) such deeds and documents as are stated by him to be in his own possession or power.

22 that the defendant shall within 28 days after personal service upon him of this Order take all necessary steps to ensure that all deeds and documents relating to the said property be delivered to the solicitors for the plaintiff Messrs ... of ...

23 ... that for the purposes of effecting such sale all deeds and documents of title (other than the map hereinafter mentioned) relating to the legal estate in fee simple in the said property and in the possession or custody or under the control of the parties or any of them be delivered to the plaintiff's said solicitors (who shall have authority to deliver the same to any purchaser of the said property or any part thereof on completion of the sale) and the said solicitors may give a good receipt for the said deeds and documents or any of them to the parties or any of them or to any person holding the said deeds and documents or any of them to the order of the parties or any of them

24 ... that a proper conveyance of the said property be settled by the Court

25 ... that the defendant shall within 4 days after service on him of this Order and tender to him of such proper conveyance execute the same and deliver the same to Messrs ... of ... the solicitors for ...

26 ... that upon an engrossment of a Transfer in the form annexed hereto being tendered to the defendant at the time of service on him of this Order he shall forthwith execute the said engrossment and deliver the same to the person serving this Order

27 ... at all reasonable times before the auction to allow prospective purchasers accompanied by the estate agents instructed on the sale to visit the said property
(NB: This is an undertaking.)

28 ... that the defendant shall on or before completion of the sale

give vacant possession of the said property to the purchaser or purchasers thereof

29 ... that the defendant shall within ... days after personal service upon him of this Order give to the plaintiff vacant possession of the said property

30 ... that the deeds and documents specified in the schedule hereto which have been deposited in Chancery Chambers be released and handed over to Messrs ... the solicitors for the ...

31 that the net proceeds of sale be placed on deposit at a bank in the name of ... and be not disposed of save by agreement between the parties or further Order to the Court

32 that the purchase money after deduction therefrom of the plaintiff's solicitors' costs of conveying the said property and £ ... for estate agents' commission be lodged in Court to the credit of this Action immediately on completion of the sale as directed in the schedule hereto
(NB: The lodgment schedule will state in the first column 'PURCHASE MONEY on sale of ...' '(amount to be verified by affidavit)' and the second column will give the name and address of the solicitors having the conduct of the sale. Sometimes the schedule provides for the amount to be verified by a certificate of the solicitors. However, it is more usual for the lodgment schedule not to be annexed to the order but to be settled by the master later.)

33 that ... be at liberty to receive the purchase money on completion of the sale and to discharge thereout the amount due on any incumbrance on the said property and to retain the balance of such purchase money and to pay thereout the debts of the partnership business remaining unpaid

34 that the net proceeds of sale of the said property after payment of what is due under a Legal Charge made ... between ... of the one part and ... of the other part and of the solicitors' costs and estate agents' fees and other expenses incurred in connection with the sale be divided between the plaintiff and the defendant in equal shares

35 that the property described in the schedule hereto be sold by public auction in such lots as Messrs ... may advise provided that within 3 days of receiving such advice they give notice thereof in writing to the solicitors for the defendant

36 that the premises at ... be sold by public auction on ... in the

two lots specified in the schedule hereto and that the conditions of sale provide for the completion not before ...

The Schedule
LOT I The ... on the Ordance Survey Sheet ...
LOT II The rest of the premises.

37 that the property described in the schedule hereto be sold by tender

38 that ... be at liberty to advertise for tenders in the form and subject to the conditions of sale which for the purpose of identification have been initialled by the Master

39 that the property described in the schedule hereto be sold by tender subject to the form of the invitation to tender the particulars ... and conditions of sale, the reserve paid and the estate agents' remuneration being approved by the Court

40 that each of the parties be at liberty to tender for and become the purchaser of the said property at the said sale.

36. ORDER NOMINATING PERSON TO EXECUTE SALE

THE COURT pursuant to Section 39 of the Supreme Court Act 1981 NOMINATES ... one of the Masters of the Supreme Court to execute the conveyance/contract/document hereinafter mentioned instead of and for and on behalf of the defendant

IT IS ORDERED

1 that a Conveyance/contract/document in the form annexed hereto initialled by the Master of exhibit ... to the ... Affidavit of ... sworn ... be executed by the said Master accordingly

2 that the defendant shall pay to the plaintiff his costs of the said application to be taxed if not agreed.

Notes

1 This form is for use when the court makes an order under s 39(1) of the Supreme Court Act 1981. That subsection is in the following terms:

Where the High Court has given or made a judgment or order directing

a person to execute any conveyance contract or other document ... then, if that person
(a) neglects or refuses to comply with the judgment or order; or
(b) cannot after reasonable inquiry be found
the High Court may, on such terms, and conditions, if any, as may be just, order that the Conveyance, contract or other document shall be executed ... by such person as the Court may nominate for that purpose.

2 The order should not be made in anticipation of a failure to execute unless the defendant has already shown by his conduct that he refuses and will refuse to execute.

3 The document to be executed must be satisfactorily identified. The precedent envisages three steps (1) the form of document is annexed to the order (2) it is initialled by the Master (3) it is identified by reference to an exhibit.

4 An order under s 39 is not the only way in which the court can deal with the problem posed by a defendant who may not sign. Section 47 of the Trustee Act 1925 provides that where the court makes an order for the sale of land it may make and order vesting the land in the purchaser or other person. Section 50 of the Trustee Act 1925 provides that 'in all cases where a Vesting Order can be made under any of the foregoing provisions the court may if it is more convenient appoint a person to convey the land ...'. It is not a condition precedent to the exercise of this power that the person concerned should have defaulted in complying with an order to execute the relevant document. It is usually more convenient to rely on the Trustee Act 1925, ss 47 or 50 ... than on the Supreme Court Act 1981, s 39 because the latter section only applies where default has been made in complying with an order to execute the relevant document, or where the party concerned cannot be found.

For orders under s 50 see Atkin, Vol 35 (1991 Issue) and Vol 41 (1986 Issue). The following is an appropriate form:
'THE COURT pursuant to Section 50 of the Trustee Act 1925 APPOINTS ... to convey the said property'.

37. POSSESSION ORDER

IT IS ORDERED

1 that the plaintiffs shall recover possession of the land described in the said Originating Summons as ... [and that the defendant do give possession of the said land on ...]

2 that the defendants shall pay to the plaintiffs [the sum of £ ... for] their costs of this action [to be taxed].

Note

1 See Ord 113.

38. PURCHASER'S ACTION (TIME FOR COMPLETION FIXED)

IT IS ORDERED

1 that the agreement dated ... in the Writ of Summons/Statement of Claim mentioned be specifically performed and carried into execution

2 that (the plaintiff accepting the defendant's title to the property comprised in the said Agreement subject to the discharge of a Mortgage thereon in favour of ...) the defendant do forthwith after service of this Order execute in escrow a Conveyance/Transfer of the said property to the plaintiff such Conveyance/Transfer to be in the form of the draft being exhibited ... to the Affidavit of ... sworn on ... a copy of which is annexed hereto

3 that the plaintiff's costs of the action be assessed in Chambers and paid by the defendant

4 that upon the plaintiff paying to the defendant the sum of £ ... (being £ ... the balance of the purchase price of the said property less £ ... the assessed costs of the plaintiff of this Action) (the sum being made up as set out in the schedule hereto) at ... on ... at the offices of Messrs ... the solicitors for the defendant at ... the defendant shall thereupon
   (a) redeem the said Legal Charge
   (b) deliver to the plaintiff the said Conveyance/Transfer duly executed together with all deeds and writings in the defendant's possession or power relating solely to the said property
   (c) give an acknowledgment and undertaking for safe custody of deeds relating to other properties as provided by Section 64 of the Law of Property Act 1925 and
   (d) give to the plaintiff vacant possession of the said property

5 that the following Inquiry be made that is to say an Inquiry as to what damages have been sustained by the plaintiff by reason of the failure of the defendant to perform the said Agreement

6 that the costs of the said Inquiry be reserved

7 that the parties be at liberty to apply.

The Schedule

39. PURCHASER'S ACTION—INQUIRY AS TO TITLE (TIME AND PLACE TO BE FIXED)

IT IS ORDERED

1 that the Agreement dated ... in the Writ of Summons/Statement of Claim mentioned be specifically performed and carried into execution

2 that the following Inquiry be made that is to say
   (1) An Inquiry whether a good title can be made to the property comprised in the said agreement

3 that in case it shall appear that a good title can be made to the said property
   (a) interest be computed at the rate of £... per annum on the sum of £... (the residue of the purchase money for the said property) from ... (when the purchase ought to have been completed according to the terms of the said Agreement) to the day to be fixed by the Court as hereinafter directed
   (b) the following Account be taken that is to say
      (2) An Account of the rents and profits of the said property received by the defendant or by any other person or persons by the order or for the use of the defendant since ...
   (c) the plaintiff's costs of this Action be assessed in Chambers
   (d) what shall be found due upon the said Account of rents and profits and the said costs when so assessed be deducted from the residue of the said purchase money and interest when so computed as aforesaid and the balance declared by subsequent Order
   (e) upon the plaintiff paying the defendant at a time and place to be fixed by the Court the said balance the defendant shall execute a proper Conveyance/Transfer of the said property to the plaintiff or to whom the plaintiff may appoint (such Conveyance/Transfer to be settled by the Court in case the parties differ) and the defendant shall at the same time and place deliver to the plantiff the said Conveyance/Transfer so executed as aforesaid together with all deeds and writings in the plaintiff's possession or power relating solely to the said property and give an acknowledgment and undertaking for production of deeds relating to other properties as provided by Section 64 of the Law of Property Act 1925

LAND AND OTHER SPECIFIC PROPERTY 439

   (f) the defendant shall thereupon give to the plaintiff vacant possession of the said property
   (g) the following Inquiry be made that is to say
      (3) An Inquiry whether the plaintiff has sustained any and if so what damages by reason of the delay of the defendant in completion of the said Agreement
   (h) that costs of the said Inquiry numbered (3) be reserved

4 that the parties are to be at liberty to apply.

40. PURCHASER'S ACTION—INQUIRY AS TO TITLE (TIME AND PLACE TO BE FIXED)—ALTERNATIVE FORM

IT IS ORDERED

1 that the Agreement dated... in the Writ of Summons/Statement of Claim mentioned be specifically performed and carried into execution

2 that the following Inquiry be made that is to say
   (1) An Inquiry whether a good title can be made to the property comprised in the said Agreement

3 that the case it shall appear that a good title can be made to the said property
   (a) the following Inquiry and Account be made and taken that is to say
   (2) An Inquiry what damages have been sustained by the plaintiff by reason of the defendant not having specifically performed the said Agreement according to the terms thereof
   (3) An Account of what is due to the defendant in respect of the purchase money for the said property
   (b) the plaintiff's costs of this Action be assessed in Chambers
   (c) what shall be found to be the amount of the said damages and the said costs be deducted from what shall be found due in respect of the said purchase money and the balance declared by subsequent Order
   (d) upon the plaintiff paying the said balance to the defendant at a time and place fixed by the Court the defendant shall execute a proper Conveyance/Transfer of the said property to the plaintiff or to whom the plaintiff may appoint (such Conveyance/Transfer to be settled by the Court in case the parties differ) and shall at the same time and place deliver to the plaintiff the said Conveyance/Transfer so executed as aforesaid together with all deeds and writings in the

plaintiff's possession or power relating solely to the said property and give an acknowledgment and undertaking for the production of deeds relating to other properties as provided by Section 64 of the Law of Property Act 1925 and shall thereupon give the plaintiff vacant possession of the said property

4 that the parties are to be at liberty to apply.

41. PURCHASER'S ACTION—GRANT OF LEASE (TIME AND PLACE TO BE FIXED)

IT IS DECLARED that the correspondence mentioned in the Writ of Summons/Statement of Claim constitutes a binding Agreement between the plaintiff and the defendant for the grant to the plaintiff of a Lease as therein alleged

AND IT IS ORDERED

1 that the said Agreement be specifically performed and carried into execution

2 that the following Account be taken that is to say
   (1) An Account of what is payable to the defendant by the plaintiff under the terms of the said Agreement on the grant of the said Lease

3 that the costs of the plaintiff of this Action be taxed and that the amount thereof be deducted from what shall be found payable on the taking of the said Account and that the balance be declared by subsequent Order

4 that the defendant shall forthwith execute in escrow a Lease in the form of exhibit ... to the Affidavit ... sworn ... and that the plaintiff be at liberty to execute in escrow a Counterpart thereof

5 that upon the plaintiff at a time and a place to be hereafter appointed paying to the defendant the said balance and delivering to the defendant the said Counterpart the defendant shall thereupon at the same time and place deliver to the plaintiff the said Lease duly executed

6 that thereupon the defendant shall give to the plaintiff vacant possession of the premises demised by the said Lease

7 that the following Inquiry be made that is to say
  (2) An Inquiry whether the plaintiff has suffered any and if any what damages by reason of the delay of the defendant in granting the said Lease

8 that the parties be at liberty to apply.

Note

1 Many variations on this form are possible.

42. PURCHASER'S ACTION—GRANT OF LEASE (TIME AND PLACE FIXED)

IT IS DECLARED

1 as a result of the said Account that there will be payable to the defendant by the plaintiff under the terms of the Agreement in the Writ of Summons/Statement of Claim mentioned on the grant of the Lease if the same be granted on the date hereinafter appointed the sum of £... made up as set out in the schedule hereto

2 that the balance due on deducting from the said sum of £... the costs of the plaintiff of this Action which have been taxed at £... is £...

AND THE COURT APPOINTS... am... pm on... at the offices of... at... as the time and place for the delivery by the defendant to the plaintiff of the Lease duly executed as provided in the said Order.

The Schedule

Premium payable on grant of the Lease	£...
Rent payable in advance in respect of period beginning on... and ending on...	£...
Conveyancing costs payable under the Agreement	£...

43. PURCHASER'S ACTION—SHORT FORM

IT IS ORDERED

1 that the Agreement dated ... in the Statement of Claim mentioned be specifically performed and carried into execution

2 that the Defendant shall pay the Plaintiff ... costs of this Action to be taxed if not agreed

3 that the parties are to be at liberty to apply in Chambers for directions for the purpose of carrying this Order into effect.

44. PURCHASER'S ACTION—SALE OF LEASE

IT IS ORDERED

1 that the Agreement dated ... in the Writ of Summons/Statement of Claim mentioned be specifically performed and carried into execution

2 that the following Account be taken
   (1) An Account of what is due to the defendant on the completion of the sale of the property comprised in the said Agreement

3 that the costs of the plaintiff of this Action be assessed in Chambers

4 that the said costs when assessed be deducted from the said amount due to the defendant on completion and the balance declared by further Order

5 that (the plaintiff by his Counsel declaring himself content with the title to the said property and it appearing that the plaintiff has executed an Assignment of the said property approved by the defendant) the defendant shall forthwith execute the said Assignment in escrow and forthwith procure the execution of licences or consents from the freeholder and the head lessee of the said property to the said Assignment and to the use of the said property as ...

6 that upon the plaintiff paying to the defendant at a time and place to be fixed by further Order the balance so declared the defendant shall thereupon at the same time and place deliver to the plaintiff the said Assignment so executed and the said licences or consents and all deeds and writings in ... custody

possession or power relating to the said property exclusively and shall thereupon give to the plaintiff vacant possession of the said property

7   that the parties are to be at liberty to apply.

45. PURCHASER'S ACTION—PURCHASER IN POSSESSION

IT IS ORDERED

1   that the Agreement dated ... in the Writ of Summons/Statement of Claim mentioned be specifically performed and carried into execution

2   that interest be computed at the prescribed rate within the meaning of the National Conditions of Sale Twentieth Edition (which apply to the said Agreement) on £ ... the remainder of the purchase money for the property comprised in the said Agreement from ... (the date on which the plaintiff went into occupation of the said property) until the date to be fixed as hereinafter directed

3   that the following Account and Inquiry be taken and made that is to say
    (1) An Account of what is due to the defendant for the remainder of the said purchase money and the said interest and for any outgoings and expenses in respect of the said property in respect of which the plaintiff is bound to indemnify the defendant
    (2) An Inquiry as to what damages have been sustained by the plaintiff by reason of the defendant not having specifically performed the said Agreement according to the terms thereof

4   that the costs of the defendant of this Action be assessed in Chambers

5   that what shall be found to be the amount of the said damages and the said costs be deducted from what shall be found due to the plaintiff on the taking of the said Account and the balance declared by further Order

6   that (the plaintiff being content with the title of the defendant to the said property) upon the plaintiff paying the said balance to the defendant at a time and place to be fixed by the Court the defendant shall execute a proper Conveyance/Transfer of the

said property to the plaintiff or to whom the plaintiff may appoint (such Conveyance/Transfer to be settled by the Court in case the parties differ) and do at the same time and place deliver to the plaintiff the said Conveyance/Transfer so executed as aforesaid together with all deeds and writings in the plaintiff's possession or power relating solely to the said property and give an acknowledgment and undertaking for the production of deeds relating to other properties as provided by Section 64 of the Law of Property Act 1925

7   that the parties are to be at liberty to apply.

46. PURCHASER'S ACTION—PAYMENT INTO COURT

IT IS DECLARED (1) that there is a binding oral agreement for the sale to the plaintiff by the defendants of the freehold property known as ... free from incumbrances at the price of £ ... made in or about the month of ... 199... between the plaintiff of the one part and the ... defendants of the other part and (2) that the said agreement was duly made by the ... defendant on his own behalf and as the duly authorised agent of the ... defendant

AND IT IS ORDERED

1   that the said agreement for sale shall be specifically performed and carried into execution

2   that the following Account and Inquiry shall be taken and made that is to say
    (1) An Account of what is due to the defendants for the balance of the said purchase money
    (2) An Inquiry as to what is the amount due to ... Building Society under a Mortgage dated ... secured on the said property

3   that on taking the Account the plaintiff be charged with interest at £... per annum on any arrears of the instalments provided for by the said agreement

4   that the plaintiff's costs of this Action be taxed

5   that the said costs when taxed and the amount found by the said Inquiry to be due to... Building Society be deducted from the amount of the balance of the said purchase money when

so computed as aforesaid and the balance (if any) declared by further Order

6   that the plaintiffs shall on or before the date specified in such further Order (a) pay to the ... Building Society the amount found by the said Inquiry to be due to it and (b) lodge in Court as directed by such further Order the balance (if any) so declared

7   that (the plaintiff being content with the title to the said property) the defendants shall execute a proper Conveyance of the said property to the plaintiff or to whom the plaintiff shall appoint (as in escrow to be delivered as hereinafter mentioned) such Conveyance to be settled by the Court in case the parties differ

8   that upon such payment to the said ... Building Society as aforesaid and upon such lodgment (if any) as aforesaid the defendants shall deliver to the plaintiffs the said Conveyance and all deeds and writings in their possession or in their power relating to the said property exclusively and give an acknowledgment and undertaking for the safe custody of deeds relating to the other properties as provided by Section 64 of the Law of Property Act 1925 and shall thereupon give the plaintiff vacant possession of the said property

9   that the parties are to be at liberty to apply.

47. PURCHASER'S ACTION—PURCHASER TO REPAY MORTGAGE AND LODGE MONEY IN COURT

IT IS ORDERED

1   that the plaintiff shall forthwith lodge in Court as directed in the schedule hereto the sum of £ ... the balance of the purchase money for the freehold property known as ... comprised in the Agreement dated ... mentioned in the Order dated ...

2   that (1) upon the service upon the defendant of this Order (2) upon the production to the defendant (a) of the Certificate of the Lodgment in Court of the said sum of £ ... and (b) of a Deed of Release or other discharge by the ... Building Society of the obligations of the defendant under the Mortgage dated ... and made between the defendant of the one part and the ... Building Society of the other part (3) upon the tender to the defendant of the engrossment of the Conveyance expressed to be made between the defendant of the one part and the plaintiff of the

other part comprising the said property known as ... which said engrossment is the exhibit marked ... to the Affidavit of ... sworn on ... and has for the purpose of identification only been initialled in the margin thereof by ... Esquire one of the Masters of the Supreme Court THEREUPON the defendant shall (A) forthwith execute the said engrossment of the said Conveyance and (B) forthwith deliver it to the person serving this Order together with all deeds and documents in the possession custody or power of the defendant relating to the said property exclusively

3 that the defendant shall within 4 days after service of this Order and production to the defendant of the documents referred to in (a) and (b) above deliver to the plaintiff possession of the said property

4 that the parties are to be at liberty to apply.

48. PURCHASER'S ACTION—RETURN OF DEPOSIT

AND the plaintiff electing to treat the Agreement in the Writ of Summons/Statement of Claim mentioned as repudiated by the defendant

IT IS ORDERED

1 that the defendant do repay to the plaintiff the deposit of £... paid by the defendant under the said Agreement together with interest thereon at the rate of £... per annum from ... until payment

2 that the following Inquiry be made that is to say
   (1) An Inquiry as to what damages have been sustained by the plaintiff by reason of such repudiation

3 that the defendant shall within 14 days after the date of the Order declaring the amount of the said damages pay to the plaintiff the said amount

4 that the defendant shall pay to the plaintiff his costs of this Action down to and including this Order to be taxed if not agreed

5 that the costs of the said Inquiry be reserved

AND THE COURT DECLARES that the plaintiff is entitled to a lien upon the property comprised in the said Agreement and described in the schedule hereto in respect of the said sum of £ ... and interest and ... said costs of this Action

AND in the case of default in payment the plaintiff is to be at liberty to apply to enforce such lien

AND the parties are to be at liberty to apply generally.

The Schedule
The ... hold property known as ... and registered at Her Majesty's Land Registry under Title Number ...

49. PURCHASER'S ACTION—SHARES

IT IS ORDERED

1 that the Agreement mentioned in the Writ of Summons/Statement of Claim for the sale of the shares described in the schedule hereto be specifically performed and carried into execution

2 that the defendant shall forthwith after service upon him of this Order execute in escrow a transfer of the said shares in the form of the draft annexed hereto

3 that upon the plaintiff paying the defendant £ ... (being £ ... the agreed price for the sale of the said shares less £ ... the assessed costs of the plaintiff of this Action) at ... am ... pm on ... day ... 199 ... at the offices of Messrs ... at ... the defendant shall at the same time and place deliver to the plaintiff the said transfer duly executed by the defendant together with the Share Certificates in respect of the said shares

4 that the parties are to be at liberty to apply.

The Schedule
... shares of £ ... each in ... plc.

Note

1 The normal stock transfer form will be used.

50. PURCHASER'S ACTION—SHARES (ALTERNATIVE FORM)

IT IS ORDERED

1 that the Agreement in the Writ of Summons/Statement of Claim mentioned for the sale of the shares described in the schedule hereto be specifically performed and carried into execution

2 that the following Account be taken that is to say
    (1) An Account of what is due to the defendant under the terms of the said Agreement

3 that the costs of the plaintiff of this Action be assessed in Chambers

4 that the amount of the said costs be deducted from what shall be found due upon the said Account Number (1) and the balance declared by subsequent order

5 that (the plaintiff being content with the title of the defendant to the said shares) the defendant shall execute in escrow proper transfers of the said shares to the plaintiff or whom he shall appoint such transfers to be settled by the Court in case the parties differ

6 that upon the plaintiff at a time and place to be appointed by subsequent Order paying to the defendant the said balance the defendant shall thereupon at the same time and place deliver to the plaintiff the said transfers together with the Share Certificates in respect of the said shares

7 that the parties are to be at liberty to apply.

The Schedule
... ordinary shares of £... each in ... plc
... preference shares of £... each in ... plc

51. PURCHASER'S ACTION—CHATTELS

IT IS ORDERED

1 that the Agreement dated ... in the Writ of Summons/Statement of Claim mentioned be specifically performed and carried into

execution but subject to such abatement in the purchase price for the chattels therein mentioned as may be proper

2 that the following Inquiry be made that is to say
 (2) An Inquiry as to what abatement ought to be allowed in the purchase price for the said chattels so that the said price shall not exceed a reasonable price therefor within the meaning of Section 123 of the Rent Act 1977

3 that what shall be allowed by way of abatement be deducted from ... (being the residue of the purchase price payable under the said Agreement and the balance (hereinafter called 'the first balance') declared by subsequent Order)

4 that interest be computed at the rate of ... per centum per annum on the first balance from ... (when the plaintiff was allowed into occupation of the ... in the said Agreement mentioned) to the day to be appointed as hereinafter directed

5 that the costs of the plaintiff of this Action be taxed

6 that the amount of the said costs be deducted from the first balance and the interest thereon and the balance if any (hereinafter called 'the second balance') declared by subsequent Order

7 that (the plaintiff being content with the title of the defendant to the said ...) the defendant shall execute a proper Assignment thereof to the plaintiff (as an escrow to be delivered to the plaintiff as hereinafter provided) such Assignment to be settled by the Court in case the parties differ

8 that the defendant shall at a time and place to be appointed by the Court and upon payment by the plaintiff to the Vendor at the same time and place of the second balance if any deliver to the plaintiff the said Assignment duly executed as aforesaid together with the Lease dated ... in the pleadings mentioned and any other deeds and writings in his custody possession or power relating solely to the said ...

9 that if the said costs exceed the total of the first balance and the said interest the defendant do pay to the plaintiff the amount of the excess

10 that the parties be at liberty to apply.

52. PURCHASER'S ACTION—VESTING ORDER

IT IS ORDERED that the Agreement made orally between the solicitors acting for and on behalf of the plaintiffs and the solicitors acting for and on behalf of the defendants on or about ... in the [Writ of Summons] [Statement of Claim] mentioned be specifically performed and carried into execution

AND IT IS DECLARED that the plaintiffs and the defendants are trustees of the leasehold properties hereinafter mentioned within the meaning of the Trustee Act 1925

AND the solicitors for the plaintiffs having certified in writing that this transaction does not form part of a larger transaction or of a series of transactions in respect of which the amount or value or the aggregate amount or value of the consideration exceeds £ ...

IT IS ORDERED

1 that the leasehold properties described in the schedule hereto vest in the plaintiffs for the estate and interest therein now vested in the plaintiffs and the defendants

2 that the defendants shall pay to the plaintiffs their costs of this Action to be taxed if not agreed

3 that the parties are to be at liberty to apply

The Schedule

1 The leasehold property demised by a Lease made ... between ... of the one part and ... of the other part and known as ... the same being held for the residue of the term of ... years from ... thereby granted.

53. PURCHASER'S ACTION—PRICE PAID INTO COURT (DEFENDANT TO EXECUTE)

IT IS ORDERED

1 that (the money specified in the schedule hereto having been lodged in Court by the plaintiff) the defendant shall within 4 days after service of this Order and tender to him of a Conveyance in the form annexed hereto deliver to the plaintiff's solicitors Messrs ... at ... the said conveyance duly executed together with all deeds and writings in his custody or power relating solely to the property hereinafter mentioned and an Acknowledgment

of the right of the plaintiff to the production of deeds relating to other properties and an Undertaking for the safe custody of the last mentioned deeds as provided by Section 64 of the Law of Property Act 1925 and shall forthwith thereupon give the plaintiff possession of the property known as ...

2 that the defendant shall pay to the plaintiff ... costs of the said application to be taxed if not agreed [£ ... assessed costs of the said application].

The Schedule
Balance of Purchase Money £ ...
Less plaintiff's costs of Action down to and including the Order dated ...

Balance lodged in court

54. VENDOR'S ACTION (TIME AND PLACE TO BE FIXED)

IT IS ORDERED

1 that the Agreement dated ... in the Writ of Summons/Statement of Claim mentioned be specifically performed and carried into execution

2 that interest be computed at the rate of £ ... per annum on the sume of £ ... (the residue of the purchase money for the property comprised in the said Agreement) from ... when the purchase ought to have been completed according to the terms of the said Agreement to the day to be fixed by the Court as hereinafter directed

3 that the following Accounts be taken that is to say:
   (1) An Account of what is due to the plaintiff for the balance of the said purchase money and interest and for ... costs of this Action
   (2) An Account of the rents and profits of the said property received by the plaintiff or by any other person or persons by the Order or for the use of the plaintiff since the ...

4 that the plaintiff's costs of this action be assessed in chambers and paid by the defendant

5 that what shall be found upon the said Account of rents and profits be deducted from the amount of the said purchase money

and interest and costs when so computed and taxed as aforesaid and the balance declared by future Order

6 that (the defendant having accepted the plaintiff's title to the said property) the plaintiff be at liberty to prepare and execute a Conveyance to the defendant (as an escrow to be delivered to the defendant as hereinafter mentioned) such Conveyance to be settled by the Court

7 that upon the plaintiff at a time and place to be appointed by the Court delivering to the defendants the said Conveyance together with all deeds and writings in his possession or power relating to the said property and giving an acknowledgment and undertaking for safe custody of deeds relating to other properties as provided by Section 64 of the Law of Property Act 1925 the defendant shall at the same time and place pay to the plaintiff the amount so declared as aforesaid

8 that the parties are to be at liberty to apply.

Notes

1 If the land is registered land the word 'transfer' should be used instead of 'conveyance' and the acknowledgment and undertaking in para 6 will not be required.

2 See Atkin, Vol 37 (1981 Issue) Form 66, p 109.

55. VENDOR'S ACTION—SHORT FORM (TIME FOR COMPLETION FIXED)

IT IS ORDERED

1 that the Agreement dated the... in the Writ of Summons/Statement of Claim mentioned be specifically performed and carried into execution

2 that (the defendant having accepted the plaintiff's title to the property comprised in the said Agreement and the plaintiff and the defendant having approved the draft of an Assignment/a Conveyance thereof the engrossment of which has been executed by the plaintiff as an escrow to be delivered to the defendant upon completion of the said Agreement) upon the plaintiff at the offices of Messrs... situated at... delivering to the defendant or to whom he may appoint the said Assignment/Conveyance together with all deeds and writings in his possession or power

relating solely to the said property and giving an acknowledgment and undertaking for safe custody of deeds relating to other properties as provided by Section 64 of the Law of Property Act 1925 the defendant shall thereupon at the same time and place pay to the plaintiff the sum of £ . . . (being as to £ . . . the balance of the purchase price and interest thereon at . . . per annum from . . . to . . . and as to £ . . . the assessed costs of the plaintiff of this Action)

3 that the parties are to be at liberty to apply.

56. VENDOR'S ACTION—FORFEIT OF DEPOSIT

AND the plaintiff electing to treat the Agreement in the Writ of Summons/Statement of Claim mentioned as repudiated by the defendant

IT IS ORDERED

1 that the deposit of £ . . . paid by the defendant under the said Agreement be forfeited to the plaintiff

2 that the following Inquiry be made that is to say
   (1) An Inquiry as to what damages have been sustained by the plaintiff by reason of such repudiation

3 that in calculating such damages the said deposit be taken into account

4 that the defendant shall pay to the plaintiff his costs of this Action down to and including this Order to be taxed

5 that the costs of the said Inquiry be reserved

6 that the parties be at liberty to apply

Notes

1 See Atkin, Vol 18 (1985 Issue).

2 Sometimes the court will, instead of ordering that the deposit be forfeited, declare that it has been forfeited. Sometimes it will declare that the plaintiff is entitled to give a valid receipt for the deposit to whoever is holding it.

57. VENDOR'S ACTION—TO GRANT MORTGAGE OF LEASE

IT IS ORDERED that the Agreement dated ... mentioned in the Writ of Summons/Statement of Claim whereby the defendant agreed to execute a legal mortgage in favour of the plaintiff be specifically performed and carried into execution

AND IT IS DECLARED pursuant to Section 48(a) of the Trustee Act 1925 that the defendant is a trustee within the meaning of the said Act of the property described in the schedule hereto and held under a Lease made ... between ... (1) and ... (2) for the term of ... years from ...

IT IS ORDERED

1 that the said property vest in the plaintiff as mortgagee for all the residue unexpired of the term granted by the said Lease less the last ten days thereof

2 that the plaintiffs are to be at liberty to add their costs of these proceedings to the moneys secured by the said Agreement dated ...

The Schedule
The leasehold property known as ... and registered at Her Majesty's Land Registry under Title Number ...

Chapter Seventeen

Partnerships: Winding Up and Receivership

1. Winding Up and Receivership

Partnerships, firms, clubs, trade unions and similar associations can be grouped as bodies having somewhat indistinct legal constitutions who may subject to qualification sue or be sued. The courts will, if asked, wind up such bodies or supervise their winding up but otherwise, unless there are impelling reasons such as to inhibit an unlawful act or protect assets, they will not enforce or interfere with their internal relations. If, for example, a partner is restrained, it will usually only be as part of dissolution proceedings; thus the court will be using its powers to protect innocent partners on what will be a temporary basis and only until the partnership assets can be sold and/or disputes resolved. However, there may be reasons, comparatively rarely, when to force the partners (or members of an association) to seek a dissolution would be inequitable or when the terms of the partnership have made provision that notwithstanding certain disputes arising the partnership is to continue; in such instances the court may be asked to make orders restraining or restricting a partner, preventing exclusion, or otherwise affecting the management or conduct of the partnership without dissolution.

Where there is a serious problem and proceedings have to be taken, especially if for dissolution, it may be essential to make early application for the appointment of a receiver and manager to take on such responsibilities as may be necessary for the daily conduct of the business. Any individual may be appointed a receiver by the court provided that he is acceptable to the partners but because of his specialised knowledge an accountant is often chosen.

Statutes

While nearly all partnerships are governed by the Partnership Act 1890, a partnership is still possible permitting a 'sleeping' partner to take a limited partnership whereby he enjoys limited liability, usually referable to the amount of capital invested; such partnerships are registerable under the Limited Partnerships Act 1907. With certain exceptions, and in particular that a limited partner cannot sue or be sued in his own name, the rules governing limited partnerships follow those of other partnerships. Trade unions and other such bodies are governed by the Trade Unions and Labour Relations Act 1974 and related legislation.

Section 32 of the Partnership Act 1890 provides for dissolution by expiration of any fixed term, by termination of the venture, or by the service of notice. Section 35 provides that on application by a partner the court may decree a dissolution of the partnership when another partner becomes permanently incapable of performing his part of the partnership contract, has been guilty of such conduct as is calculated prejudicially to affect the carrying on of the business, or has wilfully or persistently committed a breach of the partnership agreement or otherwise so conducted himself in a relation to the partnership business that it is not reasonably practicable for the other partner or partners to carry on, or when the partnership can only be carried on at a loss or when circumstances have arisen rendering it just and equitable that the partnership should be dissolved. The provisions of s 35 are important even where a written agreement or deed exists, since they will govern a situation not dealt with by the written agreement or deed.

Orders

Orders 43 and 44 relating to accounts and inquiries usually govern the course of winding up in chambers. Proceedings in or for the purpose of open court are governed by the various orders relating to writ or originating summons actions.

Parties

It is necessary for all partners to be joined in a dissolution action. In other actions it is not necessary for all partners to be joined, but any partner may request the court to join him, and the court is so empowered if it deems it fit.

Intitulement

Apart from the parties there are no particular requirements and the statute should not be included in the heading. It should however be mentioned in the text of the originating process.

The objective of the plaintiff

In a dispute between partners, in many cases the object is the urgent dissolution and winding up of the partnership because it has succumbed to serious problems. The appointment of a receiver and the taking of an account with attendant directions is therefore usually the first step to be taken in order to protect each partner and the business. On less frequent occasions the objective will be to exclude partners or else to avoid exclusion. Even where dissolution has taken place under ss 32–34 or the provisions of any written accord, a plaintiff in any proceeding is wise to seek a 'declaration' that such a dissolution has already taken place; since if such dissolution is successfully disputed the plaintiff may be denied winding up by the court.

Originating process

On practically every occasion oral evidence will be necessary so that it is usually appropriate to commence the proceedings by way of writ or summons. Where the facts are agreed and adjudication on certain items in issue only is required, the simpler form of originating process by way of originating summons could be used.

Required/have ready/on issue

(a) Originating summons and affidavit in clear cases, otherwise, (b) writ (and if so), (c) statement of claim containing a prayer for an order that the partnership be dissolved or be declared to be already dissolved and its affairs be wound up, for all necessary accounts and inquiries to be taken and made, for the appointment of a receiver, and for such other order as the court may deem fit. It may be necessary in exceptional cases to claim in addition a declaration as to some specific asset, an injunction, or specific performance. The statement of claim (or affidavit) must set out full details of the partnership and its nature, eg by deed or at will, as to when it was commenced, how it may have been terminated, the names of the partners, particulars of any retirements or new partners, and the basis on which the partnership has been, or should be, dissolved. If it is alleged that it has already been dissolved it is important so to allege in the statement of claim (or affidavit) and to include in the prayer for relief a claim for a declaration.

Sequence

(1) On or following the issue of the writ (or originating summons) an application is often made for the appointment of a receiver and such application is made on notice of motion to the judge if an injunction is also required, or if not, by summons before the master. Any such applications must be supported by affidavit evidence to satisfy the court as to the intended receiver's ability and knowledge to discharge the duties of the office, and as to his consent. On being so satisfied, the court will make an order appointing the receiver and will give, if asked, directions and consequential orders relating to his security and accounts, and also relating to accounts and inquiries to be held on the winding up; if there is an order for an account to be taken, the usual order will be for this to be taken from the date when accounts were last agreed.

The order may include a direction that no settled accounts are to be re-opened. In due course the receiver's accounts will be circulated to the parties who may require any item on which they cannot agree to be investigated by the court; ultimately they will be verified in the accounts department (room 165) and the master will then make all necessary orders thereon.

(2) Where no application is made on motion for the appointment of a receiver, a separate summons may be taken up before the master where investigation is necessary into any aspect of the conduct of the business pending trial. The master may give directions in connection with the account or orders as to inquiries relating to the winding up as wide or as limited as the applicant considers necessary and the court deems fit, including inquiry as to the debits, credits, property and effects of the partnership. The applicant himself must give careful thought to those he considers unnecessary and avoid asking for them, otherwise there will be a considerable waste of time and expense. If directions should be required, they might be as to filing evidence, producing books, discovery, access to premises, or preservation of assets; in any case the applicant should be ready to indicate in the clearest specific terms exactly what it is he wants, and should not rely on the court to give directions. If an account is ordered, it may be prepared as the master will as requested direct, but otherwise should be in any acceptable commercial form. Accounts relating to a partnership action would usually be expected to show (*a*) assets at dissolution, (*b*) what has become of the assets, (*c*) an account of mutual dealings as co-partners and (*d*) much of the information in the opening and closing balance sheets.

(3) If an order or direction of the court is not carried out, application to enforce the order can be made under Order 45, r 5 when there can be an order for attachment.

Plaintiff's/defendant's considerations

The parties must keep in sight that if there is to be a dissolution as many items as possible should be agreed so as to avoid expense and delay bearing in mind constantly that the object is to secure a dissolution on the most profitable and least expensive terms, with the court to intervene only if necessary.

Attitude of the court

While disputes between partners are dealt with by adversarial procedure when ordering investigations accounts or inquiries, the court will adopt an inquisitorial approach so as to ensure that innocent partners, and indeed all partners, are protected.

Hazards and pitfalls

Delay in taking proceedings could aggravate problems and result in loss. Despatch is desirable, particularly if the appointment of a receiver is called for. Where one partner has used some of the assets after dissolution, careful consideration will have to be given as to whether the other partners should ask for their due share of any profits made by him, or for five per cent per annum on the value of those assets. Where of course one partner is making use of the assets to the detriment of others, it may well be that proceedings should be taken immediately for the appointment of a receiver.

Costs

The usual order for costs is that they should be paid out of the jointly held fund. The court has however a discretion which it will use, where it is shown that one of the parties has behaved in an unco-operative manner, in which case he may be ordered himself to pay the costs or part of them. Costs are also likely to be awarded against any party who has committed any criminal offence.

Alternative jurisdiction

The county court has jurisdiction where the fund in question does not exceed £30,000, and for disputes involving larger funds, by consent.

Textbooks

EH Scammell & RCI Anson Banks, *Lindley on the Law of Partnership*, 15th edn, (Sweet & Maxwell, 1984).
ER Hardy Ivamy, *Principles of the Law of Partnership*, 12th edn, (Butterworths, 1986).

   A specimen statement of claim, with its defence, follows. There is then provided orders of the kind which might be made in any such proceedings.

Forms and precedents

Atkin, Vol 30, p 81.

Specimen statement of claim

Writ of Summons
(O.6, r.1)

IN THE HIGH COURT OF JUSTICE   1991 .— Ch .—**No.** F 84
Chancery Division
[**District Registry**]

Between

WILLIAM FULGENT   Plaintiff

AND

(1) MARCUS ALEXANDER   Defendants
(2) PETER BALSAM

(1) Insert name.   **To the Defendant** (¹)s MARCUS ALEXANDER and PETER BALSAM both
(2) Insert address.   of (²) 92 Parfitt Street Longley - by - Bow London E8.

This Writ of Summons has been issued against you by the above-named Plaintiff in respect of the claim set out overleaf.

Within 14 days after the service of this Writ on you, counting the day of service, you must either satisfy the claim or return to the Court Office mentioned below the accompanying **Acknowledgment of Service** stating therein whether you intend to contest these proceedings.

If you fail to satisfy the claim or to return the Acknowledgment within the time stated, or if you return the Acknowledgment without stating therein an intention to contest the proceedings, the Plaintiff may proceed with the action and judgment may be entered against you forthwith without further notice.

(3) Complete and delete as necessary.   Issued from the (³) [Chancery Chambers] [.   District Registry]
of the High Court this   6th   day of   August   1991 .

NOTE:—This Writ may not be served later than 4 calendar months (or, if leave is required to effect service out of the jurisdiction, 6 months) beginning with that date unless renewed by order of the Court.

IMPORTANT

Directions for Acknowledgment of Service are given with the accompanying form.

Specimen statement of claim

(1) Delete if inapplicable.

(¹) **Statement of Claim**

The Plaintiff claim is for damages arising out of the determination be the Defendants of a partnership with the Plaintiff in a manner not provided for by the Deed of Partnership and any variations thereto and for various accounts in connection with or incidental to the partnership and for monies had and received by the Defendants for use of the Plaintiff in respect of which the Plaintiff has suffered loss and damage and for interest thereon under Section 35A of the Supreme Court Act 1981 or pursuant to the Courts equitable jurisdiction.

And the Plaintiff specifically claims for the following release:-

(i) An order that the affairs of the partnership be wound up;

(ii). That for the purpose aforesaid all necessary accounts and inquiries be taken and made;

(iii) A declaration that the First Defendant hold 50,000 of the Loraly shares on trust for the partnership

(iv) Costs.

Mungu Kentgera

Winding up and receivership order

IN THE HIGH COURT OF JUSTICE
CHANCERY DIVISION
BETWEEN

Ch. 1991 F.No. 84

WILLIAM FULGENT

Plaintiff

- and -

(1) MARCUS ALEXANDER
(2) PETER BALSAM

Defendants

STATEMENT OF CLAIM

1. On or about 5th May 1984 the Plaintiff and the Defendants started to carry on practice as chartered accountants in partnership under the firm name of Fulgent and Co at 262 Bullham High Road, London SW2.

2. The terms of the partnership were contained in a Deed of Partnership dated 19th July 1984 and made between (1) the First Defendant (2) the Second Defendant and (3) the Third Defendant (herein called 'the 1984 Deed').

3. The 1984 Deed provided inter alia that:

(i) The terms of the partnership should be as set out in the 1978 Deed.

(ii) The Plaintiff was entitled to 50% of the net profits of the said partnership practice.

(iii) Subject as therein provided the partnership should continue during the joint lives of the partners;

(iv) All the furniture safes books boxes and other fittings in or about the partnership premises and used for the purpose of the partnership practice and the benefit of the Leases of the partnership premises should be assets of the partnership and should belong to the partners in the proportions in which they were entitled to share in the profits of the partnership;

Winding up and receivership order

(v) The Capital of the partnership should consist of such amounts as should from time to time be credited to the partners in their Capital accounts in the books of the partnership;

(vi) Each partner should at all times show utmost good faith to the other in all matters relating to the partnership;

(vii) Each partner should at all times devote his whole time and attention to the business of the partnership;

(viii) Each partner should at all times conduct himself in a proper and responsible manner and use his best endeavours to promote the partnership business;

(ix) If the partnership should be determined by any means not therein provided for, an account should forthwith be taken and settled by the partners of all the assets and liability of the partnership and thereupon such assets should be realised;

(x) The net assets should be divided between the partners in the shares in which they were at the date of such determination entitled to share in the profits of the partnership;

(xi) Upon such determination the goodwill of the partnership should be treated as an asset of the partnership.

4. The Plaintiff will at the trial of this action refer to the terms of the partnership as set out in the 1984 Deed for their full terms and effect.

5. Wrongfully and in breach of the said partnership terms the Defendants and each of them have treated their partnership with the Plaintiff as at an end.

PARTICULARS

(i) The Second Defendant wrote on a type-written Memorandum dated 16th June 1991 and sent by the Plaintiff to all the partners:

"As far as I am concerned the partnership is now at an end and we should immediately make the necessary arrangements."

(ii) At a meeting held on 6th July 1991 all the partners apart from the Plaintiff confirmed that they were treating the partnership as at an end.

Winding up and receivership order

6. By their said conduct the Defendants and each of them have evinced an intention no longer to be bound by the said partnership terms and have repudiated the same.

7. The Plaintiff, as he was entitled to do, accepted the said repudiation by letters dated 22nd July 1987 from his solicitors to each of the Defendants.

8. In the premises the partnership has been determined by a means not provided for in the 1984 Deed and the Defendants are liable to account to the Plaintiff in accordance with the provisions of the said Deed referred to in paragraph 3 hereof.

9. By letter dated 24th July 1991 the Defendants by their solicitors stated that they were prepared to agree that the date of the dissolution of the partnership was 6th July 1991-

10. In or about March 1989 the First Defendant acting on behalf of the partnership received 50,000 shares in Loraley shares.

11. Further, pursuant to Section 35A of the Supreme Court Act 1981 or alternatively pursuant to the equitable jurisdiction of the Court, the Plaintiff claims and is entitled to recover interest on the amount found to be due to him at such rate and for such period as the Court shall think fit.

And the Plaintiff claims:-

(i) An order that the affairs of the partnership be wound up;

(ii) That for the purposes aforesaid all necessary accounts and inquiries be taken and made;

(iii) A declaration that the First Defendant holds 50,000 of Loraley shares on trust for the partnership;

(iv) Further or other relief;

(v) Interest as aforesaid to be assessed;

(vi) Costs.

RICHARD DOROTHY

SERVED the 30th day of July 1991 by Lipson & Co solicitors for the Plaintiff.

Winding up and receivership order

IN THE HIGH COURT OF JUSTICE Ch. 1991 F. No. 84
CHANCERY DIVISION
BETWEEN
                    WILLIAM FULGENT
                                                    Plaintiff
                         - and -

                  (1) MARCUS ALEXANDER
                  (2) PETER BALSAM
                                                    Defendants

---

DEFENCE OF THE FIRST AND SECOND DEFENDANTS
AND FIRST DEFENDANT'S COUNTERCLAIM

---

1. The Defendants admit and aver that by the Deed of Partnership dated 19th July 1984 referred to in paragraph 1 of the Statement of Claim ("the 1984 Deed") the parties hereto agreed as from 19th July 1984 to practise in partnership as Chartered Accountants under the name of "Fulgent and Co".

2. Paragraphs 3(i) to (xi) of the Statement of Claim are subject to their precise wording and context admitted. Clause 3 of Part II of the 1984 Deed provided that the Plaintiff and the Defendants should be entitled to the net profits of the said practice in such shares as they should in any year agree and in default of agreement in specified shares 50% for the Plaintiff and 25% each between the First and Second Defendants.

3. There were also in particular express terms of the 1984 Deed by which inter alia a partner of the partnership might cease to be such (clause 17) or retire (clause 18), in which event the share and interest of the outgoing partner in the assets of the partnership should accrue to the remaining partners and he should be entitled to be paid sums calculated as set out in the First Schedule (clause 19).

4. It was further a term of the said partnership from the end of 1984 as expressly agreed at a partners' meeting at that time and as thereafter applied, that individual partners should not be obliged to account to the said partnership for "outside interests" that is, investments and opportunities connected with the said practice and its clients.

Winding up and receivership order

5. The First Defendant admits and avers that, as referred to in paragraph 11 of the Statement of Claim, there was transferred to the First Defendant from Mrs. Irene Cohen in or about the end of 1984 50,000 ordinary shares of £1 each in Loraley Shares Limited. It is denied that Mrs. Cohen transferred such shares to the First Defendant on behalf of the partnership.

6. Further or alternatively, the First Defendant disclosed his acquisition of the said shares to the Plaintiff and the other Defendant and he (and the Second Defendant) offered each of the Plaintiff and Second Defendant 10 per cent thereof (amounting in all to 20 per cent) and both of them save the Plaintiffs accepted that the said shares were an "outside interest" as aforesaid.

7. The First Defendant admits and avers that, as a result of the said loss of confidence in the Plaintiff and subsequent disputes between them, there were exchanges of memoranda dated 16th June and 3rd July 1987 as referred to in paragraph 6 of the Statement of Claim, and on 6th July 1987 the Defendants put it to the Plaintiff and the Plaintiff accepted that he should no longer be a partner in the said practice.

8. The First to Fourth Defendants admit the letters dated 22nd and 24th July 1987 referred to in paragraphs 8 and 10 of the Statement of Claim, and will refer to the same for their full terms and effect.

9. The First to Fourth Defendants deny that they acted wrongfully or in breach of the said partnership terms or evinced an intention no longer to be bound by or repudiated the same, as alleged in paragraphs 6 and 7 of the Statement of Claim. The Defendants sought to agree with the Plaintiff upon his retiring or otherwise ceasing to be a partner in the said practice as from 6th July 1987.

10. Paragraph 9 of the Statement of Claim is not admitted. The First to Fourth Defendants reserve the right to contend that the Plaintiff has or should be treated as having retired or ceased to be a partner in the practice for the purpose of clause 19 of the 1984 Deed.

11. The First to Fourth Defendants deny paragraph 14 of the Statement of Claim. The said shares were not received by the First Defendant as trustee for the partnership and neither the proceeds of sale nor the balance retained thereof belong beneficially to the partners. The Plaintiff is entitled to no part of such proceeds and shares alternatively to 6.92 per cent agreed as aforesaid (but since repudiated by him).

Winding up and receivership order

12. Save that the First to Fourth Defendants admit that the Plaintiff was paid £3444 as his said agreed part of the proceeds of sale of the said 250,000 shares as aforesaid, paragraph 15 of the Statement of Claim is denied.

13. It is denied that the Defendants are liable to account to the Plaintiff for £46562 by reason of the said partnership terms or some trust or as monies had and received, as alleged in paragraphs 16 and 17 of the Statement of Claim. The Plaintiff is not entitled to 50,000 of the said shares in Regina Health and Beauty Products Plc retained by the First Defendant nor to the transfer thereof. The First to Fourth Defendants admit that they have not acknowledged such entitlement or effected such transfer and deny that they had thereby acted wrongfully as alleged or at all.

14. The loss and damage alleged in paragraph 18 of the Statement of Claim, and the entitlement to interest asserted in paragraph 19, are denied. The First to Fourth Defendants have always been willing properly to join in an account in favour of the Plaintiff as their former partner. Alternatively, the Plaintiff has failed to mitigate his said loss and damage (if any, which is denied).

15. Save as aforesaid, the First to Fourth Defendants deny each and every allegation contained in the Statement of Claim and deny that the Plaintiff is entitled as against them to the reliefs sought or at all.

First Defendant's Counterclaim

16. The First Defendant repeats paragraphs 7 to 13 inclusive of the First to Fourth Defendants' defence above.

17. In the premises the said sum of £3444 paid by the First Defendant to the Plaintiff on or about 13th March 1987 was had and received by the Plaintiff for the First Defendant's use, and there was no consideration for same and the First Defendant seeks repayment of the sum of £3444 together with interest thereon from 13 March 1987 until repayment at 12 per cent per annum or for such period and at such rate as the Court thinks fit.

AND the First Defendant Counterclaims against the Plaintiff

(1) The said sum of £3444
(2) Interest thereon pursuant to section 35A Supreme Court Act 1981.

MURRAY ROSEN

Served the 11th day of September 1991 by Messrs Lee of 32 Sea Road, Westley
Solicitors for First to Fourth Defendants.

Partnership: Winding Up and Receivership—Orders

1. ORDER ON PARTNERSHIP ACCOUNT AND INQUIRY

UPON THE ACCOUNT AND INQUIRY directed by the Order dated ...

AND UPON HEARING Counsel/the Solicitors for the Plaintiff and Counsel/the Solicitors for the Defendant

AND UPON READING the documents recorded on the Court File as having been read

IT IS DECLARED

1 that as a result of the dealings and transactions between the Plaintiff and the Defendant as partners from ... [there is due to the Plaintiff from the Defendant the sum of £ ...] [there is due to the Plaintiff £ ... and to the Defendant £ ... from the property of the partnership and that after payment of the two said sums the balance if any of the said property after payment of all proper costs and expenses belongs to the Plaintiff and to the Defendant in equal shares]

2 that there is now no property belonging to the partnership

3 that the property belonging to the partnership consists of the items specified in the Schedule hereto

The Schedule

1 The leasehold property (valued at £ ...) known as ... and held under a lease dated ... and made between ... (1) and ... (2)

2 The goodwill (valued at £ ...) of the business of the business of ... carried on by the partners at ...

3 The chattels (valued at £ ...) listed in exhibit ... to the Affidavit of ... sworn

4 The debts amounting to valued at £ ... due to the partnership listed in exhibit ... to the Affidavit of ...

5   The sum of £ ... or thereabouts on current account with ... Bank plc at their branch at ... in the name of ... the Receiver and Manager appointed by the Order dated ...

2. APPOINTMENT OF RECEIVER

AND the parties having agreed that the partnership hereinafter mentioned was dissolved on ... and consented to this Order
   AND the plaintiff/defendant by his/her/its/their Counsel undertaking to be answerable for what the Receiver and Manager hereinafter appointed shall receive or become liable to pay until he shall have given security as hereinafter directed
   THE COURT HEREBY APPOINTS ... of ... [solicitor] [chartered accountant] [without giving security] to collect get in and receive the debts now due and owing and other assets property or effects belonging to the partnership business carried on between the plaintiff and the defendant under the title of ... in the Writ of Summons mentioned and to manage the same

AND IT IS ORDERED

1   that the said Receiver and Manager do on or before ... give security as such Receiver and Manager to the satisfaction of the court

2   that if the said Receiver and Manager shall not have given such security as aforesaid by the time aforesaid or within such further time as the court may allow his appointment as such Receiver and Manager is forthwith upon the expiration of such time to determine

3   that the plaintiff and the defendant shall forthwith deliver to the said Receiver and Manager all the stock in trade and effects of the said partnership and also all securities in their hands for such outstanding partnership estate together with all books and papers relating thereto

4   that the said Receiver and Manager shall out of the first moneys to be received pay the debts due from the said partnership

5   that the said Receiver and Manager shall submit his accounts to the plaintiff ... and the defendant ... at yearly [six-monthly] intervals

[5   that the said Receiver and Manager shall on or before ... submit to the plaintiff and the defendant his account made up to ... and that he do subsequently on or before ... in every year submit to the plaintiff and the defendant his half yearly accounts made up to the previous ... and ... respectively]

6 that the costs of the said Motion be borne by the plaintiff/defendant in any event

[6 that the costs of the plaintiff/defendant of the said Motion are to be his/her/its costs in any event]

3. DISCHARGE OF RECEIVER

UPON THE APPLICATION of the plaintiff/defendant by Summons dated ...

AND UPON HEARING ... for the plaintiff and for the defendant and for ... (hereinafter called the Receiver) the Receiver and Manager appointed by the Order dated ...

AND UPON READING the documents recorded on the court file as having been read

IT IS by consent ORDERED

1 that the Receiver be discharged from his said office without submitting/passing any further account

2 [that the Receiver shall on or before ... lodge in Chancery Chambers Thomas More Building The Royal Courts of Justice Strand London WC2A 2LL his final account and shall lodge in Court as directed in the lodgment part of the lodgment and payment schedule hereto the balance which shall by further Order be declared certified to be due from him]

3 that the Receiver be allowed remuneration in the sum of £ ... in addition to remuneration already allowed and that his assessed costs be allowed at £ ...

4 that upon the Receiver making the payments set out in the schedule hereto [upon the Receiver making such lodgment or upon its being declared certified that there is nothing due from the Receiver] the Guarantee dated ... and entered into by the Receiver and ... as his Surety be discharged

5 that the funds in court be dealt with as directed in the payment part of the said schedule

6 that the costs of the said Application be costs in the cause.

The Schedule
Lodgment and Payment Schedule if appropriate.

Notes

1 The Receiver is usually discharged first and ordered subsequently to bring in his final account and pay his balance into court or to such of the parties as the court may direct.

2 In practice it is seldom that a receiver is directed to lodge money in court so no lodgment or lodgment and payment schedule has been attached to this precedent. If such a schedule is required, the words 'BALANCE (if any) certified to be due from the Receiver A B on his final account' or similar words will go in the first column and 'The Receiver AB' in the second column. If the schedule is a lodgment and payment schedule, the 'Funds to be dealt with' will normally be 'Cash to be lodged as above'.

4. EXAMINATION OF ACCOUNT

UPON THE EXAMINATION of the Items numbered ... in the ... Account from ... to ... (both days inclusive) of ... (hereinafter called the Receiver) the Receiver and Manager appointed by the Order dated ...)

AND UPON HEARING the solicitors for the plaintiff and for the defendant and for the Receiver

AND UPON READING the documents recorded on the court file as having been read

IT IS CERTIFIED

1 that the said Items numbered ... specified in the first schedule hereto ought to be included in the said Account and are allowed

2 that the said Items numbered ... specified in the second schedule hereto ought not to be included in the said Account and are disallowed

3 that accordingly ...

AND IT IS ORDERED

1 that the plaintiff/defendant shall pay to the plaintiff/defendant £ ... being his [assessed] costs of the objections to the said Items and of the said examination [such costs to be taxed]

2 that the Receiver be at liberty to retain out of the moneys in his hands as Receiver £ ... being his assessed costs of the said objections and of the said examination.

Notes

1 This precedent is intended for use under the procedure set out in Ord 30, r 5. A receiver only lodges his account when a party is dissatisfied with an item or items. The court then examines the 'item or items' and then the result of such examination must be certified by a master ... and an order may thereupon be made as to the incidence of any costs or expenses incurred.

2 Sometimes it will be possible to refer to the items in question by reference to their numbers in the account. Where this is not possible the order can begin 'UPON THE EXAMINATION of Items in the Account ...' and the items can be set out in schedules to the order or referred to in some other way. It may be convenient sometimes to have a schedule of the items allowed and another of the items disallowed.

3 After allowing or disallowing items the master will go on to make a further certificate, eg, 'that accordingly the balance due from the Receiver on his said Account is £ ...'.

5. EXAMPLES OF ORDERS GIVING LEAVE TO DO CERTAIN ACTS

UPON THE APPLICATION OF ... (hereinafter called the Receiver) the Receiver and Manager appointed by the Order dated .../the plaintiff/ the defendant by Summons dated

AND UPON HEARING Counsel/the solicitors for the plaintiff and Counsel/the solicitors for the defendant and Counsel/the solicitors for the Receiver

AND UPON READING the documents recorded on the Court File as having been read

IT IS ORDERED

1 that the Receiver be at liberty for the purpose of carrying on the business of the defendant Company to borrow from ... a sum or sums not exceeding £ ... in the aggregate

2 [that the property and assets of the defendant Company comprised in and charged by the Mortgage Debentures issued by the defendant Company do stand charged with the payment to the said ... of the sum or sums so advanced not exceeding in the aggregate £ ... for the purpose aforesaid together with interest

at the rate of ... per centum per annum above the base lending rate of ... [at a rate not exceeding £ ... per centum per annum/ on the respective advances from the respective dates thereof subject to any over-riding Mortgage or Charge but in priority to the Charge created by the said Debentures and subject to the right of the Receiver to indemnity out of the said property and assets in respect of his remuneration to be allowed by the Court and his costs and expenses properly incurred]

3 [that the Charge hereby created be not enforced except in this Action and with the leave of the Court]

4 [that the Receiver be at liberty to take proceedings in the ... Court against ... to recover enforce ... and to prosecute such proceedings down to the completion of discovery and inspection of documents but not further without the leave of the Court]

5 [that the Receiver be at liberty to pay to the persons named in the schedule hereto the sums therein set out opposite their names in settlement of on account of the amounts due to them respectively]

6 [that the Receiver be at liberty to pay the bills specified in the schedule hereto the bills mentioned in Paragraphs ... of the Affidavit of the Receiver sworn ...]

7 [that the Receiver be at liberty to grant in the name of ... a lease of the premises known as ... in the form of the draft annexed hereto]

8 [that the Receiver be at liberty to expend not more than £ ... in carrying out the repairs described in the schedule hereto]

9 [that the Receiver be at liberty to retain Messrs ... solicitors to act for him in relation to ...]

10 that the Receiver be at liberty (a) to employ any one or more of the parties in conducting under his supervision the business ... and (b) to sell the said business]

Note

1 The receiver has to get the leave of the court to do anything beyond his primary obligation to receive the income and make payments.

Chapter Eighteen

Rectification and Rescission

1. Rectification

Courts of equity do not rectify contracts as such, but they may and do rectify instruments purporting to have been made in pursuance of the terms of a contract on the basis of common or mutual mistake of the parties to the agreement resulting in the document failing to embody their common intention. If the mistake is unilateral, then the appropriate remedy may be not rectification, but rescission. Rectification is a discretionary remedy and may not be available if the matter sought to be inserted in the agreement could itself be enforceable as a collateral agreement. Rectification and specific performance are sometimes ordered in the same proceedings.

Statute

The Supreme Court Act 1981, s 61(1) and Sched 1 assigns actions for rectifications to the Chancery Division.

Orders

There is no specific order but Ord 5, r 4 indicates that the proceedings are commenced by originating summons, and Ord 15, r 16 indicates that courts may make declaratory judgments.

Parties

The parties to the proceedings will be the parties to the document of which rectification is sought or, subject to the rights of a bona fide purchaser for value, their successors in title.

Intitulement

The title must include reference to the deed or document.

The objectives of the plaintiff

The rectification of a document which by reason of a mutual mistake is at variance with the intention of the parties. Specific performance is appropriate. Such other consequential relief as will put the parties in the position which they would have occupied if the document had originally been drawn and executed in its rectified form: where a monetary payment or transfer of title or possession has taken place, this relief will include such measure of restitution as may be required.

Originating process/required on issue

Proceedings can be commenced by writ or by originating summons under Ord 5, r 4 but because by the nature of the action there is likely to be a dispute requiring oral evidence a writ will generally be more appropriate. Oral evidence if appropriate, will suffice except where any order made would vary a settlement, since no variations of settlements can be made unless (with or without oral evidence) there is also affidavit evidence. In cases where it is agreed between the parties that the issues of fact depend solely upon written evidence which is unlikely to be augmented by oral evidence the proceedings could well be commenced by originating summons with the safeguard that the parties could be cross-examined on their affidavits if points in issue have arisen on them. Proceedings to rectify a will are most likely to arise as a counterclaim in probate proceedings. Where a will is rectified, then the probate may have to be 'rectified' as well.

Sequence

The usual sequence of an action commenced by writ (or originating summons).

Plaintiff's/defendant's considerations

The considerable burden of proof will be on the party who asserts rectification. The statement of claim or counterclaim as the case may be should show precisely the wording of the rectification required. This may extend to more than one document as where a conveyance, lease or other deed conforms with the written contract but the contract itself is at variance with the terms originally agreed between the parties; in such a case if rectification is ordered, then both the contract and the deed will require to be rectified. It is not essential that the original agreement should be an enforceable agreement; for example, if oral it may be unenforceable by reason of a statutory requirement that it should be in writing or under seal; however, provided it can be shown to represent the true intention of the parties, then it will be admissible in evidence in a claim for rectification of a document purporting to give expression to it.

The terms of an unwritten agreement if disputed will always be difficult to prove on the oral evidence of a plaintiff or defendant alone and supporting evidence is almost essential. Even if the terms are established, the court will need to be satisfied that the agreement was not intentionally modified but remained the intention of the parties as at the date the contract was concluded.

Courts will not rectify voluntary instruments without the consent of the donor if living, notwithstanding that the terms of the document are clearly shown to have been at variance with his original intentions; if rectification is sought at the instance of the donor himself, it still may not be readily granted on his unsupported testimony.

The following may be acceptable alternatives to rectification in some cases: (*a*) where part of the agreed terms mistakenly omitted from the written document can be enforced as a collateral contract, then proceedings can be taken on the collateral contract; (*b*) where the issue between the parties arises from their different interpretation of the document the court may be asked to decide the proper interpretation and to order specific performance of the terms as so construed.

Hazards and pitfalls

Rescission is often claimed as an alternative to rectification and this should be considered and the statement of claim drafted accordingly.

Costs

There may be no order as to costs if both parties are to blame. However the court cannot deprive a trustee, personal representative, or mortgagee of his right to costs out of the estate or fund provided he has not acted unreasonably.

Alternative jurisdiction

The county courts have jurisdiction.

Textbooks

PV Baker & P St John Langan, *Snell's Principles of Equity*, 28th edn, (Sweet & Maxwell, 1982).
Halsbury, Vol 32, paras 50 et seq.

Forms and precedents

Atkin, Vol 18 (1985 issue), pp 275 et seq.

2. Rescission

Rescission can only be claimed (*a*) of a voidable contract and any instrument executed in pursuance of it on grounds of (i) misrepresentation, fraudulent or innocent, (ii) mistake of fact, mutual or unilateral, (iii) misdescription, (iv) non-disclosure in the case of a contract *uberrimae fidei*, (v) deficiency of a vendor's title or other circumstances inhibiting due performance, (vi) unconscionable dealings; (*b*) of a voluntary instrument (i) on the grounds that it was induced by fraud, misrepresentation or undue influence on the part of the beneficiary (ii) executed without full knowledge of its meaning or effect. If a rescission is ordered, there will also be an order for such consequential relief as will restore the parties to the position which they occupied before the contract was formed or the instrument executed and this may include repayment of money with interest, reconveyance or redelivery, indemnity, delivery up of documents for cancellation, accounts and inquiries, or an injunction and generally all such orders and directions as may be required to effect *restitutio ad integrum: (Domb v Izoz* [1980] Ch 548). Where damages will suffice and an order for specific performance or other equitable remedy will, therefore, not be granted, an order for rescission of a contract may nonetheless be made.

Restitution involves mutual restoration of property transferred, and is a discretionary remedy which will not be granted if there has been unreasonable delay.

If an innocent misrepresentation has given a right to claim rescission, the court may award damages in lieu and declare the contract subsisting if it would be equitable to do so (s 2(2) of the Misrepresentation Act 1967).

Terms in a contract which exclude liability or remedies for misrepresentation may be declared void (s 3 of the Misrepresentation Act 1967 as amended by the Unfair Contract Terms Act 1977 which incorporates (s 11) a reasonableness test).

Statute

The Supreme Court Act 1981, s 61(1) and Sched 1 assign rescission to the Chancery Division. See also the Misrepresentation Act 1967.

Order

There is no order specific. Ord 15, r 16 enables the court to make declaratory judgments only.

Objective

An order rescinding the contract and (unless rescission is the only order available) damages which may be available by virtue of s 2 of the Misrepresentation Act 1967 or at common law. The claim will therefore be for an order for the rescission of the contract with or without damages.

Parties

The parties will be the parties to the disputed contract or instrument or, subject to the rights of a *bona fide* purchaser for value, their successors in title.

Originating process

Writ or originating summons if the facts are not materially disputed.

Required on issue/sequence:

As is usual for a writ or originating summons action.

Plaintiff's/defendant's considerations

An order for rescission normally relates back to the date of the contract or instrument and will not be made unless restitution is possible, though where a contract is severable, rescission may be sought of that part which remains unperformed.

Proof of quantified loss or damage actual or potential is not essential to a claim for rescission but will be relevant when payment of damages or compensation is claimed. An order for payment of damages in lieu of rescission under s 2(2) of the Misrepresentation Act 1967 relates only to cases of innocent misrepresentation, but the court has the general power to award compensation either in lieu of or as a condition of rescission or specific performance in favour of a party who would otherwise suffer hardship through the court's decision. The court also has power independently of that conferred by s 3 of the Act to override a condition in the contract excluding or limiting the injured parties' equitable remedies; thus a condition that an error of description shall not annul the sale will not bar an action for rescission where the misdescription is substantial: Dillon J in *Walker v Boyle* (1981) 125 SJ 724.

The remedy of rescission is properly applicable to voidable contracts which remain unenforceable until rescinded and contracts void *ab initio* can generally be repudiated without bringing an action although, of course, the party claiming repudiation may find himself a defendant to proceedings. It is always open to any party to a contract claimed to be void to apply to the court for a declaration (Ord 15, r 16).

Hazards and pitfalls

If the plaintiff purports to rescind a contract without claiming damages, he may lose his right to make a claim for damages if his rescission is accepted by the other party. Therefore it is wise for the party purporting to rescind, when rescinding, to reserve his rights to claim damages.

The measure of damages for rescission for misrepresentation under the 1967 Act is the tortious measure (ie as if there were fraud) and not the contractual measure (which would include damages for loss of bargain) (*Royscot Trust Ltd v Rogerson; The Times*, 3 April 1991).

Actions by creditors or trustees in bankruptcy for the cancellation of voluntary instruments should only be brought under s 172 of the Law of Property Act 1925 or Insolvency Act 1986 as may be appropriate.

Textbooks

PV Baker & P St John Langan, *Snell's Principles of Equity*, 28th edn, (Sweet & Maxwell, 1982).
Hanbury's Modern Equity, 13th edn, (Sweet & Maxwell, 1989).

Forms and precedents

Atkin, Vol 18 (1985 issue).

Rectification and Rescission— Orders

1. RECTIFICATION OF DEED

IT IS ORDERED

1 that the Settlement made ... between ... (1) ... (2) be rectified in the manner set out in the schedule hereto

2 that the trustees of the said Settlement shall cause a Memorandum of this Order to be endorsed on the said Settlement

3 that the defendant shall pay to the plaintiff his costs of this Action and Counterclaim to be taxed if not agreed

The Schedule

Note

1 A memorandum of the order should be endorsed on the settlement.

2. RECTIFICATION OF LAND REGISTER

IT IS ORDERED

1 pursuant to Section 82 of the Land Registration Act 1925 that the Property/Proprietorship/Charges Register of Title Number ... at Her Majesty's Land Registry (being the Title relating to the property known as ...) be rectified by cancelling entry number ... therein

2 that the defendant shall on or before ... or subsequently within 4 days after service of this Order lodge the Land Certificate of Title Number ... at Her Majesty's Land Registry ...

3 that the defendant shall pay to the plaintiff his costs of the said application (including therein his costs of the rectification to be made pursuant to this Order) to be taxed if not agreed.

Notes

1 Section 82 of the Land Registration Act 1925 states that the register may be rectified pursuant to an order of the court or by the registrar in the cases there specified.

2 Unless there is a Minute signed by counsel it is desirable for the draftsman to have a copy of the entries on the register before him when he drafts the order so that he can ensure that the order makes sense and does not give rise to any difficulty or ambiguity.

3 Sometimes the order for rectification will be preceded by a declaration, eg, that certain covenants are not subsisting or capable of taking effect or as to the construction of a transfer or other deed.

4 Section 82 (b) says 'On every rectification of the register the Land Certificate and any Charge Certificate which may be affected shall be produced to the registrar unless an Order to the contrary is made by him'. If the land certificate or charge certificate is in a party's possession and it is thought he may be reluctant to comply with the order the court may make a four-day order giving the full address of the appropriate District Land Registry.

5 Rectification comes before the Court
   (a) in ordinary proceedings for rectification (and other relief).
   (b) on appeal from the Registrar.
   (c) where the Registrar orders that the matter be referred to the Chancery Division.

6 This precedent is designed for situation (a)
   (1) In both (b) and (c) the application will probably be by originating summons.
   (2) Where there is an appeal the order below will have to be affirmed, discharged or varied and the costs of the proceedings before the registrar may have to be dealt with.
   (3) In situation (c) the costs before the registrar may have to be dealt with.

7 See Atkin, Vol 18 (1985 issue).

3. RECTIFICATION OF REGISTERS HELD BY COMMONS REGISTRATION AUTHORITY

IT IS ORDERED

1 that Entry Number ... in the Land Section of Register Unit Number ... in the Register of Common Land maintained by the ... County Council be rectified by ...

2 that the Defendant shall pay to the Plaintiff his costs of this Action such costs to be taxed if not agreed

Note

1 The action may concern the rectification of the Register of Town and Village Greens or the Rights or Ownership Sections of these registers. The order will have to be amended accordingly.

Chapter Nineteen

Trusts: General

1. Introduction

The rules of substantive law developed in relation to the long standing institution of the trust are to be found overtly or else infused covertly in nearly every action in the Chancery Division and it is pertinent that 'trust' in the Trustee Act 1925 comprehends trusts which are express, implied or constructive (s 68(17)). Such is the ambience of the institution, that aspects of the law of trust may be relevant alike to company directors, holders of joint property, owners of undivided shares in the product of oil fields, syndicated bank loans, property between contract and conveyance, advance payments for goods, personal representatives, and the taxpayer and the revenue.

Even before the Judicature Acts of the last century, courts of Chancery always exercised an inherent jurisdiction to control the administration of trusts to achieve their execution according to their terms and limitations in a manner conducive to the best interests of the beneficiaries. This jurisdiction was preserved within the Chancery Division by those Acts and as illustrated has been applied to a variety of new situations as the social and commercial life of the country has developed. The Trustee Act 1925 renewed various specific powers of the court auxiliary to the exercise of this inherent jurisdiction and additionally by s 57 enabled it to confer upon trustees either generally or in any particular instance power to effect transactions which by reason of the absence of any power vested in the trustees by the trust instrument or at law could not otherwise be effected. However (save for the Variation of Trusts Act 1958 which in limited circumstances empowers the court to alter trust limitations) neither its inherent jurisdiction, the Trustee Act or any other power enables the court to vary any limitations imposed by or any objects defined by the trust itself.

The court will expect a lay trustee to exercise in relation to the property subject to the trust the care that he would exercise in relation to his own property (*Learoyd v Whitely* (1887) 12 App Cas 727) and in the case of a professional trustee care of a possibly higher standard (*Bartlett v Barclays Bank Trust Co Ltd* [1980] Ch 515). The fascination of cases on trusts is that they often involve judgment on human conduct or the exercise by the court on appropriate evidence, of commercial wisdom.

Jurisdiction and statutes

Law of Property Act 1925, Trustee Act 1925, Settled Land Act 1925, Administration of Estates Act 1925 and Variation of Trusts Act 1958. All matters concerning the construction, execution, administration or variation of trusts and settlements, and the administration of the estates of deceased persons in the High Court has been assigned to the Chancery Division (Ord 93, rr 4 and 6). Proceedings in the High Court under the Trustee Act 1925 and Variation of Trusts Act 1958 are also assigned to the Chancery Division. By s 113(1) of the Settled Land Act 1925 proceedings under the Settled Land Act are assigned to the Chancery Division.

2. Determination of questions and orders directing acts to be done or abstained from

Order 85, r 2 bears the heading 'Determination of questions etc without administration' and it empowers the court to make such orders or give such directions concerning the administration of an estate or the execution of a trust as it could have made in or during a full administration action. The court has all attendant powers such as to require production of any documents, accounts or papers, payment into court of any funds, or the making of directions that any act shall be done or restrained. Without prejudice to this generality, Ord 85, r 2 specifically provides that an action may be brought for the determination of (*a*) any question arising from the administration or in the execution of a trust, (*b*) any question as to the composition of any class of person having a beneficial interest in or claim against the estate of a deceased person, or any property subject to a trust and (*c*) any question as to the rights or interests of persons claiming to be beneficially entitled, or claiming as creditors in the estate of deceased persons.

Order 85, r 2 further provides that an action may be brought for any of the following orders:

(1) Requiring a personal representative to furnish accounts.
(2) Requiring payment into court of money held.
(3) Directing a person to do or abstain from doing a particular act in his capacity as executor, administrator or trustee.
(4) Approving any sale, purchase, compromise or other transaction by a personal representative or trustee.

Rule 2 provides that the court will only grant an administration order if satisfied that the questions before it cannot otherwise be determined and the importance of abjuring administration and adoption of r 2 wheresoever appropriate for the determination of questions and the granting of relief can hardly be overstressed. The existence of the rule has contributed to the virtual demise of actions for the full administration of a trust or estate. Another contributory factor is the possibility of appointing the judicial trustee under the Judicial Trustees Act 1896.

Order 85, r 5 stipulates that a judgment or order for the administration or execution under the direction of the court of an estate or trust need not be given or made unless, in the opinion of the court, that question at issue between the parties cannot properly be determined otherwise than under such a judgment or order. However, when under Ord 85, r 2 the court determines a question or grants relief it may well make an order or declaration thereon. Any judgment, order or declaration made could require directions, which would then be likely to proceed in the master's chambers.

3. Applications by trustees, personal representatives or beneficiaries for the exercise of the court's jurisdiction

Applications may be made:

(1) To determine the construction or interpretation of a will or trust instrument.
(2) To authorise any sale purchase or other dealing with trust property not authorised by the trust instrument (s 57 of the Trustee Act 1925 and s 64 of the Settled Land Act 1925 are enabling provisions). The court must be satisfied that the dealing is for the benefit of the trust or settled land.
(3) To sanction any act by trustees or personal representatives for which the court's guidance or approval is required.
(4) To order the appointment or removal of a trustee.
(5) To make a vesting order.
(6) To approve an arrangement under the Variation of Trusts Act 1958.
(7) To obtain a 'Re Beddoe Order' (*Re Beddoe, Downes v Cottam* [1893] 1 Ch 557 CA) a trustee should not bring or defend an action without the sanction of the court otherwise he does so at his own risk as to costs (even if he acts on counsel's advice). The sanction should be applied for, if there is no pending action, by originating summons (note to Ord 85, r 2). The full facts should be brought before the court as to the dispute or problem. The order is known as a 'Re Beddoe Order'.

Order 15, rr 13 and 14(1)

Trustees and personal representatives may sue and be sued without their beneficiaries being joined but the court may (*a*) order a beneficiary to be made a party, (b) make a representation order under Ord 15, r 13 or (c) order that the judgment or order made shall not be binding on persons having a beneficial interest on grounds that the trustees or personal representatives could not, or did not in fact, represent the interests of persons having a beneficial interest. In the absence of an order under (a) or (c) any judgment or order made when trustees sue or are sued without joining beneficiaries shall be binding on persons having a beneficial interest (Ord 15, r 14(1)).

In an action brought by a beneficiary against trustees he is not obliged to join any other person having a beneficial interest (Ord 15, r 14(1)) and the judgment or order shall be binding on those other persons unless the court otherwise orders, but the court may order other beneficiaries to be joined or make a representation order. Additionally, if the action is for the execution of a trust the court when giving judgment or making a direction which affects persons not parties to the action may direct that notice of the judgment be served on such persons and they shall then be bound by the judgment subject to their right to make application within one month of service (Ord 44 as substituted by r 53 of RSC (Amendment No 2) 1982 (SI 1982 No 1111)).

4. Actions by beneficiaries against trustees or personal representatives

Defaults by trustees could consist of negligence, lack of accounts, refusal of information, refusal to consider exercising a discretion or power of appointment, defalcation by misappropriation, misuse of trust property whether through fraud or mistake, and in general, neglect or refusal to perform duties. Relief or redress may be granted in respect of any of these matters, and trustees or personal representatives may be compelled to perform their duties or may be prevented from the improper exercise of their powers by an order requiring them to do or abstain from doing a specific act (Ord 85, r 2); alternatively a fresh trustee or the judicial trustee may be appointed or in the last resort there may be an order for full administration under the direction of the court (Ord 85, r 1). Proceedings for relief or redress are usually commenced by writ, although if it were a case where surprise were not necessary, an originating summons could be issued.

Relief for trustees who have acted honestly

By s 61 of the Trustee Act 1925 if it appears to the court that a trustee (or personal representative) is or may be personally liable but has acted honestly and reasonably and ought fairly to be excused for breach of trust and for omitting to obtain the directions of the court, the court may relieve him either wholly or partly from personal liability; and see *Bartlett v Barclays Bank* [1980] Ch 515.

5. Appointment and removal of trustees

Under s 41 of the Trustee Act 1925, the High Court has power to appoint a new trustee or new trustees in substitution for, or in addition to, any existing trustee or trustees, or where there is no existing trustee, whenever it is found inexpedient, difficult or impracticable to make such appointment without the assistance of the court; but the difficulty must be substantial and when there is some person entitled and willing to make the appointment out of court, the court will not intervene to override his wishes or intentions unless they are manifestly objectionable.

In practice and with rare exceptions, application to the court is confined to cases where:

(1) The trust instrument has excluded the power of appointment conferred on trustees by s 36 of the Act and has named an appointor who has died or is unable or unwilling to exercise his power.
(2) No appointor has been nominated and the trustee or trustees named in the trust instrument has/have died before the trust has come into effect.
(3) The sole or last surviving trustee has died without leaving a known personal representative, or has remained out of the United Kingdom for more than twelve months, or cannot be traced, or has been removed or discharged by order of the court or in exercise of a power contained in the trust instrument, or is a minor, or has become incapable of exercising his functions as a trustee or neglects or refuses to do so, or wishes to retire but is unable to find any person willing to succeed him, or, being a corporation, has been liquidated or dissolved.
(4) The court in its inherent power, at the instance of the beneficiaries or a co-trustee, thinks fit to order the removal of a trustee who by reason of vexatious behaviour is considered to be unfit for his office.

Further to its powers of appointment, the court has wide powers under ss 44–51 of the Act to make vesting orders in respect of land, stocks and things in action. An application to the court for the appointment of a trustee or trustees will usually include an application for any consequential vesting order, but such an order may also be sought when an appointment has been made out of court and the person or one of the persons in whom the trust property or part of it is vested is unable, unavailable or unwilling to execute the necessary conveyance or transfer. Apart from cases involving the appointment or removal of trustees, the court has power to make a vesting order wherever the vesting of property in the person entitled thereto cannot otherwise be effected as, for example, when a trustee has refused or neglected to convey land in defiance of an order to do so (*Jones v Davies* [1940] WN 174) or where a contract for the sale of land has been frustrated by the dissolution of a vendor company before a conveyance could be executed.

In addition to its statutory authority the court has an inherent jurisdiction to remove or discharge a trustee where the interests of the beneficiaries so require, but the exercise of its power is discretionary and, for example, the bankruptcy of a trustee, although specified in s 41 of the Act as a ground for his removal, will not be accepted as a compelling reason if the court is satisfied that the trust assets will not be put at risk by his continuance in office. It has been held that the court has power to discharge a trustee without appointing another in his place and, if necessary, to make a vesting order in favour of the remaining trustees (*Re Chetwynd's Settlement* [1902] 1 Ch 692; *Re Stretton* [1942] WN 95).

The above sections apply to trusts generally and whether created by deed, will or statute, including trusts within the scope of the Settled Land Act 1925 and charitable trusts, but have no application to executors or administrators of the estate of a deceased person except in so far as they have assented to the vesting of the estate or some part of it in themselves as trustees. Reference should be made to (*a*) the Charities Act 1960, s 18, which confers concurrent jurisdiction on the Charity Commissioners in the matter of the appointment of trustees of a charitable trust and consequential vesting orders (*see Chapter 21*) and (*b*) the Mental Health Act 1983, which gives concurrent jurisdiction to the Court of Protection in the matter of the retirement and replacement of a trustee who is also a beneficiary and is a patient as therein defined.

Statute

Trustee Act 1925, ss 41, 44-48, 50-53, 58.

Order

Order 93, r 4.

Parties

The plaintiffs may be trustees or beneficiaries. Any trustee or beneficiary who is not a plaintiff should be named as a defendant, but a mentally disordered trustee need not be served, unless he is also a beneficiary or is a sole trustee, and the master may dispense with service upon a defendant who is out of the jurisdiction or who cannot readily be traced or whose beneficial interest is minimal or remote. Where a vesting order only is required it is not necessary

TRUSTS: GENERAL

for the beneficiaries to be made defendants, but an appointor who is not a trustee should be joined as a plaintiff.

Intitulements

'In the matter of the Will/Estate of AB deceased' or
'In the matter of AB's trust/settlement'.

Plaintiff's objective

The appointment and/or discharge or removal of a trustee where such appointment, discharge or removal cannot be obtained otherwise than by an order of the court; and/or a vesting order or appointment of a person empowered to execute a conveyance or transfer of trust property when the property cannot otherwise be vested in the person or persons entitled.

Originating process

Originating summons. The supporting affidavit should state:

(1) The death of any former trustee and any other devolution of the trusteeship.
(2) Brief particulars of the trust property, its value and the beneficial interests.
(3) The circumstances under which the appointment of a trustee is difficult or impracticable without the aid of the court.
(4) If appropriate, the circumstances necessitating an order for the discharge or removal of a trustee and/or a vesting order.

Any property situate in Scotland should be set out in a separate schedule to the originating summons and the summons should include an application for an order that the trustees be at liberty to apply to the appropriate court in Scotland for a vesting order.

Exhibits to the affidavit must include the relevant probate or letters of administration (if any) or an office copy if the original is already lodged in Chancery chambers, the trust deed (where the trust was created otherwise than by will or by statute), any deeds of appointment or retirement giving effect to the devolution of the trusteeship and any relevant death certificates.

The following documents must be lodged in chambers (room 156):

(1) Probate or letters of administration, where applicable.
(2) The written consent of the proposed trustee, attested preferably by a solicitor (Ord 38, r 11).
(3) An affidavit of witness or (where the proposed trustee is a bank or corporation) an affidavit by its secretary or other competent officer under its seal confirming its consent and authority to act as trustee and setting out its scale of charges.

(4) Where a retiring trustee is mentally disordered, an affidavit by a medical practitioner confirming his incapacity to act as trustee and (if a vesting order is required) his incapacity to execute transfers or other instruments or assignments (Practice Direction [1948] WN 273); in such circumstances the court may be asked to make a vesting order in the remaining trustee, a purchaser or some other person to carry out the court's directions.

Sequence

The master may make the order himself except in cases where the trustee of a fund significantly in excess of £30,000 (and not being a trustee under a disability or a judicial trustee) is to be removed or suspended without his consent (Practice Direction (Chancery: Masters' Powers) [1975] 1 WLR 129 as amended by Practice Direction (Chancery: Masters' Powers) (No 4) [1977] 1 WLR 1019). In all such cases and in any other case where he considers it appropriate, the master will adjourn the originating summons to the judge in chambers.

Plaintiff's/defendant's considerations

It is against the usual practice of the court to appoint as trustee the solicitor for the trust or for one of the beneficiaries but where such an appointment is made the court has an inherent jurisdiction, additionally to the provisions of the Trustee Act 1925, s 42, to authorise payment of remuneration and the master may give the required direction (Practice Direction (Chancery: Masters' Powers) [1975] 1 WLR 129).

Alternative jurisdiction

County courts have jurisdiction where the amount or value of the trust property does not exceed £30,000 and this limit may be extended by written consent between the parties.

Textbooks

D J Hayton, *Underhill and Hayton's Law of Trusts and Trustees*, 14th edn, (Butterworths, 1987).
Hanbury's Equity and the Law of Trusts, 6th edn, (Butterworths, 1989).
Halsbury (3rd edn), Vol 38, paras 1540 et seq.

Forms and precedents

Atkin, Vol 41 Notes pp 23 et seq; Forms Nos 83 et seq.

6. The judicial trustee

A judicial trustee is an officer of the court and can only be appointed by the court; as such he is accountable to the court and assumes statutory obligations beyond the inherent duties of an ordinary trustee. He may be appointed as first trustee of a newly created trust or in substitution for a trustee who has died or retired or been discharged and to act solely or jointly with another or others. Unlike an ordinary trustee, he may be appointed to administer the estate of a deceased person in place of the original executor or administrator.

An applicant for the appointment of a judicial trustee may nominate any person or body, including a beneficiary or the solicitor acting for a beneficiary or for the trustees or a trust corporation. In this respect the court, in its estimation of a fit and proper person, allows a wider choice than in the case of an appointment under s 41 of the Trustee Act 1925.

If the applicant has not named an appointee, or if his nominee is not acceptable, an official of the court may be appointed, except where the trust involves (a) persons interested as members or debenture holders of, or as having relation to, any corporation or unincorporated body or any club; or (b) the carrying on of any trade or business, unless the court, with or without special conditions to ensure its proper supervision, specifically directs. An official of the court here means a person holding paid office prior to his appointment as judicial trustee, as distinguished from a person who becomes an officer of the court by virtue of his appointment as judicial trustee. Under the Judicial Trustee Rules 1983 (SI 1983 No 370) an official of the court appointed as judicial trustee is classified as a 'corporate trustee' and in that capacity is subject to less stringent requirements as to the rendering and audit of his accounts than those imposed upon an ordinary judicial trustee.

Statute

The Judicial Trustees Act 1896 as amended by s 57 of the Administration of Justice Act 1982.

Order

The Judicial Trustee Rules 1983 (SI 1983 No 370).

Parties

The plaintiff may be a trustee or a beneficiary of an existing trust or a person creating or intending to create a trust. Any trustee who is not a plaintiff should be made a defendant together with such beneficiaries as the plaintiff may think fit. The court may give such directions as it thinks fit for the service of the summons or for the dispensing of service, but a summons issued by or on behalf of the founder or intending founder of a trust is usually not required to be served on any person (r 4 (1, 2)).

Intitulement

Unless the application is made in a pending action, the relevant statute to be cited in the body of the originating summons will be the Judicial Trustees Act 1896.

Originating process

An application for the appointment of a judicial trustee must be made by originating summons or, in the case of a pending cause or matter, by summons or motion in the cause or matter. An application for an injunction ancillary or incidental to an order appointing a judicial trustee (as where it is desired to restrain a trustee or beneficiary from dealing with trust property prior to the hearing of the summons) may be joined with the application for such an order or, in a case of urgency, may be applied for *ex parte* on affidavit. Application may be made for the appointment of (*a*) a sole judicial trustee or (*b*) two or more judicial trustees to act jointly or (*c*) a corporate trustee as defined by r 2(1) ie the Official Solicitor, the Public Trustee or a corporation either appointed by the court in any particular case to be a trustee or entitled by rules made under section 4(3) of the Public Trustee Act 1906 to act as custodian trustee.

Where the applicant has not nominated an appointee he may, if he thinks fit, give not less than four days notice of the hearing of the application to any official of the court who may be appointed judicial trustee and any official served with such notice, though not a party to the proceedings, will be entitled to attend the hearing (r 4(3, 4)).

The affidavit supporting an application for the appointment of a judicial trustee must contain the following particulars so far as they are within the applicant's knowledge:

(1) A short description of the trust and of the instrument by which it was, or is to be, created.
(2) Short particulars of the trust property with an approximate estimate of its income and capital value.
(3) Short particulars of the incumbrances (if any) affecting the trust property.
(4) Particulars of the persons in possession of the documents relating to the trust.
(5) The names and addresses of the beneficiaries and short particulars of their respective interests.
(6) The name, address and description of the proposed judicial trustee (if any) together with any proposal the applicant may make for his remuneration.

TRUSTS: GENERAL 493

Where the applicant cannot gain the required information he must mention his inability in the affidavit (r 3(5, 6)).

Sequence
(1) A copy of the order appointing a judicial trustee must be served by the party having conduct of the proceedings on such beneficiaries, former trustees and other persons as the court may direct (r 5).
(2) An order appointing a judicial trustee (other than a corporate trustee) may include such directions as the court thinks fit for the giving of security by the person appointed, but the court will not, except for special reasons, require security to be given when the application is made by a person creating or intending to create a trust. Any guarantee or undertaking ordered to be filed as security must be filed in Chancery chambers or, if the cause or matter is proceeding in a district registry, that registry (r 6).
(3) The court may give such directions as it thinks fit for the manner in which and the conditions subject to which:
    (a) the trust fund is to be held,
    (b) any title deeds, certificates or other documents which are evidence of the title to the trust property are to be disposed of,
    (c) trust property may be vested in the judicial trustee, and
    (d) any payments received or made on behalf of the trust are to be dealt with and accounts thereof are to be kept (r 7).
(4) A judicial trustee or any interested person may at any time apply to the court in writing for directions as to the trust or its administration including a direction for termination of the judicial trusteeship and the master may give directions in a written note. Otherwise the court may require the applicant or any other person to attend in chambers or may direct a summons to be issued in the proceedings or direct an issue or issues to be tried (r 8).
(5) Rules 9–13 deal with the preparation, filing and examination of accounts and the settling of the trustee's remuneration and may be summarised as follows. A judicial trustee must make up his accounts in each year to the anniversary of his appointment and endorse thereon a certificate of the approximate capital value of the trust property at the commencement of the year of account. On examination of the accounts the court will allow to the trustee such proper remuneration (not exceeding 15 per cent of the capital value of the trust property) as it thinks fit and reimbursement of expenses actually and necessarily incurred. A judicial trustee (other than a corporate trustee) must submit his accounts to the court (accounts section, room 165) for examination and

if the court considers that the accounts are likely to involve questions of difficulty, it may refer them to a qualified accountant for report and may order payment to him out of the trust funds of such remuneration as it thinks fit. Following examination by or on behalf of the court, the result must be certified by a master and an order made as to the incidence of any costs or expenses incurred. The judicial trustee must then send a copy or (if the court thinks fit) a summary thereof to such beneficiaries or other persons as the court may direct. Any person who has been served with a copy of summary or, upon application to the court, has been allowed to inspect the accounts and who remains dissatisfied therewith, may apply to the court for directions. A judicial trustee (being a corporate trustee) must submit such accounts to such persons as the court may direct. Any person so served may, on giving reasonable notice to the trustee, inspect the books and papers relating to such accounts and, if dissatisfied therewith, may give notice specifying the item or items to which objection is taken and requiring the trustee within not less than 14 days to lodge his accounts with the court and a copy of such notice must be lodged in Chancery chambers or, if the cause or matter is proceeding in a district registry, that registry. Following an examination by the accounts section of the court of the item or items to which objection is taken, the result must be certified by a master and an order may thereupon be made as to the incidence of any costs or expenses incurred.

(6) A judicial trustee's office may be terminated and a successor appointed by the court (*a*) at his own request or (*b*) upon the application by summons of any interested party or (*c*) under r 14 which provides that where a judicial trustee fails to submit his accounts in the prescribed manner or to do any other thing which he is required to do, he may be required to attend in chambers, together with such other persons as the court may direct, to show cause for the failure and the court may, either in chambers or after adjourning into court, give such directions as it thinks proper, including, if necessary, directions for the discharge of the judicial trustee and the appointment of another and the payment of costs. The Rule contains further provisions whereby a defaulting judicial trustee may be disallowed his remuneration or charged with interest on money due to the trust account which he has retained in his possession.

(7) The appointment of an official of the court as a judicial trustee operates as an appointment of the holder of that office for the time being. Upon his dying or ceasing to hold office the trusteeship passes to his successor without any further order or appointment and any property vested in him as judicial trustee vests in his successor without any conveyance, assignment or transfer (r 16).

District registries

Notwithstanding any provisions contained in the Rules of the Supreme Court, an originating summons may be issued out of a district registry for the purpose of an application to appoint a judicial trustee and where a judicial trustee is appointed on a summons or motion or in a cause or matter proceeding in a district registry all proceedings with respect to the trust and the administration thereof under the 1896 Act and Rules should be taken in that registry, provided that the court may transfer any trust of which there is a judicial trustee from a district registry to Chancery chambers or vice versa or from one district registry to another, according as it appears convenient for the administration of the trust (r 17).

Alternative jurisdiction

The jurisdiction of county courts in the matter of trusts extends to judicial trusteeships.

Textbook

Halsbury (3rd edn), Vol 38, paras 1497 et seq.

Forms and precedents

Atkin, Vol 41 (1986 issue).

7. Variation of trusts

An order for the variation of a trust is required in all cases unless all beneficiaries are *sui juris* and are parties to a deed of variation. The Variation of Trusts Act 1958 gives the court power to make an order approving any arrangement varying or revoking all or part of a trust or enlarging the powers of the trustees of managing or administering any part of the trust property. Such an arrangement may be submitted by or on behalf of any person having directly or indirectly any interest in the trust, whether vested or contingent, including (*a*) any person who by reason of infancy or incapacity is unable to give his consent, (*b*) any person (whether ascertained or not) who may become entitled directly or indirectly at a future date or upon the happening of a future event, and (*c*) a person unborn.

The court may approve the arrangement in part only. The Act should not be invoked to vary the wording of a trust instrument where the court's inherent power of rectification would suffice.

Although the Trustee Investments Act 1961 did not expressly restrict the jurisdiction of the court to enlarge trustees' powers of investment, the court has been disinclined to give trustees unfettered discretion to invest in stocks and securities outside the scope of that Act.

The court's paramount consideration is the welfare of the beneficiaries as a whole, but unless it is proposed to remove trust funds out of the jurisdiction, the court will not reject any arrangement on the ground that its objective is to avoid or reduce the liability of the settlor or of certain beneficiaries for tax or death duties (*Re Clitheroe's Settlement Trusts* [1959] 1 WLR 1159; *Re Sainsbury's Settlement* [1967] 1 WLR 476; *Re Drewe's Settlement* [1966] 1 WLR 1518).

The Act applies to both private and charitable trusts but the latter are normally dealt with by way of scheme (*see Chapter 21*).

Statutes

Variation of Trusts Act, 1958; Trustee Investments Act 1961; Trustee Act 1925, s 57; and Settled Land Act 1925, s 64.

Order

Order 93, r 6 for variations under the Variation of Trusts Act 1958.

Parties

The plaintiffs may be trustees or beneficiaries. The defendants should include the settlor or founder of the trust (if living), any trustee who is not a plaintiff and (except in the case of a discretionary trust) any beneficiaries, other than plaintiffs, who are intended to be bound by the order. If any beneficiary is under a disability or if any unborn beneficiary will be affected, evidence will be required that the arrangement is approved by his guardian *ad litem* or trustee, as the case may be. The current trustees must see that the interests of unborns are properly represented if not by separate solicitors then by separate counsel at least.

Intitulement

'In the matter of the Will/Estate of AB deceased' or
'In the matter of AB's Trust/Settlement'.

The objective of the plaintiff

To obtain the court's sanction to the variation of the terms of a trust or settlement where minors or unborns are objects.

Originating process

This is by originating summons. Particulars of the proposed variation, if not set out in a schedule to the summons, should be made an exhibit to the supporting affidavit with a copy supplied for production in court. The affidavit must state why the variation is considered beneficial. If it is desired to extend the trustees' powers of investment beyond the scope of the Trustee Investments Act 1961, special circumstances must be presented, but it is not essential to prove a financial advantage.

Sequence

(1) The originating summons comes first before the master.
(2) The application when evidence is complete is usually heard in open court. If, in order to avoid publicity or for other reasons, it is desired to have the hearing in chambers, the master will adjourn the summons to the judge in chambers who will decide whether or not to accede to that request. The master has power to make the order where the only variation sought is the removal of protective trusts (Practice Direction (Chancery: Masters' Powers) [1975] 1 WLR 129).
(3) If a person under a disability will be affected, the court usually requires evidence that the proposed variation has the approval of his guardian *ad litem* or, in the case of an unborn beneficiary, the trustees, but the judge or master may occasionally dispense with the requirement of an affidavit exhibiting a case to counsel and counsel's opinion (Practice Direction (Variation of Trusts: Counsel's Opinion) [1976] 1 WLR 884) where the advantage to the person under disability is quite clear.
(4) A memorandum of the order should be indorsed on the probate, settlement or trust instrument. And if the order is such as to attract stamp duty, the solicitor having charge of the case will be required to give an undertaking to submit a duplicate to the Inland Revenue for adjudication. Practice Note (Variation of Trusts: Stamp Duty) [1966] 1 WLR 345 contains directions for the submission of a duplicate of the order to the commissioners of inland revenue for adjudication of stamp duty, where applicable.

Plaintiff's/defendant's considerations

It has been held that the court has power to approve the reconstitution of a trust whereby the funds are transferred to trustees resident abroad (*Re Seale's Marriage Settlement* [1961] Ch 574) but power in this instance will not readily be exercised when the main or only purpose of the arrangement is the avoidance of taxation (*Re Weston's Settlements* [1969] 1 Ch 223). The court also has power to vary a trust made under foreign law where the trustees and the trust property are within the court's jurisdiction (*Re Ker's Settlement Trusts* [1963] Ch 553; *Re Paget's Settlement* [1965] 1 WLR 1046).

When considering whether to raise protective trusts the court will particularly have regard to the beneficiary's record of financial stability.

Where the only variation sought is the making or retention by the trustees of a specific investment or a specific dealing with trust property not authorised by the trust instrument or by statute, application for the court's sanction may be made under s 57 of the Trustee Act 1925, or s 64 of the Settled Land Act 1925. Section 57 provides that where in the management or administration of any property vested in trustees, any sale, lease, mortgage, surrender, release or other disposition, or any purchase, investment, acquisition, expenditure or other transaction is in the opinion of the court expedient, but cannot be effected by reason of the absence of any power for that purpose vested in the trustees by the trust instrument, if any, or by law, the court may order or confer upon the trustees, either generally or in any particular instance, the necessary power for that purpose on such terms and subject to such provisions or conditions, if any, as the court may think fit and may direct in what manner any money authorised to be expended, and the costs of any transaction, are to be paid or borne as between capital and income. Application to the court under this section may be made by the trustees or by any of them, or by any person beneficially entitled under the trust. This section does not apply to trustees of a settlement, but s 64 of the Settled Land Act 1925 contains similar provisions for the enlargement by the court of the powers of a tenant for life. The provision for conferring powers under s 57 or s 64 are that the transaction must be for the benefit of the trust or settled land. Applications for an order under the Variation of Trusts Act 1958 are made when the changes proposed are more extensive than can be dealt with by an application under s 57 of the Trustee Act 1925 or s 64 of the Settled Land Act 1925.

Hazards and pitfalls

When seeking to terminate a life interest and consequent division of the fund, actuarial evidence of the life expectancy, as to a fair division of the fund and as to the taxation consequences of the arrangement must be supplied.

Alternative jurisdiction

County courts have jurisdiction where the amount or value of the trust property does not exceed £30,000.

Textbooks

Halsbury (3rd edn) Vol 38, para 1774 et seq.
D J Hayton, *Underhill and Hayton's Law of Trusts and Trustees*, 14th edn, (Butterworths, 1987).

Forms and precedents

Atkin, Vol 41, Notes pp 48 et seq; Forms No 176 et seq.

8. Vesting orders

Pursuant to s 44 of the Trustee Act 1925 the court may in any of seven cases make an order (in the Act called a vesting order) vesting any land or interest in land in any such person in any such manner and for such estate or interest as the court may direct, or may release or dispose of the contingent right to such person, as the court may direct, provided that where the order is consequential on the appointment of a trustee, then the land or interest (for such estate as the court may direct) must be vested in the persons who on the appointment are the trustees, and where the order relates to a trustee formerly entitled jointly with another person and such trustee is under disability (or out of the jurisdiction or cannot be found or in a corporation which has been dissolved) the land interest or right must be vested in such other persons who remain entitled either alone or with any other person the court may appoint.

The seven cases are:

(1) Where the court appoints or has appointed the trustee, or where a trustee has been appointed out of court.
(2) Where a trustee entitled to or possessed of any land or interest therein whether by way of mortgage or otherwise, or entitled to a contingent right therein, either solely or jointly with any other person, (*a*) is under disability or (*b*) is out of the jurisdiction or (*c*) cannot be found or (*d*) being a corporation has been dissolved.
(3) Where it is uncertain who was the survivor of two or more trustees jointly entitled to or possessed of any interest in land.
(4) Where it is uncertain whether the last trustee known to have been entitled ... is living or dead.
(5) Where there is no personal representative of a deceased trustee who was entitled ... or where it is uncertain who is the personal representative of a deceased trustee ...
(6) Where a trustee jointly or solely entitled ... has been required by a person entitled to require a conveyance, to convey the land or interest and has wilfully refused or neglected to convey ... for 28 days after the date of the requirement.
(7) Where land ... is vested in a trustee whether by way of mortgage or otherwise and it appears to the court to be expedient.

For consequential vesting in relation to orders for specific performance see s 48 ibid, and for consequential vesting on orders for sale of mortgaged land s 47 ibid.

If the application for a vesting order is not made during the course of proceedings, the application should be commenced by way of originating summons, and appropriate evidence should be provided in an affidavit.

Trusts: General—Orders

1. BEDDOE'S ORDER

IT IS ORDERED

1 that the Plaintiffs as Executors of the Will and Codicils of the above named deceased be at liberty to institute and prosecute an action proceedings claiming ... [to defend the Action specified in the Schedule hereto and to counterclaim for ...]

2 that the Plaintiffs be at liberty to continue to prosecute [to defend] the said Action and to prosecute such Counterclaim until discovery and inspection of documents in the said Action and Counterclaim have been completed

3 that the Plaintiffs be indemnified out of the estate of the deceased in respect of all costs properly incurred by them in connection with the said Action and Counterclaim

4 that the Plaintiffs do not take any steps in the said Action and Counterclaim proceedings after the completion of discovery and inspection of documents without the leave of the Court

5 that there be taxed if not agreed down to and including this Order
   (a) on the indemnity basis the costs of and incidental to the said Application of the Plaintiffs as Executors/Trustees
   (b) the costs of and incidental to the said Application of the Defendants

6 that all the said cash be raised retained and paid out of the estate of the deceased in a due course of administration out of the funds subject to the trusts of the said Will and Codicils

7 that after the discovery and inspection of documents in the said Action and Counterclaim have been completed the Plaintiffs are to be at liberty to apply for further directions

8 that the parties be at liberty to apply

The Schedule
The Action proceeding in the ...
the short title and reference to the record whereof is ...
199...

Notes

1 A trustee should not bring or defend an action without the sanction of the court since if he does so it is at his own risk as to costs, even if he acts on counsel's advice *(Re Beddoe, Downes v Cottam* [1983] 1 Ch 547 at 557).

2 As to the parties to the action see Ord 85, r 3(2). The beneficiaries may be allowed to intervene to protect their interests.

ADMINISTRATION ACTIONS

2. CLAIM BY BENEFICIARIES

IT IS ORDERED

1 that the trusts of the Will/arising under the intestacy of the above named deceased be performed and carried into execution

2 that the following Accounts and Inquiry be taken and made that is to say
   1 An Account of the property (not specifically devised or bequeathed) of the said deceased in the hands of the Executors of his Will/the Administrators of his effects or any/either of them or in the hands of any other person or persons by the order or for the use of the said Executors/Administrators distinguishing between capital and income
   2 An Account of the debts and funeral and testamentary expenses of the deceased
   3 An Account of the legacies and annuities given by the deceased's Will
   4 An Inquiry as to what parts (if any) of the deceased's property are outstanding or undisposed of and whether any part of such property so outstanding or undisposed of is subject to any and if so what incumbrances

3 that the deceased's property (not specifically devised or bequeathed) be applied in payment of his debts and funeral and testamentary expenses and afterwards in payment of the legacies and annuities given by his Will in a due course of administration

4 that further consideration of this Action be adjourned

5 that the parties are to be at liberty to apply.

Notes

1 See Atkin, Vol 2 (1989 Issue), Ord 85 and the notes at 85/6/5 et seq. SCP.

2 In relation to para 3 of the precedent Atkin says: 'Although the matter is not beyond all doubt it is thought that it is the presence of these words which constitutes the Order one for administration: *Re Alpha Co Ltd* [1903] 1 Ch 203'. The effect of an administration order is to prevent the personal representatives from exercising any of their powers without the leave of the court.

3 When drafting the precedent must be adapted to suit the circumstances. For example, where the deceased died intestate one deletes references to the will, to executors, to property being devised or bequeathed, to legacies and annuities. One would not include the words 'distinguishing between capital and income' unless there was a life interest.

4 If the deceased died more than six years before the order, account (2) is altered to 'An Inquiry whether there is any debt of the deceased remaining unpaid'.

5 Paragraph 3 of the precedent may require attention where property specifically divised or bequeathed has to be resorted to for debts though the estate is solvent.

6 Sometimes the court will order the usual administration accounts and inquiry but not actually make an administration order. When this happens paras 1 and 3 should be omitted.

3. CLAIM BY CREDITORS

IT IS ORDERED

1 that the trusts of the Will/arising under the intestacy of the above-named deceased be performed and carried into execution

2 that the following Accounts and Inquiries be taken and made that is to say
   (1) An Account of what is due to the Plaintiff and all other creditors of the said deceased
   (2) An Account of the deceased's funeral expenses
   (3) An Account of the deceased's property in the hands of the Defendant/the Administrator of his effects/Executor of his Will or of any/either of them or in the hands of any other person or persons by the order or for the use of the Defendant or any/either of them
   (4) An Inquiry as to what parts (if any) of the deceased's property are outstanding or undisposed of and as to any part of such

property as is outstanding or undisposed of whether the same is subject to any and if so what incumbrance

[(5) An Account of what is due to such of the incumbrancers (if any) as shall consent to the sale hereinafter directed in respect of their incumbrances]

[(6) An Inquiry as to the priorities of the last-mentioned incumbrancers]

[3 that none of the above Accounts or Inquiries except ... is to be prosecuted without the leave of the Court]

4 that the deceased's property be applied in payment of his debts and funeral expenses in a due course of administration

5 that the deceased's real estate be sold subject to the further directions of the Court free from the incumbrances (if any) of such of the incumbrancers as shall consent to the sale and subject to the incumbrances of such of them as shall not consent

6 that the money to arise by the sale of the deceased's real estate be paid into Court to the credit of this Action Re ... deceased ... v ... 199...

'Proceeds of Sale of deceased's real estate subject to further Order'

7 that if such money or any part thereof shall arise from real estate sold with the consent of incumbrancers that money so arising is to be applied in the first place in payment of what shall appear to be due to such incumbrancers according to their priorities

8 that further consideration of this Action be adjourned

9 that the parties are to be at liberty to apply.

Notes

1 This follows Chancery Masters' Practice Form No 11.

2 Paragraph 3 should be omitted unless it is expressly directed to be included.

3 Account No 2(5) and Inquiry No 2(6) should be omitted unless expressly directed. Also paras 5, 6 and 7.

4 Sometimes an inquiry as to preferential debts will be added.

4. ORDER FOR ACCOUNT AGAINST PERSONAL REPRESENTATIVE

UPON THE APPLICATION of the Plaintiff by Originating Summons
 AND UPON HEARING Counsel the Solicitors for the Plaintiff and Counsel the Solicitors for the ... Defendant ...
 AND UPON READING the documents recorded on the Court File as having been read

IT IS ORDERED

1. that the following Account be taken that is to say
   (1) the Account of the property not specifically devised or bequeathed by the above named deceased in the hands of the Defendant/the Executor of his Will/Administrator of his estate or either of them or in the hands of any other person or persons by the Order or for the use of them

2. that the Defendant shall on or before ... lodge the said Account duly verified by being exhibited to an Affidavit and do within the same time serve copies of the same on the Plaintiff

3. that the Defendant shall out of his own moneys pay to the Plaintiff his costs of this Action down to and including this Order to be taxed if not agreed

4. that the further consideration of this Action be adjourned

5. that the parties be at liberty to apply.

Note

1. This form requires adaptation to the circumstances of the individual case.

5. APPOINTMENT OF RECEIVER

AND the plaintiff/defendant by his/her/its/their Counsel undertaking to be answerable for what the Receiver and Manager hereinafter appointed shall receive or become liable to pay until he shall have given security as hereinafter directed
 THIS COURT APPOINTS ... of ... [solicitors/chartered accountants] [without giving security] to receive the rents and profits of the freehold and leasehold estates and to collect and get in the outstanding personal estate of the above named deceased and to manage the business of ... lately carried on by the said deceased at ...

IT IS ORDERED

1 that the said Receiver and Manager shall on or before ... give security as such Receiver and Manager to the satisfaction of the court

2 that if the said Receiver and Manager shall not have given such security as aforesaid by the time aforesaid or within such further time as the court may allow his appointment as such Receiver and Manager is forthwith upon the expiration of such time to determine

3 that the tenants of the said freehold and leasehold estates shall attorn and pay their rents in arrear and growing rents to the said Receiver and Manager

4 that the defendants/the executors of the Will of the said deceased/Administrators of the estate of the said deceased shall deliver to the said Receiver and Manager all the stock in trade and effects of the said business and also all securities in their hands for such outstanding personal estate together with all deeds books documents and papers relating thereto

5 that the said Receiver and Manager shall submit his accounts to the plaintiff ... and the defendant ... at yearly/six-monthly intervals

[6 that the said Receiver and Manager shall on or before ... submit to the plaintiff and the defendant his account made up to ... and that he do subsequently on or before ... and ... in every year submit to the plaintiff and the defendant his half-yearly accounts made up to the previous ... and ... respectively]

7 that the costs of the said Motion be borne by the plaintiff/defendant in any event

8 that the costs of the plaintiff/defendant of the said Motion are to be his/her/its/their costs in the cause.

Notes

1 The associate must know whether security is to be given or not. If security is to be given he must then find out whether the plaintiff or defendant gives the usual undertaking in the precedent.

2 Under this form the receiver can act forthwith but it is possible to make an order under which the receiver cannot act until he has given security. When such an order is made it should not be signed until the security

has been given and that the order should contain a recital 'And the Receiver and Manager hereinafter appointed having given security to the satisfaction of the court'.

3 The consent of the receiver to act is usually required before the appointment is made.

4 It is important to be clear whether or not the receiver is also to act as manager.

5 Paragraphs (3) and (4) of the precedent should normally be included in the order as a matter of course.

6 There are alternative paragraphs (5) relating to accounts. Neither paragraph (5) goes in unless the court has actually given a direction. It is good practice when the court makes an order for accounts to direct on whom these accounts are to be served.

6. APPOINTMENT OF JUDICIAL TRUSTEE

(1) Official solicitor

THE COURT APPOINTS the official solicitor to be sole Judicial Trustee without giving security of the Will and Codicil of the above named deceased in substitution for the defendants the existing Trustees to complete the administration of the estate of the above named deceased in substitution for the ... defendants the existing ... Administrators

IT IS ORDERED

1 that the freehold and leasehold property specified in the first schedule hereto and all other (if any) the freehold and leasehold property now subject to the trusts of the said Will vested in the ... defendants as such Administrators vest in the official solicitor as such sole Judicial Trustee for all the estate and interest therein now vested in ... to be held by the official solicitor upon the trusts of the said Will/arising on the intestacy of the said deceased ...

2 pursuant to the Trustee Act 1925 that the right to transfer
  (a) the securities specified in the ... schedule hereto standing in the books of the Bank of England ... in the names and by the descriptions specified in the said ... schedule and
  (b) the securities specified in the ... schedule hereto standing in the names of ... (and to receive any interest or dividends now due and to accrue due thereon) vest in the official solicitor as such Judicial Trustee

3 that the official solicitor shall transfer the said securities into his name as the official solicitor to be held upon the said trusts

4 that the right to sue for and to recover any thing in action subject to the said trusts (and in particular the things in action specified in the ... schedule hereto) or any interest in respect thereof vest in the official solicitor as such Judicial Trustee to be held by him upon the said trusts

5 that the ... shall forthwith after service of this Order deliver up to the official solicitor as such Judicial Trustee (a) the Grant of Letters of Administration of the estate/Probate of the Will and Codicil of the deceased and (b) (upon oath if required) all securities and other property in their hands subject to the said trusts together with all deeds books (including bankers' pass books) and documents relating thereto and do forthwith after service of this Order deliver up to the official solicitor as such Judicial Trustee any sums in their hands or under their control subject to the said trusts

6 that the official solicitor shall sell the securities mentioned in the ... Part of the ... schedule hereto and hold the proceeds of sale thereof upon the trusts of the said Will/Settlement or retain the said securities until they are fully paid up in the event of the said securities being fully paid up transfer them into the names as aforesaid to be held upon the said trusts

7 that the funds in court be dealt with as directed in the payment schedule hereto the funds thereby directed to be transferred into the name of the official solicitor to be held upon the trusts of the said Will/Settlement

8 that [the defendant] do on or before ... or subsequently within 4 days after service of the order leave at Chancery Chambers room 165 Royal Courts of Justice Strand London WC2A 2LL a complete statement of the property subject to the trusts of the said Will accompanied by an approximate estimate of the income and capital value of each item

9 that the official solicitor as such Judicial Trustee is to receive such remuneration as may be directed from time to time by the Court and that he be at liberty to act as Solicitor to the trust and be allowed as part of his remuneration all proper costs in respect of professional work done by him as such solicitor as though he were not a Trustee

10 that there be taxed on the indemnity the costs of the plaintiff and of the defendants other than defendant of and incidental to the said application

11 that such costs when taxed be paid by the official solicitor out of any moneys subject to the trusts of the said Will and Codicils out of the estate of the deceased in a due course of administration.

The First Schedule
(Freehold and Leasehold Property)

The Second Schedule
(Securities standing in the Books of the Bank of England ...)

The Third Schedule
(Other Securities)

The Fourth Schedule
(Things in Action)

(2) Individual

AND the Judicial Trustee hereinafter appointed having given security to the satisfaction of the Court

THE COURT APPOINTS ... [upon first giving security] to be sole Judicial Trustee [without giving security] of the Will and Codicil of the above named deceased in substitution for the ... defendant the existing Trustee/to complete the administration of the estate of the above named deceased in substitution for the ... defendant the existing Administrator

IT IS ORDERED

1 that the said Judicial Trustee shall on or before ... give security in the sum of £ ... to the satisfaction of the Court

2 that the freehold and leasehold property specified in the first schedule hereto and all other (if any) the freehold and leasehold property now subject to the trusts of the said Will vested in the ... defendant as such Administrator vest in the said Judicial Trustee for all the estate and interest therein now vested in ... to be held by the said Judicial Trustee upon the trusts of the said Will/arising on the intestacy of the deceased

3 pursuant to the Trustee Act 1925 that the right to transfer (a) the securities specified in the ... schedule hereto standing in the books of the Bank ... in the names and by the descriptions specified in the said ... schedule and (b) the securities specified in the ... schedule hereto standing in the names of ... (and to receive any interest or dividends now due and to accrue due thereon) vest in the said Judicial Trustee

4 that the said Judicial Trustee shall transfer the said securities into his own name to be held upon the said trusts

5 that the right to sue for and to recover any thing in action subject to the said trusts (and in particular the things in action specified in the ... schedule hereto) or any interest in respect thereof vest in the said Judicial Trustee to be held by him upon the said trusts

6 that the defendant do forthwith after service of this Order deliver up to the said Judicial Trustee (a) the Grant of Letters of Administration of the estate of the said deceased/Probate of the Will and Codicil of the deceased and (b) (upon oath if required) all securities and other property in ... hands subject to the said trusts together with all deeds books (including bankers' pass books) and documents relating thereto and do forthwith after service of the Order deliver up to the said Judicial Trustee any sums in ... hands or under ... control subject to the said trusts

7 that the said Judicial Trustee do forthwith open a banking account with ... Bank plc at their branch at ... in ... name as Judicial Trustee and do pay into such account all payments received on behalf of the trust and do deposit at such branch all title deeds certificates and other documents which are evidence of the title to property subject to the said trusts

8 that the remuneration of the said Judicial Trustee is to be fixed by reference to the scales or rates of professional charges of ... provided that such remuneration shall not in any year of account exceed 15 per cent of the capital value of the trust property

9 pursuant to Rule 12(5) of the Judicial Trustee Rules 1983 that the said Judicial Trustee shall send copies of his accounts/ summaries of his accounts to each of the following persons that is to say to each of the persons named in the fifth schedule hereto

10 pursuant to Rule 13(2) of the Judicial Trustee Rules 1983 that the said Judicial Trustee shall submit its accounts for examination to each of the following persons that is to say to each of the persons named in the fifth schedule hereto

11 that there be taxed on the indemnity basis the costs of the plaintiff and of the defendant other than ... defendant of and incidental to the said application

12 that such costs when taxed be paid out of the moneys subject to the trusts of the said Will and Codicil out of the estate of the deceased in a due course of administration.

The First Schedule
(Freehold and Leasehold Property)

The Second Schedule
(Securities standing in the Books of the Bank of England)

The Third Schedule
(Other Securities)

The Fourth Schedule
(Things in action)

The Fifth Schedule
(Persons to receive copies of Accounts)

Notes

1 This is a composite form giving all the directions which may be required. Those not required should be deleted.

2 Where a judicial trustee is not an official of the court the court may require him to give security (Judicial Trustee Rules 1983, r 6). If he is not required to give security the order should read 'without giving security'. If he is to give security before his appointment is effective it is better for the order to recite that he has given it. The court may permit the judicial trustee to act before his security is completed (r 6). Security is given by bond or by undertaking where the sum required is small; the bond or undertaking must be filed (r 6).

3 Where an individual is appointed accounts are required and directions should be given in the order specifying the persons on whom the accounts should be served (r 12(5)).

4 If a professional person, ie a solicitor or an accountant, is appointed he should be given power to charge all proper costs in respect of professional work done by him as though he were not a trustee.

5 Where a corporate trustee is appointed a judicial trustee r 13 applies to service and examination of accounts. The remuneration of a corporate trustee should be fixed in the order and set out in a schedule to the order.

7. TRUSTEES

(1) New trustee

AND the Court proceeding in accordance with section 59 of the Trustee Act 1925 in relation to the ... defendant

AND ... (a solicitor) the new Trustee/one of the new Trustees hereinafter named undertaking that in the event of his becoming hereafter at any time the sole Trustee he will forthwith take steps for the appointment of a new and independent Trustee to act with him.

THE COURT APPOINTS ... a new Trustee of the Will/Settlement described in the first schedule hereto in place of ... and in addition to ... the continuing Trustee.

AND IT IS ORDERED

1 that the land specified in the second schedule hereto and all other land now subject to the trusts of the said Will/Settlement vest in the new Trustee jointly with the continuing Trustee for the estate therein now vested in the continuing Trustee and ... to be held by them upon the trusts of the said Will/Settlement

2 pursuant to the Trustee Act 1925 that the right to transfer
    (a) the securities specified in the ... schedule hereto standing in the books of the Bank of England in the names and by the descriptions specified in the ... schedule hereto
    (b) the securities specified in the ... schedule hereto standing in the names of ... (and to receive any interest or dividends now due and to accrue thereon) vest in the new Trustee and the continuing Trustee.

3 that the new Trustee and the continuing Trustee shall transfer the said securities respectively into their own names to be held by them upon the said trusts.

4 that the right to sue for and recover anything in action subject to the said trusts (and in particular the things in action specified in the ... schedule hereto) or any interest in respect thereof vest in the new Trustee and the continuing Trustee to be held by them upon the said trusts.

5 that there be taxed if not agreed
    (a) the costs of and incidental to the said application of the ... plaintiff ... defendant as Trustees and
    (b) on the common fund basis the costs of and incidental to the said application of the ... plaintiff/defendant.

6 that all the said costs when taxed or agreed be paid out of the funds subject to the said trusts.

The First Schedule
The Will and ... Codicils of ... Probate whereof was granted on ... to ... A Settlement dated ... and made between ... (1) and ... (2).

The Second Schedule
(Freehold and Leasehold Property)

The Third Schedule
(Securities standing in the books of the Bank of England)

The Fourth Schedule
(Other Securities)

... Ordinary Shares of ... each in ...
Units in ... Unit Trusts

The Fifth Schedule
(Things in Action)

Notes

1 The recital relating to s 59 Trustee Act 1925 should only be inserted where a trustee cannot be found and relief against him is only sought in his capacity as trustee. The court will indicate that it is proceeding under this section.

2 The undertaking should be included only if directed.

3 The court usually requires an affidavit of fitness of a new trustee and his written consent to act in accordance with Ord 38, r 11.

4 The order should be entitled 'In the Matter of the Estate of AB deceased'.

(2) Custodian and managing trustees

THE COURT APPOINTS (1) ... Managing Trustees of the trusts of ... and (2) ... Bank plc (hereinafter called the Bank) Custodian Trustees of the said trusts.

AND IT IS ORDERED that the Bank may charge and retain or pay out of the trust property fees not exceeding the fees from time to time chargeable by the Public Trustee as Custodian Trustee.

Notes

1 See s 4 of the Public Trustee Act 1906.

2 See Atkin, Vol 41 (1979 Issue) p 35-37.

(3) Removal of custodian trustee

IT IS ORDERED

1 that the custodian Trusteeship of [the Plaintiff] [the Defendant] be terminated.

TRUSTS: GENERAL 513

2 that the land specified in the first schedule hereto and all other the land now subject to the trusts of the said Will/Settlement vest in ... (hereinafter called the [managing] [ordinary] Trustees) for the estate therein now vested in [the custodian Trustee] to be held by them upon the trusts of the said Will/Settlement.

3 pursuant to the Trustee Act 1925 that the right to transfer.
   (a) the securities specified in the second Schedule hereto standing in the books of the Bank of England in the names and by the descriptions specified in the said Schedule.
   (b) the securities specified in the third Schedule hereto standing in the names of ... (and to receive any interest or dividends now due and to accrue thereon) vest in the [managing] [ordinary] Trustees.

4 that the [managing] [ordinary] Trustees do transfer the said securities respectively into their own names to be held by them upon the said trusts.

5 that the right to sue for and recover any thing in action subject to the said trusts (and in particular the things in action specified in the fourth Schedule hereto) or any interest in respect thereof vest in the [managing] [ordinary] Trustees to be held by them upon the said trusts.

6 that there be taxed if not agreed
   (a) the costs of and incidental to the said application of the [managing] [ordinary] Trustees.
   (b) on the common fund basis the costs of and incidental to the said application of the ... plaintiff/defendant that all the said costs when taxed or agreed be paid out of the funds subject to the said trusts.

The First Schedule
(Set out land subject to trusts)

The Second Schedule
(Set out stock standing in books of the Bank of England)

The Third Schedule
(Other securities)

The Fourth Schedule
(Things in actions)

Notes

1 Custodian Trustees are removed under s 5(2)(i) of the Public Trustee Act 1906, and a master may make such an order.

2   The Act applies both to the Public Trustee and a trust corporation such as a bank or insurance company who are entitled to act as custodian trustees.

3   On appointment, trust property is transferred to the custodian trustee as if such trustee were sole trustee. Accordingly, on the termination of a custodian trustee's appointment it may be necessary to include orders vesting the trust property in the managing or continuing trustees or in new trustees.

(4) Trustees of shares

THE COURT APPOINTS ... trustees of the 100 fully paid shares of ten pounds each numbered ... to ... (incl) in the capital of ... plc in substitution for ...

(5) Appointment of trustees of United Kingdom assets

THE COURT APPOINTS ... trustee of the shares of ... (a person of foreign domicil at present resident in England) in ... so far as represented by assets in the United Kingdom in the substitution for ...

8.   ORDER APPROVING OF SALE OF TRUST PROPERTY TO TRUSTEE

THE COURT APPROVES the conditional Contract described in the First Schedule hereto

AND IT IS ORDERED

1   that the Trustees of the Will and Codicil.../the Settlement dated ... and made between ... (1) and ... (2) be at liberty to carry the said Contract into effect notwithstanding that the purchaser thereunder is a Trustee

2   that there be taxed if not agreed
    (a) the costs of and incidental to the said application of the plaintiffs as Trustees and
    (b) on the common fund basis the costs of and incidental to the said application of the ... defendant

3   that all the said costs be raised retained and paid out of the funds subject to the trusts of the said Will/Settlement

[3   that the ... defendant shall pay to the plaintiffs and the other defendant respectively their said costs when taxed]

The Schedule
A conditional Contract made ... between ... (1) and ... (2) for the sale to ... of the ... hold property known as ...

Note

1 These applications are made under Ord 85 r 2(3)(*d*) and the form is in Atkin, Vol 41 (1979 Issue) p 217.

9. ORDER AUTHORISING TRANSACTION (TRUSTEE ACT 1925, s 57)

IT IS ORDERED

1 pursuant to Section 57 of the Trustee Act 1925 that the plaintiffs the Trustees of the Will and Codicil of .../of the Settlement dated ... between ... (1) and ... (2) be at liberty to ...

2 that there be taxed if not agreed
   (a) the costs of and incidental to the said application of the plaintiffs as Trustees
   (b) on the indemnity basis the costs of and incidental to the said application of the defendant

3 that all the said costs be raised retained and paid out of the funds subject to the trusts of the said Will and Codicil/Settlement.

Notes

1 By s 57 of the Trustee Act 1925 and s 64 of the Settled Land Act 1925 trustees may obtain the leave of the court to carry out certain transactions not authorised by the trust instrument.

2 Masters may make orders authorising trustees to acquire property not authorised by the trust instrument (Practice Direction (Chancery: Masters' Powers) [1957] 1 WLR 129). In all other cases the application is heard by a judge usually in the chambers on a Monday morning.

10. ORDER GRANTING RELIEF FROM LIABILITY (TRUSTEE ACT 1925, s 61)

IT IS ORDERED

1 pursuant to Section 61 of the Trustee Act 1925 that the plaintiffs the Trustees of the Will and Codicils of .../of the Settlement

dated ... and made between ... of the one part ... of the other part be wholly relieved if and so far as necessary from any personal liability of theirs by reason of ...

2 that there be taxed if not agreed
   (a) on the indemnity basis the costs of and incidental to the said Application of the plaintiffs as Trustees and
   (b) the costs of and incidental to the said Application of the defendants

3 that all the said costs be raised retained and paid out of the funds subject to the trusts of the said Will and Codicils Settlement.

11. VESTING ORDER (TRUSTEE UNDER DISABILITY)

AND the Court proceeding in accordance with Section 59 of the Trustee Act 1925 in relation to the ... defendant

IT IS ORDERED

1 pursuant to the Trustee Act 1925 that the right to transfer
   (a) the securities specified in the ... Schedule hereto standing in the books of the Bank of England in the names and by the descriptions specified in the ... schedule hereto
   (b) the securities specified in the ... schedule hereto standing in the names of ... (and to receive any interest or dividends now due to accrue thereon) vest in ... (hereinafter called the Trustees)

2 that the Trustees shall transfer the said securities respectively into their own names to be held by them upon the trusts of the Will and ... Codicils of ... Probate whereof was granted on ... to .../the Settlement made ... between ... (1) and ... (2)

3 that there be taxed if not agreed
   (a) on the indemnity basis the costs of and incidental to the said Application of the Trustees and ...
   (b) the costs of and incidental to the said application of the ... defendant

4 that all the said costs when taxed or agreed be paid out of the funds subject to the said trusts

The First Schedule
(Securities standing in the Books of the Bank of England)

The Second Schedule
(Other securities)

... Ordinary Shares of ... each in ... Units in ... Unit Trust.

Notes

1 Where a trustee is unfit to act or is incapable of acting then a new trustee can be appointed in his place under s 36 of the Trustee Act 1925. This is done out of court. Section 40 provides that where a new trustee is appointed in this way then the property subject to the trust vests in the new trustee together with the continuing trustees 'without any conveyance or assignment'. However, s 40(4) says that this does not extend to the three cases there mentioned (land conveyed by way of mortgage, land held under certain leases, and stocks and shares). It follows that where there are stocks and shares or land conveyed by way of mortgage subject to the trusts it will be necessary to apply to the court for a vesting order even though the new trustee has been appointed out of court.

2 Any mentally disordered person who is a trustee must be made a defendant, but he will not be served unless he is a sole trustee or has a beneficial interest. (Practice Direction [1948] WN 273). The proposed new trustee should not be a guardian *ad litem* of the mentally disordered person.

3 The master is authorised to make such an order (Practice Direction (Chancery: Masters' Powers) [1975] 1 All ER 255).

12. VESTING ORDER (TENANT FOR LIFE)

THE COURT APPOINTS ... of ... a new trustee of the Will and Codicil of ... and of the Settlement thereby created for the purpose of the Settled Land Act 1925 in substitution for ... and in addition to ... the continuing trustees

AND IT IS ORDERED ... [pursuant to Section 12 of the Settled Land Act 1925 that the land specified in the ... Schedule hereto subject to the Settlement constituted by the said Will and Codicil do vest in ... for all the estate and interest of ... at the time of his death]

AND IT IS DECLARED

1 [that the said land is vested in ... upon the trusts declared concerning the same by the Will and Codicil of ... Probate of whose said Will and Codicil was on ... granted to ... or upon

such other trusts as the same ought to be held from time to time]

2   that ... are the Trustees of the Settlement for the purposes of the Settled Land Act 1925

3   that no person is nominated by the said Will or Codicil for the purpose of appointing a new Trustee or new Trustee of the said Settlement

The Schedule

Notes

1   For forms see Atkin, Vol 41 (1979 Issue) beginning at p 234.

2   The land is vested in the tenant for life while the securities are vested in the trustees. Section 5 of the Settled Land Act 1925 requires every vesting deed of the settled land to include a description of the settled property, the names of the trustees and other details specified in the sections.

13. VESTING ORDERS (SPECIAL FORMS)

(1) Vesting the benefit of mortgages by demise

(a) that the right to sue for and recover the moneys secured by the Mortgages described in the schedule hereto and any interest in respect thereof vest in ... as ... [such Judicial Trustee as aforesaid]

(b) that the terms of years in the land comprised in the said Mortgages respectively and the terms of years in the land if any which has become subject to the said Mortgages or in so much of the land as now remains subject thereto vest in ... for the estate therein now vested in ... but subject to any equity of redemption subsisting therein respectively under said Mortgages.

(2) Vesting the benefit of a Legal Charge

that the interest created by the Legal Charge described in the Schedule hereto and all powers and remedies in respect thereof shall vest in ... for all the estate or interest therein or right thereto which was vested in the said ... immediately before his death but subject to any equity of redemption subsisting thereunder.

(3) Moneys secured by Equitable Charge

(a) that the right to sue for and recover the moneys secured by the Equitable Charge described in the schedule hereto and any interest in respect thereof shall vest in ...

(b) that the said Equitable Charge shall vest in ... for the interest therein now vested in ...

(4) Rent charges

that the rent charges described in the Schedule hereto vest in ... for all the estate and interest therein which was vested in ... immediately before his death to be held by ... as such (Custodian) Trustee.

The Schedule
Part 1

Rent Charges conveyed by a Conveyance made ... between ... (1) and ... (2)

Short Description of property out of which the Rent Charges Issue	Amount of Yearly Rent Charge
	...

...

(5) Redemption moneys

Sometimes stocks have been redeemed and the Bank of England or other body is holding the redemption moneys. The right to sue for and recover these is a 'thing in action' and the redemption moneys can be included in a Schedule of things in action, eg, the redemption moneys payable in respect of the sum of ... formerly standing in the names of ...

(6) Books of the post office

(a) that the right to transfer the Security specified in the Schedule hereto standing in the Books of the Post Office (Savings Certificate Division) in the names of ... and to receive any interest now due and to accrue due thereon vest in ...

The Schedule
... Holder's registered number ...

(b) that the right to transfer the securities specified in the Schedule hereto standing in the Post Office Register number ... in the name of ... and noted as deceased under Registered number ... and to receive any interest now due and to accrue thereon vest in ... as such [Judicial] Trustee.

The Schedule
... Register number ...

(7) Settled Land

pursuant to Section 36(3) of the Settled Land Act 1925 that the land described in the Schedule hereto vest in ... as such trustees as aforesaid for all the estate therein immediately prior hereto vested in ... to be held by them upon the statutory trusts.

(8) Scotland

that the plaintiffs as such Trustees as aforesaid are to be at liberty to take all steps that may be necessary to obtain a vesting order in Scotland relating to the securities specified in the Schedule hereto.

14. VARIOUS TRUSTEE ORDERS

(1) Securities partly paid up

that the [Official Solicitor] shall sell the securities mentioned in the ... Part of the ... Schedule hereto and hold the proceeds of sale thereof upon the trusts of the said Will/Settlement or retain the said securities until they are fully paid up and in the event of the said securities being fully paid up transfer them into his name as aforesaid to be held upon the said trusts.

(2) Funds in court

that the funds in Court be dealt with as directed in the Payment Schedule hereto the funds thereby directed to be transferred into the name of [the Official Solicitor] to be held upon the trusts of the said Will/Settlement.

(3) Security

AND the Judicial Trustee hereinafter appointed [having given security] to the satisfaction of the Court ...
    THE COURT APPOINTS ... [upon first giving security] to be Judicial Trustee ...

(4) Statement of property

that [the Defendant] shall on or before ... or subsequently within 4 days after service of this Order leave at Chancery Chambers Room 165 The Royal Courts of Justice Strand London WC2A 2LL a complete statement of the property subject to the trusts of the said Will accompanied by an approximate estimate of the income and capital value of each item.

(5) Bank account—deposit of documents

that ... shall forthwith open a separate account in their joint names as such Judicial Trustees at the ... branch of ... Bank plc and do forthwith deposit at the said branch all documents of title and other documents in their possession relating to the trusts of the said Will and not required by them for the purpose of the administration of the trusts of the said Will.

(6) Remuneration

that the Public Trustee as such Judicial Trustee is to receive by way of remuneration such fees whether by way of percentage or otherwise as are appropriate to be charged by the Public Trustee under Section 9 of the Public Trustee Act 1906 as amended by the Public Trustee (Fees) Act 1957

that the said Judicial Trustee be allowed on the examination of his accounts remuneration fixed by reference to the scales or rates of professional charges of the ... provided that such remuneration does not in any year of account exceed 15 per cent of the capital value of the trust property

that ... Bank plc be at liberty until they shall cease to be Trustees of the said Will to charge for their services as such Trustees as aforesaid the fees set forth in the Schedule hereto and to retain the said fees at the times and out of the funds in the said Schedule also specified

[The Schedule might be a reproduction of or a print of the Bank's current scale of charges].

(7) Appointment of Managing and Custodian Trustees—remuneration

THE COURT APPOINTS (1) ... Managing Trustees of the trusts of ... and (2) ... Bank plc (hereinafter called the Bank) Custodian Trustee of the said trusts

AND IT IS ORDERED that the Bank may charge and retain or pay out of the trust property fees not exceeding the fees from time to time chargeable by the Public Trustee as Custodian Trustee.

(8) Liberty to apply for revocation of grant

that the Official Solicitor as such Judicial Trustee be at liberty to take such steps as may be necessary to obtain the revocation of the Probate of the alleged Will of ... granted on ... to ...

(9) Appointment of Trustees of shares

THE COURT APPOINTS ... Trustees of the 100 fully paid shares of Ten pounds each numbered ... to ... (inclusive) in the capital of ... plc in substitution for ...

(10) Trustee of United Kingdom assets

THE COURT APPOINTS ... Trustee of the shares of ... (a person of Iraqi domicil at present resident in England) in ... so far as represented by assets in the United Kingdom in substitution for ...

(11) Adjournment into Chambers for appointment

that the said originating Summons be adjourned into Chambers for the purpose of the appointment of new trustees.

Notes

1 The question of security normally only arises where there is a Judicial Trustee who is not an official of the court. See r 6 of the Judicial Trustee Rules 1983. The Trustee's appointment may or may not be effective before he gives security—the draftsman must know what is intended.

2 The Public Trustee is in a category of his own. See the Public Trustee Act 1906 etc in SCP, Part II starting at para 4946, p 1537. Rule 11 of the Judicial Trustee Rules 1983 deals with the remuneration of Judicial Trustees (but not other Trustees).

3 The trustees here are not Judicial Trustees. As to Managing and Custodian Trustees see s 4 of the Public Trustee Act 1906.

15. VARIATION OF TRUSTS

AND the solicitors for the plaintiffs by Counsel for the plaintiffs being their Counsel for this purpose undertaking that they will within 30 days after the entry of this Order submit the duplicate thereof to the Commissioners of Inland Revenue for adjudication of the stamp duty (if any) payable thereon

[THE COURT APPOINTS the ... defendant to represent for the purpose of the said application]

AND the plaintiffs and defendants by their Counsel assenting to the Arrangement set forth in the schedule hereto

THE COURT in pursuance of the provisions of the Variation of Trusts Act 1958 APPROVES the said Arrangement on behalf of ...

AND IT IS ORDERED

1 that the Trustees of the Will dated .../Settlement dated ... in the said Arrangement mentioned shall cause a Memorandum of this Order to be endorsed on the probate of the said Will/ Settlement

2 that there be taxed
   (1) on the indemnity basis the costs of and incidental to the said application of the plaintiffs .../... defendants as Trustees and
   (2) the costs of and incidental to the said application of the plaintiffs .../... defendants

3 that the Taxing Master is to include in all such costs the costs of and incidental to the preparation and negotiation of the said Arrangement

4 that all the said costs be raised retained and paid out of the funds subject to the trusts of the said Will/Settlement [out of the estate of ...] in a due course of administration

The Schedule

The Arrangement

Notes

1 The Variation of Trusts Act 1958 gives the court jurisdiction to approve on behalf of minors, patients or unborn persons any arrangement varying an existing trust.

2 A copy of the arrangement should be supplied for the use of the associate in court.

3 The undertaking from the solicitors is required by the court. The court informs the Commissioners of Inland Revenue of the making of the order and of the undertaking to submit it for adjudication. Upon adjudication the commissioners inform the court of the amount of stamp duty if any paid. The commissioners' letter goes on the court file.

4 Masters may make these orders to the extent only of removing protective trusts where the interest of the principal beneficiary has not failed or determined (Practice Direction (Chancery Master's Powers) [1957] 1 ALL ER 255 para 3(i)).

5 The court does not always appoint someone to represent absent parties. If it does, it will usually be clear from the minutes or the originating summons who is to be represented.

6 The adult beneficiaries are stated to 'assent' but not the trustees. The originating summons will usually make it clear who the trustees are. However the minutes should be followed. The word 'assenting' rather than 'consenting' is used because this is the word used in the Act.

7 'APPROVES ... on behalf of ...'. The originating summons or minutes will normally make it clear how this is to be completed.

Chapter Twenty

Wills and Succession

1. Contentious probate

The term 'probate' is applied both to the act of proving a will and to the document issued by the probate registry in evidence that the will has been proved and that the executor is entitled to possess and administer the testator's estate.

An application for probate may be made to the principal probate registry or to one of the district probate registries of the family division of the High Court by presenting the will together with an oath testifying (*inter alia*) that the document is 'the last will and testament' of the testator and that the applicant(s) is/are the executor(s) therein named. The registrar checks that the will is duly executed and attested and contains no unauthenticated deletions or alterations and that the names therein correspond to those in the oath but, with rare exceptions, he is not otherwise concerned with its contents or with the testamentary capacity of the testator. Probate so obtained is called 'probate in common form' as distinguished from 'probate in solemn form' which is granted only after proceedings in the Chancery Division have established that the will is valid and that the applicant is entitled to the grant.

Any person who claims an interest in the estate and disputes the validity of the will on the ground, for example, that the testator was not of sound mind or acted under undue influence, may enter a caveat at the principal probate registry or at one of the district registries from which a copy will be transmitted to the principal registry. Its purpose is to ensure that any application for probate will be notified to the caveator in the form of a warning issued from the principal registry and requiring him to 'enter an appearance' there. Unless the caveator then withdraws his caveat, the applicant, if he wishes to propound the will, must institute an action for probate in solemn form by writ of summons in the Chancery Division.

Where no caveat has been entered, a person named as executor may nevertheless take proceedings on his own motion for probate in solemn form if he has reason to doubt the validity of the will or if, to his knowledge, its validity is questioned by any person claiming an interest in the estate. Conversely, a claimant who has omitted to enter a caveat, and so has allowed a grant to be obtained in common form, is not debarred from suing for revocation of that grant. The court has jurisdiction to revoke a grant of probate or letters of administration whenever it is found that the grantee was not, or has ceased to be, entitled thereto, though it may be questioned whether a costly action is justified if the end is merely to replace one administrator by another without affecting the rights of the beneficiaries.

Any action brought in the Chancery Division to determine the validity of a will or the title of any person who has obtained, or seeks to obtain, a grant of representation, falls within the class of litigation known as contentious probate. Recently that class has been extended by virtue of s 20 of the Administration of Justice Act 1982 to include applications for the rectification of a will. Such an application, though not strictly a probate action, may be made by way of counterclaim to an action for probate in solemn form. Alternatively, it may form the subject of a separate action either before or after a grant of probate.

Short probate list

This is taken after chambers summonses. It is used for the grant of probate in solemn form either in default of pleadings or by way of compromise.

On the summons for directions or on a special summons the master will order trial on affidavit evidence; order that an affidavit by one of the attesting witnesses be filed if not already done; order an affidavit in support of an order pronouncing against the last will (if required); or order trial before judge alone in Short Probate List on a Monday fixed by him.

When the action is compromised and there are persons under a disability it is usual for the summons for the compromise to be heard by the judge in chambers prior to the hearing in court; the judge will then hear the action in open court.

Statutes

Administration of Justice Act 1970, s 1(4); Supreme Court Act 1981, Sched 1, para 1(g); Administration of Justice Act 1982, s 20.

Order

Order 76, r 1 et seq.

Parties

On an application for a grant of probate in solemn form, the plaintiff will be the executor and the defendants will be any persons claiming an interest in the estate who may be disposed to contest the validity of the will. Thus caveators at least should be made defendants.

On an application for revocation of a grant, the grantee, unless himself the plaintiff, must be named as defendant and the plaintiff will usually claim as executor of another will or as the person entitled to a grant upon an alleged intestacy.

On an application for a declaration or for rectification of a will, plaintiff and defendant will be executor and beneficiary respectively or vice versa as circumstances require.

Intitulement

Chancery Division (Probate) 'In the Estate of AB deceased'.

The objective of the plaintiff

To obtain grant of probate (or letters of administration with the will annexed) in solemn form or revocation of a grant of representation and a grant in substitution therefor or a decree pronouncing for or against validity or rectification.

Originating process

Writ of summons indorsed with a statement of the parties' respective interests in the deceased's estate.

Leave to issue the writ is required and for that purpose the plaintiff must obtain in room 307/308 a provisional assignment of the case to one of the three divisions (distinguished alphabetically) of Chancery chambers and to one of the two masters in that 'division'. The plaintiff will then make an *ex parte* application to the master by leaving the unissued writ in room 307/308 with three copies. If leave is granted, the master will indorse the top copy which is to be stamped and to form the court record. Two other copies will be retained by the court on issue.

Provided the writ is formally correct, leave is rarely refused unless the plaintiff's method or purpose is seen to be an abuse of the court's jurisdiction (*Re Langton* [1964] P 163).

Sequence

Except as mentioned below, the action will be conducted in accordance with the rules of procedure common to Chancery actions commenced by writ of summons. Within those rules, differences may occur as a matter of practice. Pleadings, for example, may include a more detailed narration of family history than would be appropriate to other causes.

(1) Having obtained leave, the plaintiff will issue the writ and of the three copies one will be sent by the court to the principal probate registry of the Family Division, another retained in the Secretariat of the Chancery Division and the third issued to the plaintiff as his copy of the original. The copy served

on the defendant, or on each defendant, if more than one, must be accompanied by a form of acknowledgment of service.
(2) Unless the court otherwise directs, the plaintiff and every defendant who has acknowledged service of the writ must swear an affidavit ('affidavit of scripts') describing any will, codicil or testamentary document of which he has knowledge (including any draft of, or written instructions for, a will or any document bearing evidence of a missing will) and stating whether it is in his possession or if not, the name and address of the person having possession or control of it or, if such be the case, that he has no knowledge of its whereabouts or no knowledge of any such document. A defendant's affidavit should be filed in Chancery chambers (room 307/308) within 14 days after he has acknowledged service of the writ and a plaintiff's affidavit assuming that at least one defendant has acknowledged service within the same period. If no defendant acknowledges service, the plaintiff's affidavit must be filed before the action is set down for trial. A copy must be supplied of any script written wholly or partly in pencil, with the words which are pencilled in the original underlined in red ink in the copy. Except with the leave of the court, no party will be allowed to inspect another party's affidavit of scripts until he has himself filed an affidavit. All scripts are retained in Chancery chambers pending the hearing of the action. If the action is set down in a district registry, the plaintiff's solicitors must notify the master's secretary in writing so that the scripts will be forwarded (Practice Direction (Probate: Contentious Actions) [1974] 1 WLR 1349).
(3) A statement of claim, if not indorsed on the writ, must, unless the court otherwise directs, be served on every defendant who has acknowledged service of the writ within six weeks after his acknowledgment or eight days after his filing an affidavit of scripts, whichever is the later (Ord 76, r 7). This envisages a considerable divergence by a defendant from r 5(2) which requires him to file an affidavit of scripts within 14 days after acknowledging service.
(4) A defendant who alleges any opposing claim or entitlement must add a counterclaim to his defence. Any party may apply by summons within seven days of service for the counterclaim to be struck out or for a separate trial (Ord 15, r 5(2)).

Default proceedings

The usual procedure for judgment by default under Ords 13 and 19 does not apply to probate actions. If any defendant fails to acknowledge service of the writ the plaintiff may file in room 307/308 an affidavit of service and lodge (if none has been indorsed on the writ) in room 307/308 a statement of claim. The action will then proceed in the absence of the defaulter and the plaintiff may apply by summons for an order for trial. The master will then adjourn into court in the list marked 'short probate list'.

If the plaintiff fails to serve a statement of claim within the prescribed time, any defendant may apply by summons for the action to be discontinued or dismissed; alternatively, he may apply for leave to serve a counterclaim and the action will proceed as if the counterclaim were the statement of claim.

When a trial is ordered in default of acknowledgment of service or pleadings, the court may direct that evidence be taken by affidavit. In such case, if a grant of probate is sought, one of the witnesses to the will must swear an affidavit of due execution, and if the will has been deposited in Chancery chambers, the plaintiff's solicitor must bespeak a photocopy which will be certified as authentic by the clerk in charge and exhibited to the affidavit (Practice Direction (Probate: Contentious Actions) [1974] 1 WLR 1349).

Revocation of grant

Any person claiming entitlement to a grant of probate or letters of administration in place of an existing grant must be made a party to the action for revocation. If the existing grant is in the possession of the plaintiff, he must lodge it in Chancery chambers within seven days of the issue of the writ; if in the possession of a defendant, it must be lodged within 14 days after the writ has been served on him. Any person who fails to observe these directions may be ordered by the court to do so within a specified time and until he obeys will be unable, without the leave of the court, to take any part in the action (Ord 76, r 4(2)).

Additionally, Ord 76, r 13 (previously r 14) provides for the exercise of powers derived from s 26 of the Court of Probate Act 1857, and s 23 of the Court of Probate Act 1858. Under the former any person in possession of a will or other testamentary paper may be ordered to bring it into Chancery chambers or to attend the court for cross-examination. Under the latter the principal probate registrar is authorised to compel the production of such documents by the issue of a subpoena and the same process is available to any party to a probate action by *ex parte* application to the master. (*Note:* in the schedule to RSC (Amendment No 2) 1982 there are directions that for 's 26 of the Court of Probate Act, 1857' there shall be substituted 's 122 of the Act' and for 's 23 of the Court of Probate Act, 1858' there shall be substituted 's 123 of the Act'. There is no guidance as to what is 'the Act' referred to.)

Administration pendente lite

At any stage of a probate action application may be made by any of the parties for the appointment of an administrator *pendente lite*. The application is made by summons returnable before the master.

Two clear days before the hearing the applicant should lodge in chambers (room 307/308): (*a*) an affidavit setting out the reasons for the application, the names, address and qualification of the proposed administrator and the value of the property which is expected to come into his hands, (*b*) the written consent of the proposed administrator and (*c*) an affidavit of his fitness.

In making the order the master will set the amount of the security to be given by the administrator and will give directions as to the accounts to be rendered by him and as to his remuneration. Upon his appointment the administrator will apply to the principal probate registry for a grant of letters of administration which he should produce in Chancery chambers (room 307/308) as soon as it is issued. The grant may be limited to a specific part of the estate, but even if it is in general form, the administrator cannot distribute the residuary estate or pay any legacy or annuity given by the disputed will without the consent of all persons interested in the residue.

At the conclusion of the action, and unless all parties have agreed to dispense with formal accounts, the administrator will bring in his final account to be passed by the accounts section (room 415/416) and may issue a summons for taxation of costs and vacation of his security.

Compromise

If at any stage of the action the parties agree a compromise, the plaintiff should issue a summons for judgment, supported by affidavit and accompanied by a minute of the proposed order (Ord 76, r 12). The master will adjourn the summons to the judge in chambers for approval of the compromise, but the judgment for carrying into effect the terms which may include an order for probate in solemn form or a declaration for or against a will, must be made in court and for that purpose the action will be set down for hearing in the short probate list (Practice Direction [1972] 1 WLR 1215).

The court is empowered to approve the compromise on behalf of a minor or other party under a disability and may order that the judgment shall be binding upon persons not parties to the action (Ord 44 as substituted by r 53 of the RSC (Amendment No 2) 1982).

Discontinuance and dismissal

Application for the discontinuance or dismissal of an action may be made by the plaintiff or by any defendant who has acknowledged service of the writ. The rules contained in Ord 21 do not apply to probate actions and the leave of the court must be obtained. Application may be made by motion or summons as may be considered appropriate. Where made by summons, and if all the parties are *sui juris*, the master may make the order applied for on such terms as to costs as he thinks fit. The order may direct a grant of probate or letters of administration to the person entitled who may then apply to the probate registry of the Family Division by the usual non-contentious process. Alternatively, the master may order a stay of proceedings in the 'Tomlin' form setting out the terms of the settlement with liberty for the parties to apply for the enforcement thereof.

Conclusion of action

At the conclusion of a probate action or an action for rectification of a will, the court will send to the principal registry of the family division: (*a*) the original will or codicil (*b*) any existing grant of probate or letters of administration, whether confirmed or revoked (*c*) any documents referred to in the order, other than affidavits filed in Chancery chambers (*d*) any documents prepared for use in the Family Division and (*e*) an office copy of the court's order.

Before sending the probate or letters of administration the court will, where appropriate, indorse thereon or annex thereto a memorandum of the confirmation, revocation or rectification (as the case may be) and the probate registry will issue any confirmed or rectified grant to the person entitled.

Hazards and pitfalls

Allegations that a testator was of unsound mind or was subjected to undue influence should be supported by substantial and factual evidence. In the matter of costs the court is unlikely to look favourably upon a party who has based such allegations on inadequate evidence.

Costs

Costs in probate actions are in the discretion of the court, but an executor who from necessity or for reasonable cause has obtained a grant of probate in solemn form is entitled to his costs out of the estate without an order.

Alternative jurisdiction

County courts have jurisdiction where the net value of the estate does not exceed £30,000.

Textbooks

R B Rowe & E Heward, *Tristram and Coote's Probate Practice*, 27th edn, (Butterworths, 1989).
Halsbury, Vol 17.
Holloway, *Probate Handbook and Supplement*, 8th edn, (Longman, 1988).

2. Family provision

Whilst the county court has jurisdiction under the Inheritance (Provision for Family and Dependants) Act 1975, where the value of the deceased's net estate does not exceed £30,000, all other cases must be brought either in the Family Division or in the Chancery Division. Where proceedings are brought in the High Court but it appears to the court that the county court would have jurisdiction, then the proceedings are likely to be transferred to a convenient divorce county court.

Statute

The Inheritance (Provision for Family and Dependants) Act 1975 makes '... fresh provision for empowering the court to make orders for the making out of the estate of a deceased person of provision for the spouse, child, child of that family or dependant of that person'.

Order

Order 99, rr 1-11 with notes in AP, Vol 1 is specific to these proceedings which are assigned in the High Court to the Chancery or Family Divisions.

Parties

The claimant (plaintiff) must be one of the class of persons named in s 1 of the 1975 Act: viz (*a*) the wife or husband of the deceased (*b*) a former wife or former husband who has not remarried, (*c*) a child of the deceased (*d*) any person who was treated by the deceased as a child of the family or (*e*) any person who was being maintained wholly or partly by the deceased immediately prior to death. Where there are two or more of such claimants they should be joined as plaintiffs in the originating summons although if their interests conflict, they should be separately represented in court or the court may order one to become a defendant.

The defendants will be the personal representatives of the deceased and any beneficiary who may be affected by the court's order.

Every person whose rights under the will might be affected should either be a party or be represented by a party appointed by order to represent him (*Re Lidington* [1940] Ch 927), but a representation order (Ord 15, r 13) applicable if a person or class of persons cannot be readily ascertained, or though ascertained, cannot be found, or if expedient to save expense, may be made, usually by the judge at the hearing.

Intitulement

'In the matter of the Will of AB deceased'.

The objective of the plaintiff

The objective of the plaintiff is to satisfy the court that, seen objectively, a reasonable position has not been made (*Goodwin v Goodwin* (1969) 1 Ch 283).

Originating process

A Chancery action is commenced by originating summons. Unless it is commenced within six months from the date of the grant of representation, the leave of the court is required and should be asked for in an additional paragraph in the summons. The general form of originating summons is used with the addition of the words: 'A defendant who is a personal representative must within 21 days after service of this summons on him, counting the day of service, lodge with the court an affidavit in answer stating the particulars required by Ord 99, r 5 of the RSC'.

On issuing the originating summons, there must be lodged at the registry an affidavit exhibiting an official copy of the grant of probate and will, or grant of administration. Customarily, the affidavit gives the means of the applicant, ie the plaintiff or plaintiffs, and so far as is known the means of those who might be entitled to contest the application. Within 21 days of service of the originating summons, and accompanying affidavit, the defendant, ie the personal representative, will file an affidavit in answer in which must be given full particulars of the estate, the person beneficially interested and the value of their interests, the names of any beneficiary who is a minor (or patient) and additionally, any fact known to the deponent which might affect the exercise of the court's powers under the Act—the latter may mean quite lengthy and contentious material being contained in this affidavit, and indeed in an affidavit in reply. Practice shows that affidavits in these cases can be lengthy, and the time within which the evidence is filed, somewhat protracted.

Sequence

(1) Upon the issue of the originating summons the plaintiff must lodge in room 156 an affidavit exhibiting an office copy of the grant of representation and setting out the facts and circumstances upon which his claim is founded. Any known previous proceedings should be set out to enable the court to consider transfer from the Chancery to the Family Division (or vice versa) and indication should be given if the application will involve the taking of complicated accounts for which special facilities exist only in the Chancery division. Facts which require investigation or concerning detailed conduct are not expected in the first affidavit (note to Ord 99, r 11 in AP, Vol 1). A copy of the affidavit should be served with the summons on all the defendants. Defendants are required to give an acknowledgment of service, and within 21 days from service the personal representative must file in room 156 the original grant of representation together with an affidavit in

which he should state to the best of his knowledge and belief: (a) full particulars of the value of the deceased's estate (b) the persons or classes beneficially interested, giving their names and addresses and the value of their respective interests and identifying any beneficiary who is a minor or under a disability and in the same affidavit or if this would cause delay in providing the facts at (a) and (b) above, in a second affidavit, (c) any facts which might affect the exercise of the court's powers. A copy of the affidavit and of any affidavit filed by any other of the defendants must be served on the plaintiff and all other parties.

(2) On the first appointment the master will hear the summons in chambers and deal with questions of evidence and consideration of the mode of trial that is whether he will himself hear the originating summons in chambers or adjourn it to the judge in chambers, or if it is likely to involve a long or complex issue of fact or law by consent to the judge in court (Ord 99, r 8 and note in AP, Vol 1).

(3) The executor may seek the beneficiaries' consent to make interim payments if the plaintiff is in immediate need of financial assistance. If the personal representative is unable or unwilling to make provision without the sanction of the court, the master has power to make an interim order for the payment of a single sum or periodical sums out of the estate (Practice Direction (Chancery: Masters' Powers) [1975] 1 WLR 405).

(4) The original grant of representation must be produced at the hearing and if an order is made the grant will be retained by the court for transmission to the principal registry of the Family Division where a memorandum of the order will be indorsed. Orders which should be endorsed include a consent order staying further proceedings and an order dismissing the plaintiff's application otherwise than by consent.

(5) When a compromise is reached which is intended to be embodied in a consent order, any persons included in a representation order should be added as individual defendants and signify their approval of the compromise; otherwise they will not be bound by the order. If all the parties are *sui juris* the master has power to sanction a compromise, but he will adjourn to the judge in chambers when the court's approval is required on behalf of a minor whose claim exceeds £30,000.

(6) An order declaring the plaintiff's entitlement under the Act is not an order for the payment of money but puts him in the position of a legatee and thus enables him to enforce payment (*Re Jennery* [1967] Ch 280).

Plaintiff's/defendant's considerations

The issue before the court is not whether the testator acted reasonably but whether the disposition of the estate as at the date of the hearing makes reasonable provision for the claimant. The test is wholly objective. But it seems that the test of what is reasonable provision differs according to whether the claimant is the testator's spouse or one of the other persons named in s 1 of the 1975 Act. A spouse is entitled to a 'fair share of the family assets'; the others are entitled (if at all) to 'reasonable maintenance'. The testator's testamentary capacity, or lack of it, is not a matter for investigation for the court in these actions (*Re Goodwin* [1969] 1 Ch 283).

Attitude of the court

This will be formulated on the basis of the factors mentioned in s 3 which together with ss 1 and 2 form the core of the 1975 Act. These factors are: the financial resources and needs of all applicants and beneficiaries currently and in the foreseeable future, the obligation and responsibilities of the deceased towards applicants and beneficiaries, the size and nature of the estate, the physical and mental disability of applicants and beneficiaries, relevant conduct and age of applicants, contributions made by them to the welfare of the family, and the duration of the marriage (s 3(1) (*a*) to (*g*) and (2) (*a*) and (*b*)).

Hazards and pitfalls

Applications under the Act cannot be made after six months from the date of the grant of representation (s 4 of the Act). Leave when required is sought in the originating summons. Guidelines as to when leave would be given are contained in *Salmon, Coard v National Westminster Bank Ltd* (1981) Ch 167, and whilst leave may be given if there is no serious detriment to the defendants, it will not be if the estate has already been distributed. Applications for leave will come before the master, who at that juncture will consider the question of whether leave should be granted only, though he will also wish to be satisfied that the plaintiff has some arguable case; such applications should be supported by affidavit evidence.

At one time these applications were heard in open court by the judge, but nowadays they are heard by the master in chambers, possibly on affidavit evidence only, though directions as to evidence and as to whether there is to be orders for cross-examination will be given by the master together with a direction as to load of trial, before the hearing. When heard in court, the evidence, if oral, will be recorded in the master's chambers. If the case is to be heard by a judge, which it still of course can be, it is adjourned to the non-witness, or the witness list parts 1 or 2. The parties may seek an order adjourning the case to a judge for hearing, if they wish to do so. Considerations as to whether the case should be heard by a judge or by the master turn largely on the question of appeal, it perhaps being simpler to appeal from the master to the judge, rather than from the judge to the Court of Appeal.

The interim order, if it is sought and made, is likely to be made by the master.

Costs

Any party who has caused the unnecessary prolongation of the action is at risk on costs. But defendants who have reasonably defended will usually obtain an order for their costs to be paid out of the estate. If a claim is dismissed the plaintiff will usually have to bear his own costs and often those of the defendants. These will be usually ordered to be retained out of any legacy to the plaintiff.

Appeals

The master will adjourn to the judge in chambers any application for the cross-examination in court of a witness who has been cross-examined at the hearing of the summons (Practice Direction (Family Provision: Application) [1978] 1 WLR 585). The party seeking the adjournment must then obtain a transcript. The master may adjourn the question to the judge in chambers if there is any application for the re-examination of a witness.

Alternative jurisdiction

Under s 1 of the Inheritance (Provision for Family and Dependants) Act 1975 as read with the County Courts Jurisdiction (Inheritance: Provision for Family and Dependants) Order 1978 (SI 1978 No 176) county courts have jurisdiction when the net value of the deceased's estate does not exceed £30,000. And see Atkin, Vol 22, p 23 et seq for several full precedents.

Textbook

Halsbury, Vol 17, paras 1320 et seq.

3. Construction of wills (deeds and other written instruments)

Statute

There are no specific statutes relating to this subject.

Orders

None specific; see Ord 85, rr 2 and 3. Order 15, r 16 provides that no action or other proceeding shall be open to objection on the ground that a merely declaratory judgment of order is sought thereby.

Parties

The plaintiff may be the executor, or any person claiming a beneficial interest under a will or claiming to be interested under a deed or instrument. Any executor, beneficiary or party to an instrument whose interests may be affected by the court's findings if not joined as a plaintiff, should be made a defendant.

Intitulement

'In the matter of the Will of AB deceased dated . . .' or 'In the matter of a Deed of   made   19   between AB and CD'.

The objective of the plaintiff

To obtain the court's declaration of the proper construction of a will or codicil or any part thereof which has given rise to uncertainty, or to construe and interpret a deed or instrument.

Originating process

Writ of summons if construction will raise issues of fact, otherwise originating summons. The supporting affidavit should state the nature of the doubts and difficulties which have arisen. If construction of a will is required this is more likely to arise within a probate action, but in whatever form the action is to proceed, an office copy of the probate should be exhibited to an affidavit and the original probate and any other document which it is intended to be put in evidence should be lodged in chambers (room 307/308) and be available for production in court. The probate will be accepted as conclusive evidence of the contents of the will. A document referred to in the will may be admissible in evidence unless the testator has expressed the intention that it should not be read as a testamentary disposition.

Sequence

The master, if satisfied that the beneficiaries or other parties are sufficiently represented and having considered the defendant's evidence (if any), will adjourn the summons into court. If no defendant wishes to file evidence or no party wishes to cross-examine, the case will be assigned to the non-witness list.

Plaintiff's/defendant's considerations

The court's purpose will be to determine the testator's intentions as expressed in the will (and codicil, if any) judged upon a total reading of the document(s), or to interpret the deed or instrument. Deeds and documents are interpreted according to maxims and authorities long established and deriving in the main from those relating to interpretation of statutes. In construing wills there is a degree to which extraneous evidence may be limited; the court will rectify any patent error or omission but with that exception, the testator's words and phrases will be accorded their ordinary meaning and extraneous evidence will not be admitted to show or suggest that he intended them to bear a different meaning. Albeit, in determining the ordinary meaning of a word regard may be had to its common usage in the class or locality to which the testator belonged (*Re Rayner* [1904] 1 Ch 176, CA).

An originating summons under the above orders is the appropriate procedure only if the construction of the will is the sole issue between the parties. It should not be adopted if the validity of the will is contested (*Lewis v Green* [1905] 2 Ch 340).

Where the cause of action is a clerical error, application may be made either for construction or for rectification, but where other issues are involved, there is no such option: a case for construction arises when the testator, while knowing and understanding the contents of the will, has expressed his intentions in words which are open to misinterpretation while a case for rectification arises when the terms of the will have failed to carry out the testator's intentions. Any difficulties which might result from this apparently fine distinction are avoided by the terms of the statute (Administration of Justice Act 1982, s 20) which provides that rectification will only be granted where the failure is due to a clerical error or to a misunderstanding of the testator's instructions. Beyond these limits the equitable doctrine of rectification is still founded upon mutual mistake. It has rarely been extended to a unilateral document and never to a will (*Harter and Slater v Harter* (1873) LR 3 P & D 11; *Collins and Tuffley v Elstone* [1893] P 1; *Re Bacharach's Will Trusts* [1959] Ch 245).

In proceedings concerning construction if a person or class cannot be found or cannot be ascertained, or if he or they can be found but expense should be saved having regard to all the circumstances, the court may appoint one or more persons to represent any such person or class who is or may be interested and any judgment or order shall be binding on the person or class so represented (Ord 15, r 13). Without a representation order (Ord 15, r 13) the declaration will not be binding on persons not parties since Ord 44 (as substituted by r 53 of RSC (Amendment No 2) 1982 (SI 1982 No 1111)) does not apply to construction cases.

Settlement and execution of deeds

The procedure for settling a deed or other document pursuant to a judgment which requires or permits it to be drafted by one of the parties was formerly regulated by Ord 44, r 8 which entailed the following sequence:

(1) Plaintiff issues summons to proceed.
(2) Upon the return of the summons the master gives directions for the preparation of the draft, the service of a copy thereof on the other party or parties, the notification of objections by such other party or parties and the adjourned hearing.
(3) At the adjourned hearing the master considers the draft and any objections thereto and either settles the draft (with or without the assistance of conveyancing counsel) or adjourns to the judge in chambers.
(4) On settlement of the draft the master gives directions for preparation of the engrossment and for its lodgment in chambers together with an affidavit confirming it as a true and correct engrossment of the draft as settled.

Rule 3(1)(c) of Ord 44 which replaces r 8 is much less explicit. It provides that where a judgment given in any cause or matter in the Chancery division contains directions which make it necessary to proceed in chambers under the judgment, the court may, when giving judgment or at any time during proceedings under the judgment, give directions for the conduct of those proceedings including, in particular, directions with respect to ... (c) the preparation and service on the parties to be bound thereby of the draft of any deed or other instrument which is directed by the judgment to be settled by the court and the service of any objections to the draft.

It would appear that a summons to proceed is no longer requisite and that where objections are raised, time may be allowed to the parties to amend the draft by agreement. The agreed draft can then be lodged in chambers for the master's approval. The parties, therefore, will not be required to attend a settlement of the draft in chambers unless they have failed to agree or the master withholds his approval of the draft as agreed.

Attitude of the court

The court will strive to avoid finding testamentary provisions too uncertain to be enforced. Evidence extraneous to the will as to the full identity of a beneficiary or an asset will be received if the will gives characteristics of either which can only refer to one definite beneficiary or asset. In according to the testator's words their ordinary meaning the court has to have regard to many complex rules upon the construction of wills and the advice of counsel is nearly always necessary for the litigant.

Costs

Unless a party has unnecessarily caused the litigation the testator is regarded as the origin of the dispute and the costs of all parties will be ordered to be borne by the estate. Those of personal representatives will be ordered to be taxed on a trustee basis and those of other parties on a common fund basis.

Alternative jurisdiction

Application to a county court for a declaration as to the construction of a will or other document can only be made as ancillary to other proceedings.

Textbook

Halsbury (3rd edn), Vol 39, paras 1438 et seq.

Forms and precedents

Atkin, Vol 41 pp 190 et seq; Forms Nos 131-133.

4. Administration actions

Order 85, r 1 defines an administration action as an action for the administration under the direction of the court of the estate of a deceased person or for the execution under the direction of the court of a trust. Without divesting the personal representatives or trustees of their powers, the court is thereby enabled to exercise a wide measure of supervision, including directions for accounts and inquiries, for publication of advertisements, attendance of witnesses, production of documents and payments of moneys into court. The purpose of the full administration action is thus to enable the winding-up of an estate to take place in the face of difficulties concerning the personal representatives, or disputes over the accounts, who are creditors and beneficiaries, or concerning distribution.

Where such problems arise the court is empowered to take over the whole of the administration. This must of necessity be very expensive and protracted and the court is invariably requested to limit its activity to those aspects needing immediate attention ensuring on the one hand that the deceased's lawful wishes are carried out and on the other that expenditure in costs is kept to a minimum. The procedure for administration by the court is designed to protect those who have had placed upon them the burden of administering an estate with all the attendant duties and obligations to beneficiaries and creditors alike for although they retain the office of personal representative or trustee so long as they make full disclosure of all relevant facts within their knowledge and carry out the directions of the court they are relieved of personal liability. Nevertheless they would not be justified in loading the estate or trust with the heavy costs of such litigation if they could attain the same end by engaging professional assistance or insuring against contingent liabilities. The rules themselves discourage an excessive involvement by the court where a more limited control would suffice and Ord 85, r 2 specifically indicates a number of orders which while falling well short of a general administration order, may meet the needs of creditors or beneficiaries aggrieved by default or delay.

An administration action is thus a remedy of last resort. Where creditors or beneficiaries are aggrieved by maladministration, misconduct or incompetence on the part of executors or administrators and revocation of the grant is possible such problems can be readily and comparatively inexpensively solved by an application for their replacement by a judicial trustee under the provisions of the Judicial Trustees Act 1896. The judicial trustees if thus appointed would carry out the administration and management of the estate. The judicial trustee displaces the original personal representative though on rare occasions the court may appoint a judicial trustee to act with some of the original personal representatives.

Statutes

The administration of an estate is governed not only by the Administration of Estates Act 1925 but by many judicial authorities. See also the Trustee Act 1925, s 68(17).

Orders

The power of the High Court to make a full administration order is part of its inherent jurisdiction and the intention of Ord 85 is to assist its inherent power. Order 44 (as substituted by RSC (Amendment No 2) 1982) enables the court in any action (*inter alia*) for the administration of the estate of a deceased person to direct a copy of any judgment (or order) or direction to be served on any person who although not a party is affected by it when such person shall be bound, subject to opportunity to apply (Ord 44).

Parties

Basically any person having an interest, whether vested or contingent, in the estate or trust may sue. Administration actions are divided into 'creditors' actions' and 'beneficiaries' actions'. Each involves accounts and inquiries regarding the assets and liabilities of the estate or trust, but a person suing as a beneficiary should not be joined as plaintiff with a creditor or vice versa and, if need be, must pursue his claim by a separate action.

A creditor may sue on behalf of himself and all other creditors and it is not necessary for all the creditors to be named as parties.

A beneficiary may commence proceedings provided that he has at that time an interest in the estate. It can be a contingent as opposed to an absolute interest but not a mere hope of an interest.

All the named executors, personal representatives or trustees should be parties. Any unwilling to be joined as plaintiffs should be made defendants. They will normally be defendants to a creditor's or beneficiary's action, but they may themselves initiate an administration action in order to relieve themselves of the burden of administering an estate or trust with all its attendant duties and obligations to creditors and beneficiaries alike.

If one executor brings an action he joins in his co-executors if they consent as plaintiffs though the procedure being investigatory rather than adversarial it does not matter in administration proceedings whether the personal representatives are plaintiffs or defendants.

If the last executor of an estate dies then his executor becomes the executor of that estate and in such circumstances would need to be joined in any administration action. Representatives of deceased executors need not be brought in.

An executor de son tort or any person who has intermeddled in the management of the estate may be joined as defendant if he has intermeddled in the estate.

So far as practicable, all beneficiaries should be joined in administration proceedings though if a limited order only is sought it would be unnecessary to bring in those beneficiaries who might be unaffected by it. The court has power to add any party to the action or to appoint any person to represent any other person or class of persons who cannot be found or cannot readily be ascertained, such as, for example, unborn children, its purpose being first to ensure that everyone interested has an opportunity of being joined as a party or sufficiently represented, and secondly, to limit the possibility of any further litigation once it has made its decision on the issue presently before it.

Intitulement

(Administration of an estate)
  'In the matter of the Estate of AB deceased'.
  (Execution of trust)
'In the matter of the trusts of the Will of AB deceased' or
'In the matter of the trusts of a Settlement/Conveyance dated ... and made between ...'

The objective of the plaintiff

The plaintiff's objective is to seek an order for the full administration of an estate.

Originating process

Writ or originating summons. An originating summons with its attendant affidavit evidence is not only more appropriate to the inquisitorial procedure but enables orders to be made quickly since unchallenged evidence may at once show entitlement to an order; but a writ is necessary if either fraud or maladministration is alleged or where otherwise it would be difficult to see how the plaintiff puts his case, and would also be more appropriate if material facts were in dispute. The court may grant relief against wilful default or misconduct notwithstanding that an action has been commenced by originating summons instead of by writ. If in a creditor's action there is *prima facie* evidence that the estate is insolvent, such evidence should be disclosed in the plaintiff's supporting affidavit or in a separate affidavit.

In an action commenced by originating summons the master, being satisfied that all necessary parties are before the court and that the evidence is complete, may himself make the administration order (Practice Direction (Chancery: Masters' Powers) [1975] 1 WLR 129).

Required/have ready/on issue

By writ   The general indorsement is for the plaintiff to claim as (describe his interest in the estate such as executor or residuary legatee under the will etc) of XYZ (now deceased) of or late of (address) for an order for an account of the estate (on whatever ground may be appropriate) and to have the same administered by the court, for further or other relief and for costs. The statement of claim can be indorsed on the writ of summons or served separately. It states the interest the plaintiff has in the estate describing the basis of his claim, that the defendants are sued in their capacity intimating whether or not there is any wilful default or maladministration, giving any particulars which are relevant and requesting the relief now sought.

By originating summons   This need only state the orders specifically requested as would be on the indorsement of a writ of summons. The remaining particulars are given in the supporting affidavit. No statute need be cited in the body (or title) of the originating process.

Sequence

The kind of actions usually properly commenced by writ are claims by creditors against the estate or where there is a suggestion of wilful default on the part of personal representatives of an estate. In such actions summary procedure is available with the obvious consequences of shortening the litigation and keeping costs to a minimum. If after the statement of claim has been served (indorsed on the writ or served separately) the defendant does not defend, then a summary judgment can be taken or applied for. In some cases the court may still have to investigate by the accounts procedure what monies are due so that summary procedure may only be an essential first step. Since a summons for judgment in default may be defeated by serving a good defence, the plaintiff's best tactics may be, where applicable, an application under Ord 14. If the action is defended and summary judgment under Ord 14 is not available, it will proceed to trial in the usual way after pleadings have been closed, although on the summons for directions the court may require to be satisfied that the matter is ready to proceed to trial and that there are no other circumstances in relation to the estate which should be considered at the same time.

In an action commenced by originating summons unless there is an acknowledgment of service the court will wish to be satisfied that the parties have been served with the proceedings or as to what efforts have been made to find them. The plaintiff should swear an affidavit of service if a defendant served within this jurisdiction has failed to acknowledge service within 14 days.

In the event that parties cannot be found, the court may order the plaintiff to take such action as may be reasonable to ascertain his whereabouts. An order cannot be made against a person who has not been served with the originating process unless the order is against him in his capacity as trustee/personal representative and s 59 of the Trustee Act is satisfied. Sometimes the difficulty in service can be avoided if the person is a beneficiary and there is some other person with a similar interest in the estate who can be served and in respect of whom a representation order (see above) can be made that he do represent the missing person for the purposes of the action and if so the missing person can be struck out as a party. Subject to service, the plaintiff can swear an affidavit setting out the full facts of the case in support of the orders requested or relevant to the questions to be answered by the court and posed by the originating summons. He then takes an appointment before the master at which the court will consider the parties to the action and what further evidence is appropriate and give directions accordingly. It is usual for the appointment to be adjourned to a further date giving sufficient time for the court's directions to be carried out. In due course if the evidence is complete and the master is satisfied that all those who should be parties have been given an opportunity to place their evidence before the court the originating summons will be adjourned into court for argument with or without cross-examination. A judgment or order for the administration of an estate or, with necessary variations, for the execution of a trust, may itself contain directions; or any time during the proceedings under the judgment further directions may be given; these will proceed in chambers.

Such directions during the proceedings or under the judgment are likely to appertain to those specified in Ord 44, rr 3-11, (fully dealing with the examination of claims by creditors and beneficiaries), and they will usually include:

(1) Accounts and inquiries; the manner of their prosecution and the evidence to be adduced in support thereof.
(2) The time within which each proceeding is to be taken and the parties required to attend.
(3) The issue of advertisements for creditors and the appointment of a person who will examine the claims received, determine so far as he is able which should be admitted and which require further evidence, and furnish an affidavit stating his findings and his reasons therefor listing all other debts of the deceased which are or may be still owing. Any personal representative of the deceased other than the person so appointed, must join in the affidavit.
(4) The service of notice on creditors required to submit proof of their claims, produce documents, or attend adjudication.
(5) The service of notice on creditors who have not been required to attend the adjudication that their claim has been allowed or disallowed wholly or in part (as the case may be).
(6) Account to be furnished by the personal representatives showing all assets of the estate (capital and income) and all dealings therewith in the course of administration, including the assignment or delivery of specific gifts and payments to creditors and legatees, supplemented by a list of all debts, costs, legacies and annuities remaining unpaid and with affidavit in verification.

The master may always refer (Ord 32, r 12) any question to the judge.

All accounts and lists, with relative receipts and vouchers, are referred to the accounts section (room 415/416) for audit and preparation of the final accounts for effecting the winding up of the estate. These will include a list of apportionments where the assets are not sufficient for the full payment of debts or, after payment of debts, are not sufficient for the full payment of legacies and provision for annuities.

The result of the proceedings before the master will be stated by him in the form of an order which, subject to such directions as he may give for further consideration of the cause or matter, will be binding on all parties to the action and copies of which will be served on such of the parties as he may direct.

When giving judgment or any order or direction which affects persons not parties to the action, the court may direct notice of the judgment to be served on any such person. This direction may be made at the time of giving judgment or at any stage of the proceedings under the judgment (Ord 44 as substituted by r 53 of RSC (Amendment No 2) 1982 (SI 1982 No 1111) r 2).

If the dispute involves pedigree, the court may require one of the parties with knowledge of the family to set out in a simple diagrammatic form the whole of the relationship of all parties to the deceased.

Once the court makes an order for the administration 'in court' of the estate, proceedings are thereafter carried on in the master's chambers under (new) Ord 44, rr 3-11. A summons to proceed or application under liberty to apply must be issued by the party having carriage of the order unless full directions were given at its making.

Plaintiff's/defendant's considerations

Order 85, rr 2 and 5 categorically state that the court will not make a full administration order unless it considers that the questions at issue cannot otherwise be properly determined. The plaintiff should therefore first consider the extent of the questions which can be determined, the order which can be made and the relief which can be given under Ord 85, r 2.

It is rare to have an estate so large that costs are not relevant. It therefore behoves all parties who have any financial interest in the estate to dispose of the litigation by agreement or an agreed procedure as soon as possible. The facility afforded by the use of Ord 85, r 2 in the Chancery Division is that a dispute which has been limited by agreement will be dealt with and with reasonable expedition.

Attitude of the court

Occasionally there will be a straightforward *inter partes* dispute which must go to trial in the usual way but in the main full administration actions are fact-finding exercises which call upon the court to investigate and bring to bear the most expeditious and least costly resolution to the problem.

Hazards and pitfalls

If personal representatives recognise that their management is limited and apply to the court under Ord 85, r 2 for suitable orders at the appropriate time, intractable problems should not arise for them. Other than in simple winding-up and management of an estate procedure, personal representatives are often wise to apply to the court under Ord 85, r 2 for directions so as to avoid personal liability.

Costs

The costs of an administration action are in the discretion of the court but persons logically joined will not be personally liable and in general will be ordered to be paid out of the estate, with the following qualifications:

(1) The costs of personal representatives and trustees have priority.
(2) The costs of other parties and of creditors who have incurred costs in proving their claim will be allowed on a party and party basis or on a common fund basis as the court may direct.
(3) Costs incurred by a beneficiary in proving his title to a legacy or share of a fund cannot as of right be claimed against the estate and may be ordered to be deducted from his legacy or share (*Re Whitaker* [1911] 1 Ch 214).

See generally Supreme Court of Judicature Act 1925, s 50(1); Ord 62, rr 2(4), 28, 31.

Alternative jurisdiction

The county court has jurisdiction in proceedings for the administration of deceaseds' estates where the net value of the estate does not exceed £30,000 and may make an administration order or an order for accounts and inquiries. The county court also has jurisdiction by agreement between the parties or if the High Court remits a case to it under s 75A of the County Courts Act. Where the estate is insolvent a creditor may apply for an administration order by petition to the bankruptcy court (Bankruptcy Act 1914, s 130(1)).

Appeals

An appeal from the decision of the master on interlocutory matters goes in the usual way to the judge in chambers and from there with leave to the Court of Appeal.

Inquiries for next of kin

An order for an inquiry to ascertain the next of kin of a person who has died wholly or partially intestate may be made at any stage during an administration action or upon application by originating summons. In the latter case the plaintiff may be a personal representative and the defendant a beneficiary or vice versa, but a grant of representation is not a prerequisite and any two persons interested in the estate may be plaintiff and defendant respectively.

If the plaintiff is the only known next of kin, the Official Solicitor (subject to his prior consent) may be named as defendant to represent any unascertained next of kin. If, on the other hand, the deceased has made a will resulting in a partial intestacy and appointing an executor who has no claim as next of kin, then if no next of kin is known, the executor should name as defendant the Treasury Solicitor or (as the case may require) the Solicitor for the Duchy of Cornwall or the Duchy of Lancaster.

An application for a kin inquiry per se is unusual so long as there is at least one beneficiary who can take a grant of representation and can himself advertise for other claimants and take out insurance against the possibility of claims arising after the estate has been wound up. Where resort is had to the court, the order or the master's directions thereunder may require advertisements for claimants to be preceded by the compilation of a pedigree which in turn will necessitate the procurement of certificates of birth, death and marriage and affidavits by persons having knowledge of the genealogy of the family and the whereabouts of its surviving members. Since the record must usually cover three generations, hearsay evidence is admissible.

Where, for lack of conclusive evidence, reliance has to be placed upon a mere legal presumption as to whether a certain person is still living or is or was married or was born in wedlock, the master will not act thereon, but will record the facts and adjourn to the judge in chambers the decision whether such presumption should be given effect.

Upon the completion of the pedigree, the master will give directions for the issue of advertisements for any next of kin unaccounted for, the listing and classification of claims received in reply thereto, the service of notices on claimants required to submit proof and the fixing of a date for adjudication. With necessary variations the forms and procedure will conform with the corresponding stage of a creditor's action. The rules governing the process of advertising for claimants and adjudicating claims are given in Ord 44, rr 6 and 7.

If, at the conclusion, all possible claimants have been identified and their claims determined, the master may order the taxation and payment of costs and the distribution of the estate. If, on the other hand, the evidence has raised presumptions, application must be made to the judge in chambers for an order known as a 'Benjamin Order' (*Re Benjamin* [1902] 1 Ch 723) which, without making any binding declaration, will authorise the personal representative to distribute the estate on the footing that the unproven act or event is presumed to have taken place. The personal representative is thereby protected, but any beneficiary who may appear at a later date can claim against those beneficiaries whose shares have been augmented at his expense, as such an order in no way constitutes any kind of binding declaration.

Wills and Succession

Under Ord 43, r 8 the court may order partial distribution of an estate in cases where there is likely to be difficulty or delay in tracing some of the persons entitled (Practice Direction (Chancery Division: Miscellaneous Provisions) [1970] 1 WLR 977).

Textbook

Halsbury, Vol 17, paras 1448 et seq; Vol 37, paras 533 et seq.

Forms and precedents

AP, Vol 2, Chancery Masters' Practice Forms Nos 4 et seq.
Atkin, Vol 2, (1989 issue) and Vol 22 (1980 issue).

Wills and Succession—Orders

1. ORDER APPOINTING ADMINISTRATOR PENDING SUIT

THE COURT [by consent] APPOINTS ... of ... Administrator pending suit of the estate of the above named deceased
AND the said Administrator having given security to the satisfaction of the court
[AND the court [by consent] dispensing with the giving of security by the said Administrator]
IT IS [by consent] ORDERED that a Grant of Letters of Administration pending suit pursuant to Section 117 of the Supreme Court Act 1981 be made to the said Administrator.

Notes

1 Application is made under Ord 76, r 14.

2 If security has been directed the order should not be signed until it has been given. The court will indicate whether or not security is to be given.

3 If the court has made the order subject to the consent of the proposed administrator the order should not be signed until this has been filed.

4 If only some of the parties consent, the appropriate alterations must be made, eg 'by consent of the Plaintiff and the Third Defendant'.

5 Accounts are not usually ordered but if they are the court will give directions for the filings of accounts up to a certain date with so many days thereafter and also directions for the service of such accounts. It may be possible to adapt the precedents found under the heading 'Receiver'.

2. MASTER'S ORDER TO DISCONTINUE AND PRONOUNCEMENT AS TO VALIDITY OF WILL (ALL PARTIES *SUI JURIS*)

AND UPON READING the documents recorded on the Court file as having been read ...
AND the parties having agreed to the terms set forth in the schedule hereto [and to there being no order as to costs]

AND the court being satisfied that every relevant beneficiary within the meaning of section 49(1)(*b*) of the Administration of Justice Act 1985 has given their consent to the making of the pronouncement herein

THE COURT PRONOUNCES FOR/AGAINST the force and validity of the last Will and Testament of the above named deceased a completed copy of which is the script bearing the date ... being the exhibit marked ... referred to in the Affidavit of scripts of ... sworn ...

AND IT IS by consent ORDERED

1   that this Action [and Counterclaim] be discontinued

2   that the said terms be carried into effect but so nevertheless that execution be not issued in respect of the said terms without further order

3   that [probate of the Will] [and ... Codicil] [Letters of Administration of the estate] of the above named deceased late of ... be granted to the Plaintiff/the Defendant ... the executor named therein if entitled thereto

4   that on Application for such a grant the caveat numbered ... and entered on ... do if still subsisting cease to have effect

5   that there be taxed if not agreed
    (a) the costs of this Action [and Counterclaim] of the Plaintiff/Defendant ... the executor named in the said Will
    (b) on an indemnity basis the costs of this Action [and Counterclaim] of the Plaintiff/Defendant ... and
    (c) the costs of the Plaintiff/Defendant pursuant to the Legal Aid Act 1974

6   that the costs specified in (a) and (b) above be paid out of the estate of the deceased in a due course of administration.

The Schedule

Notes

1   Section 49 of the Administration of Justice Act 1985 empowers the court on the compromise of a probate action to pronounce for or against the validity of a will or wills provided that every relevant beneficiary consents.

2   The relevant beneficiaries are all persons who may be entitled under

the will or wills and if a pronouncement against the validity of the will might result in an intestacy, those persons who would be entitled on intestacy.

3 As a matter of policy, each will in respect of which a pronouncement is made should be set out; a pronouncement for one will being a pronouncement against any others before the court—the associate should fill in:
   (a) The date of the will
   (b) The exhibit number of the will
   (c) The deponent of the affidavit of scripts
   (d) The date of swearing.

3. COMPROMISE (IN CHAMBERS)

AND the parties having agreed to the terms set forth in the schedule hereto

IT IS ORDERED

1 that this Action and Counterclaim be discontinued

2 that the said terms be carried into effect but so nevertheless that execution be not issued in respect of the said terms without further Order

3 that Probate of the Will and ... Codicil/Letters of Administration of the estate of the above named deceased late of ... be granted to the plaintiff/defendant ... the Executor named therein if entitled thereto

4 that on application for such a grant the caveat numbered ... and entered on ... shall if still subsisting cease to have effect

5 that there be taxed if not agreed
   (a) the costs of this Action and Counterclaim of the plaintiff/defendant ... the Executor named in the said Will
   (b) on the indemnity basis the costs of this Action and Counterclaim of the plaintiff/defendant and
   (c) that the costs specified in (a) and (b) above be paid out of the estate of the said deceased in a due course of administration.

The Schedule

4. COMPROMISE (IN SOLEMN FORM)

UPON THE TRIAL of this Action and Counterclaim

AND UPON HEARING Counsel for the plaintiff and for the defendant

AND UPON READING the documents recorded on the court file as having been read

AND the parties other than the ... plaintiff/ ... defendant having agreed the terms of compromise set forth in the schedule hereto and consented to this Order

AND the court having by Order made this day but not drawn up approved the said terms on behalf of the plaintiff/... defendant

[AND the court approving the said terms on behalf of the ... plaintiff/... defendant]

THE COURT PRONOUNCES FOR the force and validity of the last Will and Testament of the above named deceased late of ... bearing date ... and ... marked '...' and of the Codicil hereto bearing date ... and marked '...'

AND THE COURT PRONOUNCES AGAINST the force and validity of the alleged last Will and Testament of the above named said deceased bearing date ... and marked '...'

AND IT IS ORDERED

1 that this Action and Counterclaim do stand dismissed

2 that the said terms be carried into effect but so nevertheless that execution be not issued in respect of the said terms without further Order

3 that the Taxing Master do tax if not agreed
    (a) the costs of this Action and Counterclaim of the ... plaintiff/ ... defendant the Executor named in the said Will
    (b) on the indemnity basis the costs of this Action and Counterclaim of the plaintiff ... /... defendant
    (c) the costs of the plaintiff ... /... defendant pursuant to the Legal Aid Act 1974

4 that the costs specified in (a) and (b) above be paid out of the estate of the said deceased in a due course of administration

5 that the plaintiff ... /...defendant shall pay to the plaintiff ... /... defendant his/her/its/their/costs of this Action and Counterclaim such costs to be taxed if not agreed.

The Schedule

Notes

1. The fifth and sixth paragraphs in the precedent No 3 are alternatives. When the court approves the terms on behalf of persons under disability at the same hearing as that at which it makes the order, then the sixth paragraph should be used. Sometimes, however, there is a separate earlier hearing at which the court considers whether the terms are for the benefit of the person under disability. When this happens the fifth paragraph in the precedent should be used.

2. Making of scripts by associates. Where a testamentary document is pronounced for or against in solemn form, the associate should mark the face of the will with a note of the effect of the judgment, eg:
'Pronounced for (or against) in an Action entitled (short title) on (date)
(Signed) ... Associate'
Where space permits this notation should be made along the right hand margin. (In practice it often has to be done along the left hand margin.) Where the document is a copy, draft or reconstruction the wording is suitably adapted, eg, 'The Will of which this is a copy (or completed draft) including the alterations and interlineations therein was pronounced ...' The Probate Registry will look at the marking when it receives the scripts.

3. Where there is a compromise to be approved on behalf of a person under a disability the master will adjourn the application to the judge in chambers on a Monday morning at the end of the list for approval of the compromise. The action is subsequently heard in the Short Probate List immediately after the hearing in chambers.

5. REVOCATION OF GRANT OF PROBATE

UPON THE TRIAL of this Action and Counterclaim
    AND UPON HEARING Counsel for the plaintiff and for the defendant
    AND UPON HEARING oral evidence
    AND UPON READING the documents recorded on the court file as having been read including the Probate of the alleged last Will and Testament of the above named deceased bearing date ... granted on ... /Letters of Administration of the estate of the above named deceased granted on ... to ...
    THIS COURT PRONOUNCES FOR the force and validity of the last Will and Testament of the deceased bearing date ... and marked ...
    AND THE COURT PRONOUNCES ... AGAINST the force and validity of

the said alleged last Will and Testament of the deceased bearing date ...

AND IT IS ORDERED

1 that the said Probate/Letters of Administration be revoked

2 that this Action and Counterclaim do stand dismissed

3 that the Taxing Master shall tax if not agreed
   (a) the costs of this Action and Counterclaim of the ... plaintiff/ ... defendant the executor named in the said Will bearing date ...
   (b) on the indemnity basis the costs of this Action and Counterclaim of the ... plaintiff/... defendant
   (c) the costs of the plaintiff ... /... defendant pursuant to the Legal Aid Act 1974

4 that the costs specified in (a) and (b) above be paid out of the estate of the said deceased in a due course of administration

5 that the plaintiff ... /... defendant shall pay to the plaintiff ... /... defendant his/her/its/their costs of this Action and Counterclaim such costs to be taxed if not agreed.

6. ORDER REFUSING REVOCATION

UPON THE TRIAL of this Action and Counterclaim
 AND UPON HEARING Counsel for the plaintiff and for the defendant
 AND UPON HEARING oral evidence
 AND UPON READING the documents recorded on the court file as having been read including the Probate of the last Will and Testament of the above named deceased bearing date ... granted on ... to ... /Letters of Administration of the estate of the above named deceased granted on ... to ...
 THE COURT PRONOUNCES FOR the force and validity of the said last Will and Testament of the said deceased
 AND THE COURT PRONOUNCES AGAINST the force and validity of the alleged last Will and Testament of the deceased bearing date ... and marked ...

AND IT IS ORDERED

1 that the said Probate/Letters of Administration be handed out to the plaintiff .../... defendant or his/her/its/their solicitors

2 that this Action and Counterclaim shall stand dismissed

3 that the Taxing Master shall tax if not agreed
   (a) on the indemnity basis the costs of this Action and Counterclaim of the plaintiff .../... the executor named in the said Will/Administrator of the estate of the said deceased
   (b) the costs of this Action and Counterclaim of the ... plaintiff/ ... defendant
   (c) the costs of the plaintiff .../... defendant pursuant to the Legal Aid Act 1974

4 that the costs specified in (a) and (b) above be paid out of the said estate of the said deceased in a due course of administration

5 that the plaintiff/defendant shall pay to the defendant/plaintiff his/her/its/their costs of this Action and Counterclaim such costs to be taxed if not agreed.

7. ORDER FOR EXAMINATION OF SCRIPTS

UPON THE APPLICATION of the plaintiff/defendant by Summons dated ...

AND UPON HEARING Counsel/the solicitors for the plaintiff and Counsel for the solicitors for the defendant

AND UPON READING the documents recorded on the court file as having been read

AND Messrs ... the solicitors for the plaintiff/defendant undertaking (1) that they will on or before ... or earlier if so directed by this court return ... the Scripts specified in the schedule hereto to Room 157 Chancery Chambers The Royal Courts of Justice and (2) that until the said Scripts ... are returned as aforesaid they will remain in the possession of Messrs ... or of Messrs ... who are handwriting experts

IT IS ORDERED

1 that the ... said Scripts be handed out to Messrs ... the solicitors for the plaintiff .../... defendant for the purpose of handwriting analysis being examined by experts by microscope and immersion tests

2 [that an officer of the Chancery Division do attend upon ... at ... and do produce to him for the purpose of handwriting analysis the Scripts specified in the schedule hereto]

3 that Messrs ... do return the said Scripts to Room ... Chancery Chambers Thomas More Building The Royal Courts of Justice Strand London WC2A 2LL on or before ... or earlier if so directed by the court

4 that the costs of the said Application are to be costs in the cause.

The Schedule

8. ORDER PRONOUNCING FOR SOME WORDS—AGAINST OTHERS

AND it appearing from an Affidavit of the plaintiffs that the scripts of which they had knowledge and which they propound in this Action included three paper writings now remaining in Court each bearing date the ...

One (hereinafter referred to as 'Script A') commencing with the words '...' another (hereinafter referred to as 'Script B') bearing the number '...' and beginning with the words '...' and a third (hereinafter referred to as 'Script C') commencing with the words '...'

THE COURT PRONOUNCES FOR the force and validity of the last Will and Testament of the above named deceased late of ... bearing date ... and of the Codicil to the said last Will and Testament being so much of Script A and Script B as is hereinafter mentioned that is to say the whole of Script A save and except the following that is to say

    (i) the words beginning with '...' down to and including the words '...'

(ii)		
	AB	£1000
	CD	£1000
	EF	£1000
	GH	£2000

and the legacy 'EF £...' in Script B and the signature of the deceased and the attestation thereof

AND THE COURT PRONOUNCES AGAINST the force and validity of (1) the said words beginning with '...' down to and including the said words '...'

2 the said four legacies to AB CD EF and GH

3 the whole of Script B save and except the words 'EF £ ... ' and

the signature of the deceased and the attestation thereof and

4   the whole of Script C.

9. ORDER PRONOUNCING FOR COMPLETED COPY OF WILL

THE COURT PRONOUNCES FOR the force and validity of the last Will and Testament of the above named deceased a completed copy of which is the script bearing date ... and marked ... referred to in the Affidavit of Scripts of the plaintiff ... /defendant ... sworn ...

AND IT IS ORDERED that Probate of the said completed copy of the said Will be granted to the plaintiff limited until the original Will or a more authentic copy thereof be proved.

10. ORDER PRONOUNCING AGAINST MISSING WILL

THE COURT PRONOUNCES AGAINST the force and validity of the Will propounded by the defendant in the Counterclaim being a Will alleged to have been executed by the above named deceased on ... but which cannot now be found

AND IT IS ORDERED

1   that the said Counterclaim shall stand dismissed

2   that Letters of Administration of the estate of the said deceased be granted to ... the lawful attorney of ... for the use and benefit of ... and until further representation be granted.

11. ORDER PRONOUNCING IN FAVOUR OF TORN UP WILL

THE COURT PRONOUNCES FOR the force and validity of the last Will and Testament of the above named deceased late of ... being the script propounded in this Action on behalf of the plaintiff and referred to in the Affidavit of Scripts of the plaintiff which Will at some time after its alleged execution was torn into pieces the remains of which now remain in the High Court of Justice and a true reconstruction of which said Will as the same was apparently executed by the deceased on ... is set forth in the schedule hereto

[THE COURT PRONOUNCES FOR the force and validity of the last Will and Testament of the above named deceased bearing date ... which Will was torn into several pieces by the said deceased at some date after its execution without affecting its validity and whereon he made numerous deletions and additions and emendations at several times after execution in ink and pencil handwriting such deletions additions and emendations not having testamentary effect the remains of which Will now remain in court and a true reconstruction of which said Will in the terms wherein the same was duly executed by the deceased on ... is set forth in the Schedule hereto.]

The Schedule
(Here set out the wording of the Will as reconstructed).

Notes

1 The precedent No 9 is based on the order dated February 26, 1975 of Walton J in the Action *Re Littler dec Littler v Rowland* 1973 W 3853.

2 It might be thought that if an order pronounces for parts of a script it would be unnecessary for it expressly to pronounce against the other parts but the practice is expressly to pronounce against the rejected parts as it is done in form No 8.

3 The form No 8 also serves as a reminder that the testator's signature and the attestation are part of a will or codicil and should not be forgotten when part is pronounced for and part against.

12. ORDER PRONOUNCING IN FAVOUR OF TORN UP WILL (ALTERNATIVE FORM)

THE COURT PRONOUNCES FOR the force and validity of the last Will and Testament of the above named deceased bearing date ... which Will was torn into several pieces by the said deceased at some date after its execution without affecting its validity and whereon he made numerous deletions and additions and emendations at several times after execution in ink and pencil handwriting such deletions additions and emendations not having testamentary effect the remains of which Will now remain in Court and a true reconstruction of which said Will in the terms wherein the same was duly executed by the deceased on ... is set forth in the Schedule hereto.

The Schedule
(Here set out the wording of the Will as reconstructed)

13. INQUIRY FOR NEXT-OF-KIN

IT IS ORDERED

1 that the following Inquiry be made that is to say
   (1) An Inquiry whether ... (a ... of the above named deceased) is living or dead and if he died after the death of the deceased on ... who are his personal representatives and if he died before the death of the deceased whether he left any and if any what issue who at the date of the death of the said deceased became beneficially entitled either absolutely or contingently to the stirpital share of the estate of the deceased to which the said ... would have become beneficially entitled had he survived the deceased and if so for what estate and interest and in what shares and proportions respectively and if any such issue have since died having attained an absolute vested interest who are their respective personal representatives

2 [that the Administrators of the estate of the deceased be at liberty subject to retention and payment out of the general estate of the costs hereinafter directed to be taxed if not agreed and all other proper costs charges and expenses) to distribute amongst the persons entitled thereto the residuary estate of the deceased except the share to which the said ... or his issue would be beneficially entitled if they respectively survived the deceased without retaining any part of the said residuary estate except the said share to meet the subsequent costs of ascertaining the persons beneficially entitled to the said excepted share (including in such last mentioned costs the costs of the said Inquiry)]

3 that there be taxed if not agreed down to and including this Order
   (a) on the indemnity basis the costs of and incidental to the said application of the plaintiffs ... as Administrators
   (b) on the common fund basis the costs of and incidental to the said application of the defendants ...

4 that the parties be at liberty to apply.

14. ANSWER TO KIN INQUIRY

UPON THE INQUIRY directed by the Order dated ...

AND UPON HEARING Counsel/the Solicitors for the Plaintiff and Counsel/the Solicitors for the Defendant and ... for the persons named in the First Schedule hereto being persons served with Notice of the said Order pursuant to Order 44 Rule 2 of the Rules of the Supreme Court

AND UPON READING the documents recorded on the Court File as having been read

AND the Master having directed that the matters set forth in the Second Schedule hereto be recorded in this Order

IT IS DECLARED UPON the footings set out in the Third Schedule hereto that the persons who upon the death of the above named deceased (who died intestate on ...) become entitled either absolutely or contingently to any property of his as to which he died intestate and the shares and proportions for and in respect of which they are respectively entitled are as set out in the Fourth Schedule hereto

AND IT IS ORDERED

1 that there be taxed from the foot of the taxation directed by the said Order
   (1) the costs of and incidental to this Action of the Plaintiff the Administrator of the estate of the deceased and
   (2) on the common fund basis the costs of and incidental to this Action of the Defendant and of the persons named in the said First Schedule
2 that all the said costs be raised retained and paid out of the estate of the said deceased in a due course of administration.

The First Schedule

Persons served with Notice of the Order dated ...
1 ...

2 ...

The Second Schedule

Matters directed to be recorded
1 ...

2 ...

3 ...

The Third Schedule

Footings upon which the inquiry is answered
1 that ...

2 that ...

The Fourth Schedule

Persons entitled

Pedigree Number	Names of persons entitled	Estate and interest of such persons	Shares and proportions to which they are entitled	Relationship to deceased

Notes

1 Certificates in answer to kin inquiries have become rare. This form is intended to help where there is an order answering the common form of kin inquiry set out in 3 of Form 200 on p 235 of Atkin, Vol 2 (1980 Issue). It is intended to be simpler than the certificate at p 250 of Atkin.

2 The order must of course show what the answer is to the inquiry. If information is recorded on the court file, however, it need not be recorded again in the order. Nevertheless if a master thinks that certain matters should be recorded in the order then they can be recorded in a schedule. For example he might wish details of advertisements or of claims disallowed or withdrawn to be recorded. He could of course also direct that the evidence be shown in a schedule. It is understood that sometimes in the past the evidence in support of each footing was identified. It does not seem essential to do this but if desired this could be done in a schedule.

3 Obviously, if no persons have been served with notice of the previous order and if the order answering the inquiry is not made on footings there will be no need for the first and third schedules.

4 It is the judge and not the master who gives leave to distribute on footings. Unless, therefore, there has been a previous order giving such leave, the parties will want to go to the judge after an order such as this making a declaration on footings. In such a situation the master's order might not deal with costs but leave them to be dealt with by the judge later.

5 Sometimes it is the costs of the inquiry rather than of the action which are directed to be taxed as (for example) if there were no other costs outstanding.

6 The first column in the fourth schedule is for the pedigree number. If however there were many persons entitled it might be convenient to have before the pedigree number column a serial number column so that the persons concerned could be numbered 1, 2, 3 etc.

15. 'BENJAMIN ORDER'

IT IS ORDERED

1 that the Plaintiff be at liberty to distribute the estate of the above named deceased on the footing that

2 that there be taxed from the foot of the taxation directed by the order dated
   (a) on the indemnity basis the costs of and incidental to the said Application of the Plaintiff/the Administrator of the said estate
   (b) the costs of and incidental to the said Application of the Defendants and of the said

3 that all the said costs be raised retained and paid out of the said estate in a due course of administration.

Notes

1 See Atkin, Vol 2 (1989 issue) and Ord 85, r 2.

2 The judge makes no declaration but merely permits personal representatives to distribute on certain findings, eg that a beneficiary is dead.

3 This order fully protects personal representatives if they distribute in accordance with the order, but a person entitled may recover from any beneficiaries who have been paid.

16. CONSTRUCTION

THE COURT APPOINTS the ... defendant to represent for the purposes of the said Application ...
AND IT IS DECLARED that on the true construction of the above mentioned Will and Codicil/Settlement and in the events which have happened ...

AND IT IS ORDERED

1 that there be taxed if not agreed
   (a) the costs of and incidental to the said Application of the plaintiffs/defendants as Executors/Trustees
   (b) on the indemnity basis the costs of and incidental to the said Application of the plaintiffs/defendants

2 that all the said costs be raised retained and paid out of the funds subject to the trusts of the said Will and Codicil/Settlement out of the estate of the said Testator in a due course of administration.

17. RECTIFICATION OF WILL

UPON the trial of this Action
   AND UPON HEARING Counsel for the Plaintiff and for the Defendant
   AND UPON READING Probate/Letters of Administration with the Will annexed of the estate of ... granted on ... to ... together with the documents recorded on the Court File as having been read
IT IS DECLARED that the Will dated ... of ... being Exhibit ... in the Affidavit of ... ought to be rectified in the manner specified in the Schedule hereto.

ORDERS ON FAMILY PROVISION APPLICATIONS

18. COMPROMISE (TERMS SCHEDULED)— TOMLIN FORM

UPON THE APPLICATION of the plaintiff by Originating Summons for an Order under The Inheritance (Provision for Family and Dependants) Act 1975
   AND UPON HEARING counsel/the solicitors for the plaintiff and Counsel/the solicitors for the defendants
   AND UPON READING the documents recorded on the court file as having been read and Probate of the Will/Letters of Administration of the estate of the above named deceased granted on ... to the ... defendants
   AND the plaintiff and the defendants other than the ... defendant having agreed to the terms of compromise set forth in the schedule hereto and consented to this order
   THE COURT being satisfied that the said terms of compromise are for the benefit of the [plaintiff] [defendant]
   HEREBY APPROVES the said terms

AND IT IS ORDERED

1 that the defendant as personal representative of the above named deceased be at liberty to carry the said terms into effect

2 that there be taxed
   (a) if not agreed on the indemnity basis the costs of and incidental to the said application of the defendant as personal representatives
   (b) if not agreed the costs of and incidental to the said application of the plaintiff and the defendant
   (c) the costs of the plaintiff/defendant pursuant to the Legal Aid Act 1974

3 that the costs specified in (a) and (b) above be paid out of the estate of the deceased in a due course of administration

4 that a memorandum of this order be endorsed on or permanently annexed to the said [Probate] [Letters of Administration]

5 that all further proceedings in this action except for the purpose of carrying the said terms into effect be stayed

6 and that for that purpose the parties are to be at liberty to apply.

The Schedule

Notes

1 There are often minutes of orders compromising claims under the Family Provision Act and the minutes should not be altered so as to make them correspond with this precedent unless it is clearly right to do so.

2 Atkin, Vol 22 (1980 Issue) contains the title on the Inheritance (Provision for Family and Dependants) Act 1975. The forms given there do not include this form but these orders are frequently made in practice.

3 By Ord 99, r 7 the grant of representation must be produced to the court at the hearing and retained until the memorandum of the order has been endorsed in accordance with s 19(3) of the Act.

4 Every final order embodying terms of compromise made under the 1975 Act must contain a direction that a memorandum thereof shall be endorsed on the probate or letters of administration and sent to the

Principal Registry of the Family Division (Practice Direction) (Family Provision: Endorsement of Order [1979] 1 WLR 1).

5 A master has power to hear any proceeding under the 1975 Act.

19. COMPROMISE—NON-TOMLIN FORM

UPON THE APPLICATION of the plaintiff by Originating Summons for an Order under The Inheritance (Provision of Family and Dependants) Act 1975

AND UPON HEARING Counsel/the solicitors for the plaintiff and Counsel/the solicitors for the defendants

AND UPON READING the documents recorded on the court file as having been read and [Probate of the Will] [Letters of Administration of the estate of] the above named deceased granted on ... to the ... defendants

AND the plaintiff and the defendants other than the ... defendant having agreed to the terms of compromise set forth in the schedule hereto and consented to this Order

THE COURT being satisfied that the said terms of compromise are for the benefit of the ... plaintiff/defendant

HEREBY APPROVES the said terms

AND IT IS ORDERED

1 that the ... defendant as personal representative of the above named deceased be at liberty to and do carry the said terms into effect

2 that there be taxed
   (a) if not agreed on the indemnity basis the costs of and incidental to the said application of the ... defendant as personal representatives
   (b) if not agreed the costs of and incidental to the said application of the plaintiff and the ... defendant
   (c) the costs of the plaintiff ... defendant pursuant to the Legal Aid Act 1974

3 that the costs specified in (a) and (b) above be paid out of the estate of the deceased in a due course of administration

4 that a memorandum of this Order be endorsed on or permanently annexed to the said Probate/Letters of Administration.

The Schedule

20. TOMLIN ORDER—ALL *SUI JURIS*

UPON THE APPLICATION of the Plaintiff by Originating Summons for an Order under The Inheritance (Provision for Family and Dependants) Act 1975

AND UPON HEARING Counsel/the Solicitors for the Plaintiff and Counsel/the Solicitors for the Defendant

AND UPON READING the documents recorded on the Court File as having been read

AND the parties having agreed to the terms set forth in the Schedule hereto

IT IS by consent ORDERED

1   that the costs of the Plaintiff and of the Defendant be taxed pursuant to the Legal Aid Act 1974

2   that a memorandum of this Order be endorsed on or permanently annexed to the Probate of the Will and Codicil/Letters of Administration of the estate of the above named deceased

3   that all further proceedings in this Action except for the purpose of carrying the said terms into effect be stayed

4   that for that purpose the parties are to be at liberty to apply.

The Schedule

21. ORDER TO MAKE APPLICATION OUT OF TIME AND INTERIM MAINTENANCE

IT IS ORDERED

1   that the plaintiff be at liberty to make his/her/their application under the said Act notwithstanding that the period of 6 months in the said Act mentioned had expired at the date of issue of the Originating Summons

2   [pursuant to Section 5 of the said Act that there be paid to the

plaintiff out of the net estate of the deceased (a) the sum of £ ... forthwith and (b) the sum of £ ... on the ... day of each month beginning on ... until the date on which the Court either makes an order under Section 2 of the said Act or decides not to exercise its powers under that Section or until further order in the meantime]

3 that a memorandum of this order be endorsed on or permanently annexed to the said Probate/Letters of Administration

4 that the further hearing of the Originating Summons is to stand over generally with liberty to restore.

Note

1 Paragraph 3 is only required if an order for interim maintenance is made.

22. ORDER RECONSTITUTING ACTION WHERE INTERESTS OF TWO OR MORE PLAINTIFFS ARE ADVERSE

AND IT APPEARING that the interests of AB ... plaintiffs are or may be adverse to those of the other plaintiff and that it is desirable that the said AB ... plaintiffs should be enabled to be separately represented for the purpose of prosecuting his/her/their claim under the said Act

IT IS ORDERD that the ... plaintiffs do forthwith cease to be a plaintiff and do henceforth be defendants in this action

AND the further hearing of the said Originating Summons is [to stand over generally with liberty to restore] [adjourned to ...]

23. ORDER FOR REASONABLE PROVISION

IT IS ORDERED

1 pursuant to Section 2(1)(a) of the Inheritance (Provision for Family and Dependants) Act 1975 that there be made to the plaintiff out of the net estate of the above named deceased monthly payments of £ ... each as from the date of the death of the deceased [until the plaintiff remarries] the arrears of such payments to be made on or before ...

2 pursuant to Section 2(3) of the said Act that the property specified

in the schedule hereto (being part of the net estate of the said deceased) be set aside for the making out of the income thereof of the said monthly payments

[pursuant to Section 2(1)(a) of the Inheritance (Provision for Family and Dependants) Act 1975 that there be made to the plaintiff [during her widowhood] out of the net estate of the above named deceased quarterly payments equal to one half of the income of the said net estate such quarterly payments to be made on 1 January, 1 April, 1 July and 1 October in every year the first such payment to be made on ... and the last to be made on ...]

[pursuant to Section 2(1)(a) of the Inheritance (Provision for Family and Dependants) Act 1975 that there be made to the plaintiff monthly payments equal to the whole of the income of that part of the net estate of the above named deceased which is specified in the schedule hereto]

[pursuant to Section 2(1)(b) of the Inheritance (Provision for Family and Dependants) Act 1975 that there be paid to the plaintiff out of the net estate of the above named deceased a lump sum of £ ... a lump sum equal to one half of the net estate of the above named deceased]

[pursuant to Section 7(1) of the said Act that the said lump sum be paid by six instalments of £ ... each on the first day of each of the six months beginning with January 199 ...]

[pursuant to Section 2(1)(c) of the Inheritance (Provision for Family and Dependants) Act 1975 that the property described in the schedule being part of the net estate of the deceased be transferred to the plaintiff] [pursuant to Section 2(4) of the said Act that the ... defendant who holds the said property do execute a Conveyance/Transfer thereof in favour of the plaintiff such Conveyance/Transfer to be settled by the Court in case the parties differ]

[pursuant to Section 2(1)(d) of the Inheritance (Provision for Family and Dependants) Act 1975 that the property described in the ... schedule hereto being part of the net estate of the above named deceased be settled for the benefit of the plaintiff] [pursuant to Section (2)(4)(c) of the said Act that the Trustees of the Settlement do have the powers set out in the ... schedule hereto] [that the ... defendants shall on or before ... issue a Summons to proceed under this Order and file an affidavit exhibiting a draft settled by Counsel of a Settlement to be executed pursuant to this Order] [pursuant to Section 2(1)(e) of the Inheritance (Provision for Family and Dependants) Act 1975 that there be acquired out of the net estate of the above named deceased at a price not exceeding £ ... a freehold property approved by the plaintiff]

[that the said property be transferred to the plaintiff]

[pursuant to Section 2(1)(f) of the Inheritance (Provision for

Family and Dependants) Act 1975 that the Settlement dated ... and made between ... be varied in the manner shown in the schedule hereto]
[that a memorandum of this Order be endorsed on the said Settlement] [pursuant to Section 2(4) of the said Act that the ... defendant who holds the property specified in the ... schedule hereto by virtue of a *donatio mortis causa* made by the deceased shall transfer the said property to the plaintiff upon receiving from the plaintiff a sum equal to the capital transfer tax paid by the ... defendant in respect of the said property]
[pursuant to Section 9 of the said Act that one half of the value of the severable share of the deceased in the property specified in the ... schedule hereto at the value thereof immediately before his death be treated for the purposes of the said Act as part of the net estate of the said deceased]

3 [pursuant to Section 2 of the Inheritance (Provision for Family and Dependants) Act 1975 that the disposition of the estate of the above named deceased effected by his Will and Codicils/by the law relating to intestacy be varied in the manner shown in the schedule hereto]
[pursuant to Section 2 of the Inheritance (Provision for Family and Dependants) Act 1975 that the Will of the above named deceased shall have effect and be deemed to have had effect as from the death of the deceased as if an annuity of £ ... payable monthly had been bequeathed to the plaintiff as from the death of the deceased during her widowhood instead of the annuity of £ ... in the said Will mentioned]

4 that there be taxed if not agreed
   (a) the costs of and incidental to the said application of the ... defendants as Personal Representatives
   (b) on the common fund basis the costs of and incidental to the said application of the plaintiff and the ... defendant
   (c) the costs of the plaintiff/defendant pursuant to the Legal Aid Act 1974

[that the costs specified in (a) and (b) above be paid out of the estate of the deceased in a due course of administration]
[that the plaintiff ... defendant do pay to the plaintiff ... defendant his/her/its/their costs of the said application such costs to be taxed if not agreed]

The Schedule

1 that a memorandum of this order be endorsed on or permanently annexed to the Probate of the Will and Codicil/Letters of Administration of the estate of the deceased.

Chapter Twenty One

Charities

1. Introduction

Charities are distinguishable from other institutions not by their form, which may be incorporated or unincorporated, but by their purposes. Apart from limited statutory exceptions, an institution of any kind which is established exclusively for purposes which are regarded as charitable under English law and (for the purposes of the Charities Act 1960) which is subject to the jurisdiction of the High Court is a charity. It has no individual beneficiaries as such. Except for exempt charities, and to a lesser degree charities excepted under statutory provisions from certain forms of control, charities are subject to the supervisory jurisdiction of the Charity Commissioners for England and Wales, to whom they are bound to submit accounts and from whom they can obtain advice and assistance on matters of charity law.

Charities, or their trustees, may of course be involved in litigation. Where it is simply a matter of (for example) recovering property or enforcing a right without the determination of any question about the trusts or constitution of the charity, or its administration, the charity or its trustees may take or defend proceedings without any constraint other than the general principle applicable to all trustees and fiduciaries that suitable advice should be obtained and that needless expense should be avoided. Special rules apply, however, when the proceedings, whether brought by or on behalf of a charity or against a charity or its trustees, either constitute 'charity proceedings' as defined in the Charities Act 1960 or take one of the other forms specifically mentioned in that Act. There are also certain appeals for which provision is made in the Act of 1960. In addition there may be proceedings for the enforcement of orders of the Charity Commissioners.

2. Charity proceedings

These are defined in the Charities Act 1960, s 28(8) as proceedings in any court in England or Wales brought under the court's jurisdiction with respect to charities or, in relation to the administration of a trust for charitable purposes, its jurisdiction with respect to trusts. They do not include proceedings to determine whether or not a charity exists, nor proceedings where charitable status is irrelevant to the issue to be decided or the relief sought, although a Beddoes Application as a preliminary step in such proceedings, the purpose of which is to protect the trustees as such, is regarded as charity proceedings.

One of the essential characteristics of charity proceedings is that, unless brought by the Attorney-General, they may not be commenced without the consent (given by order under s 28(5) of the 1960 Act) of the Charity Commissioners, or if they refuse, the leave of a judge of the Chancery Division. The reason for this restriction is that the High Court's jurisdiction is shared with the Charity Commissioners, who exercise it informally and without charge to the charity, and it is only in those cases which raise difficult or contentious issues of law or fact that it is more appropriate to invoke the jurisdiction of the court (see ss 18(9) and 28(3) of the Charities Act 1960).

Parties

Under s 28(1) of the 1960 Act the plaintiff must be the charity itself, a trustee of the charity, two or more inhabitants of the area of benefit (in the case of a local charity) or a person having an interest in the charity, ie someone directly affected by the activities of the charity, but not the estate of the founder of the charity (and perhaps not the founder personally) nor a potential beneficiary (which includes, where the charity is established for the benefit of the public at large, a member of the public). The Attorney-General, if not the plaintiff, should be made a defendant since, representing the Crown as *parens patriae*, he is concerned to protect the interests of charity generally and thus represents the beneficial interest. The trustees of the charity should be defendants if and in so far as they are not plaintiffs.

Objective of the plaintiff

The principal purpose of the plaintiff is to obtain the court's decision on a matter which cannot properly be decided under the Charity Commissioners' informal procedures and will typically involve contested questions of fact, some novel point of law or a question of mixed fact and law which cannot be resolved by agreement.

Originating process

Charity proceedings are normally commenced by originating summons, but commencement by writ will be appropriate where there are contentious issues of fact.

Sequence

Where the Attorney-General is the plaintiff no preliminary formalities are required. Otherwise, the sequence is likely to be as follows:

(1) Consultation with the Charity Commissioners. It is wise to make use of the Commissioners' statutory power to provide free advice to charities and the public, and to ascertain whether the Commissioners take the view (a) that the matter in question is suitable for reference to the court rather than being dealt with under the Commissioners' powers, and (b) that the proceedings contemplated will be 'charity proceedings', and thus (c) that the Commissioners will consider granting consent.

(2) Application to the Charity Commissioners for consent under s 28(5) of the 1960 Act. There is no special form of application, but the Commissioners usually require (a) a copy of an opinion of counsel indicating the need for the proceedings and the prospect of success, as well as (b) a draft of the originating summons or statement of claim.

(3) If the Charity Commissioners refuse consent an application may be made to a judge of the Chancery Division. Application to the court should be made within 21 days of the Commissioners' refusal to consent by lodging in Chancery Chambers the particulars set out in Ord 108, r 3(1). If the judge decides to direct the Commissioners to furnish a statement of their reasons for refusing consent, Chancery Chambers will send the applicant a copy of the Commissioners' statement. The application may be made *ex parte* in the first instance, and leave may be granted without a hearing. If there is a hearing the judge may direct that it is held in chambers.

(4) Consultation with the Treasury Solicitor, who acts for the Attorney-General, and will normally be supplied by the Charity Commissioners with a draft of their order. If the Commissioners take the view that it would be desirable for the Attorney-General himself to bring proceedings they will provide him with relevant information pursuant to s 28(7) of the 1960 Act.

(5) Issue of originating summons and affidavit evidence. The Charity Commission order should be lodged with the court.

(6) Application by motion to the judge for any urgent relief that may be required, eg the grant of an injunction to restrain a threatened breach of trust, the appointment of a receiver and manager or authority for some urgent property transaction.

(7) Hearing by a judge.

(8) Further consultation with the Charity Commissioners if (as often happens) the court refers the matter back to them under s 18(3) of the Charities Act 1960 to settle and establish a scheme.

Attitude of the court

The court's paramount concern will be to decide the issue in the interests of the charity.

Hazards and pitfalls

Proceedings commenced without obtaining the necessary consent may be struck out for this reason. Alternatively, the judge may be persuaded to grant leave if the question arises at a late stage. Failure to join the Attorney-General may deprive the plaintiff (and the court) of potentially valuable assistance.

Costs

In the absence of fault the costs will normally be made payable from the income or other funds of the charity itself and will be on the indemnity basis. Unco-operative conduct by one or more of the parties, however, may result in their being required to meet some of the costs personally.

Alternative jurisdiction

In theory, the county court has jurisdiction in matters concerning trusts (including charities) where the value of the property does not exceed the county court limit in equity. In practice, it is usually thought preferable, on grounds of expense and convenience, to rely on the Charity Commissioners to resolve the matter in such cases.

3. Appeals under Charities Act 1960

Special provisions are made in the 1960 Act as follows:

Section 5

An appeal against the Charity Commissioners' decision to enter or to refuse to enter an institution in the central register of charities set up under the Act and maintained by the Commissioners, or to remove or not to remove an institution from the register. The significance of the decision is that, so long as a charity is registered, it is conclusively presumed to be a charity for all purposes other than the rectification of the register.

Preliminary steps

Any person who is, or may be, affected by the registration of an institution as a charity may, under s 5(2) of the 1960 Act, object to its being registered or apply to the Commissioners for its removal from the register. In cases known to be contentious it is the usual practice of the Commissioners to invite and consider legal argument from the institution concerned and/or other persons interested in the question before taking a decision whether or not to accept the institution concerned for registration or to remove it from the register.

Appeal

A person aggrieved by the decision may appeal to the High Court (Chancery Division) at any time and without the necessity to seek leave. The registration remains in suspense until the appeal has been disposed of.

Parties

Where the appeal is against a refusal to register or a decision to remove from the register, the appellant is normally the institution itself, its trustees or the Attorney-General. Those most likely to object to registration or seek removal from the register are claimants to the property in question (such as those entitled to an estate in the event of intestacy), the Inland Revenue, the rating authority or the Attorney-General.

Section 18(10), (11) and (12)

Section 18 of the Charities Act 1960 is the principal section from which the Charity Commissioners derive their concurrent jurisdiction with the High Court in charity matters. These subsections are concerned with appeals to the High Court from orders made by the Commissioners in the exercise of that jurisdiction. Under subs (10) the Attorney-General is empowered to appeal against any order of the Commissioners made under s 18. Under subs (11) a charity or any of its trustees or any person removed from office or employment by the order concerned may appeal against such an order within three months of the date on which final notice is published, under s 21 of the Act, indicating that the order has been made. Under subs (12) any person interested in a charity, or the parish council or two or more inhabitants of the area of benefit (in the case of a local charity) may appeal, subject to the same time limit, against an order of the Commissioners which establishes a scheme.

Certificate

Appeals may not be brought under subs (11) or subs (12) unless the proposed appellant has obtained from the Charity Commissioners a certificate to the effect that the case is a proper one for appeal, or, if the Commissioners refuse, leave to appeal from a judge of the Chancery Division.

Appeal

The appeal should be brought by originating summons.

Parties

Unless the Attorney-General is the appellant he should be made a defendant. The Charity Commissioners themselves should not be joined unless there is a difference between their view and that of the Attorney-General.

4. Enforcement of Charity Commission orders

Section 41 of the Charities Act 1960 provides that the Charity Commissioners may apply to the High Court for the enforcement of certain of their orders. Order 108, r 4 prescribes that Ord 52, r 1(4) regarding committal for contempt of court, applies in such a case as though the reference there to a single judge of the Queen's Bench Division were a reference to a judge of the Chancery Division.

Statutes

Charities Act 1960. See also Charities Act 1985. *Note*: new legislation has been proposed in a Government White Paper, 'Charities: a Framework for the Future' (Cm 694), published in 1989.

Order

Order 108 governs proceedings under the Charities Act 1960. Owing to the comparative rarity of such proceedings it has not been necessary to update the Order. It should be noted, however, that the references to the Department of Education and Science no longer apply since the jurisdiction formerly exercised by the Department was transferred to the Charity Commissioners by the Education Act 1973. The present addresses of the Charity Commissioners are as follows:

London office: St Alban's House
57–60 Haymarket
London SW1Y 4QX
Northern office: Graeme House
Derby Square
Liverpool L2 7SB
South Western office: The Deane
Tangier
Taunton TA1 4AY

Intitulement

'In the matter of the [name of charity/institution] and in the matter of the Charities Act 1960'.

Textbooks

S G Maurice & D B Parker, *Tudor on Charities*, 7th edn, (Sweet & Maxwell, 1984).
H Picarda, *The Law and Practice Relating to Charities*, (Butterworths, 1972).
D Cracknell, *Law Relating to Charities*, 3rd edn, (Longmans, 1988).
E Cairns, *Charities: Law and Practice*, (Sweet & Maxwell, 1988).

Forms and precedents

Atkin, Vol 8 (1990 issue).

Charities—Orders

1. ORDER OF CHARITY COMMISSIONERS UNDER CHARITIES ACT 1960, SECTION 28

Sealed [date] [General] Charity [Philanthropic Society]

[Charity Commission reference]

Order authorising legal proceedings

CHARITY COMMISSION

In the matter of the Charity called the [Philanthropic Society]; and

In the matter of the Charities Act 1960.

THE CHARITY COMMISSIONERS FOR ENGLAND AND WALES BY THIS ORDER AUTHORISE the following persons, namely:

ABC, of [address]
DEF, of [address]
GHI, of [address], and
JKL, of [address]

(hereinafter referred to as the Plaintiffs) all of whom are or claim to be the Trustees of the above-mentioned Charity to take proceedings as they may be advised in the Chancery Division of Her Majesty's High Court of Justice for the following relief:

1 A declaration that the Plaintiffs are the Trustees of the aforesaid Charity.

2 Alternatively, an inquiry as to who are the Trustees of the aforesaid Charity.

3 Further or in the further alternative an Order that the Plaintiffs or some other suitable and proper person may be appointed Trustees of the aforesaid Charity.

4 An Order that the freehold land specified in the schedule hereto may be vested in the Plaintiffs to be held by them as Trustees of the aforesaid Charity.

5 A declaration that the present members of the Governing Council are the properly elected and serving members of the Governing Council of the [Philanthropy Society].

6 Alternatively, the Court do make appointments to the Governing Council for the time being or direct the holding of an election so that a Governing Council may be elected by members of the [Philanthropy Society].

7 Such further or other relief as the Court shall think fit.

8 That provision be made for the costs of this application.

The Schedule

1 Freehold land and buildings known as [Charity Hall, Benevolence Row] registered at HM Land Registry under Title No . . . .

2 Land and buildings adjoining [Charity Hall] registered at HM Land Registry under Title No . . . .

Sealed by Order of the Commissioners this . . . day of . . . .

Note

The publishers are grateful to the Charity Commissioners for permission to reproduce this form of order.

2. ORDER FOR SCHEME

IT IS DECLARED that upon the true construction of the Will of the above named deceased the bequest therein contained in favour of . . . is a valid charitable bequest

AND IT IS ORDERED

1 that a scheme for the administration of the said trusts be established

1 [pursuant to Section 18(2) of the Charities Act 1960 that it be referred to the Charity Commissioners for England and Wales to prepare and settle such scheme and that such scheme be put into effect by Order of the said Charity Commissioners without any further order of this Court]

2 that there be taxed if not agreed
(a) on the indemnity basis the costs of and incidental to the said

Application of the plaintiffs as the Personal Representative of the said deceased and

(b) the costs of and incidental to the said Application of the defendant

3 that all the said costs be raised retained and paid out of the estate of the said deceased in a due course of administration.

Notes

1 When the court refers it to the Charity Commissioners to prepare a scheme (the alternative being to settle the scheme itself) it need not also order that such a scheme be put into effect by order of the Charity Commissioners without any further order of the court. It is however a convenient course, and where appropriate the judge should be asked if he wishes to do this.

2 For examples of schemes see Atkin, Vol 8 (1990 Issue).

3. ORDER FOR INQUIRY

IT IS ORDERED

1 that the following Inquiry be made that is to say
   (1) An Inquiry whether it is practicable to regulate and administer the funds now subject to the trusts of the Will of ... in accordance with the terms of the said Will

2 that in case it be found that it is practicable so to administer the said funds a scheme be settled by the Court accordingly

3 that in case it be found that it is impracticable to administer the said funds in accordance with the said terms a scheme for the application of the said funds cy pres be settled by the Court.

Chapter Twenty Two

Companies

1. Companies

A company formed and registered under the Companies Acts is an artificial legal person closely regulated by statute and subject to the supervisory jurisdiction of the court in a number of respects. The same general rules apply whether the company is public or private and limited by shares or by guarantee or unlimited.

Where a company is a party to any proceedings it should be referred to by the name by which it is registered and in the neuter singular.

Proceedings which concern the enforcement of members' or creditors' rights under Company Law, or the internal administration of a company or its winding up are brought under specific sections in the Companies Acts 1985 or 1989 or the Insolvency Act 1986. Detailed rules about such proceedings are found in RSC, Ord 102, to which reference should be made.

There are two main reasons for the assignment of the work of the companies court to the Chancery Division: the property aspect, ie the fact that the members are interested in the property of the company through holding shares, which are themselves a form of property; and the fiduciary aspect, ie the fiduciary duties akin to trusteeship which are owed to the company by the directors.

Statutes

The Companies Act 1985, the Insolvency Act 1986, the Companies Act 1989 (not yet wholly in force).

Order

The principal order for company proceedings is Ord 102.

Parties

The parties are referred to as applicant and respondent instead of plaintiff and defendant.

Intitulement

All proceedings should be headed 'in the matter of the [name of company] and in the matter of the Companies Act 1985'.

Originating process

Proceedings should be started by originating summons (Ord 102, r 2), originating motion (r 3) or petition (r 4) according to the purpose of the proceedings. The section of the statute concerned and the rule and paragraph of Ord 102 should be expressly mentioned.

Sequence

(1) Issue of originating summons, notice of motion or petition out of the Companies Court Registry or any Chancery District Registry, with affidavit in support.
(2) Summons for directions unless this is not required (r 6).
(3) Notice to creditors, where appropriate (r 9).
(4) Advertisement of petition where appropriate (r 10).
(5) Affidavits of creditors' claims where appropriate (r 11).
(6) Interlocutory applications (various).
(7) Hearing.

Hazards and pitfalls

Company law and procedure is exceptionally detailed and technical, and there are specific requirements for different kinds of applications. Particular points to check are the *locus standi* of the applicant, the sufficiency of the evidence including whether payment of a fee (eg for copies of documents) should be proffered and whether a print of the company's memorandum and articles of association should be produced, and whether the necessary notice to other interested persons has been given.

Costs

The normal rules apply.

Appeals

Apart from certain decisions which are not appealable, there is an appeal from a registrar in chambers or a county court exercising insolvency jurisdiction to a single judge of the High Court, and from a judge of the High Court or a county court exercising other companies jurisdiction to the Court of Appeal (Ord 102, r 1, para 4).

Alternative jurisdiction

District registries of the High Court. The county court has jurisdiction as respects companies within its district having a paid up capital of not more than £120,000, and there is also the possibility of transferring High Court proceedings to the county court without jurisdictional limit.

Textbooks

Stevens, *Palmer's Company Law*.
J H Farrar, N E Furey, B M Hammick & P Wylie, *Farrar's Company Law*, 2nd edn, (Butterworths, 1988).

Forms and precedents

Palmer's Company Precedents (17th edn) Butterworths.
Atkin, Vol 9 (1990 Issue); Atkin, Vol 10 (1988 Issue) (Winding Up).

Companies—Orders

1. ORDER TO RESTRAIN ADVERTISEMENT OF WINDING UP PETITION

IN THE MATTER of ...

and

IN THE MATTER of THE INSOLVENCY ACT 1986

UPON THE APPLICATION of the above named ... (hereinafter called 'the Company')

AND UPON HEARING Counsel for the Company

AND UPON READING the documents recorded on the Court File as having been read including the Petition to wind-up the Company presented on the ... 19 ... by ...

AND the Company by its Counsel undertaking to obey any Order which this Court may make as to damages in case this Court shall be of opinion that the said ... shall have sustained any damages by reason of this Order which the Company ought to pay

IT IS ORDERED that the said ... be restrained until after the ... day of ... 19 ... or until further Order in the meantime from doing (whether by its directors or by its officers or servants or agents or any of them or otherwise howsoever) the following act that is to say advertising the said Petition

AND the Company is to be at liberty to serve Notice of Application for ... 19 ...

2. ORDER TO RESTRAIN PRESENTATION OF A WINDING UP PETITION

BETWEEN

...
Applicant

and

...
Respondent(s)

UPON THE APPLICATION by Originating Motion of ...

AND UPON HEARING Counsel for the Applicant

AND UPON READING the documents recorded on the Court File as having been read

AND the Applicant by its Counsel undertaking to obey any Order which this Court may make as to damages in case this Court shall be of the opinion that the Respondent(s) shall have sustained any damages by reason of this Order which the Applicant ought to pay

IT IS ORDERED that the Respondent(s) be restrained until after ... 19 ... or until further Order in the meantime from presenting (whether by its directors or by its officers or servants or agents or any of them or otherwise howsoever/whether by himself/herself/themselves or by his/her/their servants or agents or any of them or otherwise howsoever) a petition for the winding-up of the Applicant based upon the alleged debt referred to in ... or any part thereof

AND the Applicant is to be at liberty to serve an application for ... 19 ...

AND the Respondent(s) is/are to be at liberty to apply to discharge or vary this Order (upon giving to the Applicant ... days Notice of his/her/their/its intention so to do).

3. WINDING UP ORDER ON PETITION BY CREDITOR

IN THE MATTER OF ...

and

IN THE MATTER OF THE INSOLVENCY ACT 1986

UPON THE PETITION OF ... whose registered office is situate at ... a creditor of the above-named Company presented to this Court on the ...

AND UPON HEARING Counsel for the Petitioner [and for the said Company] [and for ... Creditors of the said Company supporting the said Petition] [and for ... Creditors of the said Company opposing the said Petition]

AND UPON READING the Evidence

IT IS ORDERED

1 that ... be wound up by this Court under the provisions of the Insolvency Act 1986

2 that the costs of the Petitioner [and of the said Company and of the said ...] of the said Petition be paid out of the assets of the said Company [but only one set of costs is to be allowed between the said Petitioner and Creditor(s) supporting] [but only one set of costs is to be allowed between the said Creditors supporting]

Note: One of the Official Receivers attached to the court is by virtue of this Order Liquidator of the Company.

Note

1 The usual practice is to give costs to the petitioner and the company (if represented). If there are supporting creditors represented by the petitioner they share one set of costs with the petitioner. Other supporting creditors separately represented share one set of costs between them. Unless the Judge otherwise directs opposing creditors do not get costs.

4. WINDING UP ORDER—SUBSTITUTED PETITIONER

IN THE MATTER of ...
and
IN THE MATTER of THE INSOLVENCY ACT 1986

UPON THE PETITION OF ... which was substituted by this Court as Petitioner on the ... 19 ... on the hearing of the said Petition in place of ...

AND HEARING Counsel for the Petitioner [and for the said Company] [and for ... Creditors of the said Company supporting the said Petition] [and for ... Creditors of the said Company opposing the said Petition]

AND UPON READING the evidence

IT IS ORDERED

1 that ... be wound up by this Court under the provisions of the Insolvency Act 1986

2 the costs of the Petitioner the said [Present Petitioner] and the said [Previous Petitioner] of the said Petition be paid out of the assets of the said Company but the costs of the said ... are to be limited to the fee incurred on presentation of the Petition [and the proper costs and disbursements of advertising the Petition]

Note: One of the Official Receivers attached to the Court is by virtue of this Order Liquidator of the Company.

5. ORDER TO STAY WINDING UP AFTER COMPULSORY ORDER GRANTED AND ENTERED

IN THE MATTER of ...
and
IN THE MATTER of THE INSOLVENCY ACT 1986

UPON THE APPLICATION dated the ... of ... the liquidator/a creditor/contributory of the above named Company

AND UPON HEARING Counsel for the Applicant and ...

AND UPON READING the documents recorded on the Court File as having been read

IT IS ORDERED

1. that all further proceedings in the winding-up of the Company under the Winding-up order dated the ... 19 ... be stayed

2. that the Applicant deliver an Office Copy of this Order to the Registrar of Companies.

6. ORDER DISMISSING PETITION WITH COSTS

IN THE MATTER of ...

and

IN THE MATTER of THE INSOLVENCY ACT 1986

UPON THE PETITION of ...

AND UPON HEARING Counsel for the Petitioner [and for the above named Company] and for ... respectively Creditors of the said Company supporting the said Petition

AND UPON READING the documents recorded on the Court File as having been read

IT IS [BY CONSENT] ORDERED

1. that the said Petition do stand dismissed

2. that the Petitioner/said Company do pay to the said Company/Petitioner its costs of this Petition such costs to be taxed if not agreed.

7. ORDER SANCTIONING DISPOSITION OF COMPANY PROPERTY AFTER PRESENTATION OF WINDING UP PETITION

IN THE MATTER of ...

and

IN THE MATTER of THE INSOLVENCY ACT 1986

UPON THE APPLICATION of the above-named ... (hereinafter called 'the Company')

AND UPON HEARING Counsel for the Company

AND UPON READING the documents recorded on the Court file as having been read including the Petition to wind up the Company presented on ...

IT IS ORDERED that notwithstanding the presentation of the Petition

1   payments made into or out of the bank account of the Company with ... Bank plc at ... for the purpose of paying debts of the Company incurred in the ordinary course of its business from the date hereof up to and including the ... and

2   dispositions of the property of the Company sold in the ordinary course of business to its customers at full market price during such period as aforesaid ... shall not be avoided by virtue of the provisions of Section 127 of the above-mentioned Act in the event of an Order for the winding up of the Company being made on the Petition

8. ORDER FOR RECTIFICATION OF REGISTER

IN THE MATTER of ...

and

IN THE MATTER of THE COMPANIES ACT 1985

UPON MOTION made by Counsel on behalf of ...

AND UPON HEARING ...

AND UPON READING the documents recorded on the Court File as having been read

IT IS ORDERED

1   That the Register of Members of the said Company be rectified by striking out the name of ... as the holder of ... shares of the said Company numbered ... to ... inclusive and by inserting the name of the Applicant as the holder of the said shares

2   That the Applicant be authorised to rectify the Register of members accordingly

3   That an Office Copy of this Order be delivered to the Registrar of Companies

9. ORDER DECLARING DISSOLUTION OF COMPANY VOID

IN THE MATTER of

and

IN THE MATTER of THE COMPANIES ACT 1985

UPON MOTION made by Counsel on behalf of ...

AND UPON READING the documents recorded on the Court File as having been read

AND IT APPEARING from the evidence that there is no objection on behalf of Her Majesty to this Order (in Right of Her Duchy of Lancaster) (The Duke of Cornwall)

THE COURT DECLARES the dissolution of the above named Company to have been void

AND IT IS ORDERED that the Applicant do within ... days from the date hereof deliver an Office Copy of this Order to the Registrar of Companies.

Note

1 Section 651 of the Companies Act 1985 states that an office copy of the Order must be delivered to the Registrar of Companies within seven days subject to the court granting an extension. It is normal practice for the time for delivering an office copy to be extended to 21 days.

10. DISQUALIFICATION OF DIRECTOR

IN THE MATTER of

and

IN THE MATTER of THE COMPANY DIRECTORS DISQUALIFICATION ACT 1986

BETWEEN

...
Applicant

and

...
Respondent(s)

UPON THE APPLICATION by Originating Summons of (the Secretary of State for Trade and Industry) (the Official Receiver)

AND UPON HEARING [Counsel for] the Applicant (in person) (and ... for ... (the Respondent(s))

AND UPON READING the documents recorded on the Court File as having been read

IT IS ORDERED

1 that pursuant to Section [(A)* (2) (3) (4) (6)] of The Company Directors Disqualification Act 1986 that the Respondent(s) the said (B)* ... shall not without the leave of the Court [be a director of a company] or [be a liquidator or administrator of a company] or [be a receiver or manager of a company's property] or [in any way whether directly or indirectly be concerned or take part in the promotion formation or management of a company] for a period of ... years beginning on (C)* ...

2 that the Respondent(s) do pay to the Applicant his costs of the said Application such costs to be taxed on the indemnity basis if not agreed

Notes

*(A)   Delete section numbers that do not apply.

*(B)   Insert Name(s) of respondent(s).

*(C)   Unless the court otherwise orders, a disqualification order takes effect at the beginning of the 21st day after the day on which the order is made (Insolvent Companies (Disqualification of Unfit Directors) Proceedings Rules 1987, r 9).

11. ADMINISTRATION ORDER ON PETITION PRESENTED BY DIRECTORS/CREDITORS

IN THE MATTER of

and

IN THE MATTER of THE INSOLVENCY ACT 1986

UPON THE PETITION of ... of ... Directors(s)/Creditor(s) of the above named Company (hereinafter called 'the Company') presented to the Court on ...
AND UPON HEARING Counsel for the Petitioner(s)
AND UPON READING the evidence

IT IS ORDERED

1 that during the period for which this Order is in force the affairs business and property of the Company be managed by the Administrator(s) hereinafter appointed pursuant to the pro-

visions of Section 8 of the Insolvency Act 1986 for the following purpose(s)
 (a) the survival of the Company and the whole or any part of its undertaking as a going concern
 (b) the approval of a voluntary arrangement under Part 1 of the Insolvency Act 1986
 (c) the sanctioning under section 425 of the Companies Act 1985 of a compromise or arrangement between the Company and any such persons as are mentioned in that section; and
 (d) a more advantageous realisation of the Company's assets than would be effected on a winding up

2 that ... of ... be appointed Administrator(s) of the Company

3 that the costs of the said Petitioner [including the costs of the report prepared pursuant to Rule 2.2(1) of the Insolvency Rules 1986] be paid as an expense of the Administration [And the Court declares pursuant to Section 231 of the Insolvency Act 1986 that any act required or authorised under any enactment to be done by the Administrators is to be done by all or any one or more of them]

Notes

1 Delete (a), (b), (c) or (d) as appropriate.

2 Delete words in brackets if not ordered by the judge.

3 The court must make such a declaration if two or more administrators are appointed.

12. ADMINISTRATION ORDER ON PETITION BY THE COMPANY

IN THE MATTER of
 and
IN THE MATTER of THE INSOLVENCY ACT 1986

UPON THE PETITION of ... (hereinafter called 'the Company') whose registered office is situate at ... presented to the Court on ...
 AND UPON HEARING Counsel for the Company
 AND UPON READING the evidence

IT IS ORDERED

1 that during the period for which this Order is in force the affairs

business and property of the Company be managed by the Administrator(s) hereinafter appointed pursuant to the provisions of Section 8 of the Insolvency Act 1986 for the following purpose(s)
  (a) the survival of the Company and the whole or any part of its undertaking as a going concern
  (b) the approval of a voluntary arrangement under Part 1 of the Insolvency Act 1986
  (c) the sanctioning under section 425 of the Companies Act 1985 of a compromise or arrangement between the Company and any such persons as are mentioned in that section; and
  (d) a more advantageous realisation of the Company's assets than would be effected on a winding up

2 that ... of ... be appointed Administrator(s) of the Company

3 that the costs of the Petitioner [including the costs of the report prepared pursuant to Rule 2.2(1) of the Insolvency Rules 1986] be paid as an expense of the Administration

[AND the Court declares pursuant to Section 231 of the Insolvency Act 1986 that any act required or authorised under any enactment to be done by the Administrators is to be done by all or any one or more of them]
  the court must make such a declaration if two or more administrators are appointed.

Notes

1 Two sealed copies of this order (one of which must be an office copy) must be sent to the administrator plus duplicates to the solicitors for the petitioner (r 2.10(4)).

2 Notice of the order must forthwith be given to the administrator (r 2.10(1)) (Form 2.4A).

3 Delete (a), (b), (c) or (d) where appropriate.

4 Delete words in brackets if not ordered by the judge.

13. ORDER FOR WINDING UP FOLLOWING ADMINISTRATION ORDER

IN THE MATTER of
and
IN THE MATTER of THE INSOLVENCY ACT 1986

COMPANIES 593

UPON THE PETITION of the above named Company by its Administrator (a) [insert name] ... presented to this Court on (b) [insert date] ...
 AND UPON HEARING Counsel for the said Company
 AND UPON READING the Administration Order dated the ... 19 ... (made on Petition No 00 ... of 19 ...) and the evidence

IT IS ORDERED

1 that the Administration Order be and the same is discharged

2 that the said (a) ... be released from his said office as Administrator [(c) ... days after sending to the Court and to the Registrar of Companies and to each member of the creditors committee the requisite Accounts of the receipts and payments of the Company]

3 that the said (d) ... be wound up by this Court under the provisions of the Insolvency Act 1986

4 [that (a) ... be appointed Liquidator of the Company]

5 that the costs of the Petitioner of this Petition be paid out of the assets of the Company.

Note

1 If a named person is not appointed liquidator, add at the end of the order the following words 'Note one of the Official Receivers attached to the Court is by virtue of this Order Liquidator of the Company'.

14. ORDER DISCHARGING AN ADMINISTRATION ORDER

IN THE MATTER of
       and
IN THE MATTER of THE INSOLVENCY ACT 1986

UPON THE application dated the ... 19 ... of (a) [insert name] ... the (Joint) Administrator(s) of the above named Company
 AND UPON HEARING Counsel for the said Applicant(s)
 AND UPON READING the documents recorded on the court file as having been read

IT IS ORDERED

1 that the Administration Order dated the ... 19 ... be discharged

pursuant to section 18 of the above mentioned Act

2 that the Applicant(s) the said (a) ... be released as (Joint) Administrator(s) of the said Company pursuant to section 20 of the above mentioned Act ([only insert if ordered by judge] ... days after sending to the Court and to the Registrar of Companies and to each member of the Creditors Committee the requisite accounts of the receipts and payments of the Company)

[3 that the costs of this application be paid as an expense of the administration]

Note

1 An office copy of this order must be sent to the former administrator and one copy to the solicitor having carriage of the order.

15. ORDER CONFIRMING REDUCTION OF CAPITAL

IN THE MATTER of
and
IN THE MATTER of THE COMPANIES ACT 1985

UPON THE PETITION of the above-named ... (hereinafter called 'the Company')

AND UPON HEARING Counsel for the Company

AND UPON READING the documents recorded on the Court file as having been read

THE COURT CONFIRMS the reduction of the capital of the Company from £ ... to £ ... resolved on and effected by a Special resolution passed at an [Annual] [Extraordinary] General Meeting of the Company held on ... 19 ...

AND THE COURT APPROVES the Minute set forth in the Schedule hereto

AND IT IS ORDERED

1 that this Order be produced to the Registrar of Companies and that an Office Copy be delivered to him together with a copy of the said Minute

[2 that pursuant to Section 139(2) of the said Act the Registrar of Companies do register this Order under Section 138(1) of the said Act notwithstanding that such Order has the effect of bringing the nominal value of the Company's allotted share capital below the authorised minimum]

3 that notice of the registration by the Registrar of Companies of this Order and of the said Minute be published once in the ... newspaper within 21 days after such registration.

The Schedule Before Referred To
...

Minute Approved By The Court
[Copy from para ... of Petition where marked]

Note

1 The company is a public company and the effect of the reduction is to reduce the allotted capital below the authorised minimum (s 118—£50,000) add the words in brackets.

16. ORDER CONFIRMING REDUCTION OF CAPITAL AND CANCELLATION/REDUCTION OF SHARE PREMIUM ACCOUNT

IN THE MATTER of ... LIMITED
and

IN THE MATTER OF THE COMPANIES ACT 1985

UPON THE PETITION of the above named ... Limited (hereinafter called 'the Company')
   AND UPON HEARING Counsel for the Company
   AND UPON READING the documents recorded on the Court file as having been read

THE COURT CONFIRMS

1 the reduction of the capital of the Company from £ ... to £ ...

2 the cancellation of the amount of £ ... standing to the credit of the Share Premium Account of the Company

3 the reduction of the Share Premium Account of the Company from £ ... to £ ... both respectively resolved on and effected by a Special Resolution passed at an Extraordinary [Annual] General Meeting of the Company held on ... 19 ...
   AND THE COURT APPROVES the Minute set forth in the Schedule hereto

AND IT IS ORDERED

1 that this Order be produced to the Registrar of Companies and that an Office Copy be delivered to him together with a copy of the said Minute

[2 that pursuant to section 139(2) of the said Act the Registrar of Companies do register this Order under section 138(1) of the said Act notwithstanding that such Order has the effect of bringing the nominal value of the Company's allotted share capital below the authorised minimum]

3 that notice of the registration by the Registrar of Companies of this Order and of the said Minute be published by the Company once in the ... newspaper within 21 days after such registration

The Schedule Before Referred To
Minute Approved By The Court
[copy from para ... of Petition where marked X-XX]

Note

1 Include para 2 if the company is a public company and the effect of the reduction is to reduce the allotted capital below the authorised minimum (s 118—£50,000) add the words in brackets.

17. ORDER FOR CANCELLATION OF SHARE PREMIUM ACCOUNT

IN THE MATTER of
and
IN THE MATTER of THE COMPANIES ACT 1985

UPON THE PETITION of ... (hereinafter called 'the Company')
AND UPON HEARING Counsel for the Company
AND UPON READING the documents recorded on the Court file as having been read
THE COURT CONFIRMS the cancellation of [the amount of £... standing to the credit of] the Share Premium Account of the Company resolved on and effected by a Special Resolution passed at an [Annual] [Extraordinary] General Meeting of the Company held on ...

AND IT IS ORDERED

1 that this Order be produced to the Registrar of Companies and that an Office Copy of it be delivered to him

2   that notice of the registration by the Registrar of Companies of this Order be published once in the ... newspaper within 21 days after registration.

18. ORDER FOR REDUCTION OF SHARE PREMIUM ACCOUNT

IN THE MATTER of
and
IN THE MATTER of THE COMPANIES ACT 1985

UPON THE PETITION of ... (hereinafter called 'the Company')
   AND UPON HEARING Counsel for the Company
   AND UPON READING the documents recorded on the Court file as having been read
   THE COURT CONFIRMS the reduction of the Share Premium Account of the Company from £ ... to £ ... resolved on and effected by a Special Resolution passed at an Extraordinary [Annual] General Meeting of the Company held on ... 19 ...

AND IT IS ORDERED

1   that this Order be produced to the Registrar of Companies and that an Office Copy be delivered to him

2   that notice of the registration by the Registrar of Companies of this Order be published once in the ... newspaper within 21 days after such registration.

19. ORDER SANCTIONING SCHEME OF ARRANGEMENT UNDER THE COMPANIES ACT 1985

[This form is not to be used for an order sanctioning a scheme of arrangement under the Insurance Companies Act 1982]

IN THE MATTER of ...
and
IN THE MATTER of THE COMPANIES ACT 1985

UPON THE PETITION of the above-named ... Limited (hereinafter called 'the Company')

AND UPON HEARING Counsel for the Company and for (1) ... (referred to in the Scheme of Arrangement hereinafter sanctioned)

AND UPON READING the documents recorded on the Court File as having been read

AND ... by [its] [their] Counsel submitting to be bound by the Scheme of Arrangement hereinafter sanctioned and (2) undertaking to execute and do and procure to be executed and done all such documents acts and things as may be necessary or desirable to be executed or done by [it] [them] for the purpose of giving effect thereto

THE COURT HEREBY SANCTIONS the Scheme of Arrangement set forth in the Schedule hereto

AND IT IS ORDERED that the Company do deliver an Office Copy of this Order to the Registrar of Companies.

The Schedule
(Only the Scheme of Arrangement needs to be scheduled not the whole scheme document)

Notes

1 Other companies represented are usually the ones giving the undertakings mentioned later in the order.

2 The wording of the undertaking may vary from one scheme to another or there may not even be an undertaking. If there is, check the wording in the preliminary to the scheme and alter accordingly.

20. ORDER SANCTIONING SCHEME OF ARRANGEMENT UNDER THE COMPANIES ACT 1985 AND CONFIRMING REDUCTION OF CAPITAL

[This form is not to be used for an Order sanctioning a Scheme of Arrangement under the Insurance Companies Act 1982]

IN THE MATTER of ...
and
IN THE MATTER of THE COMPANIES ACT 1985

UPON THE PETITION of the above-named ... Limited (hereinafter called 'the Company')

AND UPON HEARING Counsel for the Company and for (1) ... (referred to in the Scheme of Arrangement hereinafter sanctioned)

AND UPON READING the documents recorded on the Court File as having been read

AND ... by [its] [their] Counsel submitting to be bound by the Scheme of Arrangement hereinafter sanctioned and (2) undertaking to execute and do and procure to be executed and done all such documents acts and things as may be necessary or desirable to be executed or done by [it] [them] for the purpose of giving effect thereto

THE COURT HEREBY SANCTIONS the Scheme of Arrangement set forth in the First Schedule hereto

AND THE COURT CONFIRMS the reduction of the capital of the Company from £ ... to £ ... resolved on and effected by a Special resolution passed at an [Annual] [Extraordinary] General Meeting of the Company held on ... 19 ...

AND THE COURT APPROVES the Minute set forth in the Second Schedule hereto

AND IT IS ORDERED

1 that this Order be produced to the Registrar of Companies and that an Office Copy be delivered to him together with a copy of the said Minute

[2 that pursuant to Section 139(2) of the said Act the Registrar of Companies do register this Order under Section 138(1) of the said Act notwithstanding that such Order has the effect of bringing the nominal value of the Company's allotted share capital below the authorised minimum]

3 that notice of the registration by the Registrar of Companies of this Order (so far as it confirms the reduction of the capital of the Company) and of the said Minute be published once in the ... newspaper within 21 days after such registration

The First Schedule
[Only the Scheme of Arrangement needs to be scheduled not the whole scheme document]

The Second Schedule Before Referred To

Minute Approved By The Court

(copy from para ... of Petition where marked).

Notes

1 Other companies represented are usually the ones giving the undertakings mentioned later in the order.

2 The wording of the undertaking may vary from one scheme to another or there may not even be an undertaking. If there is, check the wording in the preliminary to the scheme and alter accordingly.

3 If the company is a public company and the effect of the reduction is to reduce the allotted capital below the authorised minimum (s 118—£50,000) add the words in brackets.

21. ORDER APPOINTING OFFICIAL RECEIVER AS PROVISIONAL LIQUIDATOR

IN THE MATTER of

and

IN THE MATTER of THE INSOLVENCY ACT 1986

UPON THE APPLICATION of ...

AND UPON HEARING Counsel for the ...

AND UPON READING the petition to wind up the above named Company and the evidence

AND the Applicant(s) by his/her/their Counsel undertaking to obey any order this Court may make as to damages if it shall consider that the said Company has sustained any damages by reason of this order which the Applicant(s) ought to pay (1)

[AND the Court dispensing with the requirement for lodgment of a deposit pursuant to Rule 4.27(1) of the Insolvency Rules 1986] (2)

IT IS ORDERED

1 that the Official Receiver be appointed Provisional Liquidator of the above named Company

2 that the powers of the Official Receiver as such Provisional Liquidator be limited and restricted (3) to taking possession of collecting and protecting the assets of the above named Company but such assets are not to be distributed or parted with until further Order (3)

NOTICE TO OFFICERS OF COMPANY

You are required by Section 235 of the Insolvency Act 1986 to give the Provisional Liquidator all the information as he may reasonably require relating to the Company's property and affairs and to attend upon him at such times as he may reasonably require.

Notes

1 Not given by the Crown (or bodies acting for the Crown when applying for the purpose of enforcing the law).

2 Usually only dispensed with if the order involves a Government

department application. If deposit directed order not to be issued until deposit made see Form 4.15 and Rule 4.27.

3 This can be further limited or extended.

22. ORDER ON APPLICATION TO RESTORE NAME TO REGISTER OF COMPANIES

IN THE MATTER of . . .

and

IN THE MATTER of THE COMPANIES ACT 1985

UPON THE APPLICATION by Originating Summons dated . . . the . . . 19 . . . of the above-named . . . (hereinafter called 'the Company') and of . . . a member (and director) of the Company
   AND UPON HEARING . . . for the Applicants and . . . for the Registrar of Companies (the Respondent)
   AND UPON READING the documents recorded on the Court File as having been read
   AND the Applicants by their . . . undertaking within one month of the restoration of the name of the Company to the Register of Companies . . .

IT IS ORDERED

1 that the name of the above-named . . . be restored to the Register of Companies

2 that an Office Copy of this Order be delivered to the Registrar of Companies and pursuant to the Companies Act 1985 the said is thereupon to be deemed to have continued in existence as if its name had not been struck off

3 that the Registrar of Companies do advertise Notice of this Order in his official name in the London Gazette

4 that the Applicants the said . . . and . . . do pay to the Registrar of Companies his costs of the said Application such costs to be taxed if not agreed.

23. VESTING ORDER—DISSOLVED COMPANY

AND the defendant by his solicitors not objecting to this order

IT IS ORDERED

1 that the property specified in the schedule hereto vest in the plaintiff for all the estate and interest which immediately prior to its dissolution was vested in ...

2 that the plaintiff shall pay the defendant his costs of this Application such costs to be taxed on the common fund basis if not agreed.

The Schedule

Note

1 The defendant is Her Majesty's Attorney-General and he usually acknowledges service by the Treasury Solicitor.

Chapter Twenty Three

Insolvency

1. Individual insolvency

The procedure is governed by the Insolvency Rules 1986 (SI 1986/1925 as amended by SIs 1987/1959 and SI 1989/397 and the prescribed forms must be used. The result of a petition, if it is not dismissed, is necessarily a 'bankruptcy order'.

There are two bases on which the court can make a bankruptcy order, on a creditor's petition, namely failure to comply with a statutory demand for three weeks (s 268 (1)(*a*)), or where exclusion is wholly or partly unsatisfied (s 268(1)(*b*)). A debtor's petition can only be presented on the grounds that the debtor is unable to pay his debts, and in this case, the petition must be accompanied by a statement of his affairs (rr 6167-6.72).

The prescribed forms of statutory demand are Form Nos 6.1, 6.2 and 6.3. They give the debtor a clear indication of what is claimed and why, and what he has to do to apply to set it aside (*see below*).

Rule 6.11 provides that if the creditor has taken the steps which the court would have ordered him to take if there had been an application for sub-service, then there is sufficient service but service is usually effected in the first instance by post.

Applications to set aside are to be made within 21 days of service of the statutory demand (r 6.4).

Rule 6.5(4) indicates that an application to set aside may be granted if no debt is owed, work was not properly done, or the debtor has a set-off or counterclaim. If the grounds of dispute are substantial, the court should set aside, or alternatively, the application should be adjourned for a more detailed hearing. Where there has been a judgment in default, the court should go behind it to see whether there is a triable issue, in which case the order should be to adjourn the application pending determination of the debtor's application to set aside the judgment.

If the court makes a bankruptcy order, the debtor is adjudicated bankrupt forthwith, the Official Receiver becomes receiver, and manager where appropriate (s 287) and the debtor loses control over his assets. The order cannot be rescinded, though debtors may apply for annulment.

Individual voluntary arrangements

A debtor may seek a voluntary arrangement with his creditors whereby a 'nominee', who must be a licensed insolvency practitioner appointed by the debtor, assists in drawing up a proposed composition, which is required to be approved by three-quarters in value of those who attend and vote at a creditors' meeting.

Completing bankruptcy petitions

The petition is entitled with the debtor's name, eg 'Re John Smith' and if he is 'trading as' this will be given only in the body of the petition. Date of service, as given in the affidavit of service, should be recited and it should be stated whether service is effected before or after 16.00 hours on Monday to Friday, or before or after 12.00 hours on Saturdays. If there has been substituted service, otherwise than by advertisement, the date when it is averred that service has been effected should again be recited. The date of an advertisement's appearance is treated as the date of service in those cases where there has been substituted service by advertisement. Certificates are required at the end of the petition as to three years search for prior petitions, and where the statutory demand is based on a county court judgment, a certificate that on attendance at the county court no money had been paid into court. The forms of petition are Form Nos 6.7, 6.8, 6.9 or 6.10.

Deposits are payable on presenting a petition, ie £200, or £100 if debtor presents his own petition. The court fee is £40.

Petitions are not required to be signed, witnessed or dated, as the court will seal and time/date them itself.

The appropriate court

The appropriate court is the county court for the insolvency district in which the debtor has resided or carried on business for the longest period during the six months immediately preceding presentation of the petition; county courts having 'bankruptcy' jurisdiction are listed at the back of the County Court Practice. However, if the debtor has resided or carried on business 'within the London insolvency district', then the petition must be presented to the High Court.

Hazards and pitfalls

The strictest application of the Rules and adoption of the prescribed forms is vital; there is no question of the court exercising a discretion not to require strict compliance. Pitfalls can be encountered on service of statutory demand and petition.

Textbooks

M Hunter, *Personal Insolvency*, (Sweet & Maxwell, 1988 and service 1989).
M Griffiths, *Insolvency of Individuals and Partnerships*, (Butterworths, 1988).
S Frieze, *Weaving's Bankruptcy Procedure*, 10th edn, (Longman, 1990).

2. Corporate insolvency

A decision having been made to remove those parts which dealt with corporate insolvency from the Companies Act 1985, this is now amalgamated with the Insolvency Act 1986. The law is contained in ss 122-130 of the Act, s 122(1) giving the seven grounds on which a company may be wound up; the most important being ground (*f*), the company's inability to pay its debts, and ground (*g*) that the winding up of the company is just and equitable. It is Part 4 of the Insolvency Rules which deals with members' voluntary winding up, creditors' voluntary winding up and winding up by the court. Procedure for company winding up is mirrored in the Rules for individual bankruptcy and is set out in the Insolvency Rules 1986 (SI No 1925) as amended by the Insolvency (Amendment) Rules 1987 (SI No 1919), and the prescribed forms annexed thereto.

Winding up in the case of companies is discretionary and may be declined where, for example, the majority of creditors oppose it, usually on the basis that continued trading will be more beneficial. 'Inability to pay debts' is statutorily defined (s 123(1)(*a*)) so that if a company has for three weeks neglected to pay, or come to an arrangement with a creditor who has served a written demand for a sum owed in excess of £750, it shall be presumed that there is inability to pay. This presumption also arises if there is an unsatisfied execution on a judgment, or if it can be proved that the company is unable to pay its debts as they fall due, or finally, where it can be proved that the value of the company's assets is less than its liabilities, as reflected by its balance sheet. Creditors can, and frequently do, combine to present a petition. The court may dismiss the petition, adjourn it, substitute a petition, or make an order for winding up. Once there is a winding up order, no action or proceedings can be commenced against the company.

The statutory demand must have been for a liquidated sum and must have been in prescribed Form 41. Service may be by post to or by leaving at the company's registered office.

The petition in Form 4.2 and the affidavit in Form 4.3 (which is in the prescribed forms), two copies of the petition and the affidavit verifying the petition, with a further copy of the petition annexed, together with a receipt for the deposit which is £200, and payment of the court fee of £40 are lodged with the court who will seal all copies of the petition, and give a date and venue returning two copies to the petitioner, one for service, the other for annexing to the affidavit of service. The original petition and affidavit are retained by the court. Service of the petition is at some place where the company involved has carried on business, or its last known principal place of business, on a director, officer or employee, or person acknowledging himself to be authorised by handing it to a director or other officer or employee or someone who claims to be able to accept service or by leaving it at such place that 'it is likely to come to the notice of a person attending at the registered office'. All failing, an *ex parte* application can be made by the court.

The form of petition (Form 4.2) requires the statutory grounds in para 5—these should be prefaced by a short statement of the facts supporting these grounds. Paragraph 6 requires the petitioner's statement of belief that is just and equitable to wind up the company be served. A liquidator or an administrative receiver is also entitled to receive a sealed copy of the petition.

The petition is also to be advertised. A certificate of compliance (r 4.14) must be lodged at least five days before the hearing. This certifies compliance with Rules as to service and advertisement. The advertisement is filed with the certificate.

Petitions by undefended creditors are heard in open court by the registrar.

Unlike a bankruptcy order, there is no power in the Act or Rules to annul a winding up order, though there may be some limited power to set aside (RSC Ord 35, r 2 and the note at para 4605 of SCP). Part 4, Chapter 5 of the Act deals with the provisional liquidator and the power to appoint, and r 4.25 sets out how and to whom application is to be made and how it is supported by affidavit and what the affidavit should contain.

Under s 132 of the Act it is the duty of the Official Receiver to investigate the causes of failure and generally the affairs of the company and to make a report to the court.

Administration orders may be made under the provisions contained in ss 8 - 27. Basically, if the court is satisfied that the company is unable, or unlikely to be able, to pay its debts, then the purpose is either to let the company survive and be sold as a going concern or to approve a voluntary arrangement or sanction compromise. If the court feels that an administration order will more advantageously realise a company's assets than a winding up, then it can make an administration order. The form of petition for an administration order is Form 2.1, following r 2.4, and is verified by affidavit, to which is exhibited a copy of the petition. The precise rules as to service of a winding up petition do not apply, and there is no provision for advertisement.

An administrative receiver advertises his appointment within 28 days (s 46(1)) and reports to a creditors' meeting within three months (s 48).

Textbooks

S Frieze, *Compulsory Winding Up Procedure*, 2nd edn, (Longman, 1987).
Millman and Durrant, *Corporate Insolvency, Law and Practice*, (Sweet & Maxwell, 1987).
R Pennington, *Company Liquidations: Substantive Law*, (Jordans, 1987).

Appendix A

Practice Directions

Chancery Division Practice Direction (Chancery Index No 1 of 1986) cancelled out of date Practice Directions and listed those still in force, including some Central Office and Queen's Bench Directions which are applied in the Chancery Division. Practice Directions published since then are shown in square brackets.

Practice Direction (Chancery: Index) No 1 of 1986

1   The object of this Practice Direction is to delete those Chancery (other than Companies Court) directions which are no longer required as they are out of date or found elsewhere, and to indicate those still in force which the practitioner is most likely to encounter. This is an index primarily of Chancery Practice Directions but some Central Office and Queen's Bench Practice Directions have been included which are applied in the Chancery Division.
2   The following directions are hereby cancelled:

Practice Note [1907] WN 44, Practice Note 1929 WN 105, Practice Note 1940 WN 155, Practice Note 1945 WN 210, Practice Direction (Trustees Costs) [1953] 1 WLR 1365, Practice Note (Trustees Costs) [1953] 1 WLR 1452, Practice Directions (Applications: Affidavits: Mortgages) [1955] 1 WLR 36 paras 2 and 3, Practice Direction (Title of Proceedings) [1959] 1 WLR 743, Practice Direction (Affidavit Evidence) [1969] 1 WLR 974 paras 1, 3 and 4, Practice Direction (Chancery Division: Miscellaneous Directions) [1970] 1 WLR 520 paras 3, 5 and 6, Practice Direction (Chancery Division: Miscellaneous Provisions) [1970] 1 WLR 977, Practice Direction (Hearing dates for originating summons: Expedited Form) [1974] 1 WLR 708, Practice Direction (Chancery: Setting Down) [1975] 1 WLR 321, Practice Direction (Chancery: Originating Summons) (No 2) [1976] 1 WLR 201 paras 1, 3 and 4, Practice Direction (Chancery: Speedy Trial) [1979] 1 WLR 204.
3   The following is an index of the Practice Directions now in force in the Chancery Division (other than the Companies Court).

Affidavits

Acceptance of affidavits sworn before proceedings have commenced:

Practice Direction (Affidavit Evidence) [1969] 1 WLR 974, para 2.

Appeals from masters

Notice of appeal Two copies of the notice of appeal are lodged at room 307/308 within five days after the order is made. Appeals are heard in chambers in the non-witness list:

Practice Direction (Chancery Chambers) [1982] 1 WLR 1189, para 10.

Appellant opens The appellant opens but even if the appeal is against only part of the master's order the whole of the summons is treated as being before the judge who will make such order on it as he thinks fit:

Practice Direction (Chancery: Procedure) [1983] 1 WLR 4, para 7.

Ground of appeal Notice of appeal need not state the grounds of appeal:

Practice Direction (Chancery Applications: Change of Name) [1984] 1 WLR 447, para 3.

Chancery Chambers

Administrative structure The structure of Chancery Chambers is fully explained:

Practice Direction (Chancery Chambers) [1982] 1 WLR 1189.

Termination by consent When proceedings are terminated by consent these should be reported at room 307/308 and the solicitor should collect his exhibits:

Practice Direction (Termination of Proceedings by Consent) [1963] 1 WLR 246.

Chancery Registry

Change of name Notice of change of name must be filed in room 307/308 and a copy served on every other party:

Practice Direction (Chancery Applications: Change of Name) [1984] 1 WLR 447, para 4.

APPENDIX A   611

Description of parties   Practice Direction (Central Office: Description of Parties) [1969] 1 WLR 1259.

Documents for use abroad   Where a certified copy of a judgment is required a copy must be obtained from room 307/308 and authenticated by a master:

Practice Direction (Documents for use abroad QB and Ch) [1971] 1 WLR 604.

Judgment: foreign currency   Particulars to be inserted in writ and pleadings:

Practice Direction (Judgment: Foreign Currency) [1976] 1 WLR 83.

Charging order

A judgment creditor may apply to a master *ex parte* by affidavit for an order to inspect the land register relating to the title of a judgment debtor:

Practice Direction (Land Register: Inspection) [1983] 1 WLR 150.

Consent orders

The Tomlin form   Where terms are inserted in the Schedule:

Practice Note 1927 WN 290 and Practice Direction (Minutes of Orders) [1960] 1 WLR 1168 para 2.

Orders made in court   The normal conditions for the making of a consent order in the absence of a party are set out:

Practice Direction (Chancery: Consent orders in Court) [1985] 1 WLR 593.

Cross-examination of deponents

The master may make such an order either *ex parte* or at a hearing and the form is set out in the Schedule to the Practice Direction:

Practice Direction (Affidavits: Cross-examination) [1969] 1 WLR 985.

Documentation

Directions about marking of affidavits, numbering and binding of documents and marking of exhibits:

Practice Direction (Evidence: Documents) [1983] 1 WLR 922.

Estate agents' and auctioneers' fees

Fees should normally not exceed 2½ per cent of sale price exclusive of VAT:

Practice Direction (Estate Agents' and Auctioneers' Fees) [1983] 1 WLR 86.

Grants of representation

Grants of probate and letters of administration may be accepted as evidence of death for procedural purposes but not as part of the proof of title:

Practice Direction (Chancery Division: Miscellaneous Directions) [1970] 1 WLR 520, para 4.

Execution

Notice must be given to a mortgagor if the mortgagee wishes to enforce a suspended order and a summons must be issued. Notice must also be given when leave to issue execution is required because six years have elapsed since the date of the order:

Practice Direction (Possession Order: Issue of Execution) [1972] 1 WLR 240.

Family provision

Appeals from masters Notice of appeal is given in the usual way and a transcript of any oral evidence and the judgment should be obtained:

Practice Direction (Family Provision: Application) [1978] 1 WLR 585.

Endorsement of order All orders under the Inheritance (Provision for Family and Dependants) Act 1975 including 'Tomlin' orders are endorsed on the original grant of representation and sent to the Principal Registry of the Family Division for noting:

Practice Direction (Family Provision: Endorsement of Orders) [1979] 1 WLR 1.

Judgment by default

Applications To be made to room 307/308, in the first instance, together with an affidavit of service of the writ of summons:

Practice Direction (Chancery Chambers) [1982] 1 WLR 1189, para 17.

Appendix A

Claims for interest Directions as to the manner in which claims for interest should be pleaded and what conditions must be fulfilled before a default judgment for interest can be obtained:

Practice Note (Claims for Interest) (No 2) [1983] 1 WLR 377.

Landlord and tenant

Masters will give early appointments for the hearing of joint applications to authorise agreements excluding ss 24 to 28 of the Landlord and Tenant Act 1954 on two or three days' notice:

Practice Note (Business Tenancy: Joint Applications) [1973] 1 WLR 299.

Listing Full details of the lists are contained in Practice Direction (Chancery Lists) [1983] 1 WLR 436.

Revenue listing The listing of revenue appeals is dealt with in room 163:

Practice Note (Revenue Paper: Abolition) [1982] 1 WLR 147.

Masters' powers

Practice Direction (Chancery: Masters' Powers) [1975] 1 WLR 129.

Powers under para 3(*b*), 1(ii) and (*m*) of above direction extended to cases where amount does not exceed £30,000:

Practice Direction (Chancery Procedure) [1983] 1 WLR 4, para 3.

Power to make orders authorising agreements to exclude the provisions in ss 24 - 28 of the Landlord and Tenant Act 1954:

Practice Direction (Chancery: Powers of Masters) [1971] 1 WLR 706.

Extending time for making applications under s 4, Inheritance (Provision for Family and Dependants) Act 1975:

Practice Direction (Chancery: Masters' Powers) No 2 [1975] 1 WLR 405, para 2.

Exercising powers under s 27 of Leasehold Reform Act 1967, enfranchisement where landlord cannot be found:

Practice Direction (Chancery: Masters' Powers) No 3 [1976] 1 WLR 637.

Masters' appointments Vacation of Masters' Appointments Practice Direction (No 6 of 1988).

Motions

Hearing A full code for the hearing of motions is set out in Practice Direction (Chancery Division: Motions Procedure) [1980] 1 WLR 751 and Practice Direction (Chancery Division: Motions Procedure) No 2 [1985] 1 WLR 244.

Agreed adjournment Signed consents to be lodged at room 180:

Practice Direction (Chancery Division: Motions) [1976] 1 WLR 441.

Court File must be bespoken from room 157 before application can be made:

Practice Direction (Chancery Chambers) [1982] 1 WLR 1189, para 18.

This procedure extended to cases in which an undertaking to the court has been given and is to continue unchanged:

Practice Direction (Chancery: Procedure) [1983] 1 All ER 131.

Orders

Procedure for solicitors to draw up orders made on motion by agreement:

Practice Direction (Chancery Motions: Drawing up of orders) [1970] 1 WLR 249.

By judges Details of procedure:

Practice Direction (Chancery Chambers) [1982] 1 WLR 1189, para 14.

By masters Final orders are drawn up by the court but interlocutory orders may be drawn up by the solicitors if the master agrees:

Practice Direction (Chancery Chambers) [1982] 1 WLR 1189, para 13.

Minutes of order If the drafting section does not agree with minutes settled by counsel they should be referred back to counsel through the solicitors:

Practice Direction (Minutes of Order) [1960] 1 WLR 1168, para 1.

Form of order Any party dissatisfied with the form of the order must notify room 504/514. If the differences cannot be resolved the objecting party may apply by motion or summons for the order to be amended:

APPENDIX A 615

Practice Direction (Chancery Chambers) [1982] 1 WLR 1189, para 15.

Copies of orders   Copies may be obtained from room 307/308 upon payment of the appropriate fee:

Practice Direction (Chancery Chambers) [1982] 1 WLR 1189, para 16.

Copies of scripts

When a party lodges an original script he should at the same time lodge a copy for the court file:

Practice Direction (Probate Action) [1973] 1 WLR 627, paras 6 and 7.

Transmission of scripts   It is the convenient practice for a probate action which is to be heard outside London to be set down in London so that the scripts can be sent to the district registry concerned:

Practice Direction (Probate: Contentious Actions) [1974] 1 WLR 1349, paras 3 and 4.

Verification of will

The formalities for verification are set out in:

Practice Direction (Probate: Contentious Actions) [1974] 1 WLR 1349, paras 1 and 2.

Proceedings outside London

Liverpool, Manchester, Preston, Leeds and Newcastle-upon-Tyne are places authorised for trial of Chancery actions in the Northern Area within the jurisdiction of the Vice-Chancellor of the County Palatine of Lancaster:

Practice Direction (Chancery: Proceedings outside London) [1972] 1 WLR 1.

Birmingham, Bristol and Cardiff are also places authorised for Chancery trials:

Practice Direction (Chancery Chambers) [1982] 1 WLR 1189, para 3.

Powers of circuit judge exercising Chancery jurisdiction at Birmingham, Bristol and Cardiff to be same as Vice-Chancellor of the County Palatine of Lancaster:

Practice Direction (Chancery: Proceedings outside London) [1985] 1 WLR 109.

Interlocutory applications in the Northern Area and in Birmingham, Bristol and Cardiff should be made to the judge exercising Chancery jurisdiction in the area of the circuit within which the Registry is situated:

Practice Direction (Chancery: Proceedings outside London) [1984] 1 WLR 417.

The special provisions for hearing business from Liverpool and Manchester in London on a Thursday are extended to Preston:

Practice Direction (Chancery: District Registries) [1972] 1 WLR 53, para 2.

Receivers

Accounts Directions about examination of accounts:

Practice Direction (Chancery Chambers) [1982] 1 WLR 1189, para 21.

Powers A receiver may without leave effect small repairs estimated not to cost over £1000 in one accounting period:

Practice Direction 1 July 1985.

Review of taxation

Procedure on a review of taxation:

Practice Direction (Chancery: Procedure) [1983] 1 WLR 4, para 5.

Original documents

On the construction of a will or document the original probate or original document should be available in court:

Practice Note [1949] WN 441.

Originating motion

The procedure for the issue and hearing of originating motions is contained in:

Practice Direction (Chancery: Originating Notice of Motion: case stated and similar proceeding) [1984] 1 WLR 1216.

Agreed directions for the rectification of the register of trade marks may be obtained by lodging the documents at room 307/308:

Practice Direction (Motions Procedure) Ch D [1980] 1 WLR 751, para 9.

This procedure extended to register of patents and registered designs:

Practice Direction (Application for rectification of the register of patents or designs agreed directions) [1985] 1 All ER 192.

Patent actions

Summons for directions An agreed order signed by counsel for the parties will be made without any attendance before the master. If the parties are not agreed application is made by motion to one of the assigned judges:

Practice Direction (Patent Action: Directions) [1973] 1 WLR 1425, paras 1 and 2.

Interlocutory applications Procedure when adjournment into court likely:

Practice Direction (Patent Summonses) [1970] 1 WLR 94, paras 2 and 3.

Agreed orders will be made as on a summons for directions:

Practice Direction (Patent Action: Directions) [1973] 1 WLR 1425, para 3.

Possession under Order 113

Practice set out in:

Practice Direction (Chancery: Procedure) [1983] 1 WLR 4, para 1.

Post or telephone

Details of what can be done by post and telephone are set out in:

Practice Direction (Chancery: Applications by post and telephone) [1983] 1 WLR 791.

Service by post

Service will be effected on the second working day after posting in the case of first class mail and on the fourth working day after posting for second class mail:

Practice Direction (QBD. Postal Service) [1985] 1 WLR 489.

Setting down

Leave of the court or the consent of the other parties is not required for setting down for trial out of time provided Ord 3, r 6 is complied with:

Practice Direction (Chancery: Setting down for trial) [1981] 1 WLR 322.

Speedy trial

A judge hearing a motion may give directions for pleadings and discovery and specify a date for further hearing before a master:

Practice Direction (Chancery: Expedited Trial) [1974] 1 WLR 339.

Summary judgment

A summons for judgment under Ord 14 or Ord 86 when an injunction is sought may be issued in room 157 so as to be returnable directly before a judge:

Practice Direction (Chancery Applications: Change of Name) [1984] 1 WLR 447, para 1.

Title and parties

Contents of title:

Practice Direction (Chancery: Procedure) [1983] 1 WLR 4, para 2.

Numbering and arrangement of parties in title:

Practice Note (Chancery: Deposition) [1981] 1 WLR 1560.

Trustees

Evidence on removal of trustee under disability:

Practice Direction [1948] WN 273.

Lodgment in court under s 63, Trustee Act 1925 of less than £500 must be authorised in writing by the Chief Master or Vacation Master:

Practice Direction dated 5 December 1975.

Investments of property in Scotland should be set out in a separate schedule so that trustees may apply for vesting order from the Scottish Court:

Appendix A

Practice Direction [1945] WN 80.

Variation of trusts

Undertaking required from solicitors having the carriage of the order to submit the order to Commissioners of the Inland Revenue within 30 days of entry of order for adjudication of stamp duty:

Practice Note (Variation of Trusts: Stamp Duty) [1966] 1 WLR 345.

Where any minor or unborn beneficiary will be affected by the proposed arrangement an affidavit should be filed by the guardian *ad litem* or trustees supporting the arrangement and exhibiting a case to counsel and his opinion to this effect:

Practice Direction (Variation of Trusts: Counsel's Opinion) [1976] 1 WLR 884.

Appendix B

Thomas More Building

The Chancery registry, accounts, drafting and listing sections have been moved to new permanent accommodation in the Thomas More Building within the RCJ complex. The new locations for the various Chancery functions are set out below:

Thomas More Building

2nd Floor	Chancery fees—room 204—and issue of all Chancery originating process room 211—Tel: 071 936 6715.
3rd Floor	Chancery registry—rooms 307/308—Tel: 071 936 6167/6148.
4th Floor	Chancery listing—rooms 412/413/414—Tel: 071 936 6816/6690/6678.
4th Floor	Chancery accounts—rooms 415/416—Tel: 071 936 6187/6325.
5th Floor	Chancery drafting/associates—room 508—Tel: 071 936 6216.
6th Floor	Chief Master Munrow—room 607.
6th Floor	Master Gowers—room 609.
6th Floor	Master Barratt—room 605.
7th Floor	Master Cholmondeley-Clarke—room 708.
7th Floor	Master Dyson—room 706.
7th Floor	Masters' appointments clerks—rooms 709/710—Tel: 071 936 6146.

It should be noted that these new arrangements amend the locations given in Practice Direction 1 of 1982 1 WLR 1189 [1982] 3 All ER 124.

Appendix C

The Supreme Court Fees Order 1980

Section 1: fees payable in every division of the High Court

Column 1	Column 2	Column 3
Item	Fee £	Document to be marked
A. Commencement of a Cause or Matter		
1. On sealing—		
(a) a writ of summons, or		The filed copy.
(b) an originating summons, except for the payment out of Court of a sum not exceeding £1,500 and where no other fee is specially provided, or		The filed copy.
(c) an originating notice of motion, except a notice of appeal to the High Court, or		The notice of motion.
(d) on presenting an originating petition, except where a fee under section 6 of this Schedule is payable.	60.00	The petition.
2. On sealing of an originating summons—		
(a) for approval of an infant settlement,	10.00	The filed copy.
(b) under Part III of the Solicitors Act 1974 for a solicitor's bill to be taxed,	10.00	The filed copy.
(c) under section 33(2) (or 34(2)) of the Supreme Court Act 1981 for discovery before commencement of proceedings,	10.00	The filed copy.

Column 1	Column 2	Column 3
Item	Fee £	Document to be marked
(d) under section 56 of the County Courts Act 1984 for a witness to be examined abroad.	10.00	The filed copy.
3. On presenting a petition of course.	10.00	The petition.
4. On an application for leave to apply judicial review under Order 53: Provided that where the applicant obtains leave to move, credit for this fee is to be given against the fee payable in 1.	10.00	The application.
B. Progress of Proceedings *Interlocutory applications* 5A. On taking an appointment before a master, district registrar or Admiralty registrar or before a bankruptcy registrar. This fee is not payable on an application to set aside a statutory demand or an application by the Official Receiver when applying only in that capacity.	10.00	The summons, notice or application.
5B. On lodging a summons for hearing before a Judge in Chambers in the Queen's Bench Division or an official referee.	15.00	The summons.
5C. On an *ex parte* application to a Judge in Chambers in the Queen's Bench Division, or an official referee.	15.00	The affidavit in support of the application.
5D. On lodging a motion (other than a motion for judgment) or application for hearing before a judge in the Chancery Division or the Admiralty Court.	15.00	The notice of motion or application.
5E. On an application in proceedings subsequent to the making of a wardship order or to the determination of an originating summons in guardianship or custodianship proceedings made—		

Column 1	Column 2	Column 3
Item	Fee £	Document to be marked
(a) to a registrar or district registrar	10.00	The summons.
(b) to a judge	15.00	

Provided that the amount specified in Fee No 5A, 5B, 5D and 5E shall not be payable where the application is for an order by consent.

Entering and setting down for trial or in Court—

5F. On entering or setting down any cause or matter for trial, hearing or further consideration except where it is otherwise provided in this Schedule or Fee No 1(c), 5E or 30(a) or (b) has been paid.	30.00	The *praecipe* or the filed copy of the pleadings.
5G. On setting down a commercial action in the commercial list for trial.	100.00	The *praecipe* or the filed copy of the pleadings.
5H. On entering or setting down any cause or matter for trial or hearing in the Admiralty Court except where the claim is in respect of loss of life, personal injuries or unpaid wages.	100.00	The *praecipe* or the filed copy of the pleadings.
5J. On fixing a date for the trial of a cause or matter before an official referee.	30.00	The *praecipe* or the filed copy of the pleadings.
5K. On filing an order for the hearing of a cause or matter begun by originating summons.	30.00	The order.
6. On setting down a cause on motion for judgment.	10.00	The *praecipe* or the filed motion.

Examination of witness before trial—

7. On the examination of a witness before trial.	5.00	The order.

Inquiries, trials and assessment of damages or interest by master or registrar—

8. (a) On an inquiry, reference for trial, or assessment of damages before a master, district registrar or Admiralty registrar or on any	15.00	The order, summons, judgment or certificate.

Column 1	Column 2	Column 3
Item	Fee £	Document to be marked
summons adjourned for the examination of witnesses,		
(b) on an assessment of interest before a master or district registrar.	2.00	Copy judgment.

Appeals to Judge in Chambers in the Queen's Bench Division or in the Chancery Division—

9. On sealing a notice of appeal from a master, district registrar or Admiralty registrar to a Judge in Chambers in the Queen's Bench Division or in the Chancery Division.	15.00	The notice.
10. [*Deleted by SI 1982 No. 1707*]		

Appeals to High Court—

11. On filing—		
(a) a notice of appeal to the High Court, or	15.00	The notice.
(b) a case stated or a special case for the opinion of the High Court pursuant to statute and setting the appeal or case down for hearing, or	15.00	The case.
(c) A notice of cross-appeal to the High Court, or	10.00	The notice.
(d) a respondent's notice of appeal to the High Court.	10.00	The notice.

C. Enforcement of Judgments
Writs of Execution—

12. On sealing a writ of execution.	6.00	The *praecipe*.

Applications in aid of enforcement—

13. On an application for a garnishee order *nisi*, a charging order *nisi* or the appointment of a receiver by way of equitable execution.	15.00	The affidavit or summons.
14. On an *ex parte* application to examine a judgment debtor before an officer of the Court.	15.00	The affidavit.
15. On an application for an attachment of earnings order to secure maintenance payments.	2.00	The affidavit in support of the application.

CHANCERY CHAMBERS

TO FILING SECTION - ROOM 307, T.M.B.

ACTION NO :

SHORT TITLE :

Herewith Affidavit of ....
/or if other document specify ....
filed in respect of:-

	Tick
1. Motion before Judge on	
2. Hearing before Master on	
3. Charging Order	
4. Garnishee Order	
5. Leave to issue Writ of Possession	
6. Substituted Service	
7. Service out of Jurisdiction	
8. Evidence	
9. Oral examination of Debtor	
10. To enable a Master's Order to be drawn	
11. Other (Specify)	

Signed :
Solicitors for Plaintiff / Defendant
            Other (Please specify)

Telephone No.

Ref:

JP/AFFIDAVI.FOR/L2

CHANCERY DIVISION CONSENT ORDERS

Please will you provide the following information:-

1. Is there, to the best of your knowledge, a hearing date currently fixed before the Master in this matter?

    YES

    NO

2. Is it intended that the filing of this consent Order should vacate that hearing?

    YES

    NO

3. Please give details of the pending hearing:

    (i)   Master_____
    (ii) Date:_____
    (iii) Time:_____

Signed: _____

Firm: _____

Date: _____

CHANCERY DIVISION CONSENT ORDERS

Please will you provide the following information:-

1. Is there, to the best of your knowledge, a hearing date currently fixed before the Master in this matter?

    YES

    NO

2. Is it intended that the filing of this consent Order should vacate that hearing?

    YES

    NO

3. Please give details of the pending hearing:

    (i)   Master_____
    (ii) Date:_____
    (iii) Time:_____

Signed: _____

Firm: _____

Date: _____

APPENDIX C 625

Column 1	Column 2	Column 3
Item	Fee £	Document to be marked
Registration of Foreign or Commonwealth Judgments—		
16. (*a*) Under Part II of the Administration of Justice Act 1920 or the Foreign Judgments (Reciprocal Enforcement) Act 1933—		
(i) on an *ex parte* application to register an incoming judgment or order,	10.00	The affidavit in support of the application.
(ii) on providing a certified copy of a judgment or order for use abroad.	10.00	The copy.
(*b*) Under the Maintenance Orders Act 1950 or the Maintenance Orders Act 1958—		
(i) on an *ex parte* application to register an outgoing order,	2.00	The affidavit or statement in support of the application.
(ii) on processing an incoming registration.	2.00	The affidavit of the order.
(*c*) Under the Maintenance Orders (Facilities for Enforcement) Act 1920—		
(i) on an *ex parte* application to register an outgoing order,	10.00	The affidavit or statement in support of the application.
(ii) on processing an incoming registration.	10.00	The affidavit or the order.
(*d*) Under the Maintenance Orders (Facilities for Enforcement) Act 1972—		
on an *ex parte* application to register an outgoing order.	10.00	The affidavit or statement in support of the application.
(*e*) On an application to register a judgment under the Merchant Shipping (Liner Conferences) Act 1982(c)	10.00	The affidavit.

Column 1 Item	Column 2 Fee £	Column 3 Document to be marked
(f) On an application to register an order under the Drug Trafficking Offences Act 1986(d)	10.00	The affidavit.
(g) On an application to register a custody order under Part I of the Family Law Act 1986(e)	10.00	The affidavit.
Enforcement of Arbitration Award—		
17. On an application for leave to enforce an arbitration award.	10.00	The affidavit.
D. Miscellaneous Proceedings or Matters		
Copy documents—		
18. For a photographic copy of or part of any document whether or not issued as an office copy, for each photographic sheet.	0.25	The copy or fee sheet.
19. For a typewritten copy document, per page, whether or not issued as an office copy and for each page of any additional carbon copy bespoken, half of this fee.	0.50	The fee sheet.
20. For examining a plain copy and marking the same as an office copy—for each sheet, bills of sale—	0.25	The office copy.
21. On filing—		
(a) any document under the Bills of Sale Acts 1878 and 1882, other than a fiat of satisfaction,	5.00	The document filed.
(b) a fiat of satisfaction.	5.00	The fiat.
22. (a) For an official certificate of the result of a search in one name in any register or index under the custody of the registrar of bills of sale,	2.00	
for every additional name if included in the same certificate,	1.00	

Column 1	Column 2	Column 3
Item	Fee £	Document to be marked
(b) for a continuation search, if made within one calendar month of date of official certificate (the result to be endorsed on each certificate).	1.00	The requisition for search.
Taking Affidavits—		
23. (a) On taking an affidavit or an affirmation or attestation upon honour in lieu of an affidavit or a declaration except for the purpose of receipt of dividends from the Accountant General and for a declaration by a shorthand writer appointed in insolvency proceedings, for each person making the same.	3.00	
(b) addition thereto for each exhibit therein referred to and required to be marked.	0.75	The affidavit, affirmation or declaration.
Searches—		
24. On a search of court documents (except a search for appearance or search under the Bills of Sale Act (1878) Amendment Act (1882)) including inspection for each hour or part thereof occupied.	1.00	The request.
Judge sitting as Arbitrator—		
25. (a) On the appointment of a judge of the Commercial Court as an arbitrator or umpire under section 4 of the Administration of Justice Act, 1970 and	500.00	
(b) for every day or part thereof (after the first day) of the hearing of the reference before a judge so appointed as arbitrator or umpire.	500.00	The arbitration agreement or other document produced to the judge as constituting the submission or arbitration.

Section 2: fees payable in Admiralty matters

Column 1	Column 2	Column 3
Item	Fee £	Document to be marked
In the Admiralty Registrar and Marshal's Office— 26. (*a*) On lodging with the Marshal—an instrument—under Order 75, rule 5(1),	30.00	The instrument.
(*b*) On the sale of a ship or goods—		
(i) for every £100 or fraction of £100 of the price up to £100,000,	1.00	
(ii) for every £100 or fraction of £100 of the price exceeding £100,000,	0.50	
(*c*) On entering a reference for hearing by the Registrar.	15.00	The *praecipe*.

Section 3: fees payable in the Court of Appeal

Column 1	Column 2	Column 3
Item	Fee £	Document to be marked
27. (*a*) On filing a notice of appeal—		
(i) from a County Court	25.00	The notice of appeal.
(ii) in any other case;	30.00	
(*b*) On filing a notice of cross-appeal or a respondent's notice under Order 59, rule 6(i).	15.00	The notice.
(*c*) On any application: provided that where the application is for leave to appeal and leave is granted, credit for this fee is to be given against the fee payable in (a).	15.00	The summons or form of application.

Section 4: fees payable in the funds office

Column 1 Item	Column 2 Fee £	Column 3 Document to be marked
28. On a search of the records of funds carried over to unclaimed balances—		
(a) for a period not exceeding 50 years immediately preceding the date of search,	5.00	The request.
(b) for each further period of 10 years or part thereof.	5.00	The request.

Section 5: fees payable on the taxation of costs

Column 1 Item	Column 2 Fee £	Column 3 Document to be marked
29. (a) On taking a cash account between solicitor and own client under the Solicitors Act 1974, or otherwise—for every £50 or fraction of £50 of the amounts found to have been received and paid,	0.05	The fee sheet.
(b) On the taxation of a bill of costs—	25.00	The bill.
(i) where the amount allowed does not exceed £500;	25.00	The bill.
(ii) where the amount allowed exceeds £500, for every £1 or fraction of £1 of the amount allowed:	0.05	The bill.
provided that the taxing officer may in any case require the bill of costs to be stamped before taxation with the whole or part of the amount of fees which would be payable if the bill were allowed by him at the full amount thereof (including, in cases under the Solicitors Act 1974, the		

Column 1	Column 2	Column 3
Item	Fee £	Document to be marked
fee payable in respect of the cash account).		
(c) On the withdrawal of a bill of costs which has been lodged for taxation, such fee (not exceeding the amount which would have been payable under Fee No. 29 (b) if the bill had been allowed in full) as may be reasonable having regard to the amount of work done in the court office.		The bill.
(d) On assessing costs in the Chancery Division for every £1 or fraction of £1 of the sum assessed.	0.05	The bill.
(e) On an application to a taxing officer to review his decision.	10.00	The written objection.
(f) On an application to a judge to review a taxing officer's decision.	15.00	The summons.

Section 6: fees payable on proceedings under the Companies Act 1985(a) and Insolvency Act 1986

Column 1	Column 2	Column 3
Item	Fee £	Document to be marked
30. (a) On presenting a petition for the winding up of a company by the Court, or for an order under section 459 or 456 of the Companies Act 1985		
(b) On presenting a bankruptcy petition:	40.00	The petition.
(i) if presented by a debtor or by the personal representative of a deceased debtor	15.00	The petition.
(ii) if presented by a creditor or other person	45.00	The petition.
(c) On presenting any other petition	50.00	The petition.

Column 1	Column 2	Column 3
Item	Fee £	Document to be marked
One fee only is payable where more than one petition is presented in relation to a partnership		
(*d*) On the hearing of a public examination	15.00	The application.
This fee is not payable until after a hearing on which the debtor has appeared and has been examined.		

Index

Account and inquiry—
  general order for 139-41
Account for money due—
  result of, 199
Accounts and inquiries, 170, 172-5
  attitude of court, 175
  costs, 175
  hazards, 175
  objective of plaintiff, 173
  order, 173, 193
  pitfalls, 175
  plaintiff's/defendant's considerations, 175
  procedures, 172
  section, 170
  sequence, 173-4
Acknowledgment of service—
  amendment, 42
  time for, 47-8
Action for liquidated demand—
  default judgment, 57
Action for possession of land—
  default judgment, 58-9
Action number, 125
Action relating to detention of goods—
  default judgment, 58
Administrative actions, 540-9
  compromise, 552-4
  inquiries for next of kin, 547-9
  master's order to discontinue, 550-2
  originating process, 543
  parties, 541-2
  sequence, 544--6
Administration of estates—
  intitulement, 60
Administrator pending suit—
  order appointing, 550
Advertisement—
  substituted service, by, 55
Affidavits, 264-6
  application *ex parte* by, 76-7
  binding, 265
  form, 265

Affidavits—*contd*
  headings in, 265-6
  marking, 264-5
  office copies, 266
  order of service out of jurisdiction, for, 43, 44
  reading in court or chambers, 266
  service, of, 41
Agents' accounts—
  declaration on, 142
Amendments, 42-5
  acknowledgment of service, 42
  method of making, 45
  originating summons, 42
  pleadings, 42-5
  writs, 42
Anton Piller orders, 100
  form, 110-13
Appeals, 240-62
  Commons Commissioner, from, 250-2
    disputed registration, 250-1
    unclaimed land, 251-2
  form of notice, 246-7
  judge, from, 241-4
    procedure, 242-3
    skeleton arguments, 243-4
  leave, 244-5
  master from, 240-1
    dismissed by consent, 253-4
    order on, 249-50
  revenue matters, 255-62
    alternative orders, 255-7
    dismissal, 257-8
    dismissal by consent, 258
    Inheritance Tax Act 1984, s222, 258-9
    order on case stated by Inland Revenue Commissioners, 255
    penalty appeal, 260
    stamp duty, 261-2
  stay pending, 248-9
Application *ex parte*—
  affidavit, by, 76-7

633

634 INDEX

Appointments, obtaining, 156-62
  proceedings before judge, 159-62
  proceedings before master, 156-9
Armed forces, members of service, 40

Backsheet—
  form of, 139
Beddoe's Order, 500-1
Benjamin Order, 563
Boundary disputes, 366-7
Breach of confidence, 316
Bundles of documents, 263-4
  agreed, 264
  indexes, 264
  presentation of, 263
  transcripts of evidence, 263-4
  transcripts of judgments, 263-4
  when required, 263
  when to lodge with court, 264
Business firms, 64

Caution—
  discharge, 114
Chancery Chambers, 3-13
  accounts section, 6
  court file, 6-7
  drafting/associates section, 5
  judges, 7 *See also* Judges
  listing section, 6
  masters, 7 *See also* Masters
  registry, 5
  structure, 4-7
Chancery Division—
  breadth of jurisdiction, 3-4
Chancery registry, 5
Change of name—
  intitulement, 62
Charging orders, 192
  Order Absolute, 196
  Order Enforcing, 196-8
  Order List, 195
Charities, 571-80
  Act of 1960, 574-6
  enforcement of Charity Commission Orders, 576-7
  inquiry, order for, 579-80
  order of Charity Commissioners, 578-9
  proceedings, 571-2
  scheme, order for, 579-80
  sequence, 573
Commencement of action, 14 *et seq*
Commons—
  title, 134
Commons Registration Authority—
  rectification of Registers held by, 481-2

Companies, 581-602
  administration order on petition by, 591-2
  administration order on petition presented by directors/creditors, 590-1
  disqualification of director, 589-90
  order appointing Official Receiver as provisional liquidator, 600-601
  order confirming reduction of capital, 594-6
  order declaring dissolutions void, 589
  order discharging administration order, 593-4
  order dismissing petition with costs, 587
  order for cancellation of share premium, 596-7
  order for rectification of register, 588
  order for reduction of share premium account, 597
  order for winding up following administration order, 592-3
  order on application to restore name to Register of Companies, 601
  order sanctioning disposition of company property after presentation of winding up petition, 587-8
  order sanctioning scheme of arrangement, 597-600
  order to restrain advertisement of winding up petition, 584
  order to restrain presentation of winding up petition- 584-5
  order to stay winding up after compulsory order granted and entered, 586-7
  originating process, 582
  plaintiff, as, 63, 64
  service on, 38
  vesting order - dissolved company, 601-2
  winding up orders, 585-6
Companies in liquidation intitulement, 63
Compromise, 144-5
Conduct of action, 14 *et seq*
Consolidation, 237-9
Construction of documents, 536-40
  execution, 539
  settlement, 539
Contempt of court, 212-26
  committal, order for, 212-14
  enforcement of forfeited recognisance, 225-6

Contempt of court—*contd*
  order for payment of fine and enforcement under s16(1)(a), Act of 1981, 215–16
  order for release of contemnor, 215
  order for suspended committal upon payment of fine, 218–19
  order refusing application for committal, 215
  order refusing committal and accepting apology, 214
  payment of fine and enforcement under s16(1)(b), Act of 1981, 216–18
  release on bail on giving recognisance, 224
Contentious probate, 525–31
  administration *pendente lite*, 529–30
  compromise, 530
  conclusion of action, 531
  default proceedings, 528–9
  discontinuance, 530–1
  dismissal, 530–1
  originating process, 527
  revocation of grant, 529
  short probate list, 526
Copyright, 305–8
  alternative jurisdiction, 307
  hazards, 307
  objective of plaintiff, 306
  pitfalls, 307
  sequence, 306–7
  statute, 305
  tribunal, 307
Corporations aggregate—
  service, 40
Costs, 269–97
  add to security, 288
  'as a contribution', 289
  as if a trustee, 288
  assessed, 289
  assessment, 228
  bases, 273–4
    indemnity, 273
    standard, 273
  cause, in, 282–3
  claim, on, 270–1, 274–5
  counterclaim, on, 270–1, 274–5
  disallow, 289–90
  discretion, 271–3
  down to and including, 286
  fixed, 289
  from the foot, 286
  in any event, 283–4
  including and excluding, 288
  legal aid, 281–2
  legal aid taxation, 271
  liability, 269–73
  no order, 271, 285

Costs—*contd*
  occasioned by, 285–6
  order by consent on client's application, 297
  order for review of taxation, 296–7
  order on application by person interested in funds, 296
  order on application by persons liable to pay bill, 294–6
  order on assessment by master, 290
  order on client's application for taxation, 293–4
  order that unsuccessful defendant pay successful co-defendant direct, 271
  order to deliver bill, 290–1
  particular claim or issue, 287
  pay a proportion, 288
  payment, 284
  personal liability of solicitor, 279
  'personally', 286–7
  plaintiff's/defendant's, 270, 271
  reserved, 270, 284–5
  security for, 35–6, 280–1
  set-off, 287
  solicitor and own client, 289
  solicitor's application for taxation, 291–3
  stage of proceedings at which to be taxed, 275–9
  standard indemnity, 289
  usual directions in trustees cases, 287–8
Counterclaims—
  title, 132–3
County court jurisdiction, 231–2
Court of Protection, 66
Cross-examination of deponents
  order for, 89
    both parties, 90
    one party, 89–90
Crown, 64
  service, 39

Damage—
  assessment by master, 192
  order on, 193–4
Damages—
  undertaking as to, 81
De-consolidation, 239
Declaration, 129
  agent's accounts, on, 142
  partnership accounts, on, 141–2
  trustees' accounts, on, 142
Deed—
  rectification of, 480
Deeds, construction of
  intitulement, 60

Default judgment, 45-7
  action for liquidated demand, in, 57
  action for possession of land, 58-9
  action relating to detention of goods, 58
  action for unliquidated damages, in, 58
  discovery, 46
  four-day orders, 46-7
  interest, and, 37
  pleadings, 45-6
Defendants, proceedings between title, 132
Directions for hearing, obtaining, 156-62
  proceedings before judge, 159-62
  proceedings before master, 156-9
Disability, persons under, 66-8
Discontinuance, 47
Discovery—
  default judgment, 46
  order for, 86
Dismissal of action—
  order for, 146-7
    chambers, in, 147
    trial, at, 146-7
District registries, 227-30
  applications in Chancery Division, 228
  jurisdiction, 228
  practice, 228-30
  procedure, 228-30
  restricted jurisdiction, 227-8
  unrestricted jurisdiction, 227
Documents, construction of
  intitulement, 60

Easements, 368-9
Enforcement applications, 75-98
Enforcement of orders and judgments, 170-2
Estates, proceedings against, 130-1
European Court—
  reference to, 254
Examination of judgment debtor—
  order for examination of, 200
Exhibits, 266-8
  general rules, 266-7
  legibility, 268
  marking, 267
  numbering, 267
Expert evidence—
  order for, 91

Family provision, 531-6
  application out of time, 567-8
  attitude of court, 535
  compromise, 564-7

Family provision—*contd*
  interim maintenance, 567-8
  order for reasonable provision, 568-70
  order reconstituting action where interests adverse, 568
  originating process, 533
  parties, 532
Fees, 621-32
  Admiralty matters, 629
  Chancery orders, 628
  Companies Act 1985 proceedings, 631-2
  Court of Appeal, 629
  every division of High Court, 621-8
  Funds Office, 630
  Insolvency Act 1986 proceedings, 631-2
  taxation of costs, payable on, 630-1
Females—
  intitulement, 63
Forms—
  originating process, for, 19-20
Four-day orders, 46-7
Funds, 181-5
  attitude of court, 183-4
  carry over, 209
  costs, 184, 208
  hazards, 184
  interest on payments into court on satisfaction, 190
  investment, 205-6
  lodgment schedule, 204
  notes for guidance on completion of payment schedules, 190-1
  orders, 182
  originating process, 183
  particulars of payments, 206-8
  payee, 209
  payment schedule, 204
  payments, 184-5
  payments into and out of court, 182
  persons under disability, 190
  pitfalls, 184
  recitals, 205
  requirements, 183
  restraints, 204-5
  sale, 206
  sequence, 183
  statutes, 181-2
  transfer, 206
Funds in Court—
  title, 133
Further and better particulars—
  orders for, 85
Future proceedings—
  title to, 126-8

Garnishee orders—
  absolute, 210-12
  nisi, 209-10
Garnishee proceedings, 191-2
Government departments—
  service, 39
Grant of probate—
  revocation, 554-5
  order refusing, 555-6
Guardian *ad litem*—
  order appointing, 69-70
Guardian of minor's estate—
  appointment, 200-3
    compensation for Criminal Injuries Compensation Board, where, 203
    damages paid into court, where, 201-2
    legacy paid into court, where, 200-1
    legacy paid to trustees, where, 202-3
Guardianship of estate of minor title, 134

House of Lords—
  making order of, 252

Injunctions, 99-117
  interim, 81
  mandatory, 103
  Mareva, 99-100
  nature of, 99
  no order on motion, 107
  order for directions, 113-14
  order to stand over motion, 107
  prohibitive, 103
  specimen interim affidavit, 102
  undertaking as to evidence, 107
  undertakings in lieu of, 81
Insolvency, 603-7
  corporate, 605-7
  individual, 603-5
Intellectual property, 305-35
  examples of directions, 319-23
Interest, 36-7
  claims for, 36-7
  contractual, 36
  default judgments, and, 37
  judgment, 36-7
  pleading of, 37
Interim injunction, 81, 110
  intended action, 109-10
  specimen, 101
Interlocutory applications, 30, 75-98
  application to amend, 77
  ex parte by affidavit, 76-7
  motions *See* Motions
  procedural questions, to determine, 83

Interlocutory applications—*contd*
  procedure for obtaining hearings or appointments, 82
  summons, by, 75-6
Interlocutory motion—
  treated as motion for judgment, 108
Interpleader, 34
  notes to orders in proceedings, 35
Interpleader proceedings—
  orders in, 92-8
Interrogatories order—
  for, 85-6
Intitulement, 60-3
  administration of estates, 60
  change of name, 62
  companies in liquidation, 63
  construction of wills, deeds and documents, 60
  females, 63
  mentally disordered persons, 63
  minors, 62
  numerous defendants, 61
  parties added, 61
  parties suing or sued in representative capacities, 61
  probate actions, 60
  statutes, 60
  substituted names, 62
  transmission of interest, 61-2

Joint property, 336-40
  affidavit, 343-5
  order for sale, 346-7
  originating summons with endorsement, 341-2
Judges, 7-8
  appeals from, 241-4
  orders for judge in chambers, 8
  orders made by, 118
  orders only for judge in court, 7-8
Judicial trustee, 491-5
  appointment, 506-10
    individual, 508-10
    Official Solicitor, 506-8
  district registries, 495
  originating process, 492-3

Land charge—
  discharge of, 114-15
Land Register—
  rectification, 480-1
Landlord and tenant—
  certificate that improvement is proper, 406
  certificate that works duly executed, 406
  compensation for improvements, 405

Landlord and tenant—*contd*
  declaration that consent to
    assignment unreasonably withheld,
    405
  order appointing manager, 414-15
  order authorising agreement for
    surrender of tenancy, 412-13
  order determining interim rent, 411
  order for compulsory acquisition of
    landlord's interest, 415-16
  order for new tenancy, 407-8
  order for possession, rent, mesne
    profits, 403
  order for relief from forfeiture, 404
  order giving leave to take
    proceedings, 407
  order on joint application to exclude
    provisions of ss24-28, Landlord and
    Tenant Act 1954, 412
  order permitting discontinuance of
    application, 411-12
  order refusing new tenancy, 409-11
  order revoking order for new tenancy,
    409
  order substituting date, 411
  order to confer right of first refusal
    on tenants, 413-14
  order under Leasehold Reform Act
    1967, 416-17
Landlord and Tenant Act 1954—
  joint applications under title, 133
Landlord and Tenant Act 1954, Part II,
  378-87
  alternative jurisdiction, 382
  attitude of court, 381
  exclusion of provisions, 383
  interim rents, 382
  landlord's notice to terminate, 384
  landlord's notice under s40, 386-7
  parties, 378
  required/have ready/on issue, 379
  tenant's counter notice by solicitor's
    letter, 385
Leapfrog Order, 252-3
Leasehold enfranchisement, 388-90
Leasehold Reform Act 1967
  application under, 133
Legal aid—
  costs, 281-2
Listing, 151-6
  categories, 152
  estimates of duration, 155-6
  non-witness list, 152, 156
  practical observations, 153
  Practice Direction, 154-6
  responsibility for, 154
  short probate list, 153
  warned list, 153

Listing—*contd*
  withdrawal of case, 153
  witness actions: fixed and 'floating'
    dates, 155
  witness actions set down and warned,
    154-5
  witness lists, 152

Mareva injunctions, 99-100
Mareva order—
  form, 115-17
Masters, 8-13
  allocation of cases to, 12
  appeals from, 240-1
  assessment of damage by, 192
    order on, 193-4
  judgments and orders likely to be
    made in chambers, 9-11
  location of, 12-13
  matters and proceedings not to be
    dealt with by, 11-12
  orders made by, 118
  orders to be made with specific
    authority of judge, 12
  trial before—
    order for, 91-2
    order on, 92
Mental patients—
  service, 40
Mentally disordered persons—
  intitulement, 63
Mesne profits—
  assessment of interest, 194-5
Minors—
  intitulement, 62
  service, 40
Month—
  meaning, 48
Mortgages, 390-5
  considerations for defendant, 393-4
  declaration of freedom from
    incumbrances, 417-18
  equitable enforcement, 418-20
  order for disclosure of title, 423-4
  order for foreclosure absolute, 421-2
  order for foreclosure nisi, 420-1
  order for payment, 423
  order for possession, 422-3
  originating summons (mortgagee's
    possession), 398-9
  parties, 391-2
  plaintiff's affidavit (possession), 400-2
  power of sale and foreclosure, 394-5
Motions, 77-82
  agreed adjournment of, 80
  attitude of court, 79-80
  by consent as trial of action, 78-9
  'by order', 78-9

Index

Motions—*contd*
  evidence, 79
  ex parte applications on, 78
  hazards, 81
  hearing of, 77-8
  listing of, 78
  pitfalls, 81
  procedure, 79
  saving, 78-9
  trial, treated as, 83-4
Musgrave Inquiries—
  result, 428
Musgrave Order, 424-8

Next friend—
  order for discharge and appointment, 69
Notices of motion to commit service, 41

Official Referee—
  transfer to, 236
  trial by, 236-7
Order 113—
  title, 134
Order to carry on, 71-4
Orders, 118-50
  account and inquiry, for, 139-41
  action number, 125
  agreed, 120
  alteration, 122-4
    after entry, 122-4
    before entry, 122
    clerical errors, 122
    inherent jurisdiction, 123-4
  amendments to, 121
  carriage of, 124
  consent absence of party, in, 121
  contents, 124
  backsheet, 124
    heading, 124
    operative part, 124
    recitals, 124
    upon application, 124
    upon hearing, 124
  copies of, 120
  correction, 122-4
    after entry, 122-4
    before entry, 122
    clerical errors, 122
    inherent jurisdiction, 123-4
  drawing up of, 121-8
    duties of draftsman, 122
  headings, 130
  judge, made by, 119
  lodging of documents when made by court, 120
  master, made by, 118

Orders—*contd*
  masters'—
    solicitors, drawn up by, 118
  motions by agreement, on, 121
  not required, when, 118
  openings to operative parts, 138-9
  operative parts, 139-44
  parties, 125-8
  partnership account, 141
  previous order, varying, 148-50
  proceedings against estates, 130-1
  title, 125-8
    examples, 131-3
  wording of, 120
Originating motions, 17-18
Originating process—
  forms for, 19-20
    completion of, 20
  issue by post, 298-9
  selection of, 15-21
  sequence of proceedings, 24-32
  service on persons, 37-8
  title to, 125-6
Originating summons, 18-19
  amendments, 42
  commencement by, 25-7
  defendant failing to attend, 26
  discovery, and, 26-27
  first appointment, 25
  general provisions, 21-4
  issuing, 22-3
  lease to issue, 20-1
  oral hearing, 26
  orders for directions on examples, 49-51
  service, 23-4
  supporting documents, 22
  timetable for procedure, 27-8
  titles, 133-4

Parties, 63-8
  business firms, 64
  Crown, 64
  members' clubs, 63
  order to carry on, 71-4
  partnership, 64
  persons under disability, 66-8
  plaintiff limited company, 63
  plaintiff residing out of England and Wales, 63
  representation orders, 65
  transmission of interest, 65
  trustees in bankruptcy, 64-5
Partners—
  service, 40
Partnership account—
  declaration on, 141-2
  order for, 141

Partnerships, 64
  examination of account, 471-2
  order on account and inquiry, 468-9
  orders giving leave to do certain acts, 472-3
  receivership, 455-73
    order, 462-7
  specimen statement of claim, 460-1
  winding up, 455-73
    order, 462-7
Passing off, 315-16
Patents, 308-12
  declaration of validity, 323-4
  examples of orders in appeal from Comptroller General, 324-5
  interim order: leave to amend specification, 326-7
  leave to amend specification, 326
  order dismissing appeal by consent, 327-8
  order on trial of infringement action, 328-9
  order where infringement action fails, 329-31
  title, 133-4
Payment—
  order for, 195
Payment into court—
  form for, 187-9
Personal representative—
  order for account, 143
Personal service, 39
Persons under disability—
  funds, 190
Petitions, 17
Place of trial, 30, 164-8
  appeals from district registrars, 167
  Birmingham, 165
  Bristol, 165
  circuit administration, 167-8
  Crown, 167
  motion days outside London, 166-7
  Northern Area, 166
  practice procedure, 167-8
  South Wales, 165
Plaintiff—
  limited company, 63, 64
  residing out of England and Wales, 63
Pleadings—
  amendment, 42-5
  default judgment, 45-6
  order giving leave to amend— examples, 57
Possession—
  originating summons, 375
  plaintiff's affidavit, 376-7
  summary applications for, 370-7
    Ord 113 not applicable, 373-4

Possession—*contd*
  trespass, 370-3
Possession order, 436-7
Post, 298-301
  acknowledgment of service, 299
  adjournment by consent, 300
  agreed orders, 300
  appeals from masters, 300
  drawing up of orders, 301
  filing documents by, 300
  issue of summons, 299-300
  legal aid taxation, 300
  office copies, 301
  originating process, issue of, 298-9
  writ, issue of, 298-9
Postal service, 38-9
  order for, 55
Practice Directions—
  index, 609-19
Preservation orders, 104-6
Probate—
  contentious, 525-31
Probate actions—
  intitulement, 60
Procedural questions—
  application to determine, 83

Receivers, 175-7
  appointment, 469-70
  discharge, 470-1
Receivership, 192
Recitals, 138
Rectification, 474-6
  deed, of, 480
  Land Register, of, 480-1
  originating process, 475
  Registers held by Commons Registration Authority, 481-2
Registered designs, 308-12
  appeal orders, 332-3
  order on trial of infringement action, 331-2
Registered land, 396-7
Representation orders, 128-9
  parties, 65
Representative capacities, parties suing or sued in intitulement, 61
Request for lodgment, 186
Rescission, 476-9
Rules of the Supreme Court—
  application to Chancery, 14

Sale of land—
  common form order, 429-35
  order nominating person to execute sale, 435-6
  order on sale at auction, 429

INDEX 641

Sale of land—*contd*
  purchaser's actions, 437-51
    chattels, 448-9
    payment into court, 444-5
    price paid into court, 450-1
  purchaser in possession, 443-4
  purchaser to repay mortgage and lodge money in court, 445-6
    return of deposit, 446-7
    sale of lease, 442-3
    shares, 447, 448
    vesting order, 450
  vendor's actions, 451-4
  Sales by order of court, 177-81
    binding effect of order, 180
    enlargement of powers of trustees, and, 180-1
    mortgage actions, 180
    Order 31, r1, 178-80
    Order 85, r2(3), 178
    section 30, Law of Property Act 1925, 178
Scientific adviser—
  order appointing, 319
Security for costs, 35-6
Sequestration, writ of—
  directions to sequestrators, 220-2
  discharge of, 222-3
  order for, 219
Service, 37-42
  acknowledgement, 42
  amendment, 42
  affidavit, 41
  armed forces, members of, 40
  companies, on, 38
  corporations aggregate, 40
  Crown, 39
  documents other than originating process, 38
  government departments, 39
  mental patients, 40
  minors, 40
  notices of motion to commit, 41
  originating process, of, 37-8
  outside jurisdiction, 41-2
    affidavit, 43, 44
    order for, 56
    order setting aside, 57
  partners, 40
  personal, 39
  postal, 38-9
  subpoenas, 41
  substituted, 40
Setting down, 162-4
  cases in which obviated, 163
  order for, 169
  originating summons, 163
  originating summons actions, 164

Setting down—*contd*
  procedure on, 163-4
  'squatters' actions, 163
  writ actions, directions for, 162
Sheriff claim—
  barred, 92-3
  conditional order to withdraw, 93-4
  order for sale, 94-7
  order for trial of issue, 94-7
  order to withdraw, 93
Slip Rule, 148
Solicitor—
  ceasing to act, 69
Specific performance, 348-52
  defence, 363-4
  defandant's affidavit, 360-1
  minutes of order, 365
  order giving leave to defend, 362
  plaintiff's affidavit, 358-9
  statement of claim, 355-6
  summons for summary judgment, 357
  writ of summons, 353-4
Stakeholders—
  summary determination, 97
Statutes—
  intitulement, 60
Stay or proceedings—
  order for, 145-6
  consent by, 145
  Tomlin form, 145
Subpoenas—
  service, 41
Substituted names—
  intitulement, 62
Substituted service, 40
  advertisement, by, 55
  fixing to property, by, 55
  orders for, 55
  post, by, 55
Succession, 525-70
  answer to kin inquiry, 561-3
  inquiry for next-of-kin, 560
Summary judgment, 82-3
Summons—
  interlocutory application by, 75-6

Taxation of costs—
  title, 133
Telephone, 301
Telex, 301-2
Third party directions—
  form, 70-1
Third party notice, 30-2
  specimen, 33
Third party proceedings—
  title, 131
Thomas More Building, 620

642 INDEX

Time, 47-8
  acknowledgment of service, 47-8
Tomlin form, 145
Tomlin Order, 564, 567
Trade marks, 312-15
  examples of orders for rectification of Register, 334-5
  orders on appeal from Registrar, 333-4
  title, 133
Transfer of actions, 232-9
  county court to High Court, 236
  county court order, 232-3
  High Court order, 232
  Crown, 233
  district registry, to, 234-5
  district registry to London, from, 234-5
  High Court to county court, 233
  Official Referee, to, 236
  one division to another, 235
Transmission of interest—
  intitulement, 61-2
  parties, 65
Trespass, 370-3
Trial—
  interlocutory motions treated as, 83-4
  master, before, 156
  order for, 91-2
  order on, 92
Trial of issue—
  order for, 97-8
  order on, 98
Trustees *See* Trusts
Trustees' accounts—
  declaration on, 142
Trustees in bankruptcy, 64-5
Trusts, 483 *et seq*
  actions by beneficiaries, 486-7
    relief for trustees who have acted honestly, 486-7
  applications for exercise of court's jurisdiction, 485-6
  appointment of receiver, 504-6
  appointment of trustees, 487-90
  Beddoe's Order, 500-1
  claim by beneficiaries, 501-2
  claim by creditors, 502-3
  custodian trustee, 512-14
  determination of questions, 484-5
  judicial trustee *See* Judicial trustee
  legislation, 483-4
  managing trustee, 512-13
  new trustee, 510-12
  order approving sale of trust property to trustee, 514-15
  order authorising transaction, 515

Trusts—*contd*
  order for account against personal representative, 504
  order granting relief from liability, 515-16
  orders directing acts to be done or abstained from, 484-5
  removal of trustees, 487-90
  trustee orders, 520-2
  variation, 495-8. *See also* Variation of trusts
  vesting order—
    special forms, 518-20
    tenant for life, 517-18
    trustee under disability, 516-17
  vesting orders, 498-9

Unless order, 86-7
  defendant, against, 86-7
  plaintiff, against, 86
'Upon application' paragraphs—
  examples, 134-7
'Upon hearing' paragraphs
  examples, 137-8
'Upon reading' paragraphs
  examples, 138

Variation of trusts, 495-8, 522-4
  originating process, 496

Wills, 525-70
  construction, 536-40
  missing, order pronouncing against, 558
  order for examination of scripts, 556-7
  order pronouncing for completed copy, 558
  order pronouncing for some words - against others, 557-8
  pronouncement as to validity, 550-2
  rectification, 564
  torn up, 558-60
Wills, construction of—
  intitulement, 60
Witness—
  order for examination of, 87-9
    examiner abroad, before, 88-9
    examiner, before, 87
    judicial authority abroad, before, 87-8
Witness statements exchange of, 16-17
  order for exchange, 89
Writ—
  amendments, 42
  commencement of proceedings by, 28-30

Writ—*contd*
  directions in actions—
    examples, 52-5
  general provisions, 21-4
  issue by post, 298-9
  issuing, 22-3
  leave to issue, 20-1
  order to convert to, 52
  service, 23-4

Writ—*contd*
  supporting documents, 22
  timetable for procedure, 30
  title to, 125-6

Writ of possession—
  order giving leave to issue, 199

Writ of summons—
  proceedings which must be commenced by, 18